Entrepreneurial Politics in
Mid-Victorian Britain

Entrepreneurial Politics in Mid-Victorian Britain

G. R. SEARLE

OXFORD UNIVERSITY PRESS

1993

Oxford University Press, Walton Street, Oxford OX2 6DP

Oxford New York Toronto
Deehi Bombay Calcutta Madras Karachi
Kuala Lumpur Singapore Hong Kong Tokyo
Nairobi Dar as Salaam Cape Town
Melbourne Auckland Madrid
and associated companies in
Berlin Ibadan

Oxford is a trade mark of Oxford University Press

Published in the United States
by Oxford University Press Inc., New York

British Library Cataloguing in Publication Data
Data available

Library of Congress Cataloging in Publication Data
Searle, G. R. (Geoffrey Russell)
Entrepreneurial politics in mid-victorian Britain / G. R. Searle.
p.   cm.
Includes bibliographical references and index.
1. Great Britain—Politics and government—1837–1901.   2. Middle
classes—Great Britain—Political activity—History—19th century.
3. Entrepreneurship—Great Britain—History—19th century.
I. Title.
DA560.S39 1993   941.081—dc20   92-28432
ISBN 0-19-820357-8

1 3 5 7 9 10 8 6 4 2

Typeset by Best-set Typesetter Ltd., Hong Kong
Printed in Great Britain
on acid-free paper by
Bookcraft Ltd., Midsomer Norton, Bath

Acknowledgements

IN writing this book I have accumulated many debts, not least to all the archivists and librarians who have helped me in my researches. I should like to thank the following institutions for permission to quote from documents in their custody: British Library; Guildhall Library, London; Manchester Central Library; University of Southampton Library; University College Library, London; St Deniol's Library, Hawarden (access via the Clwyd Record Office); West Yorkshire Archives, Bradford; West Yorkshire Archives, Leeds; Lancashire Record Office; Bradford City Library.

In addition, the Association of British Chambers of Commerce, the Bradford Chamber of Commerce, and the Manchester Chamber of Commerce have kindly allowed me to draw upon the minutes of their respective organizations. For permission to include quotations from the Palmerston Papers, I am grateful to the Trustees of the Broadlands Archives Trust, which also holds the copyright in Lord Palmerston's letters. Permission to quote from the letters of William and Robertson Gladstone has kindly been given by Mr. C. A. Gladstone.

I am also grateful to my university, the University of East Anglia, which has facilitated the writing of this book by granting me study leave and helping over travelling expenses. Finally, I would like to thank John Ashworth, John Charmley, Michael Hickox, Terry Jenkins, and Roger Virgoe, who have read earlier versions of the typescript and offered helpful advice and criticism as well as encouragement. Needless to say, I am wholly responsible for any errors that remain.

Norwich   G.R.S.
August 1992

Contents

Contents

There is a prevailing and well-founded belief that our Government, since the Reform Act, has been virtually in the hands of the middle classes.

(*The Economist*, 28 April 1855)

In England, the bourgeoisie never held undivided sway. Even the victory of 1832 left the landed aristocracy in almost exclusive possession of all the leading Government offices. . . . Thus, even after the repeal of the Corn Laws, it appeared a matter of course that the men who had carried the day, the Cobdens, Brights, Forsters, etc., should remain excluded from a share in the official government of the country, until twenty years afterwards a new Reform Act opened to them the door of the Cabinet.

(Engels, *Socialism*)

Neither contemporaries nor historians have doubted that the capitalist middle class were the 'real' rulers of mid-Victorian England, in the sense that the laws which were passed and executed by landed Parliaments and Governments were increasingly those demanded by the business men and—which is not necessarily the same people—their intellectual mentors. . . . It was by persuading the rest of society, or the great majority of it, to accept their ideal of a class society based on capital and competition, not by personally capturing the institutions of government, that the capitalist middle class was able to achieve its aims: free trade in nearly everything, from commerce, through land, labour, and appointments under the State, to education and religion.

(Perkin, *Origins*)

The peculiar flexibility of the English aristocracy snatched a class victory from the brink of defeat, and helped alter the course of national development. At the moment of its triumph, the entrepreneurial class turned its energies to re-shaping itself in the image of the class it was supplanting. That self-conscious spokesman of a bourgeois revolution, Richard Cobden . . ., watched with dismay his troops deserting the cause.

(Wiener, *English Culture*)

Introduction

In the immediate aftermath of the repeal of the Corn Laws in 1846 and for some years to come, there was a mood of triumphalism in advanced Radical circles. The *Norfolk News* believed that the Anti-Corn Law League had taken effective control of the government of the country: 'The seat of power on the great question of the day has been transferred from Downing street to Manchester,' it proclaimed; there were now 'TWO PARLIAMENTS', one in London, the other in Manchester. 'Practically the cotton lords have drawn [*sic*] the land lords out of office. The mills have beaten the aristocracy . . . The one is marching from victory to victory, the other is retrograding lamely from discomfiture to defeat.' Which Parliament would the nation obey?[1]

In fact, the leading spokesman for the Anti-Corn Law League, Richard Cobden, was far too sensible to imagine that the northern industrialists, whose interests he largely represented, were on the point of overthrowing the institutions of the aristocratic state. He well understood that the Conservative Prime Minister, Sir Robert Peel, supported by a landowner-dominated Parliament, had made a timely surrender to the League, the better to safeguard the established order. As Peel himself had put it in a private letter earlier in 1846: 'The worst ground on which we can *now* fight the battle for institutions, for the just privileges of Monarchy and Landed Aristocracy, is on a question of food.' The army promotions system, the game laws, and the Church, he warned, were already 'getting attacked with the aid of the league'.[2] Repeal of the Corn Laws would therefore be in the long-term interest of Britain's 'territorial Constitution'.

Yet Peel had good reason to be fearful for the survival of his traditional world. For Cobden and other leading Anti-Corn Law Leaguers believed that something far more substantial was at stake than an attempt to change a mistaken fiscal regime: they saw themselves as being at war with aristocratic England. Indeed, the very existence of the Corn Laws symbolized the privileged position occupied by the big landowners—privileges from which flowed both social prestige and various kinds of material advantage. Middle-class Radicals like Cobden were keen to destroy these privileges, while at the same time trying to vindicate their own claims to be something other than second-rate citizens. In particular, they wanted to defend the new industrial cities of the north from their gentlemanly detractors. It was a battle between two civilizations, two sets of values, perhaps even two races: for some League

---

[1] *Norfolk News*, 10 Feb. 1849.
[2] Cited in Donald Read, *Peel and the Victorians* (Oxford, 1987), 163.

publicists were accustomed to portray the industrial work-force as peace-loving 'Saxons' and their aristocratic rulers as a 'Norman' military caste.

In this campaign against 'feudal' privilege, Richard Cobden, a self-made entrepreneur and calico printer, had quickly emerged as the dominant figure. Significantly, when he launched his first important pamphlet on the world, it bore the pseudonym 'A Manchester Manufacturer'. Cobden and his circle were thus differentiated from many other contemporary Radical politicians. For example, both class and political beliefs kept them aloof from most of the working-class and plebeian Radical movements of their day. Yet neither did the 'Cobdenites' come into frequent contact with the Philosophic Radicals who, though anti-aristocratic, were personally detached from the world of the manufacturing north and, if they represented a class interest at all, seemed to be speaking for the expanding *professional* middle classes, especially those public officials whose sense of 'service' insulated them from the crude play of market forces; in this particular metropolitan coterie the Mancunian manufacturers had no place.[3] By contrast, Cobden, in the opinion of the well-placed observer Walter Bagehot, was 'altogether a man of business speaking to men of business'.[4] That is why historians have called Radicals of this type 'the entrepreneurial Radicals', and their quest to reshape the world in the image of the new manufacturing class 'entrepreneurial politics'. It is in this sense that both terms are used in the present book.

What, in particular, did the entrepreneurial Radicals hope to achieve? Their main concern was to undermine the foundations of the aristocratic state. After all, many features of the *ancien régime* had been left largely untouched by the 1832 Reform Act. For example, the distribution of parliamentary seats still grossly favoured the agricultural districts and small towns, leaving the newer industrial cities seriously under-represented; this was particularly galling to the northern manufacturers. Many members of the Victorian middle class also resented intensely the prevalent assumption that 'government' was some arcane mystery best left to a hereditary caste of landowners and higher professionals. Such considerations of status played an important part in nineteenth-century politics, where, arguably, they counted for quite as much as calculations of economic advantage. The issue was well formulated by the Victorian biographer of William Byles, the proprietor and editor of the *Bradford Observer*: 'When these sturdy yeomen by dint of thrifty living and keen adventure in business found themselves established as manufacturers and merchants, they felt they were just as good as the squirearchy which still

---

[3] But note Cobden's defence of professional men drawing 'precarious incomes', Ch. 2. One of the few Benthamite organizations which Cobden joined was the Law Amendment Society, to which Brougham and J. S. Mill, among others, were also attached.

[4] Walter Bagehot, 'Mr. Cobden', *Economist*, 8 Apr. 1865; reprinted in *The Collected Works of Walter Bagehot*, ed. N. St John Stevas (1968), iii. 296.

expected to rule the countryside.'[5] What the League leaders were demanding, then, was that people from their 'order' should be accorded a position of political influence commensurate with their economic importance.

But the entrepreneurial Radicals went further in contending that the country was currently in the grip of a sinister aristocratic *system*, which controlled almost all branches of public life, particularly the administration of the colonies, the armed services, and diplomacy. Thus we find Cobden fulminating against 'that great juggle of the "English Constitution"—a thing of monopolies, and Church-craft, and sinecures, armorial hocus-pocus, primogeniture, and pageantry!'[6] Underlying this outburst, of course, was the characteristically Radical view of history as a nightmare—a mere jumble of folly, ignorance, and mystification.

The entrepreneurial Radicals, then, were advocates of institutional modernization. But they also hoped that their success in contributing to the demise of the Corn Laws would shortly lead to a more general infusion of market rationality into public policy. What had made the Corn Laws so offensive was that they seemed to suggest that land somehow differed from other kinds of property. It was precisely to destroy this 'superstition' that many merchants and manufacturers had first thrown themselves into political life. Why, they asked, should 'business methods' and the 'principles of political economy'—the two things were often confused—not be introduced into all branches of public administration? Such Radicals hoped to construct a world in which monopoly would be replaced by competition and merit would take precedence over inherited position. Even though the *Norfolk News* may have allowed its heart to run away with its head, in the late 1840s the entrepreneurial Radicals had reason for looking with some confidence to the future.

Yet, in the event, as Cobden and his close political friend John Bright were later to concede, nothing dramatic like this ever happened. Britain underwent no 'bourgeois revolution' in the course of the Victorian period, and many of the appurtenances of aristocratic privilege survived into the next century.

This was particularly the case with respect to the personnel of those running the British State. At the national level, the mid-Victorian system continued to be one in which industrialists were grossly under-represented. Even as late as 1865, businessmen comprised less than a quarter of the House of Commons, and the true proportions were probably much less. By contrast, well over half of all MPs still came from land-owning families, many being

---

[5] Cited in David James, 'William Byles and the *Bradford Observer*', in D. G. Wright and J. A. Jowitt (eds.), *Victorian Bradford* (Bradford, 1981), 118.

[6] Cobden to F. Cobden, 11 Sept. 1838, in J. Morley, *The Life of Richard Cobden* (London, 1881; 1896 edn.), i. 130.

related to the peerage.[7] Moreover, as Cobden and Bright complained, most mid-Victorian *Cabinets* had an even more heavily aristocratic complexion. For, paradoxically, the repeal of the Corn Laws was followed by the emergence of Ministries headed by Russell, Derby, Aberdeen, and Palmerston, which in their upper ranks were almost as aristocratic as any in the country's history. Lord John Russell's Government of 1846, for instance, contained twenty-one Ministers of whom twelve were the sons of aristocrats and five had inherited baronetcies.[8] The 'Sacred Circle of the Great Grandmotherhood' reigned supreme. As for Palmerston, he formed a Cabinet in 1859 in which eleven out of fifteen posts were assigned to territorial magnates.[9] This situation remained little changed until the very end of the century.[10]

Why did so few businessmen force their way to the top in politics? On this issue, at least, historians are in broad agreement. The rules of the parliamentary game undoubtedly militated against the success of the great 'captains of industry'. For example, discrimination against the newer industrial cities in the allocation of seats made it difficult for urban men of wealth to get nominated to constituencies that they stood a chance of winning—unless, that is, they were prepared to accept aristocratic patronage, in which case they risked perpetuating their own subordination.

But the problem was not so much that businessmen wanting to sit in Parliament faced various kinds of obstacles, but rather that they were unwilling to embark upon such a career at all. Thus, in his study of Rochdale, Salford, Bolton, and Blackburn, John Garrard has shown that the parliamentary representation of these towns was dominated by just four well-known business families: the Fieldens, the Turners, the Hornbys, and the Pilkingtons.[11]

Financial timidity goes some way to account for this general reluctance on the part of businessmen to commit themselves to a political career. Take, for example, the case of Cobden, who became an easy target for the ridicule of his opponents after he twice had to be bailed out by his friends from the financial difficulties into which he had stumbled. But the first of these collapses came about because the problems of combining a business and a political career had obliged him to hand over the management of his firm to his amiable, but ineffectual, brother.[12] This was a dilemma which faced most

---

[7] W. L. Guttsman, *The British Political Élite* (1963; 1968 edn.), 41.

[8] Donald Southgate, *The Passing of the Whigs 1832–1886* (1962), 195.

[9] F. B. Smith, *The Making of the Second Reform Bill* (Cambridge, 1966), 15. See figures in John Vincent, *The Formation of the British Liberal Party 1857–68* (1966; 1972 edn.), 41. More generally, see Guttsman, *British Political Élite*, 35–40. On Palmerston's policy with regard to the promotion of businessmen to Ministerial office, see the discussion in Ch. 4.

[10] e.g. see James Cornford, 'The Parliamentary Foundations of the Hotel Cecil', in R. Robson (ed.), *Ideas and Institutions of Victorian Britain* (1967), 268–311.

[11] John Garrard, 'The Middle Classes and Nineteenth Century National and Local Politics', in John Garrard *et al.* (eds.), *The Middle Class in Politics* (1978), 38.

[12] Though Howe thinks that ruin such as Cobden experienced was not the usual fate of manufacturers who went into Parliament; Anthony Howe, *The Cotton Masters 1830–1860* (Oxford,

industrialists in this period. Later, with the establishment of the joint stock company and the move to larger units of production, mechanisms were developed by which routine day-to-day management could be devolved on to others. But so long as the family firm remained the dominant economic enterprise, many businessmen found that, though entrepreneurial activities could be combined with local politics, involvement in national politics was a distraction in which they could indulge only at some risk. This may be why, in industrial towns like Halifax in the 1850s and 1860s, it was *second-generation* textile masters who tended to seek a parliamentary seat.[13]

Many businessmen simply felt that they could not afford to devote sufficient *time* to national politics. As Oliver Heywood protested when attempts were made to draft him as a parliamentary candidate, 'his duties and engagements in Manchester wholly prevented him from acceding.'[14] Even businessmen otherwise very active in their localities in the Liberal cause tended to shy away from parliamentary involvement. Robert Hyde Greg, of the famous textile firm, *was* returned for Manchester in 1839, but only because he was recovering from a nervous breakdown brought about by overwork and had not been consulted; he was much annoyed by what had been done in his name, and at the 1841 election declined to defend his seat.[15]

Greg's two-year stint as an MP was exceptionally brief. But businessmen *as a group* had shorter parliamentary careers than professional men or 'gentlemen', something which remained true throughout the century and beyond. This was because many businessmen, especially successful pioneers of their fortunes, were obliged to build up their firms *before* they could think of going into the Commons, and so became MPs for the first time when they were quite elderly. To take four examples of businessmen who will feature later in this study, Samuel Morley and Titus Salt made their début at the age of 55, Thomas Bazley at 61, and Duncan McLaren at 65.[16] Indeed, Anthony Howe has shown that cotton masters who were returned to Parliament for Lancashire seats between 1832 and 1859 did so at an average age of 45.6 (as against 32.7 for MPs from the landed gentry),[17] in many cases only after they had retired from active business. The situation was summed up by Cobden

---

1984), 95. For examples of how some Victorian businessmen coped with the problem of combining their business interests with a parliamentary and a ministerial career, see H. L. Malchow, *Gentlemen Capitalists: The Social and Political World of the Victorian Businessman* (Basingstoke and London, 1991), 372, 276.

[13] J. A. Jowitt, 'Parliamentary Politics in Halifax, 1832–1847', *Northern History*, 12 (1976), 199.

[14] Garrard, 'Middle Classes', 41.

[15] Mary B. Rose, *The Gregs of Quarry Bank Mill: The Rise and Decline of a Family Firm, 1750–1914* (Cambridge, 1986), 131–2. On the dilemma of Alfred Illingworth, see Margaret Holden to Isaac Holden, 7 Aug. 1868, in *The Holden–Illingworth Letters* (Bradford, 1927), 416.

[16] See J. B. Mackie, *Life of Duncan McLaren* (Edinburgh, 1888), ii. 80–1. 'He was unhampered by official connections or the desire for office,' Mackie adds.

[17] Howe, *Cotton Masters*, 95.

with his usual clarity: 'The misfortune is generally that men of business come into Parliament too late in life, after their powers are exhausted.'[18] Exhausted or not, many business MPs found that their relatively short parliamentary careers reduced their chances of being given office.[19]

The existence of business ties could also limit an MP's effectiveness in other ways. Take the case of the shipowner William Schaw Lindsay. Writing to his friend Cobden in July 1857, Lindsay said that, although he had just put down a Commons motion, 'I am very busy at the "shop" just now, and I have only once been in the House since it opened.'[20] Many politicians from similar backgrounds would have echoed the cry from the heart of A. J. Mundella, the Nottingham hosiery manufacturer: 'To be in Parliament, a man ought to be independent of business.'[21]

Moreover, some mercantile and industrial MPs found the rituals and procedures of the House of Commons exasperatingly cumbersome, by comparison with the more 'businesslike' procedures of the local municipality, with which they felt much more at home. Thus, according to his daughter, William Rathbone's 'instincts as a man of business and as a lover of thorough work were outraged by the ineffective and slovenly character of much of the legislation'.[22] Some businessmen were only too happy to escape from these frustrations. Northern industrialists also disliked having to present improvement legislation before Commons committees, for which they were obliged to take costly legal advice and to receive what they considered inadequate courtesy from MPs. 'People who might think that they were very important in Bolton found themselves very little boys when in London,' bitterly remarked the mill-owner Thomas Thomasson.[23] As for actually becoming an MP, this, for many businessmen, meant an exchange of the real power and influence which they exercised in their localities for a social position entailing subordination and marginality.[24]

A particularly poignant case of a businessman conscious of being 'out of

---

[18] Cobden to Absalom Watkin, 6 Mar. 1857, in Sir E. W. Watkin, *Alderman Cobden of Manchester* (n.d.), 167.

[19] But Howe says that the average length of service of Lancashire cotton masters entering Parliament was 12.8 years, compared with 13.7 for the gentry—not a big difference (Howe, *Cotton Masters*, 95–7).

[20] Lindsay to Cobden, 10 July 1857, Cobden Papers, Add. MS 43,669, fo. 165; also, Lindsay to Cobden, 9 June 1857: 'I have enough, I am about to retire to some extent from business, and then I will be able to attend to politics which I cannot do when engaged as at present' (ibid., fo. 153).

[21] Mundella to Leader, 31 July 1870, in W. H. G. Armytage, *A. J. Mundella 1825–1897: The Liberal Background to the Labour Movement* (1951), 84. Before the end of the following year he had taken the plunge and abandoned all connection with the Nottingham manufacturing company: 'From now on I shall go in for unprofitable politics exclusively,' he told Leader (ibid. 105–6).

[22] Eleanor F. Rathbone, *William Rathbone: A Memoir* (1905), 226.

[23] John Garrard, *Leadership and Power in Victorian Industrial Towns 1830–1880* (Manchester, 1983), 101.

[24] Malchow, *Gentlemen Capitalists*, 1, 58.

his depth' at Westminster is furnished by Titus Salt, the Bradford alpaca manufacturer, who in 1859 was persuaded against his better judgement to stand as Liberal candidate for his adopted city. He was, of course, elected without difficulty. But, as his pious biographer sadly relates, Salt felt unsuited to his new position by both habit and previous training. He seldom spoke in the Commons, except on formal occasions, and though he felt honoured at having the opportunity to mingle with other leading Radicals whom he admired, he feared that the late nights and unhealthy atmosphere were undermining his health. Suffering from 'broken sleep . . . shattered nerves and gouty twinges', he resigned his seat—although in the event he still had over fifteen years to live.[25]

Moreover, businessmen who sat in the Commons suffered from a disability that has been memorably described by Walter Bagehot. Such men, Bagehot argues, enjoyed less influence than other MPs because they lacked the kind of social cohesion to be found among the landed classes:

The merchants and manufacturers in Parliament are a motley race—one educated here, another there, a third not educated at all. . . . Traders have no bond of union, no habits of intercourse; their wives, if they care for society, want to see not the wives of other such men, but 'better people', as they say—the wives of men certainly with land, and, if Heaven help, with the titles.[26]

This is a slight exaggeration, because there was a tendency for Dissenting MPs to have come from certain key schools, and many of them also belonged to important business networks created by chapel connections and intermarriage.[27] Indeed, one historian has even claimed that some commercial men, many of whom were Quakers, formed a kind of great cousinhood of their own.[28] None the less, Bagehot's point generally holds good.

Moreover, the problems of getting into the House of Commons and succeeding in it were dwarfed by the problem of then securing Ministerial promotion, because strong social prejudices still existed at Court and among the aristocracy against giving high offices of State to men from 'unsuitable' backgrounds. Of course, many businessmen were not looking for office in the first place. But it is interesting that of the so-called Manchester School politicians, the first two to serve as Ministers both came from landed families: Milner Gibson and Charles Villiers, the younger brother of the Earl of Clarendon (the latter was an ally rather than a member of the 'School').

---

[25] R. Balgarnie, *Sir Titus Salt Baronet* (1877; new edn., Settle, 1970), 189–90. By way of contrast, Isaac Holden became an MP after his doctors told him that his health required a complete change of occupation! ('Memoir of Isaac Holden', *Holden–Illingworth Letters*, 802).

[26] Walter Bagehot, *The English Constitution* (1867; Fontana edn., 1963), 174.

[27] For examples of family networks centred around the chapel, see Patrick Joyce, *Work, Society and Politics: The Culture of the Factory in Later Victorian England* (Brighton, 1980), 12.

[28] Malchow, *Gentlemen Capitalists*, 6–7.

Cobden turned down the Presidency of the Board of Trade in 1859;[29] and although John Bright would undoubtedly have welcomed an offer, he was denied any such opportunity until 1868, the ostensible reason for his rejection being that he had attacked 'classes'.[30] Politicians on the Conservative side of the House faced equal difficulties. The newspaper wholesaler W. H. Smith, 'the Bookstall Man', did get into the Conservative Cabinet as First Lord of the Admiralty in 1877; but the Queen queried the suitability of the appointment, saying she feared that it 'may *not please* the Navy in which service so many of the *highest rank* serve . . . if a man of the Middle Class is placed above them in that very high Post'.[31]

A Ministerial career would anyhow involve most businessmen in financial sacrifices. Some back-benchers at least had the option of subsidizing their political hobby by acquiring a clutch of company directorships. Indeed, Sir Charles Wood positively encouraged the ambitious Hugh Childers to take up this option. Other business MPs received useful investment tips, or were occasionally able to lobby on behalf of their own industries. Even so, looked at from a narrowly pecuniary point of view, a parliamentary career was not usually profitable. But promotion to office usually entailed a further loss of income—even though there were no clear rules defining what 'outside interests' a Minister could legitimately retain.[32]

Another handicap from which many businessmen suffered was a certain lack of confidence as debaters and orators, such as we have already seen in the case of Salt. 'I must apologise to the House for troubling them, although I seldom detain them long,'[33] began the Liverpudlian merchant and banker William Brown with characteristic diffidence. Many businessmen were content to make brief one-minute interjections to express their approval or disapproval of some technical proposal on which they felt their position gave them the authority to pronounce. Some even took the view that they were performing a public service in confining themselves to these 'business-like' interventions and in eschewing time-consuming oratory. Cobden and Bright were shining exceptions here; so, too, was W. E. Forster, whose nomination as a parliamentary candidate to succeed Salt was welcomed by the *Bradford Observer* with the argument that a commercial city needed to be represented

[29] Morley, *Cobden*, ii. 228–36. See Ch. 4.

[30] This was Palmerston's explanation of why John Bright could not be made an offer (Morley, *Cobden*, ii. 232).

[31] Viscount Chilston, *W. H. Smith* (1965), 86, 94. But William Cowen, the Radical MP and businessman, expressed his delight: 'The large mercantile and trading classes will regard your appointment with especial satisfaction' (ibid. 96).

[32] Spencer Childers, *The Life and Correspondence of the Right Hon. Hugh C. E. Childers, 1827–1896* (1896), i. 99, 117–18. Thomas J. Spinner, jun., *George Joachim Goschen. The Transformation of a Victorian Liberal* (Cambridge, 1973), 19–20.

[33] Parl. Deb., 3rd ser., vol. 114, 762: 17 Feb. 1851.

by a local businessman who was at the same time something more than a local businessman.[34]

For the cardinal point was that the House of Commons was an assembly which lived by debate, and even junior Ministers were expected to have attained a certain level of fluent advocacy, while great Commons reputations were seldom won without exceptional displays of ability in public speaking. One reason why so many businessmen looked with admiration upon Gladstone was the latter's conspicuous possession of gifts which they themselves lacked. Not, of course, that businessmen were alone in providing the House with tongue-tied Members—landed society contributed its fair quota! But it is probably true that the education, training, and experience acquired by most industrialists and commercial men meant that they were less fitted for parliamentary life and for Cabinet office than were, say, lawyers.[35]

Neither did their often skimpy education help businessmen to shine in their new surroundings. There is a broad truth in Engels's verdict, made in his 1892 Introduction to *Socialism: Utopian and Scientific*:

The meekness with which the wealthy middle class submitted to [their exclusion from high political office] remained inconceivable to me until the great Liberal manufacturer, Mr. W. A. [sic] Forster, in a public speech implored the young men of Bradford to learn French, as a means to get on in the world, and quoted from his own experience how sheepish he looked when, as a Cabinet Minister, he had to move in society where French was, at least, as necessary as English!

In fact, argues Engels, 'the English middle class of that time were, as a rule, quite uneducated upstarts, and could not help leaving to the aristocracy those superior Government places where other qualifications were required than mere insular narrowness and insular conceit, seasoned by business sharpness'.[36]

Yet the very things that hampered businessmen in their attempts to pursue a career in Westminster and Whitehall also gave an edge and purpose to entrepreneurial politics, and so contributed towards its survival. Businessmen who strove to secure a parliamentary seat, as some did, were invariably motivated by an urge to win social recognition and outside acknowledgement of the worth of the local communities in which they were men of consequence.[37] This sort of touchy 'class pride' may, in many cases, have set limits to their ambitions once they actually arrived at Westminster. But it also

[34] 'For statesmanship we want men of wider views than a factory can produce; of broader and deeper insight into human wants and human rights than a mere business training can furnish' (quoted in Jack Reynolds, *The Great Paternalist. Titus Salt and the Growth of Nineteenth Century Bradford* (1983), 207–8).

[35] See comments of B. Clyde Binfield, *So Down to Prayers: Studies in English Nonconformity 1780–1920* (1977), 122–3.

[36] In Karl Marx and Frederick Engels, *Selected Works* (Moscow, 1958), ii. 111.

[37] This is one of the main themes in Malchow, *Gentlemen Capitalists*.

denoted the existence of social strains and tensions which were likely to have serious political consequences.

Moreover, the fact that few businessmen enjoyed a conventionally success-ful political career does not preclude the possibility that those who made it to Westminster exercised considerable *influence*. Nor, for the 'entrepreneurial ideal' to prevail, was it perhaps necessary for the manufacturing class itself to capture the institutions of government. If businessmen in mid-Victorian Britain did indeed 'fail' politically, what did this 'failure' really signify?

This is an issue which divides the history profession down the middle. But over the last twenty years or so, most historians have inclined to the view not only that mid-Victorian businessmen failed to make a major impact in national politics, but that the entrepreneurial ideal itself grew weaker as the century proceeded. Among the most influential originators of this line of thought were Perry Anderson and Tom Nairn of the *New Left Review*, who in the mid-1960s wrote a series of influential papers in which they argued that Britain, despite its pioneering experiences during the Industrial Revolution, had somehow failed to achieve true maturity as an industrial nation because, unlike other European States, it had never undergone a 'bourgeois revolution' such as the Jacobin revolution in France.

Indeed (according to Anderson) when a new manufacturing middle class later came into existence in the north of England, it lacked the self-confidence to challenge this powerful aristocracy. After a 'brief and inglorious' high watermark in the campaign to repeal the Corn Laws, the industrial bourgeoisie sank back into apathetic acquiescence, being 'bent exclusively on integrating itself into the aristocracy, not collectively as a class, but by individual vertical ascent'.[38] Anxieties created by the French Revolution abroad and by working-class disaffection at home further contributed to the emasculation of the middle class, as, later in the century, did the rise of Imperialism. The outcome of all this was a sluggish industrial sector and the poor economic performance of subsequent decades.

But the Marxist Left has not been alone in lamenting the survival of older traditions of hierarchy and status. Many members of the 'Thatcherite Right' have also drawn attention to similar 'attitudinal' factors—hence the popularity of Martin Wiener's scholarly philippic *English Culture and the Decline of the Industrial Spirit 1850–1980* (1981). Wiener agrees with Anderson that Britain's distinguishing characteristic has been that the middle classes who made the Industrial Revolution then lacked the self-confidence to seize the cultural and political leadership to which their economic wealth seemingly entitled them. The bourgeoisie was 'civilized' in the image of landed society,

---

[38] Perry Anderson, 'Origins of the Present Crisis', *New Left Review*, 23 (Jan.–Feb. 1964), esp. 28–32.

argues Wiener, and thereafter the country's élite separated itself 'from the sources of dynamism in existing society and [strove] to attach itself to an older way of life'.[39]

More recently the debate has been enlivened by W. D. Rubinstein's claim that an important divide separated the financial and commercial sectors of the economy from the manufacturing centres of Victorian Britain. Merchants, and especially bankers, he contends, not only amassed larger fortunes than manufacturers, but, in their social affiliations and life-styles, had more in common with the aristocratic world of London 'Society' than with the textile magnates, the colliery proprietors, and other industrialists from such regions as northern England, South Wales, and Clydeside.[40] Cain and Hopkins have taken this insight further with their concept of 'gentlemanly capitalism'.[41]

The prevailing emphasis upon the *social subordination* of the manufacturing and industrial classes has also drawn sustenance from the work of urban historians. The important feature of the mid-Victorian years, according to this school, was the growing differentiation of classes in big cities like Manchester. As the major manufacturers moved their residences away, not only from the neighbourhood of the poor, but also from proximity to humbler members of the middle-class community like shopkeepers, they became more conservative in their social attitudes—and in time in their political attitudes too. Meanwhile, growing prosperity and the removal of the more glaring injustices against which they had complained earlier were producing an atmosphere hostile to the politics of middle-class assertiveness. This leads naturally to a discussion of the 'gentrification' of the industrial middle class—what many historians see as its new-found interest in social status and in the acquisition of titles and posts, an interest which allegedly signalled its rapprochement with the old pre-industrial establishment.

In a recent book, *Class, Sect and Party*, dealing with the 'making of the middle class in Leeds', R. J. Morris has taken issue with such interpretations. He argues that 'middle class formation was as much about competition for loyalty and dominance within the middle classes as it was about conflict with other social groups'. He stresses the hierarchical nature of the Leeds middle-class community, of which an 'élite' of professional men and well-established merchants formed the apex. Divided by religion and by party loyalty, this

---

[39] Martin J. Wiener, *English Culture and the Decline of the Industrial Spirit 1850–1980* (Cambridge, 1981), 43. For a critical account of Wiener's book and of the reasons for its popular success, see James Raven, 'British History and the Enterprise Culture', *Past & Present*, 123 (1989), 178–204.

[40] See, e.g. W. D. Rubinstein, 'Wealth, Élites, and the Class Structure of Modern Britain', *Past & Present*, 76 (1977), 99–126.

[41] P. J. Cain and A. G. Hopkins, 'Gentlemanly Capitalism and the British Expansion Overseas. I. The Old Colonial System, 1688–1850', *Economic History Review*, 39 (1986), 501–25. See also their follow-up article, 'Gentlemanly Capitalism and British Expansion Overseas. II. New Imperialism, 1850–1945', *Economic History Review*, 40 (1987), 1–26.

middle class came to a sense of its own identity largely through participation in a network of voluntary societies which countered the disruptive effects of party allegiance by creating 'a neutral area of civil society within which class formation could take place'. Morris accordingly rejects the idea of a middle-class 'failure'; that class's acceptance of status and hierarchy, he argues, arose from within the middle-class community itself, and should not be seen as an 'aping' of aristocratic values.[42] But even here the emphasis is on a kind of subordination, albeit one that was self-imposed.

A pessimistic view of the political prospects of both the mid-Victorian businessman and the 'entrepreneurial ideal' has also been encouraged by many economic historians. For example, it has been claimed that business organization changed decisively in the latter half of the century with the spread of the joint stock company and the advent of limited liability. The effect of these developments, it is said, was to create a separation between managers and shareholders. And this in turn meant not only the end of the family firm and the small partnership as the dominant business units, but also the death of entrepreneurial politics, which presupposed the existence of a class of small capitalist entrepreneurs.[43] Such an interpretation dovetails neatly with the line taken in H. L. Malchow's recent *Gentlemen Capitalists: The Social and Political World of the Victorian Businessman*, which charts the progress of a group of Victorian businessmen who, starting off as social 'outsiders', later secured election to Parliament and, basing themselves in London, eventually became assimilated into a 'national wealth-owning elite'.[44]

A second kind of economic explanation is the one provided by Gatrell, who argues that when the 'Manchester School' collapsed eventually in the town of its birth, this happened because of the changing needs of the textile industry, whose accelerated production made it increasingly dependent on selling goods in Middle Eastern and Far Eastern markets, where traders needed the assurance that, if need be, they would receive naval protection. In these circumstances, Cobdenite cosmopolitan pacifism seemed economically irrational, as well as politically unacceptable, whereas Palmerston's foreign policy had much more to offer.[45] The first step had been taken on the road to business support for Imperialism—something which, it is generally agreed, finally put

---

[42] R. J. Morris, *Class, Sect and Party. The Making of the British Middle Class: Leeds, 1820–1850* (Manchester, 1990), esp. 151, 329. A very different study, but one which also focuses on 'internal' affairs, is Garrard, *Leadership and Power*.

[43] J. D. Y. Peel, *Herbert Spencer: The Evolution of a Sociologist* (1971), esp. 218–23. Joyce, *Work, Society and Politics*, 28. Harold Perkin, *The Origins of Modern English Society 1780–1880* (1969, 1972 edn., 438). Perkin also argues that the land campaign drove many businessmen into the same camp as the landowners, so uniting 'active' and 'passive' property (ibid. 451–4).

[44] Malchow, *Gentlemen Capitalists*, passim.

[45] V. A. C. Gatrell, 'The Commercial Class in Manchester c.1820–1857', Ph.D. dissertation, Cambridge University, 1971, 351–413.

paid to the earlier kind of entrepreneurial politics, since Imperialism led to the revival of 'militarism', with all its aristocratic associations.[46]

All these 'pessimistic' interpretations are true as far as they go. Nor are they mutually exclusive. Yet somehow they do not quite cover the case. One problem is that the chronology does not fit. For example, despite the advent of limited liability in 1856, the small-scale family firm remained the norm until the 1880s, if not later.[47] But most would agree that Cobden's revolutionary agenda had collapsed long before then. The same difficulty applies to those interpretations which emphasize the 'rise of Imperialism'. R. J. Morris's explanation is open to criticism for the very opposite reason. If what he says is true, it is hard to see how entrepreneurial politics could ever have taken root at all.

It is here that many historians would wish to challenge the premisses underlying all the accounts which have been discussed so far. For there are grounds for taking a much more 'optimistic' view of the role of the industrialist in mid-Victorian Britain. In particular, too much importance, according to some historians, has recently been placed on what was happening at Westminster, to the neglect of local politics. This has distracted attention from the crucially important consideration that the 1835 Municipal Corporations Act had made it possible for industrialists to capture political power in their own localities. Thus, between 1835 and 1860, textile masters alone comprised one-third of all Lancastrian councillors;[48] and John Garrard, in his study of four northern towns, has shown that after 1835 local government largely passed into the hands of wealthy businessmen, the only serious threat to their domination coming from shopkeepers.[49] Indeed, being a good businessman was held to be a strong qualification for public office, since, as major ratepayers, such men were thought to have a vested interest in securing efficient and economical administration. Thus, in 1865, one Birmingham businessman anxious to establish his own political credentials reminded electors that the council was, in fact, 'a large manufactory. If there was a good

---

[46] Paul Warwick, 'Did Britain Change? An Inquiry into the Causes of National Decline', *Journal of Contemporary History*, 20 (1985), 99–133.

[47] P. L. Cottrell, *Industrial Finance, 1830–1914* (1980), Ch. 6.

[48] Howe, *Cotton Masters*, 143. They also contributed a disproportionate number of aldermen and mayors (ibid. 151). In Birmingham, by contrast, small businessmen formed the largest group in the 1850s and early 1860s, with bigger businessmen coming to the fore thereafter (E. P. Hennock, *Fit and Proper Persons: Ideal and Reality in Nineteenth-Century Urban Government* (1973), 27, 34–5; Linda J. Jones, 'Public Pursuit of Private Profit? Liberal Businessmen and Municipal Politics in Birmingham, 1865–1900', *Business History*, 25 (1983), 240–1. Businessmen also played an important role on Nottingham Council (Roy Church, *Economic and Social Change in a Midland Town: Victorian Nottingham 1815–1900* (1966), 181–2, 370–2).

[49] Garrard, 'Middle Classes', 35–66. See also Garrard, *Leadership and Power*, passim. On the importance of the shopocracy, see T. J. Nossiter, *Influence, Opinion and Political Idioms in Reformed England: Case Studies from the North East 1832–74* (Hassocks, 1975), esp. Ch. 9.

system and careful management, at the lowest possible cost, the results must be satisfactory.'[50]

Moreover, for businessmen, too, the rewards for involvement in local politics were considerable. Municipal office, the mayoralty in particular, was a confirmer of social status, which reinforced the position of businessmen as a kind of urban squirearchy, the 'natural' leaders of the new industrial Britain.[51] In addition, industrialists had an obvious interest in influencing the policy of their municipality—for example, by determining the level of rates. Indeed, as Daunton points out, it was the 'local state' which 'provided the setting where a self-confident middle class built its characteristic institutions and culture'.[52] In short, even if the industrialists had little prestige or influence at Westminster, they were able to control their own localities, which is what would have mattered to them most.

This leads on to a wider point. Many detailed investigations of social relationships within particular localities have tended to give a picture of the social role of the mid-Victorian entrepreneur rather different from that purveyed by writers like Wiener. 'Industrialists', writes Richard Trainor of the Black Country, 'were neither swamped by landed influence nor spurned by aloof aristocrats: manufacturers were too strong for the first outcome, the landed élite too flexible for the second.'[53] And Theodore Koditschek, in his analysis of early nineteenth-century Bradford, makes the same point even more strongly, saying that 'it was not the weakness but the very strength of liberal entrepreneurial identity which . . . constituted the industrial bourgeoisie's most striking characteristic'.[54]

But the 'pessimists' can also be bearded in their own lair. For it is possible to demonstrate that even at Westminster and Whitehall the entrepreneurial ideal exercised considerable influence throughout the Victorian period. This is precisely the view of Perkin, who believes that 'the entrepreneurial class ruled, as it were, by remote control, through the power of its ideal over the ostensible ruling class, the landed aristocracy which continued to occupy the

---

[50] L. Jones, 'Public Pursuit of Private Profit?', 242.

[51] John Garrard, 'Parties, Members and Voters after 1867', in T. R. Gourvish and Alan O'Day (eds.), *Later Victorian Britain 1867–1900* (1988), 136. But Howe also suggests that, in so far as involvement in local government was valued as a means of achieving status, there was a tendency for businessmen to withdraw from local politics when this had been achieved or if other avenues opened up for gratifying their social ambitions: e.g. gaining a seat on the county bench (Howe, *Cotton Masters*, 161).

[52] M. J. Daunton, '"Gentlemanly Capitalism" and British Industry 1820–1914', *Past & Present*, 122 (1989), 152.

[53] Richard Trainor, 'The Gentrification of Victorian and Edwardian Industrialists', in A. L. Beier, David Cannadine, and James M. Rosenheim (eds.), *The First Modern Society* (Cambridge, 1989), 196.

[54] Theodore Koditschek, 'The Dynamics of Class Formation in Nineteenth-Century Bradford', in Beier *et al.* (eds.), *First Modern Society*, 547. However, Koditschek goes on to say that this 'ultimately proved to be the greatest impediment in its efforts to stabilize social relations in the town'.

main positions of power down to the 1880's and beyond'.[55] Did the social background of the country's élites much matter, as long as the Parliaments of the day, though seemingly dominated by the landed interest, nevertheless repealed the Corn Laws and the Navigation Laws, legalized limited liability, and facilitated commercial growth in dozens of small ways? Even in nineteenth-century Germany, if David Blackbourn and Geoff Eley are to be believed, middle-class interests suffered little from a Junker-dominated regime.[56]

It may be a mistake, then, to attempt to determine the location of class power by the simple expedient of counting the proportions of Cabinet Ministers (or county councillors or magistrates or whatever) who had been educated at Eton or who came from families listed in *Bateman's*.[57] A country's political system, it can be argued, should be judged by what it does, not by the social composition of its leadership; its class character is determined by its *functions*, not its *personnel*. This is a perspective applicable not only to Germany but also to Britain, where policy, it can plausibly be shown, also tended to reflect prevailing commercial interests. Of course, much of all this was first said many years ago by Karl Marx, when he asserted that the British middle class, confident that capitalist values were in safe hands, had been content to *delegate* the technicalities of administration to the great Whig families, who acted as the '*aristocratic representatives* of the bourgeoisie'.[58]

But this, in turn, suggests the importance of supplementing the many regional studies which explore the interrelationship between various élites, landed, commercial, financial, and industrial, with an investigation of what was happening at the level of national politics—specifically in the crucial formative years separating the repeal of the Corn Laws and the passing of the Second Reform Act in 1867. For what is largely missing in the various studies of particular towns and industries, excellent though most of them are,[59] is any adequate consideration of the wider national context. Morris and Koditschek, for example, deliberately concentrate on 'internal' affairs to the almost com-

---

[55] Perkin, *Origins*, 271–2.

[56] David Blackbourn and Geoff Eley, *The Peculiarities of German History: Bourgeois Society and Politics in Nineteenth-Century Germany* (Oxford, 1984), e.g. 246.

[57] E. P. Thompson, 'The Peculiarities of the English', in *The Poverty of Theory* (1978), 61–4.

[58] Karl Marx, review of Guizot's *Why has the English Revolution been Successful?* (March 1850), in Karl Marx and Frederick Engels, *On Britain* (Moscow, 1962 edn.), 349. Marx also argues that the landowner had become a kind of agrarian capitalist. This last argument is one which much recent economic history seems to support. See the copious illustrations in J. V. Beckett, *The Aristocracy in England 1660–1914* (1986), Part 2.

[59] In particular, see Howe, *Cotton Masters*, passim. Richard Trainor, 'Peers on an Industrial Frontier: The Earls of Dartmouth and of Dudley in the Black Country, *c*.1810 to 1914', in David Cannadine (ed.), *Patricians, Power and Politics in Nineteenth-Century Towns* (Leicester, 1982), 70–132. Trainor, 'Gentrification', 167–97. Joyce, *Work, Society and Politics*, passim. Theodore Koditschek, *Class Formation and Urban-Industrial Society: Bradford, 1750–1850* (Cambridge, 1990).

plete exclusion of 'foreign policy'; that is to say, they tend to treat their respective towns (Leeds and Bradford) as though they formed a world apart, and they say little about the involvement of their urban élites in national politics. Indeed, with the partial exception of Howe's, all these regional studies are silent on the subject of what happened to industrialists after they became drawn into the 'alien' world of Westminster and Whitehall. Needless to say, this issue is also one of marginal interest to most students of 'High Politics'.[60]

In any case, the sort of political history which is primarily concerned with a struggle for place and office will not throw much light on the entrepreneurial Radicals of mid-Victorian Britain, few of whom were ambitious in a conventional sense. A more promising approach is to look at the ideas and values of these men, in an attempt to see what difficulties, ideological as well as practical, they encountered when they tried to apply them to the complex problems confronting Parliament and Government. The present study, therefore, is issue-oriented. It re-examines the great political controversies of the middle decades of the nineteenth century by asking what contribution was made to their resolution by Radical industrialists and merchants once they had forced their way into Westminster. At the same time, it also deals with a somewhat wider group of politicians (including Robert Lowe), not all of whom came from business backgrounds, but who, like the entrepreneurial Radicals proper, self-consciously sought to replace aristocratic traditions of government by the 'rational' criteria of the market as embodied in the 'laws' of political economy.

When this approach is adopted, it becomes apparent that one of the main obstacles facing those attempting such change was less the hostility of opponents or the seductive power of a 'gentlemanly' way of life but rather the difficulty of deciding what it actually was that they were trying to achieve. Were the entrepreneurial Radicals primarily concerned to further their material interests? Or was it more important for them to vindicate the claims of people of their 'order' to be treated with the respect to which they thought themselves entitled? Secondly, what did their beloved laws of political economy really *mean*? And were they really willing to follow the implications of these 'laws' to their logical conclusion? More basically still, to what extent did the needs of 'capitalism' coincide with the actual political and economic demands that were being advanced by flesh-and-blood capitalists?

[60] But for two recent studies of national politics which have important implications for class relations in the mid-Victorian period, see Peter Mandler, *Aristocratic Government in the Age of Reform: Whigs and Liberals, 1830–1852* (Oxford, 1990), and E. D. Steele, *Palmerston and Liberalism, 1855–1865* (Cambridge, 1991).

I

Class Politics in the 1840s

Whose interest was it to have the Corn Laws repealed? It was the interest solely of the manufacturing capitalist.

(Disraeli, 1848)

The manufacturers having beaten the land on the corn question, the land said, 'We will retaliate a little on mills.'

(Lord Brougham, 17 May 1847)

THE CLASS IMPLICATIONS OF THE CORN LAW STRUGGLE

The Anti-Corn Law League, at least in its inception, was very much a 'business organization', the only major political movement to have been launched from within a Chamber of Commerce.[1] Cobden was a calico printer, and the comrades-in-arms with whom he was associated in this venture were nearly all of them successful Lancastrian businessmen: John Benjamin Smith, a cotton dealer; George Wilson (the movement's organizing genius), a corn merchant who later became a glue manufacturer with important railway interests; and John Bright, a second-generation cotton spinner from Rochdale. The 'second-string leaders' on the executive committee[2] also tended to come from the ranks of the mill-owners; among the latter was the Quaker Henry Ashworth of Bolton, Cobden's close friend.

Moreover, it was as an articulator of the wishes and needs of the manufacturing centres that the Anti-Corn Law League often chose to present itself. For example, after Cobden, at a big League rally at Covent Garden Theatre in December 1845, had made a soothing speech about free trade ensuring harmony between the classes, John Bright began his oration on a quite different note:

Notwithstanding the hope that my Friend who has just addressed you has expressed, that [our agitation] may not become a strife of classes, I am not sure that it has not already become such, and I doubt whether it can have any other character. I believe

---

[1] See material in the John Benjamin Smith Papers, MS 923.2, S338.
[2] Howe, *Cotton Masters*, 215.

this to be a movement of the commercial and industrious classes against the lords and great proprietors of the soil.[3]

Cobden must have winced at the aggressive impetuosity of his younger colleague. But the activities of the Anti-Corn Law League make much more sense if Bright's, rather than Cobden's, characterization of the movement is accepted. Later, with the 'cause' making notable headway, Cobden himself was prepared to admit that, at least initially, those who created the League had 'entered upon this struggle with the belief that we had some distinct class interest in the question'.[4]

Yet what can this 'class interest' have been? What impelled a textile manufacturer like Henry Ashworth to devote at least one-quarter of his time to Anti-Corn Law League business[5] at a time when the work of a factory owner could not conveniently be delegated to others? And why did the various League appeals raise so much money so quickly from its key supporters, most of them manufacturers? Or again, why, in the middle of the Corn Law crisis, did a thousand Bradford merchants, bankers, professional men, worsted spinners, manufacturers, shopkeepers, and other tradesmen write a letter to *The Times* in support of Repeal?[6]

There may, of course, have been 'hidden' class interests at work which the Leaguers could not avow, even to themselves. For example, it certainly seems as if many manufacturers, like Henry Ashworth, found it convenient to blame the Corn Laws for bad living conditions and for the low wages which they paid their 'hands'.[7] Confronted by Chartist and working-class hostility to the Repeal programme, Cobden was inclined to attribute that, too, to aristocratic misgovernment: 'Every instance of violence or turbulence in the great multitude of work-people ought to be laid to the charge of the aristocracy, who have drawn the utmost from their labour to spend in wars and extravagance abroad and at home, and neglected to return any portion for the expense of educating them.'[8] The one class that was entirely blameless for the sufferings of working men, it seems, was the employing class. This casting of the aristocracy in the role of scapegoat was to enjoy a long life: Lloyd George was still putting it to effective use during the constitutional crisis of 1909–11.

[3] James E. Thorold Rogers (ed.), *Speeches on Questions of Public Policy by John Bright, M.P.* (popular edn., 1883), 415. Hereafter *Bright's Speeches*.

[4] Speech at Manchester, 19 Oct. 1843, in John Bright and J. E. Thorold Rogers (eds.), *Speeches on Questions of Public Policy by Richard Cobden, M.P.* (1870; 1908 edn.), 49. Hereafter *Cobden's Speeches*.

[5] Rhodes Boyson, *The Ashworth Cotton Enterprise: The Rise and Fall of a Family Firm 1818–1880* (Oxford, 1970), 202.

[6] *The Times*, 3 July 1846; cited in Read, *Peel and the Victorians*, 241.

[7] See Boyson, *Ashworth Cotton Enterprise*, 216; also William C. Lubenow, *The Politics of Government Growth: Early Victorian Attitudes towards State Intervention 1833–1848* (Newton Abbot, 1971), 154; J. T. Ward, *The Factory Movement, 1830–1855* (1962), 247.

[8] Cobden to J. Sturge, 1 Mar. 1839; cited in Wendy Hinde, *Richard Cobden: A Victorian Outsider* (New Haven, Conn., 1987), 69.

Yet although the Leaguers clearly believed that they would derive tangible economic benefits from Repeal, a scrutiny of their public explanations does not make it entirely clear what these were supposed to be. The Chartists always suspected that the whole purpose of the exercise was to lower the level of wages.[9] Understandably enough, Cobden was anxious to dissociate himself from any such suggestion. But his reasoning varied from one occasion to another. Thus, in one big speech he argued that 'the rate of wages ha[d] no more connection with the price of food than with the moon's changes';[10] yet he sometimes made a rather different claim: namely, that 'in the manufacturing districts, whenever food is dear, wages are low; and that whenever food is low, wages rise'.[11] But Cobden's main contention (which became official League policy) was that Repeal would enable manufacturers to increase exports to foreign countries and that the general opening up of trade which Repeal would bring in its wake would therefore increase *general* prosperity by cheapening the cost of bread and creating more employment.[12] He also predicted that the prosperity of the manufacturing districts would spill over into the agricultural areas by raising urban demand for agricultural products. Repeal, therefore, would be in everyone's interest: manufacturer, operative, and agriculturist alike.

Historians have disagreed over whether or not the outcome justified these predictions.[13] Yet narrow economic calculations were probably not that important to *either* side in the controversy. For what the Anti-Corn Law League represented was an assault by an 'excluded' urban élite on the social dominance and virtual monopoly of political power of the aristocratic Establishment. The original petition of the Manchester Chamber of Commerce had made this clear. 'The Commerce and Manufactures of Great Britain are the chief cause of the wealth and power of the country,' began its proud statement, 'and afford an important resource for the employment of the population.' Cotton, it went on, was 'the staple manufacture of the Empire'. 'Any laws which establish[ed] a distinction between the *rights* of landowners

[9] This charge was used against pro-League candidates in the 1841 general election: T. L. Crosby, *Sir Robert Peel's Administration* (Newton Abbot, 1976), 30–1. See Ian D. C. Newbould, 'Whiggery and the Dilemma of Reform: Liberals, Radicals and the Melbourne Administration, 1835–9', *Bulletin of the Institute of Historical Research*, 53 (1980), 229–41.

[10] 25 Aug. 1841, *Cobden's Speeches*, 4.

[11] 13 Mar. 1845, ibid. 143.

[12] Though this, of course, could only have happened if Britain took in *large* quantities of foreign wheat. See Betty Kemp, 'Reflections on the Repeal of the Corn Laws', *Victorian Studies*, 5 (1961–2), 193. The Leaguers argued that, by artificially raising the price of bread, the Corn Laws damaged the efficiency of the labourer, whose industry, skill, and intelligence were 'the capital of the English nation' (W. Cooke Taylor, *Notes of a Tour in the Manufacturing Districts of Lancashire* (based on 2nd edn. of 1842; reissued 1968), 153.

[13] Read, *Peel and the Victorians*, 259; Norman McCord, *The Anti-Corn Law League 1838–1846* (1958), 208–9; S. Fairlie, 'The Nineteenth-Century Corn Law Reconsidered', *Economic History Review*, 18 (1965), 544–61.

and Manufacturers', said the Chamber, were 'unjust and offensive.'[14] In short, in a 'class struggle' of the kind in which the League was engaged, considerations of immediate pecuniary advantage played only a small part.

The northern manufacturers, then, saw themselves as locked in a power struggle for the control of society.[15] Another way of thinking about this elemental conflict was to portray the 'progressive' cities as being at war with the 'feudal' countryside. In *Bleak House* (1853) Dickens perceptively shows his great aristocrat Sir Leicester Dedlock confusing Watt, the engineer, with Wat Tyler, the leader of the Peasants' Revolt! Manufacturers and landowners, it almost seemed, were engaged in a kind of civil war. Indeed, at moments of high tension, as during the climacteric of the Repeal campaign, the Leaguers were inclined to talk as though the two groups belonged to different *races*, with a subject race, the Saxons, having risen up in revolt against the Norman feudal caste that had quartered itself on British soil.[16] Hence the fight against 'feudalism' could be portrayed as the attempt by a subject people to throw off the 'Norman yoke'.[17] The *Norfolk News* argued in precisely these terms as late as 1855.[18]

Opponents frequently expressed dismay at such displays of 'class feeling'. But Cobden and his friends saw no reason to desist as long as the existing aristocratic system remained in place. It is significant that at several stages in the 1840s League leaders should have seriously considered resorting to lock-outs, in order to put pressure on the Government. For a time Cobden was also quite interested in the idea of organizing a deliberate withholding of taxes; this, he told Bright, 'would terrify the enemy far more than pikes or pistols'.[19] Eventually he came out against both these stratagems (which Bright favoured); but he did so because he doubted, and with good reason, whether they could be planned with sufficient thoroughness to be effective. He did not question their morality. In fact, Peel's Government believed that some of the textile magnates had initially encouraged the working-class disturbances that culminated in the 1842 'Plug Plot'; and for a time the authorities treated the

---

[14] Manchester Chamber of Commerce petition, 27 Dec. 1837, John Benjamin Smith Papers, MS 923.2, S338.

[15] McCord, *Anti-Corn Law League*, 185–6. Taylor, *Notes of a Tour*, 52–5.

[16] McCord, *Anti-Corn Law League*, 185–6. See also D. G. Wright, 'The Second Reform Agitation', in D. G. Wright and J. A. Jowitt (eds.), *Victorian Bradford* (Bradford, 1981), 166.

[17] See Christopher Hill, 'The Norman Yoke', in *Puritanism and Revolution* (1958), 50–122. But Hill does not realize that this myth was used, not just by working-class Radicals, but by Radical manufacturers in the early 19th cent.

[18] *Norfolk News*, 3 Feb. 1855. Thomas Carlyle in *Past and Present* (1843; Ward Lock & Co. edn., 1910), 245–6, portrayed the English aristocracy as facing a crisis similar to that faced by the French aristocracy on the eve of the Revolution.

[19] Hinde, *Richard Cobden*, 109. In 1841 Cobden advised caution on the idea of a 'tax strike' (McCord, *Anti-Corn Law League*, 109–10); and a year later he ruled out the plan of mill-owners closing down their factories, on the ground that it would not work (ibid. 124).

League as though it constituted a revolutionary threat only slightly less serious than Chartism.[20]

To the manufacturers who supported the Anti-Corn Law League, then, the landowners constituted 'the enemy', and in early 1843 they moved out from the cities into the countryside, and started attacking the enemy in its main bastions.

The most effective of their campaigns was perhaps the freehold purchase movement, whereby supporters of the League were helped to purchase small plots of land that would entitle them to qualify as 40s. freeholders in county elections.[21] When, somewhat surprisingly, the Appeal Court ruled, in the cases of *Marshall* v. *Bown* in February 1845 and *Alexander* v. *Newman* in January 1846, that votes created in this way were valid, the path was open for the League to flood the county constituencies with its urban adherents.[22]

To the Leaguers this stratagem held a double attraction. On the one hand, it would foster among working men and shopkeepers those qualities of prudence and thrift to which the middle classes attributed so much importance.[23] But at the same time freehold purchase would have the effect of 'contaminating' the counties with Radical urban voters. There is no doubt that many Radical activists believed that in the course of a few years enough 40s. freeholders could be created 'to rescue half the counties of England from the domination of the landlords'.[24] The mere prospect of this happening, according to the Cobdenite *Manchester Examiner and Times*, 'would alarm the landlords into large concessions of fiscal and financial reform'—an optimistic view of the situation which Cobden, initially at least, shared.[25]

How successful such activities were in purely electoral terms is an issue over which historians have differed.[26] But since it was only in the counties with large urban agglomerations that the freehold purchase scheme could be expected to work, the Leaguers knew that they could not win over Parliament until they had broken the social dominance of the great landowners in the small boroughs and the *rural* counties. Hence the League's second ploy, aimed at winning over the farmers. As we have seen, Cobden thought this to be quite feasible; indeed, he assumed that the farmers were his natural

---

[20] Nicholas C. Edsall, *Richard Cobden: Independent Radical* (Cambridge, Mass., 1986), 111–14.
[21] 26 Nov. 1849, *Cobden's Speeches*, 553.
[22] John Prest, *Politics in the Age of Cobden* (1977), 90–3.
[23] See Ch. 6.
[24] *Sheffield Independent*, 18 Nov. 1848.
[25] *Manchester Examiner*, 3 Feb. 1849. Cobden, 11 Dec. 1844, 13 Nov. 1845, *Cobden's Speeches*, 122–3, 171.
[26] Prest, *Politics*, 95–102. See also D. A. Hamer, *The Politics of Electoral Pressure: A Study in the History of Victorian Reform Agitations* (Hassocks, 1977), 84–6. On the Protectionists' vigorous counter-attack, see Angus Macintyre, 'Lord George Bentinck and the Protectionists: A Lost Cause?', *Transactions of the Royal Historical Society*, 39 (1989), 143–4.

allies and only needed encouragement to speak out against the Protectionist aristocracy.

A main plank in this strategy was to try to persuade farmers that their standard of living need not suffer under Repeal provided they went over to 'high farming'. On the contrary, said the Leaguers, the 'threat' of Repeal would provide just the stimulus to greater competitive effort that, in the long run, would be the salvation of British agriculture. 'We are the great agricultural improvers of this country,' Cobden proclaimed audaciously. 'Amongst the other glories which will attach to the name of Manchester will be this, that the Manchester men not only brought manufactures to perfection, but that they made the agriculturists also, in spite of themselves, bring their trade to perfection.'[27] This would happen because Free Trade in corn would 'stimulate the cultivation of the poorer soils by compelling the application of more capital and labour to them'.[28]

Time and again Cobden asked agriculturalists to follow the example of Lancashire. Had the cotton manufacturers created their industry by looking to Parliament for assistance, he asked? No, they owed their achievements to hard work, the judicious application of skill and capital, and commercial acumen.[29] 'You must have men of capital on your land; you must let your land on mercantile principles,' said Cobden in March 1849.[30] Indeed, in his famous Commons speech of March 1845, he had even suggested that the Anti-Corn Law League might form a joint stock association, with the aim of purchasing an estate and running a model farm on proper business lines.[31] At present the main impediment to agricultural efficiency was 'a want of capital'. Once that deficiency had been remedied, Cobden said, tenant farmers 'would be as successful men of business and traders and manufacturers as their countrymen'.[32] However, he claimed, capital shrank instinctively from insecurity of tenure.[33] The answer lay in the granting of long leases, which, in the words of *The League*, would be 'marketable securities' upon which the farmer could raise money, if need be; agriculturalists would then be placed on the same level as 'other industrious employers of capital'.[34] At the very least, there should be recognition of 'tenant right'.[35]

But that, in turn, would mean a social revolution in the countryside,

---

[27] 19 Oct. 1843, *Cobden's Speeches*, 52.

[28] 8 Feb. 1844, ibid. 63.

[29] e.g. 12 Mar. 1844, ibid. 86–7. See Bright's later observations, 11 Apr. 1851, *Bright's Speeches*, 434.

[30] 8 Mar. 1849, *Cobden's Speeches*, 207.

[31] 13 Mar. 1845, ibid. 137–8. Cheshire, he once observed, could treble its agricultural output if only it were run more efficiently (24 Oct. 1844, ibid. 114).

[32] 13 Mar. 1845, ibid. 134.

[33] 13 Mar. 1845, ibid. 135.

[34] *The League*, 20 Sept. 1845, p. 825. See Cobden's speech of 13 Mar. 1845, *Cobden's Speeches*, 137.

[35] 9 Jan. 1850, *Cobden's Speeches*, 228.

something which Bright and Cobden thought desirable in any case. The tenant farmers to whom these two Radicals looked for a regeneration of agriculture would be not just 'men of capital', but also 'men of independence', men who could think for themselves and would contemptuously spurn the notion of social or political subservience to a landlord. Cobden was always reminding his audience that landowners were not themselves agriculturists; they were merely rent-owners.[36] Farmers would first have to learn to stand up for their rights. Subsequently landowners and tenants could come together 'in their separate capacity as buyers and sellers; so that they might deal together as other men of business'.[37] But if that were to occur, farmers would have to feel more pride in their class, and recognize that in certain respects their interests conflicted with those of their landlords. At a more basic level, farmers, like the rest of the community, would have to abandon what Cobden liked to call their 'superstitious' attitude to land: the false belief that, somehow, land differed radically from other kinds of property.

This led the Leaguers to broaden their strategy by launching an attack on the aristocratic ethos of landed society, symbolized in particular by the existence of field sports. Interestingly, when Cobden entered into ownership of his little estate, he authorized his tenants to kill and eat all the rabbits and hares they could find: 'I must confess', he said, 'that I have no taste whatever for the preservation of such vermin, which I believe to be utterly inconsistent with good farming, and the greatest obstacle to the employment of the labourers.'[38] Bright, who felt even more strongly on the matter (calling the Game Laws 'abhorrent to the civilization of our day'[39]), succeeded in 1845 in forcing the Government to set up a Select Committee to look into the subject, upon which he was joined by his fellow-Leaguers Milner Gibson and Villiers. Soon they were locked in battle with landed society (one of whose spokesman was the Protectionist Lord George Bentinck).[40]

The dispute over the Game Laws really centred on a fundamental difference of values. While Colonel Sibthorp fulminated against impertinent Quakers who sought to undermine one of the pillars of the landed estate,[41] Bright stepped up his attacks on the Game Laws, his determination strengthened by a recent case in which a poacher had been hanged:

Surely Manchester may yet again lead the crusade against the wretches who learn nothing from revolutions abroad, and who are blindly intent on their own destruction

---

[36] 17 Feb. 1843, ibid. 16.

[37] 9 Jan. 1850, ibid. 228. Bright, too, suggested that 'the old retainer and chieftain theory' be replaced by a commercial relationship (11 Apr. 1851, *Bright's Speeches*, 436).

[38] 9 Jan. 1850, *Cobden's Speeches*, 226.

[39] 11 Apr. 1851, *Bright's Speeches*, 435.

[40] Chester Kirby, 'The Attack on the English Game Laws in the Forties', *Journal of Modern History*, 4 (1932), 18–37; see also Parl. Deb., 3rd ser., vol. 97, 919–49: 23 Mar. 1848; Kirby, 'Attack', 29–30; *The League*, 1 Feb. 1845.

[41] Parl. Deb., 3rd ser., vol. 97, 951–3: 23 Mar. 1848; see Kirby, 'Attack', 37.

[he exploded to George Wilson]. We are the slaves of a privileged class—brutal in its propensities, assured of its power, and blind to the retribution which may, and I believe will, overtake them.[42]

Bright seems to have enjoyed some success with farmers over the Game Laws issue. But in other respects the farming community proved to be very difficult to seduce.[43] Indeed, the 'Anti-League', which came into existence in 1844 to combat the Cobdenites, though it accepted the Duke of Richmond and the Duke of Buckingham as its national leaders, was really the creation of angry tenant farmers, who continued to provide its main impetus.[44] Cobden affected to believe that the agricultural Protectionists were rarely farmers, but more often lawyers, land valuers, and auctioneers.[45] On other occasions, and with better justification, he spoke of farmers having been 'talked to and frightened by their landlords'.[46]

But here, too, there was much wishful thinking. The fact is that the tenant farmer had the most to lose from Repeal. Big landowners, like the Earl of Ducie, might have possessed the resources to engage in high farming; but most tenant farmers did not. As Robert Stewart says, whereas Cobden presented 'high farming' as an alternative to Protection, tenant farmers themselves, with good reason, tended to see Protection as the precondition for embarking upon this costly gamble.[47] But, once again, more than economic calculations were at issue. Significantly, livestock farmers (admittedly annoyed at the ending of the ban on imports of live farm animals in 1842) stood by the Corn Laws with as much fervour as the cereal farmers, though they seemingly had nothing to gain by doing so.

In one respect, however, the class politics of the 1840s were more complex than has so far been admitted. For although Cobden never wavered in his allegiance to 'his' order, the manufacturing and commercial class, he also genuinely believed that the inauguration of Free Trade would usher in an era of *universal* prosperity. Underpinning this optimism lay a body of theory which Cobden, himself no theoretician, seems to have derived mainly from James Wilson, the editor of *The Economist*, founded in 1843, initially as a pro-Repeal organ. Wilson's importance to Cobden was that he supplied an alternative economic model to that of the other classical economists, like Ricardo. The latter had argued that, were the Corn Laws to disappear, corn prices would

---

[42] Bright to George Wilson, 25 Mar. 1848, George Wilson Papers.

[43] See Southgate, *Passing of the Whigs*, 126.

[44] Travis L. Crosby, *English Farmers and the Politics of Protection 1815–1852* (Hassocks, 1977), 130–5.

[45] 8 May 1844, *Cobden's Speeches*, 89; a line repeated in *The League* and reprinted in Crosby, *English Farmers*, 134.

[46] 27 Feb. 1846, *Cobden's Speeches*, 195.

[47] Robert Stewart, *The Politics of Protection: Lord Derby and the Protectionist Party 1841–1852* (Cambridge, 1971), 38–9.

fall; but so, *pari passu*, would the labourer's wages, so Repeal would not materially benefit the working class and would actually damage the farmers. Wilson, however, set out to demonstrate that a free exchange of goods and services (involving a total commitment to laissez-faire) would minister to the prosperity of *everyone*. He developed this thesis in two pamphlets published in 1839. The Corn Laws, he argued, had brought about sharp fluctuations in price which benefited no one and hurt the agriculturalists especially. Moreover, European corn producers enjoyed no cost advantage which would enable them to flood the British market. So British farmers had no need to worry about Repeal; on the contrary, they would actually be enriched by it.[48] At an economic level, the same applied to the land-owning class.

It seems clear that these pamphlets, which received much publicity, quickly came to the attention of the League leaders. Before long, Cobden in particular was using very similar arguments. As a result, he was able to hold out a promise of economic progress from which adversarial conflict had been banished—in that there would be no economic 'losers'.[49] But Cobden combined this belief in the possibility of a harmonious reconciliation of the economic interests of all social classes—indeed, of humanity itself—with a very hard-headed awareness of the inevitability of social conflict, the very thought of which actually filled him with exhilaration. How could two such seemingly contradictory beliefs be held?

The answer may lie in an important letter which Cobden wrote to James Wilson in May 1839. Replying to Wilson's characteristically sanguine expression of belief that the League's land-owning opponents would shortly see the desirability, even for themselves, of promoting Repeal, Cobden pointed out:

I think you have lost sight of one *gain* to the aristocratic landowners—the *political* power arising out of the present state of their tenantry—and political power in this country has been pecuniary gain.... There is also another point: We say, and justly, that the land would increase in value through the increase of trade by freeing commerce. But we forget the jealousy that feudal lords have to the growth of plebeian fortunes. If the agriculture is only to increase in profit through the extension of the trading interest, then the landlord takes his proper place secondary to the merchant or cotton-spinner. But the aristocracy prefer their present relative position at the expense of some positive loss.[50]

---

[48] Cobden, too, argued that the British farmer would be protected by *distance* (12 Mar. 1844, *Cobden's Speeches*, 72).

[49] Thus, Cobdenite economic theory, in so far as there was such a thing, seems to owe less to Ricardo or even Smith than to James Wilson and to Cobden's contemporary and enthusiastic admirer Frédéric Bastiat, author of 'Harmonies Économiques'. On the importance of the writings of James Wilson to the propaganda of the Anti-Corn Law League, see Scott Gordon, 'The London *Economist* and the High Tide of Laissez-Faire', *Journal of Political Economy*, 6 (1955), 465–7. One of Wilson's heroes was Bastiat.

[50] Cobden to J. Wilson, 3 May 1839, in Emilie I. Barrington, *The Servant of All: Pages from the Family, Social and Political Life of My Father James Wilson* ... (1927), i. 27–8.

In other words, even though the landowners might not benefit economically from agricultural protection, the very existence of the Corn Laws betokened their occupation of a privileged position from which flowed both social prestige and other kinds of *economic* advantage. Cobden was obviously thinking here of the exploitation by landed society of the political patronage to which it had easy access, especially in the Army and the Navy: 'How could your aristocracy endure without this expenditure for wars and armaments?', he once asked.[51] Such activity was, of course, perfectly legal; but Cobden thought it to be *illegitimate*, and wanted it excluded from the untrammelled pursuit of economic advantage. He knew, however, that this could not be achieved without a fierce political struggle.

True, there were occasions on which Cobden could be found making adroit appeals to his 'class opponents'. For example, in March 1845, in one of his most influential Commons speeches in support of Repeal, he nonplussed the Conservative front bench by saying: 'You, gentlemen of England, the high aristocracy of England, your forefathers led my forefathers; you may lead us again if you choose.... But this is a new era.... If you identify yourselves with the spirit of the age, you may yet do well.'[52] Although Cobden occasionally spoke this way in *public*, also acknowledging the support that the League was receiving from enlightened aristocrats, his softer tone was clearly intended to embarrass his opponents.[53] In any case, although the Free Traders repeatedly attempted to reassure the landed and agricultural interest about the consequences of Repeal, it was to little avail. Even if the Leaguers' promises were believed, they were not sufficient to reconcile a large section of the landed classes to the threatened loss of their dominant social and political position.[54]

To the farming community, on the other hand, Cobden might have been expected to have had a greater appeal. Some historians think it highly significant that in 1846, with his business interests in ruin as a consequence of his political commitments, Cobden should have used most of the £76,000 voted him by his grateful supporters for the purchase of his original family home and its estate, where, as he later put it, he was to be found 'deep in mangolds and pigs'.[55] Indeed, most of Cobden's adult life (as well as of his youth) was spent in 'rural isolation' in Sussex, rather than in Lancashire,[56] though, of course, he continued to represent northern constituencies: the West Riding between 1847 and 1857 and Rochdale after 1859.

Although poor health (which rendered him ill-suited to the Lancashire

[51] Cobden to Ashworth, 27 Aug. 1860, John Morley, *Cobden*, ii. 362.
[52] 13 Mar. 1845, *Cobden's Speeches*, 145. But this speech can also be construed as a threat.
[53] Edsall, *Cobden*, 149.
[54] Stewart, *Politics of Protection*, 38–40.
[55] Cobden to Parkes, 28 July 1857, Morley, *Cobden*, i. 200.
[56] Edsall, *Cobden*, 27. For Bright's anxiety over the political consequences of Cobden's 'rural isolation', see Bright to Cobden, 1 Jan. 1855, John Bright Papers, Add. MS 43,384, fo. 4.

climate) had much to do with Cobden's retreat to the Sussex Weald, the latter also testifies, as many historians rightly observe, to his lifelong interest in the countryside and in agricultural pursuits. This, they say, marked him off from almost all other members of the Manchester School, and goes some way to account for his effectiveness as an advocate of Repeal; alone among the League leaders he was able to address audiences of farmers with first-hand knowledge of their problems. A close supporter of Cobden's, the Revd Henry Dunckley, could describe him as 'a thorough Englishman, true to the traditions and sentiments which he inherited as the descendant of a race of Sussex yeomen, never more at home than when in company with farmers, discussing the state of their crops'.[57] Indeed, Cobden often chose to portray himself in just this way.[58] He told the Commons on one occasion that he had 'something like an hereditary right to identify [him]self with farmers'.[59] This made him a very formidable antagonist to the 'landed interest' which dominated mid-Victorian Parliaments.

Cobden also differed from his political partner, John Bright, according to Read, in that his knowledge of the agricultural south as well as the industrial north gave him a 'national' perspective on politics, which was missing in Bright, the archetypal 'northerner'.[60] This, in turn, is used to explain Cobden's habit of presenting Repeal not just as something due to the textile industry and the population it employed, but as the precondition of the welfare of *all* classes in the community, including farmers and even landlords.[61]

How much substance is there in this line of argument? First of all, it is misleading to give the impression that Cobden's social background was particularly unusual for a first-generation manufacturer of his period. Crouzet, for example, has shown that 12 per cent of fathers of founders of large industrial undertakings in Britain between 1750 and 1850 were either owner-occupiers or tenant farmers, a proportion which rises to over 14 per cent in the case of textiles.[62] (This is not altogether surprising, since at a time of industrial take-off the new entrepreneurs had to come from *somewhere*!)

It is true that, probably as a result of his family background, Cobden took a concerned interest in the problems of agriculture. But his speeches on this

---

[57] Revd Henry Dunckley, *Richard Cobden and the Jubilee of Free Trade* (1896), 63.

[58] e.g. 3 July 1844, *Cobden's Speeches*, 99.

[59] See his interesting speech of 9 Feb. 1844, ibid. 65; also his speech of 13 Mar. 1845: 'I have as wide and extensive an acquaintance with farmers as any Member in this House' (ibid. 141).

[60] Donald Read, *Cobden and Bright: A Victorian Political Partnership* (1967), 95–6. See Bagehot's observations in 'Lord Palmerston at Bradford', *Economist*, 13 Aug. 1864; reprinted in *Collected Works*, iii. 281.

[61] Edsall, *Cobden*, 150–2.

[62] François Crouzet, *The First Industrialists: The Problem of Origins* (Cambridge, 1985), 122–3, 147. Another entrepreneurial Radical from this background was the great contractor Samuel Morton Peto. See the biographical sketches by Clyde Binfield in the *Biographical Dictionary of Modern British Radicals*, vol. 2: 1830–1870 (Hassocks, 1984), ii. 407–11, and by P. L. Cottrell in *Dictionary of Business Biography*, 4 (1985), 644–52.

subject are instructive. He believed that British farming stood in need, not of protection, but of technical improvement, under the supervision of 'men of capital and energy'. A fine example had been set, he said, by the enlightened Earl of Ducie, a convert to Free Trade: one of those men 'who look upon land as we manufacturers do upon the raw material of the fabrics which we make'.[63] Such appeals (they were normally addressed to farmers) are interesting. But they hardly seem to constitute evidence that Cobden, as a 'southerner', had some viewpoint which distinguished him from the textile manufacturers. On the contrary, someone who could seriously suggest that cornfields be modelled on cotton factories must surely be seen as an extreme ideologist of the entrepreneurial middle class.

Nor, for all his undoubted love of the Sussex countryside, was Cobden in any doubt as to where his allegiance lay in the 'battle of civilizations': in that struggle between urban and rural England which was so pronounced a feature of the early Victorian period. In his campaign to secure the incorporation of Manchester in 1838, Cobden had urged the necessity of placing 'for ever the population of our town and neighbourhood beyond the control of a booby squirearchy, who abhor us not more for our love of political freedom, than for those active and intellectual pursuits which contrast so strongly with that mental stupor in which they exist—I had almost said—vegetate'.[64] And later, in the summer of 1848, he expressed fury when Disraeli attacked the urban population to the cheers of his supporters: 'I intend to turn the tables upon the majority who so vociferously applauded his buffoonery by taking up the gauntlet in the name of the great towns,' he told George Wilson.[65] Like one of his famous contemporaries, Cobden was liable to be contemptuous of 'the idiocies of rural life'.

Cobden also resembled other entrepreneurial Radicals in taking a great pride in the wonders of modern technology to which the manufacturers owed so much of their wealth, and was always ready to sing its praises.[66] Thus, the only way in which Cobden can really be called a 'national' figure is that he did at least *address* the question of the fate of the agriculturalists after Repeal and try to fit this into his system of thought; but, in the battle of civilizations, his prime allegiance always lay with the manufacturing North.

For the real issue was whether agriculture should be treated as central to British social and political life. Most Tories thought that it should be. Disraeli, for example, called upon the Government to 'maintain [a] balance

---

[63] 12 Mar. 1844, *Cobden's Speeches*, 86.

[64] Richard Cobden, *Incorporate Your Borough* (1838), 6.

[65] Cobden to George Wilson, 24 June 1848, George Wilson Papers. See Cobden's outburst in the Commons on Disraeli's second budget of 1852 (13 Dec. 1852, *Cobden's Speeches*, 272–3). For the context of this speech, see Ch. 2.

[66] For Cobden's excitement over the new cable link with America, see Cobden to J. B. Smith, 25 Aug. 1858, John Benjamin Smith Papers, MS 923.2, S345, fo. 73.

between the two great branches of national industry', manufacturing and agriculture; but he then went on to argue that England ought to give a 'preponderance, for that is the proper and constitutional word, to the agricultural branch', because 'in England we have a territorial Constitution', and such a Constitution is 'the only barrier against that centralising system which has taken root in other countries'. Repeal would mean a subjection to 'the thraldom of Capital', Disraeli predicted.[67]

It was on precisely this ground that many landowners rejected Free Trade, even when they had something to gain from the process of urban and industrial growth. Lord George Bentinck is reputed to have said that, although he had been told that Free Trade would personally save him £1,500 a year, he could not bear to be 'sold'—testimony, as Angus Macintyre says, to his passionate belief in an aristocratic code which emphasized duty, consistency, and honesty.[68] Moreover, as Kitson Clark has noted, even in the mid-Victorian period agriculture was not organized for profit, but rather 'to secure the survival intact of a caste'.[69] Landowners did not see their estates simply as an economic resource, but more as an inheritance which guaranteed the perpetuation of a particular way of life, carrying with it onerous responsibilities but also legitimate privileges.

Thus, a gulf of sentiment separated the two sides. Free Trade, opined the *Quarterly Review* in December 1849,

is in its very essence a mercenary, unsocial, democratising system opposed to all generous notions, all kindly feelings. Based on selfishness—the most pervading as well as the most powerful of our vicious propensities—it directs that impulse into the lowest of all channels, the mere sordid pursuit of wealth. It teaches competition and isolation, instead of co-operation and brotherhood; it substitutes a vague and impractical cosmopolitanism for a lofty and ennobling patriotism; it disregards the distress of the poor . . . Wealth is its end and Mammon its divinity.

In short, Free Trade was 'a selfish, sordid, and degrading creed'.[70] This, too, was the message of the 'Young Englanders'. Lord John Manners, for

---

[67] Parl. Deb., 3rd ser., vol. 83, 1346–7: 20 Feb. 1846. Cited and discussed in Bernard Semmel, *The Rise of Free Trade Imperialism* (Cambridge, 1970), 155–6. For similar sentiments, see Disraeli's speech in Parliament on 14 Feb. 1843, cited in William Flavelle Monypenny, *Life of Benjamin Disraeli Earl of Beaconsfield*, vol. 2: 1837–1846 (1912), 138.

[68] Cited in Monypenny, *Disraeli*, 360. Bentinck thought that such bad behaviour would shock 'the mind of the Middle Classes' (Macintyre, 'Lord George Bentinck', 146). For the agriculturalists' appreciation that Repeal was not a narrowly economic question but was essentially about the political domination of the landed gentry, see Robert Stewart, *Party and Politics 1830–1852* (1989), 85.

[69] G. Kitson Clark, *The Making of Victorian England* (1962), 218. However, as Macintyre says, it has never been demonstrated that Protectionist landowners were any less interested in 'high farming' than those who supported Repeal (Macintyre, 'Lord George Bentinck', 155).

[70] *Quarterly Review*, 86 (1849), 182; cited in Stewart, *Politics of Protection*, 46. *Blackwood's Magazine* took a similar line; see 'The Late and the Present Ministry', *Blackwood's Magazine*, 60 (Aug. 1846), 251; cited in Macintyre, 'Lord George Bentinck', 158.

example, believed that 'commercialism' was the enemy of civilization, whereas 'feudalism' was something to be admired, the very reverse of Cobden's position.[71]

THE FACTORY QUESTION

The contempt felt by many sections of landed society for the world of the northern mill-owners found expression in the 'factory movement', which can be seen, in part, as a 'feudal' counter-attack on its middle-class detractors. Lord Ashley, the leader of the reformers, bewailed 'the National Sin of this accursed system' (meaning the factory system),[72] and the 'Tory Radical' Richard Oastler defiantly proclaimed: 'Cotton Mills are not a necessity—fields are. England was a great nation when Manchester was a little hamlet.'[73] So disgusted was Oastler with the factory system and with the 'Manchester philosophy' which that system had spawned that he even managed to convince himself that the old handicrafts could be revived. If that proved impossible, he at least wanted to protect the exploited mill-hands from their capitalist masters; so he became an enthusiastic proponent of the legislative limitation of the working day in factories (the Ten Hour Day).[74]

The Tory Radicals, like Oastler and his fiery disciple, William Busfeild Ferrand, combined their campaign for a Ten Hours Bill with attacks on the New Poor Law, seeing both as attempts to destroy the traditional rights of the poor so that a handful of rich capitalists could get richer.[75] Initially Oastler and his friends assumed landowners to be the natural allies of the working class against the capitalists. But by the end of the 1830s, events had led them to the conclusion that the landed magnates, by their unwillingness to shoulder their traditional responsibilities for the poor, had dissolved 'the social contract' and that, in consequence, the working class was morally entitled to resist its oppressors.[76]

Yet disillusionment with the aristocracy did nothing to weaken the Tory Radicals' commitment to an idealistic paternalism, which they associated

---

[71] Geoffrey Faber, *Young England* (1987), 138. Manners, however, also used the same term in a hostile sense about the mill-owners (ibid. 106). Disraeli also defended 'feudalism' in his parliamentary speech of 14 Feb. 1843; cited in Monypenny, *Disraeli*, 141–2. On the links between 'the protectionist mentality' and the revived interest in medievalism and chivalry, see Macintyre, 'Lord George Bentinck', 153–4, n. 39.

[72] Ward, *Factory Movement*, 265.

[73] Ibid. 393.

[74] On Oastler, see Cecil Driver, *Tory Radical: The Life of Richard Oastler* (New York, 1946).

[75] On how the anti-Poor Law campaigners came into conflict with the factory owners, especially Henry Ashworth, see Nicholas C. Edsall, *The Anti-Poor Law Movement, 1834–44* (Manchester, 1971), 51–2, 60; Boyson, *Ashworth Cotton Enterprise*, 190–1. Oastler opined: 'Had there been no New Poor Law, there would have been no Anti-Corn Law League' (Ward, *Factory Movement*, 268).

[76] Edsall, *Anti-Poor Law Movement*, 177–9.

with the best traditions of rural society. Still less did it soften their hostility either to political economy as a creed or to the mill-owners. Against the latter, in fact, they launched a series of intensely bitter class attacks. Thus, in September 1841 Ferrand, newly elected as Conservative MP for Knaresborough, lashed out against the northern manufacturers, accusing Cobden and the mill-owners of making fortunes out of the misery of their operatives and creating 'a land of slavery'—to rapturous applause from many landed gentlemen.[77] Cobden was able to vindicate his record as an employer, but, as he commented privately, 'Nothing seems to be considered so decided a stigma as to brand a man a millowner.'[78] Ferrand resumed the attack on the capitalists of the Anti-Corn Law League in February of the following year.[79]

Lord Ashley, heir to the Earl of Shaftesbury's extensive Dorset estates, took a more moderate line, at least in public. When he went on a tour of the manufacturing districts in 1844, he emphasized that he was an enemy of the *abuses* of the factory system, not of the system itself.[80] But privately he was complaining that his campaign for the institution of a Ten Hour Day was being opposed by 'the most powerful array of capitalists'.[81]

It is true that most textile manufacturers reacted with fury to the very notion that the hours of adult workers in their mills should be subject to legislative restriction. The 'Manchester Men' certainly took this line. The young Cobden, for example, countered complaints about bad factory conditions by suggesting that discontented operatives could always go to America if they did not like Lancashire.[82] And Bright, whom Ashley called 'ever my most malignant enemy', was threatening as late as 1855 to close his factory down altogether if 'we mill-owners' were subjected to further interference.[83] Significantly, the Central Committee, which organized resistance to factory legislation, was led by Henry Ashworth, and its membership overlapped to a considerable extent that of the Anti-Corn Law League.[84]

Why did most mill-owners—as we shall see, there were some notable exceptions—feel so bitterly about the Factory Acts? On a theoretical level, they believed that any restraint on the behaviour of adult males (as distinct from women and children) was a grotesque violation of the plain truths of

---

[77] Parl. Deb., 3rd ser., vol. 59, 941–9: 28 Sept. 1841.

[78] Hinde, *Richard Cobden*, 104. See Ward, *Factory Movement*, 231.

[79] Ward, *Factory Movement*, 238–9; Parl. Deb., 3rd ser., vol. 60, 420–32: 14 Feb. 1842.

[80] Geoffrey B. A. M. Finlayson, *The Seventh Earl of Shaftesbury 1801–1885* (1981), 223–4, 212.

[81] 19 Mar. 1844, in Edwin Hodder, *The Life and Work of the Seventh Earl of Shaftesbury* (1887), ii. 34.

[82] See Cobden to W. C. Hunt, 21 Oct. 1836, Morley, *Cobden*, i. 464–8. He later took a more moderate position.

[83] Parl. Deb., 3rd ser., vol. 137, 613: 15 Mar. 1855. Edward Baines, jun., called the Factory Acts 'as despotic as any thing in the Prussian or Austrian system' (Edward Baines, *Letters to the Right. Hon. Lord John Russell on State Education* (1846), 123).

[84] Howe, *Cotton Masters*, 180.

political economy. Bright, for example, greeted the Ten Hours Bill with incredulity: Why did the operatives work long hours?, he asked the House. Because, he replied, like everyone else—lawyers, for example—they wished to increase their income in order to provide for their families or to improve their station in life.[85] How dare MPs interfere with this 'natural right'!

The cotton lords also expressed anxiety about the effects of foreign competition, which, they said, had not been nearly so evident earlier in the century when the pioneering Factory Acts had been passed. To retain their overseas markets, they warned, they would be forced into savage wage reductions in order to recoup the losses which they would experience under a future Ten Hours Bill.[86] But it is significant that once again the factory question became linked in many people's minds with the cause of Repeal. A Minister like James Graham thought it perverse that Parliament should be attempting to regulate factory labour so soon after abolishing the Corn Laws, and Bright agreed that the same basic principle was at stake in both issues.[87]

Self-interest, of course, must have played its part. Ward, for one, believes that manufacturers like Ashworth and Greg who strenuously opposed the factory reformers were behaving as they did only because they were bad employers.[88] In this he is echoing the complaints of Ferrand, who once accused Ashworth of being a 'trafficker in white slaves'.[89] Howe, on the other hand, argues that these men were, by the standards of the day, 'benevolent employers who stood to gain if competitors working excessive hours were brought into line'.[90] Cobden himself certainly seems to have been a considerate master, though, when Ashley introduced legislation in 1845 to regulate calico printing, he was painfully aware of his own firm's reliance on child labour, and deemed it prudent to keep a low profile when Parliament debated the matter.[91]

The case of Bright is instructive. In the Commons he presented himself as a paternalist who had provided schools and other benefits for his workforce. Yet he warned MPs that 'if they now armed the workmen against the capitalists by fixing by law ten hours, or any other number of hours for

---

[85] Parl. Deb., 3rd ser., vol. 89, 1140–2: 10 Feb. 1847. Taylor called the Ten Hours Bill 'a remedy . . . which assuredly has no parallel in the annals of quackery' (Taylor, *Notes of a Tour*, 131).

[86] Lubenow, *Politics of Government Growth*, 159. *Report of the Central Committee of the Association of Mill Owners and Manufacturers Engaged in the Cotton Trade for the Year 1844* (Manchester, 1845), 14.

[87] Parl. Deb., 3rd ser., vol. 90, 780: 3 Mar. 1847. For Bright's views, see ibid., vol. 89, 1147–8: 10 Feb. 1847; also ibid., vol. 91, 126: 17 Mar. 1847.

[88] Ward, *Factory Movement*, 202, 211.

[89] Ibid. 319.

[90] Howe, *Cotton Masters*, 182. See also Michael Sanderson, 'Education and the Factory in Industrial Lancashire, 1780–1840', *Economic History Review*, 20 (1967), 278–9.

[91] Hinde, *Richard Cobden*, 137–8. However, Cobden did speak briefly when Ashley asked leave to introduce his Bill (Parl. Deb., 3rd ser., vol. 77, 662–3: 18 Feb. 1845).

the duration of labour ... it would be impossible that the feeling which hitherto existed on the part of the manufacturers towards the operatives would continue'.[92] What Bright clearly resented was less the infringement of an abstract principle than what he saw as the singling out of industrialists for exceptional restriction by representatives of the aristocratic state.[93] In this he was following the line of the Central Committee, which expressed its sense of outrage at the 'slander and falsehood' to which mill-owners had been exposed. Not to counter these attacks, it warned, would betray an absence of 'self-respect' and a neglect of their 'duty to the order to which they belong'.[94]

Thus, in the 1840s class feeling ran high. The spokesmen for the northern manufacturers were genuinely affronted by what they saw as the hypocrisy of their land-owning opponents. In Cobden's opinion, the 'Young Englanders' were 'sad political humbugs'.[95] Why, asked the Manchester men, did these self-professed philanthropists not do something to improve the lot of the farm labourer, which, on every objective test, was far more wretched than that of the operative? Indeed, as Cobden pointed out, 'the farther you travel from the much-maligned region of tall chimneys and smoke', the lower agricultural wages tended to be.[96] Yet no one was suggesting that the hours of *agricultural* workers should be restricted.[97] When consideration was also taken of the fact that most of the aristocratic participants in the factory movement were vocal defenders of the Corn Laws, which artificially raised the cost of bread to the detriment of both rural and urban poor, what right did these 'bogus philanthropists' have to seek to protect the factory hands from their employers?[98]

A similar counter-attack was launched by Edward Baines, junior, spokesman for the West Riding industrialists. In a pamphlet of 1843 he wrote 'to vindicate the Manufacturing Districts from the aspersions cast upon them' by the likes of Lord Ashley. His pamphlet contains an eloquent panegyric on the great urban centres of northern England, praising 'that energetic and

---

[92] Ibid., vol. 89, 1146–7: 11 Feb. 1847.

[93] With perfect consistency, Bright also opposed the Government audit of railway accounts as an intolerable interference in the operation of private industry (Bright to G. Wilson, 12 July 1849, George Wilson Papers).

[94] *Report of Central Committee*, 4, 16.

[95] Cobden to Absalom Watkin, 9 July 1844, Watkin, *Alderman Cobden*, 131. Cobden was anxious lest the 'aristocracy of industry' throw itself upon 'the patronage of the landed aristocracy'. Shortly afterwards he made a public appeal to the pride of what he called 'Young Manchester'—i.e. the 'natural leaders' of industrial society (ibid. 139).

[96] 12 Mar. 1844, *Cobden's Speeches*, 78.

[97] See also Milner Gibson and Hume, Parl. Deb., 3rd ser., vol. 78, 1377, 1382: 2 Apr. 1845.

[98] See Bright's famous speech about Ashley and his friends looking at the manufacturing districts through the magnifying end of the telescope, the rural districts through the other end (Parl. Deb., 3rd ser., vol. 73, 1148–9: 15 Mar. 1844). For Peel's view of the connection between the two issues, see Robert Stewart, 'The Ten Hours and Sugar Crises of 1844: Government and the House of Commons in the Age of Reform', *Historical Journal*, 12 (1969), 42.

persevering industry, which, combined with the highest mechanical skill, large
capital, and mercantile intelligence and enterprise, constitutes the main
spring of all the foreign commerce of England'. But Baines was no less keen
to make a comparison with country districts like Ashley's Dorsetshire, where,
in respect of immorality, ignorance, and wretchedness, a state of affairs
existed far worse than anything that could be found in the much criticized
manufacturing areas.[99]

Ashley, who eventually accepted the case for Repeal, though not until 1845,
was very vulnerable to such an attack, since conditions on his father's Dorset
estates (which had recently been publicly exposed in *The Times*) were among
the worst in the country. Moreover, he was not on good terms with his family,
and for a long while he was 'happily blind to the scandals on his father's
estates', as his biographer puts it.[100] Cobden was determined to exploit
Ashley's weakness. On 17 March 1843 he reminded the House that a recent
Return had shown that one out of seven of the population of Dorset was a
pauper, a much higher ratio than in any manufacturing district.[101] And later
that year Ashworth was sent off to Dorset with instructions from Cobden to
collect 'a battery of facts which will enable us to turn the tables completely on
Lord Ashley and Co. in the next session'. 'We want you to get leave of
absence for a week to run down into Dorsetshire . . . on a tour of inspection
into those agricultural districts from which Lord Ashley goes to Parlt to *care*
for the poor manufacturers.'[102] On 12 March 1844 Cobden put this information to devastating parliamentary use.[103]

The intensity of the quarrel between the factory reformers and the textile
manufacturers can be seen in the so-called Dodd affair,[104] which was typical
of the bad-tempered exchanges which passed between the two sides. On
another occasion Lord John Manners complained to Ashworth that League
speakers, in dealing with landowners, had used terms like 'Vampires,
Bloodsuckers, calling them a class of men living upon the Bones and sinews of

---

[99] Sir Edward Baines, *The Social, Educational and Religious State of the Manufacturing Districts*
(1843), esp. iii, 54, 58–60. All this despite the general view that Baines was of a 'Whiggish'
disposition and sought 'partnership' with landed society, not, as with the League, middle-class
'pre-eminence' (Derek Fraser, 'Edward Baines', in Patricia Hollis (ed.), *Pressure from Without in
Early Victorian England* (1974), 183–209, esp. 192. A similar apologia was Taylor's *Notes of a Tour
of 1842.*

[100] J. L. and Barbara Hammond, *Lord Shaftesbury* (4th edn., 1936), 90–1.

[101] 17 Feb. 1843, *Cobden's Speeches*, 16.

[102] Cobden to Ashworth, 1 Dec. 1843, Cobden Papers, Add. MS 43,653, fos. 64–5.

[103] 12 Mar. 1844, Hodder, *Seventh Earl of Shaftesbury*, ii. 23; 12 Mar. 1844, *Cobden's Speeches*,
80–2.

[104] George Macaulay Trevelyan, *The Life of John Bright* (1913), 157. William Dodd, *The
Factory System Illustrated*, ed. W. H. Chaloner (1968; original edn. 1842). As Chaloner points out,
there is no evidence that Dodd was ever employed in the cotton industry at all (p. v); Ward,
Factory Movement, 232; Parl. Deb., 3rd ser., vol. 73, 1149–58: 15 Mar. 1844; Hammond and
Hammond, *Lord Shaftesbury*, 94–5; Finlayson, *Seventh Earl of Shaftesbury*, 212.

the labouring class etc. etc.'. Ashworth replied that he personally had never spoken this way, but he pointed out that Ashley and Oastler were frequently abusive about the factory masters and that in the Commons the mere mention of the word 'Trade' or 'the Manufacturing or Mercantile interests' was enough to cause howls of derision from the Protectionists.[105] Even Cobden, basically a sweet-natured man, fell short of his normal standards of conduct when he commissioned Thackeray to produce a cartoon depicting Ashley as snatching bread from a small child and putting a larger share in his own pocket while proclaiming 'I will never rest until the poor factory child is protected by a ten hours bill from the tyranny of the *merciless and griping millowner*.'[106] This was class war with a vengeance! Ferrand, indeed, would have been pleased had it actually come to a physical contest:

Mr. Cobden the other day said that he would back Stockport against Steyning. Good God, gentlemen, if the League are so mad as to attempt to come to blows, the forces which they could muster would speedily be annihilated by the brawny arms of the agriculturalists.[107]

TOWN VERSUS COUNTRY?

But clearly the class politics of the 1840s were more complicated than has been admitted so far. For the struggle between 'agriculturalists' and the cotton lords had no clear outcome. In fact, it might seem as if each side triumphed and each was defeated. For in 1846 Repeal was carried, only for the same Parliament to pass the Ten Hours Bill in the following year—though, admittedly, some of the gains won by the factory employees in the 1847 Bill were cancelled out by Grey's amending measure of 1850.

Marx provided a famous explanation of why these startling twists and turns occurred in his account to an American newspaper of the 'exoteric history of the Ten-Hours Act'. In Marx's view, the landed aristocracy, which had received 'a deadly blow by the actual abolition of the Corn Laws in 1846, took its vengeance by forcing the Ten-Hours Bill of 1847 upon Parliament', only for the 'industrial bourgeoisie' to recover by judicial authority in 1850 much of what it had lost by parliamentary agitation, the process of 'tit for tat' ending only when 'the wrath of the Landlords had gradually subsided' to the point where they were prepared to make 'a compromise with the Mill-lords'.[108]

This explanation has been emphatically rejected by many historians, who have produced the inevitable exceptions and anomalies. But it is perhaps worth acknowledging that Marx's 'explanation' follows quite closely what

---

[105] Boyson, *Ashworth Cotton Enterprise*, 207.
[106] McCord, *Anti-Corn Law League*, 69–70.
[107] Ward, *Factory Movement*, 314.
[108] *New York Daily Tribune*, written 25 Feb. 1853; reprinted in Marx and Engels, *On Britain*, 382.

many contemporary observers of British politics were saying, among them the former Lord Chancellor, Lord Brougham, and the Birmingham MP, George Muntz.[109] Ashley, too, believed that the majority who voted for the Ten Hours Bill in 1847 'were governed, not by love to the cause, but by anger towards Peel and the Anti-Corn Law League'.[110]

An analysis of the evidence of the division lobby shows that the situation was actually more complex than this. Some Conservative MPs did indeed vote for the Ten Hours Bill for the first time in 1847, out of a sense of 'betrayal' over the Corn Laws, and this might have been enough to tilt the balance in favour of the reformers, although without Whig support the Bill would not have been carried.[111] On the other hand, the Protectionists had *always* been more favourable than any other parliamentary group to factory reform, evidence of the logical connection between Protectionism and the Ten Hours cause.[112] True, too much should not be read into this commitment, since, leaving aside 'extremists' like Oastler and Ferrand, most mainstream Protectionists took a view of the rights of property that was not irreconcilable with that of their opponents; indeed, Tory 'paternalists', with their attachment to the small-scale locality, were particularly hostile to central interference and regulation.[113] All the same, there was a body of Conservative MPs who consistently supported the Ten Hours cause; the Peelites and the Radicals, by contrast, were mostly hostile, whereas the Whigs were divided.[114] In short, though Marx's explanation of why the 1847 Bill became law is not satisfactory, the tie-up between Protectionism and factory reform, despite considerable cross-voting, really did exist: it is not just a 'historical myth'.

To what extent can these differences in the profiles of the parties' voting records be explained in *class* terms? 'Revisionist' historians have tried to demolish the idea that there was any such connection by showing that the proponents of Ten Hours legislation were by no means drawn exclusively from the ranks of the 'agriculturalists'. Is their case a persuasive one?

The 'factory reformers' were certainly a motley group; they comprised hand-loom weavers, middle-class 'experts', North of England clergymen (mostly Anglicans), and even some factory owners, as well as aristocrats like

---

[109] Parl. Deb., 3rd ser., vol. 92, 920: 17 May 1847.

[110] Ward, *Factory Movement*, 415.

[111] Lubenow, *Politics of Government Growth*, 147. For the important, but neglected, role of the Whigs in sponsoring factory reform, see Peter Mandler, 'Cain and Abel: Two Aristocrats and the Early Victorian Factory Acts', *Historical Journal*, 27 (1984), 83–109.

[112] J. T. Ward (ed.), *Popular Movements c.1830–1850* (1970), 64. 57% of Protectionists supported the Ten Hours cause in 1844, 70% in 1846, 94% in 1847. On the logical connection between Protectionism and Ten Hours, see Stewart, 'Ten Hours and Sugar Crises', 40.

[113] Ward, *Factory Movement*, 160–1. David Roberts, *Paternalism in Early Victorian England* (New Brunswick, NJ, 1979), passim.

[114] Lubenow, *Politics of Government Growth*, 214. See also William O. Aydelotte, 'The House of Commons in the 1840s', *History*, 39 (1954), 260–2.

Ashley and country squires like Ferrand. The sponsor of the 1847 Act (Ashley himself being out of Parliament at the time) was William Fielden, owner of the largest textile firm in the world, yet also a keen Radical and Repealer— even a mild Chartist.[115] Fielden's case seems to totally invalidate the 'class interpretation' of the politics of the 1840s. Moreover, among the mill-owners of West Riding there was significant support for a restriction of the operatives' working day.[116] On the other hand, only four cotton lords played a prominent part in the factory movement (Fielden, Charles Hindley, Joseph Brotherton, and William Kenworthy); and since the Ten Hours Act was greeted by petitions of protest signed by 353 firms (employing 123,226 hands) in February and by 483 firms (employing 129,256 hands) in May 1847, the class unity of the cotton manufacturers clearly remained almost solid until the very end.[117] Ashley himself later declared: 'In very few instances did any mill-owner appear on the platform with me.'[118] A 'class' interpretation of the factory controversy is therefore not lacking in plausibility.

The fiscal issue, by contrast, *did* cut across class lines to a much greater extent. For by 1846 a substantial part of the landed aristocracy had accepted the case for free trade, some out of sympathy with the sufferings of the poor, some out of fear of revolution, while others, through marriage or investments, had come to identify their own interests, at least in part, with the commercial and industrial sectors of the economy.[119] Such considerations impressed 'agriculturalists' on both sides of the House: traditional Tories like Ashley, as well as many Whigs. Of course, given the composition of mid-Victorian Parliaments, there was no way, had such a 'conversion' not occurred, in which the Corn Laws could ever have been abolished.

Conversely, not all manufacturers and merchants favoured Repeal. Forgetting that this was so, Ferrand, who had perhaps taken his own propaganda too literally, 'went for' a textile owner at a meeting of the Truck Committee in June 1842, thinking that he had felled an 'enemy', only to find that the 'culprit', Dugdale, was a good Tory and an opponent of the League—much to Cobden's amusement.[120]

The politics of the 1840s were complicated by another set of considerations. The more intelligent and flexible of the Protectionists had from an early stage recognized the need to build a political base wider than that furnished

---

[115] Fielden thought restriction of hours would reduce overproduction which was the main cause of distress, not foreign competition (Stewart Angus Weaver, *John Fielden and the Politics of Popular Radicalism, 1832–1847* (Oxford, 1987), passim).

[116] On the pro-Reform petition of two Bradford mill-owners, William Walker and William Rand, see Samuel H. G. Kydd ('Alfred'), *The History of the Factory Movement* (1857; revised edn., New York, 1966), ii. 167–8, 173–85.

[117] Howe, *Cotton Masters*, esp. 187.

[118] Hodder, *Seventh Earl of Shaftesbury*, ii. 209.

[119] Semmel, *Free Trade Imperialism*, 139.

[120] Cobden to Ashworth, 7 June 1842, Cobden Papers, Add. MS 43,653, fos. 35–6.

by landed society. Bentinck, in particular, had been quick to see that an alliance might be constructed between agriculture and other economic interests threatened by the application of Free Trade: shipping, for example, and businesses involved in the colonial trade.[121] From this perception there developed a distinctive brand of economic nationalism, which later found institutionalized expression in groups like the National Association for the Protection of British Industry and Capital and Ferrand's Lancashire, Yorkshire, and Cheshire Labour League for the Protection and Regulation of the Interests of Native Producers.[122]

Nor did such a policy of co-operation with urban businessmen present serious difficulties for a man like Bentinck, who, far from being a bucolic squire, fully understood the need for 'modern' methods of political agitation. Significantly, Bentinck was also an enthusiast for railway development, seeing this as providing a wholesome boost to agricultural production both in England and in Ireland.[123] Thus, notwithstanding the important political differences between agriculture and industry in the 1840s, there were also ties of interest and sentiment uniting the two sides. As for Disraeli, instinct and calculation alike told him that some sort of reconciliation between town and country would sooner or later have to be effected.[124]

How, then, if at all, did class and social background shape attitudes towards Repeal? William Aydelotte, who exhaustively analysed the 1841 Parliament, has concluded that on the Corn Law issue a Conservative MP's social background and economic interests had very little to do with whether or not he supported Peel in 1846.[125] Yet his researches have also led him to the conclusion that the *type of constituency* an MP represented played a significant part in determining political behaviour: 'Members of Parliament tended to take lines . . . that were, so far as we can tell, appropriate for the needs of their own constituencies.'[126]

---

[121] Macintyre, 'Lord George Bentinck', 149–50.

[122] Ibid. 163. Ward, *Factory Movement*, 398.

[123] On Bentinck's recognition of the need to master statistics in a statistical age, see Macintyre, 'Lord George Bentinck', 147, and on his interest in railways (on which subject he was prepared to take advice from a railway magnate like Samuel Laing), ibid. 151, n. 32.

[124] In *Coningsby* (1844), for example, Disraeli provides a sympathetic portrait of the wealthy mill-owner Millbank, thought by some to be modelled on Cobden, by others on Ashworth; and in the marriage between Millbank's daughter and Coningsby which ends the novel, Disraeli optimistically predicts the eventual reconciliation between 'Saxon industry and Norman manners'.

[125] William O. Aydelotte, 'The Country Gentlemen and the Repeal of the Corn Laws', *English Historical Review*, 82 (1967), 47–60. However, as Stewart notes, Aydelotte reaches this conclusion by looking at the Conservative Party, not at the House of Commons as a whole (Robert Stewart, *The Foundation of the Conservative Party 1830–1867* (1978), 216).

[126] William O. Aydelotte, 'Constituency Influence on the British House of Commons, 1841–1847', in William O. Aydelotte, *The History of Parliamentary Behaviour* (Princeton, NJ, 1977), 237. Other historians have reached the same conclusion. See Read, *Peel and the Victorians*, 113; Stewart, *Conservative Party*, 216; G. S. R. Kitson Clark, 'The Electorate and the Repeal of the Corn Laws', *Transactions of the Royal Historical Society*, 1 (1951), 125.

It also seems as if 'enlarged views' were most commonly to be found among MPs and peers who, in the present or the past, had had to take a Ministerial view of the national interest. Thus, by the mid-1840s the Whig leaders had come round on pragmatic grounds to acceptance of the inevitability of Repeal, while several prominent Whigs, including Russell, were quick to embrace the case for a restriction of working hours in the factories. What, though, of Peel and other members of the *Conservative* front bench?

It is tempting to suppose that, in finally deciding on the repeal of the Corn Laws, Sir Robert Peel was influenced by his family background. In his essay entitled 'The Character of Sir Robert Peel', Walter Bagehot suggests that, like Cobden, the Conservative Leader illustrates the truth of the adage that 'the grain of the middle class will always come out'.[127] Indeed, long before the fateful decision to end agricultural protection had been taken, the leaders of the Anti-Corn Law League were publicly suggesting that Peel might in time join their side. 'I do not altogether like the idea of giving Peel up. He is a Lancashire man,' Cobden told one League meeting, while on another occasion he claimed a personal affinity with the Prime Minister: 'He is the son of a cotton-printer.'[128]

Once Repeal had been carried, there was speculation among Sir Robert's friends and foes about the contribution which his 'class' had made to that outcome. G. H. Francis, in a critical biography published in 1852, expressed the 'ultra-Tory' view of Peel: namely, that his treachery towards the landed classes had been 'long-planned': 'The manufacturer's son was now to raise up his order by destroying the aristocracy.'[129] From a diametrically opposed political viewpoint, the Free Traders tended to agree. One thinks of Cobden's famous appeal to Sir Robert to cut himself adrift from all party ties and to act as the spokesman and leader of the middle class. Peel, he claimed, was 'the idea of the age, and it has no other representative among statesmen'.[130]

Peel's untimely death provided a further occasion for outpourings of this kind, especially in the industrial North, where some mill-owners in Manchester showed their respect by shutting their factories for a day and giving their workers a paid holiday.[131] Indeed, the Manchester Chamber of Commerce, in its message of condolence to Lady Peel, went so far as to announce that upon itself had devolved the sacred duty of upholding 'those

---

[127] In *Collected Works*, iii. 250. See also *Morning Post*, 19 Mar. 1845; Greville, Diary, 22 Jan. 1846: both cited in Read, *Peel and the Victorians*, 148, 220.

[128] 13 Nov. 1845, *Cobden's Speeches*, 171. See also John Bright's speech, in Henry Ashworth, *Recollections of Richard Cobden M.P. and the Anti-Corn Law League* (1878; 2nd edn.), 198. 8 Feb. 1844, *Cobden's Speeches*, 604.

[129] Cited in Read, *Peel and the Victorians*, 306.

[130] Cobden to Peel, 23 June 1846, Morley, *Cobden*, i. 390–7.

[131] Read, *Peel and the Victorians*, 271.

counsels which he has left to us as a legacy, never to be forgotten'.[132] (On whether the unhappy widow was consoled in her bereavement by this assurance, history is silent!) Many large towns, including Birmingham, Leeds, Bradford, and Glasgow, later erected Peel monuments.[133] So, of course, did Manchester itself. And the kind of local and class pride which Mancunians felt in 'the Lancashire Premier' is nicely captured by the editorial which appeared in the *Manchester Guardian* on the inauguration of the new statue:

There is peculiar appropriateness in the choice of Sir ROBERT PEEL for the first niche in our local PANTHEON . . . We are not surrounded here by the associations which, in some places, fill the youthful mind with dreams of martial exploits. We cannot pretend to accord spontaneously the highest place in our appreciation to those by whom the philosophy and poetry of our own language has been enriched. Least of all, are we prone by habit or education, to magnify the lustre of even the brightest hereditary fortune . . . Sir ROBERT PEEL's career is, we suppose, exactly what a wealthy Manchester merchant might consistently set before his sons, if he proposed to hold up to their view the very highest ambition which he conceived it possible for their age and country to afford them.[134]

Conscientious almost to a fault (did his middle-class ancestry show through *here?*), Peel seems to have spent a considerable time in the 1820s in a systematic study of the 'classical economists', achieving a mastery of their works which was later to stand him in good stead; he could fluently cite Adam Smith, Ricardo, Say, and Hume, although his convictions also owed much to an Evangelical view of the world which saw the principles of political economy as part of God's Providential design.[135] It may also be significant that Peel had a great faith in railways as a means of promoting 'the moral and social welfare of this country, and add[ing] to its political security'.[136] Again, like members of the Manchester School, he saw the Press as a particularly remarkable triumph of capitalist enterprise.[137]

Indeed, both before and after Repeal, Peel was making speeches about the economy which could almost have come from a Joseph Hume or a Cobden. Seldom has the economic case for free imports and against 'legislative interference' been so clearly and unequivocally stated.

The principles which should govern the commercial intercourse of nations do not differ from those which regulate the dealings of private individuals. It is the same law

---

[132] Message of condolence to Lady Peel, 11 July 1850, Manchester Chamber of Commerce Papers, fo. 143.

[133] Read, *Peel and the Victorians*, 294.

[134] *Manchester Guardian*, 15 Oct. 1853.

[135] 'I have read all that has been written by the gravest authorities on political economy on the subject of rent, wages, taxes, tithes', Peel told the Commons in 1839 (Semmel, *Free Trade Imperialism*, 143).

[136] Read, *Peel and the Victorians*, 9.

[137] Ibid. 37. See also Boyd Hilton, 'Peel: A Reappraisal', *Historical Journal*, 22 (1979), 585–614.

which determines the planetary movements and the fall of the slightest particle of matter to the earth. It is the same law which determines the accumulation of wealth by the private trader and the powerful kingdom.[138]

By the end of his life, Peel was even urging farmers, in language reminiscent of Cobden's, to concentrate on ways of increasing their productivity, rather than looking for legislative protection. 'Your interests are inseparably inter-woven with the general prosperity,' he declared during the important debate on agricultural distress in February 1850, in one of his last major parliamen-tary speeches. 'It would be impossible to reinvest the land now with the privileges which it possessed at the time when the feudal system was broken up.'[139] Like Cobden, then, Peel was a convinced advocate of 'high farming'.[140]

But whether such 'dogma' significantly influenced Peel's Ministerial con-duct is quite another question. Arguably Peel felt driven to do what he did by inherited responsibilities; for, as he told Croker in a famous letter of 1842, whereas one might 'on moral and social grounds prefer cornfields to cotton factories, an agricultural to a manufacturing population', Britain's lot had been cast, 'and we cannot recede'.[141] Similarly with the Ten Hours agitation. Peel explained to the Queen that he could not take risks with the textile industry because it constituted £35 million out of a total of £44 million of the country's exports.[142] It was this intense practicality which, though it enfuriated some, endeared him to many sectors of opinion. Peel was, moreover, a party leader, who set less store by party than by his sense of what he owed to his country in his capacity as the 'Queen's Minister'.[143] From such responsibilities, rustic Conservative back-benchers were entirely free.

It is probably these considerations, not his alleged affinities with the industrial middle class, that best explain Peel's behaviour in 1846. True, he never apologized for his family background,[144] and he even seems to have retained what some contemporaries thought to be a Lancashire accent—though, more likely, it was the lilt of Staffordshire, where he had set up house. Nevertheless, as Gash has noted, he had been sent off as a young boy to

---

[138] Parl. Deb., 3rd ser., vol. 106, 1450: 6 July 1849.

[139] Ibid., vol. 108, 1251–2: 21 Feb. 1850.

[140] D. C. Moore, 'The Corn Laws and High Farming', *Economic History Review*, 18 (1965), 561. Peel tried to put his own ideas into practice on his own estates, granting fixed leases and financial inducements to tenants who improved the drainage, consolidated small fields, and collected manure (Read, *Peel and the Victorians*, 260).

[141] Peel to Croker, 27 July 1842, in Charles Stuart Parker (ed.), *Sir Robert Peel: From his Private Papers*, ii. (1899), 529.

[142] Read, *Peel and the Victorians*, 107–8.

[143] Angus Hawkins, ' "Parliamentary Government" and Victorian Political Parties, c.1830–c.1880', *English Historical Review*, 104 (1989), 654–6. Hawkins calls the 1841 general election 'a great triumph for an anti-party view of executive authority' (ibid. 654).

[144] For Peel's revealing letter of thanks to Baines, who had sent him a copy of his *History of the Cotton Manufacture*, see Peel to Edward Baines, jun., 22 Feb. 1835, Baines Papers.

Harrow and then Oxford, whence he had embarked on a career of lifelong involvement in Westminster politics. Peel was thus 'severed from the practical framework' of his father's world.[145]

Moreover, even if we were to follow Kebbel in his view of Peel as 'the great Minister of the middle-classes',[146] the fact remains that the party which Peel led lacked significant middle-class support.[147] For Conservatism in the 1840s was based on the English agricultural counties and smaller boroughs, not the larger urban and manufacturing centres. 'Peel's alleged middle-class leanings', Robert Stewart concludes, 'reaped no greater reward in the manufacturing towns than the more aristocratic Conservatism of Lord Derby in the 1850s and 1860s.'[148] Primarily based as it was on the agricultural districts, Peel's Conservative Party showed little concern for urban sensitivities.

Moreover, Peel himself did not really *want* to act as a mouthpiece for the industrial towns, since he took a 'traditional' view of the role of the Conservative Party and, indeed, of politics generally. His famous credo of February 1843 bears repeating:

I believe it to be of the utmost importance that a territorial aristocracy should be maintained. I believe that in no country is it of more importance than in this, with its ancient constitution, ancient habits, and mixed form of government. I trust that a territorial aristocracy, with all its just influence and authority, will long be maintained. I believe such an aristocracy to be essential to the purposes of good government. The question only is—what, in a certain state of public opinion, and in a certain position of society, is the most effectual way of maintaining the legitimate influence and authority of a territorial aristocracy.[149]

Although Peel went on to say that he regarded the interests of the manufacturing and the agricultural classes to be the same, there is little doubt as to where his primary allegiance lay. Thus, most historians now agree that Peel's action in 1846 was a considered concession designed to protect the aristocracy from further radical assault.[150] Peel retrospectively justified what he had done in precisely these terms.[151] But did he succeed in his objectives?

---

[145] Norman Gash, *Mr Secretary Peel: The Life of Sir Robert Peel to 1830* (1961), 3.

[146] T. E. Kebbel, *A History of Toryism* (1886), 299; however, Kebbel also sees that Peel's 'own order' was that of landed society.

[147] Compare Robert Blake, *The Conservative Party from Peel to Churchill* (1970; 1972 edn.), 50.

[148] Stewart, *Conservative Party*, 159–60. See also Norman Gash, *Reaction and Reconstruction in English Politics 1832–1852* (Oxford, 1965), 134–6. Aydelotte claims that MPs with business interests divided almost equally between Whigs and Conservatives. He omits to mention, however, that the latter outnumbered the former by 368 to 289! ('House of Commons', 258).

[149] Cited in Gash, *Reaction and Reconstruction*, 139.

[150] Aydelotte, 'Constituency Influence', 202. G. Kitson Clark, 'The Repeal of the Corn Laws and the Politics of the Forties', *Economic History Review*, 4 (1951–2), 12; Kemp, 'Reflections on Repeal', 195–204.

[151] Read, *Peel and the Victorians*, 163.

CONSEQUENCES

The best place to start an examination of this issue is with the views of the Anti-Corn Law Leaguers themselves. Cobden himself never took so sanguine a view of the Radicals' prospects in the aftermath of Repeal as did the excitable *Norfolk News*.[152] While the agitation against the Corn Laws was still taking place, he had had a premonition that Repeal might come about, as a result not of 'agitation from without', but of 'conversion from within' through the medium of 'some statesman of established reputation'.[153] But is that what he *wanted* to happen? Clearly, Cobden was none too happy when Lord John Russell issued his 'Edinburgh Letter', a sign that the 'aristocratic Establishment' was about to embrace Free Trade. The country's difficulties, he publicly observed at the time, 'will not be got rid of . . . because a lord has written a very ambiguous sort of a letter'. Reform, he told his Mancunian audience, 'will have to be done by your own right arm, if it is done at all'.[154]

Two months later, by which time it was clear that Peel's Government would probably move to abolish the Corn Laws, the Radical leader revealed what was passing through his mind: 'We should have liked to have had another year of qualification for counties. If we had had another year or two, we could have shown the monopolist landowners that we can transfer power in this country from the hands of a class totally into the hands of the middle and industrial classes of this country.'[155] Four years later he was making the same claim.[156] In fact, Prest thinks that Cobden was boasting, though not idly, when he said that with the 'tremendous engine' of the 40s. freeholder, he could have unseated 100 monopolists in three years.[157] As it was, Peel, through his timely concession, brought the League's campaign to an abrupt halt before the registration drive and the purchase of 40s. freeholds had got into full swing. The outcome was a Parliament still heavily under aristocratic control.[158]

So, at one level, Cobden may have been sincere when he later assured Russell that he was so pleased with the disappearance of the hateful Corn Laws that he could view with comparative indifference having the prize of 'total victory' snatched from his grasp.[159] But his observations to Ashworth in January 1848 reveal a mood of disappointment which had deepened during the intervening period: 'I thought Free Trade was the beginning of a new era,

---

[152] *Norfolk News*, 10 Feb. 1849. See Introduction. For the League journal's greeting of Peel's (temporary) resignation in December 1845, see *The League*, 13 Dec. 1845, 158–9.

[153] 28 Sept. 1843, *Cobden's Speeches*, 40.

[154] 28 Oct. 1845, ibid. 160.

[155] 17 Dec. 1845, ibid. 175.

[156] 26 Nov. 1849, ibid. 554.

[157] Prest, *Politics*, 96.

[158] Ibid. 96–7; see McCord, *Anti-Corn Law League*, 208.

[159] Cobden to Russell, 6 Feb. 1846, in G. P. Gooch (ed.), *The Later Correspondence of Lord John Russell 1840–1878* (1925), i. 107–8.

but it is evident we repealed the Corn laws by accident, without knowing what we were about. The *spirit* of Free Trade is not yet in us.'[160]

Such pessimism was perfectly compatible with faith in Peel as a person. Encouraged perhaps by the Prime Minister's famous encomium to him in the House of Commons, Cobden appealed to Peel to put himself at the head of the great middle class. But if the Radical Leader really believed that this appeal would meet with a sympathetic response, he was guilty of a sad self-deception.[161]

As for the long-term political consequences of Repeal, these are difficult to determine. Some historians argue that the events of 1846 ushered in an 'Indian summer of the British aristocracy'[162] in which the landed classes preserved their privileged status at a time of dramatic technological change.[163] Perkin, on the other hand, contends that Repeal was 'tantamount to accepting the middle-class view of the national interest, which placed the needs of consumers and the prosperity of producers before the unearned incomes of the landlords, or at any rate saw the last as secondary to and dependent upon the other two'.[164] In Perkin's view, the aristocracy may have retained its near monopoly of political authority, but only at the cost of making itself the instrument of the ideas and ideals of another class. Which of these two lines of interpretation is the more convincing?

There is a sense in which both interpretations are true. Peel's dilemma was that his economic 'principles' did not harmonize with his political convictions. In consequence, when he tried to bludgeon the Conservative Party (dominated, as it was, by the 'country gentlemen') into accepting the necessity for Repeal, he broke it in two and destroyed, however heroically, his own ministerial career. The class reconciliation which Peel desired had to await more propitious times.

Arguably such a reconciliation took place after Peel's premature death in 1850, under the man who consciously projected himself as his natural heir, William Ewart Gladstone, another businessman's son who was trained for political leadership within the aristocratic state only to find himself in the position of having to force painful readjustments on the old order he was so anxious to save. But, as we shall see later, Gladstone, by temperament and family circumstance, was much better fitted for the role.

All this had important consequences for the history of the British party system. For although at one level Peel may have 'saved' the aristocratic

---

[160] Cobden to Ashworth, 8 Jan. 1848, Cobden Papers, Add. MS 43,653, fo. 99.
[161] Bright was also deceiving himself when, in December 1852, he described Peel as having been 'a follower of Villiers' (Bright to J. B. Smith, 27 Dec. 1852, John Benjamin Smith Papers, MS 923.2, S344, fo. 9).
[162] Kitson Clark, 'Repeal of Corn Laws', 13.
[163] Moore, 'Corn Laws', 561.
[164] Perkin, *Origins*, 373.

order, his actions during the crisis of 1845–6 had the effect of putting the Conservatives out of the running as a party of government for the next generation. Theoretically, of course, there was no reason why an aristocratic party like the Tories could not have pursued a policy of 'modernization' through a selective resort to the policies recommended by the political economists. But few members of the Conservative Party outside Peel's own devoted band of followers had the stomach for such an enterprise. The result was a party schism which, in retrospect, has an air of inevitability about it. And this schism left the main body of the divided Conservative Party at a very considerable disadvantage. For, as Disraeli was quick to realize, the Protectionist impulses of the country gentlemen did not offer a broad enough base for the government of a rapidly industrializing society like Britain.

Yet victory did not go to the Cobdenites. Instead, it was the Whigs, the group which, above all others, the Manchester School most despised, which emerged as the dominant group in the mid-Victorian years. This is significant. For although the Whigs themselves were also a largely aristocratic party, they had no intention of throwing in their lot with Tory country gentlemen. In 1846 there were indeed rumours of an impending alliance between Palmerston and the Protectionists, but rumours they remained.[165] For the Whigs were determined to hold on to their political hegemony, and a sufficiently large number of them viewed the problems of the day with the sort of detachment which allowed them to give ground to the urban Radicals when it seemed patriotic or expedient to do so. Indeed, the decay in the course of the 1840s of the Whig approach to social policy, once epitomized by Young Whigs like Morpeth and more loosely endorsed by Russell himself, was bringing about the coalescence of Whiggery and liberalism within a creed which many urban Radicals were likely to find congenial.[166]

Such a strategy made good political sense anyway, since from the start there existed a group of urban Radicals who had abandoned Cobden's revolutionary politics in favour of a policy of co-operation with the Whigs. A good example of this kind of middle-class 'permeator' was James Wilson, the son of a wealthy Quaker textile manufacturer, someone who as a young man had set himself up in the hat-making trade. In 1843 Wilson founded *The Economist*, and he continued not only to own and manage but also edit this weekly journal for the next sixteen years, before passing on the editorship to his son-in-law Walter Bagehot.

James Wilson, as we have already seen, believed in the existence of a 'natural harmony of interests' in society. This economic outlook had political consequences which were quickly to estrange him from the Manchester School. For if, reasoned Wilson, Free Trade and laissez-faire were beneficial

---

[165] See Monypenny, *Disraeli*, 392–3.
[166] Mandler, *Aristocratic Government*. See also Conclusion, p. 295.

to all mankind, what reason was there for supposing that the 'traditional ruling class'—at least its more intelligent members—would not champion the new economic creed?

Of course, certain of the great Whig landowners had indeed supported the League from its early days. Not surprisingly, therefore, two of these men, having read and admired Wilson's books, professed a desire to become acquainted with him. One of them, the Wiltshire landowner Lord Radnor, actually helped Wilson to set up *The Economist*. The other was the Earl of Clarendon, who secured an introduction through his younger brother, Charles Villiers, the pioneering advocate of Repeal, who, of course, had known Wilson since the start of the Corn Law campaign.[167]

Clarendon himself, though rejecting the doctrinaire position of the League, had long considered himself a Free Trader, and he soon emerged as perhaps the most prominent of those Whig landowners working for good relations with the urban Radicals. In 1846, for example, he urged Russell to keep open the possibility of making Cobden the offer of a Cabinet place (Cobden was then travelling on the continent).[168]

The calculations underlying Clarendon's advice are made clear in a lengthy memorandum which he wrote to his colleagues at that time. 'There is nothing which more requires the true conservative process of reform than the Whig party,' he said. 'It is considered to be aristocratical in its opinions, exclusive in its personnel, and guided by historical reminiscences rather than by present public opinion.' While he thought that 'nothing should be done to offend or alarm the aristocracy or the landed interest', Clarendon also wanted to see established 'a government fairly representing the industrial mind and conservative progress of the country'. Clarendon went on to argue: 'The country will not stand still: an impetus has been given to men's minds that cannot be checked; wants and hopes have been excited that must be satisfied; commercial, financial and social reforms have been commenced and must be continued.' He also warned that Peel had 'not broken up his party and embarked on a *middle-class* policy without being prepared to carry it out to its full results', so that there was a real risk of the ex-Prime Minister 'rally[ing] round him the free-traders, manufacturers and middle classes, who are already better disposed to him than to Lord J. R.[ussell].'[169]

To a Whig who thought in this way, James Wilson was a man of considerable usefulness. On becoming President of the Board of Trade in 1846,

---

[167] Ronald K. Huch, *The Radical Lord Radnor: The Public Life of Viscount Folkestone, Third Earl of Radnor (1770–1869)* (Minneapolis, 1977), 157. Lord Radnor's brother-in-law was one of the heads in Barings (Barrington, *Servant of All*, i. 91). On Radnor's educational interests, see Ch. 7.

[168] Gooch (ed.), *Later Correspondence of Russell*, i. 83–4.

[169] Herbert Maxwell, *Life and Letters of Fourth Earl of Clarendon* (1913), i. 265–7. See Mandler, *Aristocratic Government*, 252–3. Compare his uncle, the Third Earl, who objected to the London and Birmingham Railway traversing his park (J. T. Ward and R. G. Wilson (eds.), *Land and Industry* (Newton Abbot, 1971), 21).

Clarendon felt himself particularly in need of the commercial intelligence and economic expertise which Wilson was able to supply. 'I would be much obliged by your sending me this afternoon to the Board of Trade any information respecting the quantities of sugar used in the Breweries and Distilleries' ran a typical message of June 1847, Clarendon being at the time deeply embroiled in the negotiations that would eventually culminate in the equalization of the sugar duties, a long-standing proposal of the Free Trade lobby.[170] Indeed, as Walter Bagehot later put it, Wilson became so fully a master of the sugar question that 'some people fancied he must have been in the trade'.[171] Wilson also gave the Ministry advice on the repeal of the Navigation Acts (he is said to have converted no less a personage than the Duke of Wellington to its necessity) and other measures for removing impediments to industry. After Clarendon had been moved to the Irish viceroyalty, Wilson continued to give him help, for example, over the Encumbered Estates Act, a welcome first step, in the view of the urban Radicals, to removing the privileged position of landed property so that it could be treated on a par with other forms of wealth.[172]

By this time Wilson was himself in office. For in July 1847, after 'an accidental conversation at Lord Radnor's table',[173] he was elected as a Whig for the small borough of Westbury. To win, he had had to fight a tough contest, but his newly acquired aristocratic friends (Radnor, Villiers, and the neighbouring magnate Lord Lansdowne) had rallied to his support. A year later he was made Secretary of the Board of Control, before eventually becoming Financial Secretary of the Treasury. 'As no man has done what you have to rectify public opinion and diffuse correct information upon commercial questions,' wrote Clarendon encouragingly, 'the people will feel secure that nothing wrong with respect to them can be done so long as you remain a member of the Government.'[174] That, in a nutshell, was why Wilson had been given office in the first place, though some Whig notables also courted Wilson because they wanted him to give their work sympathetic coverage in ·his newspaper articles and leaders.

From the very foundation of *The Economist*, Wilson and his closest friends had been at variance with the 'impracticables' of the League who wanted to subject the journal to their own control.[175] Over the next few years the rift widened. Time and again, *The Economist* gave the Cobdenite critics of aristocratic mismanagement patronizing little lessons in the complexities of

---

[170] Barrington, *Servant of All*, i. 89.
[171] Walter Bagehot, 'James Wilson', *Collected Works*, iii. 345.
[172] See his friendly letter to Wilson about the Famine (Barrington, *Servant of All*, i. 122–3).
[173] Bagehot, *Collected Works*, iii. 342.
[174] Barrington, *Servant of All*, i. 141.
[175] Though Cobden himself was perhaps converted away from this position (see Barrington, *Servant of All*, i. 41).

government, mocked them as doctrinaire extremists, and told them to trust in the good will of the Whig leadership. A 'modern' commercial policy, readers were assured, could be carried out smoothly by the powers that be, without any disturbance of the political or constitutional status quo.

Understandably, the Manchester School took exception to these strictures. In fact, from the moment he became a 'ministerialist' in association with the aristocratic Whigs, Wilson alienated many of the influential Radical leaders. Cobden, writing to Bright about 'our good friend, James Wilson', observed: 'I fear it is too much to expect any man to live in London in the atmosphere of the clubs and political cliques, and preserve the independent national tone in his paper, which we had hoped for in the *Economist*.'[176] And when Wilson accepted office, Cobden privately took the view that his one-time ally had 'committed political suicide'.[177] As for Bright, he initially wanted the Radicals to run a candidate against Wilson (and other new Ministers) at Westbury when he sought re-election![178] Moreover, when *The Economist*, still under Wilson's editorial control, defended successive Ministries from their Radical assailants, as it frequently did, the Radicals savagely denounced Wilson as a 'placeman' and 'backslider' who had sold his convictions for the rewards of office.[179]

Yet contemporaries were agreed in assigning particular importance to *The Economist*. Disraeli called it the 'able organ' of 'the middle classes';[180] and a few years later Gladstone spoke of it as a journal 'which carries great weight among the most intelligent and instructed commercial classes'.[181] In light of this, Wilson's policy of supporting friendly co-operation between the business community and the enlightened wing of landed society acquires a considerable significance.

Nor was *The Economist* alone in taking this line. The *Manchester Guardian*, for example, pursued a parallel path—not surprisingly, since Wilson acted for many years as one of its London correspondents—and the two journals often quoted approvingly from one another.[182] There was a further link with Manchester's industrial élite in that W. R. Greg, the 'millowner-turned-*littérateur*', was in the habit of working up many of Wilson's speeches into his own articles (he subsequently married one of Wilson's daughters).[183] Indeed,

---

[176] Cobden to Bright, 24 Oct. 1846, Morley, *Cobden*, ii. 12.

[177] Barrington, *Servant of All*, i. 139.

[178] Bright to Wilson, 5 May 1848, George Wilson Papers.

[179] Administrative Reform Association, pamphlet no. 10, 24–5.

[180] Disraeli to Stanley, 10 Feb. 1859, in George Earle Buckle, *Life of Disraeli*, vol. 4 (1916), 198.

[181] Parl. Deb., 3rd ser., vol. 174, 570: 7 Apr. 1864.

[182] David Ayerst, *Guardian: Biography of a Newspaper* (1971), 104–5.

[183] Howe, *Cotton Masters*, 167. Greg's prize essays on Free Trade so impressed Radnor that he had them reprinted for wider distribution (Barrington, *Servant of All*, i. 84).

Howe implies that Greg's furious opposition to the Factory Acts may have helped to shape the editorial line taken by *The Economist*.[184]

Like Wilson, Greg was a convinced 'permeator'. In a famous letter to Cobden of May 1848, protesting the emergence of parliamentary reform, he urged the importance of working 'with the tools we have', rather than spending 'years of contest in obtaining new tools'. The pressing need, he said, was to promote 'real reforms, practical, legal, and administrative'. Greg saw no difficulty in achieving this: 'The repeal of the Corn Laws, wrung by reason from a Protectionist Parliament,' he argued, 'shows that *any* real reforms demanded of the People headed by [trusted] Reformers . . . must be promptly granted by any Parliament, however chosen.'[185] Greg developed this line of thought in an article in the *Edinburgh Review*, a journal of similar persuasion to his own (Cornewall Lewis edited it between 1852 and 1855),[186] in which he dissociated himself from the old class animosities, saying that the important social distinction of the day was no longer between businessmen and landed society but between 'the educated portion of the community' and the mass of unskilled and ill-informed labourers.[187] The corollary of all this was Greg's publicly expressed view that Cobden and Bright were 'doctrinaires', stranded by 'the entire and nearly universal secession from them of that part of the community which they used to influence so specially'.[188]

In fact, Cobden had been on bad terms with the *Manchester Guardian* almost from the start of his career. Archibald Prentice, the pioneer Leaguer, was soon calling the *Guardian* people 'Tories who are pleased to call themselves reformers . . . with a horror of a too rapid march of improvement'.[189] The paper's editor and partner Jeremiah Garnett did his best to stop Bright being nominated for Manchester in 1847, and ten years later took the lead in putting up Palmerstonian candidates against him and Milner Gibson.[190] Moreover, a very sharp ideological battle raged from 1848 onwards between the *Guardian* and the *Manchester Examiner*, which Bright and the railway magnate Absalom Watkin had set up as the mouthpiece of the 'Newall Building' set.[191] Yet the *Guardian*, in taking its pro-Palmerston line in the mid- and late 1850s, could claim, with some justification, to be the journal which reflected the opinions of Manchester's commercial class more accurately than did the *Examiner*.

---

[184] Howe, *Cotton Masters*, 167.

[185] Greg to Cobden, 11 May 1848, Cobden Papers (MCL).

[186] See Wilson to Aberdeen, 24, 26 Sept. 1854, Aberdeen Papers, Add. MS 43,254, fos. 117, 121. Edinburgh had long been the home of 'advanced Whiggery'.

[187] *Edinburgh Review*, 96 (Oct. 1852), 452–508.

[188] *National Review*, 1 Oct. 1855, cited in Howe, *Cotton Masters*, 229.

[188] Ayerst, *Guardian*, 73.

[190] Ibid. 125–6.

[191] Ibid. 99–102. Its joint proprietor was George Wilson, who also wrote articles for it (Stephen Koss, *The Rise and Fall of the Political Press in Britain*, vol. 1: *The Nineteenth Century* (1981), pp. 99, 107).

For the paradox is that the events of 1846–7 had made possible the sort of moderate Radical politics represented by both *The Economist* and the *Manchester Guardian*. 'Class', as we shall see, did not disappear from the political agenda in the 1850s. But the stark antagonisms which had divided Cobden from Ferrand in 1841–2 were never again to occur. And those fierce town/country antipathies which had shaped so much of the politics of the 1840s gradually abated. This was not as obvious in 1846 as it seems in hindsight, and entrepreneurial politics still had a very long way to run. Nevertheless, the events of 1846 were to shape the politics of the next few decades. For what had happened was the triumph of Free Trade but the defeat of the Free Traders.

2

Financial Reform, 1848–1853

Cut down the army and navy expenses 5 or 6 million and you do much more than save the money! . . . if the free traders will work it out the game is in their own hands and the time not distant when they will be the real rulers of the country.

(Woolley to Wilson, 1848)

INTRODUCTION

Peel seems in 1846, to have presided over a lasting 'national' settlement of the country's commercial problems. The Anti-Corn Law League had had its teeth drawn by the Premier's timely concession, while, at least for the time being, the Protectionists, even though they remained the largest single party in the Commons, were routed. Peel's resignation in June, which led to the formation of Lord John Russell's Whig Ministry, simply set the seal on his triumphant achievement. Not surprisingly, the 1847 election was a torpid affair; fewer seats were contested than at any other Victorian election. With Peel backing the Whig Government, no serious alternative was on offer, several of the Protectionist leaders, including Disraeli, making little secret of their belief that a restoration of the Corn Laws lay outside the realm of practical politics.

But all this was to end shortly after the new Parliament had been elected. In late 1847 the country was in the throes of a commercial depression; many banks failed, among them the Royal Bank of Liverpool, which closed its doors in October. In that same month the Government temporarily suspended the Bank Charter Act. With the bank rate as high as 12 per cent, businessmen were badly hit, and in all the major commercial and industrial centres a spate of bankruptcies occurred.[1] There was thus only a slight exaggeration in the claim of a Norwich merchant in March 1848 that the country was 'in a state of commercial disaster and manufacturing distress, which was unparalleled in the knowledge of man'.[2]

Moreover, in the course of 1847, while industry was depressed, corn prices tumbled. And until they rose again in late 1852, many farmers faced

---

[1] Sydney Buxton, *Finance and Politics: An Historical Study, 1783–1885* (1888), 87–8. D. Morier Evans, *The Commercial Crisis 1847–1848* (2nd edn., 1849).
[2] *Norfolk News*, 4 Mar. 1848.

acute difficulty, even ruin. Together, these set-backs dented confidence in the durability of Peel's 'national settlement', since the commercial distress reawakened the militancy of the class-conscious urban Radicals, while the agricultural depression stimulated a pronounced Protectionist revival.[3]

Political complications followed upon these economic difficulties. In February 1848 the Whig Government put forward a budget under which the income tax, due to expire, was renewed for another five years and its rate actually increased—from 3 per cent to 5 per cent. Faced by public outcry and parliamentary opposition, the Government beat a hasty retreat.

The circumstances which made this budget so unpopular and so untimely were, of course, the main cause for its introduction in the first place. The commercial recession had depressed tax yields, leaving the luckless Chancellor, Sir Charles Wood, with an estimated deficit of £8 million if the income tax were not renewed and a deficit of £3 million if it were[4]—hence the need for tax increases. So began what Charles Greville called in his diary 'Charles Wood's income tax agony'.[5] However, this short-term crisis was superimposed on a problem of much longer standing. Peel had revived the income tax in 1842 as a temporary measure to tide the country over until such time as the commercial prosperity produced by his reductions in customs and excise duties would cover the initial loss of revenue. Three years later the Conservative Government renewed the income tax and also initiated a further radical revision of the country's antiquated tariff structure. But the 1845 budget *abolished* many duties, rather than simply *reducing* them. And as Bulwer Lytton noted later, the old argument about the regenerative capacity of tax cuts thereafter became increasingly untenable.[6] Notwithstanding ministerial assertions about its temporary nature, the country was becoming dependent on the income tax, unless, of course, ways could be found to drastically reduce public expenditure.

But in 1848 the latter course was ruled out, since not only did the country face the cost of the late Kaffir War, but the Whig Ministry had recently been pressurized by the Duke of Wellington's discovery of gaps in the national defences into proposing major schemes of fortification and defence, and this, too, was cited in justification of the proposed income tax increases. In fact, Russell's addition of half a million to the defence estimates had brought spending on defence to an all-time peak of £18 million in 1847.[7]

The public reacted angrily, and the Government soon found itself assailed

---

[3] On agricultural depression, see Stewart, *Politics of Protection*, 117, 142.

[4] Buxton, *Finance and Politics*, 90–1.

[5] 2 Mar. 1848, in Charles C. F. Greville, *A Journal of the Reign of Queen Victoria from 1832 to 1852* (1885), iii. 146.

[6] Parl. Deb., 3rd ser., vol. 126, 456: 25 Apr. 1853.

[7] Buxton, *Finance and Politics*, 92. On the background to this, see M. S. Partridge, 'The Russell Cabinet and National Defence, 1846–1852', *History*, 72 (1987), esp. 240–5.

on two fronts, in Parliament and in the major urban centres. On 28 February, to appease restless MPs, it brought in a revised budget, which renewed the income tax for three (rather than five) years and left the existing rates unchanged. At the same time three parliamentary committees of inquiry into Government expenditure were set up. Ministers also had to beat off Joseph Hume's attempt to confine the income tax increase to *one* year.[8] Eventually, in the autumn, Wood announced savings of over £800,000, mostly at the expense of the Navy. Even so, the budget deficit could be bridged only by issuing a loan, an expedient to which Cobden and others raised strong objections.[9]

This imbroglio had long-term political consequences. For a start, it confirmed the public in its suspicion that the Whigs were incompetent financiers;[10] Wood had been appointed to the Treasury only because he was Lord Grey's relative, complained one Radical paper.[11] It also precipitated a Radical breakaway. In April 1848 some fifty or sixty Cobdenites formed themselves into a separate party, advocating retrenchment and parliamentary reform, and, to quote Gash, 'though the endemic Radical vices of quarrelsomeness and individualism soon asserted themselves, the breach between them and the Whigs was a running sore for the remainder of Russell's Administration'.[12]

But more worrying to the Government in the short run was evidence that most middle-class electors were enraged by the budget. Wood made it clear that he believed the public to be misinformed, but he also conceded that he had no alternative but to bow to the weight of opinion in the country. 'The country is roused, and the press is unanimous,' reported the *Illustrated London News*. 'There never was an instance of the people and the Press being so strongly and completely united against any former tax.'[13] Three months later the outcry had still not abated:

Associations formed with the sole object of urging financial reform upon the attention of the legislature are arising in all the great manufacturing and commercial districts. They hold meetings, prepare petitions, disseminate information, and ripen the mind of the country on this all-important topic.[14]

The income tax increases were especially unpopular. Quite apart from the hardship caused by the commercial crisis, it had been felt, even before the

---

[8] Parl. Deb., 3rd ser., vol. 97: 6 Mar. 1848. For its effects on the Whig Ministry, see Mandler, *Aristocratic Government*, 252–3.

[9] Parl. Deb., 3rd ser., vol. 101, 647: 29 Aug. 1848.

[10] Buxton, *Finance and Politics*, 95.

[11] *Norwich Mercury*, 10 Feb. 1849. Wood was the son-in-law of Lord Grey of the Reform Bill (who had died in 1845) and a close ally of the Third Earl, currently Colonial Secretary.

[12] Gash, *Reaction and Reconstruction*, 195.

[13] *Illustrated London News*, 26 Feb. 1848, p. 112. See also the comments in *Annual Register*, 1848, p. 34.

[14] *Illustrated London News*, 20 May 1848, p. 324.

proposed increases, that the imposition of this tax was unjust. Moreover, a week after the introduction of the first budget, revolution broke out in France, and though initially this seemed to the Government to offer a welcome distraction, it also made nonsense of the Ministry's 'invasion scare', and so mobilized large sectors of the middle class against the 'extravagance' of the aristocratic state.

Petitions [on the subject] poured in from all the principal towns in the country, constituencies instructed their Members to oppose, on pain of forfeiting their future support, the Ministerial measure, and it became evident, from a variety of symptoms, that a formidable agitation was rising up in the country, which if resisted might sweep away the Income Tax and the Ministry together.[15]

Public reaction took two forms: first, a belief that aristocratic mismanagement had encouraged gross waste and extravagance which could be overcome only by a fierce economy drive; and, second, a more wide-ranging political attack on the armed services, seen as a refuge for the incompetent younger sons of landed families. Cobden combined the two by demanding that the estimates be reduced to their 1835 level, largely at the expense of the Army and the Navy.

And so, in a year of revolutions, Britain's ruling class had to cope not only with Chartist disturbances[16] and the botched Irish 'rising', but also with a renewal of the bourgeois revolt, which, some contemporaries thought, constituted Britain's real contribution to the European revolutionary ferment.[17] And 'revolt' is hardly too strong a word for what was taking place: Wood's proposed budget, said the Cobdenite *Manchester Examiner*, constituted an outrage to which the great towns would 'only submit when every form of resistance that morality will sanction has proved unavailing to avert the evil'.[18]

Leagues sprang up all over the place. In March Cobden announced the birth of the Political Reform League, and in the following month a body called the 'Equitable Taxation League' was formed.[19] This was also the time when Hume launched his 'Little Charter' movement.[20]

But the agitation in the country owed little to such bodies, and occurred

---

[15] *Annual Register*, 1848, p. 43.
[16] See Roland Quinault, '1848 and Parliamentary Reform', *Historical Journal*, 31 (1988), 831–51, for a different view. See also Henry Weisser, *April 10: Challenge and Response in England in 1848* (Lanham, Md., 1983), and John Saville, *1848: The British State and the Chartist Movement* (Cambridge, 1987).
[17] See George Dixon, *Liverpool Mercury*, 25 Apr. 1848.
[18] *Manchester Examiner and Times*, 22 Feb. 1848.
[19] The former was dedicated to free trade, removal of indirect taxes, a fairer and more equitable representation of the people, justice for Ireland, land reform, a fairer system of promotions in the armed services, and a pacific foreign policy (*Norfolk News*, 18 Mar. 1848). The Equitable Taxation League also wanted suffrage extension, the secret ballot, triennial parliaments, and equal electoral districts (*Illustrated London News*, 20 May 1848, p. 325).
[20] Quinault, 'Parliamentary Reform', 836–9.

spontaneously in most of the major urban centres, with businessmen very often to the fore. The events in Norwich were not untypical. Here the Chamber of Commerce unanimously passed four resolutions: regretting the proposed income tax increase, lamenting the unfair mode of its operation, urging the reduction of national expenditure, and calling for the extension of the income tax to Ireland. According to press accounts, the meeting which the Chamber summoned 'was attended by a large number of the most responsible merchants and traders in the city'; at its conclusion the deputy mayor was given a petition to hand on to the borough's two MPs. A requisition was also presented to the mayor for the summoning of a 'Common Hall', in which the wishes of the inhabitants could be expressed. This meeting was not so well attended, perhaps because people could hardly leave their businesses in the middle of the day. But shortly afterwards the town council assembled to adopt a resolution on the income tax, and was actually in session when news came through of the ministerial climb-down.[21]

There was, in fact, hardly a town of any size which did not hold a big public rally. In Sheffield a committee was convened to produce a memorial for its MPs; the town hall was taken over for a protest meeting, and the borough electors put on record their total opposition to the 'increase of taxation upon the industry of the middle classes, and [the] needless amount of expenditure for apparently warlike purposes'.[22] Cobden, fearing that Leeds was about to direct the protest movement, urged George Wilson to action. The agitation, he wrote, 'legitimately belongs to the free trade party, whose head-quarters are in Manchester'.[23] Wilson responded by organizing a memorial which was signed by over 5,000 electors in the space of twelve hours.[24] The Manchester Chamber of Commerce also passed a resolution on the subject.[25] Perhaps the fact that the home of Free Trade did not take a more prominent role in the agitation had something to do with the threat posed by Chartist disturbances.[26] In addition, one of Manchester's two MPs, Milner Gibson, was hardly in a position to participate because he was serving as vice-president of the Board of Trade, an embarrassing situation which caused the other Member, John Bright, to lament that Gibson was becoming 'a martyr to Whig imbecility'.[27]

In fact, it was in Liverpool that the most impressive demonstrations were held. In late February 'what the Americans call "An Indignation Meeting"'

---

[21] *Norwich Mercury*, 26 Feb., 4 Mar. 1848; *Norfolk News*, 26 Feb., 4 Mar. 1848.
[22] *Sheffield and Rotherham Independent*, 26 Feb. 1848. On the protest meetings in the West Riding, see *Bradford Observer*, 2 Mar. 1848.
[23] Cobden to G. Wilson, 17 Jan. 1848, George Wilson Papers.
[24] *Manchester Examiner and Times*, 4 Mar. 1848.
[25] See *Manchester Guardian*, 15 Mar. 1848.
[26] The alarms set off by Chartism in Manchester from March to July 1848 are vividly captured in the diary of the old Leaguer Absalom Watkin (A. E. Watkin, *Absalom Watkin: Extracts from his Journal 1814–1856* (1920), 251–6).
[27] Bright to G. Wilson, 6 Apr. 1848, George Wilson Papers.

took place in the Sessions house which attracted such a throng of people, mainly businessmen, that not all could gain admission. This was the start of a series of public meetings in Liverpool,[28] which continued, as in other cities, well into the spring of 1849.

All these demonstrations shared a number of features. First, they were non-party occasions. Though the feeling behind the agitation may have been 'Radical', prominent Conservatives took part. In Norwich, for example, one of the principal speakers was Samuel Bignold, who was elected six years later as Conservative Member for the city. And in Liverpool the February demonstration was presided over by the mayor, T. B. Horsfall, a local merchant but also an active Conservative (and, again, a future Conservative MP), while one of its highlights was the reading out of a letter denouncing the budget from the pen of John Gladstone.[29] 'Banish the nicknames of Whig and Tories which now men bore', said a speaker at one of the later Liverpool meetings, 'and let them henceforth . . . be a mercantile and trading party, and thus . . . they would best serve the interests of the people and of the merchant, and best secure, likewise, the safety of Crown and country.'[30]

Secondly, all these meetings were dominated by businessmen furious at what they saw as aristocratic incompetence and exclusiveness. 'If there was one sentiment more than another rather prevailing than specifically dwelt upon,' reflected the *Liverpool Mercury*, 'it was this—and it was derived from the effects of class legislation—that for a commercial country like Great Britain, members of aristocratic families are not necessarily the wisest nor the most disinterested of governors.'[31] Robertson Gladstone, one of the leading Liverpudlian 'rebels', played upon this feeling when, turning to his predominantly mercantile audience, he said: 'You are looked upon as suspicious characters . . . and therefore it is [?imperative]—as this is a great mercantile manufacturing country—that we should require a larger proportion of the Government to be selected from amongst gentlemen such as I see before me (loud and reiterated cheering).' The very success of the demonstrations also did something to boost middle-class self-confidence. Wood and his friends had found to their surprise, said the *Manchester Examiner*, 'that calico-printers and cotton-spinners really are possessed of intellects which can see into other things than the exigencies of trade, and of eloquence, which can cope successfully, not on one, but on all subjects, with the most thoroughbred aristocratic statesman!'.[32]

A third feature of these meetings was the way in which, time and again,

[28] *The Times*, 1 June 1848; *Liverpool Mercury*, 25 Feb. 1848.
[29] *Liverpool Mercury*, 25 Feb. 1848.
[30] A. H. Wylie, *The Times*, 1 June 1848.
[31] *Liverpool Mercury*, 25 Feb. 1848.
[32] *Manchester Examiner and Times*, 25 Feb. 1848.

parallels were drawn between private commercial establishments and Departments of State. This became a favourite theme of the Radical Press:

John Bull is a commercial creature, and, spite of prejudices, a very fair judge, as well as a very severe critic, of money transactions and money accounts. He has come to see, and to feel too, that Government is in fact very much a matter of pounds, shillings, and pence, and that English statesmanship is little better than an elaborate and very successful experiment on the taxability of the English people.... If England were a private estate, would I, or any gentleman in his senses, pay fifty million a year for its management? Why then should not the same principle of economy be applied to the national property as are held necessary in reference to a farm, a shop, or a profession?[33]

The businessmen who packed the financial reform meetings were regaled with the same message. George Dixon of Birmingham, for example, appealed directly to the interests of his Norwich audience:

He counted that this financial matter was a grand battle as to whether the nation should be governed on genteel principles, or the vulgar principles of shopkeeping and commerce. It was a stale thing to tell them that Bonaparte had said that they were a nation of shopkeepers. All he would say was that at any rate they kept their books in a very disgraceful manner (laughter).... Now, the truth was, that they must become vulgar shopkeeping men after all.[34]

Similarly, John Williams, MP for Macclesfield, treasurer of the National Parliamentary and Financial Reform Association and himself a retired linen draper and silk merchant, told a meeting at Marylebone that there was one Government department employing 220 clerks in which the accounts had not been balanced for eight years; the accountant subsequently called in had declared that, through the adoption of double-entry bookkeeping, the work could have been done efficiently with only twenty-two clerks.[35]

THE LIVERPOOL FINANCIAL REFORM ASSOCIATION

The most effective and long-lived of the provincial pressure groups which sprang up to channel this angry movement of middle-class protest was the Liverpool Financial Reform Association (LFRA). It came into existence, ostensibly as a non-political body, during the excitement following Wood's first two 1848 budgets in April of that year. But as W. N. Calkins has shown, it had a forerunner in the Liverpool Association for the Reduction of the Duty on Tea, founded two years earlier.[36] The Government's refusal to accede to

---

[33] *Norfolk News*, 26 Feb. 1848. The paper returned to this theme the following month (18 Mar. 1848).

[34] *Norwich Mercury*, 10 Feb. 1849.

[35] *Illustrated London News*, 3 Mar. 1849, p. 142.

[36] W. N. Calkins, 'A Victorian Free Trade Lobby', *Economic History ·Review*, 13 (1960–1), 95–7. See Robertson Gladstone's letters to William Gladstone, Glynne–Gladstone MSS (hereafter, Hawarden Papers).

the demands of this pressure group had shown financial reformers that they must cease bidding against one another and form a common front. The new organization never attracted significant working-class support (membership fees were 5s. per annum). Instead, the membership was dominated by local Liverpool worthies, often active on the town council and in the Chamber of Commerce, with tea and coffee brokers being especially prominent. Robertson Gladstone, William Gladstone's elder brother, took on the presidency of the Association.[37]

It was an appropriate choice. Whereas the other Gladstone brothers had received an 'élite' education, Robertson had been quickly pulled out of Eton by his father, who realized that this was the son who would succeed him in business. In time Robertson became a partner in his father's firm and an important figure in the Liverpool mercantile community. At the same time, he began sloughing off his inherited Tory convictions and embracing 'advanced' Liberalism. Even as early as September 1841 we find Robertson complaining that Peel's commercial policy showed that the Prime Minister was 'not acquainted with the feelings, at the present moment, of the mercantile constituency of the country'.[38] By 1853 such feelings had crystallized; public affairs, he now argued, should be conducted by men of humble birth with a grasp of practicalities, 'those who gain their subsistence by their own exertions, and who form the backbone of the *trade* of the country—these are the men to speak—not the money mongers.... The wrong class of society is in office.'[39] Bright, with whom Robertson Gladstone had earlier begun a correspondence, noted approvingly to Cobden in November 1848 that the Liverpudlian merchant prince was 'very liberal—quite ready to go for reform'.[40]

Like many businessmen, Robertson Gladstone viewed the conventions and rituals of parliamentary life with impatience: 'the long, tiresome speeches, the talk about themselves—and their technical observations of 'Right Hon. Gentlemen' and 'Noble Lord', and so forth.[41] To him it was 'painfully clear' that 'the Government and the House of Commons [were] foreigners to the real condition of trade and of the position of the great mass of the people'.[42] 'We in the middle classes', he told William, 'have daily acquaintance' with the social problems of the big cities, 'and therefore are qualified to deal with

---

[37] Calkins, 'Victorian Free Trade Lobby', 91–8. Another body was also set up in Liverpool, the National Confederation for the Equitable Adjustment of Taxation, which dealt with local as well as national finance. There was some overlap in membership between the two bodies.

[38] Robertson Gladstone to William Gladstone, 18 Sept. 1841, Glynne-Gladstone MSS, vol. 661. There is much valuable information on the Gladstone family and on Robertson Gladstone in S. G. Checkland, *The Gladstones: A Family Biography 1764–1851* (Cambridge, 1971).

[39] Robertson Gladstone to William Gladstone, 30 Nov. 1853, Hawarden Papers, vol. 663.

[40] Bright to Cobden, 21 Dec. 1848, John Bright Papers, Add. MS 43,383, fo. 185.

[41] Robertson Gladstone to William Gladstone, 24 May 1847, Hawarden Papers, vol. 661.

[42] 22 Mar. 1848, ibid., vol. 662.

them ... far better than the man who never once even looks out of [a] window.'[43] It is significant that, while taking an affectionate interest and pride in his younger brother's political career, Robertson was still looking in the late 1840s and early 1850s to *Cobden* as a political leader, and it was Cobdenite prescriptions which came most readily to his lips. 'What does this Balance of Power mean, but a struggle for aristocratic distinction, place and position!,' he exclaimed in a characteristic outburst in November 1853.[44]

This vehement Radicalism was faithfully expressed in the programme of the LFRA. Its stated objectives were: 'to promote, by all legal and constitutional means—1. ECONOMICAL GOVERNMENT. 2. ABOLITION OF CUSTOMS AND EXCISE DUTIES, AND SUBSTITUTION OF DIRECT, IE HONEST, TAXATION. 3. PERFECT FREEDOM OF TRADE.'[45]

Although Cobden thought it unrealistic to press for the substitution of *all* customs and excise duties by direct taxation, he quickly saw the importance of the LFRA, and drew it to the attention of the Commons on 6 July. The fact that its president was a Conservative, the brother of the MP for Oxford University, said Cobden, showed that this was not a recklessly radical body, though he added that it was disgraceful that the House of Commons should need to be told how to perform the duty of reforming the financial system and reducing expenditure by an outside assembly, and one headed by a Conservative at that![46]

Recognizing that he and the Association were 'separately working to accomplish similar objects',[47] Cobden went up to Liverpool in early December 1848; he met leading members like William Brown (MP for Lancashire South) and Lawrence Heyworth, and joined the Council Board of the Financial Reform Association, which Robertson Gladstone continued to chair. The Liverpudlians were 'earnest men', Cobden informed his wife, even if he did not see which of them was 'capable of directing so great an undertaking'.[48]

Nevertheless, Cobden felt sufficiently encouraged to write up his own schema for taxation reform, which was later published as the sixth of the Financial Reform Association's tracts and became commonly known as the

---

[43] 6 Mar. 1853, ibid., vol. 663.

[44] Robertson Gladstone to William Gladstone, 30 Nov. 1853, Hawarden Papers, vol. 663. On Robertson's continuing infatuation with Cobden, see Richard Shannon, *Gladstone*, vol. 1: *1809–1865* (1982), 395. Later, after Cobden's premature death, Robertson asked William whether he could get him a photograph of his great hero (Robertson Gladstone to William Gladstone, 30 Dec. 1865, Hawarden Papers, vol. 666).

[45] These objectives were defined at a meeting on 20 Apr. 1848.

[46] 6 July 1848, *Cobden's Speeches*, 548. For Robertson Gladstone's reactions, see his letter to his brother, 15 July 1848, Hawarden Papers, vol. 662.

[47] LFRA pamphlet no. 6, p. 1.

[48] 8 Dec. 1848, Morley, *Cobden*, ii. 31–2.

'National Budget'.[49] As Cobden later explained to a sceptical Bright, he had 'put forth that plan to raise the standard of discussion upon financial Reform, and to prevent the financial Reformers from wasting time upon trifles'.[50] He also hoped that his budget would enable the Manchester men to join in the agitation which Liverpool had so effectively started without their being 'committed to all the crude and in some cases absurd publications they [i.e. the LFRA] have put forth'.[51] In fact, Cobden well understood that beneath Bright's objections lay a contempt for Liverpool's political capacity and wisdom, a prejudice which he partly shared. Yet Cobden also saw that any 'new agitation . . . would have greater force if it did not *seem* to spring from Manchester—because it would look like the restless cravings of old agitators for continued excitement', and he knew that it would be both curmudgeonly and 'unpatriotic' to allow petty jealousy to damage a promising agitation for which the country seemed 'ripe'.[52]

Following Cobden's intervention, a public meeting was held in Liverpool on 20 December at which the 'budget' was read out to tremendous applause. It proposed 'economies' of £10 million, mainly at the expense of the armed services and the ordnance, coupled with the raising of another £1 million from the introduction of a probate and legacy duty upon real estate, entailed or unentailed. These changes would allow the giving away of about £11 million through the abolition or reduction of a whole range of customs duties (on tea, timber, butter, and cheese), excise duties (on malt, hops, soap, and paper), and taxes (window tax and advertisement duty).[53]

The commercial men of Liverpool, once more in an intensely class-conscious mood, were enraptured by this message. One enthusiastic gentleman called out that they should make Cobden Prime Minister of England. (Robertson Gladstone from the Chair agreed that this would be a good thing, but told his audience that the 'people' already had it within their power to direct the policy of the House of Commons by maintaining pressure on it.[54]) The Liverpudlians especially appreciated the foreign policy implications of retrenchment: 'pounds, shillings and pence, he thanked God, knew nothing of frontiers,' said one member of the audience, coarsening Cobden's message somewhat![55] But it was perhaps Robertson Gladstone, introducing the meeting, who really got to the heart of the matter:

What we contend for is this—that the affairs of the nation shall be conducted, in every respect, precisely as every sensible, sound-thinking member of this community, with a

---

[49] See Robertson Gladstone's acceptance of it (Robertson Gladstone to William Gladstone, 8 Jan. 1849, Hawarden Papers, vol. 662).

[50] Cobden to Bright, 27 Dec. 1848, Cobden Papers, Add. MS 43,649, fo. 128.

[51] 22 Dec. 1848, ibid., fo. 110.

[52] Ibid. 109.

[53] LFRA pamphlet no. 6, pp. 8–12.

[54] Ibid. 15.

[55] Ibid. 14.

due regard to economy, would organise his own business (loud cheering). Every man wants to know how cheaply he can get his work done (applause). We want to get value received for our money (loud applause).[56]

Although Cobden provided the movement for financial reform with a credible national spokesman,[57] Gladstone's family name also counted for something. Wrote one friendly critic:

Nothing could have been more graceful and more happy than that Liverpool and Gladstone should have completed what Manchester and Cobden had begun; that a name occupying the foremost place in our commercial annals, ranking with the Greshams and the Fuggers of the past, should have declared, in the name of our first seaport, that our merchants could do with fewer floating batteries, and that our colonial system was a profitless delusion.[58]

At first all went well. At the Liverpool meeting of 20 December the Secretary of the LFRA spoke of the enormous progress that the Association was making, and several Radical MPs and businessmen, including the Chairman of Manchester's Chamber of Commerce, Thomas Bazley, announced their support.[59] A number of big rallies were subsequently held in January 1849, notably one at Manchester, where Cobden elaborated on what he meant by 'economic reform'.[60] The *Illustrated London News* thought that these demonstrations portended a revival of the Anti-Corn Law League.[61] Though this did not happen, it was announced at the annual meeting of the Association, held on 18 April 1849, that thirty-six local groups from all over the country had already affiliated.[62]

The Association also achieved valuable publicity when on 26 February Cobden took the opportunity of moving an amendment to the motion for going to the Committee of Supply to air the LFRA's programme. The financial reformers were beaten in the division lobby by 275 to 78, but Cobden, Bright, and Milner Gibson were able to rehearse their grievances against high expenditure on armaments and the colonies and to press for a return to the spending levels of 1835.[63] On 23 March Cobden informed MPs that branches in imitation of Liverpool's were springing up in London, Edinburgh, Manchester, and many smaller towns; he hoped that in the

---

[56] Ibid. 3.

[57] '"The Cleverest Cob" in England', *Punch*, 13 Jan. 1849, p. 6; 'The Schoolmaster at Home', ibid., 10 Feb. 1849, p. 49.

[58] 'Economist', *Letter to Robertson Gladstone, Esq., on the Publications of the Financial Reform Association* (1849), 5.

[59] LFRA pamphlet no. 6, pp. 6–7.

[60] See *The Times*, 11 Jan. 1849; 10 Jan. 1849, *Cobden's Speeches*, 242–51; Morley, *Cobden*, ii. 36.

[61] *Illustrated London News*, 13 Jan. 1849, p. 17.

[62] LFRA pamphlet no. 16, pp. 11–12.

[63] Parl. Deb., 3rd ser., vol. 102, 1218–1303: 26 Feb. 1849.

interests of retrenchment every town and village would soon have one.[64]

Robertson Gladstone reported excitedly to his brother on the progress of the movement: 'The demand for the Tracts (by purchase) is unprecedented. I find that about *140,000* of them are now in circulation.'[65] A month later he returned to this theme: 'You see what a stir Financial Reform has made throughout the kingdom; they may attend Cobden, but he had nothing to do with it originally; the game was made, before his Budget appeared . . . I believe about 60 Financial Reform Associations are now in existence.'[66] This could be dimissed as childish boasting. Yet the *Annual Register* was able to declare that by the close of the 1848 Session, financial reform had taken 'a considerable hold upon the public mind' and 'obtained a general acquiescence'.[67]

Most historians have dismissed the movement for financial reform as a nine-day wonder.[68] It is certainly true that, after a flurry of public meetings in 1848 and 1849, the LFRA fell back largely on the publication of a series of tracts. Nor did all members of the 'Manchester School' share Cobden's commitment to financial reform as an end in itself. Bright, in particular, remained sceptical, because he was still hankering after a suffrage agitation. In his message to the LFRA, he included the significant words:

The policy hitherto has been to spend all they can raise, instead of spending as little as possible. But this springs naturally from the fact that the tax-payers do not form the Parliament. Our representation is a juggle, and, without a change in it, I doubt if we shall be able to apply a remedy to the extravagance of our rulers.[69]

But Cobden disagreed, and tried to impress on Bright the potential possessed by Liverpool's financial reformers:

However defective in men and money at present, they are in as good a position as we were a year after the League was formed; and they have far more hold upon the public mind than we had even after three years' agitation. I rather think that you do not fully appreciate the extent to which the country is sympathizing with the Liverpool movement.[70]

---

[64] Parl. Deb., 3rd ser., vol. 103, 1190–6: 23 Mar. 1849. These remarks came during a debate initiated by a Conservative back-bencher, who protested at the LFRA's 4th pamphlet attacking the 'clothing colonels', which, he said, gave the common soldier the impression that 'the Army was created and maintained for the benefit of the aristocracy'. The LFRA was defended by Hume, Cobden, and Milner Gibson, the latter (no longer a Minister) calling it 'a respectable association' ('Oh!, oh!').

[65] Robertson Gladstone to William Gladstone, 8 Jan. 1849, Hawarden Papers, vol. 662.

[66] n.d. (probably Feb. 1849), ibid.

[67] *Annual Register*, 1849, pp. 152–3.

[68] e.g. Norman McCord, 'Cobden and Bright in Politics, 1846–1857', in Robert Robson (ed.), *Ideas and Institutions of Victorian Britain* (1967), 89–90. For a disparaging view of the LFRA, see P. R. Ghosh, 'Disraelian Conservatism: A Financial Approach', *English Historical Review*, 99 (1984), 275.

[69] LFRA pamphlet no. 6, p. 7.

[70] Cobden to Bright, 23 Dec. 1848, Morley, *Cobden*, ii. 38. See also Hinde, *Richard Cobden*, 194–5. Cobden to Ashworth, 23 Dec. 1848, Cobden Papers, Add. MS 43,653, fo. 119.

Bright and George Wilson, who had originally envisaged a rather different kind of agitation,[71] were not so easily persuaded. In fact, the episode brought about one of the severest disagreements between Cobden and Bright which the two men ever experienced. Bright poured out his grievances to Wilson. Cobden, he said,

is for one thing at a time, and so am I, if it be a thing well defined, which I think financial reform is not. . . . Financial reform will be given with double speed by the ruling class if they see we have a strong association to back us, and which threatens to take the power from them . . . Agitation without registration is worth little.[72]

Two months later the disagreement remained unresolved. Grumbled Bright: 'Cobden is still wrong on these points, and Walmsley and the reformers here [i.e. London] are not willing to put everything aside for 'financial', and they can't see their way to do it.'[73] This was true, for most of the London Radicals continued to insist that parliamentary reform be given precedence.[74]

THE ECONOMY CAMPAIGN

But the financial reform movement certainly achieved two things. First, it put pressure on the Government to instigate an economy drive. Select committees on expenditure were set up in the spring of 1848. Cobden was naturally disappointed, though hardly surprised, when the Government ignored his suggestion that these committees should have 'what there is not in the Cabinet—an equal proportion of merchants, manufacturers, professional men, and landed proprietors, or other possessors of realized property'.[75] Nevertheless, he and Hume were both appointed to two of these bodies.

The committee examining the Navy estimates later came up with a number of suggestions for savings in the dockyards; it also called for further enquiry 'with the view to ascertaining whether new work may not be done more cheaply by contract'.[76] A separate committee charged with investigating the Army and Ordnance expenditure similarly looked to private business establishments as models for emulation. Was it necessary, asked this com-

---

[71] Bright to Cobden, 21 Dec. 1848, John Bright Papers, Add. MS 43,383, fos. 182–3.

[72] Bright to G. Wilson, 24 Dec. 1848, George Wilson Papers.

[73] 15 June 1849, ibid.

[74] e.g. see reports of the meeting at St Pancras in March and the first public meeting of the Metropolitan Financial and Parliamentary Reform Association in May (*The Times*, 18 Mar., 23 May 1849). But many of the branches of the LFRA had also disconcerted its officers by opting to go 'far beyond us' in the matter of parliamentary reform (LFRA pamphlet no. 16, pp. 11–12). On metropolitan developments, see N. C. Edsall, 'A Failed National Movement: The Parliamentary and Financial Reform Association, 1848–54', *Bulletin of the Institute of Historical Research*, 49 (1976), 108–31.

[75] Parl. Deb., 3rd ser., vol. 97, 508: 13 Mar. 1848.

[76] Report on Navy Estimates from Select Committee on Navy, Army and Ordnance Estimates, XXI (1847–8), pp. xcv–xcvi.

mittee, that the Ordnance should keep such large stocks in reserve when modern means of conveyance enabled a speedy replenishment in the event of an emergency?[77]

That savings could be made in the dockyards by putting employees on piece-work was a proposition that commanded widespread support. So keenly was this advocated by *The Economist* that the labour unions feared for the future of their members' jobs, especially once Wilson had joined the Government.[78] Robertson Gladstone had reform ideas of his own; merchant ships and steamers, he suggested, could, when necessary, be converted to war uses.[79] Other economists recommended subcontracting in the naval shipyards as a way of improving standards and reducing waste and extravagance; even *The Times*, usually no friend of the financial reformers, thought that this proposal merited closer consideration.[80]

Meanwhile, Sir Charles Trevelyan, Secretary of the Treasury, had begun his own investigations, which were specifically aimed at giving his department control and supervision over all government spending.[81] As Jenifer Hart has observed, Trevelyan was not a Whig in his sympathies, but he 'co-operated in some economy drives with Hume'.[82] Much was achieved in this way, especially in respect of dockyard economies.[83]

Still more might have been done had Cobden, who believed that national policy, like household policy, should be determined by income and not vice versa, not committed the financial reformers as a group to the reduction of State expenditure to the level of 1835.[84] *The Times* was not alone in protesting against this idea: 'Every man's common sense tells him that one year's budget of a great country cannot be arbitrarily fixed as a standard for budgets 15

---

[77] Second Report from Select Committee on Army and Ordnance Expenditure, IX (1849), p. lxxi.

[78] S. Maccoby, *English Radicalism, 1832–1852* (1935), 405–6.

[79] See Robertson Gladstone to William Gladstone, 26 Feb. 1853, Hawarden Papers, vol. 663.

[80] *The Times*, 31 July 1849.

[81] As was also recommended by the Third Select Committee on Miscellaneous Expenditure, XVIII (1847–8), p. ix.

[82] Jenifer Hart, 'Sir Charles Trevelyan at the Treasury', *English Historical Review*, 75 (1960), 109. On Trevelyan's attitude to military organization, see Hew Strachan, 'The Early Victorian Army and the Nineteenth-Century Revolution in Government', *English Historical Review*, 95 (1980), 795–7.

[83] According to the *Manchester Guardian* (30 Jan. 1849), the report on the Admiralty came up with 30 economy proposals, of which the Government accepted 28, most of them affecting the dockyards. On investigations into different Government departments, see Jenifer Hart, 'The Genesis of the Northcote–Trevelyan Report', in Gillian Sutherland (ed.), *Studies in the Growth of Nineteenth Century Government* (1972), 69–71. On the 'customs scandal' of 1851, see John Masterman, MP, *Report of Proceedings at the Public Meeting of Merchants, Bankers, and Traders of the City of London, Held at the London Tavern on Wednesday, Dec. 3, 1851, for a Reform of the Board of Customs* (1851).

[84] This was in stark opposition to Disraeli's later dictum that 'expenditure depends on policy' (Ghosh, 'Disraelian Couservatism', 284).

or 20 years later'.[85] Gladstone objected to the 'National Budget' on the same grounds, complaining that Cobden 'puts the cart before the horse in determining first what he will repeal and then, with much less detail, how he will support the establishments of the country'.[86] *The Economist* joined in the criticisms of Cobden, adding that the financial reformers' gloomy interpretation of the growth in public expenditure ignored the underlying strength of the expanding British economy.[87]

None the less, public expenditure *did* fall significantly between 1848 and 1850, with armaments spending dropping from £18 million in 1847 to just over £14 million in 1851, before increasing once more until in 1853 it had reached £16 million out of a total expenditure of £55 million.[88] Well might Cobden claim that this would not have occurred but for the efforts of the Liverpudlian financial reformers.[89]

Significantly, however, the urban Radicals were not alone in promoting 'economies', for leading Protectionists sometimes supported them too. Indeed, as *The Times* noted, Colonel Sibthorp was often a far more effective critic of the Admiralty's estimates than anyone from the Manchester School.[90] True, most Tory MPs shrank from doing anything that might damage national security; but at least they had no compunctions about attacking extravagance within the *civil* administration. Thus, Joseph Henley called in 1849 for the salaries of all civil servants to be cut by 10 per cent.[91]

Of course, there was never much likelihood of a warm *rapprochement* between Radicals and Protectionists. On the contrary, the start of the 1848 crisis saw some Protectionist papers explicitly blaming the country's mishaps on free trade.[92] And in 1851, such was the tension between the two groups that disgruntled East Anglian farmers proclaimed that they would rather march on Manchester, the capital of free trade, than on Paris![93] For its part, the Manchester School viewed the Protectionist revival with alarm. Cobden, for example, told a Leeds audience in December 1849 that it would be folly to attempt to restore Protection, since this could only have the effect

---

[85] *The Times*, 15 Apr. 1850. Moreover, Cobden also had to face criticism from middle-class newspapers from whom he might have expected support. See the *Manchester Guardian's* sneers at 'amateur Chancellors' (3 Jan. 1849) and Cobden's quarrel with Baines (Cobden to Baines, 28 Dec. 1848, Cobden Papers, Add. MS 43,644, fos. 205–6).

[86] William Gladstone to Robertson Gladstone, 27 Dec. 1848, Hawarden Papers, vol. 569, fo. 13.

[87] *The Economist*, 27 Jan. 1849, p. 89; also 6 Jan. 1849, pp. 1–2. It also argued that the growth in expenditure was partly caused by the one-off expense of converting the Navy to steam and other 'exceptional' items (ibid., 20 Jan. 1849, p. 60).

[88] Buxton, *Finance and Politics*, 92–3.

[89] 8 Mar. 1850, *Cobden's Speeches*, 254.

[90] *The Times*, 15 Apr. 1850.

[91] See Stewart, *Politics of Protection*, 151.

[92] e.g. *Liverpool Mail*, 18 Mar. 1848.

[93] Asa Briggs, *Victorian People* (1954; 1965 edn.), 29.

of unleashing a new onslaught on the whole aristocratic system. Cobden was only slightly less hostile to Disraeli's scheme for 'compensation' for the agriculturalists, which he characterized as 'robbery' and as a device for reimposing the old Corn Law in another guise.[94] As we shall see, the only assistance which he was prepared to give agriculture was a reduction of the malt duty, in the hope of separating the farmer from the landowner—a traditional Radical ploy.

Such friction notwithstanding, Disraeli did on occasion try—or at least pretend to try—to edge the Conservative Party in the direction of the LFRA by taking up the issue of 'retrenchment', as, for example, in the course of 1849.[95] And four years later, Robertson Gladstone received intimations that similar overtures were being made. In a transparent attempt to put pressure on his brother, Robertson wrote him a letter, telling him that 'a member of the Carlton Club [was] in correspondence with the Council of the Financial Reform Association in connection with the objects of the Association and with a view to their furtherance'.[96]

But, as we shall see shortly, Disraeli's experiences with his second budget were to show the difficulties in the way of a Cobdenite–Protectionist *rapprochement*.

THE ATTACK ON THE ARMED SERVICES

In any case, barriers to such co-operation had already been erected by the LFRA through its attacks on the monarchy and the armed services, activity which was especially likely to cause offence in Conservative quarters. The first two pamphlets issued by the Association had dealt respectively with the Civil List, the proposal being to reduce it in two stages from 385,000 to 150,000, and with the expenses of the royal household, some of whose minor ceremonial offices were itemized and held up to ridicule.[97] With the wisdom of hindsight, the officers of the LFRA conceded that this might have been an error of judgement, in that the size of the Civil List was hardly 'the greatest financial grievance' which the country had to bear; the issue had been highlighted, they explained, only because the Court infected 'every department with a mean ambition to ape its multitude of useless officials, its parades and ceremonialism, the worthless legacy of a half-civilized age'.[98] None the less,

---

[94] See his speech at Leeds, 18 Dec. 1849, *Cobden's Speeches*, 211–22, in which he warned the aristocracy that they would be 'torn to pieces' if the struggle over the Corn Laws was resumed. Cobden to Jos. Ellison, 12 Dec. 1849, Cobden Papers, Add. MS 43,668, fos. 51–2. On Disraeli's six proposed alternatives to Protection, see Ghosh, 'Disraelian Conservatism', 269–70.

[95] See Stewart, *Conservative Party*, 235. Disraeli's attitude to 'economy' is well discussed in Ghosh, 'Disraelian Conservatism', 286–8.

[96] Robertson Gladstone to William Gladstone, 26 Feb. 1853, Hawarden Papers, vol. 663; he repeated the claim on 6 Mar. (ibid.).

[97] LFRA pamphlet nos. 1 ('Civil List') and 2 ('Curtailment of Allowances to Royal Family').

[98] LFRA pamphlet no. 35, p. 8.

a would-be supporter had good cause to complain of what he called 'an undercurrent of radicalism, with its flippant, conceited, arrogant sneer',[99] while *The Times*, a persistent enemy of the organization, was able to lambast it for its 'low taste'.[100]

The Association soon switched its attacks from the monarchy to the armed services. The tone was set early on when, at a meeting in Liverpool on 17 November ('a simple-minded Liverpool audience', *The Times* called it), speaker after speaker hurled insults at the military. Officers were described as 'men who spurn an honest trade or the profession of a merchant, but who, nevertheless, dabble in the common market for their own aggrandisement'. It was alleged that this scandal was allowed to continue only because the House of Commons was full of officers or their close relatives (381 in all, according to one estimate).[101] Such attacks were repeated in Manchester before a capacity audience, numbering some six or seven thousand, chaired by George Wilson, the old Anti-Corn Law League organizer. Cobden claimed that it would be possible to reduce the tea duty and abolish duties on timber, butter, malt, hops, and house windows if only they could put a stop to the 'waste' of £10 million on 'an unproductive service like our fighting establishments in peacetime'.[102]

Soon afterwards the LFRA published its fourth pamphlet, whose principal author seems to have been Robertson Gladstone himself. It included a vigorous denunciation of the system whereby certain army officers ('the clothing colonels') profited from their task of supplying uniforms to their men. This soon involved Robertson Gladstone in a bad-tempered exchange with Major-General Napier. Had these insults been uttered by an individual, said Napier, his officers would have vindicated their 'honour' by physically chastising the author.[103] *Punch* rallied to the Association's side.[104] But in a House of Commons full of army officers, MPs lined up in February 1849 to express their indignation. Unfortunately for the LFRA, the impression conveyed by this episode was that the Association was not entirely in command of its facts.[105] And although the Select Committee examining armed services expenditure later looked into the question of whether 'clothing colonels' should be abolished, it reached no clear conclusions on the matter.[106]

---

[99] 'Economist', *Letter to Robertson Gladstone* (1849), 6.

[100] *The Times*, 3 Oct. 1848.

[101] Ibid., 18, 19 Nov. 1848.

[102] Ibid., 11 Jan. 1849.

[103] LFRA pamphlet no. 4. *The Times*, 29 Dec. 1848, 6, 10, 25 Jan. 1849.

[104] e.g. 'Foozle, Colonel and Tailor', *Punch*, 27 Jan. 1849, p. 39. However, by publishing Napier's attacks on the financial reform tracts, *The Times* only succeeded in giving them greater publicity. See Strachan, 'Early Victorian Army', 793.

[105] Parl. Deb., 3rd ser., vol. 102, 1218–1303: 26 Feb. 1849.

[106] Report from Select Committee on Army and Ordnance Expenditure, X (1850). The Committee issued no recommendations, but discussed the clothing question on 26 Apr. 1850; see esp. qs. 4685–97, 4748–9, 4777–83.

The LFRA was on much stronger ground when it raised the issue of the narrow social composition of the officer corps.[107] But it may be doubted whether it was a wise ploy to couple these attacks with complaints about the emoluments of army officers. As *The Times* correctly pointed out:

It is perfectly true that the country is served by gentlemen, but it is wholly false that those gentlemen are pecuniary gainers by their service. On the contrary, ours is the only army in the world which is thus partially exempted from a mercenary character, and which is led by officers by whom the profession and calling itself is in most cases esteemed a sufficient reward. Yet this is the point of our system which is selected by the Liverpool financiers as the fittest and most prominent object of denunciation and abuse![108]

Unfortunately for the LFRA, this part of its campaign effectively put paid to its claim to be a non-party organization, and potential Conservative sympathizers began to shy away from it. One such person wrote an open letter to Robertson Gladstone, saying that 'the capitalist, whether manufacturer or merchant, ha[d] been sorely pinched these last three years, and ha[d] silently cursed Income-Tax and Poor Rates' and so was yearning for retrenchment. But he protested at the LFRA's insinuations that to 'improve' was to '*Americanise*'. 'In an association such as yours one Tory is worth a dozen Liberals,' wrote this pamphleteer; 'Mr. Cobden and the League well knew this, and, accordingly, they gave the chief seats in the synagogue to all who joined them.'[109]

Also unpopular was the 'pacifist' note which the Association was always striking. 'There is no such defence against invasion as ports ever open to all comers' was characteristic of its utterances.[110] Similarly Cobden told a Manchester audience that there 'must be a smaller manifestation of brute force in the eyes of the world';[111] meanwhile, the *Liverpool Mercury* thought it a 'fundamental error' to suppose that the maintenance of a large war establishment in times of peace would impress foreigners, who took far more account of evidence of 'our permanent means of providing for war when it comes'.[112]

The Whigs were especially annoyed by this sort of propaganda. Lord John Russell, for example, thought that the 'plans of Hume and Cobden' were 'destructive of the Empire'.[113] But many businessmen were also contemptu-

---

[107] However, some military historians think that the Radicals exaggerated the socially exclusive nature of the office corps. See Hew Strachan, *Wellington's Legacy: The Reform of the British Army 1830–54* (Manchester, 1984), 110.

[108] *The Times*, 19 Nov. 1848.

[109] 'Economist', *Letter to Robertson Gladstone*, esp. 4, 8, 14.

[110] LFRA pamphlet no. 35, p. 11.

[111] *The Times*, 11 Jan. 1849.

[112] *Liverpool Mercury*, 16 Jan. 1849.

[113] Russell to Bedford, 18 Dec. 1849, Gooch (ed.), *Later Correspondence of Russell*, i. 198. Cornewall Lewis was equally contemptuous (Lewis to Sir Edward Head, 4 Sept. 1849, in Gilbert Frankland Lewis (ed.), *Letters of Sir George Cornewall Lewis* (1870), 211).

ous of the doctrinaire Radicals. The *Manchester Guardian*, for example, alleged that Cobden had taken far too optimistic a view of French intentions, and suggested that the Radical leader had been 'misled by his own benevolent feelings'.[114] Moreover, as Sir Charles Wood pertinently observed in the Commons debate of February 1849, all these strictures on the military came ill from the citizenry of Liverpool, who had pleaded with the Government for troop reinforcements during the Chartist disturbances of the previous year. 'Gentlemen connected with the manufacturing interests must remember that they would be the first to suffer from the effects of tumult and plunder,' he said.[115]

There was even an *economic* case that could be mounted against the financial reformers' view of foreign affairs. As one pamphleteer put it in 1849:

I will venture to affirm, that false economy like yours has lost this country more in one year than all your tailor colonels and drunken captains would in a century! . . . You may carry on free trade in politics to any extent you please abroad; but at home, though we adopt your recommendations in commerce, we shall not feel disposed to deprive the constitution of Protection![116]

Finally, it is probably true, as modern military historians have pointed out, that the penny-pinching campaigns of the 'economists' did nothing whatever to help the cause of military efficiency—rather the reverse, in fact.[117]

THE PROBLEM OF INCOME TAX REFORM

But what really brought down the financial reform movement was a fundamental indecision about the kind of fiscal outcome it favoured. All could agree that the existing income tax was unsatisfactory because it failed to distinguish between what, in the jargon of the day, were called 'permanent' and 'precarious' incomes. This, complained the entrepreneurial Radicals, involved favouritism to landowners and those living off the 'Funds' (those assessed under Schedules A and C) at the expense of businessmen and professional men (assessed under Schedules D and E) whose income was constantly at risk from ill health and other vicissitudes of life.

As Cobden explained in the House of Commons on 13 March 1848:

Between those whose incomes are derived from realised property and those whose incomes depend on trades and professions, there is a tangible, visible, marked line of

---

[114] *Manchester Guardian*, 13 Jan. 1849. Cobden's strictures also led to a breach with the Radical faction, of which the 'Radical General', George de Lacy Evans, was a key figure (Edward M. Spiers, *Radical General: Sir George de Lacy Evans 1787–1870* (Manchester, 1983), 132–3).

[115] Parl. Deb., 3rd ser., vol. 102, 1243: 26 Feb. 1849. And the Protectionist, Herries, deprecated the violent language used at the LFRA's meetings (ibid. 1266).

[116] 'Harry Holdfast', *A Short Letter to Mr. Cobden in Reply to his Long Speech at Manchester, from his Quondam Admirer* (1849), 9–12.

[117] Strachan, 'Early Victorian Army', 793. John Sweetman, *War and Administration: The Significance of the Crimean War for the British Army* (Edinburgh, 1984), 35–40.

demarcation.... [Take the case] of a man of business, who has £10,000 of capital. He gets £500 a year for the interest of his capital, and 5 per cent more as the produce of his skill and industry. Is that man, getting £1,000 a-year by the application of his talents, to pay the same as the man who derives £1,000 a-year from real property, worth £25,000?

'Professional men, and men of business, and the labourers whom they employ', Cobden boldly asserted, 'are the classes which have the first claim upon the sympathy and justice of the State. The industrious classes put in motion the wheels of the social system, and upon their activity and enterprise all the value of realised property depends.'[118] Underlying such remarks as these, there lurked the view, never explicitly formulated, that Schedule D should be entirely abolished in order to release more investment capital, this being seen as the key to national prosperity.[119]

Criticism of the income tax merged naturally with the articulation of another demand: that the probate and legacy duty levied on 'personalty' should be extended to real estates, which were still exempt. All the financial reformers were enfuriated by this 'anomaly'. As Cobden said in his 'National Budget' letter: 'In the last year upwards of two millions was paid into the Exchequer by the heirs to personal property, converting many of the hard-earned accumulations of our merchants, manufacturers, professional men, traders, and mechanics; whilst the ducal domain, or the estate of the great landed proprietor, passed untaxed from the dead to the living.'[120] Bright took the same line, as, of course, did the Liverpool reformers.

Yet how were the hardships allegedly being inflicted upon the earners of 'precarious' incomes to be remedied? Two possible strategies emerged, and both were discussed by the Select Committee on the Income Tax which Hume chaired in 1848. The first strategy was simply to vary the rates as between those covered by Schedules A and C, on the one hand, and those covered by Schedules B, D, and E, on the other. The second way of tackling the problem was to capitalize all incomes and make this the basis of assessment, thereby taking into account the *duration* of income and its *regularity*. This had long been advocated by William Farr, who presented arguments in its favour before Hume's committee, where he made a convert of the chairman but failed to convince the majority of its members.[121] Many businessmen

---

[118] Parl. Deb., 3rd ser., vol. 97, 506–7: 13 Mar. 1848.

[119] This issue is interestingly discussed by Shehab, who argues that the income tax reformers might have been more successful had they urged the State to encourage the creation and accumulation of new capital, rather than attempting to demonstrate the existence of 'double taxation', which is what they did when the matter came before the 1861 Select Committee (F. Shehab, *Progressive Taxation: A Study in the Development of the Progressive Principle in the British Income Tax* (Oxford, 1953), 153).

[120] LFRA pamphlet no. 6, p. 9.

[121] Shehab, *Progressive Taxation*, 107–11. Meta Zimmeck, 'Gladstone Holds His Own: The Origins of Income Tax Relief for Life Insurance Policies', *Bulletin of the Institute of Historical Research*, 58 (1985), 172–3.

liked this solution; after all, capitalization was a familiar feature of insurance transactions (hence its nickname, the 'actuaries' scheme'). What it might have meant in practice can be seen from the abortive amendment moved by a Liberal back-bencher in the spring of 1848, which provided for a scheme under which realized property would have been assessed at 8*d*. in the £; trade, commerce, and manufactures at 6*d*.; and income from professional and other precarious sources at 4*d*.[122] Such a differentiation of income for tax purposes struck many businessmen as inherently fair. But was it practicable?

Moreover, the Radicals' common commitment to the cause of the earners of 'precarious' incomes concealed a more fundamental uncertainty about what kind of fiscal system they actually *favoured*. As we have seen, the LFRA wanted to move towards a situation in which customs and excise duties as a whole would be swept away, so that *all* revenue would derive from direct taxation. This led Jeffery, one of the LFRA's spokesmen, to urge that the income tax be made permanent and be extended until it became the *only* source of public revenue.[123] Similarly, when in 1853 Gladstone proposed the abolition of income tax in seven years' time, Heyworth, another Liverpudlian financial reformer, pleaded with the House not to 'stultify itself' by foregoing the advantage of a fiscal device from which *all* classes of the community ultimately benefited.[124]

The Liverpool reformers would also have liked to put an end to the income tax *threshold*, so that *all* citizens would have an interest in the conduct of financial policy.[125] Heyworth pointed out that only half a million people were currently paying income tax, whereas three million were subject to indirect taxes.[126] Making income tax universal would, he thought, encourage everyone to become a good bookkeeper, something that would be an educative experience in itself.[127]

Unfortunately the Liverpool reformers did their case no good by frequently presenting their 'solution' to the fiscal difficulty in excited terms as if it were an answer to all the problems of society:

The taxation of industry is an evil and a sin which the world cannot, if it would, endure much longer; happy the nation which shall first be emancipated from such barbrous

---

[122] Parl. Deb., 3rd ser., vol. 97, 162–231: 3 Mar. 1848. The proposal proved too much for most MPs, who rejected it by 141 votes to 316.

[123] Report of Select Committee on Income and Property Tax, XX (1852), qs. 5679–5753.

[124] Parl. Deb., 3rd ser., vol. 126, 1343–4: 9 May 1853. All this was bound up, in Heyworth's mind, with a pure *laissez-faire* ideology (ibid., vol. 140, 1528: 28 Feb. 1856). Heyworth's commitment to the income tax led to his later expulsion from the inner councils of the LFRA (see Ch. 4).

[125] Report of Select Committee on Income and Property Tax, q. 5751.

[126] Parl. Deb., 3rd ser., vol. 126, 1343: 9 May 1853. Compare Lord Cranborne's complaint about the financial reformers' attempts to alter this ratio, Apr. 1866, in Paul Smith (ed.), *Lord Salisbury on Politics: A Selection from his Articles in the Quarterly Review, 1860–1883* (Cambridge, 1972), 215.

[127] Report of Select Committee on Income and Property Tax, q. 5751.

thraldom; happy the people who first proclaim and practise the truth, that all right to labour and to exchange the produce of labour is as much the gift of God to every human being as the right to *think* and to communicate his thoughts, and that it ought to be held equally sacred by individuals and by nations.[128]

Indirect taxes were a 'sin', claimed the LFRA, because of the inducement they gave to smuggling.

Cobden, by contrast, while equally enthusiastic about the 'emancipation of commerce', was noticeably more cautious in his references to direct taxation, which, of course, involved 'inquisition' into an individual's private affairs. In 1845 he had referred sarcastically to 'those men with sharp noses, and ink-bottles at their buttons,—who have gone prying about your houses and at your back-doors, to learn how many dinner-parties you give in a year, and to examine and cross-examine your cooks and foot-boys as to what your style of living may be'.[129] And although he later came to feel that, on balance, direct taxes were preferable to indirect taxes, because the latter were, in Dunckley's words, 'thoroughly unbusinesslike and anti-commercial',[130] he still urged caution upon the Liverpool reformers:

It would be far easier [he wrote in his National Budget letter] to effect a reduction of expenditure to the extent of £10,000,000, and apply the whole of that sum to the removal of the Excise and Customs duties, than to transfer the same amount from indirect to direct taxation. Excepting in Liverpool and a few of our largest trading towns, there is not, at present, a very great force of public opinion in favour of direct taxation. It has yet to be created and organized.[131]

Indeed, many Cobdenite journals shared the view, expressed in the *Norfolk News*, that 'the Income Tax in its present form [was] robbery, its renewal, still more its enlargement, [was] madness, indicative of a fatal futurity'.[132] Even if the 'unjust' treatment of 'precarious incomes' could be rectified, which (as we shall see) would be far from easy to achieve, did the commercial men who supported the financial reform movement really want to see the income tax made a permanent part of the country's fiscal system? This would, of course, be going far beyond the Peelite orthodoxy (also subscribed to by most Whigs): namely, that there was no point in 'refining' the income tax since it would expire once the short-term emergency which had called it into existence had passed away.

---

[128] LFRA pamphlet no. 35, 12.

[129] 15 Jan. 1845, *Cobden's Speeches*, 127. But he added that at least the revenue so generated did go to the Queen, not like the corn duty which went to the tithe and the landowner. For the depth of Cobden's hostility to income tax at this time, see Cobden to Baines, 14 Dec. 1844, Cobden Papers, Add. MS 43,664, fos. 177–8.

[130] Revd Henry Dunckley, *The Charter of the Nations; or Free Trade and its Results* (1854), 373.

[131] LFRA pamphlet, no. 6, 8. See also his letter to Robertson Gladstone, 7 Jan. 1850, Hawarden Papers, vol. 579.

[132] *Norfolk News*, 26 Feb. 1848.

Hume, in particular, remained an inveterate critic of the income tax. In fact, it was he who in 1851 flouted Cobden's advice and sought to persuade the House of Commons to confine the renewal of that tax to just one year. Perhaps, Hume ruminated, the tax was no longer necessary now that the country was running an estimated budget surplus of £2 million. Hume also secured the establishment of a Select Committee on the Income Tax, under his own chairmanship, to examine ways in which it could be made more equitable.[133]

Bright, too, had a long history of opposition to the income tax. In 1842 he had condemned its reimposition in the strongest possible terms. The tax, he claimed, was a heavy burden 'upon all honest men who honestly declare the amount of their income, whilst knaves can often get off by a lie or a false oath'. Moreover, said Bright, the tax bore down upon income 'from whatever source derived', without taking it 'in proportion to the amount of property'; this was unjust since it helped landowners, whose land retained its value, while damaging manufacturers, whose machinery depreciated. Instead of the income tax, Bright advocated a 'property tax', which should, he said, 'be an assessment upon all land and buildings, and canals and railroads, but not on property such as machinery, stock in trade, etc.'.[134] This idea, as we shall see, re-emerged, in more detailed form, in the tract *The People's Blue Book*, published anonymously in 1857.

In March 1848 Bright followed Hume's lead in urging that the extension of the income tax be confined to one year, ignoring the warning of other Radicals that this would entail his going through the same lobby as the Protectionists: 'I shall never shrink from a right vote for fear we should be in a majority—at least I hope not,' he told George Wilson.[135] By 1851 he had changed tack, and this time he voted against Hume's spoiling motion. Nevertheless, whereas Cobden's initial hostility to the income tax abated, Bright's did not. Nor did the two men entirely see eye to eye over the 'property tax', an innovation which Cobden seems never to have endorsed. All this was to prove significant in the future.

Yet these disagreements among the business Radicals surfaced only occasionally in the late 1840s and early 1850s, because the movement for 'financial reform' succeeded in focusing their common resentment against the 'privileges' enjoyed by the landed interest, especially its exemption from legacy duties. Moreover, whether they wanted the abolition of the income tax or its conversion into a permanent part of the country's fiscal system, the Radicals

---

[133] See H. C. G. Matthew, 'Disraeli, Gladstone, and the Politics of Mid-Victorian Budgets', *Historical Journal*, 22 (1979), 620; Buxton, *Finance and Politics*, 94; Zimmeck, 'Gladstone Holds His Own', 170–2.

[134] Trevelyan, *Life of Bright*, 72–3.

[135] Bright to G. Wilson, 7 Mar. 1848, George Wilson Papers.

could all agree that, in its existing form, it discriminated unfairly against people employed in trade, industry, and the professions. Consequently there was an outcry whenever attempts were made to renew the income tax in the middle of a recession when a budget deficit threatened, as in 1848. But renewal proved equally unpopular in years of comparative prosperity, as in 1851, when its necessity could legitimately be questioned. As long as this fiscal uncertainty remained, most businessmen would have concurred with Cobden's verdict that the history of taxation in Britain was, taken all in all, the history of feudal oppression.[136]

It is hardly an exaggeration, therefore, to say that the country's future, both financial and political, would, to a considerable extent, be determined by whichever party or statesman succeeded in resolving this problem in such a way as to secure widespread satisfaction. In the event, two attempts were made: one by Disraeli in his second budget of 1852 and one by Gladstone in his budget of the following year.

DISRAELI AND HIS 1852 BUDGET

Disraeli faced by far the more difficult task. Not least, he was unlucky in having to make a financial statement in November, midway through the financial year, when the fiscal situation was not clear. Gladstone, by contrast, found himself to be the fortunate inheritor of a surplus, which might have been Disraeli's, had his government lasted longer. The new Chancellor also showed poor judgement on certain issues, and he was inexperienced and ill served by his Treasury officials. But Disraeli's fundamental dilemma has been well stated by Robert Blake: 'He could not please the landed interest without risking destruction in a Parliament which that interest no longer controlled. He could not resist it without risking the break-up of his party.'[137]

Faced by the income tax difficulty which had plagued the life of his Whig predecessor, Disraeli embarked on a characteristically audacious gamble. In Colin Matthew's words, he initiated 'a pincer movement against the centre by the two extremes of Westminster politics, the country party and the radicals'. In other words, he offered concessions to the agriculturalists *and* the urban middle classes.[138]

At first sight this looks like an attempt to square the circle. But Disraeli's gambit had a certain logic to it; for although the Cobdenite Radicals and

---

[136] 17 Dec. 1845, *Cobden's Speeches*, 177. The remark had been made before the income tax renewal, but this had always been, and long remained, Cobden's opinion of the country's fiscal system.

[137] Robert Blake, *Disraeli* (1966; 1969 edn.), 347–8. The most recent discussion of Disraeli's budget is to be found in Ghosh's important and controversial article 'Disraelian Conservatism'.

[138] Matthew, 'Disraeli, Gladstone', 621–2. For a quite different interpretation, see Ghosh, 'Disraelian Conservatism', esp. 281, 275–6. Ghosh claims that income tax differentiation was more a Whig than a Radical demand.

the Protectionist Party clearly represented distinct—even opposing—social and economic interests, they had certain things in common at the level of parliamentary politics. For a start, neither had much chance—in the immediate future, anyway—of winning a Commons majority for itself, and both chafed at the Whig ascendancy. A coming together by the 'outs' in an effort to oust the 'natural party of government' therefore had much to recommend it. Moreover, Disraeli had always liked and admired Cobden, and Bright was amused, as well as mistrustful, of the Conservative leader, which made the enterprise that much less hopeless. Nor would such a juncture have been entirely unprincipled. For, as we have seen, there were times when, despite the chasm between the two groups over free trade versus protection, each found itself advocating retrenchment. To understand the background of Disraeli's second budget, it is therefore necessary to examine more closely the relationship which had developed between Disraeli and the Radicals during the previous four years.

In public, of course, the relationship was an antagonistic one, not least on fiscal matters. Thus Disraeli (not yet acknowledged as leader of the Opposition) was warning the Commons in 1848 that what he called 'the Manchester confederation' planned to impose 'class legislation' of a brutal kind through the existing government, which—Bright had recently admitted as much—was an avowedly 'middle class government'. Since great fortunes were not to be found among the landed proprietors of England—or so Disraeli claimed—it was unjust that Cobden should be trying to make taxation fall entirely upon 'the realised property of this country'.[139] Moreover, from March 1849 onwards, Disraeli initiated a series of annual motions calling for an inquiry into the burdens on land, suggesting that some of the rates be transferred to the Consolidated Fund.[140] Relief was urgent. 'The landowners of this country might be rather supposed to be a conquered race than a predominating legislative interest,' so ran the *Annual Register's* summary of his speech of March 1849; 'in no European country was the land so heavily burdened.'[141] This was the old 1840s class rhetoric, in which the interests of agriculture were set against those of industry.

Yet Cobden reacted with subtlety to Disraeli's motions. Clearly, he had no intention of consenting to 'compensations' for the landowners, but he did see certain advantages in exploiting the prevailing agricultural depression and trying to win over the tenant farmers to his side. In fact, his 'National Budget', as he explained to Bright, had been deliberately framed so as to bring 'into one agitation the counties and the towns'.[142] That is why this manifesto contained a proposal to secure the total repeal of the malt tax, which was

---

[139] Parl. Deb., 3rd ser., vol. 97, 437–8: 10 Mar. 1848.
[140] See Stewart, *Politics of Protection*, 151.
[141] *Annual Register*, 1849, p. 51. In February 1851 Disraeli's motion was lost by only 14 votes.
[142] Morley, *Cobden*, ii. 34–5.

rapidly becoming to farmers a symbol of class oppression rather as the corn tax had been to the manufacturers prior to 1846.[143]

Admittedly, there was a price to be paid for this preferred 'bribe', since, in a speech to the Commons on 15 March in which he mocked Protectionist talk about the 'burdens on land', Cobden had made it clear that the abolition of the malt and hops duty would involve the speedy reduction of armaments expenditure.[144] Nevertheless, in 1849 the Conservative leadership was nervously noting that farmers in some parts of the country seemed tempted by the Cobdenite programme.[145] Cobden jubilantly reported to Bright that his farmer friend Lattimore had told him that at his local farmers' club, home of the local Anti-Malt Tax Committee, there was even talk about 'the propriety of joining the Liverpool Financial Reform movement'.[146] Interestingly, the Cobdenite *Norfolk News* was claiming in January 1849 that the 'most revolutionary part' of Cobden's recent speech at Manchester was its offer to help farmers rid themselves of the malt tax:

Monopoly has raised a feud between commerce and agriculture, for the purpose of pillaging both, and the day which sees them once more heartily united for the common good, will assuredly see also the end of unjust taxes, and of their source, large military establishments, colonial jobbery, and foreign intermeddling. . . . What do the Norfolk farmers say to them?

Let there be an alliance between the plough and the shuttle, the farmer and the shopkeeper.[147] Many farmers must also have welcomed Cobden's advocacy of rent reduction in a speech delivered at Aylesbury, near Disraeli's own constituency.[148]

But at the same time as Cobden was trying to insert a wedge between landowner and farmer, the more intelligent of the Protectionists were attempting something similar: namely, to broaden their party's social base by enticing some of their urban opponents into its fold. For example, in March 1849, in the course of urging compensations (he preferred to talk about 'recognition') for the suffering agriculturalists, Disraeli came up with a scheme for shifting half the rate burden on to the Consolidated Fund; among the beneficiaries, he said, would be 'the owners of real property in towns', with whose grievances he claimed to sympathize deeply. Rating reform, in fact, would 'put an end to those complaints of which we have heard so much from Manchester, Bradford, and other great seats of manufacturing industry', he cleverly

---

[143] Heyworth acknowledged as much; see Parl. Deb., 3rd ser., vol. 109, 796: 12 Mar. 1850.

[144] Ibid., vol. 103, 846: 15 Mar. 1849.

[145] Newdegate was warning Lord Stanley in February 1849 that farmers were saying that they would 'with much regret join the Cobdenite party, as the only men who manifest any practical intention of assisting them in their difficulties' (Stewart, *Politics of Protection*, 144).

[146] Cobden to Bright, 16 Nov. 1848, Cobden Papers, Add. MS 43,649, fo. 95.

[147] *Norfolk News*, 20 Jan. 1849.

[148] Maccoby, *English Radicalism*, 306.

added. When Disraeli came up with another version of this proposal a year later, Cobden, who had hoped to debate the merits of free trade with his Protectionist opponents, was visibly disconcerted. Clearly this was an ingenious attempt, as Avner Offer says, 'to separate the shopkeeper and house-capitalist from the mill-owner and merchant, thus isolating the urban patriciate within its own bastions'.[149] All the more surprising, then, that Disraeli did not attempt a reform of local taxation along these lines when he became Chancellor.

However, when Disraeli drew up his second budget in 1852, he did make an effort to win over the entrepreneurial Radicals. He did so by acceding to their long-standing demand that the income tax distinguish between 'precarious' and farm incomes, on the one hand, and income from rentals and from the funds, on the other. Moreover, the tax threshold was left at £100 for those earning 'industrial incomes', whereas other taxpayers were now liable as soon as their earnings reached £50. Reductions in the tea duty were also likely to please the Cobdenites. At the same time, the agriculturalists would be appeased not only by the proposed abolition of the duties on malt and hops but also by the provision that farming profits would henceforth be assessed on one-third, rather than one-half, of rental. Since all these 'bribes' were costly, Disraeli also lowered the exemption limit on inhabited house duty, in the hope of avoiding a deficit.

Yet, for all its ingenuity, Disraeli's budget was not a success. In particular, the attempt at income tax differentiation soon ran into difficulties. True, the Chancellor had recently been a member of Hume's Committee, but he had not mastered the complexities of the tax system, apparently. Rejecting the 'actuaries' scheme', which he had never liked, Disraeli opted instead for a differentiation by income tax schedules; but he failed to realize that, for example, schedule A (land) covered profits from collieries, quarries, and canal companies, and schedule D covered income from personal or real property outside England and Scotland.[150] Disraeli's enemies were quick to pounce on such anomalies.

Nor did the scheme make much political sense. Disraeli's belated overture to Bright does indeed confirm the suspicion that he was hoping to squeeze his budget through a Commons in which his party lacked a majority by wooing the Cobdenite Radicals.[151] But the manœuvre did not succeed. True, Cobden acknowledged, it was a 'remarkable' fact

that a Government supported almost exclusively by county Members—representing territorial interests only—should be the first Government to deal—at all events, in

---

[149] Avner Offer, *Property and Politics 1870–1914: Landownership, Law, Ideology and Urban Development in England* (Cambridge, 1981), 167–70. Angus Macintyre claims that Lord George Bentinck had earlier foreshadowed this move of Disraeli's ('Lord George Bentinck', 150–1).

[150] Blake, *Disraeli*, 332–3. Matthew agrees, but thinks that the injustices and anomalies of the unreconstructed tax were as bad (Matthew, 'Disraeli, Gladstone', 622).

[151] Matthew suggests that Hume tried to 'catch' Disraeli (ibid. 621).

principle, if not going to the full extent—fairly with the income-tax, as it relates to trades and professions. Most assuredly that proposal should have come from a Government representing this side of the House.

But Cobden would have preferred a capitalization scheme. And he furiously denounced those elements in the budget which had been put forward as 'compensation' for the abandonment of Protection: 'We are entering on the old controversy between town and country, and you compel us to go into this controversy in a spirit that I thought was never to have been revived.' Cobden particularly disliked the house duty, from which small urban property owners would have been the main sufferers, contrasting this provision of the budget with the favour being shown to the land; the towns would never put up with such unfair treatment, he said. Indeed, Cobden's speech contained a savage indictment of the ground landlord, which seems to prefigure the later rhetorical exercises of David Lloyd George.[152]

In fact, Cobden's remarks indicate the extent of Disraeli's failure in 1852. What the latter was *trying* to achieve is clear from his intervention in the budget debate of the following year. Disraeli then defended country gentlemen as a class from Bright's attacks by arguing that they had done more than any other class for the rights and liberties of the people. He also urged the representatives of the big towns to respect the institutions as well as the material prosperity of the countryside, both, in his opinion, being necessary to national greatness. Radicals who ignored this truth would soon find that 'they ha[d] changed a first-rate Kingdom for a second-rate Republic'. Yet Disraeli saw no reason why this should happen, since he claimed that there was no longer any 'difference of material interests between the people of the great towns and the people of the country', which meant that it was illogical to attack land, as distinct from other forms of property.[153] Thus did Disraeli stand Cobden on his head by singing the praises of 'his own' class and then universalizing its values.

But Disraeli's attempt to further this vision through the second of his 1852 budgets had ended in abysmal failure. All he had achieved was to demonstrate that, in fiscal matters at least, there was no possibility of creating class harmony through the reconciliation of the polar opposites of British society. Indeed, in the course of promoting his budget, the Conservative leader had made dangerous concessions at the expense of his own class and party, which his opponents would shortly exploit. Yet he had not succeeded in detaching the Radicals from the Whigs and winning them over to his side. And so, with the Peelites contemptuously hostile to a financial measure which they thought eccentric and irresponsible—'quackish' was Gladstone's description—the budget was doomed to defeat, and with it the Derby Ministry itself.

---

[152] 13 Dec. 1852, *Cobden's Speeches*, esp. 276, 272.
[153] Parl. Deb., 3rd ser., vol. 126, 992–3: 2 May 1853.

It was thus left to Disraeli's successor, Gladstone, to try another formula for the resolution of the fiscal dilemma.

GLADSTONE'S 1853 SETTLEMENT

Gladstone had opposed the setting up of Hume's Committee and had refused to sit on it, perhaps because he disliked Hume's commitment to differentiation.[154] Moreover, the subsequent failure of Disraeli's budget had simply confirmed him in the view which he had always held: that differentiation was not a practical proposition. What, Gladstone irritably asked his Cobdenite brother, Robertson, did the financial reformers '*mean*' by 'precarious' incomes? (Robertson promptly put him in touch with the appropriate 'experts'![155]) Tackling politics as he did from the point of view of someone involved in executive government, Gladstone was clearly exasperated by Radical sloganizing. Moreover, as he told the Commons, differentiation of the income tax would mean an intolerable amount of extra work for the Treasury.[156]

Gladstone also made good use of three lines of argument with which Sir Charles Wood had vainly attempted to defend himself against his critics in March 1848. There was, Wood had suggested, an immense amount of 'evasion and fraud' under schedule D, since official returns indicated that there were only 9,000 persons in Great Britain deriving incomes exceeding £1,000 a year from trades and professions. 'Can anyone believe that?', asked Wood. 'Why, it is notorious that, with the exception of a very few landed proprietors, the great amount of wealth in this country is to be found amongst the manufacturing and commercial classes.'[157] In short, the middle classes did not have a genuine fiscal grievance at all. Wood had also argued that the income tax was *already* differentiated, in that schedule A was based on gross income, schedule D on net income. What was more, the landowners, said Wood, were being more heavily taxed than other sectors of the community if *local* as well as imperial taxes were taken into consideration.[158]

Gladstone repeated all these arguments, but to much greater effect, in defence of his 1853 budget.[159] Although it had a small provision exempting savings which had been invested in deferred annuities or in life assurance,[160]

---

[154] J. B. Conacher, *The Aberdeen Coalition, 1852–1855* (1968), 61.

[155] William Gladstone to Robertson Gladstone, 3 Mar. 1853, Hawarden Papers, vol. 570, fos. 1–2. Robertson Gladstone to William Gladstone, 6 Mar. 1853, ibid., vol. 663.

[156] Shehab, *Progressive Taxation*, 116.

[157] Parl. Deb., 3rd ser., vol. 97, 1031–4: 27 Mar. 1848.

[158] Parl. Deb., 3rd ser., vol. 97, 1031–4: 27 Mar. 1848. See the *Manchester Guardian*'s irritable rejoinder to this argument, 29 Mar. 1848.

[159] Professional men, he argued, paid only one-twelfth of the income tax, and, but for the difficulty of 'weeding them out', there was even a case for excluding them from liability entirely (Shehab, *Progressive Taxation*, 119).

[160] Ibid. 119–20. It has been shown that Gladstone's insertion of premium relief into his budget was an attempt 'to satisfy in part the grievances of the tax reformers without making any

this was the nearest it came to income tax differentiation. The new Chancellor did not, on the other hand, feel that all was well with the existing form of the income tax. In 1853 he told Manchester businessmen that he recognized how unsatisfactory that tax still was, hence his decision to work towards its eventual abolition, which was planned for 1860.[161] The occasion for this statement was the Chancellor's unveiling of the Peel memorial in Manchester, which was appropriate, since Peel had revived the income tax only on the understanding that it should never become part of the country's permanent fiscal system.

But more than a pious devotion to Peel's memory was involved here. For it seems that Gladstone genuinely disapproved of the income tax, and did so on grounds which were broadly similar to those invoked by his businessman father. As early as 1841 he had advised Peel against restoring the income tax on a number of grounds: among them, that such a move would strongly offend the mercantile class.[162] He had been led to this opinion, he later explained, 'by vivid recollections of descriptions I have often heard my father give of the effect of the old income tax in a commercial community'.[163]

Moreover, whereas the LFRA worried lest indirect taxes would encourage smuggling, Gladstone saw even greater moral dangers in the income tax: schedule D, he told Robertson in 1859, was 'full of pitfalls and traps against which even honesty, such as is generally found, cannot be proof'.[164] He also thought the tax inquisitorial and an encouragement to high expenditure. This became almost an *idée fixe* of Gladstone's over the following decade. 'I seriously doubt', he later told Cobden, 'whether the spirit of expenditure will give place to the old spirit of economy, as long as we have the Income Tax.'[165] This, of course, was a complete rejection of the contention of the Liverpool reformers and of Cobden, who obstinately clung to their belief that direct taxation would of itself *discourage* extravagance by bringing home its consequences in an unmistakable way to the electorate.[166]

In fact, Gladstone was convinced that the Liverpool reformers were barking up the wrong tree when they tried to move the country towards a total reliance upon direct taxation. As a practical financier, he came to feel that a mixture of direct and indirect taxes better served the country's interests. Nor had he ever been impressed with the 'National Budget'; what a pity, he had told Robertson in December 1848, that Cobden was apparently 'too great a man to

concessions of principle and thus to cut the ground from beneath their feet' (Zimmeck, 'Gladstone Holds His Own', 168). There was also a small element of graduation: see Matthew, 'Disraeli, Gladstone', 627.

[161] *The Times*, 13 Oct. 1853.

[162] Gladstone to Peel, 4 Nov. 1841, Parker (ed.), *Sir Robert Peel*, ii. 500.

[163] Gladstone to Peel, 16 Nov. 1841, in Francis Edwin Hyde, *Mr. Gladstone at the Board of Trade* (1934), 18.

[164] William Gladstone to Robertson Gladstone, 18 Aug. 1859, Hawarden Papers, vol. 572; cited in Checkland, *Gladstones*, 398–9.

[165] Gladstone to Cobden, 5 Jan. 1864, Cobden Papers, Add. MS 44,136, fo. 214.

[166] e.g. Cobden to Bright, 14 Apr. 1858, ibid., Add. MS 43,650, fo. 287.

fight details in the House of Commons—he rarely attended during the discussion of the Estimates, differing from Hume who is always at his post'.[167] What mattered most, Gladstone believed, was the achievement of economy.

Yet Gladstone had much in common with his brother and also with Cobden in the matter of seeking further ways of 'emancipating' commerce from its burdens. He wanted to achieve this, as his admirer F. W. Hirst later explained, less because he wanted to help consumers than because he sought to provide a stimulus to employment—another Peelite legacy.[168] The temporary renewal of the income tax in the 1853 budget was accordingly presented as a necessary accompaniment to a further wholesale reduction and abolition of customs and excise duties, including duties on tea, soap, and timber, proposals which were bound to go down well with the business Radicals, who also welcomed the extension of the income tax to Ireland, something for which the LFRA had been calling in its big meetings in 1848–9.[169]

How, though, did Gladstone view the fiscal responsibilities of land? Here his attitude was complex, as befitted someone whose own personal relationship to landed society was ambivalent. On the one hand, he did actually believe that the land was currently overburdened with taxes, as the landowners themselves had always claimed. 'You say and I agree', he wrote to Robertson in January 1853,

that the income tax bears unequally on the professional class: a landed proprietor of £500 per annum (holding in fee) is better able to pay it than a medical man with the same income from his profession. But I should be glad to know whether you think that these two persons are on the average *equally able* to save a given amount out of their incomes. I think not. I think that the calls of society as to scale of living and otherwise on a man with a permanent income to a given amount, are as a general rule considerably higher than those on a man with a precarious income.[170]

In fact, ironically enough, Gladstone's budget of that year was in several respects softer towards the landed interest than Disraeli's had been, since it kept the threshold for schedule A taxpayers at £100, whereas Disraeli had proposed to lower it to £50.

On the other hand, Gladstone promised in his budget that legislation would shortly be introduced to extend the probate and legacy duties to real estate: a long-standing Radical demand.[171] This commitment caused him considerable trouble with his Cabinet colleagues, Palmerston being a particularly persistent

---

[167] William Gladstone to Robertson Gladstone, 27 Dec. 1848, Hawarden Papers, vol. 569, fo. 14.

[168] Francis W. Hirst, *Gladstone as Financier and Economist* (1931), 186.

[169] But Disraeli's second 1852 budget would also have made Ireland liable to Schedules C and D.

[170] William Gladstone to Robertson Gladstone, 21 Jan. 1853, cited in Hyde, *Mr. Gladstone*, 24 (where the recipient is erroneously given as J. Gladstone).

[171] See Gladstone to J. Wilson, 1 Apr. 1853, cited in Barrington, *Servant of All*, i. 230.

critic. Moreover, when the budget came before Parliament, it was the landed
gentlemen on the Conservative benches who expressed most indignation.
'When were the boons to Manchester to end?', asked Newdegate. 'For the last
ten years they had been doing nothing but legislating for Manchester,' while
agriculture had been left to languish; he regarded the budget as 'another
blow at the agricultural interest'.[172] When the Succession Duties Bill came
before Parliament, another violent outcry ensued, with county members talking darkly about the spoliation of landed property, and some even predicting
the destruction of landed society itself.[173]

But it was in the House of Lords that opposition to Gladstone's policies
was fiercest. Lord Malmesbury tried to get the question of succession duty
referred to a Parliamentary Select Committee,[174] and the Earl of Winchilsea
'looked back to the time when the bold Barons of England resisted the
imposition of those oppressive taxes which were sought to be levied on the
people in feudal times'.[175] At first the Prime Minister felt that the Government
might have to accept Malmesbury's motion, though in the end it was defeated
by 139 to 126, thanks to thirteen votes from the episcopal benches.[176]

In fending off the Opposition attacks, an important role was played by
Aberdeen and other great Whig and Peelite landowners who came forward to
argue that Gladstone, like Peel, was really a true friend of the land.[177] Indeed,
by a nice irony, it was Charles Wood, speaking as a landowner, who made one
of the most telling defences of the budget, arguing that the landowners were
bound to share in the prosperity of 'the trading, mercantile, and manufacturing population', in whose well-being they had an inextricable stake.[178] In any
case, said Wood, Disraeli's December budget, with its tax differentiation,
had posed much greater dangers to land than anything which the present
Government was proposing.[179] This was a shrewd thrust. For Disraeli
occupied a very vulnerable position in 1853, since, as several Ministerialists
reminded him, he had made two observations when in office which suggested
that the *Derby* Ministry was about to extend the legacy duties.[180]

In any case, the more the Conservatives were driven to fury by a budget

[172] Parl. Deb., 3rd ser., vol. 126, 497–8: 25 Apr. 1853.

[173] In the debate on the Succession Duties Bill, Sir John Pakington also spoke of Gladstone's
'pandering to Radical prejudices and Radical exactions. . . . [He] thought it was high time that this
war of classes was at an end' (ibid., vol. 128, 75: 13 June 1853). Viscount Galway, Lord Lovaine,
and Thomas Booker all made similar complaints (ibid. 325: 16 June 1853; vol. 126, 735–6: 28
Apr. 1853; ibid. 467: 25 Apr. 1853).

[174] Ibid., vol. 127, 659–70: 27 May 1853.

[175] Ibid., vol. 129, 708: 25 July 1853.

[176] Conacher, *Aberdeen Coalition*, 76.

[177] Parl. Deb., 3rd ser., vol. 127, 672: 27 May 1853. See also Lord Lansdowne, ibid., vol. 129,
736: 25 July 1853.

[178] Ibid., vol. 126, 741: 28 Apr. 1853.

[179] Ibid. 746.

[180] See ibid., vol. 123, 1651: 16 Dec. 1852.

which they detested but felt unable to defeat, the more the Radicals warmed towards it. The one source of anxiety in Radical circles was the continuation of the income tax in an undifferentiated form. Muntz, the businessman who represented Birmingham, even declared his intention of voting against the 1853 budget out of sympathy for the many small traders in his constituency, calling the income tax 'a foul blot on the whole scheme of the Government'.[181] Heyworth, speaking for the LFRA, welcomed the budget, by contrast, but wished that Gladstone had had the courage to commit himself to a 6 per cent or even a 10 per cent income tax: 'The country was daily becoming more enlightened upon the subject, and was daily becoming more in favour of direct taxation, which was in fact the only scientific and systematic mode of raising the national revenue.'[182] The same line was taken by Robertson Gladstone; in a private comment on the 1853 budget, he said that the Liberals of Liverpool positively *disliked* the stoppage of the income tax in 1860, though in general they were very pleased with the package as a whole.[183]

Cobden's position was more complex. Originally he had opposed the income tax, since he disliked the retention of the corn and sugar duties; but the balancing introduction of a legacy tax now caused him to change his mind. Although he regretted the failure to distinguish between 'precarious' and 'permanent' incomes, Cobden admitted that, in Lancashire and Yorkshire at least, there was 'more feeling of resistance and of suffering under the inquisitorial character of the tax among mercantile men and trading capitalists than there is upon the score of the unjust assessment of the tax'; in any case, businessmen submitted to income tax as the price to be paid for 'the extension of commerce and the freeing of industry from the fetters that bound it'. Cobden ended his speech to the Commons with an accurate prophecy: indirect taxes would and should continue to be remitted, he said, which meant there was little 'prospect of our being able to do away with the income-tax in 1860'.[184]

What really reconciled all the Radicals to the budget and made them enthusiastic in its support was the extension of legacy duties to land. This pleased even Hume, understandably disappointed that his draft report on the income tax had been entirely ignored; he called the succession duties 'by far the best part of the Ministerial scheme'.[185] Hume's disciple William Williams,

---

[181] Ibid., vol. 126, 507–8: 25 Apr. 1853.

[182] Ibid., 1343: 9 May 1853.

[183] Robertson Gladstone to William Gladstone, 23 Apr. 1853, Hawarden Papers, vol. 663.

[184] 28 Apr. 1853, *Cobden's Speeches*, 283–93, esp. 289 and 293. He went on: 'As an advocate of direct taxation, I would, as an abstract principle, levy [the income tax] upon everybody, where the tax could be collected with a profit'; but since the poor paid proportionately far more in indirect taxes, they must, in equity, be exempted from income tax.

[185] Parl. Deb., 3rd ser., vol. 126, 471: 25 Apr. 1853. Robertson Gladstone told his brother that the LFRA had urged Hume not to attempt to jeopardize the budget (Robertson Gladstone to William Gladstone, 23 Apr. 1853, Hawarden Papers, vol. 663).

who had for some time past been pressing hard for the extension of the legacy duties to the landed classes,[186] was also delighted. Gladstone, he said, 'had, in proposing this tax, shown more political virtue, more moral honesty, than any of his predecessors had done for more than a century'.[187] And, predictably, Bright, 'speaking for the large population of the towns', was so heartened by this new blow to the hated 'land monopoly' that he was prepared to tolerate for the time being the continued existence of the 'unpalatable income tax'.[188]

Press comment followed a similar track. The *Manchester Guardian* said that nothing had more pleased 'the middle classes in our large towns' than the succession tax: 'This is, in fact, the key-stone of the popularity of the budget.' The *Guardian* thought that the extension of death duties to landed property was an expression of recent developments

which have thrown so much larger a share of political influence and power into the hands of the great middle classes. Indeed, it would be difficult to conceive a stronger evidence of the potent and undue share of influence which the landed class had acquired under our constitution as it existed prior to the Reform Bill, than the existence of so monstrous an abuse as that caused by the distinction between personal property and real property—between the hard earnings of careful and self-denying industry and inherited broad acres of land,—in the relation in which they stood with regard to the legacy duties.

In an outburst of uncharacteristic class feeling, the *Guardian* declared that it was hardly a matter for surprise 'that country gentlemen should feel sore at being so rapidly stripped of all the immunities which they have so long enjoyed, and which have been looked upon as a badge of their own peculiar position'; but it observed that people from this class should be 'thankful that nothing [had been] said as to compensation for the past'.[189]

The Cobdenite papers sounded a similar note. The *Norfolk News*, for example, declared its approval of the budget '*as a whole*'. 'It will be remembered by our readers that the entire eradication of every trace of the feudal distinction between land and money, which has for so many centuries given to the owners of the soil an unfair predominance in legislation and so many unjust privileges and exceptions in fiscal arrangements, has ever been to us a most important object.' The *Norfolk News* called the destruction of this distinction through the succession duties the budget's most striking feature: 'We are so much pleased with it,' ran its editorial comment, 'that we could on its account overlook many minor defects and incongruities.' And although cross that the income tax should have been renewed on an unreformed basis, the *Norfolk*

---

[186] His motion of 1 Mar. had been defeated by 124 votes to 71 (Parl. Deb., 3rd ser., vol. 124, 805–35).
[187] Ibid., vol. 128, 98: 13 June 1853.
[188] Ibid., vol. 127, 366: 13 May 1853.
[189] *Manchester Guardian*, 13 June 1853.

News expressed relief over its gradual reduction and ultimate repeal.[190] The *Liverpool Mercury* reacted similarly, calling the budget the best since the one which made the reputation of Peel, Gladstone's 'great master'.[191] The *Manchester Examiner* also enthused, but located the inspiration of the budget elsewhere, seeing it as 'a large embodiment of those views and principles which have especially characterised what has been called the "Manchester School" of politicians'.[192]

In conclusion, there can be little doubt that Gladstone had brought off a remarkable *coup* with his 1853 budget, establishing himself as a statesman of the front rank and laying down principles of public finance which were to continue for at least another generation. In particular, as Conacher says, many contemporaries were impressed by the fact that Gladstone, unlike his predecessors, seemed to have a coherent plan, one which covered a span of eight years.[193] In the words of the *Manchester Guardian*: 'For the first time in our day, we begin to see it as a thing that is practicable, that our financial system should assume a fixed and settled state, and that it should no longer be subject to violent and uncertain changes every year.'[194]

CONCLUSION

In retrospect, we can see that this was also one of the budget's weaknesses, since the future could not be bound so easily. In fact, a little over a year after the passing of the 1853 budget, Britain's involvement in the Crimean War wrecked the Chancellor's step-by-step approach to the abolition of the income tax, which, in the event, was never abolished at all. But even if the Crimean War had not taken place, it seems unlikely that Gladstone would have followed the advice of the Liverpool reformers and moved towards a total reliance on direct taxes. By 1861 he was protesting his undying affection for *both* the beautiful sisters, direct and indirect taxation, and Gladstonian policy dictated that a judicious balance should be struck between them.[195]

But this takes us to the nub of the issue. Gladstone was beginning to exercise a fascination over the urban Radicals, but he did not belong to their school at all. Opposition protests about the budget being dictated by Manchester simply made Gladstone seem more radical than he really was, which obviously helped him to get his measures through the Commons. This was particularly true in the case of the succession duties. Even in 1853 some

---

[190] *Norfolk News*, 23 Apr. 1853. But it reported displeasure from local grocers, tea dealers, coffee merchants, tobacconists, and chemists over the increase in duties on licenses to sell these commodities.

[191] *Liverpool Mercury*, 22 Apr. 1853.

[192] *Manchester Examiner and Times*, 23 Apr. 1853.

[193] Conacher, *Aberdeen Coalition*, 64.

[194] *Manchester Guardian*, 20 Apr. 1853.

[195] Hirst, *Gladstone*, 205.

Radicals, like Bright, were pointing out that Gladstone had gullibly 'bought' the Opposition's claim that the land was unfairly burdened, and that, as a result, the new succession duties were not sufficiently stringent: 'While money in the funds, property in banks, machinery, or merchandise, would have to pay from 1 to 10 per cent, according to the degrees of consanguinity, real or rateable property would only have to pay $\frac{1}{2}$ to 5 per cent.' Bright protested vehemently against such a distinction.[196] But, along with other Radicals, he liked the principle that had been established too well to wish to damage Gladstone's chances of carrying his measures.[197]

The 1853 budget thus marked the start of a strange love affair between Gladstone and the great urban and industrial centres. The relationship can be seen taking shape in the visit he made to Manchester in October to inaugurate the Peel memorial. During this visit, in the first major speech which he ever made to a 'popular' audience, Gladstone presented himself, and was accepted, not only as Peel's disciple and successor, but also as a statesman blessed with a peculiar insight into the nature of industrial communities. He received three addresses of welcome, one from the mayor and the Corporation of Manchester, one from the Chamber of Commerce, and a third from the Commercial Association. Later that same day, in the town hall, he was praised as the author of the budget and of the 'commercial freedom' of the city, especially by Thomas Bazley, on behalf of the Chamber of Commerce. Gladstone returned the flattery, calling Manchester the centre of a region which had 'perhaps accumulated greater wealth than any commercial or manufacturing emporium known in history' and praising it for its world-famous 'advanced intelligence' and patriotism.[198]

Unlike his brother Robertson, William Gladstone was not, of course, an entrepreneurial Radical from the business world. But his family and social ties made it possible for sympathizers to cast him in this role. Moreover, in the words of an admiring contemporary, 'Mr. Gladstone has never attempted to sever the link between his original trade-surroundings and his subsequent political life, and, while devoting himself with all the ardour of his being to the latter, has always been ready to acknowledge his obligations to the former.'[199] This was true in the sense that, for all his affiliations with landed society, Gladstone always referred to himself publicly as 'middle class'.[200] Further, his

[196] Parl. Deb., 3rd ser., vol. 127, 367: 13 May 1853.

[197] Buxton explains how it was that real property was still treated more tenderly than personalty (Buxton, *Finance and Politics*, 119–20).

[198] Gladstone also denounced war, though at the same time claiming that his budget would prepare the country for war should one break out. He expressed an anxiety to get rid of more customs and excise duties, but said it was 'our duty to conform our measures to the exigencies of State'. He also hinted at the future abolition of paper duties (*The Times*, 13 Oct. 1853). See also Shannon, *Gladstone*, 276–7.

[199] *Fortunes Made in Business*, vol. 2 (1884), 112–13.

[200] H. C. G. Matthew, *Gladstone 1809–1874* (Oxford, 1986; 1988 edn.), 53. For Gladstone's pride in being connected with a famous mercantile family, see his famous speech to the Liverpool

recent unhappy experiences in unravelling the tangled business affairs of his brother-in-law Stephen Glynne may have helped him acquire that patient but thorough mastery of financial detail which was to be a large part of his success as Chancellor and perhaps brought out in him some kind of hereditary financial flair. Robertson certainly believed in such a thing; thus he responded to William's expressions of anxiety concerning his aptitude for the work of Chancellor by reassuring him that he was 'the son of a thoroughly practical man'. (In any case, he added, how much better prepared he was than his predecessor, Disraeli, 'a novel writing Book Seller, whose life and atmosphere have been only in the region of Fiction and who knows as much of Finance and Arithmetic as to enable him to add up two columns of his publisher's accounts'.[201])

The task of sorting out the affairs of the bankrupt Oak Farm company, together with the settlement of his father's finances following the latter's death in 1851, had also brought Gladstone into much closer contact with his businessman brother than he had had during his earlier parliamentary career.[202] In fact, when he became Chancellor, Gladstone requested Robertson to 'supply me as occasion offers with such information as may be at your command, and rest assured it will always have my best attention'.[203] Robertson responded with relish, bombarding William with advice, commercial intelligence, and LFRA tracts. Scarcely a week elapsed in which a letter, generally crowded with information and political gossip, did not arrive on the Chancellor's doormat. 'You will admit, I think, that the House of Commons, as at present constituted, with so few mercantile men amongst its members, are [sic] scarcely at the moment competent to determine what will injuriously oppress trade *in its details*, or will not do so,'[204] he later said, in justification of the latest piece of advice which he was pressing upon his brother.

Robertson Gladstone's 'knowledge of trade matters was very extensive', wrote the anonymous contributor to *Fortunes Made in Business*, published in 1884, 'and it is said that on many questions of fiscal and commercial policy, the experience and knowledge of the Liverpool merchant was of great service to his brother when, as Chancellor of the Exchequer, he had to deal with

---

Collegiate Institution in December 1872 (*The Times*, 23 Dec. 1872). Moreover, although Gladstone had been put through an educational experience which largely removed him from the world of his father's activities, he had also, as Checkland says, been brought up in the belief that 'waste was close to sin'; and these puritanical notions of economy and accountability he later applied, with remarkable intensity, to the field of public finance (Checkland, *Gladstones*, 398).

[201] Robertson Gladstone to William Gladstone, 1 Jan. 1853, Hawarden Papers, vol. 663.

[202] e.g. William Gladstone to Robertson Gladstone, 12 Mar. 1845, Hawarden Papers, vol. 568, fo. 161. Robertson gave his brother a substantial sum in 1847 to tide him over the Oak Farm difficulty.

[203] William Gladstone to Robertson Gladstone, 27 Dec. 1852, Hawarden Papers, vol. 569, fo. 215.

[204] Robertson Gladstone to William Gladstone, 21 Apr. 1860, Hawarden Papers, vol. 665.

financial and trading concerns'.[205] Although this may be true, there can be no suggestion that William acted upon all the advice which he received from this source; little notice, for example, was paid to Robertson's suggestion that William's budget speeches consist of 'a few terse pithy passages'![206] Robertson's usefulness was as a conveyor of the opinions and prejudices of one of the country's great mercantile communities. For this helped Gladstone establish himself as the great class reconciler, the one senior statesman who could interpret the cities to the country's ruling élite and vice versa. Such a role he assumed in earnest in 1853.

But Gladstone's first budget was also important for a quite different reason: it exposed the limitations of the entrepreneurial Radicals. The class agitation which had erupted in 1848 and which threatened to disturb the country's rulers in the years that followed came to nothing. This was in part the consequence of a paradoxical situation. The urban Radicals could only be brought out on to the streets in times of economic adversity. Hence, the advent of commercial prosperity, which Cobden's friends felt had materialized because of their own successful campaign for 'the liberation of commerce', deprived them of further occasions for political self-assertion.

More fundamental, however, was the failure of the Radicals to agree on a positive programme of fiscal reform. Should they oppose the income tax, accept it on condition that it be refined and improved, or work for its retention as a permanent feature of the country's finances? There were sound 'business' reasons for espousing any of these three courses of action. But the ensuing arguments separated Cobden from Bright, on the one hand, and from his friends in the LFRA, on the other, just as they drove a wedge between the Radicalism of Birmingham and that of Liverpool.

This left the Cobdenites with little to offer in the fiscal field except retrenchment. But this, involving as it did drastic economies in expenditure on the armed forces, had popular appeal only at times when the threat of foreign war seemed remote. Events in the Crimea were soon to expose the vulnerability of this part of the Radical credo.

---

[205] *Fortunes Made in Business*, 2, p. 175.
[206] Robertson Gladstone to William Gladstone, 1 Jan. 1853, Hawarden Papers, vol. 663.

3

The Crimean War and Administrative Reform

IMPACT OF THE CRIMEAN WAR

Visiting Constantinople in late 1854, in the company of the editor of *The Times*, John Delane, Austen Henry Layard was one of the first British civilians to recognize that a tragedy was about to unfold in the Crimea: 'The mismanagement has been far above anything I could conceive,' he wrote to a friend in England, 'and it has lead [sic] to a dreadful sacrifice of human life, from sickness and to the most fatal delays.'[1] Before long *The Times*, through the graphic reports being sent home by its correspondent William Henry Russell, was starting to awaken British public opinion to the enormity of what was happening. Its campaign reached a climax on 23 January of the following month: 'Failure, failure, failure,' it fulminated. Charles Dickens, in his *Household Words*, gave further publicity to what he called 'a confused heap of mismanagement, imbecility, and disorder, under which the nation's bravery lies crushed and withered'.[2]

'Towards the end of January', as the *Annual Register* later recalled,

public sympathy and indignation were roused to the utmost by the conviction that the soldiers of the finest army Great Britain had ever sent forth were ingloriously perishing of disease, overtasked and underfed, from the absence of the most ordinary calculation and foresight. The nation was greatly excited.[3]

The stridency of the press attacks shocked Charles Greville, who noted in his diary: 'People are furious at the untoward events in the Crimea, and cannot make out the real causes thereof, nor who is to blame, and they are provoked that they cannot find victims to wreak their resentment on.'[4] Discontent spread through all classes. As one former Conservative Minister told the Commons on 26 January: 'The universal cry from one end of the country to the other was, "Why are things so mismanaged?" The conversation in railway carriages, on board steam-boats, among high or low, rich or poor, whatever might be their politics, was all in the same strain—one universal shout of mismanagement.'[5]

---

[1] Layard to Lady Huntly (his cousin), 8 Sept. 1854, Layard Papers, Add. MS 38,944, fo. 28.
[2] 'That Other Public', in Charles Dickens, *Miscellaneous Papers* (1914), 496.
[3] *Annual Register*, 1855, p. 2.
[4] Greville's Diary, 19 Feb. 1855, Greville, *Journal*, i. 244.
[5] Parl. Deb., 3rd ser., vol. 136, 1142: 29 Jan. 1855.

Nor could public disquiet simply be blamed on an unscrupulous press agitation.[6] After all, had not Lord John Russell himself, in his resignation speech of late January, confirmed everyone's worst fears when he pointed out that troops were dying of disease at a rate of ninety to a hundred a day?[7] *The Economist* believed that there had been gross exaggeration in the newspapers; yet it conceded that 'our Crimean campaign presents a scene of inconceivable mismanagement and resulting disaster such as Europe has not witnessed since the expedition to Walcheren and the retreat to Corunna'. 'We must have a searching investigation and unsparing reform,' it concluded.[8]

As a junior member of the Aberdeen Government, *The Economist*'s editor, James Wilson, had additional grounds for concern. One of his daughters recorded in her diary at about this time: 'Papa and Mr. Greg much excited at the mismanagement of the Army; Papa called this War "the death-blow of the Aristocracy".'[9] Greville, reflecting the concerns of senior Cabinet Ministers, was even more worried at the emergence of what he called the 'revolutionary doctrine' that 'it is not this or that Minister who can restore our affairs, but a change in the whole system of government, and the substitution of plebeians and new men for the leaders of parties and members of aristocratic families, of whom all Governments have been for the most part composed'.[10] Karl Marx, on the other hand, was correspondingly delighted; in March he gleefully prophesied the breakdown of the 'superannuated compromise' which had followed the 1832 settlement, a compromise whereby the middle class had delegated the actual work of executive government to the aristocracy. Now, under the pressure of war, wrote Marx, the aristocracy 'has been compelled to confess its incapacity any longer to govern England'.[11]

THE ADMINISTRATIVE REFORM MOVEMENT

The bare outlines of the agitation can soon be given. On 26 January the Commons passed (by 305 to 148 votes) Roebuck's motion of censure, which destroyed the Aberdeen coalition and led to the setting up of the Sebastopol Committee. The movement for administrative reform then switched to the country, where Layard, a back-bench Liberal MP, made a succession of well-publicized speeches. On 5 May, rather late in the day perhaps, a pressure group came into existence, the Administrative Reform Association (ARA). It held two big meetings in the Drury Lane Theatre, on 13 June and 27 June (at the second of which Dickens was the star performer). Several public demon-

---

[6] Parl. Deb., 3rd ser., vol. 136, 1528: 19 Feb. 1855 (Layard).
[7] Ibid. 961: 26 Jan. 1855.
[8] *Economist*, 27 Jan. 1855, p. 83.
[9] Barrington, *Servant of All*, i. 249.
[10] Greville, *Journal*, i. 244.
[11] Karl Marx, 'The Crisis in England and the British Constitution', Mar. 1855, in Marx and Engels, *On Britain*, 423–4.

strations had already taken place in provincial cities, most of them during the previous month. These were intended to provide backing out of doors for the resolution which Layard was to move in Parliament on 15 June. However, this resolution, which deplored 'the manner in which merit and efficiency have been sacrificed, in public appointments, to party and family influence, and to a blind adherence to routine', was comprehensively rejected, by 355 to 46.[12]

Thereafter Layard receded into the background, to be replaced by the wealthy hosiery manufacturer Samuel Morley, who became the ARA's chairman in August. Morley tried to work out a practical programme of administrative reform, the result being a series of anonymous pamphlets, which (perhaps unfairly) were generally dismissed as unreadable.[13] This particular stage in the agitation culminated in the presentation of a petition to Parliament, calling upon it to ensure that Civil Service posts were filled by means of an open examination. The ARA was then remodelled with a view to attracting less affluent subscribers. Finally, in June 1856, an exhausted Morley admitted defeat, and the organization came under the control of Roebuck (not in very good health himself), whose attempts to use it to put pressure on MPs were widely resented and led to many defections.[14] It collapsed when Parliament was dissolved in 1857; but it had lost its importance long before then. Anderson describes well the meteoric rise and fall of the ARA, which had been 'founded in May 1855, [was] a mass movement by June, and by August [was] quite insignificant'.[15]

But the movement for administrative reform in 1855 had an importance which far transcended the deficiencies of the short-lived ARA. As Anderson puts it, the main significance of the events in the Crimea was that they supplied the occasion for a vigorous display of 'middle-class assertiveness'.[16] True, there were other dimensions to the agitation. For example, many of the administrative reformers looked back nostalgically to the heyday of the independent MP, invoking the concept of an 'ancient constitution' whose balance had been upset by the intrusion of 'corruption' and 'faction'.[17] At a practical level this led to such proposals as the 'Goderich Pledge', an attempt to persuade MPs to commit themselves in advance not to accept office, and to Layard's suggestion that all Civil Service appointments be dependent on the approval of the House of Commons.

[12] Parl. Deb., 3rd ser., vol. 138, 2040–1: 15 June 1855.
[13] Olive Anderson, 'The Administrative Reform Association, 1855–1857', in Patricia Hollis (ed.), *Pressure from Without in Early Victorian England* (1974), 270.
[14] Among them Charles Dickens, who worked off his spleen by satirizing the aristocratic 'Tite Barnacles' in *Little Dorrit*.
[15] Olive Anderson, *A Liberal State at War: English Politics and Economics during the Crimean War* (1961), 104.
[16] Ibid. 105.
[17] Olive Anderson, 'The Janus Face of Mid-Nineteenth-Century English Radicalism: The Administrative Reform Association of 1855', *Victorian Studies*, 8 (1964–5), 231–42. See Torrens McCullagh's invocation of the principles of 1688 in *Norwich Mercury*, 16–19 May 1855.

There was also another 'face' to 'administrative reform': a traditionalist, *Conservative* face. Of course, an element of opportunism coloured the attempts by Conservative MPs to exploit the Ministry's Crimean War embarrassments. But in fairness one must add that Disraeli had been contemplating far-reaching administrative changes while a member of the minority Tory Ministry of 1852.[18] Such Conservative 'reformers', if they can be called that, had a distinctive case to argue. According to them, everything that had gone wrong in the Crimea could be attributed to the exclusiveness of the great Whig families, who, in the words of G. M. W. Peacocke, MP for Maldon, 'sought to confine the Government within the limited circle of their own relations, and to exclude from it the gentry of England, with acres broader and pedigrees more ancient than their own'.[19]

'BUSINESS PRINCIPLES'

But by far the most important aspect of the movement for administrative reform was the claim that the Army and the Government both needed to be organized on good, sound 'business principles'. Bringing 'public management to the level of private management in this country' was the ARA's main goal. It also spoke of the need to apply to public offices 'those principles of common sense which the practical experience of private affairs suggests as essential to avert failure and ensure success',[20] and claimed that the 'whole system of Government offices is such as in any private business would lead to inevitable ruin'.[21] Such remarks were usually a prelude to attacks on aristocratic monopoly and exclusiveness, with frequent charges of jobbery, favouritism, and nepotism. Thus J. Lewis Ricardo wrote to George Wilson:

There is not a clerk in Manchester or the City of London that would not have known how to supply the Army with what it wanted when he had unlimited capital at his command. . . . Whatever may be the composition of the new ministry they will have plenty of Dukes Lords and Baronets but they will most carefully eschew any man of business.[22]

To save the country, there needed to be 'businessmen in government'; indeed, there were even those who claimed that the 'techniques of government should be but the techniques of commerce writ large'.[23]

It became a cliché of the Radical Press to contrast the marvels of modern industry and commerce with the backwardness of both military and administrative life. The *Manchester Examiner* said that it was hardly surprising that

---

[18] Buckle, *Life of Disraeli*, iv. 32–3.
[19] Parl. Deb., 3rd ser., vol. 138, 2096: 15 June 1855.
[20] ARA paper no. 3, p. 21, and 'General Aims'.
[21] Ibid., no. 1, p. 4.
[22] Ricardo to G. Wilson, 26 Jan. 1855, George Wilson Papers.
[23] Anderson, 'Janus Face', 241.

the Army had given so poor an account of itself in the Crimea, since it had escaped the influence of all the reforming movements of the day and remained 'where it was half a century ago, under the "cold shade of the aristocracy"; the perquisite of a class, a perquisite which has cost the nation during the intervening period no less than a thousand millions sterling'.[24] But, for an example of what Anderson has called 'the poetry of business',[25] one cannot do better than cite this account by the *Daily News*, in which the wonders of private enterprise are contrasted with the archaism of government:

Who that has seen our mechanical and engineering exploits—who that has heard of the Menai bridges, mammoth steamers, our network of railways, Crystal Palace built almost in a night, steam hammers, steam guns &c &c—who that has seen or heard, in short, of our civil engineering, would have expected that the concentrated will of our people, the Government, acting through our concerted strength, the army, would fail to make use of the concentrated mechanical and engineering knowledge and skill of the nation? No foreigner could have expected this; but every Englishman knows well enough that in most things which it undertakes Government is beaten by private enterprise.[26]

Layard spoke in a similar vein: while 'all that concerned the private relations and private enterprise of this country had made a progress unexampled in national history . . . the government of the country had been standing still'.[27]

Layard was not himself a businessman, but many of his close associates in the ARA were, and several of them came forward to testify to the nation's needs. For example, W. S. Lindsay, a wealthy shipowner, told his Norwich audience why he had become involved in the movement: 'I felt as a merchant, and a man of business, that the fame and power of England, as a commercial nation, was fast slipping away from that high position she had so long occupied, and that this country was in danger of becoming a second-rate state.' Was it not extraordinary, he continued, 'that while we as a nation had been able to meet the combined competition of the whole world, and to carry out the greatest enterprises—the government, with power to select the best men for all purposes, and with almost unlimited means, could not carry on the war beyond a disgraceful and calamitous manner'. 'My business is easily done,' he boasted, 'because done on a proper system, and with regularity.' Before coming to Norwich he had spent an hour and a half in his London counting-house: 'Should not the government conduct the business of the nation equally well as that of a private individual?'[28]

The great railway contractor Samuel Laing made a similar point, this time directed at the 'amateurishness' of the military establishment:

[24] *Manchester Daily Times*, 29 Jan. 1855.
[25] Anderson, *Liberal State*, 108.
[26] *Daily News*, 2 Aug. 1855.
[27] Ibid., 14 June 1855.
[28] *Norwich Mercury*, 16–19 May 1855.

If a merchant, possessing a large establishment, were to attempt the purchase system in the appointment of his clerks, how long would it be before his name appeared in the *Gazette*? If a railway company adopted the same system in the appointment of servants to take charge of the express train, what length of time would elapse before a verdict of manslaughter would be returned against them? The mainspring of all the business affairs of life was a rigid system of promotion by merit.[29]

The way in which administrative reform often served as a focus of class feeling, just as financial reform had recently done, is well brought out by the meeting which Layard addressed in Liverpool in April. This took place at a *déjeuner* held on board a newly launched clipper, and was put on by the shipowner T. M. Mackay, owner of the Black Ball line of packets (later chairman of the Liverpool Chamber of Commerce), so that Layard could meet leading members of the local mercantile community. The financial reformers of the city seem to have stayed away, but many of the merchant princes were present, along with the American consul and the mayors of Birmingham and Salford and other large towns. Mackay, in introducing his guest, asked his audience to think about what constituted 'a distinguished man':

Few would think of the merchant or manufacturer, who, by years and years of toil, enriched the commerce of the country—few of the enterprising shipowners who sent their vessels into every part of the world, and upon whose flags the sun never sets, few would think of those amongst us whose open-handed liberality has not been the less because unseen.

Mackay's point was that, although he had no quarrel with the aristocracy, he felt that the middle classes should be given 'a clear stage, and no favour'. Layard, in his predictably sympathetic response, combined his views on the war with praise of the business community, and pointed to the decline of the commercial cities of the Middle Ages as a warning to modern Britain, before concluding with a toast to 'the Town and Trade of Liverpool'. (Many of the other toasts managed to include complimentary references to the Black Ball line![30]) This blend of civic pride, class resentment, patriotism, and commercial promotion captures quite accurately the mood of this particular phase of middle-class consciousness.

Yet what, in practical terms, would bringing the standards of public service up to those of private business *mean*? The leaders of the ARA were unable to

[29] Parl. Deb., 3rd ser., vol. 137, 1220: 27 Mar. 1855. The great contractor Sir Samuel Morton Peto, who went out to the Crimea to build 39 miles of railway line for the use of British troops, regaled the Commons in 1859 with stories of the confusion he had discovered there, and these faults of organization, he declared, were still rife in military camps (Parl. Deb., 3rd ser., vol. 154, 1270–2: 14 July 1859).

[30] *Daily News*, 23 Apr. 1855; Gordon Waterfield, *Layard of Nineveh* (1963), 264–5. Layard was delighted with the occasion and with his host: 'an excellent specimen of one of our merchants' (Layard to Lady Huntly, 22 Apr. 1855, Layard Papers, Add. MS 38,944, fo. 35).

come up with any clear answers. Samuel Morley suggested that Ministers should concentrate on one line of work to the exclusion of all else: 'They never heard of a timber merchant becoming a colonial broker, or changing from one sort of business to another like this.' At the Civil Service level, he thought, much red tape could be cut away if responsibility for a particular line of business were concentrated in the hands of an individual, as happened in commercial life.[31] Moreover, there was general agreement that public servants who displayed incompetence should be sacked, as, said Lindsay, they would be in *his* firm.[32] In particular, the practice of civil servants failing to keep proper records of their activities on the grounds of 'confidentiality' should be ended: 'Recordation is in the public service what account-keeping is in private business.'[33]

Better still would be the installation of a selection procedure which would exclude incompetent people from the very start. Here, open examinations were commended—though, as we shall see, critics objected that examinations were seldom, if ever, used in this way by private firms. It was also suggested that civil servants be paid the 'market rate' for their work, but be given no favours or perquisites, 'a simple commercial law from which there is no escaping'.[34] More basically, the Association suggested that 'a non-parliamentary commission of commercial men ... be appointed to investigate the present condition and arrangement of the whole of the departments under Government direction and control'.[35]

In no way did belief in the superiority of business methods come over more strongly than in the commitment to what would nowadays be called 'privatizing' public work. Layard told the Commons on 24 July 1854: 'I have often heard it said ... why does not the Government allow some great firm to contract for carrying on the war? This question, however ludicrous it may appear, is based upon a very good common-sense view of the war.' His parliamentary friends Laing and Stevenson, the engineer, would not have made the mistakes which Whitehall was making, he observed.[36] In the Commons on 12 March 1855 Laing himself offered the Ministry advice on how the troops could have been efficiently and economically supplied with provisions; perhaps after the estimates had been agreed, he suggested, the matter could have been 'referred to a Committee of business men upstairs to determine how far the contract system could be adopted'.[37]

And so it was that general approval greeted the Government's decision in February 1855 to use the contractor Sir Joseph Paxton to organize the

[31] *Daily News*, 14 June 1855.
[32] *Norwich Mercury*, 16–19 May 1855.
[33] ARA paper no. 3, p. 21.
[34] *Liverpool Mercury*, 22 June 1855.
[35] 'Administrative Reform', Layard Papers, Add. MS 39,053, fo. 7.
[36] Parl. Deb., 3rd ser., vol. 135, 652: 24 July 1854.
[37] Ibid., vol. 137, 447–8: 12 Mar. 1855.

building of huts and roads in the Crimea. Later, another contractor, Sir Thomas Peto, was asked to build the Balaklava railway. As the First Lord of the Admiralty, Sir Charles Wood, conceded: 'You cannot find any adequate substitutes for the stimulus of private and individual interest.'[38]

THE ARA'S PREDECESSORS

Of course, this kind of thinking did not originate in the Crimean War. In some ways the movement for administrative reform in 1855 was but a continuation of certain strands in the programme of the financial reformers.[39] Writing to Robertson Gladstone in May, Cobden pointed out how recent events had vindicated the earlier views of the Liverpool 'economists':

I have often thought of you since the *Times* led off its onslaught against the aristocratic misdeeds in the management of the army. I recollect [that] when you put your name to similar views, but much more mildly expressed, a few years ago, you and your Association were assailed by the *Times*, and were told that the army was as open to Leeds and Liverpool as to the families of the landed aristocracy. But it is always so. It requires some great calamity to convince the people of the country that any reform is necessary.[40]

The ARA also followed the precedent of the LFRA in holding public meetings in the provinces, which were often presided over by the mayor at the request of prominent local citizens. This happened at Norwich, Sheffield, and doubtless many other cities.[41]

Moreover, it is interesting to observe that many contemporaries also saw similarities between the ARA and the Anti-Corn Law League. For example, the Norwich Radical Tillett, in a public letter to Morley at the height of the administrative reform agitation, wrote:

The Anti-Corn Law League proceeded on the simple principle that it is positively wicked for man's laws to obstruct God's benificence; and that, therefore, to every market where corn was to be found there should be perfect freedom of access, all the world through. So you should say, wherever there is a capacity to serve one's country there is a 'divine right to employment'; and if human laws or systems oppose that right, those laws or systems are manifestly unnatural and impious.[42]

---

[38] Anderson, *Liberal State*, 116–18.

[39] The links between 'financial reform' and the later attempts to reform the Civil Service are well discussed by Hart, 'Northcote–Trevelyan Report', 68–72.

[40] Cobden to Robertson Gladstone, 3 May 1855, Hawarden Papers, vol. 579.

[41] But Anderson also notes that the ARA's organization was largely based on John Ingram Travers's 'City Committee for the Reform of the Customs' (Anderson, 'ARA, 1855–1857', 269). On the 'customs scandal' which gave rise to this organization, see Masterman, MP, *Report*. Interestingly, one of the speakers was W. S. Lindsay, while entrepreneurial Radical MPs like James Clay and William Williams were also associated with the protest. Bright, too, sent a message of support, in which he referred to 'the many grievances to which the mercantile body is subjected under the present arrangements and policy of the Customs'.

[42] *Norfolk News*, 26 May 1855.

In addition, the ARA emulated many of the *methods* of the Anti-Corn Law League, which was not surprising since some of its ardent supporters were former Leaguers. Torrens McCullagh, for one, made public reference to this at the second Drury Lane meeting in late June:

He had been a member of another association that succeeded: he meant that for the liberation of foreign commerce; and he perfectly remembered the first meeting held at Manchester in a room not one-fourth the size of that theatre, and how the originators of the movement exalted in such a sign of success as the room being full.[43]

As had been the case with the League, the agitation for administrative reform depended on holding large public meetings, two of the big London ones taking place at theatres. By-election interventions were also important in both movements. Thus, a great fillip to administrative reform was Sir William Tite's victory over a Tory opponent at a by-election in Bath on 5 June—an event which, Marx sardonically observed, was being publicized with 'no less ostentation than [were] . . . the bloodless successes on the Sea of Azov'.[44]

In fact, a self-conscious manipulation of the Press also played an important part in the administrative reform movement. Dickens, for example, was involved in the agitation from the beginning, helping Layard draft his initial resolutions and offering help in securing favourable publicity in such papers as the *Illustrated London News*, as well as directly promoting the movement in *Household Words*.[45] The paper of which Dickens had previously been editor, the *Daily News*, threw its weight behind the ARA with great gusto, as did *The Times* initially. It was, of course, the reports submitted by *The Times*'s military correspondent which had alerted the public to the importance of the issue in the first place.

THE MANCHESTER SCHOOL AND ADMINISTRATIVE REFORM

But in other ways the ARA differed quite sharply from the old Anti-Corn Law League. For a start, the Manchester School held aloof from the agitation for administrative reform, disgusted by the war fever which had seemingly engulfed all classes. Henry Ashworth, for example, noted with dismay that the tradesmen and manufacturers of Manchester, 'who lead a life which they measure in effect by accumulations of money', were 'as fanatical as the rest'. As he wrote to Cobden, 'In 1851 we were rejoicing in our strength and in our control over the passions which lead to warfare. Nothing was so gratifying at our ·Great Exhibition as when we were pluming ourselves on the progress of

---

[43] *Daily News*, 28 June 1855. Thackeray likened the ARA to the League, and suggested that Layard might turn out to be another Peel! (Gordon N. Ray, *The Letters and Private Papers of W. M. Thackeray* (1946), iii. 683).

[44] Marx, 'Crisis in England', 428.

[45] Dickens to Layard, 7 Apr. 1855, Layard Papers, Add. MS 38,947, fos. 14–15.

the peaceful arts and the impossibility of any future war.' Ashworth blamed the reaction on the Duke of Wellington's funeral, the Press, 'the countenance of sacerdotal favour (dissenters included)', and 'the authority of fashion'.[46]

What especially mortified men like Ashworth was the fact that many *Radical* politicians, following the example of Roebuck, rushed to support the war. In fact, to a Radical manufacturer like W. E. Forster of Bradford, the fight against Tsarist autocracy was a righteous cause.[47] Others, faced by a national crisis, simply put their country first, believing, as did Laing, that they had to accept war 'as a last resort' and fight that war 'with the utmost vigour'.[48] In Manchester itself, Bright's views on the war were publicly assailed by a former League stalwart Absalom Watkin, a Mancunian businessman who had seconded Bright's nomination for the borough in 1847.[49] In Leeds, Cobden's attempt to deliver an anti-war speech was interrupted by shouts of 'Gammon'.[50] The unity of the 'Radical Party' was broken, and its commitment to peace exposed as an illusion.

With so many of their former Radical allies and constituency supporters openly supporting the war, Cobden and Bright were in despair; indeed, Bright later experienced a prolonged nervous collapse. Cobden wondered whether the world had gone mad or merely himself: the war, he told Baines, had brought him 'to the most complete state of scepticism—I have no faith left'.[51] True, Cobden initially took comfort in the thought that 'the discredit and slaughter to which our patricians, civil and military, have been exposed, will go far to make real war unpopular with that influential class to come, whilst the swift retribution likely to fall on the cabinet will tend to make Governments less warlike in future'. And when the storm over military and administrative incompetence was at its height in early January, he wrote to Bright: 'The break-down of our aristocratic rulers, when their energies are put to the stress of a great emergency, is about the most consolatory incident of the war.' But he also expressed doubts as to whether the middle class had the self-assurance 'to venture on the task of self-government. They must be ruled by lords.'[52]

Predictably, the Manchester School was obsessed with the effect that war would have on the national finances. Some, including Dunckley, argued that free trade had at least made the country better able to enter the war—an ironic situation which they ruefully savoured.[53] But they all expressed alarm

---

[46] Ashworth to Cobden, 15 Dec. 1855, Cobden Papers, Add. MS 43,653, fos. 247–8. Cobden's earlier delusions about the pacifism of the middle class were irrevocably destroyed.

[47] T. Wemyss Reid, *Life of William Edward Forster* (1888), i. 301–2.

[48] Parl. Deb., 3rd ser., vol. 136, 849: 22 Dec. 1854.

[49] Watkin, *Absalom Watkin*, 288 and Appendix.

[50] Cobden to Bright, 5 Jan. 1855, Morley, *Cobden*, ii. 166.

[51] Steele, *Palmerston and Liberalism*, 51.

[52] Cobden to Edward Baines, jun., 11 Dec. 1854, Baines Papers.

[53] Dunckley, *Charter of the Nations*, 439–40.

about the possibility that fiscal progress might be endangered by a furtherance of hostilities. Bright told the Commons in June:

We have had for twelve years past a gradual reduction of taxation, and there has been an immense improvement in the physical, intellectual, and moral condition of the people of this country; while for the last two years we have commenced a career of reimposing taxes, have had to apply for a loan, and if this war goes on extensive loans are still in prospect. Honourable members may think this is nothing. They say it is a 'low' view of the case. But these things are the foundations of your national greatness.[54]

Cobden and Robertson Gladstone shared Bright's worries about the economic burdens being imposed by the war, and viewed every small symptom of financial crisis with a mixture of apprehension and satisfaction. In *What Next—and Next?* (1856) Cobden warned that the Crimean War had not only inflicted suffering upon the labouring poor (to say nothing of the wretched troops), but that it had also threatened the capitalists with 'heavy loss' by absorbing so much of that 'floating capital without which our mills and furnaces, our steam engines, docks, and railways become as valueless as if the timber and iron of which they are constructed were still in their native mines or forests'.[55]

'It is evident that the Towns and Trade are to bear all the burdens of the war—far more than the farmers' taxes are paid by the higher price of corn,' grumbled Bright.[56] He wrote with bitterness, conscious that his *own* firm was being badly damaged by the stupidity of his countrymen.[57] Yet, there seemed to be 'a paralysis over the Mercantile body'. He had written to Bazley and Henry Ashworth to summon a meeting of the Manchester Chamber of Commerce, but his friends had replied that the idea met with little favour.[58] In fact, as Ashworth incredulously reported to Cobden, the cotton manufacturers were indifferent to higher income tax, in the hope of '*crippling the power of Russia*'.[59] In the event, to the discomfiture of the Manchester School, the anticipated economic collapse did not occur.[60]

---

[54] Trevelyan, *Life of Bright*, 247.

[55] *The Political Writings of Richard Cobden* (1886), 523–5.

[56] Bright to W. B. Smith, 19 Oct. 1855, John Benjamin Smith Papers, MS 923.2, S344, fo. 18.

[57] Bright to Smith, 31 Dec. 1855, ibid., fo. 21.

[58] Bright to Smith, 4 Nov. 1855, ibid., fo. 19.

[59] Ashworth to Cobden, 15 Dec. 1855, Cobden Papers, Add. MS 43,653, fo. 248. Bright's letter on the war (29 Oct. 1854) concentrated on its wickedness; but it also made great play of the expense and the disturbance to trade. His Mancunian assailant replied, however, by scoffing at 'the sages of the "penny-wise and pound-foolish" school, who displayed their knowledge of arithmetic in pompous calculations of the great saving which would accrue to the nation from the reduction of our means of defence to some obsolete standard' (Watkin, *Absalom Watkin*, 318–19, 307).

[60] Steele, *Palmerston and Liberalism*, 53–4. Cobden quickly dropped the fallacious argument that the war was economically damaging because trade with Russia was more important than trade

Nor did Cobden or Bright have any clear idea of how to cope with the parliamentary crisis occasioned by the war. In January 1855 the latter confessed to being 'sorely puzzled' as to how to respond to the Roebuck motion.[61] As for Cobden, he voted for Layard's June resolution, only one of forty-six MPs to do so, just as he later voted for Vincent Scully's proposal in support of instituting a system of open competitive examinations for Civil Service posts. But this was essentially the limit of his involvement. '*The people are to blame for this*,' he told Colonel Fitzmayer; there was no point in making the aristocracy or the Court scapegoats.[62] To an overture from Walmsley, who claimed that the war was going badly because the aristocracy were not men of business, Cobden replied bluntly: 'It is a pity that our quarrel with the aristocracy does not spring from some other cause than the complaint that they don't carry on *war* with sufficient vigour.'[63] Bright agreed: 'I am one of those who believe the fundamental error to be in the *policy* rather than the management' of the war, he told his brother-in-law.[64]

Cobden took his criticisms further. If Britain wished to fight Continental wars, he argued, it should adopt conscription, thereby forcing the middle classes in areas like West Yorkshire, who were so zealous in support of the war, to take part, which they were not doing at present.[65] He repeated some of these observations in the House of Commons, saying that although he had not 'dealt always very gently with the aristocracy of this country', he would 'never truckle so low to the popular spirit of the moment' when what mattered was that the people consider how far *they* were 'responsible for the evils which may fall upon the land'.[66] In fact, as Edsall notes, the irony was that during the Crimean War Cobden found himself 'looking to an aristocratic Parliament as a check on the people rather than the other way round'.[67]

There were other reasons why Cobden chose to keep a low profile over the war. As he reminded a friend in January 1855, 'There is now a general

with Turkey. In fact, the textile industry *benefited* from the war—hence its general popularity with the Mancunian business community (Gatrell, 'Commercial Middle Class', 429–35).

[61] Bright to G. Wilson, 27 Jan. 1855, George Wilson Papers.

[62] Cobden to Fitzmayer, 11 May 1855, Hinde, *Richard Cobden*, 254.

[63] Cobden to Walmsley, n.d., in Hugh Mulleneux Walmsley, *The Life of Sir Joshua Walmsley* (1879), 298. For Cobden's clashes with the reforming general, de Lacy Evans, see Spiers, *Radical General*, 170. Evans wanted the war to continue until such time as Russia had been totally defeated.

[64] Bright to McLaren, 5 Mar. 1855, in Mackie, *McLaren*, ii. 19. Layard was contemptuous of the lack of patriotism shown both by the Manchester School and by such Peelites as Gladstone (Layard to Lady Huntly, 25 July 1855, Layard Papers, Add. MS 38,944, fo. 39).

[65] Cobden to Walmsley, 27 Sept. 1855, Walmsley, *Life*, 300–1. Evans, too, thought that the Treasury deserved a large share of the blame for the Army's disorganization (Spiers, *Radical General*, 167).

[66] 5 June 1855, *Cobden's Speeches*, 335–6.

[67] Edsall, *Cobden*, 289. There was, Cobden told Bright, 'no out-of-doors support for the party of peace and non-intervention', so they would have to work through the Commons (Steele, *Palmerston and Liberalism*, 51).

complaint that we allowed our army to fall to too low a standard, in consequence of the cry of the financial reformers for a reduction of the expenditure.'[68] (Incidentally, Gladstone, too, knew himself to be vulnerable to the charge of having contributed to the catastrophe through his parsimonious management of the national finances. Indeed, the most criticized department of the Army, the Commissariat, had been under the direction of the Treasury, whose Secretary, Charles Trevelyan, must also take much of the blame for the Crimean War break-downs.[69]) The Manchester men also had to face Palmerston's unfair gibe (aimed specifically at Bright) that they reduced 'everything to the question of pounds, shillings and pence', and, in considering the defence of their country's liberty and independence, first drew up a balance sheet to see whether the cost of defence contributions would or would not be outweighed by the contributions which the general of the invading army might levy upon Manchester.[70]

So it was that the Manchester School (and also the Liverpool financial reformers) held aloof from the movement for administrative reform. This refusal of Cobden and Bright to take serious notice of the ARA undoubtedly weakened the impact of that organization.

WHO SUPPORTED ADMINISTRATIVE REFORM?

Yet there may be another way in which the ARA differed from the Anti-Corn Law League: the two organizations operated from rather different social bases. Thus, Anderson has argued that the ARA was *not* an expression of 'the mercantile, manufacturing, nonconformist radicalism of Manchester, Liverpool, and the West Riding'.[71] Is this true? Of course, one of the leading spokesmen for the Association was Samuel Morley, a prominent Dissenter and Nottingham manufacturer. Also, as we have seen, prior to the foundation of the ARA, Layard was given a great reception in Liverpool, where, to quote his words, 'nearly 300 of the leading men of this part of England, representing more wealth, enterprise, intelligence and influence than any similar body of men in England perhaps, including the Mayors of all the great surrounding cities', turned up to applaud him—an occasion on which he was sounded out about his willingness to stand for Liverpool as a parliamentary candidate.[72] Moreover, according to the *Norfolk News*, branches of the organization were

---

[68] Cobden to Fitzmayer, 10 Jan. 1855, Morley, *Cobden*, ii. 169.
[69] Strachan, 'Early Victorian Army', 797.
[70] Jasper Ridley, *Lord Palmerston* (1970; 1972 edn.), 576–7.
[71] Anderson, 'ARA, 1855–1857', 275.
[72] Layard to Lady Huntly, 22 Apr. 1855, Layard Papers, Add. MS 38,944, fo. 35; *Daily News*, 23 Apr. 1855, from which, however, it seems that Layard had been invited to stand prior to the 1852 election.

formed in Liverpool and Manchester, and a public meeting was held in Birmingham.[73]

But a month later the London correspondent of the *Liverpool Mercury* was lamenting that Liverpool had not yet moved in the matter.[74] And it has been claimed that no meetings were held or branches established in any part of Lancashire except Rochdale, whose MP, Miall, was not a Lancashire man anyway.[75] It may also be significant that, although the Cobdenite *Manchester Examiner* expressed sympathy with the movement, it adopted a somewhat detached attitude towards what it clearly saw as a metropolitan agitation.[76] Even when public meetings on administrative reform *were* held in northern cities, like the one in Sheffield in June, they did not always lead to affiliation with the ARA itself.[77]

When provincial meetings did stimulate the establishment of branches of the ARA, they tended to be in non-industrial cities like Norwich and Gloucester.[78] But, in contrast to the old League, London was where the ARA originated and where its most impressive rallies were held. It may well be, as Layard conceded, that 'many of the leading men of the City were not connected with this movement',[79] but it is noteworthy that both the chairman (Morley) and the secretary (John Travers) were 'City princes',[80] and that among the best-known subscribers were the Rothschilds and Samuel Courtauld.[81] William Schaw Lindsay, the Scottish shipping magnate, also operated out of the City.

Who attended these meetings? Some forty MPs (about eight of them Independent Irish) were associated with the ARA at one stage or another, and of these most were businessmen or from the professions. Although the organization had the potential to appeal to sections of the working class, the high subscription of one guinea clearly prevented many from actually joining. Anderson thinks that the movement's base was comprised of City merchants, brokers, wholesalers, agents, and bankers, plus London professional men.[82] In the provinces the membership was also solidly middle class. Thus, the *Norwich Mercury* noted of the big St Andrew's Hall meeting of mid-May 1855 that it 'was, perhaps, more entitled to be considered a purely middle class

---

[73] *Norfolk News*, 26 May 1855; see Waterfield, *Layard*, 270. In Birmingham the speaker was Muntz.

[74] *Liverpool Mercury*, 19 June 1855.

[75] Howe, *Cotton Masters*, 233, n. 141.

[76] e.g. *Manchester Examiner and Times*, 28 June 1855.

[77] *Sheffield Independent*, 23 June 1855.

[78] Anderson, 'ARA, 1855–1857', 275. It is also noteworthy that few of the MPs supporting the Association were returned by industrial cities.

[79] *Daily News*, 14 June 1855.

[80] Anderson, 'ARA, 1855–1857', 269.

[81] Anderson, 'Janus Face', 232, n. 2.

[82] Anderson, 'ARA, 1855–1857', 273.

movement than almost any we remember'.[83] In his notes for his (undelivered) speech to the ARA, Thackeray, too, observed that it was the very class of men who had acted as 'special constables' at the time of the Kennington Common rally in April 1848 who were now heading the agitation: 'quiet peaceful educated citizens quitting their everyday occupations shops chambers city-desks and what not to show front against a menacing danger'.[84] But it seems to have been a section of the middle class hitherto unattracted by politics which was particularly prominent in the ARA—hence, perhaps, the naïve, even jejune, character of much of its activity.

THE CRITICS OF 'BUSINESS PRINCIPLES'

Why, then, did the ARA not make the impact on either the urban middle class or the country at large which the Anti-Corn Law League had made a decade earlier? In part this was because, understandably enough, the organization soon ran into fierce opposition. Indeed, the very extravagance of the claims which it made on behalf of the business community was almost bound to provoke a reaction. There was certainly no dearth of Conservative MPs ready to point out that businessmen, too, had their faults. For example, the MP for Surrey West, Henry Drummond (who was a friend of Admiral Dundas, whom the ARA had attacked and who thus had his own motives for joining in the fray), amused the House on 18 June by subjecting the middle classes to critical scrutiny. Self-government in the big cities hardly suggested, he said, that the middle class had much administrative capacity. In Newcastle upon Tyne the council was run by 'the very elect of the middle classes',

yet they have not sufficient administrative talent to clean and drain their own town.... Croydon is another place in which the middle classes boast that they are competent to self-government, and the end of the administrative faculties was, that they produced a virulent fever which destroyed hundreds of human lives, owing to their bungling and incompetence. As to London, we know what a mess that is in, and has been ever since the shopkeepers had the management of their lighting, and drainage, and supply of water.

Moreover, alleged Drummond, businessmen were not that good at running their own concerns. As for the railroads, 'Look at the immense amount of capital which has been expended, and the average return upon it is said to be under 2 per cent.'[85]

Other newspapers took up this cry. The *Globe* treated the adulteration of foodstuffs as indicative of middle-class morality, while the *Saturday Review*, a

---

[83] *Norwich Mercury*, 16–19 May 1855.

[84] Ray, *Letters of Thackeray*, iii. 681.

[85] Parl. Deb., 3rd ser., vol. 138, 2182–3: 18 June 1855. See rejoinder in *Daily News*, 22 June 1855.

constant critic of the efficiency of large-scale business, had the pleasure of pointing out in March 1856 that the boots which civilian contractors had supplied to the Army were of very poor quality and that the privately constructed Balaklava railway was in poor shape, since the rails had been laid down on mud![86] It also proved embarrassing to the commercial Radicals that, slap bang in the middle of the administrative reform campaign, the banking firm of Messrs Strahan, Paul & Co. went bankrupt, a juicy scandal which got extensive press coverage.[87] The fraudulent activities exposed in this case hardly suggested that all would be well if political and administrative authority were handed over to the business world. As one MP observed, it might well be unfair to charge 'the middle classes with the bankruptcies and failures which had happened in the country during the last few years', but it was equally unfair to blame the aristocracy as a whole for the follies of particular subordinate officers.[88]

Interestingly, certain spokesmen for the *professional* middle class, like John Stuart Mill, also queried the supposed capacity of businessmen to come to the rescue of the State.[89] More surprisingly, by June 1855 even *The Times* was arguing such a case: two of the worst bunglers in the Crimea, it noted, were Admiral Boxer, manager of the transport service, and Major Sillery, supervisor of hospitals at Scutari, both of whom had risen through the ranks. Well might the 'Thunderer', in one of its more reflective moods, wonder whether the nation would really be improved if 'stockbrokers, railway directors and "Heaven knows who" were made the ruling class'.[90] The administrative reformers were certainly embarrassed by the fact that two of the most inefficient branches of the Army, the Commissariat and the Army Medical Service, were the *least* aristocratic.[91]

Moreover, the businessmen who had criticized the Government and the Army soon came under fire themselves. For example, Sir Charles Wood, now First Lord of the Admiralty, enjoyed a minor parliamentary triumph when he claimed in the Commons that two years earlier Lindsay had been brought before the courts for failure to fulfil a contract; Lindsay, he said, was demonstrably less efficient than the Government in managing his own affairs.[92] This personal assault on Lindsay was probably, as one pamphleteer

---

[86] Anderson, *Liberal State*, 120, 122–3. A decade later, criticizing Cobden's proposal for 'privatizing' government manufacturing establishments, the *Bradford Observer* commented: 'The rotten gunboats, the worthless tools, the shoddy clothing, and pasteboard boots supplied by contractors during the Crimean War have not been forgotten' (28 July 1864).

[87] See account in *Manchester Examiner and Times*, 27 June 1855.

[88] Parl. Deb., 3rd ser., vol. 138, 2190: 18 June 1855 (J. G. Phillimore).

[89] Anderson, *Liberal State*, 121–2.

[90] James Winter, *Robert Lowe* (Toronto and Buffalo, 1976), 82–3.

[91] Anderson, *Liberal State*, 115–16. On the working of the Commissariat, see Sweetman, *War and Administration*, 41–59.

[92] Parl. Deb., 3rd ser., vol. 139, 704–12: 10 July 1855.

claimed at the time, a deliberate attempt by the Government to discredit administrative reform: 'Government touts were going about the City for days, after Mr. Lindsay's speech at Drury Lane was delivered, seeking not for means of dispelling the charges which he had made against the Admiralty, but for any stories bearing on that gentleman's past career by which his character might be damaged!'[93] Lindsay furiously defended himself, and the war of words rumbled on throughout the summer.[94] But even the *Daily News* conceded that, though Lindsay was bound to defend himself against his parliamentary detractors, 'the discussion . . . could not possibly be productive of any advantage to the public'.[95]

THE FAILURE OF LEADERSHIP

This whole episode points to a second reason for the ARA's failure: a weakness of leadership. Looking back over 1855, the *Annual Review* bluntly concluded that the Association had been 'unsupported by names carrying any considerable intellectual weight or political influence, either upon the sympathies of the masses, or the convictions of the intelligent portion of the community'.[96]

In the absence of the Manchester School, the task of administrative reform fell upon those whom Palmerston once referred to as 'the three Ls': Layard; Samuel Laing, the railway magnate; and W. S. Lindsay.[97] Austen Henry Layard, the discoverer of Nineveh, established himself in the summer of 1855 as the movement's star performer, drawing large and enthusiastic crowds to his provincial meetings. Layard's strength was that he could speak with personal knowledge about conditions in the Crimea (where, incidentally, he had a brother serving in the Army who later died of dysentery while on the point of leaving Balaklava). He was also spurred on by a sense of destiny— perhaps also by a sense of grievance—after Palmerston had been obliged, at the Queen's behest, to withdraw his offer of the under-secretaryship at the War Office.[98]

Unfortunately for the cause of reform, Layard was not popular in the Commons, and, from the start, was prone to get into hot water by making personal allegations against individuals which he was unable to substantiate[99]

---

[93] Jacob Omnium, *A Letter on Administrative Reform* (1855), 6.

[94] See W. S. Lindsay, *A Confirmation of Admiralty Mismanagement . . . with Reply to the Charges of Sir C. Wood* (1855).

[95] *Daily News*, 25 June 1855.

[96] *Annual Register*, 1855, p. 144.

[97] Winter, *Robert Lowe*, 87.

[98] Ridley, *Lord Palmerston*, 594. But Layard himself blamed the outcome on the Cabinet and on Whig exclusiveness (Layard to Lady Huntly, 27 Feb. 1855, Layard Papers, Add. MS 38,944, fo. 34; Waterfield, *Layard*, 258).

[99] See his partial retraction to the Commons (Parl. Deb., 3rd ser., vol. 136, 1043–4: 26 Jan. 1855; Waterfield, *Layard*, 269–70).

but which he refused to withdraw gracefully. He cannot, it is true, be blamed for the way in which his private criticisms of Admiral Dundas entered the public domain;[100] but, far from learning from this experience and in defiance of the good advice of his friends, he then involved himself in a public altercation with Lord Hardinge. The military Members took particular exception to his strictures on aristocratic exclusiveness in the Army, and so rough a ride did he get in April that some papers thought that Palmerston should have protected him against the rowdies.[101] A month later the enfuriated army officers were again on the rampage, accusing Layard of killing one Captain Christie with an unjust accusation. *The Times* thought that 'the whole process resembled too closely the operation of hunting down a bag fox, or putting to death an obnoxious dog who had been dropped in the lock of a canal', and observed: 'One or two more such field nights, and Mr. Layard is a martyr, with all the immunities of the class'.[102]

Such treatment did indeed win Layard sympathy among his out-of-doors supporters, as his post-bag shows. But inside Parliament his sobriquet, 'Mr Lie-Hard', suggests the distrust which he inspired; and when he introduced his big motion in June, in a rambling three-hour speech, it was contemptuously voted down, MPs preferring Bulwer Lytton's amendment, which did not threaten the Palmerston Government.[103] In any case, Layard lacked stamina. For much of 1855 he was in a highly emotional state, attributed by some to the after-effects of malaria which had left him a little light-headed. By mid-July he was writing to his cousin: 'I shall shake the dust off my shoes and turn my back upon England. I feel that I want complete change. The wear and tear of the last six months begin to tell upon me.'[104] Soon afterwards he left the country to study fresco paintings in Italy, leaving others to carry on the crusade as best they could. He subsequently became chairman of the Ottoman Bank. In the 1857 election Layard was thrown out by his constituents—'punished because he had a year or two ago deceived them into admiring him', as *The Economist* caustically put it.[105]

Despite his later business ventures, in 1855 Layard could not be truly described as a businessman—though he was undoubtedly middle class and Palmerston thus had a point when he said that his successful career demonstrated that in the British system of government merit *did* often win recognition.[106] But William Schaw Lindsay was an authentic 'Liberal commercial',

---

[100] Waterfield, *Layard*, 252.

[101] Ridley, *Lord Palmerston*, 595–6.

[102] *The Times*, 19 May 1855. All this rebounded on Graham; see Arvel B. Erickson, *The Public Career of Sir James Graham* (Oxford, 1952), 368–9. Bright said privately that he felt compelled to come to Layard's defence, thinking him 'shabbily used' (Bright to G. Wilson, 18 May 1855, George Wilson Papers).

[103] Parl. Deb., 3rd ser., vol. 138, 2040–2133, 2154–2225: 15, 18 June 1855.

[104] Layard to Lady Huntly, 15 July 1855, Layard Papers, Add. MS 38,944, fo. 38.

[105] *Economist*, 4 Apr. 1857, p. 362.

[106] Ridley, *Lord Palmerston*, 596.

someone who well deserved his place in Samuel Smiles's pantheon of fame: an orphan at the age of 14, who as a boy had worked his passage in a steamer by trimming coals, before going on to found his own shipping firm, W. S. Lindsay & Co., which by the 1850s was perhaps the largest shipping house in the world. Later he was to write a standard history of merchant shipping.[107]

But the 'sharp treble Scotch tones' which had delighted the *Daily News* reporter at the Drury Lane meeting[108] were not to the liking of his fellow MPs. Moreover, like Layard, Lindsay weakened his attacks (specifically on the Admiralty contracting system) by larding them with personal charges that he was later obliged to retract. Some of his complaints seem also to have been rooted in a concern to extend his own firm's business.[109] In May 1855 Layard was complaining that 'Lindsay is a conceited active fellow—eaten by vanity— with few of the tastes or feelings of a gentleman'.[110]

Most MPs were delighted when Sir Charles Wood gave the bumptious Scotsman a taste of his own medicine: 'Nobody expected these tactics, but all enjoyed them, except the victim, who sat with knees crossed and sunken head, with barely a friend beside him,' according to one journalist's account.[111]

A weightier figure was Samuel Laing, who had served as a high-ranking official in the Railway Department at the Board of Trade in the 1840s before embarking on a successful career as a railway manager. Not only was Laing a doughty defender of railway interests in the House; he soon established himself as an effective spokesman for entrepreneurial Radicalism, and on all matters affecting finance and commerce (on limited liability, for example), his was a lucid and informed voice. Palmerston recognized his abilities in 1859 by appointing him Financial Secretary to the Treasury, in succession to James Wilson. But in 1854–5 Laing was too junior an MP for his strictures on the Government's want of 'business methods' to make a major impact.

Moreover, the '3 Ls' made a cardinal strategic error. Reversing the usual practice of Cobden and Bright, they spent a great deal of time attacking

---

[107] Lindsay also became a friend of Cobden, whom he helped with his financial affairs and with whom he wrote a pamphlet about maritime law. For their relationship, which dates back to 1854, probably earlier, see Cobden Papers, Add. MS 43,668, fos. 268–72. He was a guest at Midhurst in January 1854 (Cobden to J. B. Smith, 12 Jan. 1854, John Benjamin Smith Papers, MS 923.2, S345, fo. 23).

[108] *Daily News*, 14 June 1855.

[109] See his attack on the West India Mail Co. (Parl. Deb., 3rd ser., vol. 136, 1894: 26 Feb. 1855).

[110] Layard to Lady Huntly, 7 May 1855, Layard Papers, Add. MS 38,944, fo. 37. However, as Anderson says, this description could equally well be applied to Layard himself ('Janus Face', 242, n. 28).

[111] *Manchester Examiner and Times*, 25 June 1855. Lindsay had been quite ill in the autumn of 1854 (Lindsay to Cobden, 27 Sept., 16 Oct. 1854, Cobden Papers, Add. MS 43,668, fos. 268, 270; Cobden to J. B. Smith, 12 Jan. 1854, John Benjamin Smith Papers, MS 923.2, S345, fo. 23). A few years later Bright was writing to Cobden knowingly about Lindsay's 'failing'—a want of prudence and judgement (Bright to Cobden, 10 Feb. 1861, John Bright Papers, Add. MS 43,384, fo. 247).

individuals, while protesting, not too convincingly, that they had no animus against the aristocracy as a class. Thus Layard claimed that he wanted 'to save the aristocracy'.[112] And Lindsay, speaking 'as one of the people', declared himself proud of the aristocracy, 'proud of them when he compared them now with what they were formerly, and also when he compared them with the aristocracy of other countries'. 'The people did not complain of the aristocracy,' he said; 'nor did they care whether a scion of the house of Bedford or the child of some unknown man held the reins of Government. All they required was that the destinies of this country should be intrusted to men of ability and energy, who would carry us through the fearful crisis in which the country now was.'[113] These protestations, did nothing, of course, to disarm the social groups who stood to lose from the success of the ARA's campaign; so in a sense the Association got the worst of all worlds.

The consequences of all this bungling were explained by Lord John Russell in a letter to his father-in-law: 'Layard and Lindsay have done much harm by desecrating the good cause of administrative reform.'[114] The movement also acquired an unsavoury reputation as a happy hunting ground for careerists like William Tite and Torrens McCullagh, both of whom were clearly looking for a 'cry' that would gain them a parliamentary seat. Little wonder, then, that some earnest administrative reformers like Vincent Scully actually set out to discredit the ARA spokesmen, in the interest of the cause which they had at heart.[115] In fact, when over the next few years it came to the serious business of instituting practical changes, the ARA leaders played a small, almost negligible role. The solid work was done by General de Lacy Evans in respect of the Army and Viscount Goderich in respect of opening up the Civil Service by means of examinations—to say nothing of the Northcote–Trevelyan group of reformers.

It is interesting to speculate as to what Cobden or Bright would have made of 'administrative reform' had they not been sulking in their tents in 1855. And how would the campaign in the country have fared if the organizer had been George Wilson, not the amiable but harassed Samuel Morley? Presumably Cobden, Bright, and Wilson would have selected one particular aspect of administrative reform that seemed to be of central significance and to possess symbolic resonance, and would then have campaigned single-mindedly for its implementation. This, after all, was what had brought success

[112] Parl. Deb., 3rd ser., vol. 136, 1528: 19 Feb. 1855.

[113] Ibid. 1894–5: 26 Feb. 1855. See also ARA paper no. 3, p. 7. The resolutions to be proposed at the London Tavern in April 1855 contained one which read: 'That while we disclaim any desire of seeing the Aristocracy deprived of their reasonable share in the Councils of the Crown; we feel it our duty to protest against the pretensions of any section of the community to monopolise the functions of Administration' (Layard Papers, Add. MS 39,053, fo. 6). See Lord Goderich's remarks (Parl. Deb., 3rd ser., vol. 138, 2161: 18 June 1855).

[114] Anderson, 'ARA, 1855–1857', 285, n. 46.

[115] Ibid. 285.

to the Anti-Corn Law League. True, the ARA had a slogan 'THE RIGHT MAN IN THE RIGHT PLACE', but it was a slogan which simply begged the crucial question. As the young W. E. Forster complained to Layard, his friends in Bradford were 'discontented, dissatisfied and suspicious' with the existing state of affairs, and 'would cry out loud enough for the right man in the right place, if we knew where were the right men, or indeed if we knew exactly who were the wrong men'.[116]

Lacking a proper focus, the Association failed to make the impact it should have done. One day its spokesmen were attacking nepotism in the Army or the purchase system; another day they were arguing the need to replace the patronage system in the Civil Service by a selection system based on open examinations; then the concern would switch to a purification of the parliamentary system. True, a common thread ran through all these issues: the need to fill public offices on the basis of pure merit, without reference to political considerations or social connections. But Layard and his friends found themselves discoursing on many more subjects than they could properly master, and, as a result, they often gave the impression of being 'amateurs'—which was ironical, since it was the alleged 'amateurishness' of the existing system that they had set out to attack. In Forster's words, there was 'a vagueness about the whole affair' which perplexed would-be supporters.[117] The unsympathetic Whig MP, E. F. Leveson Gower sneeringly observed that the members of the ARA, 'assuming to represent the commercial classes, and holding themselves out as practical men, had not as yet laid down any practical plan to attain the objects they had in view'.[118]

THE POLITICAL DILEMMA

In a wider sense, too, the ARA lacked a political strategy. It was never entirely clear, for example, whether it was aiming to pressure the Administration into adopting a particular line of reform or to turn the Government out. Some of the anti-aristocratic feeling in *early* 1855 had been stimulated by the (well-justified) belief that the Aberdeen Government's heart was not in the war,[119] and this goes far to explain the success of Roebuck's motion. There was also anger over the delays in finding a successor to Aberdeen, which some of the reformers blamed on the cliquishness of the great Whig families in general and on Lord John Russell in particular.

But Palmerston's arrival in 10 Downing Street presented the critics with a problem. The new Prime Minister soon gave office to the up-and-coming MP Robert Lowe, who, shocked by the record of aristocratic mismanagement, had

---

[116] W. E. Forster to Layard, 18 May 1855, Layard Papers, Add. MS 38,983, fo. 399.
[117] Ibid., fo. 399.
[118] Parl. Deb., 3rd ser., vol. 138, 2092: 15 June 1855.
[119] Anderson, *Liberal State*, 111.

earlier in the year told his Kidderminster constituents that he wanted to stop public men making appointments except to candidates whose ability and knowledge had 'been previously tested by a sufficient examination'.[120] In fact, this appointment almost certainly represented a move to silence the criticisms being made of the Government in *The Times*, for which Lowe was a regular leader-writer.[121] The manœuvre was successful since, like that other middle-class 'renegade' James Wilson, Lowe had to content himself with subordinate office in a Whig-dominated Ministry. In such matters Palmerston was a pragmatist. Nor did he have any principled objection to employing business-men in order to improve the efficiency of the war machine; for example, he ordered his War Secretary to put a railway manager in charge of the Commissariat in the Crimea.[122] On the other hand, most of Palmerston's appointees to high office were aristocrats. As Marx observed on 27 February, 'The outcry against the aristocracy has been answered ironically by Palmerston with a ministry of ten lords and four baronets, eight of the former sitting in the House of Lords.'[123] Three years later, in May 1858, with Palmerston now out of office, 120 Liberal MPs, many of them Radicals from the big towns, assembled to express their disquiet. With T. E. Headlam, MP for Newcastle, in the chair, they passed a resolution (moved by M. T. Bass and seconded by William Baxter, both businessmen) to the effect that a future Liberal Ministry would forfeit their confidence 'unless it [rested] upon a wider basis than that upon which recent Governments have been constructed'. (Palmerston later promised to turn over a new leaf.[124]) But while the war was in progress, the Premier largely escaped public criticism.

In other respects, too, Palmerston was a doughty believer in the aristocratic virtues, as he showed when, defending British army officers against Layard's imputations, he waxed lyrical about the gallantry and bravery which they had shown at Balaklava.[125] This, of course, superbly missed the point that the critics were making: that these traditional aristocratic virtues would not by themselves prevail in modern war, which now required the application of science and up-to-date business methods, the very qualities of efficiency that supposedly characterized the businessman.[126]

So Cobden and Bright had some grounds for believing Palmerston to be

---

[120] *The Times*, 22 Feb. 1855.

[121] See discussion in Winter, *Robert Lowe*, 83–7. This was not Lowe's first spell in office. He had earlier worked on Indian reform at the Board of Control under Sir Charles Wood.

[122] Ridley, *Lord Palmerston*, 592–3.

[123] Marx, 'Crisis in England', 418.

[124] *The Times*, 8 May 1858. Other Liberal MPs taking part in this meeting were James Clay, Aspinall Turner, and William Jackson, all of them commercial Members. The meeting also urged the importance of reforming institutions like the War Office and the Foreign Office (Steele, *Palmerston and Liberalism*, 80–1, 83–4).

[125] Parl. Deb., 3rd ser., vol. 136, 1535: 19 Feb. 1855.

[126] Laing made precisely this point (ibid. 1796: 23 Feb. 1855).

the embodiment of 'the old aristocratic order' at its most benighted. On the other hand, his 'earnestness' about the war was never in doubt. As Forster told Layard on 18 May, his Radical friends in Bradford wanted to help the cause of reform in every way, 'but at present what gain would there be in changing Lord Palmerston for Lord Derby or Lord Panmure for Lord Grey or Lord Ellenborough?'[127] In similar vein, Laing wrote to Morley in May, saying that 'a majority of Independent Liberal Members of the House of Commons' agreed with Layard's motion, but asked whether it should be pursued, even if it produced the fall of the Government, followed by paralysis or by a Derby Administration.[128] The dilemma became even more acute with Lord John Russell's resignation on 7 July. It was probably this event which persuaded some 'reformers', including Delane of *The Times* and Robert Lowe, that Palmerston would now have to be given whole-hearted support if the war was to be won.[129] It certainly explains why in July Roebuck failed to persuade the Commons to censure Ministers for the conditions revealed in his recently published Sebastopol Committee Report.[130]

But some contemporaries took a wider view of the matter, and interpreted Palmerston's rise to the premiership not as an accidental by-product of the war, but as evidence of the 'impermeability' of Britain's aristocratic system of government to any genuine reforming programme. Prominent figures within the ARA who believed this to be the case therefore agreed with Thackeray that their Association would be 'mere Bosh' if nothing were done to secure the 'reform of the Chiefs as well as the Subordinates'.[131]

Yet how realistic was it to expect the existing Parliament to pass legislation that would annul the privileges of its dominant aristocratic caste? One of the ARA's own 'papers' drew attention to this difficulty in an interesting way. It showed that Vincent Scully's motion on administrative reform (discussed below) attracted significantly more support from Members representing the more populous constituencies than from those returned by 'rotten boroughs': its 127 supporters represented 276,501 electors and 6,126,249 people, its 142 opponents only 216,749 electors and 4,750,406 people.[132] The deduction to be drawn was obvious.

And so, once again, the cry was raised that nothing could be achieved until Parliament itself had been reformed. Morley gave his authority to this

---

[127] W. E. Forster to Layard, 18 May 1855, Layard Papers, Add. MS 38,983, fo. 400.

[128] Edwin Hodder, *The Life of Samuel Morley* (1887), 123–4. See also *Leeds Mercury*, 16 June 1855.

[129] Winter, *Robert Lowe*, 82–7. But there are other explanations for this volte-face. See also J. B. Conacher, *Britain and the Crimea, 1855–56* (1987), 66, 239, n. 25.

[130] It later transpired that Palmerston, a former Secretary at War, knew much more about the Army than most of his press critics (Edward M. Spiers, *The Army and Society, 1815–1914* (1980), 115).

[131] Anderson, 'Janus Face', 234; Ray, *Letters of Thackeray*, 253.

[132] ARA paper no. 10, pp. 12–14.

demand.[133] True, he also argued that, even without 'organic' changes, the electorate could achieve much by taking responsibility on itself for the return of 'honest' and 'independent' Members. But the chimera of a new Reform Bill once again made an appearance in 1855, distracting attention from the main issue, as it had when the financial reform agitation was at its height. At Sheffield, for example, the meeting convened by the mayor was narrowly prevented from pressing a demand for franchise extension, a demand understandably popular with those working-class elements attracted to the administrative reform movement.[134] Likewise, the *Manchester Examiner* pityingly dismissed the ARA because of its attempt to deal with administrative reform in isolation from constitutional reform: 'The disease it seeks to remedy is not functional, but organic; and if aristocratic privilege and incompetence are no longer to monopolise the executive or fill the administrative offices of the state, we must have such a reform of the House of Commons as will give to the people a real ascendancy in their own branch of the legislature.'[135] But even if this diagnosis were true, it offered no remedy, in the short run, to the nation's difficulties.

ENTER THE NORTHCOTE–TREVELYAN REFORMERS

All depended, of course, on what was meant by administrative reform. In fact, a reorganization of the Civil Service had been on the agenda *before* the outbreak of the Crimean War, ever since the publication of the famous Northcote–Trevelyan report in February 1854.

This Report owed something to the financial reform movement of the late 1840s and the consequent search for a more 'economical' administration. Between 1848 and 1853 Sir Charles Trevelyan, Secretary to the Treasury, had investigated at least half a dozen public establishments, among them the War Office, the Foreign Office, and the Home Office, with a view to their 'modernization'. A customs scandal in 1852 provided the pretext for a more general inquiry, of which Gladstone was the main Ministerial supporter. The result was the Northcote–Trevelyan Report, which identified the 'patronage system' as the source of most of the administrative ineptitude and political corruption of the day, for which the remedy was said to be the institution of open competitive examinations.[136]

---

[133] Hodder, *Life of Morley*, 126.

[134] *Sheffield Independent*, 23 June 1855. Many of the latter (some ex-Chartists included) attached themselves to the State Reform Association, with its programme of manhood suffrage. See Anderson, *Liberal State*, 105. By late 1855 it is arguable that parliamentary reform had come to dominate the activities of the ARA (John R. Greenaway, 'Parliamentary Reform and Civil Service Reform: A Nineteenth-Century Debate Reassessed', *Parliamentary History*, 4 (1985), 161).

[135] *Manchester Examiner and Times*, 16 June 1855.

[136] Hart, 'Trevelyan at Treasury', 103–4. The origins of the Northcote–Trevelyan report are

The notion of employing this method of filling public offices was not new. Indeed, a year earlier Trevelyan's brother-in-law Macaulay had made it the central component in his Government of India Bill. However, this did not make the Northcote–Trevelyan Report any more acceptable when it came out in February 1854. When the Cabinet considered it, all the Peelites, bar Graham, came out in favour, and all the Whig Ministers, bar Granville, raised objections.[137] As Conacher notes, the Peelites, several of whose members were sons of prosperous businessmen who had been accepted into the aristocratic establishment as a result of their education and ability (the late Sir Robert Peel, Gladstone, and Cardwell, for example), were quicker than the Whigs to appreciate the need for efficient, modern government, even though, ironically, it was the Peelite Ministers who were later to be responsible for many of the Crimean War fiascos.[138]

But for the outbreak of the Crimean War, matters might have progressed no further. True, after February 1855 the Ministers most eager for administrative reform, Gladstone in particular, were out of office. But Palmerston's Government, confronted by a public outcry and by the agitation that was shortly to lead to the formation of the ARA, realized that *something* had to be done. On 21 May, in advance of the debate on Layard's motion, it rushed out an Order-in-Council setting up a Civil Service Commission from which all nominees for public office would have to receive a certificate of fitness. Such a system of *qualifying* examinations fell far short of the demands of the Northcote–Trevelyan reformers, since it merely modified, without abolishing, the abuses inherent in patronage methods of appointment. The *Liverpool Mercury*, along with other Radical organs, denounced it as 'the greatest *sham* in the shape of a reform ever attempted to be put upon even a public so largely credited by knaves with gullibility as the English'.[139] Yet, even at the time, the Order-in-Council could be seen as a hesitant first step towards the bolder scheme articulated in the Northcote–Trevelyan report. Eventually, of course, in 1870, Gladstone's Ministry finally sanctioned the new Order-in-Council under which open competitive examinations became the normal mode of entry into the Home Civil Service.[140]

well discussed by Hart in 'Northcote–Trevelyan Report' and in the fullest and most recent account, Hans-Eberhard Mueller, *Bureaucracy, Education, and Monopoly: Civil Service Reforms in Prussia and England* (Berkeley, Calif., 1984), ch. 5.

[137] Shannon, *Gladstone*, 282–3. There is evidence that Graham, too, initially voted for the adoption of Northcote–Trevelyan (Edward Hughes, 'Sir Charles Trevelyan and Civil Service Reform, 1853–5', *English Historical Review*, 64 (1949), 62).

[138] Conacher, *Aberdeen Coalition*, 550.

[139] *Liverpool Mercury*, 22 June 1855.

[140] Nevertheless, by the early 20th cent., open competition was used for only about one-third of Civil Service appointments; and before 1914, transfers between departments were very rare. The theory underlying Northcote–Trevelyan report 'remained in many respects at odds with the *practice* of the period' (Richard A. Chapman and J. R. Greenaway, *The Dynamics of Administrative Reform* (1980), 16–17).

THE NORTHCOTE−TREVELYAN REPORT AND
THE ARA

But was this the road down which the businessmen active in the ARA wanted to proceed? It was one of the main failures of that body that it never gave a clear answer to this question. Naturally the ARA latched on to those passages in the Northcote−Trevelyan report critical of the patronage system, whole chunks of which it reproduced in its second 'Official Paper'. In his eagerness to carry his proposals, Trevelyan may well have grossly exaggerated the defects in the existing administrative system;[141] but that would not have worried businessmen who were already convinced of Whitehall's incompetence and aristocratic ineptitude. Moreover, the idea of filling public offices by means of examinations struck a responsive chord in the breasts of many commercial men. Samuel Morley believed that life itself was 'really a continued competitive examination'; and, like others of his class, he seems to have viewed examinations as a kind of adjunct to the market economy, with which it shared the function of objectively distributing rewards and punishments without reference to a person's birth or connections.[142]

However, the ARA laid itself wide open to the taunt that, although it purported to be concerned to introduce 'business methods' into public life, it was here *departing* from business practice, since private firms did not recruit their own staff on the basis of examination performance. Palmerston, for one, took great pleasure in twitting the ARA with this alleged inconsistency:

We have often been told in this House, that Government ought to shape its course according to the example of private individuals, of merchants, of shipowners, and of railway and other great companies. Now, I have yet to learn that merchants, bankers, railway companies, or any other private associations fill up their appointments in the manner thus recommended.[143]

The new chancellor, George Cornewall Lewis, made the same point.[144]

Gladstone thought that there was a simple answer to these objections: private firms did not have examinations because 'the principle of private interest which presides over the management of these institutions is a self-acting security'.[145] Moreover, as the *Leeds Mercury* observed, merchants and joint stock companies did make searching enquiries into their employees' competence, and were able to dismiss them should they prove incompetent, which governments could not.[146]

---

[141] Chapman and Greenaway, *Dynamics of Administrative Reform*, 20−2.

[142] Hodder, *Life of Morley*, 448; see Conclusion.

[143] Parl. Deb., 3rd ser., vol. 146, 1483: 14 July 1857.

[144] Ibid., vol. 139, 690−2: 10 July 1855; also vol. 141, 1420: 24 Apr. 1856, when he also noted that competitive examinations were not being proposed as a way of recruiting municipal functionaries or magistrates.

[145] Ibid., vol. 139, 726: 10 July 1855.

[146] *Leeds Mercury*, 14 July 1855.

None the less, some of the ARA's supporters were sufficiently worried by Palmerston's taunts to argue defensively that the attainment of examination certificates could perhaps serve as a kind of objective 'testimonial' or 'reference', and thus be of service to both commercial establishments *and* public departments. This later became a definite proposal, published in the ARA's sixth and eighth official papers: preliminary, open qualifying exams acceptable to both private and public employers should be set in provincial cities. The examination papers could perhaps test vocational skills, as was now being done for doctors and solicitors.[147] Lord Goderich took a different line: he wanted the new examinations to be competitive. Yet, in a speech in the Commons, he, too, claimed that many commercial establishments would be willing to recognize examination certificates. The Society of Arts (which ran its own system of examinations) had, he said, elicited a favourable response from, among others, several railway companies, Mr Akroyd of Halifax; Titus Salt; Francis Crossley, the carpet manufacturer; Sir Elkanah Armitage of Manchester; Sir Samuel Morton Peto; and Messrs Truman, Hanbury, & Buxton, the brewers.[148] Of course, as Lord Robert Cecil observed, this did not meet Lewis's point at all: the issue was whether the result of such examinations should be *binding* upon government departments.[149]

It was here that a serious divergence opened up between the ARA and the group promoting the Northcote–Trevelyan report. Of the latter, Sir Charles Trevelyan was perhaps the man closest to the radicalized middle-class reformers, since he shared their commitment to 'economical' government and the 'principles of political economy'. On the other hand, Trevelyan was a staunch Whig in his political views. Significantly, he had not initially placed great emphasis upon open examinations, and only came to do so under pressure from Gladstone.[150] Moreover, himself an Evangelical who had risen to the top of his profession from a genteel professional background and a public school education, Trevelyan could hardly be expected to take the view that the country's salvation lay in importing business talent and business methods directly into Whitehall.[151]

Still less was this the viewpoint of Gladstone, perhaps the key figure in this 'reforming' circle. As the Member for Oxford University, Gladstone had recently sponsored a Bill to 'modernize' his Alma Mater.[152] Now, to university reformers like Gladstone, examinations, which were being increasingly

---

[147] Anderson, *Liberal State*, 115.
[149] Parl. Deb., 3rd ser., vol. 141, 1405–6: 24 Apr. 1856.
[149] Ibid. 1435–6.
[150] Hart, 'Northcote–Trevelyan Report', 73–80.
[151] Hart, 'Trevelyan at Treasury', 109.
[152] Matthew, *Gladstone 1809–1874*, 84. To quote Gladstone's own words, this measure had been framed on 'the principle of working with the materials which we possess, endeavouring to improve our institutions through the agency they themselves supply, and giving to reform in cases where there is a choice the character of return and restoration'.

employed in the 'liberal professions', offered a perfect way of raising educational standards. But, as Colin Matthew puts it, 'Gladstone [also] saw competitive examination as the means of achieving the ascendancy of a Coleridgean clerisy in the secular world.'[153] In short, his beloved Oxford University was to be 'saved' by adaptation to what Gladstone perceived to be the requirements of the modern world.

The Northcote–Trevelyan proposals fitted well into this scheme of things, because the examinations which Gladstone had in mind would be geared to the syllabuses of the ancient universities and public schools, whose pupils would therefore be given the opportunity of an enlarged public usefulness.[154] This is why headmasters like Vaughan of Harrow and dons like Benjamin Jowett of Balliol were, from an early stage, deeply involved in the Northcote–Trevelyan inquiry. The reform of the Civil Service, in conjunction with the modernization of the country's ancient educational institutions, represented a way of perpetuating aristocracy and an aristocratic set of values in a modern industrial society.

These objectives were clearly expressed in the famous letter which Gladstone sent to a sceptical Russell in January 1854:

> I do not hesitate to say that one of the great recommendations of the change in my eyes would be the tendency to strengthen and multiply the ties between the higher classes and the possession of administrative power. . . . I have a strong impression that the aristocracy of this country are even superior in natural gifts, on the average, to the mass: but it is plain that with their acquired advantages, their *insensible* education, irrespective of book-learning, they have an immense superiority.

The separation that was being proposed between mechanical and intellectual work, argued Gladstone, would 'open to the highly educated class a career and give them a command over all the higher parts of the civil service, which up to this time they have never enjoyed'.[155] Trevelyan took the same view of the matter.[156] Gladstone and his friends also believed that the abolition of patronage would *strengthen* the aristocracy and the traditional Constitution, not, as the critics of Northcote–Trevelyan said, *weaken* them.[157]

What sort of Civil Service was being envisaged here? The Northcote–Trevelyan report spoke of creating a senior body of permanent officials

---

[153] Matthew, *Gladstone 1809–1874*, 85. The Coleridgean influence on Gladstone at this time has been emphasized by Peter Gowan, 'The Whitehall Mandarins', *New Left Review*, 162 (1987), 24–7.

[154] In fairness, one should say that the Northcote–Trevelyan report itself expressed an impartial interest in *all* academic subjects; see Mueller, *Bureaucracy*, 172.

[155] Gladstone to Russell, Jan. 1854, in Edward Hughes, 'Civil Service Reform 1853–5', *History*, 27 (1942), 63.

[156] For Trevelyan's belief that the tendency of the measure would be 'decidedly *aristocratic*', though 'in a good sense', see Trevelyan's 'Reply to Remarks by Captain O'Brien', in Hughes, 'Sir Charles Trevelyan', 72. Gladstone later repeated his claims in public (Parl. Deb., 3rd ser., vol. 139, 731: 10 July 1855).

[157] Gowan, 'Whitehall Mandarins', 20.

'possessing sufficient independence, character, ability, and experience to be able to advise, assist, and, to some extent, influence those who are from time to time set over them'.[158] But this goal was light-years away from the thinking of the ARA. For although Gladstone and his associates all valued efficiency and economy, there was, particularly in Gladstone, an 'étatiste' strand, a deep sense of involvement in the running of the Queen's Government. Their particular conception of the State necessitated a cadre of highly educated officials, recruited from the élite educational institutions shortly after graduation, men who could work with their political chiefs on terms of social equality because they had shared a similar education. And that education, it was assumed, would be a predominantly classical one. The 'feelings and habits of gentlemen' that Trevelyan valued were supposedly fostered by exposure to a liberal education in one of the country's traditional centres of excellence; vocational training and technical qualifications had no real part in this scheme of things.

This undervaluing of 'expertise' was to have profound long-term consequences, leading eventually to a policy of subordinating 'specialists' (medical officers of health, statisticians, engineers) to what would later be called 'general administrators'. As that self-constituted expert Edwin Chadwick complained at the time, the proposed scheme would exclude 'a candidate who was pre-eminent in the practical administrative reform, although he had never taken an academic degree'.[159]

But were the ideas of the Northcote–Trevelyan group any more congenial to the businessman entrepreneur? Samuel Morley, in his address at the Drury Lane theatre, declared his commitment to 'less rather than more government' and to lessening rather than increasing the role of departments.[160] But it seems doubtful if he and Gladstone really meant the same thing by this. A further difference separated the two groups, as Palmerston shrewdly noted: some reformers (the Northcote–Trevelyan set) were trying to make the Civil Service a permanent profession, while others (the ARA) decried routine and called for 'selection from commercial men, men of sagacity and practical experience'.[161]

More fundamental still was the antipathy felt by most businessmen to 'bookish' examinations, at which aristocratic youths would anyhow have an advantage. What did any of this have to do with that practical common sense upon which the commercial classes prided themselves? It is significant that the original objectives of the ARA included the declaration: 'All examinations, whether for appointments or promotions, shall be public—competitive—in a prescribed course of subjects, *not of books*, and shall not include examination

---

[158] Report on the Organization of the Permanent Civil Service, XXVII (1854), 3.
[159] 1 Aug. 1854, Reports and Papers Relating to the Civil Service, XX (1854–5), 165–6.
[160] Hodder, *Life of Morley*, 126; *Daily News*, 14 June 1855.
[161] Parl. Deb., 3rd ser., vol. 138, 2214: 18 June 1855.

in the dead languages.'[162] As he later explained, Layard was 'by no means an advocate of our Greek and Latin system'.[163] The ARA also urged that there 'be no restriction as to age at which persons shall enter the public service',[164] another divergence from the Northcote–Trevelyan scheme. Finally, the entrepreneurial Radicals wanted officials to be accountable to Parliament, rather than to the Executive Government, in defiance of conventional notions of Ministerial responsibility.[165]

W. R. Greg spoke for many businessmen when he criticized the premisses of the Northcote–Trevelyan report:

In the 'permanent Civil Service' do not let us fall into the pedantic and Chinese error which has been lately recommended of a 'competitive literary examination' for posts the qualification for which no literary examination could possibly determine; but require each nominee to pass such a board of investigation as will test at least alert intelligence and moderate education, and will stop absolute incapacity upon the threshold.[166]

A junior civil servant was even more outspoken: commenting on Jowett's role in the affair, he opined that 'black silk [was] ten times more pedantic and impracticable than red tape'. 'The senior wrangler', he sneered, 'may be an intellectual giant as compared with the government clerk, but one would not be more out of place in the academical senatus than the other at the office-desk.'[167] And a 'Practical Man' expressed the view 'that a young man from school, full of classics and mathematics, is totally unfit for a public office ... In short, placing a highly educated youth in a Government Office is like putting a thorough-bred horse in a dung-cart—he is sure to leap the traces, his official hours; kicks the cart, his duty; and defies the driver, his superior'.[168] The City Committee for Customs Reform, a committee of London businessmen formed in April 1851, expressed similar objections.[169]

But it was the LFRA which voiced the greatest contempt for the work of the Civil Service Commissioners. While the financial reform movement had always been mainly concerned with cheapening government, its spokesmen had never given much practical thought to improved methods of recruitment.[170]

---

[162] ARA, printed address entitled 'Administrative Reform', Layard Papers, Add. MS 39,053, fo. 7.

[163] Layard to Lady Huntly, 10 Apr. 1856, Layard Papers, Add. MS 38,944, fo. 46. Layard felt that the Scottish universities prepared their students better 'for the practical business of life'.

[164] ARA, 'Administrative Reform', fo. 7.

[165] This particularly incurred the displeasure of Lord Goderich (Goderich to Layard, 3 May 1855, Layard Papers, Add. MS 38,983, fos. 343–6).

[166] W. R. Greg, *The One Thing Needful* (2nd edn., 1855), 21–2.

[167] *Administrative Reform: The Re-Organisation of the Civil Service by a Subordinate therein* (1855), 8, 10.

[168] *Civil-Service Examinations for, and Promotion therein, Considered by a PRACTICAL MAN* (1855), 3. Anderson, *Liberal State*, 115.

[169] Hart, 'Northcote–Trevelyan Report', 71.

[170] Ibid. 70–2.

But an article appearing in the *Financial Reformer* later in the decade indicates how the public offices might have been staffed and run, had true entrepreneurial values prevailed:

Civil Service Examinations [it declared] are the prettiest things of this kind that we have seen for some time. They are not continued in the interests of financial economy, or anything half so vulgar and common-place, but to test the ability of an army of applicants by a highly ornamental and fanciful standard of education. Such education is common to the members of the upper ten thousand, who do not get their living by rude contact with the world; but the great middle class of the country . . . knows little, and cares less, about those things which Civil Service Commissioners have decided to consider so needful. . . . There is nothing like it in the whole trading and commercial world. A knowledge of the classics, of ancient and modern history; of algebra and mathematics; of Shakespeare, taste, and the musical glasses, is not demanded of every clerk who applies at the door of a merchant's counting house. He is asked if he knows the difference between Debtor and Creditor,—between his right hand and his left; if he can cast up a column of figures, or balance an intricate account; if he can write legibly, and spell correctly; his testimonials are looked into, and, if these are satisfactory, he is engaged at once, but only upon trial. The moment he fails in his work, he is discharged.

The LFRA thought that 'one half of the civil expenditure of Government might be swept away at a blow, and the Civil Service be improved' by the drastic remedy of lengthening the hours of work, abolishing pensions and 'life appointments', and hiring superintendents who would 'be paid by a percentage upon the savings of their offices, and not by a premium upon the waste'.[171]

Gladstone and his friends responded by pouring scorn on this distinctive business ideology. Stafford Northcote, for example, questioned the validity of the analogy between public departments and private firms. It was impossible, he contended, to reorganize the former along commercial lines, since 'the public departments were liable to such changes and rechanges' that routine work was at a premium, something which distinguished them from most commercial establishments.[172]

More basically, Gladstone took exception to what he saw as the crudity and demagoguery of the attacks on the aristocratic system mounted by the ARA (and the financial reformers before them). In January 1855 he vigorously defended the Aberdeen coalition against Roebuck's motion, seeing the proposal for a committee of inquiry as a threat to 'the power, dignity, and usefulness of the Commons of England'.[173] Indeed, soon afterwards he was

[171] *Financial Reformer*, Nov. 1858, pp. 62, 66–7. The employers' organization, the National Federation of Associated Employers of Labour, later took a similar view of the inappropriateness of literary examinations; administrative capacity, it argued, depended almost entirely on practical experience and the possession of certain personal qualities (*Capital and Labour*, 26 Aug. 1874).

[172] Parl. Deb., 3rd ser., vol. 138, 2082: 15 June 1855.

[173] Ibid., vol. 136, 1205–6: 29 Jan. 1855.

provoked into resignation by Palmerston's decision to accept the spirit of the House of Commons's motion by setting up the Sebastopol inquiry. Nor did Gladstone feel at all friendly to Layard and company, men who had destroyed the career of dear colleagues of his like Lord Aberdeen.

Further, Gladstone genuinely disliked the attacks which the ARA was making against the aristocracy and its claim that the commercial middle class was the repository of all wisdom and virtue. All this ran counter to Gladstone's attempt to effect a historic compromise between a reformed, modernized aristocracy and the business community. True, during the debate of 15 June, Gladstone did wish Layard 'God speed' in his campaign to reform the diplomatic, consular, and civil services. But he coupled this with a strong defence of aristocracy and of the aristocratic principle, both of which he thought were indelibly associated with the greatest chapters in the country's history.[174] In the excitement of the moment, he even denied that the highly aristocratic Aberdeen Ministry, of which he had recently been a member, had put obstacles in the way of administrative reform![175]

The most intelligent attempt to build a bridge between the two sets of reformers was made by an Irish Liberal Member, Vincent Scully, a lawyer, who moved a motion on administrative reform in July 1855 which was only narrowly defeated, by 140 votes to 125. It congratulated the Government on setting up the Civil Service Commission, but called for open competitive examinations held in public that would apply to the diplomatic and consular services, as well as the home departments. This proved acceptable to Northcote and Gladstone, both men speaking in support of the motion, as well as voting for it. But Scully, a member of the ARA, was eager to point out that 'he had never proposed a mere literary examination, but one which should be a true test of fitness for office', an assurance repeated by the deputy chairman of the ARA, Tite.[176] Eighteen members of the ARA then voted for the Scully motion, among them Lindsay and Roebuck, as well as Cobden. But it was a confused vote, and the compromise was not likely to survive for long.[177]

CONCLUSION

What, then, were the long-term administrative consequences of the Crimean War? Undoubtedly, the set-backs in the Crimea gave a boost to the activities of the military reformers. In particular, Lord Goderich, son of the former

---

[174] Parl. Deb., 3rd ser., vol. 138, 2114, 2099: 15 June 1855.

[175] Shannon, *Gladstone*, 311–12.

[176] Parl. Deb., 3rd ser., vol. 139, 742: 10 July 1855. Tite declared his commitment to 'an examination of candidates for initiatory appointments—not in the dead languages, but a practical examination', ibid., 737.

[177] Moreover, although on 24 Apr. 1857 the House of Commons passed a resolution moved by Goderich, accepting the *principle* of an extended examination system, it remained unclear what kind of examination system MPs had in mind (ibid., vol. 146, 1463–86: 14 July 1857).

Prime Minister but at this stage in his career an 'advanced' Liberal, worked hard to abolish the purchase system, in the hope of opening up a military career to men of talent, regardless of their background.

When Goderich's motion of 1 March 1855 was defeated, interest momentarily switched back to the overhaul of the civil departments. However, agitation for reform of the Army was later sustained by that incongruous figure, the Radical general George de Lacy Evans, the wounded 'hero of Alma'. Like other reformers, Evans pointed out that a higher level of efficiency prevailed in the 'Scientific Corps' (the Artillery and Engineers), in which the purchase of commissions played no part, than it did in the cavalry and infantry. Indeed, though no military man was happy admitting this, the Army was probably in a worse state than the Royal Navy, which, like the Scientific Corps, possessed a higher proportion of middle-class officers. Reformers like Lacy therefore presented the abolition of purchase as a way of opening up a path to merit and of promoting a greater spirit of professionalism in the Army.[178]

This line of argument did not entirely fit with the more general attacks on aristocratic domination of public life. The purchase system, Lord Panmure informed the Court, was very well suited to the not inconsiderable number of army officers who came from 'the commercial portion of Your Majesty's subjects'.[179] Indeed, as Lord Elcho (the later 'Adullamite') pointed out, 'the purchase of commissions was not in itself aristocratic'; commissions in the Army were open to *all* classes, and the 'reason why they were not sought by manufacturing and mercantile men was simply that they considered them a very bad investment for their money'.[180] This was to ignore the intense social discrimination practised in the crack regiments against officers of 'inappropriate' backgrounds. All the same, Elcho had a point: the system of purchase seems in many ways to have been a method of selection and promotion more plutocratic than aristocratic.

Be that as it may, Evans's campaign was widely viewed as yet another attack on the aristocratic order, and was resented as such. Sidney Herbert, himself trying to reform the Army administration under the remorseless pressure of that archetypal middle-class figure Florence Nightingale, continued to press the traditional argument that soldiers were more willing to 'obey men whom they look up to as gentlemen than men who have risen from among themselves'.[181]

Meanwhile Palmerston hit upon a way of 'muzzling' Evans which was simplicity itself: he set up a Royal Commission of Inquiry into the purchase

---

[178] Parl. Deb., 3rd ser., vol. 140, 1791–4: 4 Mar. 1856. See Spiers, *Radical General*, chs. 7–8.
[179] Cited in Steele, *Palmerston and Liberalism*, 53.
[180] Parl. Deb., 3rd ser., vol. 136, 2135–6: 1 Mar. 1855.
[181] Ibid., vol. 140, 1843: 4 Mar. 1856. But Herbert wanted to combine purchase with the employment of examinations.

system, of which Evans was the only reforming member.[182] In this way the abolition of purchase was deferred by over a decade, though, in hindsight, the *ancien régime* looks as if it were merely living on borrowed time.

Whether or not the Crimean War made a significant contribution to the process of military reform remains unclear. In its wake a Staff College was set up, and the education offered by both Sandhurst and Woolwich was over-hauled.[183] Moreover, during the next twelve years there were seventeen Royal Commissions, eighteen Select Committees, and nineteen internal War Office committees investigating various aspects of military administration.[184] But, as one historian puts it, 'Peace reawakened traditional prejudices, which pre-cluded completion of the task until continental sabres began to rattle in earnest a decade hence.'[185] Other historians have taken a different line, arguing that the work of military reorganization had already begun *before* 1855, though not in time to raise standards of efficiency for the war emergency.[186]

There is another irony. Despite the mishaps of the war, it seems that the traditional officer caste emerged with enhanced prestige, a view expressed with characteristically gloomy realism by Cobden when he took stock of the situation in September 1856: 'The aristocracy have gained immensely since the people took to soldiering.'[187] Certainly, whatever the inadequacies of the military high command and the failures of its organizational machinery, the tragic events in the Crimea not only shattered the Radical Party into fragments, but also helped to impress upon Britons of all classes and persuasions the heroism of soldiering. Without the Crimean War experience, it seems unlikely that the Volunteer Movement of 1860 on would have enjoyed such widespread support, sweeping even a former Quaker like Forster into its ranks.[188]

Finally, whereas in early 1855 the popular mood was strongly critical of the aristocracy, that mood soon softened. The destruction of the Aberdeen coalition did something to appease the critics, and Palmerston's Ministry survived because few wanted another change of government while the war was still in progress. In fact, Palmerston benefited from his relative lack of responsibility for the Crimean fiasco (he had previously been Home Secretary), and this made it possible for people to believe that there was an alternative, aristocratic Minister competent to take over the conduct of a war

[182] Spiers, *Army and Society*, 145; *idem, Radical General*, ch. 8.

[183] Brian Bond, *The Victorian Army and the Staff College 1854–1914* (1972).

[184] Sweetman, *War and Administration*, 132.

[185] Ibid. 132. The same view is taken by Bond, *Victorian Army*, 82–3.

[186] e.g. examinations were established in 1849 for first commissions and in the following year for promotion to captain. See Strachan, *Wellington's Legacy*, esp. 139, which also emphasizes the innovative work of Wellington's successor as Commander-in-Chief, Viscount Hardinge (1852–6), and the reforming efforts of Viscount Howick, later Third Earl Grey.

[187] Cobden to Wilson, 23 Sept. 1856, McCord, 'Cobden and Bright', 114.

[188] Reid, *Life of Forster*, 320–1.

which was generally popular. In this way the new Prime Minister was able to dictate the pace and direction of reform. Shortly afterwards, the outbreak of the Indian Mutiny further deflected public attention from the work of military reform.[189]

As far as the home Civil Service was concerned, once the immediate wartime crisis had passed, the sophisticated programme of the Northcote–Trevelyan reformers began to look more attractive than the sloganizing and practical vagueness of the ARA. Interestingly, it was Lowe, who had briefly sided with the 'administrative reformers' in 1855 before becoming disillusioned with their crudities, who, as Gladstone's Chancellor of the Exchequer, later drew up the Order-in-Council of 1870 which belatedly gave effect to the broad essentials of the Northcote–Trevelyan scheme. By this time Lowe, anxious about the implications of the recent franchise extension, was working to create a privileged élite, a new aristocracy of talent, to counter the democratizing tendencies of the day. Even as a young man serving at the Board of Control, Lowe had been converted to Benjamin Jowett's belief that the Civil Service should be staffed not by 'full, free, and fair' competition, as he had urged at Kidderminster in 1855, but by the élite of the older universities.[190] For Lowe was essentially a member of the intellectual professional class, and, to quote his biographer, he emphatically did not want to hand over the direction of the nation to Congregational bankers or Methodist linen drapers. He 'never confused entrepreneurship with statecraft' and, despite his worship of market forces, he wanted national life to be directed by 'guardians' and administrators whose university education had given them a wider moral perspective on life.[191] How far removed all this was from the thinking that had inspired Layard, Lindsay, and Morley fifteen years earlier!

In truth, the ARA contributed little to the creation of the late Victorian Civil Service. Its activities should rather be seen as the culmination of the movement which had recently found expression in demands for 'financial reform'. Later in the century, many middle-class fathers began to look to the Civil Service for career openings for their sons, but this pressure did not make itself felt in the 1850s. Indeed, the ARA leaders, like the financial reformers before them, wanted 'cheap government'—hence the *fewer* officials employed in the public service the better, as far as they were concerned. Unable to agree upon a practical scheme for staffing and organizing the Whitehall departments, the ARA was in any case at its most effective when operating as a protest movement, campaigning against the aristocracy and exposing official abuses.

[189] Spiers, *Radical General*, 186. But since it was thought that the middle-class generals in charge of the Indian Army had given a better account of themselves than the aristocrats responsible for the Crimean blunders, the Mutiny did, in some respects, vindicate the case of those agitating for Army reform.

[190] Winter, *Robert Lowe*, 73–4.

[191] Ibid. 82–3.

The impact of the Crimean War on this campaign is difficult to assess. On the one hand, the war aroused public anger in a way that dockyard scandals and even an increase in the income tax could never do. On the other hand, it deprived the protesters of their 'natural' leaders, Cobden and his friends, who fastidiously refused to exploit patriotic indignation for short-term political gain and would do nothing that had as an objective increased efficiency in the waging of war. At the same time, events in the Crimea, while in some respects discrediting the existing officer corps, also raised the prestige of soldiering. So, once the traditional military caste had demonstrated its attainment of moderate levels of efficiency, it stood to gain, rather than lose, from the recent national crisis.

This was a consideration not lost on Gladstone, as ever concerned to 'modernize' landed society and safeguard the public usefulness of a purified aristocracy. True, Gladstone himself had a passion for 'economical' government. But in other respects, his objectives were diametrically opposed to those of the ARA. This was significant, because, to be effective, the entrepreneurial Radicals crucially depended on Gladstone's co-operation and goodwill. But when it came to the attempt to import 'business principles' into public life, the future Liberal Leader proved to be highly unsympathetic.

The issue of examinations eventually brought these differences into sharp relief. The businessmen of the ARA, in so far as they wanted public examinations at all, tended to see them as a mechanism for the creation of an 'internal market', thereby reinforcing entrepreneurial values. Gladstone and his friends, by contrast, favoured examinations of a kind that would make the ancient universities and the public schools the principal educators of the new administrative élite.

Far from constituting a blow to the *ancien régime*,[192] the Northcote–Trevelyan reforms can therefore better be seen as 'a way of consolidating the landed interest within the state while presenting this political reorganization in the colours of the urban middle-classes, as a purely administrative-efficiency reform based on objective tests and meritocratic criteria'.[193] Apart from the aristocracy and the gentry, the other main beneficiaries were 'well-educated' professional men. In Noel Annan's words, Northcote–Trevelyan was the 'intellectual aristocracy's "Bill of Rights", the eventual institution of competitive open examinations its "Glorious Revolution"'.[194] Conversely, the losers by the Civil Service reforms were administrative experts of one kind or another, men like Chadwick and Kay-Shuttleworth; for with the disappearance of the tradition of 'programme commitment', a new breed of

---

[192] For a different view, see Oliver MacDonagh, 'The Nineteenth-Century Revolution in Government: A Reappraisal', *Historical Journal*, i (1958), 64.

[193] Gowan, 'Whitehall Mandarins', 33.

[194] N. G. Annan, 'The Intellectual Aristocracy', in J. H. Plumb (ed.), *Studies in Social History* (1955), 247.

'Whitehall Mandarins' began to emerge: influential officials like Ralph Lingen whose primary concern was retrenchment and control.[195]

But the other losers from this change were the entrepreneurial Radicals, who, in the late Victorian period, found themselves effectively cut off from the institutions of the State. The outcome was not pre-ordained. In the 1850s it was quite conceivable that Britain might develop an administrative structure somewhat resembling that of the United States, so much admired by many of the Radicals. But the opportunities offered by the crisis of the Crimean War were not seized on, and the eventual triumph of the alternative set of ideas embodied in the Northcote–Trevelyan report signalled a decisive defeat for the entrepreneurial ideal, in education as well as public administration. For good or ill, we are still living with the consequences.

---

[195] See Richard Johnson, 'Administrators in Education before 1870: Patronage, Social position and Role', in Gillian Sutherland (ed.), *Studies in the Growth of Nineteenth-Century Government* (1972), 110–38. Gowan, 'Whitehall Mandarins', 12.

4

The Primacy of Palmerston? 1855–1865

> Lord Palmerston received with open arms at Manchester is a living
> illustration of the additional force which has been given to our foreign
> policy, and the higher force which has been imparted to our commercial
> transactions by uniting the interests and the operations of both. . . . Trade
> is now much more than the acquisition of lucre; it is a great political
> engine, and our merchants are princes not merely by the vastness of their
> riches but also by the extent of their power.
>
> (*The Times*, 10 November 1856)

A view generally accepted among present-day historians is that by the late
1850s and early 1860s entrepreneurial politics was losing its cutting edge.
This has been ascribed to three causes. First, it is claimed that the working
out of the repeal of the Corn Laws led to a closer *rapprochement*, 'fusion'
even, between land and business, the classes that once opposed one another.
Bernard Cracroft put the case forcefully in his 1866 'Essay on Reform':

> Trade, since the abolition of the Corn Laws, has tended more and more to coalesce
> and blend with Land, and the landed interest. The reason is plain: the bulk of English
> merchants and mercantile men are also in different degrees landowners. Protection
> was the only wall of separation between land and trade. That wall removed, the
> material interests of the two classes have become, and tend to become, every day more
> indissolubly connected and inseparably blended.[1]

Because they were ambitious for social promotion, most businessmen had no
fundamental objection to landed government, despite being critical of some of
its abuses. Indeed, many were busily engaged in purchasing land on their own
behalf, and so had little to gain, but much to lose, from following Cobden in
an assault on the land system.[2]

Secondly—and this was one of Cobden's favourite themes—the trade
prosperity of the late 1850s and early 1860s may have blunted discontent and
made it difficult to mobilize the middle classes in a new political campaign. As
Cobden wrote in December 1861:

---

[1] W. L. Guttsman (ed.), *A Plea for Democracy. The 1867 Essays on Reform and Questions for a
Reformed Parliament* (1967), 124–5. See also the similar views of Goldwin Smith, in R. T.
Shannon, *Gladstone and the Bulgarian Agitation 1876* (1963), 226.
[2] Steele, *Palmerston and Liberalism*, 117, 228, 205–6

People can bear and thrive under adversity, but wealth demoralises them sadly. Where are the vigorous self-relying and self-respecting spirits in the rising generation to fill the places of those robust natures who stood forth 22 years ago to fight for commercial freedom. It is only the sufferings and trials of monopoly that could produce such men. Free Trade destroys the energy of the rising world, for every thing but accumulation.[3]

It required a return to the sort of economic depression ('bad trade or deficient harvests—from which heaven defend us!') which had existed during the 1840s, he privately observed, before the middle classes would bestir themselves and renew the fight for their own emancipation.[4] As it was, Cobden told another of his friends, 'the great increase of our manufacturing system has given such an expansive system of employment to the population, that the want of land as a field of investment and employment for labour has been comparatively little felt. So long as this prosperity of our manufactures continues, there will be no great outcry against the landed monopoly.'[5]

But, thirdly, there was the growing popularity of Lord Palmerston, still viewed by Cobden and Bright as the great 'impostor', but now treated with respect by many one-time Radical businessmen.

What caused this change? Gatrell has argued that, as far as Manchester was concerned, it owed much to the realization that the textile industry needed to find new overseas markets, such as China. As a result, the Palmerstonian policy of 'Imperial Free Trade' seemed to offer the business community more than Cobdenite non-interventionism.[6] Others have argued that businessmen in the big industrial centres also realized that the maintenance of Free Trade required that Britain be strong enough to be capable of intervening, if need be, in European affairs.[7] The Cobdenite stress on peace and retrenchment consequently fell on deaf ears: 'Do we require vast armies and ... navies?', Bright asked rhetorically at his big Birmingham meeting in April 1859: 'Yes,' came the reply![8] More generally, as the legitimacy of Britain's political institutions became less subject to questioning and a new patriotic pride began to take hold, Palmerston won support for his doughty defence of Britain's world interests.

Important in registering the changed attitudes among businessmen, it is said, was the Volunteer Movement, which many of them supported. Well might Cobden lament the growth of the martial spirit fostered by Palmerston and its corrupting effect on the 'class pride' of 'his order'. For the glorification of military life (which the Crimean War had also done much to stimulate) involved the re-establishment of many of those aristocratic values and

---

[3] Cobden to Ashworth, 13 Dec. 1861, Cobden Papers, Add. MS 43,654, fo. 129.
[4] Cobden to Hargreaves, 6 June 1857, Cobden Papers, Add. MS 43,655, fo. 6.
[5] Cobden to White, 22 Nov. 1857, cited in Morley, *Cobden*, ii. 215.
[6] Gatrell, 'Commercial Middle Class', Ch. 10.
[7] Steele, *Palmerston and Liberalism*, 192.
[8] Ibid. 125.

practices against which the Anti-Corn Law League had railed in the 1840s. Cobden seems to have seen this development largely in terms of the servility and social deference of manufacturers and merchants. For like Herbert Spencer (the political theorist with whom he had most in common[9]), he seems to have subscribed to a two-stage model of progress, which postulated a necessary transition from 'military' to 'industrial' types of social organization. From this he drew the erroneous deduction that in modern industrial societies ritual, ceremonial, and military pride and pomp could have no legitimate place.[10] That a new alliance between industrialism and militarism was in the making was something which could no more be encompassed by Cobden's view of the world than it could by Herbert Spencer's theories. This explains his uncomprehending contempt when, contrary to what he had earlier predicted, the new Manchester Corporation, with the prominent Unitarian businessman John Potter as mayor, introduced maces, cloaks, and chains, and held municipal banquets. The crowds which turned out in Manchester to greet the Queen when she visited the town in 1851 also grated on his nerves. To Cobden all this childish behaviour belonged to the world of 'feudalism'.[11]

Yet military analogies were now permeating even the idiom of self-help. Thus, while Samuel Smiles (himself an enthusiastic Volunteer) still professed his admiration for trade, he now did so in language which must have grated on the ears of the Manchester School:

Trade tries character perhaps more severely than any other pursuit in life. It puts to the severest tests honesty, self-denial, justice, and truthfulness; and men of business who pass through such trials unstained are perhaps worthy of as great honour as soldiers who prove their courage amidst the fire and perils of battle. And, to the credit of the multitudes of men engaged in the various departments of trade, we think it must be admitted that on the whole they pass through their trials nobly.[12]

Moreover, Smiles made it clear that he deprecated riches for their own sake:

The power of money is on the whole over-estimated. The greatest things which have been done for the world have not been accomplished by rich men, nor by subscription lists, but by men generally of small pecuniary means. . . . The highest object of life we take to be to form a manly character, and to work out the best development possible, of body and spirit—of mind, conscience, heart, and soul.[13]

---

[9] See Peel, *Herbert Spencer*, Ch. 3.

[10] Greenleaf also makes this point (W. H. Greenleaf, *The British Political Tradition*, Vol. 2: *The Ideological Heritage* (1983), 48 and passim).

[11] See Peel, *Herbert Spencer*, Ch. 8. Derek Fraser, *Urban Politics in Victorian England* (1976; 1979 edn.), 204–5. See also Cobden's contempt for the 'mummeries' of the Lord Mayor of London's procession: 'I never saw anything half so absurd, or half so offensive to intelligence or common sense' (23 Jan. 1851, *Cobden's Speeches*, 536).

[12] Samuel Smiles, *Self-Help* (1859, 1910 edn.), 336. Smiles himself became an enthusiastic admirer of the Volunteers, and even gave theoretic support for compulsory conscription, thinking it an aid to thrift and sobriety! (see Briggs, *Victorian People*, 136).

[13] Smiles, *Self-Help*, 365, 367.

Historians have argued (how plausibly we will see in due course) that underlying such utterances was a new mood of class relaxation, as successful merchants and manufacturers achieved social acceptance. Moderate reforms in the administrative structure and fiscal system had muted (if not removed) the main complaints of the entrepreneurial middle class. And many of the barriers against men of urban wealth, which had once caused so much resentment, began to be lowered—witness the acquisition by businessmen of titles, deputy lieutenancies, and other such honours. Thus S. M. Peto received a baronetcy from Palmerston's hands, as did Francis Crossley, though the former was a Baptist and the latter a Congregationalist.[14]

Cobden and Bright (and many subsequent commentators) viewed this as evidence of 'flunkeydom', a servile spirit leading many of the mercantile class to 'ape' the land-owning classes.[15] But more recently, it has been interpreted as a determination on the part of the middle classes to assert themselves as persons of consequence in the new industrial society.[16] Whichever explanation is accepted, the development was hardly helpful to Bright's attempts to rally 'the people' in a middle-class-led assault on aristocratic privilege.

Nowhere did this transformation of class relations assume so striking a form as in Leeds, where Baines's *Mercury* became increasingly aligned with *The Times* and other pro-Palmerstonian papers. And the new social and political moderation of one-time Leeds Radicals was powerfully exemplified by the Lord Mayor, Peter Fairbairn, a wealthy self-made engineering magnate, who in November 1858 spoke out strongly against Bright's campaign for parliamentary reform. What Fairbairn objected to was less an extension of the franchise than the *tone* of Bright's speeches, with their uncritical adulation of America and their tendency, as he saw it, to 'set the working classes against the middle classes, and the middle classes against the aristocracy' when what was needed was for all classes to 'be one family and live together in brotherly love'.

Earlier in 1858 the Queen had knighted Fairbairn when she visited Leeds to open its new town hall, and she and Prince Albert had been delighted with its 'loyal' sentiments. Carried away by his pan-class enthusiasms, Fairbairn soon afterwards held a civic banquet in honour of Lord Fitzwilliam's son, only to be put in his place by the Earl who insisted on the need to preserve proper distinctions of rank between noblemen and commoners. Nevertheless, it is sobering to recall that a decade earlier Fairbairn had been a fierce Repealer, a

---

[14] Steele, *Palmerston and Liberalism*, 181.
[15] Ibid. 120.
[16] Howe, *Cotton Masters*, 262–9. See the attitudes of the old Leaguer, Absalom Watkin, diary, 10 Oct. 1851, Watkin, *Absalom Watkin*, 268. For the bitterness of one Radical businessman over what he saw as 'the evident deadness, to all ideas of progress towards liberty of thought and action, at present observable in our comfortably off and rich classes, from the £10 voter upwards' (see S. C. Kell, *The Political Attitude of our Law-Making Classes towards the Unenfranchised and the Duties Incumbent upon these in Consequence* (Bradford, 1861), 9).

franchise reformer, and, though an Anglican, an educational voluntarist who had supported Sturge's candidacy for Leeds in 1847.[17] Class reconciliation, it seems, had proceeded a long way during the period of Palmerstonian domination.

Moreover, changing circumstances were bound to modify the political attitudes of former Radical businessmen. In the 1840s and early 1850s the cry had been for the 'liberation of commerce'. This had been achieved with the repeal of the Corn Laws and Navigation Acts and also through the 'rationalization' of the fiscal system. True, the land was not yet 'free', and as long as that was the case, entrepreneurial politics were always likely to revive. But in other respects, the self-appointed leaders of the middle classes were faced with a transition not dissimilar to that experienced by labour leaders half a century later when, as Keir Hardie put it, issues of political emancipation gave way to issues of administration.

One symptom of that transition has already been touched upon. So long as many businessmen perceived the State as an extension of aristocratic society, as Cobden never ceased do, so long would they tend to fight almost all attempts to regulate adult labour in the factories as an insult to their order. But by the early 1860s, if not earlier, few manufacturers viewed the Factory Acts in this black-and-white way, while some acknowledged that there were distinct commercial advantages to be reaped from well-considered proposals for industrial regulation. This is an interesting development, since it suggests a growing confidence on the part of the commercial and industrial classes in their ability to impose their views on, or even capture, the State.[18]

Moreover, it was now apparent to most businessmen that more was involved in the establishment of a modern capitalist society than simply removing the fetters from industry in the expectation that the economy would then regulate itself. Even those who believed, in a doctrinaire way, in the virtues of laissez-faire (which was not, in fact, the dominant belief that historians once supposed it to be) could not agree on what laissez-faire entailed on a *practical* level. Historians have been equally bemused.

The fact is that the problems engaging the interest of businessmen were becoming more technical and complex. The London conference summoned in January 1857 by the Law Amendment Society gives a good idea of the range of these problems. Its agenda comprised the following items:

the Law of Partnership; the Bankruptcy Laws; the Local Dues on Shipping; the Consolidation and Revision of the Statutes of Commercial Law; Tribunals of Com-

---

[17] E. D. Steele, 'Imperialism and Leeds Politics, *c.*1850–1914', in Derek Fraser (ed.), *A History of Modern Leeds* (Manchester, 1980), 329–31. Further information on Fairbairn comes from Derek Fraser's essay in the same anthology, 'Politics and Society in the Nineteenth Century', 294.

[18] On changing attitudes to the factory question, see Ch. 8.

merce; Assimilation, as far as possible, of the commercial laws of England, Ireland, and Scotland; Uniformity of Weights and Measures; the Law of Banking.[19]

The heroic age of entrepreneurial politics, it seems, had well and truly ended. Indeed, if *The Economist* is to be believed, two-party conflict had itself expired because of a lack of 'issues' to sustain it:

Where all are reformers of the law, where all are educators of the people, where all are purifiers of the military and civil services, we—whether as electors or as senators—are chiefly called upon to consider the honesty of a man's purpose, the vigour of his will, and the sagacity of his plans. Where all think so much alike, it matters much less what a man *thinks* than what he *can do*.[20]

There is indeed a sense in which the Manchester School was beginning to look decidedly dated by the start of the 1860s. Only Cobden, by far its most intelligent member, kept his reputation fresh with the business community by his part in the negotiation of the French Commercial Treaty. But to many businessmen active in the Chamber of Commerce movement the main public issue was the revision of bankruptcy law, which, for all its undoubted importance, was highly technical and certainly not capable of being reduced to a political slogan. In this new world neither Cobden nor Bright felt at home.[21]

Take, too, the case of Samuel Morley, who had first entered politics as a warm admirer of Cobden; we are told by his biographer that 'for many years a bronze statuette of Richard Cobden stood upon the mantelshelf in Mr. Morley's library'.[22] But by this stage of his career Morley was fighting hard for other, more prosaic reforms in which he took a personal interest, particularly the amendment of the bankruptcy laws and changes in the banking system. And significantly, when Morley attempted to solicit Cobden's views on banking and currency reform, the great spokesman for the entrepreneurial middle class declined, implying that he did not know much about the matter and was anyhow too involved in his crusade to alter the Maritime Code.[23] As for Bright, he had the misfortune to outlive Cobden and last into an age in which most of the new commercial politicians would dismiss him as 'useless'.[24]

Given this background, it is not surprising that many historians have treated the 1857 general election as though it marked the virtual end of the influence

---

[19] G. Henry Wright, *Chronicles of the Birmingham Chambers of Commerce, A.D. 1813–1913, and of the Birmingham Commercial Society A.D. 1783–1812* (Birmingham, 1913), 139.

[20] *Economist*, 1 Nov. 1856, p. 1202. Interestingly, this was written in response to Gladstone's famous anonymous article in the *Quarterly Review*, 'The Declining Efficiency of Party', which called for a resurrection of party, based upon a two-party system.

[21] On the bankruptcy question, see Ch. 5.

[22] Hodder, *Life of Morley*, 153.

[23] Cobden to Morley, 8 Nov. 1861, ibid. 151–2.

[24] On Bright's 'ignorance', see G. C. Lewis to J. Wilson, 27 Dec. 1858, cited in Barrington, *Servant of All*, 197–8.

of the Manchester School. For this election saw Milner Gibson and Bright
ejected from their parliamentary seats by their Mancunian constituents, while
Cobden, escaping from the West Riding, failed to find a new berth in
Huddersfield. Moreover, Bright, distraught by his failure to win over the
public in his denunciations of the Crimean War, was still slowly recovering
from a nervous breakdown.

Nor did this betoken a mere personal tragedy, it can be argued. For,
according to some historians, the 1857 election indicated that deep sea
changes were taking place within the middle-class community, especially
in Manchester.[25] As the social structure of that city became more and
more stratified, the Manchester School, it is maintained, grew increasingly
unpopular in the town of its birth. It is this that explains Bright's defeat at the
hands of his Manchester constituents in 1857, an event which had been long
brewing.[26] The *Manchester Guardian*, which helped engineer that defeat, took
the view that Bright was simply sitting for the wrong constituency, and saw it
as necessary that he be defeated so that he 'did not misrepresent Manchester
and thereby cause the state of opinion prevalent here to be misconceived
throughout Europe'.[27]

Many contemporary observers of the political scene took a rather similar
view: 'The Manchester party is extinguished,' declared Bagehot's *Economist*.
Itself a powerful articulator of this new mood, *The Economist* combined conventional regrets over the loss which the Commons would sustain by the
absence of Cobden and Bright with pleasure at the well-deserved popular
repudiation of an unpatriotic faction. The election result had shown 'how
hollow and unwarrantable were their boasts that they and only they were the
true representatives of the middle and industrious classes', it said.[28] Lowe,
who had himself nearly stood for Manchester, also offered a gloating com-
mentary on the rout of the Manchester School in an anonymous article in the
Edinburgh Review. 'In Manchester itself, the authority of the sect calling itself
the Manchester School has come to be regarded as an intolerable oppression,'
Lowe wrote. The ablest of its MPs (did he mean Cobden but not Bright?)
would doubtless return to Parliament in due course, the better for having
been taught the lesson that factious opposition to all government would not
be tolerated by the electorate. Interestingly enough, Lowe had very nearly
accepted the invitation of the Manchester Whigs to stand against Bright and
Gibson in the 1857 general election, causing Bright to remark privately of his
rival: 'Lowe has had a sharp eye on the political market, and has made two
bargains of himself already, in the 5 years he has been in Parliament—and

[25] Gatrell, 'Commercial Middle Class', Ch. 10.
[26] See Fraser, *Urban Politics*, 205–10. Gatrell, 'Commercial Middle Class', Ch. 10.
[27] Ayerst, *Guardian*, 126–7.
[28] *Economist*, 4 Apr. 1857, p. 362.

possibly if I had done the same, I might have had the hearty support of Neild, Garnett etc!'[29]

In his recent, important study of Palmerston, Steele powerfully reinforces this interpretation. During the years of Palmerston's two premierships, he argues, Liberal businessmen fitted comfortably into the Palmerstonian party.[30] But Steele believes that the political 'tranquillity' of the mid-Victorian years owes less to the subservience of the once Radical middle classes than to Palmerston's skill in imposing his political priorities on the country. Acutely conscious of the importance of public opinion, the elderly Premier shocked Gladstone in the late 1850s and early 1860s by touring the northern cities and making orations there in which the susceptibilities of his middle-class audience were skilfully 'stroked'.[31] Palmerston also used his powers of patronage adroitly to integrate excluded social groups like Nonconformists into the existing order. He even tried to bestow a peerage on two northern industrialists (R. H. Greg and J. G. Marshall), only to be overruled by the cautious Lord Granville.[32] Well might Cobden complain that the leading capitalists, out of whom he had once hoped to form his own Radical party, had been 'used' by Palmerston.[33]

But, more controversially, Steele also diverges sharply from the conventional view of Palmerston as a 'reactionary' in domestic affairs by presenting him as a cautious but constructive reformer who on many issues was ahead of Gladstone himself: 'He [Gladstone] followed where Palmerston led.'[34] When, on certain issues—for example, parliamentary reform and the abolition of church rates—Palmerston held back, this was not so much an expression of innate conservatism, but rather a recognition of the impracticality of attempting large measures of reform at a time of public apathy and contentment. Indeed, so little interest was there in parliamentary reform for most of his years in power, that when in 1858–9 Bright tried to whip up popular interest in the subject, the response of his middle-class audiences was one of annoyance and derision.[35] Nevertheless, according to Steele, Palmerston should be credited with preparing the country for the form of democracy it was later to enjoy with the establishment of the household franchise in 1867, and deserves to be seen as one of the chief architects of the late Victorian Liberal Party.

How valid is this interpretation? A good place to start might be the Prime

---

[29] Anon. (Lowe), 'The Past Session and the New Parliament', *Edinburgh Review*, 105 (Apr. 1857), 571, 576. A. Patchett Martin, *Life and Letters of Robert Lowe, Viscount Sherbrooke* (1893), ii. 171; Bright to Cobden, 21 Mar. 1857, John Bright Papers, Add. MS 43,384, fo. 89.
[30] Steele, *Palmerston and Liberalism*, 134.
[31] Ibid. 15.
[32] Ibid. 28, 225.
[33] Ibid. 134.
[34] Ibid. 24.
[35] Ibid. 122–3.

Minister's 'triumphant' visits to Manchester in 1856, Leeds in 1860, Sheffield in 1862, and Bradford in 1864. These triumphs have often been used to support the view that the northern middle class had, if anything, transferred its allegiance from the entrepreneurial Radicals to the elderly aristocrat.[36] This, of course, was also the burden of Bright's and Cobden's bitter complaints. The invitation to Palmerston to lay the foundation stone of the new Bradford Wool Exchange in 1864 caused Cobden particular pain: 'The highest aim of too many of our capitalist class is to throw themselves at the feet of a feudal aristocrat. The more prosperous we make them the greater is their servility to the ruling class.'[37] Do these visits really bear out the view that an accommodation was occurring during the 1850s and 1860s between the entrepreneurial middle class and landed society under the aegis of Palmerston, in which the former was content to play a subservient role?

PALMERSTON AND THE NORTHERN MIDDLE CLASSES

Let us start with the Manchester visit of November 1856. There is no doubt that Palmerston was given a very warm welcome by all sections of Mancunian society, nor that businessmen vied with one another to demonstrate their affection and respect. The City Council, the Chamber of Commerce, and the Commercial Association all presented him with effusive addresses, in which they emphasized that, although they were delighted over the attainment of peace, their commercial interests had in no way lessened their patriotic support of the Government in the recent 'just and necessary war'.

Aspinall Turner, the President of the Manchester Commercial Association, welcomed Palmerston to Manchester with a speech which expressed all these sentiments, but also showed a concern to defend the local business community from the charge of 'materialism':

Your Lordship may think that we are devoted to cotton-bags and calico, to unfenced machinery and shaftings (laughter), to banking and money-making. These are, indeed, the instruments with which we work, but they are by no means the sole object of our thoughts and attentions (cheers).[38]

However, it is interesting to note that the Manchester Chamber of Commerce, by contrast, took a rather more robust line; after a few courteous opening flourishes, its address was given over largely to the city's commercial grievances: its anxiety about the failure to open up new sources of cotton

---

[36] Bright to Cobden, 25 Oct. 1860, John Bright Papers, Add. MS 43,384, fo. 229.

[37] e.g. Vincent, *British Liberal Party*, 182–3. Cobden to Ashworth, 27 Aug. 1864, Cobden Papers, Add. MS 43,654, fo. 317. See also Cobden's comments on Palmerston's visit to Manchester, Cobden to J. B. Smith, 8 Nov. 1856, John Benjamin Smith Papers, MS 923.2, S345, fo. 56.

[38] *The Times*, 7 Nov. 1856.

supply, its unhappiness over the recent loss of the Local Dues upon Shipping Bill, and so forth. The Council, too, complained of the 'impolitic and unjust' burdens being suffered by the local shipping interests.[39] In short, the Mancunian businessmen may have enjoyed the chance of 'hobnobbing' with a lord, but many of them saw the visit primarily as an opportunity to bend the Prime Minister's ear and secure economic favours for their region.

Palmerston handled the situation with great tact. Flattered, apparently, by the local business community, he responded by flattering his hosts in an equally extravagant way. Manchester and the surrounding district, he proclaimed, was a 'hive of industry', 'one of the great sources of national wealth', and 'the cradle and the nursery of genius'; and he declared his gratitude at being given the opportunity to become acquainted with its leaders. Speaking later in the day at the newly opened Free Trade Hall, Palmerston was careful not only to praise the building, 'which in its splendour is worthy either of an emperor of the present day or of one of those great commercial States which in the earlier periods of history played so powerful and prominent a part in the affairs of the world', but also to show his understanding of its symbolic significance. Moreover, while at Manchester he gave the most emphatic possible declaration of his support for a policy of extending the free trade system throughout the world; indeed, his various speeches were peppered with liberal invocations of progress worthy of a Macaulay.[40] The occasion, taken as a whole, hardly seems to justify Bright's bitter complaints about the Mancunians' 'flunkeyism'.

In fact, there were occasions when Palmerston's eagerness to ingratiate himself with northern businessmen landed him in trouble. For example, making a hurried visit to Liverpool at the end of his Lancastrian trip, he gave the shipowners of that city the clear impression that he favoured a policy of 'free seas and free ports' in a public declaration which won him the applause of his mercantile audience but which, as we shall see, he later had cause to regret.[41]

The Leeds visit of October 1860 is equally instructive. Scarcely had Palmerston disentangled himself from the cheering crowd at the railway station than he was whisked away to the Mayor's parlour, where representatives from the Chambers of Commerce throughout the West Riding successfully pressed him in language which, though polite, was very firm, to commit himself to a speedy reintroduction of the Bankruptcy Bill. Again, while it is undoubtedly true that most local businessmen felt flattered at having such a great personage in their midst, the general tone surrounding Palmerston's visit was anything but sycophantic. The occasion was rather one in which Yorkshire capitalists

---

[39] Manchester Chamber of Commerce Papers, 3 Nov. 1856, fos. 540–1.
[40] *The Times*, 4, 7 Nov. 1856.
[41] Ibid., 8 Nov. 1856.

publicly gave thanks for all the wonderful things that they had collectively achieved, an exercise in self-congratulation in which the Prime Minister was expected to participate. Arguably, we have here that curious mixture of 'bragging self-praise and insecurity' which one scholar has identified as characteristic of Bradford's prominent citizens.[42] But a kind of regional and class *pride* was the dominant emotion, and Palmerston received a warm Yorkshire welcome precisely because he was being welcomed on *his hosts' own terms*.[43]

The Sheffield visit of August 1862 also took place amid great popular excitement, with the enthusiastic crowds almost mobbing their distinguished visitor. Moreover, at the opening banquet in the Cutlers' Hall, Palmerston and the Mayor, who had organized the visit, both agreed, to the applause of the assembled dignitaries, that no one would begrudge the paying of taxes, however large, if the money were spent wisely on a prudent but effective defence of the country's vast world-wide commercial interests and its honour and independence. But such unanimity is hardly surprising since the Mayor, John Brown, was the proprietor of the Atlas Steel and Spring Works, which was making armoured plating for Royal Navy vessels! (Palmerston toured the establishment on his second day, and declared himself impressed.) Even so, the Prime Minister did not have everything his own way since, after making his speech at the banquet, he had to listen to the local MP, Roebuck, deliver one of his famous slashing speeches in which he called upon the Government to come to the aid of the South in the American Civil War. The Mayor of Manchester, who had been invited to the meeting, then took the opportunity of trying to press Palmerston to alter or abolish the labour test in order to alleviate distress in the stricken Lancashire cotton towns.[44]

Palmerston's later visit to Bradford showed even more clearly that there were difficulties as well as rewards in wooing the big cities. Palmerston had been invited to lay the foundation stone of the new Bradford Wool Exchange —apparently an odd choice of visiting dignitary. In fact, however, the entire affair had been stage-managed by H. W. Ripley, a wealthy dyer, local celebrity, and current president of the Bradford Chamber of Commerce.[45] Ripley had brought Palmerston to Bradford on his own initiative, and later put him up at his home, in part to promote his own influence in the borough, but also, by staging a pro-Palmerston demonstration, to weaken the position of the

[42] Igor Webb, 'The Bradford Wool Exchange: Industrial Capitalism and the Popularity of Gothic', *Victorian Studies*, 20 (1976–7), 46.

[43] *The Times*, 26 Oct. 1860. See Asa Briggs's account of the Queen's opening of the Leeds town hall in Sept. 1858, in *Victorian Cities* (1963; 1968 edn.), 170–9, esp. 179.

[44] *The Times*, 11 Aug. 1862.

[45] Webb, 'Bradford Wool Exchange', 57–8. Malcolm Hardman, *Ruskin and Bradford: An Experiment in Victorian Cultural History* (Manchester, 1986), 176–7. On Ripley, see William Cudworth, *Manningham, Heaton and Allerton* (Bradford, 1896), 244–9; Reynolds, *Great Paternalist*, 68–9, 177, 329–30; Hardman, *Ruskin and Bradford*, 160–4.

Radicals who controlled the Bradford Liberal Association, among them the recently elected MP for the town, W. E. Forster.

But the stratagem misfired badly. A 'Working Man's Palmerston Reception Committee', angry at the Ministry's inactivity over franchise reform, organized a demonstration; and some 30,000 workmen greeted their visitor with stony silence. (Palmerston, who privately thought the Bradford visit 'a Bore', had earlier asked his Chief Whip if some other person who was 'more generally acceptable to the working men' could be found to lay the foundation stone.[46]) But many of the local *businessmen* were also less than friendly. In fact, when the Bradford Chamber of Commerce had discussed making an address to Palmerston, as Ripley urged, some businessmen had opposed the idea, one saying that the Chamber of Commerce was a purely commercial body, and that it would be inappropriate to honour Palmerston, 'who, in the whole course of his life, had never been favourably associated with commerce'. Why not honour Cobden, he wondered? There had also been some opposition to the Palmerston invitation in the town council, though an address was agreed on almost unanimously.[47]

It is true that, on his arrival in Bradford, the Prime Minister was effusively thanked for the French Treaty of 1860, which local businessmen believed responsible for the current prosperity of the Yorkshire textile industry. But the Treaty was known to be mainly the handiwork of Cobden, backed by Gladstone, not of Palmerston. An even more backhanded compliment was the gratitude expressed by Forster for the pacific policy of the British Government which had kept the country out of a European war over the Schleswig–Holstein question!

The nadir came with the banquet following the stone-laying ceremony. Forster, in a speech welcoming visitors from other Yorkshire towns, took the opportunity to remind Palmerston that 'the people of Bradford had extreme opinions', a theme taken up by Francis Crossley, the carpet manufacturer and MP for Halifax, who in his reply to Forster's toast said that 'on some occasions he had listened with pain' to the Prime Minister's depreciation of 'political and ecclesiastical reforms'—clearly a reference to the extension of the franchise and the church rates issue. Although Crossley intended his insult mainly for Ripley, it came over as a public rebuke of Palmerston from a member of his own parliamentary party. True, his remarks had been greeted by cries of 'Shame', and the majority seems to have agreed with Byles that, in agreeing to lay the foundation stone, the Prime Minister was paying a tribute 'to the genius of commerce and indirectly to the skill and labour from which commerce springs'.[48] Even so, only the Prime Minister's good-humoured

---

[46] Palmerston to Brand, 3 July 1864, Brand Papers.

[47] Bradford Chamber of Commerce Minutes, 27 July 1864, fos. 220–1; *Bradford Review*, 4 Aug., 23 July 1864.

[48] *The Times*, 10 Aug. 1864; *Bradford Review*, 13 Aug. 1864; *Bradford Observer*, 11 Aug. 1864.

nonchalance saved the visit from disaster. In fact, Palmerston again made a strongly 'liberal' speech; perhaps, as the *Spectator* cynically observed, because he had 'felt the cold current amidst all the balmy breezes'. Had he only had the presence of mind to compare Bradford favourably with Leeds, it added, a workman's guard would have escorted him home![49]

What all these episodes show is how mistaken it is to describe the northern industrialists as abasing themselves before Palmerston. The Prime Minister's various visits to the northern towns were seen by both sides as symbolic encounters between the 'old' and the 'new' England. Byles, for example, said that Palmerston should be welcomed to Bradford as 'the sole living link between England's heroic age and the commercial epoch'.[50] But Palmerston was quite as much concerned to ingratiate himself with his hosts as they were to impress upon him their loyalty and patriotism.[51] Thus there is something unsatisfactory about an interpretation which views Palmerston's flattery of industrialists as evidence of the elderly Premier's supreme skill at 'managing' the middle classes, while taking at face value the flattery which the northern industrialists heaped on him and automatically assuming that it denoted subservience. Quite who was manipulating whom?

THE RADICAL REVIVAL

A similar ambiguity hangs over political life generally during the late 1850s and 1860s. No one doubts that Palmerston was a generally popular Prime Minister, among the middle classes of the industrial cities as elsewhere. But this does not mean that the period of his ascendancy marks the death of 'entrepreneurial Radicalism'. The 1857 election, for example, was not quite the political watershed that *The Economist* presented it as being, and those who celebrated the obsequies of the Manchester School were doing so very prematurely. In 1859 Cobden returned to Parliament as Member for Bright's home town of Rochdale, while Bright himself, his health partly restored, had won a by-election in Birmingham the previous year. The third of the leaders of the 'School', Milner Gibson, now MP for Ashton, became President of the Board of Trade in Palmerston's second Ministry in 1859.

Even in Manchester there was a Radical revival. Eighteen months after the 1857 disaster, a by-election took place in which the victor was Thomas Bazley, an old League stalwart (he was later one of the pallbearers at

---

[49] Cited in *Bradford Observer*, 18 Aug. 1864. After the Bradford meeting in 1864, even the *Financial Reformer* found itself, to its evident surprise, heartily welcoming the Prime Minister's liberal speech, which it hoped presaged the final destruction of the custom-house! (Sept. 1864, p. 493).

[50] *Bradford Observer*, 4 Aug. 1864.

[51] As Steele rightly says, whereas Gladstone lectured the middle classes, Palmerston flattered them (*Palmerston and Liberalism*, 36).

Cobden's funeral).[52] Further doubt is cast on the deep structural explanations put forward for what happened in 1857 by the by-election victory in Manchester in 1867 of John Bright's brother, Jacob, who promptly proclaimed the resurrection of the ideals of peace, retrenchment, and reform associated with the names of Cobden and Manchester.[53] True, Manchester was never again to play the central role in promoting 'advanced Radicalism' which it had for the previous twenty years. But this did not mean the death of entrepreneurial politics, and to claim as much is to attach exaggerated importance to a single industrial city.

In Cobden's view, the Radical torch had passed from Manchester to Birmingham. In a famous letter to Joseph Parkes, written on the eve of Bright's by-election victory, Cobden argued that Birmingham's 'exemption from aristocratic snobbery' arose

from the fact that the industry of the hardware district is carried on by small manufacturers, employing a few men and boys each, sometimes only an apprentice or two; whilst the great capitalists in Manchester form an aristocracy, individual members of which wield an influence over sometimes two thousand persons. The former state of society is more natural and healthy in a moral and political sense.[54]

But Birmingham's greatest period of fame as a national centre of Radicalism was yet to come. In many respects the town which played that role in the 1860s was Bradford. Although it had acquired a charter only as recently as 1848, Bradford was currently undergoing a remarkable economic expansion. And perhaps because, unlike Manchester or Leeds, it was a purely manufacturing town with a relatively simple social structure ('the largest of the factory towns rather than the smallest of the industrial cities'), it provided an environment in which many brands of entrepreneurial Radicalism could flourish.[55]

Admittedly, divided as they were between several factions, the Radicals of Bradford failed to set up their own 'School'. By the late 1850s, mainstream Radicalism in the town was being articulated by William Byles's *Bradford Observer*, now a moderate organ rather like the *Leeds Mercury*, which tended to celebrate past triumphs such as Repeal and the incorporation of the borough, instead of looking to the future. However, in reaction to this political

[52] In his account of the 1868 election, Hanham calls Bazley a 'Palmerstonian' (H. J. Hanham, *Elections and Party Management: Politics in the Time of Disraeli and Gladstone* (1959; 1978 edn.), 310), which hardly seems accurate, although it is true that by this time he had mellowed considerably and was even the owner of more than 5,000 acres of land in Lancashire and Gloucestershire (Briggs, *Victorian Cities*, 132).

[53] *Financial Reformer*, 1 Jan. 1868, p. 260.

[54] Cobden to Parkes, 9 Aug. 1857, Morley, *Cobden*, ii. 199.

[55] Gary Firth, 'The Bradford Trade in the Nineteenth Century', in D. G. Wright and J. A. Jowitt (eds.), *Victorian Bradford* (1981), 7–36; Joyce, *Work, Society and Politics*, 26. But it has been argued that Bradford can better be seen as the smallest of the industrial cities (Koditschek, *Class Formation*, 429, n. 52).

approach, leading textile magnates like the Kell brothers and Alfred Illingworth founded the *Bradford Review* in 1858.[56] Although these Radicals later came to be best known for their zeal in the cause of Disestablishment, they were also associated with the causes of financial reform and an extension of the franchise. Bradford, in fact, made a major contribution to the two big 'Woodhouse Moor' reform demonstrations in nearby Leeds in October 1866 and April 1867.[57] Yet another strand in the borough's Radicalism, a highly innovative one, was represented by W. E. Forster, the borough's MP from 1861 to 1885, whose career achieved national importance, as we will see later in this chapter. The point to be made here is that Bradford's politics, however confused, show how resilient Radicalism still was in the 1860s and how wide and deep was the support it enjoyed from businessmen.

FINANCIAL REFORM: THE SECOND PHASE

But although Bradford has some claim to be the 'shock city' of the 1860s, it was a pre-industrial city—and a Tory-controlled one at that—which provided the impetus for a new phase of Radicalism in the aftermath of the 1857 reverses. For at precisely this moment the Liverpool Financial Reform Association awoke from its semi-hibernation. In fact, on 10 March 1857, about three weeks before Manchester went to the polls, the Association's secretary, Charles Macqueen, had approached George Wilson and suggested the launching of a new campaign for financial reform.[58] Over the next few years the LFRA returned to its former practice of holding rallies and issuing pamphlets. In July 1858 it also brought out a regular monthly periodical, *The Financial Reformer*. Papers were read to the various annual meetings of the Social Science Congress,[59] and influential recruits were won, including Duncan McLaren, John Bright's brother-in-law, the future Radical MP for Edinburgh.[60] In the early 1860s a host of distinguished entrepreneurial Radicals attached themselves to the LFRA: for example, Ashworth, Bazley, and Samuel Morley, the latter organizing its Lecture Fund in 1861 and later serving as its Vice-President. (Perhaps, it has been suggested, the LFRA was now becoming less 'provincial' in its orientation and rather more 'an expected Radical Liberal credential'.)[61]

---

[56] James, 'Byles and *Bradford Observer*', 123.

[57] Wright, 'Second Reform Agitation', 185–8. See material in W. S. Nichols Papers.

[58] Macqueen to G. Wilson, 10 Mar. 1857, George Wilson Papers.

[59] e.g. *Report on Taxation: Direct and Indirect: Adopted by the Financial Reform Association, Liverpool, and Presented to the Annual Meeting of the National Association for the Promotion of Social Science, held at Bradford, October, 1859* (Liverpool, n.d.). In the previous year the secretary of the LFRA, Macqueen, had given a paper on indirect taxation to the same body (*NAPSS*, 1858, pp. 672–81). In 1863 Macqueen again spoke to the National Association during its annual meeting in Edinburgh (ibid., 1863, pp. 863–8).

[60] *Financial Reformer*, Nov. 1860, p. 445.

[61] Ibid., June 1860, p. 411. Malchow, *Gentlemen Capitalists*, 304.

Financial reform revived as an issue in the late 1850s when it became apparent that Gladstone's great budget of 1853 had not, as had once been hoped, settled the fiscal difficulty for good and all. In the following year the Crimean War had forced Gladstone to increase the income tax from 7*d.* to 1*s.* 2*d.*, thereby raising once more the larger question of the 'fairness' of that tax and the apportionment of the burdens which it imposed on the different classes. Gladstone's successor, Cornewall Lewis, had added only another 2*d.* to the income tax, and had instead placed greater reliance on borrowing as a way of financing the war.[62] The business Radicals, who were alarmed by this, also disliked the imposition of new, small duties for revenue-raising purposes, which were begun by Gladstone himself in his second 'War Budget', and carried on by Lewis in April 1855 and again in 1857. Even a pro-war businessman Radical like Laing argued that it would be folly, at a time when there was so much popular anger against 'the upper classes for their mismanagement, to reverse a financial policy from which the labouring population had reaped such advantage'.[63] The impending expiry of the income tax in 1860 (unlikely though its realization seemed) also placed financial policy very much in the forefront of people's minds.

One manifestation of the new concern was the publication in 1857 of an anonymous pamphlet, *The People's Blue Book* (actually written by Charles Tennant[64]), which called for the total abolition not only of all customs and excise duties, but also of the income tax and the succession duty! Instead, necessary revenue should be raised almost entirely through, first, a 'Capitation Tax' (remarkably like the modern 'community charge', though levied nationally) and, second, a 'property tax'. The latter would be fixed at 20 per cent of the annual value of income deriving from both real estate and personal estate (in the form of annuities, dividends, and so forth), with exemption for those whose income was less than £2 from houses and landed property and less than £1 from personal investments. Wages and salaries were not to be taxed at all until such time as they had been 'converted into capital'.[65] Significantly, the valuation was also to exclude 'all mines and minerals, and all works, and manufactories, of every description; and also all canals, and railways', though not the houses and other buildings on which manufactories were built, nor the land through which the canals and railways passed.[66]

---

[62] Olive Anderson, 'Loans versus Taxes: British Financial Policy in the Crimean War', *Economic History Review*, 16 (1963–4), 318. Angus B. Hawkins, 'A Forgotten Crisis: Gladstone and the Politics of Finance during the 1850s', *Victorian Studies*, 26 (1983), 296–7, 306–8.

[63] Parl. Deb., 3rd ser., vol. 137, 1795: 26 Apr. 1855. Anderson, 'Loans versus Taxes', 320–1.

[64] [Charles Tennant], *The People's Blue Book: Taxation as it is and as it ought to be* (1857), passim. Tennant claimed in his preface that he had been working on his book when the LFRA pamphlets fell into his hands. He said that he had voted for the first Reform Bill, and acknowledged a debt not only to the LFRA, but also to Adam Smith, Archbishop Whately, James Mill, Dr Chalmers, S. T. Coleridge, Tooke, and others (pp. viii, xi–xii).

[65] Ibid. 206–7.

[66] Ibid. 207.

The People's Blue Book was a remarkably successful, quickly running through several editions; but what gave it considerable political significance was that its proposals were, for a time, taken up by Bright, who, as we have seen, had been flirting with the notion of a property tax as far back as 1842.[67] So much became apparent when, in the course of 1858, against the advice of Cobden, Bright launched his campaign for parliamentary reform, concentrating on such archetypally middle-class issues as the need for a measure of redistribution.[68] To this campaign, financial reform became closely linked.

In July 1859, shortly after the fall of the Derby Government, Bright delivered a grand oration in the Commons in which he lambasted the succession duty for its inadequacy and bitterly complained about the income tax ('odious beyond all others that I know of'), which, he said, pressed 'upon all capital employed in shops or manufactures with double the weight that it does upon that which is employed strictly in the cultivation of the land'.[69]

The message was repeated even more stridently in early December, when Bright came forward as the main speaker at a big rally in Liverpool organized by the LFRA. This meeting, which was attended by some three or four thousand people, opened in an excited mood, with the Secretary telling his audience that 'the mission of the Anti-Corn Law League is still unfulfilled'. Bright then made a direct appeal to the class feeling of the meeting ('ye of the middle classes'): let us look at the problems of the world, he urged, 'with the eyes of men of business and of common sense'. His appeal was to the conscience but also the self-interest of the trading community: 'I say the poor are taxed oppressively to spare the rich, and I say that trade is taxed oppressively to spare the proprietors of the soil.' After calculating the different contributions made by each of the classes under the income tax, to dramatize its unfairness, Bright ended his speech with a call for electoral reform, but not before he had attacked the inadequacies of the succession duty and floated the idea of a property tax, which he thought should be a tax of 8*s*. per £100 on all property whose owners had an income of £100 per annum.[70]

For the time being, anyway, Bright was identified with the programme of the *People's Blue Book*, as Cornwall Lewis and others rightly perceived.[71] But where did the LFRA stand on this issue? The concept of a property tax had had no place in its original objectives, which were confined to the abolition of

---

[67] For Cornwall Lewis's worried reaction, see *Edinburgh Review*, 111 (Jan. 1860), 252; Cranborne was also much disturbed (Smith (ed.), *Salisbury on Politics*, 215).

[68] See Ch. 6.

[69] 21 July 1859, *Bright's Speeches*, 481–4. A recent publication, the *Papers of the Birmingham Income Tax Reform Association* (1857), had fiercely denounced the tax for being inquisitorial. Bright, however, preferred to emphasize the injustice involved in the refusal of successive governments to differentiate between fixed and permanent incomes.

[70] *The Times*, 2, 3 Dec. 1859.

[71] Lewis to Henry Reeve, 4 Dec. 1859, Lewis (ed.), *Letters of Cornwall Lewis*, 373–4. See also *The Times*, 1 Dec. 1859.

all customs and excise duties. Moreover, in the past, its leading officers, including Heyworth and Jeffery, had always sung the praises of the income tax, which Bright had now come to their rally to denounce! Once again, albeit in a more critical guise, the entrepreneurial Radicals had run up against the problem of precisely how they expected the nation's revenues to be raised.

This dilemma particularly affected the organizers of the LFRA. They were under pressure from a number of different quarters. On his return from the United States, Cobden saw the officers of the Association, and he and Bright favoured the Association with another visit in September 1859. They used these occasions to applaud the LFRA's 'principles' (Bright said he 'reverenced the Association . . . for its steady and expanding adherence to principle'), while making it clear that they regarded the total abolition of all customs and excise duties as utopian. Cobden dilated on the importance of organization, and Bright suggested as an attainable objective the immediate abolition of all duties on tea, coffee, and sugar, along with other duties which brought in only small amounts of revenue.[72]

While an agitated Council debated the expediency of sponsoring this minimal programme, which some of its members would clearly regard as a betrayal, the author of *The People's Blue Book*, who had insisted on attaching himself to the organization, deprecated the adoption of anything falling short of his own grand scheme.[73] After much agonizing, the Council agreed to do nothing!

Its members certainly did well to keep clear of the property tax notion, which was open to a multitude of objections,[74] many of which were forcibly mobilized by *The Economist*:

A certain fallacy runs through all Mr Bright's speeches on the subject. . . . He thinks that all people with visible 'property' are rich, and all who are without it are poor. But such is not the truth. A man who earns a large income for his station in life, a lawyer or a physician, is rich; but one who has only a small income is poor, though its source be visible and tangible.

Was it seriously being suggested that the poor widow with money in the Funds be heavily taxed, while the Lord Chancellor, for example, escape scot-free? *The Economist* raised another objection. What, it asked, 'would be the effect of this scheme on the savings of the country? So long as a man simply

---

[72] *Financial Reformer*, Aug. 1859, pp. 215–16. Ibid., Oct. 1859, pp. 243–4.

[73] *Financial Reformer*, Oct. 1859, p. 253. But in its *Report on Taxation*, presented to the annual meeting of the National Association for the Promotion of Social Science held at Bradford in October 1859, the LFRA coupled its by now familiar diatribe against the wickedness and folly of customs and excise duties with a tentative commendation of what it called 'that valuable contribution to the service of Political Economy, "The People's Blue Book"', the salient features of which it then went on to outline (pp. 17–18).

[74] The Council of the Association could not fully understand the proposal (*Financial Reformer*, Dec. 1860, p. 460). Macqueen later made it clear that Bright's commendation of the property tax had never been endorsed by the LFRA (*The Times*, 2 Jan. 1865).

earns much and spends the whole of it, he is not to pay, according to this proposal; but the moment he begins to save it and have "property", he is taxed.'[75]

The LFRA was not alone in steering clear of the property tax. Bright, too, quickly abandoned it. What, then, was left for 'financial reformers' to do, except wring their hands at the iniquities of the status quo? Heyworth continued to sing the praises of the income tax, even in its undifferentiated form; but this eventually led to his being forced to resign the presidency of the Association.[76] Meanwhile, other Liverpool reformers insisted on the continuing need for reform of the income tax so as to bring relief to those on 'precarious' incomes. But, interestingly, this time the attempt to achieve such an objective devolved on a *Conservative* MP, the banker John G. Hubbard, Member for Buckingham. Indeed, the LFRA's request in 1861 to be permitted to submit evidence to the Select Committee examining the subject was politely rejected. In any case, nothing could be achieved on this front in the face of the Treasury's opposition.[77]

An inability to devise a constructive money-raising alternative did not stop the LFRA, however, from continuing to press for a total abolition of all customs and excise duties. Indeed, so doggedly did it pursue this objective that in late 1864 it stumbled into an unfortunate public altercation with its great hero, Cobden. The background to this incident was the famous Rochdale speech of 23 November, in which Cobden declared that 'as regards the question of protection, Mr Gladstone has finished his work' and all that the Chancellor need do now to complete his work as a financial reformer was to secure drastic cuts in public expenditure.[78] For this utterance Cobden was sharply rapped over the knuckles by the Association, which asked how the 'liberation of commerce' was compatible with the survival of customs and excise duties that still raised £40 million a year? Through his secretary, Cobden replied that his own particular mission had been 'nothing more than the abolition of *protective* duties', not *all* duties, though others might well wish to press for the latter objective. This exchange greatly amused *The Times*, which was confirmed in its views as to the LFRA's total lack of practical common sense.[79]

Faute de mieux, the entrepreneurial Radicals thus found themselves thrust

[75] *Economist*, 3 Dec. 1859, p. 1341. Later in the month *The Economist* returned to the charge, querying the meaning of 'visible property' (17 Dec. 1859, p. 1400; ibid., 31 Dec. 1859, p. 1455).

[76] *Financial Reformer*, 1 Apr. 1865, p. 63.

[77] On this later phase of the differentiation question, see B. E. V. Sabine, *A History of Income Tax* (1966), 82–7. Shehab, *Progressive Taxation*, Ch. 8.

[78] *Cobden's Speeches*, 495.

[79] *Financial Reformer*, 2 Jan. 1865, pp. 11–12. *The Times*, 23 Dec. 1864, 2 Jan. 1865. Yet the attack on customs and excise was still capable of eliciting a favourable response from businessmen; e.g. the Bradford Liberals declared in 1864 that they would 'no longer submit to have £41 million a year wrung from struggling industry' (*Bradford Review*, 16 Jan. 1864).

back once more on two well-tried courses of action: retrenchment and reliance on Gladstone. Never at home with the detail of fiscal policy, Bright was undoubtedly relieved to return to 'economy' as the principal answer to all the country's fiscal difficulties; cut public spending, and then neither the income tax nor any conceivable replacement would be needed. Thus, for the rest of his life, Bright continued to hammer away at the theme of government waste and extravagance.[80]

The other pillar of the financial reformers' programme in the early 1860s was to offer general support to Gladstone, who had returned to the Exchequer in June 1859,[81] following the failure of his recent attempt to re-unite the Conservative Party on this basis of his own 1853 settlement.[82] Indeed, a year later, in his great 1860 budget, Gladstone managed, by coupling a renewal of the income tax with a bold programme of tariff reduction, to please nearly everyone. *The Economist* thought the budget's popularity to be well justified, and it welcomed the sensible balance that had been struck between direct and indirect taxation, observing, with justice, that although the income tax in its existing form pressed 'very hardly on incomes that are *earned* in trade and industry', those who earned them were quite willing to pay the tax 'to obtain the advantages of the simple tariff which Mr Gladstone has offered them'.[83] The entrepreneurial Radicals, including most members of the LFRA, agreed with this assessment.[84]

In fact, the excited Liverpool reformers were quick to greet the budget as '*our* budget'. 'As Manchester stood nobly forward to win the first free-trade battle, Liverpool may now claim the credit of winning the second.'[85] Robertson Gladstone proudly told his brother that the budget inaugurated 'a new era', and enclosed a letter which he had received from Jeffery, in which the budget was called 'a Financial Reform document'.[86] This was, of course, a piece of self-delusion. But Tory journals like the *Quarterly Review* encouraged such wishful thinking by claiming to believe that Gladstone was but putty in Bright's hands and by dubbing the 1860 budget 'this Liverpool budget'—a measure which had originated with the LFRA, that 'elegant periphrasis . . . for the imposing personality of Mr. Robertson Gladstone'.[87] Lord Cranborne

---

[80] See Vincent, *British Liberal Party*, 202–3.

[81] Heyworth felt that the Council did not need to produce a positive programme of its own, and 'had no right to tread upon the functions which properly belonged to the Government'. Robertson Gladstone agreed, communicating to the Council his brother's aspirations and difficulties! (*Financial Reformer*, Dec. 1861, p. 547).

[82] Although, during the short-lived Conservative Ministry of 1858–9, Disraeli was to produce a budget which adhered to Gladstonian principles in many respects, the political basis for a Conservative-Peelite rapprochement was missing (Hawkins, 'Forgotten Crisis', 298–320).

[83] *The Economist*, 3 Mar. 1860, p. 224.

[84] See e.g. Robertson Gladstone's observations, *Financial Reformer*, Feb. 1862, p. 573.

[85] *Financial Reformer*, Mar. 1860, p. 349.

[86] Robertson Gladstone to William Gladstone, 11 Feb. 1860, Hawarden Papers, vol. 665.

[87] *Quarterly Review*, 109 (1861), 216–17.

propounded a similar argument.[88] As usual, Bright took an unduly complacent view of the situation; the Chancellor's 1860 budget speech, he observed to Cobden, had 'more sound doctrine in it, of our sort, than any I have ever heard from the Treasury bench'.[89]

Moreover, when the paper duties clauses were thrown out by the House of Lords, the Liverpool reformers joined Bright in indignantly rushing to the Chancellor's defence.[90] The local merchant Charles Holland told a cheering audience: 'As a Liverpool man, he was proud of him [Gladstone], and gloried in him. The industrial classes of Liverpool should stand by him to a man.'[91] The Mancunians, too, were now inclined to claim Gladstone as one of their own. In 1862, for example, the Manchester Chamber of Commerce publicly conveyed its feelings 'of respect and esteem towards one whom Lancashire regards amongst the most gifted of her sons, and England places amongst the foremost of her statesmen'.[92] Meanwhile, Gladstone's employment of Cobden in the negotiation of a commercial treaty with France offered yet another reason why the doctrinaire financial reformers should have been tempted to 'toe the line' and not make too many difficulties for the Government. Finally, because Gladstone shared the Radicals' keenness to eliminate waste and curb public expenditure, the latter were denied any easy opportunity to launch a frontal attack on the Government as a whole, even had they wanted to do so.

That the Liverpool reformers were wise to fall in behind Gladstone becomes apparent in the light of their later attempt to remonstrate mildly with him on the occasion of his visit to Liverpool in October 1864. At a meeting at which the Liverpool Chamber of Commerce made the Chancellor an honorary member, the LFRA presented him with a long petition, in which, mixed up with the flattery appropriate to the occasion, was censure of the recent budget. Why had it been decided to reduce income tax by a penny, rather than abolish the registration duty on corn? Gladstone, clearly nettled, spoke witheringly in his reply of 'those who would ascend . . ., if they could, into the seventh heaven of speculation'. No Government, he added, should seek popularity by sponsoring 'abstract, extensive, sudden and sweeping reforms' which might endanger public credit or throw the finances of the country into confusion.

[88] Robert Stewart, ' "The Conservative Reaction": Lord Robert Cecil and Party Politics', in Lord Blake and Hugh Cecil (eds.), *Salisbury: The Man and his Policies* (1987), 104–5.

[89] Bright to Cobden, 26 Feb. 1860, Bright Papers, Add. MS 43,384, fo. 187. On Gladstone's 'politicization' of the chancellorship and seduction of the Radicals, see P. M. Gurowich, 'The Continuation of War by Other Means: Party and Politics, 1855–58', *Historical Journal*, 27 (1984), 617.

[90] *Financial Reformer*, July 1860, p. 415. But Robertson Gladstone thought it better not to get involved publicly in the issue (Robertson Gladstone to William Gladstone, 19 May 1860, Hawarden Papers, vol. 665).

[91] 19 June 1860, recorded in *Financial Reformer*, July 1860.

[92] Manchester Chamber of Commerce Papers, 24 Apr. 1862. See also the characterization of Gladstone in the anonymous *Fortunes Made in Business*, vol. 2, 113–14.

The manner of the LFRA's remonstrance was as unfortunate as its substance. The Liverpool Chamber's president had earlier said that his organization did 'not wish to be mixed up with the Financial Reform Association'. And his apprehensions were undoubtedly confirmed when Jeffery delivered his prolix petition, which took nearly half an hour to deliver. Impatient members of the audience shouted 'Time' and hissed when criticisms of their distinguished guest were read out. Many newspapers had much to say about the folly and bad manners displayed by the LFRA.[93]

What all this suggests is that the financial reformers, and indeed the entrepreneurial Radicals generally, fell into a heavy dependence on Gladstone, and could make absolutely no progress in those areas where he was flatly hostile to their ideas. One example of this is the failure of Hume's old disciple William Williams to give the succession duties 'real teeth'. In 1861 Williams attempted to ensure 'that real property should be made to pay the *same* duty as that now payable on personal property'; but for his pains he was flattened by Gladstone. Although the issue was to be raised again by a Liberal Chancellor thirty-three years later, the issue could not be revived immediately. Williams himself was so bewildered by Gladstone's dialectics that he never moved another motion on the subject in the House![94]

In the late 1850s and 1860s the Association of Chambers of Commerce began to interest itself in the reform of the income tax, despite an initial desire to steer clear of anything politically controversial.[95] But it was by and large left to a younger generation of Radicals to carry on the battle for fundamental change in the taxation system, and this campaign did not begin in earnest until the 1880s. Meanwhile Gladstone's creative compromise held the field in as much as fiscal controversies never again threatened to precipitate class war as they had in the late 1840s and early 1850s—except, perhaps, much later in the very different circumstances surrounding Lloyd George's 'People's Budget'.

COBDEN'S LAST CRUSADE

Gladstone's financial policies had a somewhat different effect on Cobden. Ever since the 'Arrow Incident' (and perhaps from an even earlier date) Gladstone and Cobden had found themselves moving closer to one another on issues of foreign affairs and on how best to handle colonial problems and

---

[93] *Financial Reformer*, Nov. 1864, pp. 534–42.

[94] David Evans, *The Life and Works of William Williams*... (Llandyssul, 1939), 156–9. Parl. Deb., 3rd ser., vol. 161, 615–24: 19 Feb. 1861.

[95] On the Chambers of Commerce, see Ch. 5. See the petition of the Birmingham Chamber of Commerce, which was sent on to Gladstone, 14 Feb. 1860 (Wright, *Birmingham Chambers of Commerce*, 165–6). For another business critique of the income tax, see Sir S. Morton Peto, *Taxation: Its Levy and Expenditure Past and Present* (1863), esp. 86.

armament expenditure. Cobden's convictions about the Whigs' hereditary incapacity in finance also drew him to Gladstone.[96] True, as most recent historians have emphasized, Cobden and Gladstone viewed public life from quite different perspectives. For example, Cobden was a secular optimist, who believed that making trade completely free would promote unlimited economic expansion and usher in an era of universal peace; by contrast, Gladstone, with his belief in original sin, saw free trade as 'static (or cyclical), nationalist, retributive, and purgative, employing competition as a means to education rather than to growth'.[97] Moreover, Bright and other Radicals were undoubtedly misled in many ways by Gladstone's apparent identification with the big cities (as Shannon and others have observed); for, in fact, the Chancellor never really subscribed to entrepreneurial Radical ideals. Nevertheless, for the time being, these profound ideological differences were largely concealed by a general agreement on many day-to-day political issues.

When Gladstone came back into Government in 1859, he actually persuaded Palmerston to offer Cobden the Board of Trade, and was disappointed when the offer was turned down. (Instead, the post went to Milner Gibson.) He 'was exceedingly sorry', he told his brother, 'to find that Cobden [did] not take office. It was in his person that there seemed to be the best chance of a favourable trial of the experiment of connecting his friends with the practical administration of the government of this country.'[98] Austerely independent to the end, Cobden also declined Gladstone's offer of the chairmanship of the Board of Audit, where he could have indulged his passion for 'economy' in an official capacity. As he later explained to Gladstone, 'To lose my individuality would to me be a moral death.' Seeing what Cabinets sometimes did, he was 'almost induced to add a word to our litany and, in addition to "plague, pestilence and famine", to pray for deliverance from a seat in the Cabinet'.[99]

Instead, of course, Gladstone employed Cobden in the negotiation of the French Commercial Treaty. Both men later saw this as a joint triumph, though Gladstone was generous in his praise of Cobden's 'great and signal service' to 'the great commercial classes of this country' and to the nation.[100] Thus a convergence in policy between Cobden and Gladstone seemed to be taking place in these years, and the later tendency to conflate the two men was encouraged by Gladstone himself when he agreed to appear as the main speaker at the inaugural dinner of the Cobden Club on 21 July 1866. Indeed, it is interesting to note that when, in 1866, Liberal activists set out to create a new Liberal club, they advertised the venture as one that was aimed at 'that

[96] Cobden to Bright, 10 Jan. 1861, Cobden Papers, Add. MS 43,651, fo. 212.
[97] Boyd Hilton, *The Age of Atonement: The Influence of Evangelicalism on Social and Economic Thought, 1795–1865* (Oxford, 1988), 69–70.
[98] John Morley, *Life of William Ewart Gladstone* (1903), i. 626.
[99] Cobden to Gladstone, 15 Jan. 1862, Gladstone Papers, Add. MS 44,136, fo. 160.
[100] Letter of 4 Dec. 1860, Shannon, *Gladstone*, 429.

influential and rapidly increasing section of our countrymen who revere the memory of Richard Cobden, and support the enlightened views of William Ewart Gladstone'.[101]

The French Treaty not only marked the apogee of the Cobden–Gladstone relationship: it also helped to restore Cobden's one-time reputation as the great spokesman for the values and interests of the industrial and commercial classes. True, there are some historians who believe that Cobden received very little support from the increasingly important Chambers of Commerce; Manchester, says Vincent, refused to assist Cobden with experts to negotiate the details of the cotton duties.[102] But that hardly gives a fair impression of the overall position. After all, the brains behind the Association of Chambers of Commerce, Jacob Behrens of Bradford, was in constant attendance on Cobden in Paris, and other Chambers freely co-operated with him in the arduous work of negotiating the complicated tariff schedule.[103]

Moreover, when Cobden returned to England in triumph after the conclusion of his labours, the great manufacturing centres vied with one another to do public honour to their great hero. As John Morley puts it, 'The commercial class were compelled to forgive him what they called his crotchets, to one who had opened for them new channels of wealth.'[104] The exhausted Cobden, who disliked ceremonial and feastings, fled to Algiers in search of peace and quiet.

Indeed, for a time the Government's ratification of the 1860 Treaty persuaded some members of the Manchester School that *they* now controlled the destinies of Palmerston's administration. The *Saturday Review* observed this manifestation of 'bourgeois triumphalism' with a mixture of amusement and exasperation. George Wilson, the former chairman of the Anti-Corn Law League, it noted, had recently made a speech good-humouredly comparing Lord Palmerston's Administration to 'a prosperous mercantile house largely engaged in the Manchester trade':

Mr. Gladstone and Mr. Milner Gibson, if we remember rightly, were the active managing partners, whose ability and enterprise commanded public confidence, though the more quiet senior members of the establishment were spoken of with conventional civility. The firm was doing a 'roaring business', especially in com-

---

[101] George Wilson Papers. A year later, the National Reform Union produced a pamphlet, *The Radical Party: Its Principles, Objects and Leaders—Cobden, Bright, and Mill*, in which Gladstone was presented as the statesman who 'more or less combined' the qualities of its three Radical heroes (cited in *Financial Reformer*, 1 May 1867, p. 96).

[102] Vincent, *British Liberal Party*, 207.

[103] *Sir Jacob Behrens, 1806–1889* (privately printed, n.d.), 58–9. On Bradford's contribution to the French Treaty, see Firth, 'Bradford Trade', 18.

[104] Morley, *Cobden*, ii. 371. The Bradford Chamber of Commerce had hoped to give a dinner to Cobden, as well as to Gladstone and Milner Gibson, with the Leeds, Huddersfield, and Batley Chambers asking to be associated with the occasion (Bradford Chamber of Commerce 10th Annual Report, 1861, 26; Bradford Chamber of Commerce 11th Annual Report, 1862, 6).

modities suited to the French market. Mr. Cobden had fortunately been engaged as a 'commercial traveller', and was cultivating the foreign connexion with extraordinary success. We forget the precise terms in which the orator indicated the gratifying fact that Mr. Bright's services had been secured in the capacity of touter for home consumers. It was sufficiently explained, however, that the member for Birmingham, though not ostensibly a partner, was the life and soul of the whole concern, and drew a large share of the profits; and that all was sure to go well so long as it had the benefit of his co-operation, and the support of his extensive and influential circle of friends.

Wilson, in short, apparently believed that 'the Manchester School was in safe possession of the government of the Country'.[105]

Cobden himself never took so sanguine a view of the matter. His pleasure in the French Treaty soon gave way to alarm as the Palmerston Government embarked upon a naval arms race with the Second Empire. The whole purpose of the Treaty, Cobden complained, had been to reduce tension between the British and French peoples in the interests of commercial stability, and his suspicious mind suggested to him that the various 'scares' about a French invasion emanating from the Prime Minister could only be a deliberate bid to undermine the Treaty and recreate the sort of international tension upon which the aristocracy throve.

To counter this threat, Cobden tried hard to mobilize businessmen behind a new economy campaign. Realizing the wisdom of taking a back seat on the issue, he entrusted the organization of the protest manifesto to Samuel Morley, who was invited to get up a memorial among leading bankers and City merchants in favour of arms talks with the French.[106] This Morley declined to do, but back-bench Radical MPs were persuaded to sign an 'economy manifesto', which duly reached the Government in January 1861.[107] Fifty-one 'rebels' signed this 'round-robin'—a mixed bunch which included Quaker pacifists and men with a grudge against the Ministry. But, significantly, something like 60 per cent of the signatories were Radical businessmen who represented the great urban constituencies. As we have seen, Cobden and Bright did not sign this letter themselves, but the list of those who did includes the names of such well-known entrepreneurial Radicals as Baines, Bazley, Crossley, Lindsay, Moffatt, Peto, J. B. Smith, and Titus Salt.[108]

[105] *Saturday Review*, 12 (10 Aug. 1861), 131–2.

[106] Edsall, *Cobden*, 368–9.

[107] Printed letter to Palmerston from Liberal MPs, in Brand Papers. For further information on this episode, see Brand to Palmerston, 7 Jan. 1861, Broadland Papers, GC/BR/7; Palmerston to Brand, 18 Jan. 1861, Brand Papers; Brand to Palmerston, 20 Jan. 1861, Broadland Papers, GC/BR/8 (with enclosure of private letter to Palmerston from Liberal MPs and list of signatures, dated 15 Jan. 1861, with Brand's annotations); Cobden to Morley, 29 Jan. 1861, with enclosed address, Cobden Papers, Add. MS 43,670, fos. 89–96; Morley to Cobden, 25 Mar. 1861, ibid., fos. 118–20.

[108] Enclosure of 15 Jan. 1861, Brand Papers. But in the Commons the 'economists', especially Bright, chose to emphasize *parliamentary* reform, not armaments cuts, when they moved their amendment to the address (Parl. Deb., 3rd ser., vol. 161, 105: 5 Feb. 1861).

The more doctrinaires members of the LFRA would have liked to go farther. They regretted the supplicatory tone which the petitioning MPs had used, and demanded the setting up of a Commons Finance Committee, to which the following year's estimates could be sent, a proposal which was said to enjoy the Chancellor's support.[109]

But where did Gladstone really stand on the question of 'economy'? It is of interest that Bright had been in touch with him from the very start, explaining the origins of the round robin and suggesting that he might like to use the document in negotiations with other members of the Cabinet! 'The Towns and our great populations', Bright concluded, would 'regard the government with increased favour if they see them having some regard to the pressure of taxes upon them.'[110] In his reply two days later, Gladstone said that Bright's letter and its enclosure had afforded him 'the highest pleasure. It is the very thing I could have longed for, and it is admirably timed.' He hoped that 'all the men of weight and likelihood at least will have the opportunity of signing it', and asked Bright's permission to make use of the paper with his colleagues.[111] Bright wrote back on 9 January saying that he saw no harm in that idea and that he was encouraging his friends to sign the address, which he thought likely to attract some fifty to sixty names. Meanwhile Gladstone and Milner Gibson, he suggested, should be working for an arrangement with France on the question of naval armaments.[112]

A similar sort of collusive relationship existed between Gladstone and Cobden. In fact, during the early 1860s Cobden persisted in treating Gladstone as if they were both fellow conspirators in league against Palmerston's policies of aristocratic reaction. Gladstone did not exactly encourage this notion, but neither did he show much loyalty to the head of the Ministry of which he formed a part. Conversely, when Gladstone became locked in conflict with Palmerston over the proper level of defence spending, Cobden felt that he and his friends had a duty to support the Chancellor. Gladstone 'has thrown out repeated signals of distress on this subject', Cobden told Ashworth, 'and if he had been supported as he ought to have been by the manufacturing and commercial classes, he would have been able to have fought a more successful battle in the Cabinet against the "services" which there rule supreme'.[113] The closeness of the Chancellor's views on retrenchment and high armaments to Cobden's much publicized views produced an embarrassing moment in the spring of 1862 when an irritated Palmerston accused Gladstone of making remarks in a recent speech which seemed to be an endorsement of Cobden's recently published *Three Panics*.

[109] *Financial Reformer*, Feb. 1861, p. 472.

[110] W. E. Williams, *The Rise of Gladstone to the Leadership of the Liberal Party, 1859 to 1868* (Cambridge, 1934), 46–8.

[111] Ibid. 49.

[112] Ibid. 51–3.

[113] Cobden to Ashworth, 16 Apr. 1862, Cobden Papers, Add. MS 43,654, fo. 193.

Gladstone produced a rather evasive reply, which Palmerston graciously accepted, but this did not stop mischievous MPs from raising the issue in the House of Commons.[114]

Indeed, it seemed as if retrenchment might actually break up the Government after Forster held a breakfast party at which many leading entrepreneurial Radicals drafted an economy resolution.[115] On 3 June 1862 this resolution, moved by James Stansfeld of Halifax, came before an excited House of Commons. With Disraeli on record deploring the excessive expenditure on armaments,[116] a defeat for the Government was a real possibility. Gladstone was in a particularly difficult situation. In the end, he turned down an appeal for support from the 'economico-radical party';[117] but he also declined Palmerston's suggestion that the Government support a more friendly resolution to be moved by Horsman. When Walpole, for the Conservatives, put down an economy resolution of his own, it seemed as though a juncture was about to be effected between the Opposition and the Radical economists.

Fortunately for the Government, Walpole, contrary to Disraeli's wishes, withdrew his resolution, after Palmerston had made it clear that he would treat all the critical resolutions as votes of confidence in his Ministry. Stansfeld's motion was then defeated by 367 to 65.[118] The Commons then went on to unanimously agree to a resolution concocted by Palmerston which congratulated the Government on its reduction of national expenditure and also spoke of 'the necessity of economy in every Department of the State'. Gladstone, of course, had no option but to vote with his Cabinet colleagues. Cobden, in despair, vented his feelings by threatening the Government with all-out opposition and making the implausible prediction that high expenditure was about to ruin the cotton industry and with it the whole British economy.[119]

But the demonstration, though Forster privately called it a 'fiasco', had not been entirely in vain.[120] Sixty-five back-benchers (not including Bright, who

---

[114] For more details, see Shannon, *Gladstone*, 457–9; Philip Guedalla (ed.), *The Palmerston Papers, Gladstone and Palmerston, 1851–1865* (1928), 205–14. But, for a different interpretation of the Gladstone–Palmerston relationship, see Steele, *Palmerston and Liberalism, passim*.

[115] Reid, *Life of Forster*, 350.

[116] Donald Southgate, *'The Most English Minister...': The Policies and Politics of Palmerston* (1966), 493.

[117] Shannon, *Gladstone*, 459. Gladstone had wanted to move resolutions of his own (Guedalla (ed.), *Palmerston Papers*, 221–9).

[118] Parl. Deb., 3rd ser., vol. 167, 306–94: 3 June 1862. For a vivid description of the debate, see Trelawny's diary, 3 June 1862, in T. A. Jenkins (ed.), *The Parliamentary Diaries of Sir John Trelawny, 1858–1865* (1990), 208–11. On how Palmerston won over prominent Conservatives, see Gurowich, 'Continuation of War', 626. Steele emphasizes Conservative disunity and Palmerston's rout of his critics (*Palmerston and Liberalism*, 161–3, 218).

[119] Parl. Deb., 3rd ser., vol. 167, 381: 3 June 1862. (But Cobden's speech actually came before the crucial vote.)

[120] Reid, *Life of Forster*, 350.

unaccountably absented himself when it came to the division) had made a public stand for retrenchment, and of these, twenty-five had signed the round robin of the previous year. Their defiance had extracted from Palmerston half a promise that reductions in expenditure might be effected during the following year.[121] ('That is the first time I ever heard he was' concerned with economy, Disraeli commented.[122]) And when a few days later a similar agitation arose on the subject of the Fortifications Bill, Brand, the Chief Whip, urged the Prime Minister to meet his critics half-way: 'Although you gained, & deservedly, a signal victory on Tuesday last, we must not shut our eyes to the fact that the cry for retrenchment is strong & growing, & that the H. of C. requires humouring just now upon this point.'[123] Palmerston fell in with this advice. Indeed, Cobden, seeing that Palmerston had been forced on to the defensive, soon recovered his optimism. As his biographer puts it, in 1862, as in the 1840s, 'Cobden was foretelling the imminent demise of a system that he abhorred.'[124]

What is more, Cobden then joined his ship-owning friend William Schaw Lindsay in an intensified campaign for changes to be made in international maritime law, which he believed formed the next stage in the emancipation of commerce. As Cobden put it in his *Letter to Henry Ashworth Esq.* of 1862:

Free trade, in the widest definition of the term, means only the division of labour, by which the productive powers of the whole earth are brought into mutual co-operation. If this scheme of universal dependence is to be liable to sudden dislocation whenever two governments choose to go to war, it converts a manufacturing industry, such as ours, into a lottery, in which the lives and fortunes of multitudes of men are at stake.[125]

Cobden therefore called for the exemption of *all* merchant ships from capture at sea in the event of war and for the abolition of the right of blockade (thus exempting neutral ships from search).[126] Fellow manufacturers were urged to take the lead in this new crusade: 'As the greatest merchants and carriers in the world *we* are more interested than any other in putting an end to this system of feudal spoliation. If the political parties in the trading community would unite they might (but not otherwise) put an end to this practice, and make the ocean free.'[127]

This was indeed a matter about which certain sections of the business community felt strongly. For example, in February 1860 the Liverpool Shipowners

[121] Parl. Deb., 3rd ser., vol. 167, 322–33: 3 June 1862.
[122] Southgate, 'Most English Minister', 494.
[123] Brand to Palmerston, 7 June 1862, Broadlands Papers, GC/BR/13. Palmerston agreed (Palmerston to Brand, 10 June 1862, Brand Papers).
[124] Edsall, *Cobden*, 375.
[125] Cobden, *Political Writings*, 389.
[126] A good account of the exact legal position is found in *Morning Star*, 25 Oct. 1862. On the problems caused by Palmerston signing the Declaration of Paris in 1856, see Ridley, *Lord Palmerston*, 609–10.
[127] Cobden to Ashworth, 17 Oct. 1861, Cobden Papers, Add. MS 43,654, fos. 117–18.

had sent a solemn memorial to Lord John Russell on the question of maritime international law;[128] and both the Liverpool and the Manchester Chambers of Commerce had passed resolutions on the subject. This was *before* the outbreak of the American Civil War. The resultant Federal blockade of the South, cutting off the cotton-producing areas from their main suppliers, then made this a highly practical issue as far as the Lancashire business community was concerned. Among other consequences, it furnished Cobden with the argument that before Britain could protest at the American blockade of Southern ports, she would herself have to renounce the right of blockade.[129]

Cobden's hope was that he might be able to use his new prestige in the eyes of the Chambers of Commerce to enlist these bodies in his support. As early as 1856 he had sent the Manchester Chamber a letter on international maritime law, pleading with it to 'throw the weight of its great influence into the scale of humanity and progressive civilisation'.[130] Later, in October 1862, he personally addressed a special meeting of the Chamber, to which Liverpool shipowners had also been invited. The reform of maritime law should be discussed, Cobden urged, 'from a modern point of view'; that is to say, not as a discussion about 'Grotius, who lived in the time of Queen Elizabeth (laughter)'.[131] He also took the occasion to remind his audience of the historic part which the Manchester Chamber had played in the repeal of the Corn Laws and urged them to rise once more to a historic opportunity, remembering that the whole question of maritime law and commercial blockades particularly affected their district:

Where are the young men who have come into active life since the time when their fathers entered upon the great struggle for Free Trade? . . . They have inherited an enviable state of prosperity from their fathers. For fifteen years there has hardly been a serious check to business—scarcely a necessity for an anxious day or night on the part of the great body of our manufacturing and trading population. But let not the young men of this district think that the possession of such advantages can be enjoyed without exertion, watchfulness, and a due sense of patriotic duty. We must not stand still, or imagine that we can remain stereotyped, like the Chinese.[132]

The Manchester Chamber, he urged, should take the *lead* in this campaign.[133]

That the Manchester Chamber proved so receptive to Cobden's message owed much to the fact that he had earlier persuaded his friend Henry

---

[128] *Economist*, 11 Feb. 1860, p. 143.

[129] Cobden to Chevalier, 25 Oct. 1862, Morley, *Cobden*, ii. 401. Cobden to Ashworth, 9 Sept. 1864, ibid. 452–3.

[130] Manchester Chamber of Commerce Papers, 20 Nov. 1856, fo. 552.

[131] Oct. 1862, ibid. 416–18.

[132] 25 Oct. 1862, *Cobden's Speeches*, 461. Henry Ashworth later wrote a book on the subject: *International Maritime Law, and its Effect upon Trade* (Manchester, 1864).

[133] Manchester Chamber of Commerce Papers, Oct. 1862, fos. 418–19.

Ashworth to take on its presidency with a view to 'politicizing' its deliberations: a strategy which he tried in vain to 'sell' to a sceptical Bright.

But the Association of Chambers of Commerce (to which neither Liverpool
nor Manchester were formally affiliated) proved a tougher nut to crack,
because its constitution enjoined upon it a strict neutrality in all 'political'
issues. Even so, some delegates tried year after year to commit the Association
to a Cobdenite resolution on international maritime law affecting private
property at sea. However, these attempts were usually beaten down at the
instigation of the Hull Chamber, on the ground that the issue was 'not suited
to the discussions of the Chambers'.[134]

Nevertheless, in 1862 the Liverpudlian merchant Horsfall initiated a
Commons debate on the subject (Cobden tactfully withdrew his own rather
similar motion), which showed that the movement was beginning to make
significant progress. For two days MPs seriously discussed the whole question
of international maritime law. Unfortunately, Cobden, who had intended to
open the second day's debate, contracted a serious cold, and Lindsay, who
took his place, was a poor substitute. The *Illustrated London News* commented
sarcastically on 'the asservations in a rough Ayrshire dialect of a shipowner
who very naturally professed a dislike to the capture of merchandise at sea'.[135]

What the debate on international maritime law showed was that, on matters
of this kind, party allegiance was less important than 'class background'. Most
of the commercial Members, Conservatives as well as Liberals, supported
Horsfall's motion. By contrast, the lawyers who spoke (the Attorney-General
and the Solicitor-General included) came out in opposition—a symptom of
the tension between the business community and the legal profession which
took many forms during this period.[136] Predictably, there was also opposition
from MPs enjoying close links, personal or sentimental, with the armed
services. Baillie-Cochrane, for example, complained that Horsfall had concentrated too much on the commercial aspect of the question and had ignored
the fact that the development of the country's commerce had only been made
possible in the first place by British naval supremacy.[137]

Palmerston went further, saying that Horsfall's motion, if adopted, would
'level a fatal blow at the naval power of this country, and would be an act of
political suicide'.[138] In this he was doing only what other commentators had
done: effectively accusing the commercial Members of a want of patriotism. In
fact, though, the Prime Minister was in a somewhat difficult position, since, as

---

[134] Papers of the Association of British Chambers of Commerce, 24 Feb. 1864. This was one
of several attempts to get the Association to commit itself on the issue. On the apparently
unsuccessful attempt to involve the Bradford Chamber, see Bradford Chamber of Commerce
Minutes, 25 Nov. 1861, fo. 548.

[135] *Illustrated London News*, 22 Mar. 1862.

[136] See Ch. 5.

[137] Parl. Deb., 3rd ser., vol. 165, 1379: 11 Mar. 1862.

[138] Ibid. 1392.

several MPs reminded him, he had entirely agreed with the views of the Liverpudlian merchants and shipowners when visiting their city in late 1856.[139] With his customary insouciance, Palmerston simply announced that he had changed his mind! But, very cleverly, he also turned the arguments of the Cobdenites back upon his assailants. Horsfall's motion, he said, was 'an attempt to set up the assumed interest of one class of persons against the general interests of the country'. War, for example, might indeed hamper British *shipping*, as Horsfall claimed, but it would not damage British *commerce*. 'The shipping interests', he jeered, now wanted to be relieved from the pressure of war, just as they had earlier wanted to preserve the special position given them by the Navigation Acts. Such special pleading even reminded Palmerston of the arguments employed before 1846 by the advocates of the Corn Laws! To this accusation no cogent reply was forthcoming, and Horsfall's motion was not put to the vote.[140]

Thus Lindsay's private prediction that there was a majority in the House in favour of exempting private property from capture at sea seems to have been over-optimistic, and Cobden, though confident that the cause would triumph sooner or later, was left to rue that the country was still being 'governed by men whose ideas have made no progress since 1808—nay, they cling to the ideas of the middle ages!'[141]

THE AMERICAN CIVIL WAR

Meanwhile, the American Civil War, though it furnished additional reasons for the reconstruction of the international maritime code, also presented the entrepreneurial Radicals with a very complex dilemma. Along with many others of all classes, members of the Manchester School felt the tug of conflicting loyalties and sympathies. On the one hand, Cobden, who had visited the United States when a young man, was a lifelong admirer of the American system of government and even more of America itself, which he always presented as a model of a progressive, dynamic modern society. 'Our only chance as a nation is in knowing in time what is sure to come from the United States,' he characteristically observed to Bright.[142] 'I have never missed an opportunity', he wrote on another occasion, 'of trying to awaken the emulation and even the fears of my countrymen, by quoting the example of the United States.'[143]

Obviously it was the northern industrial states which Cobden so greatly admired—just as it was in the north (more specifically the Midwest) that he

---

[139] *The Times*, 8 Nov. 1856.

[140] Parl. Deb., 3rd ser., vol. 165, 1696–7: 17 Mar. 1862.

[141] Cobden to Chevalier, 4 Mar., 7 Aug. 1862, Morley, *Cobden*, ii. 398, 401.

[142] Cobden to Bright, 1 Nov. 1853, cited in Vincent, *British Liberal Party*, 70.

[143] Cobden to Watkin, 14 Jan. 1852, in Watkin, *Alderman Cobden*, 167.

had made his fateful Illinois Railways investment. Yet, in the eyes of many 'radical' British businessmen, admiration for the North was tempered by disapproval of its high tariff system—which, as even Bright admitted, had alienated 'men who care more for trade than for any broad question of liberty affecting mankind at large'.[144] 'The old protectionist fallacies seem to be rife there,' Cobden reflected sadly in January 1865, 'and it is impossible to make the Americans believe that a session of prostration must follow their present saturnalia of greenbacks and government expenditure. However, I have great hopes that the intelligence of the country will prove equal to all trials.'[145] Paradoxically, it was the 'backward' South which, through its free trade practices, was the better integrated into the world economic system.[146]

In addition, by blockading the southern ports, the Federal Government found itself blamed for the 'Lancashire cotton famine', which hit many, though not all, the big cotton manufacturers, as well as the luckless operatives. Were the British Government to have attempted a breach of the blockade (as some cotton brokers and merchants in Liverpool were demanding in 1861),[147] the problems of Lancashire might have been resolved. But, of course, such a course of action would have carried a real risk of war with the Federal Government, which in turn threatened the mercantile and manufacturing community with disaster. No wonder that the cotton lords were divided in their response to the American crisis.

For Bright the choice was relatively simple. Long before Lincoln's Emancipation Proclamation, which first made the institution of slavery the central issue, Bright had come out as a partisan supporter of the North, which he believed to be involved in a clear-cut crusade against evil. As his letters to his friend William Hargreaves reveal, Bright saw his own firm's commercial prospects severely smitten,[148] but, as the Federal armies advanced to victory, he praised the Lord. Others of the Manchester School reacted similarly, among them the businessmen grouped in the Manchester Union and Emancipation Society, co-founded by the Cobdenite Thomas Bayley Potter (later to serve as the first secretary of the Cobden Club), whose vice-president was that mainstay of northern entrepreneurial politics, George Wilson.[149]

But to Cobden the matter was not clear-cut at all, and it took Bright some time to win him round to his own point of view, if, indeed, he ever really did so. Initially Cobden doubted the North's ability to prevent the secession of the

---

[144] Bright to Hargreaves, 30 Sept. 1861, Bright–Hargreaves Papers, Add. MS 62,079, fo. 46.
[145] Cobden to J. B. Smith, 6 Jan. 1865, John Benjamin Smith Papers, MS 923.2, S345, fo. 96.
[146] Morley, *Cobden*, ii. 372–3.
[147] Mary Ellison, *Support for Secession: Lancashire and the American Civil War* (Chicago, 1972), 150–1.
[148] e.g. Bright to Hargreaves, 14 Nov. 1861, Bright–Hargreaves Papers, Add. MS 62,079, fo. 50.
[149] Ellison, *Support for Secession*, 46, 79.

South—an expression, no doubt, of his assumption that, in the modern world, nothing could be achieved by fighting, a view also held by his collaborator in the campaign to reform the maritime code, W. S. Lindsay.[150] As the war escalated, Cobden's gloom deepened. What probably tipped his sympathies in favour of the northern cause was less his moral concern about the slavery issue than the suspicion, which he shared with Bright, that a Southern victory would be welcome to the reactionary aristocratic clique within the British Government. Cobden was also horrified at the prospect of Britain becoming involved in a war with the United States, something he had long felt would be the supreme catastrophe.

In the event both Bright and Cobden were to play a useful role in persuading the American Secretary of State that the British people meant well by the Federal cause, thereby reducing the risk of an Anglo-American conflict. But the entire episode shows that, so far as Cobden (and Henry Ashworth and Lindsay) were concerned, commercial considerations tended to bulk larger than 'moral principle' when the two came into conflict with one another—though they themselves would not have seen it in this light. Significantly, both Bright and Benjamin Smith privately expressed anxiety lest some of Cobden's pronouncements (for example, his insistence on the North's duty to raise the blockade) be misconstrued as sympathy with the South.[151]

The American Civil War also split the business community by region and sector. In the West Riding, opinion was more unequivocally on the side of the North than was the case in Lancashire.[152] But it may be significant that Bradford, fervent for the Federal cause, was gaining economically from Lancashire's difficulties—so much so that at one point rumours of peace caused a crisis of confidence on the Bradford Exchange![153] Thus, when Forster spoke out strongly in favour of the North, he did not have to face the difficulties encountered by his counterparts on the other side of the Pennines.

The main impact of the American Civil War, at least in its early stages, was to damage Cobden and his friends. 'We were told that Manchester and the Cotton towns ought to govern England and that principles of government ought to be learnt in America,' jeered *The Times* in August 1862; 'but America

---

[150] Lindsay to Cobden, 21 Oct. 1861, Cobden Papers, Add. MS 43,670, fos. 170–1. The *Morning Star* (8 Jan. 1861) also began by accepting that the Southern States had a perfect right to secede from the Union if they wanted to do so.

[151] Bright to J. B. Smith, 13 Jan. 1862; J. B. Smith to Cobden, 22 Jan. 1862, John Benjamin Smith Papers, MS 923.2, S344, fo. 43; MS 923.2, S345, fo. 91, respectively. On Cobden's despairing, detached view of what was happening in America, see Cobden to Paulton, 18 Jan. 1863, in Morley, *Cobden*, ii. 410–11.

[152] Though here, too, the *Leeds Mercury* was initially inhibited in its expression of support for the North by dislike of the tariff (D. G. Wright, 'Leeds Politics and the American Civil War', *Northern History*, 9 (1974), 118). A critical view of the North was also taken by the *Bradford Observer* under the editorship of William Byles (D. G. Wright, 'Bradford and the American Civil War', *Journal of British Studies*, 8 (1969), 74–6).

[153] Wright, 'Bradford', 80–1.

is now in the agony of dissolution, and has involved Manchester in its ruin.'[154] Yet in the long run entrepreneurial Radicalism may perhaps have been *helped* by events in the United States. For the pro-Northern cause drew together many employers and working-class politicians in a common enterprise which prefigured the movement for an extension of the franchise, a movement in which many northern Radical businessmen took leading roles, particularly in the West Riding.[155] But the impact of that development on the course of entrepreneurial politics must be left for consideration later.

COBDEN AND PALMERSTON

Shortly before the formal conclusion of the American Civil War, Cobden died unexpectedly (on 2 April 1865). Despite their recent disagreements over the war,[156] Gladstone and Cobden had struck up a kind of respectful friendship. Even before Cobden's death, Gladstone had paid tribute to Cobden as one of the 'teachers in the school of true economy' to whom he owed much (the others being Adam Smith and the younger Pitt). Certainly, Gladstone was quick to pay public tribute to the dead Radical leader.[157] Privately, to Robertson, he made his famous remark: 'What a sad, sad loss is this death of Cobden...ever since I really came to know him, I have held him in high esteem and regard as well as admiration; but till he died I did not know how high it was.'[158] These were diplomatic sentiments to express to his brother. But it is surely significant that Gladstone acted as one of the twelve pallbearers at Cobden's funeral, the only 'official' person to do so, all the rest being close personal friends of Cobden or colleagues from the Anti-Corn Law League days. Afterwards Gladstone sat down and wrote in his private journal: 'Cobden's name is great: & will be greater.'[159]

The significance of Cobden's career was well understood, not least by Disraeli, who, in a gracious tribute to the Radical, said of him that he was 'without doubt, the greatest political character the pure middle class of this country has yet produced'.[160] Others drew attention to his fierce spirit of independence and total unconcern with office: 'Richard Cobden refused to be muzzled,' wrote *Reynolds's Newspaper*; 'and, in this, he presents a most brilliant

---

[154] *The Times*, 11 Aug. 1862.

[155] See Ch. 6.

[156] This led to a break in the correspondence between the two men in 1862, lasting over a year (Edsall, *Cobden*, 388).

[157] *Financial Reformer*, Nov. 1864, 540. Parl. Deb., 3rd ser., vol. 178, 1102–3: 27 Apr. 1865.

[158] William Gladstone to Robertson Gladstone, 5 Apr. 1865, Morley, *Life of Gladstone*, ii. 143.

[159] A remark not quoted by his latest biographer. Gladstone's diary, 7 Apr. 1865, in H. C. G. Matthew (ed.), *The Gladstone Diaries*, Vol. 6: *1861–1868* (Oxford, 1978), 347. When George Wilson sent him a bust of Cobden later that year, Gladstone received it with warm thanks (George Wilson to Gladstone, 29 May 1865, George Wilson Papers).

[160] Parl. Deb., 3rd ser., vol. 178, 677: 3 Apr. 1865.

contrast to the Layards, the Gilpins, the Wilsons, the Villierses, the Gibsons, and the rest of the frail and fallen Radicals, whose apostasy has contributed to make the very name of Liberal a stench in the national nostril.'[161] Long after his death, Cobden served as a kind of 'role model' for a later generation of businessmen, who saw him as an inspiring example of what a 'mere' manufacturer could achieve. As late as 1890, Mundella was offering as a school prize copies of a hagiographical biography of Cobden entitled *Life of an English Hero*.[162] But it was Forster, at the ceremony to mark the unveiling of Cobden's statue in the Bradford Wool Exchange in 1877, who best expressed Cobden's importance: 'We are proud of him because he belonged to ourselves. We are manufacturers, and he has made the name of manufacturer famous in English statesmanship.'[163] With Cobden's death, entrepreneurial Radicalism had lost its great leader and spokesman; it would never find an adequate replacement.

Yet, although he was almost twenty years Cobden's senior, Palmerston survived him by more than six months. Some historians have seen a symbolic significance in that. Palmerston's ascendancy, it is often said, testifies not only to the continuing strength of the British aristocracy, but also to the hold that the Prime Minister had acquired over the affections of important sectors of the middle class. As we have seen, this case has been elaborated by Steele, who ascribes to Palmerston genuinely Liberal credentials, which made him a natural leader for his age.

However, one can exaggerate the extent of the class harmony that prevailed in these years. For a start, Palmerston was not particularly successful in 'incorporating' new middle-class men into his Administrations. In his first Government he did, it is true, promote Matthew Talbot Baines to Cabinet office; but this was not a particularly daring appointment, since Baines (the elder brother of Edward Baines, jun.) had already deserted his family's Congregationalism for the Church of England and was a 'gentrified' career lawyer.[164] Indeed, the narrowness of the social composition of this Government provoked a veiled protest from Liberals in the big cities once Palmerston had left office. When he returned to the premiership in 1859, Palmerston tried to propitiate his critics. In particular, he vainly attempted to put Cobden at the head of the Board of Trade, a post that in the event was filled by Milner Gibson, a fellow pupil of the Manchester School. But Gibson came from a landed family, as did Villiers, another old Leaguer, who also joined the Cabinet.

---

[161] *Reynolds's Newspaper*, 9 Apr. 1865.

[162] Armytage, *A. J. Mundella*, 327.

[163] *The Times*, 26 July 1877. Given the middle class's general concern to deny its own existence, Cobden is interesting, as one historian says, because of his willingness to 'own up' (Morris, *Class, Sect and Party*, 8).

[164] See Ch. 7.

True, as Steele points out, a number of business Liberals were muzzled by being brought into the Government; but, significantly, they were all fobbed off with minor offices: Charles Gilpin served as a junior Minister at the Poor Law Board under Villiers; Samuel Laing became Financial Secretary of the Treasury; and in April 1863 James Stansfeld was made Civil Lord of the Admiralty.[165] Robert Lowe and Layard, both from middle-class backgrounds, were also found junior postings. But, far from representing a significant new departure, this seems rather more like a continuation of the traditional Whig policy of 'co-opting' useful middle-class men to junior office. After all, Russell (who had made a half-hearted attempt to 'land' Cobden way back in 1846) had earlier found minor berths in his Administration for James Wilson and M. T. Baines. The commercial middle classes achieved a real political breakthrough only after Palmerston's death, during Russell's second Administration and under Gladstone.

Neither is Palmerston's domestic record particularly impressive. Steele rightly draws attention to the Prime Minister's achievements in the matter of divorce law reform and his far-sighted, though unavailing, attempt to institute a system of life peerages; he also believes that Palmerston might well have taken action to abolish church rates and extend the franchise but for the fact that public opinion was not yet 'ripe' for such initiatives. On the other hand, there is little doubt that Palmerston personally blocked reform of the Civil Service and the Army. Moreover, the policies which were particularly gratifying to the commercial middle classes mostly derived from Gladstone at the Treasury and from Robert Lowe, first at the Board of Trade (the establishment of limited liability) and later at the Council of Education (the Revised Code).[166] Again, what we seem to be confronting here is a continuation of the policy of pragmatic concessions to the industrial and commercial classes which had already occurred during the Administrations of Palmerston's predecessors, Aberdeen and Russell.

In any case, as the inauguration of the Bradford Wool Exchange in 1864 shows, towards the end of his premiership Palmerston's policy of encouraging class co-operation within the framework of an aristocratic state was clearly breaking down. But, then, his hold over the political life of the big cities had never been entirely secure. Indeed, the problem of trying to give an account of the relationship between Palmerston and the business community during the late 1850s and the early 1860s is rather similar to the problems confronting those who have written about industrial relations during this same period. In each case contradictory influences seem to be at work, making the story a complicated one, involving both conflict and reconciliation.[167] The

---

[165] Steele, *Palmerston and Liberalism*, 119, 126–7.
[166] On Lowe's activities in these fields, see Chs. 5 and 7.
[167] See Neville Kirk, *The Growth of Working Class Reformism in Mid-Victorian England* (1985), esp. Ch. 6; also the discussion below, Ch. 8.

general movement may have been towards greater class integration, as the commercial middle classes became more assimilated, socially and politically, into 'respectable' society; but this trend was frequently interrupted by a recrudescence of animosities. The resulting tension gave Bright and, still more, Cobden (the latter basking in the glory of his triumph in the matter of the Anglo-French Treaty), continuing opportunities for embarrassing the Palmerston Government. Entrepreneurial Radicalism had by no means died out by the 1860s. It was, however, in the throes of a process of transition.

ENTREPRENEURIAL POLITICS AT THE CROSSROADS

For, as Palmerston's life and career slowly drew to a close, entrepreneurial politics stood at the crossroads. Cobden himself, shrugging off his disappointments in what proved to be his valedictory address to his Rochdale constituents in November 1864, pointed the way to a new militant phase in Radical politics:

If I were five-and-twenty or thirty, instead of, unhappily, twice that number of years, I would take Adam Smith in hand . . . and I would have a League for free trade in Land, just as we had a League for free trade in Corn. You will find just the same authority in Adam Smith for the one as for the other; and if it were only taken up as it must be taken up to succeed, not as a political, revolutionary, Radical, Chartist notion, but taken up on politico-economic grounds, the agitation would be certain to succeed; and if you can apply free trade to land and to labour too—that is, by getting rid of those abominable restrictions in your parish settlements, and the like—then, I say, the men who do that will have done for England probably more than we have been able to do by making free trade in corn.[168]

Although they ignored Cobden's suggestion that a land campaign should 'have no politics in it', both Joseph Chamberlain (first elected to Parliament nearly a dozen years later) and Lloyd George were later to find this great speech an inspiration.

But quite how many Radicals would be prepared to follow Cobden? Already, it seemed, the younger businessmen Radicals who professed to revere Cobden's name were striking out along different paths, among them the worsted manufacturer W. E. Forster, returned as MP for Bradford at a by-election in 1861. By upbringing a Quaker (though he had taken leave of the Society of Friends in 1850 when he married the daughter of Dr Arnold of Rugby[169]), Forster was a complex figure. To the end of his days he revered Cobden as a role model; but in the late 1850s he came to admire Palmerston's foreign policy, dismissing the internationalism of the Manchester School as

---

[168] 23 Nov. 1864, *Cobden's Speeches*, 493.
[169] According to his biographer, Forster's marriage had the 'inevitable' outcome of 'widening his sympathies and modifying his judgments' (Reid, *Life of Forster*, i. 264).

'impracticable and un-English'.[170] Significantly, Forster had responded to the formation of the Volunteers by himself learning to handle arms and to drill, and he even formed a company composed of his own work-force, in the belief that the new movement 'would do great indirect good by bringing masters and men together, giving them good-fellowship and *esprit de corps*'.[171] 'Even our friend Forster, born in my sect,' grumbled Bright to Cobden, 'ran into the *Volunteer* trap like the rest—which does not say much for his penetration.' (Bright, in fact, had never trusted Forster, writing to Byles in April 1846, 'Mr Forster, whom I know very well, is totally unsound and inexperienced as a politician.'[172])

Forster also dissociated himself at an early stage from Disestablishment, so putting himself at loggerheads with the 'Illingworth set' in the town, before finally discrediting himself in the eyes of *most* Nonconformists by sponsoring the 1870 Education Act.[173] Moreover, influenced by the writings of Thomas Arnold (his father-in-law) and Carlyle (and later by the Christian Socialists), Forster soon developed heterodox views on trade unionism and factory legislation, in which he displayed what one historian has called his 'statist leanings'.[174]

But in other respects Forster was an ardent Radical. His strong feelings on the subject of slavery (appropriate in a relative of the Buxtons) had led him to play an important role in preserving good relations with the American Federal Government during the most difficult period of the Civil War. Moreover, so strong was his attachment to parliamentary reform that he made the Government's commitment to this objective a condition of his taking office in 1865. Like that other up-and-coming business Radical A. J. Mundella, he was also alive to the economic importance of education.[175]

But Forster's main involvement in entrepreneurial politics came through his participation in the Chamber of Commerce movement. Speaking to the Bradford Chamber of Commerce (of which he was a vice-president) in 1863, he declared that he was not simply answerable to his constituents, but also 'had a duty to perform to this large borough in promoting to the utmost the interests of those who were so largely engaged in commerce'.[176] Moreover, as one of the three regular delegates of the Bradford Chamber, Forster had played an important part in the creation of the Association of Chambers of Commerce. Indeed, on becoming an MP, he worked tirelessly as the

---

[170] Forster to wife, 1863?, ibid. i. 362.

[171] Ibid. i. 320–1. But for Alfred Illingworth's sharp attack on the Volunteer Movement in January 1864, see *Bradford Review*, 30 Jan. 1864.

[172] Bright to Cobden, 6 Sept. 1861, John Bright Papers, Add. MS 43,384, fo. 264. James, 'Byles and *Bradford Observer*', 126.

[173] Reynolds, *Great Paternalist*, 207, 329–32.

[174] Ibid. 38, 130. Koditschek, *Class Formation*, 519–20.

[175] See Ch. 7.

[176] Bradford Chamber of Commerce Minutes, 19 Jan. 1863, fo. 76.

Association's parliamentary spokesmen, urging reforms in the consular service, an extension of free trade, and heading deputations to Government Ministers—services for which the Association formally thanked him.[177] When he later entered the Government, he thus brought to it a perspective shaped by a successful business career. So Forster can certainly be categorized as a 'business Radical', even though he lacked the revolutionary fervour and conviction of a Cobden or a Bright.

But the abandonment of revolutionary politics by Radical businessmen can be traced even more clearly through the career of George Joachim Goschen, the son of a well-established City banker. Like many other bankers, Goschen had received an élite education, in his case at Rugby and Oxford University. Yet, when he entered Parliament for the City of London in June 1863, Goschen did so on a Radical platform, espousing parliamentary reform, the ballot, and the abolition of church rates.[178] His main interest at this time was in the ending of university tests.

But when, eight months later, he was selected to second the address, Goschen quickly made clear the moderation of his views by obliquely dissociating himself from the non-interventionist policies and the 'class attacks' of the Manchester School,[179] a stance which led him into a tetchy exchange of letters with an angry Cobden. Goschen stood his ground, reiterating his disagreement with Bright's 'dangerous' views concerning 'the motives and intentions of the governing class'. 'Mr. Bright believes...in a degree of selfishness on the part of the governing classes which in my humble opinion is a libel on them.'[180] Goschen's speech displeased Bright as well as Cobden: 'This Oxford "young man of great promise" has, I suppose, already found out the way to please the Aristocratic Order,' he wrote in his diary.[181] Bright was correct; a year later Goschen had become Vice-President of the Board of Trade, and a few months later, to everyone's surprise, entered the Cabinet as Chancellor of the Duchy of Lancaster after a mere two and a half years in the Commons.

Goschen's famous speech has another significance, in that it gives a foretaste of the kind of entrepreneurial politics that would develop over the next few decades, especially in the 'solution' it offered to 'the question of the condition of the working classes'.

---

[177] See Ch. 5. But Forster gave up his vice-presidency of the Bradford Chamber on becoming a Minister because of pressure of work (Bradford Chamber of Commerce Minutes, 29 Jan. 1866, fo. 402).

[178] Arthur D. Elliot, *Life of George Joachim Goschen, First Viscount Goschen* (1911), i. 51–2.

[179] Parl. Deb., 3rd ser., vol. 173, 80–6: 4 Feb. 1864.

[180] Elliot, *Goschen*, i, 66–76. For Cobden's anger towards Goschen, see Cobden to J. B. Smith, 6 Feb. 1864, John Benjamin Smith Papers, MS 923.2, S345, fo. 92.

[181] 4 Feb. 1864, in R. A. J. Walling (ed.), *The Diaries of John Bright* (New York, 1930), 267.

I hope the day will come when the doctrine of free trade, which has been applied with such signal success to capital and commerce, and from which such wonderful results have flowed, will be brought to bear upon other factors of our national prosperity—for instance, upon labour—when the restrictions which now impede the free circulation of labour as well as of land will be temperately reconsidered.[182]

This sounds superficially like Cobden's later oration at Rochdale. But, of course, the emphasis is different. Cobden was proposing a radical assault on the 'land monopoly'. Goschen's priority, as he had put it in an earlier speech, was the establishment of 'as full and perfect freedom of contract as was consistent with the interests of commerce and morality'.[183] Cobden's was the utterance of a man of the Left. Goschen was giving voice to the sort of 'economic liberalism' which soon afterwards found expression in his famous Poor Law Minute of 1869 (aimed at stopping poor relief in support of wages and at drawing a sharper line between private charity and the Poor Law). Such views were already beginning to make a distinct appeal to many members of the Conservative Party.

Indeed, even in the 1860s, one can detect the start of a drift of disaffected businessmen into the Conservative Party. Among them was a figure we have already encountered, Henry Ripley of Bradford, who had already abandoned Congregationalism for the Anglican creed and was now moving rapidly towards his eventual absorption into the Conservative Party—a path that was also being taken by prominent manufacturers in neighbouring towns, like Edward Akroyd of Halifax.[184] Yet this was a trend that was not to affect British life significantly until after the passing of the Second Reform Act. The temptation must be resisted of allowing the wisdom of hindsight to colour our perceptions of political life in the preceding decade.

[182] Parl. Deb., 3rd ser., vol. 173, 86: 4 Feb. 1864.
[183] Ibid., vol. 172, 835–6: 15 July 1863.
[184] On Akroyd, see Edward Akroyd, *The Present Attitude of Political Parties* (1874). J. A. Jowitt, 'Copley, Ackroydon and West Hill Park: Moral Reform and Social Improvement in Halifax', in J. A. Jowitt (ed.), *Model Industrial Communities in Mid-Nineteenth Century Yorkshire* (Bradford, 1986), 73–81.

5

The Development of Commercial Politics,
1850–1870

Look at the statute book for 1865 . . . You will find, not pieces of litera-
ture, not nice and subtle matters, but coarse matters, crude heaps of
heavy business. They deal with trade, with finance, with statute-law
reform, with common-law reform; they deal with various sorts of business, but with business always. And there is no educated human being
less likely to know business, worse placed for knowing business than a
young lord. . . . A young lord just come into £30,000 a year will not, as a
rule, care much for the law of patents, for the law of 'passing tolls', or the
law of prisons.

(Walter Bagehot, *English Constitution*)

What's everybody's business is nobody's. The manufacturers of this
country are very neglectful in these matters. There is not much combination among manufacturers.

(Robert Macfie, 21 May 1863).

THE CHAMBERS OF COMMERCE MOVEMENT

In 1860 many, though not all, of the provincial Chambers of Commerce, some
of which had a long history, decided to form a federation, in order to increase
the influence of businessmen on Parliament and the Government. With the
emergence of the Association of Chambers of Commerce (hereafter ACC), a
new era in entrepreneurial politics had begun.

The Association owed much to the Bradford Chamber of Commerce and
its vice-president Jacob Behrens, the textile merchant and German immigrant,
though the Hull and Birmingham Chambers also gave valuable support.[1]
From modest beginnings, the ACC quickly made its mark on political life,
since despite the patchiness of its geographical spread, it had affiliated to it

---

[1] *Jacob Behrens, 1806–1889* (based on a record begun by Behrens in 1873 and continued until
his death), 64. In 1859 the annual meeting of the National Association for the Promotion of
Social Science met at Bradford, where the local Chamber of Commerce met with representatives
from other Chambers. Together, they decided that the Chambers of Commerce needed a
national association of their own (Bradford Chamber of Commerce 9th Annual Report, 1860,
p. 23).

the Chambers of most of the important industrial and commercial areas, particularly in Yorkshire and the Midlands.

The Association saw its own role as being 'a most useful medium of communication between the commercial, manufacturing and trading classes and the Government of this country'. With increasing numbers (so run the minutes following the first annual meeting), 'the Association (as representing the collective influence, experience, and practical knowledge of the various great centres of commerce and manufactures) cannot fail to exercise a powerful and beneficial influence in the diffusion of sound principles on the various and most important commercial questions constantly occupying the attention of the Legislature'.[2]

As it developed, the Association tended to concentrate on topics many of which were technical, even dry. Bankruptcy and imprisonment for debt dominated the agenda for the first decade and a half of its existence. But the Association also spent much time on issues like patents and trade marks (this led to an early success, the Merchandise Marks Act of 1862); improving the postal facilities for merchants and traders;[3] attempting to reform the financial basis of the lighthouse service; and so on. The annual meeting did not disdain passing such resolutions as the one in favour of the use of adhesive stamps for inland bills of exchange.[4] Indeed, as its organization and procedures became formalized, the Association speedily acquired an expertise in handling such questions. More and more Chambers affiliated to it (the number was up to 50 by 1874), and affiliation fees were raised, enabling the Association to employ a London agent.[5]

The ACC was important in another respect, in that involvement in its affairs offered a way into national politics for the new, post-Cobden generation of businessmen. The most notable of these was Forster; but it is striking how many of the activists in the movement secured election as MPs over the next ten to fifteen years: Monk and Norwood in 1865, Whitwell and Ripley in 1868, Sampson Lloyd in 1874, and so on. In addition, by 1867, Mundella, who was elected for Sheffield a year later, had emerged as a leading figure in the Association, where he hammered away at his two specialized interests, industrial arbitration and technical education. It is difficult to say whether involvement in the Association sharpened the desire of these businessmen to launch out on a parliamentary career, or whether, as seems more likely,

---

[2] ACC Papers, 6 Feb. 1861. In practice, this meant 'making life a burden' for the Board of Trade!

[3] The Association welcomed the State's acquisition of the telegraph system in 1868, and worked closely with the civil servant chiefly responsible for its subsequent administration (A. R. Ilersic and P. F. B. Liddle, *Parliament of Commerce: The Story of the Association of British Chambers of Commerce, 1860–1960* (1960), 124).

[4] ACC Papers, 26 Nov. 1867.

[5] James Hole, a former Owenite (Briggs, *Victorian Cities*, 141–2).

ambitious, energetic, and public-spirited businessmen were naturally attracted both to the Association's work and to seeking a seat in the Commons. In any case, the two lines of activity soon began to converge. Significantly, Behrens rejected the offer of the presidency of the ACC in 1883, on the grounds that he was too old to think of becoming an MP.[6]

Most active members of the Association in the 1860s and 1870s were Liberals. Of those MPs who attended its meetings or became honorary members during the first decade, forty-four (75.5 per cent) sat on the Liberal side of the House, as compared with only fifteen (24.5 per cent) on the Conservative side. Even after the Conservatives had made their breakthrough in the 1874 general election, Liberal MPs still outnumbered Conservative MPs on the honorary members' list by forty-nine to twenty (68 per cent to 28 per cent), with three Irish Nationalists making up the total.[7]

Such a Liberal preponderance, however, simply reflected the fact that the Liberal Party continued to be the dominant force in those large commercial and industrial centres where the local Chambers of Commerce were located. There is no question of Conservative businessmen being in any way at a disadvantage within the organization. In fact, for most of this period (from 1862 to 1880, to be precise) the office of president was held by a Conservative, Sampson S. Lloyd, who became Conservative MP for Plymouth in 1874.

Outside the Association, these activists often played a prominent part in the affairs of their particular party. But within it, a strict political neutrality was enjoined. Members attending the annual dinner in 1869 cheered John Bright, the new president of the Board of Trade, when, addressing his audience about the social problems which necessitated a poor-rate, he appealed to them to take the lead in finding a solution.[8] But since the very survival of the organization depended on its steering clear of anything that savoured of party controversy, his words went largely unheeded.

Some *individual* Chambers were prepared to take greater risks. For example, the Leeds Chamber repeatedly called for legislation facilitating the transfer of land; it also responded sharply to a proposal from the Cheshire Chamber of Agriculture to compensate farmers who had been hit by the cattle plague.[9] Even in the 1860s the old industry–agriculture rivalry, it seems, had not entirely abated. And when a Bill to preserve salmon fisheries by preventing river pollution was before the House in 1861, a Leeds delegate pointed out, with some force, that 'manufacturing operations ha[d] contributed more to the wealth of this country than can ever be the case of trout and salmon'.[10] But

---

[6] Ilersic and Liddle, *Parliament of Commerce*, 140–1. Joseph Chamberlain was also active in his local Chamber of Commerce for a couple of years, before retiring. See Wright, *Birmingham Chamber of Commerce*, 178, 189–90.

[7] ACC Papers, loose paper dated 1874.

[8] *The Times*, 25 Feb. 1869.

[9] M. W. Beresford, *The Leeds Chamber of Commerce* (Leeds, 1951), 49, 62–3.

[10] Ibid. 62.

usually contentious issues were tactfully side-stepped. Indeed, the Constitution of the Bradford Chamber specifically declared that the organization had been 'instituted solely for Commercial purposes' and that 'questions of party politics [were] excluded'.[11]

The National Association took even greater care to ensure that the issues it dealt with, though sometimes controversial, had no party flavour about them. The non-party nature of the organization was scrupulously observed, and anything that smacked, however slightly, of party feeling was usually stamped on without ceremony. Leone Levi, an academic outsider who had helped to set up the Liverpool Chamber in 1849 and who continued to provide an intellectual rationale for the movement, had insisted from the very start that Chambers of Commerce must be 'uninfluenced by party feelings or conflicting notions of commercial policy'.[12]

Light on this situation is once again shed by the career of Samuel Morley. We have already seen him as a crusading entrepreneurial politician in the 1840s and early 1850s. By the end of the decade, however, much of his activity was centred on a metropolitan reform group called the Mercantile Law Amendment Society, which was supported by several banking houses and some of the leading firms in the wholesale trade. In his concern to change the current Bankruptcy Laws, Morley soon found himself co-operating closely with the Chambers of Commerce (London as yet having no Chamber of its own); and by the end of the decade he was a leading figure in the Association, acting, for example, as its main spokesman on the 1869 Bankruptcy Bill.

All this while, Morley was taking a leading part in the efforts to remove the grievances of the Dissenters, among whom he was one of the leading lay figures. But his sectarian crusades had obviously to be kept separate from his role as a proponent of commercial reform, and vice versa. No one could doubt the zeal with which he threw himself into these two separate campaigns, but, in contrast to his hero and role model Cobden, whose career had been all of a piece, Morley was obliged by the necessities of the day to compartmentalize his activities. Looked at from the practical point of view, this was an eminently sensible course to take. But it marked a retreat from the entrepreneurial politics practised by the Manchester School at the height of its influence.

ATTITUDES TOWARDS COBDENITE REFORMS

There were, it is true, occasions when the Association did show a modicum of courage. For example, it decided in 1865 to adopt a resolution on the need to

[11] Bradford Chamber of Commerce 8th Annual Report (1859), 19.

[12] Leone Levi, *Chambers and Tribunals of Commerce and Proposed General Chamber of Commerce in Liverpool* (Liverpool, 1849), esp. 5. Levi was also associated with the Bradford Chamber, serving for a time as its paid London agent (*Monthly Journal of the Bradford Chamber of Commerce*, Jan. 1924, p. 164). He also gave periodic addresses to the Bradford Chamber.

reorganize the administration of government manufactories. Cobden had made a big speech on the subject in the Commons the previous July in which he had urged the reduction, or even the abandonment, of the country's manufacturing establishments, his argument being that government 'should not be allowed to manufacture for itself any article which can be obtained from private producers in a competitive market'. MPs, Cobden had argued, should in future 'place [them]selves entirely in dependence upon the private manufacturing resources of the country', so that they could say to the British people, 'Our fortunes as a Government and nation are indissolubly united, and will rise or fall, flourish or fade together, according to the energy, enterprise, and ability of the great body of the manufacturing and industrious community.' The public interest, according to Cobden, could only be guaranteed by competition:

You can never make the conductors of these Government establishments understand that the capital they have to deal with is really money. How should it be real money to them? It costs them nothing, and, whether they make a profit or a loss, they never find their way into the *Gazette*. Therefore to them it is only a myth—it is a reality only to the taxpayers.[13]

Mischievous critics pointed out that the existence of government manufactories at least lessened the power of business interests which stood to gain from war![14] But this consideration apparently mattered little to Cobden, who continued to insist that 'privatization' (to use the modern term) would produce a kind of 'social contract' between Government and people, between the State and civil society.

Six months later, faced by a motion on the subject from the Birmingham Chamber, the president of the Association was in communication with Cobden over the line which the annual conference should take.[15] But the outcome was significant. The Association rejected Birmingham's own motion[16] in favour of a much more moderate one which merely advocated an annual audit of stock, on the basis of which prices would be determined, subject to the approval of the House of Commons.[17] The main reason for this display of caution was that many delegates were clearly unhappy with the prospect of being publicly associated with a man of Cobden's reputation. Thus, Colonel Akroyd (Cobden's conqueror at Huddersfield in 1857) warned that 'the resolution would be viewed with great jealousy as coming from such a source'. And another delegate said that the subject was one 'with which the meeting ought not to deal. It was more a political than a commercial question, and affected the people as taxpayers rather than as makers of goods.'[18]

---

[13] 22 July 1864, *Cobden's Speeches*, 294–309.
[14] *Bradford Observer*, 28 July 1864.
[15] *The Times*, 23 Feb. 1865.
[16] ACC Papers, 22 Feb. 1865.
[17] Ibid. But these were Cobden's own words.
[18] *The Times*, 23 Feb. 1865. Ripley of Bradford also opposed the proposal, saying that

It was precisely this concern to separate 'commercial' from 'political' issues which set severe limits on what the Association was usually prepared to attempt. For example, some delegates tried year after year to commit the Association to a Cobdenite resolution on international maritime law affecting private property at sea; but, usually at the instigation of the Hull Chamber, these attempts were beaten down, on the grounds that the issue was 'not suited to the discussions of the Chambers'.[19] Moreover, although Ashworth, the Manchester president, was the guest of the Association in 1864, the Manchester Chamber's minutes record with dismay that many of the national delegates at that meeting were 'absolutely prohibited from expressing an opinion' on the subject of international maritime law.[20]

The Association also moved cautiously on financial questions. All could agree in deploring the system of delegating the collection of the income tax to men who might be a businessman's trade competitor: 'This means of enabling one tradesman to acquaint himself with the affairs of another has been, in many cases, found to be most inquisitorial and unjust.'[21] But a resolution attacking the income tax in so far as it was imposed on trades and the professions and calling for its repeal was decisively rejected.[22] In 1870 many delegates once again took up the age-old grievance about the income tax falling on 'fluctuating and terminable Income', this time with success, except that the resolution failed to get enough of a majority for it to become official policy[23] (though later in the year a motion was carried calling for a Select Committee to examine the issue[24]). Not until 1871 was the Association able to carry a motion castigating the unfairness of the income tax on those employed in the trades and professions, as compared with its effect on realized property;[25] and only in 1873 did delegates finally screw up the courage to pass a motion condemning the income tax itself.[26]

THE GOVERNMENT AND FOREIGN TRADE

It helped the Association at this early stage of its existence that Free Trade enjoyed virtually unanimous support from the mercantile classes. All delegates, whatever their party affiliations, could unite in deploring the perverse

government manufactories acted as a check on the profit-making eagerness of private establishments. On John Holms's later attack on government arsenals and naval yard manufactories in 1873, see Malchow, *Gentlemen Capitalists*, 284–5.

[19] ACC Papers, 24 Feb. 1864.

[20] Manchester Chamber of Commerce Papers, 9 Mar. 1864, fos. 497–8. This should not have surprised Ashworth, however, considering the difficulty he had had in getting his *own* Chamber to move in colonial and defence matters (Boyson, *Ashworth Cotton Enterprise*, 232–5).

[21] ACC Papers, 28 Nov. 1867.

[22] Ibid., 24 Feb. 1869.

[23] Ibid., 23 Feb. 1870.

[24] Ibid., 24 Nov. 1870.

[25] Ibid., 26 Sept. 1871.

[26] Ibid., 18 Feb. 1873.

behaviour of foreign and—what annoyed them still more—colonial countries which persisted in accepting the Protectionist fallacy. By the same token, trouble was later to hit the organization when first the Fair Trade movement, then Tariff Reform undermined this consensus.[27]

Even so, the ACC was divided in the early 1860s over just what the British Government should do to bring about the world-wide adoption of Free Trade.[28] What the Chambers could largely agree upon was to deplore the amateurishness of the Foreign Office. Indeed, many businessmen had a very fundamental quarrel to pick with that department, since they shared Cobden's belief that diplomacy served little purpose in the modern world.[29] As Forster put it, trade matters were now far more important to the country than 'dynastic intermeddling'.[30]

Unsurprisingly, the Foreign Office was compared unfavourably with the Board of Trade, whose officials from the 1830s onwards had included several self-educated and self-made men, some of whom, like Bowring and G. R. Porter, had pursued mercantile careers (albeit unsuccessfully!) before becoming civil servants.[31] A few of the Ministers who served in that department—for example, Poulett Thomson and Henry Labouchère—could also boast some commercial experience.[32] Even Cobden was happy to pay tribute to the Board of Trade's work: 'During the last fifty years, [it] has taken the most enlightened views upon questions of commerce, and has always been in advance of the community in its appreciation of our true interests with regard to commercial policy.' Would that the Foreign Office, which also had responsibility for questions of trade with foreign countries, had been imbued with the same spirit, he said![33]

What especially angered the Chambers of Commerce in the early 1860s was, to use their own words, the Government's 'want of watchfulness over the changes which from time to time take place in the Tariffs of other nations'.[34] The Bradford Chamber, in particular, was incensed when the French began negotiating a series of trade agreements with other countries, including Belgium and the Zollverein, which put British exporters at a comparative disadvantage.

---

[27] On the changes within the initially pro-Free Trade Bradford Chamber, as foreign competition in the worsted trade intensified, see Eric M. Sigsworth, *Black Dyke Mills. A History* (Liverpool, 1958), 91–107.

[28] e.g. ACC Papers, 25 Feb. 1863, 22 Feb. 1865. Forster was again the key figure.

[29] Parl. Deb., 3rd ser., vol. 174, 1117–18: 15 Apr. 1864. The least the Foreign Office could do, he said, was to ensure that its clerks had studied Adam Smith and understood commercial policy!

[30] Ibid., vol. 177, 1858: 17 Mar. 1865.

[31] Lucy Brown, *The Board of Trade and the Free Trade Movement 1830–42* (Oxford, 1958), 26–8, 30–2.

[32] Roger Prouty, *The Transformation of the Board of Trade, 1830–1855* (1957), 104. Prouty says they tried to apply the canons of business to government itself (ibid. 106–7).

[33] Parl. Deb., 3rd ser., vol. 174, 1116–17: 15 Apr. 1864.

[34] ACC Papers, 25 Feb. 1863.

The commitment to Free Trade, the delegates grumbled, did not mean that the British Government should stand by and 'hold their hands'; it should, rather, 'make itself a propagandist of the principles of free trade'.[35] Unfortunately, Ministers seemed insufficiently concerned with Britain's trading interests, and were slow to respond to overtures from such bodies as the Chambers of Commerce.

But this failure, alleged the critics, was largely attributable to the fact that there was a division of labour in such matters between the Board of Trade, which had an intimate acquaintance with the requirement of the country's foreign commerce but little power, and the Foreign Office, which had the power but lacked the information (and perhaps even the will-power) necessary for the protection of Britain's overseas trading interests.[36] To put an end to this dual responsibility became one of the ACC's most pressing goals. In February 1864, goaded by the Bradfordians, the Association sent the Foreign Secretary a memorial outlining their discontents. Commercial men wanted to be 'put in immediate and direct communication with those who [were] responsible' for Government policy, said the Association; as for the 'double act' performed by the two Whitehall departments, this simply produced confusion and delay.[37] Naturally, the Foreign Office mandarins begged to differ. Palmerston, confronted by a delegation of Chamber of Commerce delegates, also 'poo-pooed the whole matter, and stated that the arrangements between the Foreign Office and the Board of Trade were perfect'![38] But in April, Forster, who had quickly established himself as the Association's main parliamentary spokesman, forced the Commons to set up a Select Committee to examine the whole matter. Surprisingly, perhaps, Forster himself was then elected committee chairman over the heads of much more senior backbenchers, Cobden and Bazley included.[39]

The 1864 Select Committee made a number of recommendations for improving the situation.[40] Russell responded by creating a new commercial department at the Foreign Office, and there is some evidence that this change had the effect of making the Foreign office much more receptive to future Chamber of Commerce pressure. However, the report itself was otherwise

[35] The words were Forster's (Bradford Chamber of Commerce Minutes, 19 Jan. 1863, fo. 75).

[36] Bradford Chamber of Commerce 11th Annual Report, 1862, p. 29. The Foreign Office had consulted the Board of Trade only at the last moment over the French Commercial Treaty (Ilersic and Liddle, *Parliament of Commerce*, 31).

[37] Correspondence with the Association of Chambers of Commerce, 1864, LVIII (1864).

[38] Bradford Chamber of Commerce Minutes, 23 Mar. 1864, fo. 172.

[39] Forster himself expressed surprise at being offered the chairmanship over the head of Cobden (Parl. Deb., 3rd ser., vol., 177, 1851: 17 Mar. 1865). He quickly began organizing his Bradford friends, who were summoned to give evidence to the Committee: e.g. Forster to Darlington (secretary of the Bradford Chamber), 20 Apr. 1864, West Yorkshire Archives, Bradford, DB 16/3/7. Report from Select Committee on Trade with Foreign Nations, VII (1864).

[40] Report from Select Committee on Trade with Foreign Nations, p. vi.

ignored. Forster, not a man to be fobbed off in this way, insisted on knowing what steps the Government had taken or proposed to take. But, as we shall see, the ensuing debate proved something of a disaster for the entrepreneurial Radicals.

The Association continued to press for other improvements in the way in which Governments handled issues of foreign trade. The adequacy of the consular service particularly engaged its attention. A delegate from Hull called for consuls to be drawn from 'mercantile men of high standing', not 'the hangers-on of aristocratic families and . . . novelists who had written themselves out'. The country, he said, was not getting its money's worth for the £140,000 it annually spent on the service: 'Let us have men who understand commercial matters as Consuls.'[41] Such sentiments were widely approved. Specifically, the Association urged that consuls be appointed by the Board of Trade. But not till 1880 did the Foreign Office create the office of commercial attaché, a development the Association generally welcomed.[42]

More fundamentally still, in 1869 the ACC began its long campaign (originally instigated by Akroyd of Halifax) to establish a real Ministry of Commerce.[43] The President of the Board of Trade, complained the Association, was sometimes a junior Minister outside the Cabinet; and in any case the holders of that office carried far too many responsibilities to deal adequately with the problems of commerce and industry. Conversely, many commercial matters were still being controlled by other departments, like the Treasury, the Colonial Office, and the India Office.[44] Although not all businessmen favoured the creation of a Ministry of Commerce, the campaign testifies to the widespread feeling among traders and manufacturers that the Whitehall 'system' was not dealing sympathetically with their concerns.

THE DECIMALIZATION ISSUE

In some respects decimalization posed a very similar sort of question: was an industrialized society like Britain prepared to throw aside tradition and espouse policies which seemed 'rational' to the commercial mind?

Decimalization had been on the political agenda since the 1820s, but it owed its revival to the activities of the Manchester Chamber of Commerce, which in 1852 produced a very long memorial on the subject.[45] The follow-

---

[41] Ilersic and Liddle, *Parliament of Commerce*, 25.

[42] Ibid. 25–6. In 1870 the Radical manufacturer John Holms was urging the transfer of the consular service from the Foreign Office to the Board of Trade and complaining that the existing system was geared more to prestige than to the promotion of the interests of British traders (Malchow, *Gentlemen Capitalists*, 283).

[43] ACC Papers, 17 Nov. 1869. The proposal was taken up by Behrens (Bradford Chamber of Commerce 19th Annual Report, 1870, p. iv).

[44] In 1871 Gladstone heard a deputation from the Association expound its views on this matter, but he evinced little sympathy with its complaints (ACC Papers, 27 Sept. 1871).

[45] Manchester Chamber of Commerce Papers, 25 Mar. 1852, fos. 255–6.

ing year the Commons established a Select Committee (chaired in its later stages by the great shipping magnate William Brown), which unanimously recommended the adoption of a pound divided into 1,000 mills or farthings.[46] A second commission looked into the possibility of a metric system of weights and measures.

In fact, it was increasingly the idea of a metric system of weights and measures which held the limelight. The very first annual meeting of the ACC passed a resolution urging Britain to fall into line with other European countries in this respect: the 'present complicated system', delegates agreed, was 'very inconvenient to us as a great commercial nation', and reform would lead to 'the saving of time in trading and other accounts'.[47] The result was the setting up of a Select Committee, including, among others, Cobden and Benjamin ('Corn Law') Smith, which produced a report that the reformers could claim as a victory.[48]

Smith, who became almost obsessed with its importance,[49] and another 'Liberal Commercial', William Ewart, MP for Dumfries, continued to hammer away at the subject. Thanks to their efforts, permissive Bills were enacted in 1864 and 1868. But a dissatisfied ACC continued, without success, to press for a compulsory measure, their complaints becoming louder as foreign competition intensified.[50]

Why did businessmen feel so strongly on the matter? Cobden, a staunch believer in decimalization, saw it as a way of promoting international harmony and averting the risk of war, as did Smith.[51] Another reason for supporting decimalization came out in Cobden's memorable speech to the Commons in 1864, when he talked of his experience as a negotiator during the French Commercial Treaty talks, when, he said, he had felt 'humiliated' by the contrast between Britain's confusing, complicated system and the clear, 'rational' system which had been adopted by the French. Cobden suggested that adoption of the metric system would make it much easier for school-children to cope with their sums, noted the approval of it registered by the Chambers of Commerce, and appealed to his old friend Milner Gibson, now President of the Board of Trade, to add still further lustre to his name by establishing 'free trade in arithmetic'.[52] Other businessmen rushed to Cobden's support, Bazley, for example, claiming that decimalization would 'materially economize time and promote the wealth of the country'.[53]

---

[46] Report of Select Committee on Decimal Coinage, 422 (1853), pp. iv–viii.
[47] ACC Papers, 6 Feb. 1861.
[48] Report of Select Committee on Weights and Measures, 1862 (251), p. x.
[49] See Bright to Cobden, 10 Feb. 1861, John Bright Papers, Add. MS 43,384, fos. 248–9.
[50] Ilersic and Liddle, *Parliament of Commerce*, 137. W. A. Munford, *William Ewart, M.P. 1798–1869: Portrait of a Radical* (1960), 148–50.
[51] See Cobden's letters to J. B. Smith of 5 and 23 Sept. 1853, John Benjamin Smith Papers, MS 923.2, S345, fos. 15, 18.
[52] Parl. Deb., 3rd ser., vol. 172, 28–34: 1 July 1863.
[53] Ibid. 38.

This was a line of argument very commonly heard in favour of the reform. Metrication, in the words of Baines, was 'one of the most striking and important of modern improvements'.[54] 'The fact is,' argued Ewart, 'the metric system is the complement and corollary of Free Trade. By adopting it, we shall extend the commerce of England and the commerce of the world.'[55] And Smith declared, 'We are the first commercial nation in the world, we must maintain our position—to stand still is to be left behind; let us press on then until an international language is established by the use of the same pound weight, the same yard measure, the same gallon, and the same money thoughout the world.'[56]

The importance of the decimalization debate lies in the fact that it provided the occasion for a straightforward clash between businessmen seeking to 'rationalize' the country's commercial procedures and those who clung to 'customary practice', invoking Magna Carta and the like. Typical of the latter group was Palmerston, an outspoken opponent of metrication, who observed in a private letter that 'nothing [was] so difficult to change as the traditional habits of a free people in regard to such Things' and who then went on to sneer at attempts 'to Frenchify the English Nation'.[57]

BUSINESSMEN AND THE LEGAL PROFESSION

But it was with the old-established legal profession that the businessmen in politics found themselves most often in dispute. And the state of the law of bankruptcy provided the arena for some of the fiercest battles between the two groups.

As commerce expanded in the 1850s, the inadequacy of the means of legal redress available to traders became increasingly apparent. To quote Ilersic and Liddle, 'A revision of the legal code applicable to commercial and industrial matters was as necessary to the expansion of industrial England as were Watt's steam engine and the Bessemer process.'[58] The specific grievance which stirred the commercial classes into action concerned the cost and complexity of the administration of bankruptcy. Sampson Lloyd spoke in 1863 of an earlier case in which an insolvent man had had assets of £956,114; but before his creditors could get their hands on this sum, £299,061 had been absorbed in administrative expenses, with £111,000 alone going in solicitors' fees.[59]

To end such abuses, the Chambers of Commerce backed a Bill which had

---

[54] Parl. Deb., 3rd ser., vol. 173, 1740: 9 Mar. 1864. See Cobden's letter to Chevalier, his co-worker during the negotiation of the French Treaty, 5 Nov. 1864, in Morley, *Cobden*, ii. 450.

[55] Parl. Deb., 3rd ser., vol. 192, 179: 13 May 1868.

[56] Ibid. 201.

[57] Ridley, *Lord Palmerston*, 681. But Gladstone also remained a sceptic on decimalization.

[58] Ilersic and Liddle, *Parliament of Commerce*, 67.

[59] i.e. before the 1861 Act (ibid. 68).

been introduced in 1859 by Headlam, MP for Newcastle, and by Lord John Russell, MP for the City of London, emanating from the National Association for the Promotion of Social Science.[60] The Bill ran into the sands. Palmerston then tried to squeeze time for another Bill in 1860, calling it 'a Measure of very great importance to all the trading and Commercial Interests'.[61] When this attempt failed, the Chambers of Commerce continued to keep up the pressure on the Prime Minister. And on his visit to Leeds in October 1860, delegates from the various Yorkshire Chambers extorted from Palmerston a promise that Headlam's Bill would be reintroduced in the following session.[62] In 1861, perhaps in fulfillment of this pledge, the Government duly passed its own Bankruptcy Act.

But this legislative measure left untouched the problem of excessively high administrative costs. And so the Association pressed, year in, year out, for a radical simplification of the entire legal procedure and for unification of all the provisions affecting those who were bankrupt or insolvent, such as existed in Scotland. The *Bradford Observer* spoke for most traders and manufacturers when it alleged (in February 1865) that 'the Bankruptcy Acts have proved the greatest legislative failures of our time'.[63]

Eventually, in 1869, the Attorney-General, Collier, a politician with a record of sympathy towards the claims of the commercial world, told the Chambers of Commerce in an apologetic speech that the Government was about to introduce a Bankruptcy Bill. To approving cheers from his audience, he admitted that 'lawyers, who had most to do with the settling of such Bills, were more or less prejudiced in favour of keeping things as they were'.[64] Collier's Bill of 1869 pleased the Association by giving increased powers to creditors. Yet even this measure proved to be a failure, because many creditors lacked the time or the money to pursue their claims and bring defaulters to justice. Hence the issue continued to rumble on until eventually, in 1900, businessmen achieved what they regarded as a broadly acceptable settlement.[65]

Allied to the bankruptcy issue was the attempt by businessmen to prevent the abolition of imprisonment for debt as a remedy against insolvent people who defrauded their creditors or showed other kinds of gross irresponsibility. As a delegate complained to the Leeds Chamber of Commerce, the Commissioners in Bankruptcy seemed 'to show a marked leniency towards bankrupts and . . . to look on creditors as persecutors'.[66] Again, it was decades

---

[60] See *Transactions of the National Association for the Promotion of Social Science*, 1861, pp. 227–8. On this Association, see below.

[61] 18 May 1860, cited in Southgate, '*Most English Minister*', 476.

[62] *The Times*, 26 Oct. 1860. See Ch. 4.

[63] *Bradford Observer*, 23 Feb. 1865.

[64] *The Times*, 25 Feb. 1869.

[65] Ilersic and Liddle, *Parliament of Commerce*, 69–73.

[66] Beresford, *Leeds Chamber of Commerce*, 43.

before Parliament could be persuaded to pass legislation which commercial Members thought even remotely reasonable. Well might one historian see in these difficulties 'evidence of industrial middle-class alienation'.[67]

The massive difficulties involved in correcting what most businessmen saw as glaring abuses, when such abuses worked in the financial interests of members of the legal profession, pushed the leaders of the Chambers of Commerce into more radical proposals. Important in this respect was the agitation launched by the powerful Liverpool Chamber as early as the 1850s for the establishment of so-called tribunals of commerce, such as existed in many Continental towns, including Paris.[68]

In fact, a parliamentary Select Committee on the subject was set up in 1858, but its members had time to do no more than gather information about how tribunals operated elsewhere before it was disbanded; to the annoyance of many businessmen, a recommendation that the Committee be reappointed was simply ignored.[69] But the Hull and Newcastle Chambers were determined not to let the matter drop.[70] Indeed, by the middle of the 1860s an insistence on the re-examination of the desirability of tribunals had become one of the issues which aroused most interest at meetings of the ACC, which drew up petitions and pestered the Board of Trade to act.[71] Eventually, in 1871, the Government agreed to establish another Select Committee. Its members included many prominent figures from the Association, such as Norwood, Akroyd, Monk, and Whitwell; and it heard representations from other Chamber activists, including Behrens and Lloyd, the latter claiming that he had only ever heard *one* delegate at the Association's annual meetings express hostility to the proposal.[72]

Faced with this impressive testimony, the Committee ended up recommending that, in large towns that also served as centres of the surrounding district, tribunals should be established, consisting of one member of the legal profession as president and two 'members selected from the commercial classes for the office of commercial judge, with a registrar to carry on the routine

---

[67] Victor M. Batzel, 'Parliament, Businessmen and Bankruptcy, 1825–1883: A Study in Middle-Class Alienation', *Canadian Journal of History*, 18 (1983), 186.

[68] H. W. Arthurs, *'Without the Law': Administrative Justice and Legal Pluralism in Nineteenth-Century England* (Toronto, 1985), 57. Significantly, Levi's call to the merchants of Liverpool to set up their own Chamber of Commerce in 1849 was linked to his proposal for the establishment of a local tribunal of commerce (Levi, *Chambers and Tribunals*, 25–31). Behrens also linked together the two issues: see J. Behrens, *Tribunals of Commerce: A Paper Read before the Members of the Bradford Chamber of Commerce at their Annual Meeting, 19 January 1865* (Bradford, 1865).

[69] Report of Select Committee on Tribunals of Commerce, IX (1873), which includes the report of the 1858 Committee.

[70] Behrens, *Tribunals of Commerce*, 3–4.

[71] But the Association, though it consulted a barrister on the legal bearings of the case, thought it 'desirable to have as much freedom from the interference of lawyers as would be consistent with legal practice'! (ACC Papers, 14 June 1870).

[72] Report of Select Committee on Tribunals of Commerce, XII (1871), q. 753.

business of the court'. The commercial judges were to be appointed from among *local* businessmen and were to serve in rotation or whenever a case arose upon which they had special experience. It also recommended that procedures be 'of the simplest and most summary character' and that the jurisdiction of the courts be compulsory and exclusive over all commercial disputes in the district.[73]

In 1872 four of the Association's MPs introduced a Bill to give effect to these recommendations, but the Lord Chancellor simply referred the whole matter to the Judicature Commission. In 1874 this Commission rejected anything that approximated the Select Committee's scheme, on the rather odd grounds that businessmen could not agree on exactly how a tribunal was to be constituted. Instead, the Commission proposed the creation of a tribunal in which a judge would be assisted by two skilled assessors who could give advice on any technical matter coming before the court.[74] Even this proposal was too radical for the legal profession, and was accordingly ignored.[75] After sporadic attempts to revive the issue, the ACC effectively admitted defeat, and switched its attention to an equally unsuccessful campaign to extend the jurisdiction of the County Courts.[76]

Why did businessmen feel so strongly about tribunals of commerce? The answer can be found in the Select Committee Report of 1871. 'General dissatisfaction exists among the commercial community at the manner in which justice is administered in commercial cases by the Superior Court,' said the report; and it instanced delays, expense, and 'the difficulty of bringing the real question in dispute before the court in a satisfactory manner'.[77] Businessmen particularly disliked the current legal provision that all debts exceeding £20 be taken before the Superior Courts in Westminster. More basically still, many merchants were out of patience with the legal profession. That helps explain the backing given by many Chambers to the establishment of a tribunals system, on the French or Belgian model, from which lawyers would be *entirely excluded*.[78]

But behind this story of disagreement between the Chambers of Commerce and the legal profession lurk far more important issues. H. W. Arthurs has placed the whole controversy surrounding tribunals of commerce in a wider perspective. Before the creation of the County Courts in 1846, he shows, most civil disputes of a minor nature had been handled by special local 'courts',

[73] Ibid., pp. v–vi.

[74] Third Report of Royal Commission on the Judicature, XXIV (1874), 7–9.

[75] Arthurs, *'Without the Law': Administrative Justice*, 60. See also Robert B. Ferguson, 'The Adjudication of Commercial Disputes and the Legal System in Modern England', *British Journal of Law and Society*, 7 (1980), 143.

[76] Ilersic and Liddle, *Parliament of Commerce*, 83, 85–90.

[77] Report on Tribunals of Commerce, XII (1871), p. iii.

[78] Third Report of the Royal Commission on the Judicature, XXIV (1874), 7–8.

called 'courts of requests' (or sometimes 'courts of conscience').[79] These 'courts', outside the formal legal system, were well equipped to deal with commercial cases, since they were sensitive to local customs and saw their role as one of mediation and conciliation rather than the delivery of decisive judgments.

But during the 1830s the legal profession launched an increasingly aggressive attack on these bodies, arguing that they did not administer 'real' law,[80] and in 1846 they were largely replaced by the new County Courts, which lawyers welcomed as a step towards the establishment of a centralized, uniform legal system.

But all this brought lawyers into conflict with businessmen, whose norms of conduct were rather different. To businessmen, the main consideration was the speedy resolution of disputes. This predisposed them to favour a system of informal or semi-formal arbitration, since they believed that the law 'should reflect the demands of common sense, conscience, and trade custom'.[81] Moreover, since most commercial disputes were seen by businessmen merely as an unwelcome interruption in an ongoing relationship, the adversarial procedures of the law courts did not strike them as a suitable remedy for their day-to-day difficulties. As one legal journalist observed:

The legal and commercial notion of justice are distinct, and the real complaint of the man of business against the lawyer proceeds upon a sense of this opposition. Justice in the lawyer's sense is adherence to a rule . . . Justice in the sense of the man of business is the attainment of a result satisfactory to the feelings of a benevolent bystander who takes an interest in both parties.[82]

Failing to get the tribunals of commerce for which so many commercial pressure groups were agitating, businessmen continued to avoid the courts entirely, whenever possible, and to employ a variety of informal systems of arbitration, some entirely *ad hoc*, some organized through a trade association— for example, the Liverpool Cotton Brokers' Association and Liverpool's Corn Trade Association.[83] Certain Chambers of Commerce, including Bradford, even tried to turn *themselves* into arbitration bodies, though, of course, they lacked effective sanctions to enforce their judgements.[84] What all this shows is

---

[79] H. W. Arthurs, '"Without the Law": Courts of Local and Special Jurisdiction in Nineteenth Century England', in Albert Kiralfy, Michele Slatter, and Roger Virgoe (eds.), *Custom, Courts and Counsel* (1985), 130–7.

[80] Ibid. 140.

[81] Arthurs, *'Without the Law': Administrative Justice*, 83.

[82] Cited in ibid. 79.

[83] Report on Tribunals of Commerce, XII (1871), q. 1445; Ferguson, 'Adjudication', 145.

[84] e.g. the Leeds arbitration panel; see Beresford, *Leeds Chamber of Commerce*, 49; Bradford's Chamber had a standing arbitration committee. Moreover, from the 1870s onwards, commodity associations started issuing standard contract forms, a practice stimulated by 'forward trading' (Ferguson, 'Adjudication', 150).

the marked preference of businessmen for adjudication procedures which took account of trade custom. Indeed, the only helpful contribution made by the law was to provide for its own circumvention, as when the 1854 Common Law Procedure Act allowed judges to refuse to hear a case if the party initiating proceedings had previously contracted to go to arbitration.[85]

On one level, the dispute was an ideological one. At stake was a disagreement over whether business practice should conform to legal norms or vice versa. But the dispute also represented a clear-cut conflict of interest. The Royal Commission on the Judicature made the point with the utmost clarity in its dismissal of the suggestion that commercial tribunals would be competent to handle commercial disputes:

We fear that merchants would be too apt to decide questions that might come before them (as some of the witnesses we examined have suggested that they should do) according to their own view of what was just and proper in the particular case, a course which from the uncertainty attending their decisions would inevitably multiply litigation, and with the vast and intricate commercial business of this country would sooner or later lead to great confusion. Commercial questions, we think, ought not to be determined without law, or by men without special legal training.[86]

Clearly, as Arthurs puts it, the legal profession resented the advocacy of arbitration systems as an affront to its own competence and indispensability.[87]

But social tensions also entered into the quarrel. In Beresford's words:

The lawyers themselves were drawn from a social group different from that of the new industrialists, and it would have been easy for the business man to see the lawyer as at once a creature of hereditary privilege and, at the same time, a parasite taking unnecessary fees from such business men as were careless enough to let their disputes come as far as litigation.[88]

The quarrel between the two groups was also of political significance, since many of the new commercial MPs were confirmed in their suspicion that the legislature was a bumbling assembly dominated by lawyers mainly concerned to protect their own interests. This in turn led to attacks on the 'amateurishness' of parliamentary procedures, particularly as these affected Private Bills. Some businessmen went even further, and burst out angrily against the whole system of Westminster politics, in which party rivalries always seemed to take precedence over commercial legislation.[89]

---

[85] Ferguson, 'Adjudication', 147–8. Many businessmen also avoided the law, and resorted to informal arbitration procedures to deal with the problem of bankruptcy (Batzel, 'Parliament, Businessmen and Bankruptcy', 186).

[86] Report on the Judicature, 8.

[87] Arthurs, *'Without the Law': Administrative Justice*, 78; the *Law Times* once dismissed tribunals of commerce as yet another 'hit at the lawyers' (ibid. 57).

[88] Beresford, *Leeds Chamber of Commerce*, 47.

[89] For evidence of mounting frustration, see Ilersic and Liddle, *Parliament of Commerce*, 90–2.

BUSINESS DISPUTES

Unfortunately, the Chambers of Commerce movement was often hampered in its dealings with the outside world by its own internal disputes. It was, of course, inevitable that conflicts of material interest should divide the business community.[90] True, the entrepreneurial crusades of the 1840s and early 1850s had temporarily papered over these divisions, at least to a considerable extent. But in the more relaxed social and political atmosphere of the Palmerstonian years, business disagreements came out into the open once more.

Particularly serious were disputes between the railway companies and the merchants and manufacturers who relied upon their services. By the late 1850s the railway companies had organized themselves into a formidable parliamentary pressure group. In 1867 no fewer than 162 MPs and 53 peers were railway directors, while in the same year there came into existence the United Railway Companies Committee, renamed two years later the Railway Companies Association, a body which soon achieved a friendly working relationship with the Board of Trade.[91]

The railways had been seen earlier as a symbol of the new industrial Britain, deplored by reactionary Tory squires like Sibthorp, but welcomed as agencies of social and political progress by the urban Radicals. 'I like railways,' Cobden proclaimed in 1845.[92] But twenty years later they were beginning to be viewed in quite a different way: as semi-monopolistic bodies exploiting the rest of the community. It is significant that, at its very first meeting, the ACC should have debated a resolution protesting at the amalgamation of railways; and it continued to worry away at the issue for many decades.[93]

What annoyed merchants and industrialists were the inequalities of charges on goods transported by rail. In 1865 the Association claimed that the existing system was unjust, 'not being regulated by the exigencies of Trade, but generally by the ability to combine which exist amongst the leading Companies, and which operates prejudicially not only upon the trade of inland towns (where competition by shipping is impossible) but upon some of the most important manufacturing interests of the Country'.[94] The Government,

---

[90] The divisions were especially apparent between the City and the manufacturing districts. Cobden later recalled that 'the City magnates were almost as difficult to convert [to the League] and cost us nearly as much trouble to beat, as the Duke of Richmond and his farming friends' (Cobden to S. Morley, 25 Mar. 1861, Cobden Papers, Add. MS 43,670, fo. 118).

[91] Philip S. Bagwell, 'The Railway Interest: Its Organisation and Influence, 1839–1914', *Journal of Transport History*, 7 (1965), 83–4, 69–71.

[92] 28 Oct. 1845, *Cobden's Speeches*, 161.

[93] ACC Papers, 2 Feb. 1860. For the suspicions entertained of railway companies, see the views of Duncan McLaren, himself a former railway director (Mackie, *McLaren*, ii. 61–2).

[94] ACC Papers, 22 Feb. 1865.

under pressure from the Chambers of Commerce, set up a Royal Commission of Inquiry, but this body, dominated as it was by railway interests, failed to tackle the problem to the satisfaction of traders and manufacturers.[95] Meanwhile, there was also discontent in the business world at the quasi-monopolistic position of the telegraph companies. The Edinburgh Chamber raised the matter in 1865; the National Association took it over in the following year; and a campaign was launched which culminated in 1870 in the nationalization of the telegraphs, under Post Office control.[96]

Superimposed on these conflicts of interest between different economic sectors was a rivalry between the various big cities and industrial regions. It is noticeable that it was the Birmingham Chamber of Commerce which sponsored the resolution on the damage inflicted on inland towns by the 'railway monopoly'. At least this was a grievance with which almost all the big urban centres could identify. But it was quite otherwise when, for example, the ACC sat down to consider motions deploring the levying of extra duties on goods bonded in inland towns. This motion could not be carried by the necessary majority because most delegates from ports like Bristol opposed it! What this obviously shows is that individual Chambers were spending much of their time trying to secure advantages for their own towns at the expense of their neighbours.

How bitter such disputes could be became apparent when Lowe, Vice-President of the Board of Trade between 1855 and 1858, brought forward his Local Dues on Shipping Bill. Following a Royal Commission recommendation, Lowe boldly set out to sweep away a mass of corporate privileges which enabled certain municipal corporations to levy dues on shipping which used their ports. This won him the support of Cobden,[97] and his policies were also much to the liking of the Mancunian business community, which had long complained of the way these dock and town dues were damaging the manufacturing interests.[98] But other shipowners disliked the attempt to abolish differential port duties, which gave a measure of protection to British companies vis-à-vis their foreign rivals. The angry Liverpudlians, led by Horsfall, the shipowner who represented the city in Parliament, vented their anger on the tactless Lowe and his Board of Trade officials: not coming from a business background, they complained, these men were not fit to 'preside

---

[95] Ilersic and Liddle, *Parliament of Commerce*, 103–5. See also Beresford, *Leeds Chamber of Commerce*, 66–70.

[96] For a much fuller discussion of the entire issue, see Ira J. Cohen, 'Towards a Theory of State Intervention: The Nationalization of the British Telegraphs', *Social Science History*, 4 (1980), 175–83.

[97] Parl. Deb., 3rd ser., vol. 141, 214–18: 14 Mar. 1856.

[98] Manchester Chamber of Commerce Papers, 4 Feb. 1856, fo. 475. Bradford strongly supported Manchester on this, Titus Salt agreeing to give evidence favourable to reform to the Select Committee of Inquiry (Bradford Chamber of Commerce 6th Annual Report, 1857, p. 14; Bradford Chamber of Commerce Minutes, 26 Jan. 1857, fos. 85–6).

over the commercial interests of the country'. Lowe's political career was
dented by his having unwittingly involved himself in this civic vendetta.[99]

Given these clashes of interest, it not surprising, that the various Chambers
of Commerce found it difficult to combine into a national organization. Thus
London, lacking a Chamber of Commerce before 1881 (it affiliated to the
Association in 1882), initially went its own way,[100] while Liverpool almost
immediately disaffiliated because it believed that it had been committed
to policies without adequate consultation. Meanwhile the major cities of
Glasgow, Edinburgh, and Manchester contemptuously kept themselves to
themselves.[101]

In fact, when Leone Levi, Professor of Commerce at King's College,
London, wrote to the Manchester Chamber proposing the holding of an
annual conference of all the Chambers of Commerce, he received the frosty
reply that 'the Directors of this Chamber much prefer to act independently of
all other Bodies whatsoever and do not at present perceive any advantage
would flow from the proposed arrangement'.[102] Five years later a Mancunian
delegation attended the ACC's annual dinner, but the Manchester Chamber,
in subsequently acknowledging the kind hospitality which its men had
received, commented patronizingly that during the recent debate on international maritime law most delegates had not 'devoted that amount of time
and attention to the subject which its importance demand[ed]'.[103] Such
attitudes had important consequences, given the fact that the Manchester
Chamber of Commerce represented not just Manchester itself, but also the
entire cotton industry of Lancashire and Cheshire.[104]

These displays of mutual ill will allowed *The Times* to sneer at the
Association's pretensions to be a 'representative' body. Pertinently, it also
noted how intensely sectional were most of the resolutions which the Association was considering, and it questioned whether any 'national' policy could be

[99] Winter, *Robert Lowe*, 101–3, 109. 'A peer and a lawyer were not exactly the persons to
preside over the commercial interests of the country' (Parl. Deb., 3rd ser., vol. 145, 1137–8: 4
June 1857). But the question was partly settled the following session with the Mersey Commerce
and Docks (no. 2) Bill, based on the recommendations of a Select Committee which had been set
up in the wake of the previous year's disaster.
[100] For a disparaging view from a contemporary of London's commercial class, see W. L.
Sargant, *Essays of a Birmingham Manufacturer* (Birmingham, 1869), ii. 14–27.
[101] Ilersic and Liddle, *Parliament of Commerce*, ch. 2. Liverpool eventually affiliated in 1900,
Glasgow in 1910, Edinburgh in 1893, and Manchester in 1898. The Edinburgh Chamber held
aloof for so long because so much of the legislation which the Association sponsored did not
cover Scotland. See Mackie, *McLaren*, ii. 64–5.
[102] Manchester Chamber of Commerce Papers, 7 Nov. 1859, fo. 104.
[103] Ibid., 17 Feb., 9 Mar. 1864, fos. 478–9, 497–8. If anything, Manchester thereafter tended
to co-operate with its old enemy, the Liverpool Chamber, and also with Glasgow, both of which
were also pursuing an 'independent' line, while giving the Association a wide berth. On the old
rivalry between Manchester and Liverpool, see above.
[104] Report from Select Committee on Trade with Foreign Nations, VII (1864), q. 905
(H. Ashworth).

shaped from the 'pressure of local grievance'.[105] The point was made more brutally by Layard in rejecting Forster's attempts to reform the relationship between the Board of Trade and the Foreign Office:

It should . . . be borne in mind that when the hon. Member for Bradford pretended to speak on the part of the Chambers of Commerce of this country, he, in truth, represented only a certain number of them, in which several large commercial countries [sic], such as London, Liverpool, Manchester, and Glasgow, as well as others of great importance, were not included.[106]

Moreover, in addition to these *regional* conflicts were important commercial issues on which businessmen simply could not be brought to agree. Among the most important were patents and limited liability.

THE ISSUE OF PATENTS

Many Victorian businessmen would have liked to see the total abolition of all patent legislation. The system did not even seem to be helping the inventor, the supposed beneficiary; Dickens memorably satirized its expense and dilatoriness in *Little Dorrit*.[107] More fundamentally, many found it anomalous that the 1624 Statute of Monopolies should have survived into the nineteenth century. Free Trade could readily be invoked to demonstrate that patents were an impediment to free competition and had the effect of raising costs. A former president of the Liverpool Chamber of Commerce, the Liberal MP for Louth, a sugar refiner by trade, Robert Andrew Macfie, spearheaded the attack, writing a book on the subject, *Patent Monopolies*; in May 1869 he brought the issue before Parliament itself.[108]

Macfie enjoyed the backing of *The Economist*, which argued that, although constant improvement of existing technology would obviously continue, important new inventions were unlikely in the future! 'The inventor must be a man who is closely associated with capitalists, or be a capitalist himself,' it said. 'In no other way can he have the means of knowing the thousand improvements of machinery and processes which have culminated in the present factories and machines.' Most British manufacturers, harried by patent litigation, would welcome abolition, *The Economist* claimed. In any case, 'The more that invention falls into the hands of great capitalists the more likely is it to strengthen the manufacturing of a country which is already most

---

[105] *The Times*, 21 Feb. 1865.
[106] Parl. Deb., 3rd ser., vol. 177, 1874: 17 Mar. 1865.
[107] Also in his short story *A Poor Man's Tale of a Patent*.
[108] Parl. Deb., 3rd ser., vol. 196, 888–92: 28 May 1869. Macfie had earlier outlined his objections to patents in May 1863 in his evidence to the Royal Commission on Patents, qs. 1935–2024.

powerful.'[109] In short, the abolitionists wanted to end 'the existence of a legal monopoly in a society formally committed to the free play of market forces'.[110]

On the other hand, it was generally recognized that there *was* such a thing as 'intellectual property'. This formed the basis for the belief of such authorities as Adam Smith and John Stuart Mill that patents were legitimate.[111] Moreover, some businessmen, including Mundella, argued that many inventions originated with the skilled artisan, rather than the capitalist, and that it would be unjust to deprive these intelligent working men of the financial reward to which their ingenuity entitled them.[112] The abolitionists themselves recognized the force of this argument by proposing that inventors be recompensed for their labours by the allocation of government grants. But this ran into predictable opposition from other businessmen worried about so dangerous an enlargement of the authority of the State.[113] Perhaps patents were the lesser of two evils.

The parliamentary debate of May 1869, which ended inconclusively without Macfie's motion being put to the vote, demonstrated that no united view within the business community existed on the patents issue, since manufacturers (like lawyers) spoke on both sides of the question. However, by this time, opinion was clearly beginning to move in favour of *reform* of the patent system, rather than its abolition, a process which had begun with the Patent Law Amendment Act of 1852. By the 1860s, the reformers had achieved an ascendancy in the relevant professional associations, like the Institution of Civil Engineers; they enjoyed the support of the formidable Lord Brougham; and they carried their proposals through the National Association for the Promotion of Social Science in 1859 and through the Society of Arts shortly afterwards.[114] In fact, by the time of the parliamentary debate, opinion seemed to be polarizing between (as Lord Elcho put it) the 'philosophers' who advocated abolition on doctrinal grounds and the 'practical men' who took a

---

[109] 'The Debate on the Patent Laws', *Economist*, 5 June 1869, pp. 656–7. This was largely a repetition of the arguments used by the engineer William Armstrong in his evidence to the Royal Commission on Patents in 1863 (q. 1105).

[110] Victor M. Batzel, 'Legal Monopoly in Liberal England: The Patent Controversy in the Mid-Nineteenth Century', *Business History*, 22 (1980), 189.

[111] Ibid. 191. For a lawyer's view on the subject, see W. R. Cornish, *Intellectual Property: Patents, Copyright, Trade Marks and Allied Rights* (1981).

[112] Parl. Deb., 3rd ser., vol. 196, 914: 28 May 1869.

[113] Batzel, 'Legal Monopoly', 192. But, as Forster realized in his cross-examination of Armstrong before the Royal Commission on Patents, Armstrong's position was really that 'in the absence of any Patent Law, the law of supply and demand would give [the inventor] such a reward for his services that he would be rewarded without a Patent Law if it was a really useful invention' (q. 1113). And if that were the case, then it would be superfluous for the State to step in and give its *own* reward.

[114] Batzel, 'Legal Monopoly', 192–5. The National Association for the Promotion of Social Science created a Special Committee to investigate the subject; see *Transactions of the National Association for the Promotion of Social Science*, 1861, pp. 229–39.

'rational and sensible view of the question'.[115] The ACC also came to accept that what Britain most wanted was an *efficient* patent system such as was enjoyed in the United States.[116]

The reformers eventually triumphed in 1883, when an important piece of legislation (originating with the Society of Arts) led to the reorganization of the Patent Office. As one historian puts it: 'Custom and a growing sense of traditional practice seem to have been at work, solidifying the place of patents in industrial England.'[117] Through a long process of discussion and debate, businessmen, lawyers, social scientists, and legislators had edged their way to a viable compromise on the patents question. For once, it was *The Economist* which seemed to be ignoring the practical needs of commerce and relying on abstract arguments which eventually came to look archaic.

LIMITED LIABILITY

As on the patents question, it took businessmen a long time to make up their minds as to whether they wanted limited liability. Before 1856 Britain had the most restrictive company legislation in the industrial world. Gladstone's Joint Stock Registration and Regulation Act of 1844 had granted joint stock companies certain privileges; but these could be secured only by complying with various conditions laid down by the Board of Trade. Moreover, the Act itself did not legalize limited liability, this 'privilege' being reserved for big concerns, like railway companies, that could afford to acquire a private charter.[118]

Then, quite suddenly, in 1856, Parliament affirmed the principle of limited liability when Robert Lowe (who had taken over from his predecessor, Bouverie) carried his famous Bill on the subject. Limited liability was extended in 1858 to banks (thanks to the exertions of the Newcastle MP, Headlam), and finally, in the great consolidating measure of 1862, to insurance companies as well. Indeed, the pendulum swung so far in the opposite direction that the remaining years of the century were given over to attempts to reinstate the safeguards which Parliament had so blithely thrown away in 1856 (all bar the publication of the annual return of shareholders).[119]

---

[115] Parl. Deb., 3rd ser., vol. 196, 917: 28 May 1869.

[116] This, in particular, was the view of Mundella, who attributed America's technical inventiveness to her excellent patent laws (ibid. 915). See also ACC Papers, 21 Feb. 1866, where the principle of patents was approved, but it was agreed that enquiries should first ascertain whether the invention being patented really *was* new. Not until the Patent Act of 1907 did the Chambers of Commerce get a settlement which they believed to conform to modern industrial requirements (Ilersic and Liddle, *Parliament of Commerce*, 101).

[117] Batzel, 'Legal Monopoly', 199.

[118] P. L. Cottrell, *Industrial Finance, 1830–1914* (1980), 44–5. See P. S. Atiyah, *The Rise and Fall of Freedom of Contract* (Oxford, 1979), 562–6.

[119] Bishop Carleton Hunt, *The Development of the Business Corporation in England, 1800–1867* (New York, 1936; 1969 edn.), 153–4. However, it took much longer for opinion to accept the desirability of the société en commandite (Ilersic and Liddle, *Parliament of Commerce*, 77–8).

Yet, among businessmen, no clear consensus on the question of limited liability emerged for a very long time; indeed, opinion was sharply divided. On the one hand, supporters claimed that the institution of limited liability would remove unnecessary and arbitrary barriers to freedom of trade. In February 1856 Laing, for example, called the restrictions then prevailing 'an impertinent interference with the natural rights of individuals'; provided that the rest of the world knew that a company had been formed on a limited liability basis, there was no need for State intervention.[120] Lowe took the same line: 'I hold that it is not the business of the State to save men from the effects of their own improvidence.' 'Artificial restraints' were unnecessary for the honest trader, and easily circumvented by the dishonest.[121] Cobden, too, saw no need for the House 'to legislate to protect the very intelligent people on the other side of Temple-bar from losing their property by giving too easy credit. That was a matter which might fairly be left to themselves.'[122] Some business MPs were also pleased at the prospect of commerce being emancipated from a judicial interference which had caused it many difficulties in the past.[123]

It was also argued that limited liability would effect a marriage between skill and capital, which could not happen under the current restrictive system.[124] Finally, there were appeals to experience. Not only did other countries enjoy the advantages of limited liability without the dire consequences predicted by its opponents, claimed the reformers; but it had already proved its worth in Britain through the construction of docks and railways. Indeed, according to Laing, Britain herself owed her very means of conveyance to limited liability.[125] Without it, said another MP, we would all still be travelling in stage-coaches and sailing packets.[126] But since, before 1856, only wealthy companies could afford the cost of acquiring a charter,[127] the law had to be reformed before the advantages of this trading system could come within the reach of men of smaller means.

On the other side, the opponents of limited liability were equally sure of their case. These men denied that the country was suffering from a want of outlets for investment. Joint stock companies trading under limited liability might have been necessary for the construction of major public works like railways or in highly speculative enterprises like mining, they said, but this was neither necessary nor desirable for the majority of manufacturing and mercantile firms. Opponents were equally unimpressed by the invocation of

[120] Parl. Deb., 3rd ser., vol. 140, 488–9: 8 Feb. 1856.
[121] Ibid. 114, 124–8: 1 Feb. 1856.
[122] Ibid., vol. 119, 681: 17 Feb. 1852. See also Cobden's remarks, Parl. Deb., 3rd ser., vol. 134, 781: 27 June 1854.
[123] e.g. J. G. Phillimore (ibid., vol. 140, 146: 1 Feb. 1856).
[124] See e.g. Cobden, ibid., vol. 119, 682: 17 Feb. 1852.
[125] Ibid., vol. 139, 1392–3: 26 July 1855.
[126] Collier, cited in Hunt, *Development of the Business Corporation*, 133.
[127] A charter cost about £402 (Cottrell, *Industrial Finance*, 43).

the example of foreign countries. Archibald Hastie, a Scottish merchant, claimed that limited liability had actually proved injurious in America and France by encouraging speculation and fraud.[128] Britain's commercial pre-eminence, it was often claimed, rested on the integrity of her business class, and this would be undermined by the general adoption of limited liability. France and the United States supplied many examples of fraud and commercial failure, which Britain should heed as a warning. This was also the point repeatedly made by the Liverpool shipowner William Brown, who claimed that 'he had always been ready to adopt any measure which could be advantageous to the middle classes',[129] but said that he saw nothing good in limited liability, which would, in fact, put in jeopardy the 'high character of its merchants'.[130] The *Leeds Mercury* agreed, dismissing limited liability as meaning nothing more nor less than 'freedom to trade without paying one's debts'. In any case, it asked, could so many of the great capitalists in the House of Commons be wrong on a matter about which they had so much knowledge?[131]

It was this division of opinion among businessmen which caused the Royal Commission on Mercantile Law to reject limited liability in its 1854 Report (by five votes to three), after having heard conflicting testimony from representatives of commerce and industry.[132] Of course, the subsequent success of the Limited Liability Bill (almost 2,500 companies had become incorporated by 1862)[133] may imply that this measure did indeed meet a need—at least a need that was recognized once the Bill had come into force. But *prior* to enactment this could not easily have been predicted. Muntz, the businessman who represented Birmingham, protested that limited liability 'emanated from the Board of Trade, the head of which knew nothing about trade. Those Bills would introduce a system of trades' unions, which would be most dangerous to the public and of no benefit whatever to the parties them-selves.'[134] And T. Potter ('Manchester Man') flatly denied that 'capitalists' wanted the Government Bills: 'The middle classes have knowledge sufficient to work their own capital successfully, and they have not asked for limited liability,' he declared.[135] The Leeds Chamber also came out in opposition.[136]

In fact, as Cottrell shows, there was little provincial support for changes in the law, though the degree of opposition varied from city to city.[137] Even

---

[128] Parl. Deb., 3rd ser., vol. 139, 1393: 26 July 1855.
[129] Ibid., vol. 134, 795: 27 June 1854.
[130] Ibid., vol. 139, 355: 29 June 1855.
[131] *Leeds Mercury*, 31 July 1855.
[132] First Report of Royal Commission on Mercantile Laws, XXVII (1854), 5–7.
[133] Hunt, *Development of the Business Corporation*, 143.
[134] Parl. Deb., 3rd ser., vol. 139, 1350: 24 July 1855. Muntz's Metal Company was itself converted in 1863 (Hunt, *Business Corporation*, 152).
[135] Cottrell, *Industrial Finance*, 50.
[136] Beresford, *Leeds Chamber of Commerce*, 40.
[137] Cottrell, *Industrial Finance*, 51.

Cobden tacitly admitted that this was so when he likened the debate over limited liability to earlier controversies. Classes, he thought, often failed to grasp what was in their own best interest: the farmers had opposed Repeal, the shipowners had clung to the bitter end to the Navigation Acts, and many capitalists, who stood to *gain* from limited liability, were now expressing their fear of it.[138]

Nor can such a division of business opinion be neatly categorized. For example, the Manchester Chamber of Commerce came out as an opponent of limited liability. Edmund Potter, the calico printer, told members that he thought it

a rather suspicious thing when a cabinet came forward with propositions for improving the country in commercial matters, especially when there had been no solicitation from the country for such facilities for the employment of capital as it was proposed to give. The whole thing was in the hands of the lawyers and certain capitalists in London.

But Bright, one of the City's two MPs, at once stood up and told him that his fears were 'almost altogether imaginary'.[139] Nevertheless, after further discussion, the Manchester Chamber resolved that the legalisation of limited liability would 'lead to reckless speculation, and encourage dishonesty, and so disturb the equable current of trade as, eventually, to place in jeopardy the regular employment of the people'.[140]

In Birmingham the reverse situation applied; whereas, over many years, the Chamber of Commerce had pressed for the widest possible extension of the principle of limited liability, its veteran MP George Muntz, as we have seen, made powerful speeches attacking it. Liverpool, too, was divided. Its MP, J. C. Ewart, claimed that there was 'a very strong feeling' in his city favouring limited liability, but in fact the Liverpool Chamber came out against it by 209 votes to 107.[141]

The dispute later carried over into the arena of the ACC. Nearly all delegates agreed on the need to have a registration of the names of partnerships, so that traders could know precisely with whom they were dealing and, in case of default, whom they should sue.[142] But the persistent attempts of the Birmingham Chamber to extend a form of limited liability to private partnerships ran into persistent opposition. 'People must not expect to have the profits of trade without its risks and inconveniencies,' observed one of the Leeds delegates.[143] The Association's secretary laconically summed up the situation thus: 'The expediency of further extending the principle of Limited

[138] Parl. Deb., 3rd ser., vol. 134, 784: 27 June 1854. In this respect he resembled Robert Lowe.
[139] Manchester Chamber of Commerce Papers, 4 Feb. 1856, fo. 474.
[140] Ibid., 12 June 1856, fo. 512.
[141] Parl. Deb., 3rd ser., vol. 139, 358: 29 June 1855; ibid., vol. 134, 795: 27 June 1854 (W. Brown).
[142] Ilersic and Liddle, *Parliament of Commerce*, 73–4.
[143] ACC Papers, 19 Feb. 1862.

Liability is a subject on which great difference of opinion prevails among Chambers of Commerce.'[144] Indeed, the Chambers only gradually united in an acceptance of the system; and even then, worried by the huge numbers of failures and frauds in the 1860s, they pressed for publicity clauses and other safeguards that would minimize the danger of abuse.[145]

Why were manufacturers and merchants unable to agree on the question of limited liability? Some historians believe that opposition to change came primarily from large capitalists wishing to protect their existing quasi-monopolistic position. Cobden's own support for reform certainly owed much to his hatred of monopolies; indeed, he even seems to have supposed that limited liability might enable energetic working men to set up business enterprises of their own, something which he hoped would 'bridge over the gulf which now divided different classes, ... [so diminishing] that spirit of alienation between employers and employed which they all deplored'.[146] Cobden, of course, was mistaken in his belief that the proposed legislation would lead to a wider diffusion of capital; on the contrary, its long-term consequence was the facilitation of large, complex, impersonal amalgamations.[147]

But in any case, there is little firm evidence to support the view that resistance to limited liability was rooted in a desire to protect existing privileges. The *Leeds Mercury* was not alone in finding it incredible that a great shipowner like William Brown, in opposing the reform, should really have been animated by fear of upstart competitors.[148]

In fact, the probability is that these divisions of opinion cannot be explained in purely economic terms at all. That is certainly the view of Boyd Hilton, who has suggested that underlying the triumph of limited liability were shifts in moral and theological perspective, involving a 'retreat from retributive or evangelical economics'. There was now a new secular confidence in the desirability of economic expansion, and 'speculation' ceased to be a pejorative word. Hilton also sees the adoption of limited liability

as the moment when the middle classes suddenly opted out of the capitalist system *at the point where it stood to damage themselves*. ... More people would be admitted to the share-holding élite, but the élite itself would be cushioned against danger. To this extent limited liability can be stigmatized as a gross example of middle-class selfishness.[149]

---

[144] Ibid., 24 Feb. 1863.

[145] Ilersic and Liddle, *Parliament of Commerce*, 78–9.

[146] Parl. Deb., 3rd ser., vol. 134, 785: 27 June 1854. In fact, it was the Christian socialist Robert Slaney who did much to push forward the case for limited liability in the first place. Like many other MPs, he saw this as a way of helping smaller enterprises compete with larger ones (John Saville, 'Sleeping Partnership and Limited Liability, 1850–1856', *Economic History Review*, 8 (1955–6), 419–22).

[147] Parl. Deb., 3rd ser., vol. 119, 681–2: 17 Feb. 1852. Winter, *Robert Lowe*, 100.

[148] *Leeds Mercury*, 31 July 1855.

[149] Hilton, *Age of Atonement*, 259, 262–3, 267.

This is an ingenious interpretation, but perhaps it takes too little account of the sharp division of middle-class opinion on the subject in the 1850s. A simpler explanation is that businessmen were moving into terrain where the slogans of the 1840s no longer provided clear guidance. The future was obscure, and businessmen as a class could no more read it than anyone else. As we shall later see, similar differences of opinion were opening up in the field of education and factory reform.[150]

Outside the business world, too, the distribution of political opinions was not one that could easily have been predicted. Thus Gladstone sponsored the Bill which abolished the Usury Laws, saying that he wanted to establish 'entire and unrestricted freedom in trade in all that related to the borrowing and lending of money',[151] yet he continued to harbour doubts about the wisdom of limited liability, which, at the very least, he wanted to surround by stringent safeguards.[152] Palmerston's view of limited liability was far more optimistic. In 1855 he was recommending Lowe's measure as a reform which complemented the recent repeal of the Corn Laws, since it was 'a question of Free Trade against monopoly'.[153]

Finally, it may be significant that the prime mover in sponsoring limited liability legislation was Robert Lowe, not himself a businessman, but someone whose profoundly pessimistic cast of mind led him to the conviction that *all* social groups (not just the aristocratic establishment) would corruptly favour their own selfish interests unless their behaviour were regulated by a complicated system of rewards and punishments. As an extravagant admirer of the political economists, Lowe unashamedly accepted the concept of 'economic man' as the basis upon which most public action should be based: 'Once place a man's ear within the ring of pounds, shillings, and pence, and his conduct can be counted on to the greatest nicety,' he argued in 1878; deviations from this rule, he added, were so slight as not to invalidate the conclusions of political economy.[154]

The free working of the market, Lowe believed, provided the most efficient method of distributing these pecuniary rewards and punishments. Thus, not only did he cleave to Free Trade with a doctrinaire passion, he was also, like James Wilson, deeply committed to the theory of laissez-faire. Lowe's contribution to the carrying of the 1856 measure legalizing limited liability should be understood as an expression of these convictions. Earlier in 1852, while still on the back-benches, he had intervened in a Commons debate with

---

[150] See Chs. 7 and 8.

[151] Parl. Deb., 3rd ser., vol. 134, 931: 29 June 1854.

[152] See Hilton, *Age of Atonement*, 360. Gladstone to Lord Cranworth, 1 Dec. 1854, Gladstone Papers, Add. MS 44,529, fo. 187.

[153] Parl. Deb., 3rd ser., vol. 139, 1390: 26 July 1855. On Palmerston's attitudes, see discussion in Steele, *Palmerston and Liberalism*, 214.

[154] Robert Lowe, 'Recent Attacks on Political Economy', *Nineteenth Century*, 4 (1878), 864.

a vehement defence of the 'natural right' of everyone to adopt this form of trading free from government regulation or interference. 'It was no part of our laws to settle people's private affairs, or to interfere to prevent the public from protecting themselves,' he insisted,[155] and in his written evidence to the Royal Commission on Mercantile Law he went on to develop his views with his customary lucidity:

The only case in which the state is justified in prohibiting parties from contracting is, where a contract arises out of a breach of law and morality, as gambling, or is made for the purpose of a future breach of law or morality, as smuggling, or is in itself a breach of some other substantive law, as insuring an enemy's ship . . . The received principle in commercial legislation is, to leave people to act for themselves and not to restrict competition. The burden of proof lies on those who introduce an exception to this principle, in favour of large capitalists, and maintain that the law should interfere by prohibitive enactments on behalf of those best able to take care of themselves. Every enterprise which the law of unlimited liability prevents—and in my small experience, I know of many—is so much given to capital already invested at the expense of the public—so much taken from the consumer to increase the profits by diminishing the competition of the producer.[156]

The fact that the business community itself was deeply divided on the wisdom of limited liability counted for nothing with a man of Lowe's temperament and outlook on life. He believed limited liability to be a logical extension of Free Trade, and that was that. It is, of course, arguable that the all-important Act of 1856 laid the precondition for industrial and commercial expansion later in the century; but, if so, this represents the triumph of theoretical faith over practical experience. As we have seen, many economic historians now believe that Lowe's principles served to foist upon the country a dangerously lax set of company laws which it took several decades to modify—something that would have been avoided had Lowe been prepared to listen more carefully to what many Chambers of Commerce and other mercantile spokesmen were trying to tell him.[157] But, in Lowe's defence, it could equally well be argued that the Chambers of Commerce had already fatally weakened themselves by their inability to form a coherent strategy on this, as on other, important national questions.

THE ROLE OF GOVERNMENT

But did the Chambers of Commerce even have a *right* to take part in the formulation of public policy? On this, the most basic issue of all, the

---

[155] Parl. Deb., 3rd ser., vol. 123, 1081: 7 Dec. 1852.

[156] First Report on Mercantile Laws, 84.

[157] See Winter, *Robert Lowe*, 98–9. Cottrell, *Industrial Finance*, 54. To be fair to Lowe, the legislation had been largely initiated by his predecessor, Edward Bouverie, who was the second son of Lord Radnor.

entrepreneurial Radicals again found themselves at loggerheads with one another. This became painfully obvious when Forster insisted on the Commons debating his Committee's Report on Foreign Trade in 1865. The surprising thing about this occasion was that prominent Liberal businessmen and their sympathizers failed as a group to come to his support—to the obvious delight of members of the Government, including Layard, now Under-Secretary at the Foreign Office, his days as an angry middle-class Radical well and truly behind him.[158]

On the surface, the disagreement was a narrow one concerning the practicality of the Committee's recommendations. The businessmen, as Layard rightly pointed out, were not able to agree on the respective roles they wanted the Foreign Office and the Board of Trade to assume; indeed, the Committee's final proposals had only been carried on the casting vote of the chairman.[159]

But the Commons debate also drew attention to a much more fundamental disagreement within the business world. Forster, on behalf of the Chambers of Commerce, was advocating an improvement in the mechanism by which commercial men transmitted their opinions to the officials responsible for regulating the country's foreign trade. But Cobden's old friend James White, a London merchant, did not think this at all a *desirable* objective; he suspected (probably unfairly) that the Association was actually trying to push the Government into negotiating more trade treaties, something he thought contrary to the doctrine of Free Trade.

Together with Robert Lowe, White also expressed alarm at what he saw as attempts to enhance the role of the Board of Trade. To all intents and purposes, Lowe came out in favour of the Board's *abolition*, portraying it as an anachronistic survival from the mercantilist era, with regulatory responsibilities that were trivial and a consultative role that, in the new era of commercial enlightenment, was redundant.[160] White went further, and hinted at the possibility that Forster's attempts to strengthen the Board of Trade betokened a revived Protectionism: 'What was that but teaching the people to look to the Government to do for them that which they ought to do for themselves? That was one of the worst and most insidious forms of protection.'[161]

Baines and Bazley angrily repudiated these insinuations. Bazley actually

---

[158] Parl. Deb., 3rd ser., vol. 177, 1873–82: 17 Mar. 1865. Layard had himself been a member of the Select Committee.

[159] Ibid., 1873–4 (Layard), 1865 (White). Lindsay, when giving evidence before the Select Committee, was by no means hostile to the Foreign Office, and Horsfall, speaking in the Commons, was highly complimentary (ibid. 1859). Even the Bradford businessmen could not agree initially on precisely what they wanted (Bradford Chamber of Commerce Minutes, 2 Sept. 1861, fo. 530).

[160] Parl. Deb., 3rd ser., vol. 177, 1862: 17 Mar. 1865 (Lowe). This represented a volte-face from the position which Lowe had adopted in 1857 when he himself was Vice-President and the department was under attack (ibid., vol. 145, 1162, 1164, 1173: 4 June 1857).

[161] Ibid., vol. 177, 1869: 17 Mar. 1865 (White).

called for the Board to be strengthened, 'so as to render that Department capable of taking cognizance of the whole commercial enterprise of the Empire, and become what it ought to be, the great organ of industry in this country'.[162] Similar aspirations lay behind the later campaign to create a Ministry of Commerce. Here was a division of opinion within the business community that was to assume a profound significance over the next few decades.

The parliamentary debate of February 1865 is also interesting, because it reveals that, with changing economic circumstances, Cobden's old Free Trade disciples were losing their cohesion. Cobden himself was absent from the House on this occasion, and died only a few weeks later. What role, if any, then, did Cobden (and Bright) generally envisage for the new Chambers of Commerce movement?

THE CHAMBERS OF COMMERCE AND ENTREPRENEURIAL POLITICS

The Chambers of Commerce movement, in fact, raised political issues on which Cobden and Bright did not quite see eye to eye. Bright was hostile to the new development. His hostility clearly owed something to his personal disagreement with the dignitaries of the Manchester Chamber, whom he held responsible for his own defeat for the borough in 1857. Moreover, when in the following year the Chamber coalesced with the Manchester Association, which included Aspinall Turner, one of the men who had displaced him as MP for Manchester, Bright's alienation was complete. Whereas he had been a regular speaker at the Manchester Chamber up until the mid-1850s, thereafter he avoided its meetings entirely (of course, after 1857 his connections with Manchester came to an end). His contempt for the Manchester Chamber soon developed into a contempt for Chambers of Commerce as such. The following outburst is typical:

I suspect your friends of the Bradford Chamber [he wrote to Cobden in September 1861] would believe anything that Palmerston and Russell told them in preference to anything you or I could say. There is an inveterate flunkeyism which pervades nearly all the newly-rich in the money-making men in these districts—and I have little faith in their *latent* power. When it ceases to be *latent*, we shall probably find it against us. However, I shall willingly work with them when I can, but I dare say they will be afraid of being suspected of being too radical if they are seen acting with us.[163]

Cobden took a rather different view of the matter. On the one hand, he distrusted all employers' organizations;[164] on the other, he had the shrewd-

---

[162] Ibid. 1900.
[163] Bright to Cobden, 6 Sept. 1861, John Bright Papers, Add. MS 43,384, fo. 264.
[164] Howe, *Cotton Masters*, 163–4.

ness to see the significance of the Chambers of Commerce movement. While working on the details of the French Treaty, he showed a particular interest in the responses of the various Chambers: '*These are the only parties whose judgment is of much worth*,' he opined.[165] (Incidentally, Bradford played a particularly prominent role during the French negotiations, a committee of its Chamber of Commerce sitting almost daily either in Bradford or in Paris to deal with the complicated tariff schedule in so far as it affected the worsted industry.)[166] Moreover, Cobden later encouraged his friend Henry Ashworth to become president of the Manchester Chamber in 1862, telling him that such bodies were the 'only power in the State possessed of wealth + political influence sufficient to counteract in some degree the feudal governing class of this country'.[167] A year earlier, desperately hoping to find support for his campaign to cut armaments expenditure, Cobden had also tried to reason Bright into a less hostile attitude to the new movement. 'The trading classes' on whom the country's hopes depended, he told his friend, were now those represented in the Chambers of Commerce.

They may not be all that we could wish but they have no sinister interest except their snobbery to mislead them, and this latter failing may be cultivated into something better by an appeal to their self-esteem. I still think it a mistake your keeping aloof from these bodies.... Depend on it, our only chance of keeping the dominant class in order and preventing great evils is through the union of the industrious and trading classes. The working classes may play their part hereafter, but unless the employers can be kept right now, we have no security against the combination of powerful interests which are ready to coalesce the moment they find the game of Whig and Tory played out.[168]

But Bright was not convinced:

Now, candidly tell me, could you expect that I should present myself at a meeting of merchants in Manchester, after what occurred in 1857, or to endeavour to reason with a body of men, with whom you and I have striven for 20 years without effect, to give them some knowledge of their own interests and to appeal to their self-respect? It would only be to subject myself to further insult to mix with them in the discussion of questions which they cannot comprehend, and I should feel it a deep humiliation to assume a friendship for men whom I hold in utter contempt.[169]

'I observe that you are very savage with the class represented in these bodies,'

---

[165] Cobden to Watkin, 3 Nov. 1860, Watkin, *Alderman Cobden*, 187.

[166] Bradford Chamber of Commerce 10th Annual Report, 1861, pp. 7–9, 22–5. Cobden was duly grateful for their help (ibid. 25).

[167] Boyson, *Ashworth Cotton Enterprise*, 234.

[168] Cobden to Bright, 19 Oct. 1861, Cobden Papers, Add. MS 43,651, fos. 267–8. Cobden particularly regretted that Bright had not been present to deal with an 'offensive' speech made by Laing (on which, see Manchester Chamber of Commerce Papers, Sept. 1861, fos. 343–4).

[169] Bright to Cobden, 24 Oct. 1861, John Bright Papers, Add. MS 43,384, fos. 271–2.

Cobden replied 'and you have good reason to feel so. But *cui bono?* Besides, in your districts, at least, this is not the time to talk of old grudges.'[170]

As we have seen, Cobden practised what he preached. In 1862 he went out of his way to address the Manchester Chamber on the subject of international maritime law. And, interestingly, in the course of his speech he expressed the hope that, instead of forming a new pressure group to deal with this subject, the leading Chambers of Commerce do the organizing themselves. Others 'will join you, and we will make short work of it, I promise you.'[171]

Arguably, Bright was showing, for once, the greater realism. The Chambers of Commerce were not likely to embark upon the kind of controversial political crusade beloved of the old Leaguers. Nevertheless, Bright's attitude to them still seems rather perverse.[172] Shortly after he became President of the Board of Trade, for example, he consented to be the main speaker at the Association's annual dinner. It cannot have been an entirely comfortable occasion for the assembled businessmen. Bright tactlessly told his audience that 'many of the subjects which take up a great deal of time and strength probably after all are not of great importance, and ... there are greater questions which affect the commerce of the country which, for some cause, the Chambers have thought beneath, above, or beyond their province'. Bright went on to recall the way in which the Manchester Chamber had initiated the Corn Law campaign thirty years previously, and observed: 'The Manchester Chamber of Commerce might have gone on discussing some question like the registration of partnerships, and the great question of the repeal of the Corn Laws and all the vast results that followed it might have been postponed for years or for generations.' Some Chamber delegates may have felt flattered at Bright's suggestion that they might become 'truly the saviours of their country'. But his vision of the Association's future role stood little chance of realization, and was likely to cause annoyance.[173]

Bright repeated the offence eight years later when he was invited to unveil a statue of Cobden in the Bradford Wool Exchange. Subsequently, at a lunch given in his honour by Jacob Behrens and attended by local worthies and by outside Association dignitaries, he again urged his audience not to be obsessed with 'small things—the mint, anise and cummin', but to take on responsibilities more worthy of their position, such as a crusade to make Free Trade a global reality.[174] 'Another speech on Free Trade and higher duties of

---

[170] Cobden to Bright, 31 Oct. 1861, Cobden Papers, Add. MS 43,651, fo. 273.

[171] Manchester Chamber of Commerce Papers, Oct. 1862, fos. 418–19. 25 Oct. 1862, *Cobden's Speeches*, 449–61. See Ch. 4.

[172] e.g. he complained that the Chambers of Commerce were not 'legal bodies, elected by somebody' (Bright to Cobden, 24 Oct. 1861, John Bright Papers, Add. MS 43,384, fo. 272).

[173] *The Times*, 25 Feb. 1869.

[174] Ibid., 26 July 1877.

Chambers of Commerce', Bright noted in his diary.[175] But Behrens, writing his memoirs in old age, was still smarting over this speech.[176]

It took Gladstone to show that it was possible to court the Chambers of Commerce while at the same time rebuffing their more absurd pretensions without causing offence. This he did, with great skill, on his famous tour of Lancashire in October 1864, when the Liverpool Chamber made him an honorary member for life. The president of the Chamber, Grainger, in making the award, waxed eloquent on the subject of such organizations, seeing in them 'a form of self-help, part of the genius of the English character'. Grainger went on:

As in classic ages, with which Mr. Gladstone was so familiar, their heroes proudly wore a simple wreath of laurel as a reward for their success, and as in modern days we welcomed our countrymen, illustrious in arts and arms, by conferring on them the franchises of our cities and universities, so now the merchants of Liverpool would honour themselves and him by enrolling in their Chamber of Commerce the conqueror of financial difficulties—(cheers,)—the liberator of commerce—(renewed cheers,)—and the enlightened friend of the working classes (Great applause).

But Gladstone, in his gracious acceptance of the honour, chose his language with circumspection. He cheerfully acknowledged the usefulness—indeed the necessity—of Chambers of Commerce; but he was careful to delineate what he considered the limits of their influence:

It is among you, it is by your mutual communications that opinions are gradually brought into being, under the influence of that light which experience gives you, that they, from time to time, acquire more and more substantive form and power until at length—having passed the test of searching and protracted examination by a free press, the free assemblies, and the free conversations of the country—they reach to the condition of maturity in which the legislature may safely and wisely adopt them.[177]

Gladstone clearly felt that the Chambers of Commerce were too one-sided in their approach for them to be allowed to shape public policy.

NATIONAL ASSOCIATION FOR THE PROMOTION OF SOCIAL SCIENCE

Here an interesting contrast can be drawn between the Chambers of Commerce and the National Association for the Promotion of Social Science,

---

[175] 25 July 1877, in Walling (ed.), *Diaries of Bright*, 397.

[176] *Jacob Behrens*, 68–9. Behrens recalls Bright (erroneously, I think) urging the Chambers to devote their undivided attention to the land question.

[177] *The Times*, 15 Oct. 1864; *Financial Reformer*, Nov. 1864, pp. 537, 539. The following year Edinburgh made Gladstone an honorary member of its Chamber of Commerce (Mackie, *McLaren*, ii. 63). For Gladstone's polite, but cautious, handling of Chamber of Commerce delegates, see his encounter with the Bradfordians (Bradford Chamber of Commerce Minutes, 23 Mar. 1864, fo. 172).

founded in 1857.[178] The relationship between the two bodies was initially quite close. In fact, the ACC arose out of dissatisfaction with the way in which commercial issues had been handled at the Social Science Association's third annual meeting in Bradford in 1859.[179] But this did not lead to a total withdrawal of businessmen from the Social Science Association. On the contrary, for the next decade there was a considerable overlap between the two bodies, with prominent businessmen playing a particularly active part in the 'Social Economy' section of the latter body; moreover, in 1862, its council included such familiar entrepreneurial Radicals as Bazley, Samuel Morley, W. S. Lindsay, and John Benjamin Smith. Further, some Chambers of Commerce were directly affiliated to the Social Science Association, like Birmingham's (whose representative was George Dixon).[180] Nor is it surprising to find Henry Ripley as one of the two 'national' representatives of the Bradford Branch Association. For in the 1860s 'social science', in the eyes of some of its devotees, meant little more than what intelligent businessmen were thinking.

In addition, the annual meetings of the Social Science Association, which took place by turns in the great provincial cities of the country, Sheffeld, Bradford, Glasgow, and so on, provided businessmen with a very effective platform from which to air their views. Thus the Liverpool financial reformers made great efforts to win converts to their cause, papers on the evils of indirect taxation being presented every year between 1858 and 1864, with contributions from Macqueen, Jeffery, Samuel Morley, and Duncan McLaren.[181] Similarly, the 'Jurisprudence' section was an arena in which businessmen could air their grievances against the legal system and propound their schemes on nearly all the issues discussed in this chapter: tribunals of commerce, reform of the Patent Laws, the International Maritime Code, the Bankruptcy Laws, and so on.

Yet, although the big employers were well represented in the National Association for the Promotion of Social Science, they in no way dominated its affairs. The presiding genius of the organization was the former Lord Chancellor, Lord Brougham, who was also the leading light in the Law Amendment Society, founded in 1844, which merged its identity in the Association in 1864;[182] its principal organizer and secretary, George W. Hastings (later a Liberal MP) was also a lawyer. Other professional groups

---

[178] See the important article by Lawrence Goldman, 'The Social Science Association, 1857–1886: A Context for Mid-Victorian Liberalism', *English Historical Review*, 101 (1986), 95–134.

[179] Ilersic and Liddle, *Parliament of Commerce*, 1, 7.

[180] *Transactions of the National Association for the Promotion of Social Science*, 1862, pp. xx–xxi, xxiii.

[181] Goldman, 'Social Science Association', 109; see also Ch. 4. Goldman also shows that prominent members participated in the work of the Administrative Reform Association (pp. 117–18).

[182] Ibid. 96–8. Batzel, 'Legal Monopoly', 194.

like doctors and social investigators played an increasingly important role. According to one historian, 'The commercial bourgeoisie certainly came to the Association but the real work was done by the "service middle class"—the doctors, lawyers and civil servants who were finding positions in an expanding bureaucracy and who supplied the dynamic in late Victorian social investigation and in the formulation of social policy.'[183] Though this slightly exaggerates the role which professional men played in the 1860s, it also contains an essential truth. Edwin Chadwick, Sir John Simon, Kay-Shuttleworth, and Dr Southwood Smith were the kind of public figures who found the Association particularly congenial.

More to the point, the Social Science Association represented an attempt to foster 'social integration'. Its annual meetings often included visits to nearby aristocratic houses, which aimed to bring the middle classes and the landowners to a clearer understanding of each other's point of view. It also provided a national platform for the spokesmen of the trade' union movement. Indeed, the Social Science Association was often referred to as an 'unofficial parliament'.[184]

This emphasis on 'bringing together' helps to explain the Association's initial success. Gladstone held the organization in some respect, and other up-and-coming Liberal politicians like Bruce chose to associate themselves with its activities because they recognized that its purpose was to facilitate the emergence of some sort of informed *consensus* on issues of public importance. In so far as the Association managed to fulfil this ambition, it helped to determine the legislative agenda of the 1870s and 1880s, and even to shape the contents of legislation.[185] Interestingly, the Association went out of its way to draw attention to this aspect of its work, the official record speaking, for example, of how, by reconciling the different points of view, it was entitled to much of the credit for the passing of the 1861 Bankruptcy Act.[186]

Now the Chambers of Commerce had an indispensable *contribution* to make towards the establishment of an enlightened Liberal consensus; but, as an avowedly sectional organization, the Association's contribution needed to be 'balanced' by that of others. This is simply another way of saying that the Social Science Association had a legitimacy in the eyes of the political world to which the Chambers of Commerce could never aspire. Cobden and Bright

---

[183] Goldman, 'Social Science Association', 132. See also S. E. Finer, *The Life and Times of Sir Edwin Chadwick* (1952), 490–1.

[184] Goldman, 'Social Science Association', 112–14, 106–9. J. S. Mill, a member of its governing Council, said: 'It really brings together persons of all opinions consistent with the profession of a desire for social improvement' (ibid. 96–7).

[185] Ibid. 121, 123–7.

[186] *Transactions of the National Association for the Promotion of Social Science*, 1861, p. xxvi. The Law Amendment Society, dedicated to reform of the legal system along Utilitarian lines, was another organization which drew together men from different walks of life, its prominent members including Brougham, Mill, Cobden, and Lowe.

were therefore mistaken in supposing that what hampered the Chambers of Commerce movement was the timidity of its leadership. On the contrary, the success of the Social Science Association shows that, while businessmen could influence the formulation of policy, they could only do so, in normal circumstances, after reaching compromises with other sectional groups (the much-despised lawyers included) possessing interests which intersected with their own. The political culture of mid-Victorian Britain was one in which the idea of an objective 'scientific' solution to social difficulties made a wide appeal: businessmen had to accommodate themselves to that dominant fact and to abandon all notions of imposing *their* solutions on the country's political leaders.

6

Parliamentary Reform

The Reform Bill has disappointed the hopes of the middle classes. It has not secured that purity of governmental administration which was expected as its legitimate consequence. The influence of the aristocracy in the Reformed House of Commons was as overwhelming as in the old borough-mongering Parliament. Jobbery and corruption still inhered in the system. National interests were sacrificed to aristocratic prejudices. Trade and commerce languished in consequence of unequal taxation and unjust monopolies.

(*Liverpool Mercury*, 18 April 1848)

Now no one can justly say after the Repeal of the Corn Laws and the alteration of the Navigation Laws, to say nothing of other changes, that the commercial and manufacturing interest has not effective weight in the House of Commons; and it seems to me that in making changes in our Constitution we ought to look to the great and permanent interests of the country rather than to momentary considerations or individual opinions.

(Lord Palmerston to Lord John Russell, 10 December 1851)

Now, you are told, and some of you persuade yourselves, that the middle-class govern the House of Commons. It is a great delusion. The middle-class element is very small in the House of Commons, and it is getting less and less.... What you want is a greater infusion of the popular element, and you cannot have that unless you have an enlargement of the political rights of the people. And I would advise the middle class not to allow this to be dealt with as a working man's question. The middle class themselves are interested in having a reform of Parliament, in order that their influence should be felt there, for it is not much felt there now, I assure you.

(Cobden, 23 November 1864)

THE REFORM DEBATE, 1848–65

When businessmen sought to carry the reforms they believed to be necessary if commerce and industry were to flourish, they often came up against the hostility of an aristocratic legislature unsympathetic to their endeavours. Inevitably, therefore, many urban Radicals were driven to wonder whether limited reforms were worth pursuing at all until such time as the basis of representation had itself been changed. Joshua Walmsley, a businessman who declined to back the Liverpool Financial Reform Association, gave his reasons in a public letter to his brother-in-law, James Mulleneux, a well-to-do merchant from that city, thus: 'It appears to me that you and your colleagues are proposing to raise a superstructure without a foundation.'[1] ·As we have seen, the same point was also made at the height of the Administrative Reform Association's campaign.

Bright drew a more general moral in 1858 when he said in one of his public speeches: 'The great body of the middle classes, if not excluded, are so arranged that they may be said to be almost altogether defrauded.... Depend upon it, a real measure of Reform is as much wanted for the security and for the welfare of the middle classes of society as it is for the operative classes.' The current House of Commons, he complained, was 'diametrically opposed to all the great principles of political economy, which we and you struggled for so many years to place on our statute books in the shape of a wiser legislation in matters of trade'.[2] Cobden reiterated these sentiments in the last of his speeches to his Rochdale constituents in November 1864.[3]

The majority of the middle-class reformers, however, drew back from initiating a campaign for parliamentary reform because they doubted whether so ambitious an objective was for the moment attainable. The sceptics deployed two lines of argument. Some said that the success of the Anti-Corn Law League had demonstrated that even an aristocratic-dominated Parliament and Government *could* be successfully pressured when 'opinion out of doors' had been mobilized on an issue possessing popular appeal.[4] Others argued that the existing system was on trial; *if* it failed to respond to contemporary business needs, then changes would have to be sought in the franchise requirements, but the time for such agitation had not yet arrived.[5]

As far as businessmen were concerned, the great blemish in the post-1832 settlement was the allocation of seats, which discriminated unfairly against the manufacturing and commercial districts and gave a grotesquely inflated weighting to the agricultural and landed interests. As one angry Radical pointed out, twenty-two small boroughs with a combined population of only 100,000 returned the same number of MPs as London, Liverpool, Leeds, Lancaster, Manchester, Marylebone, Finsbury, Lambeth, Tower Hamlets, Sheffield, and Edinburgh, whose residents numbered over 3,750,000.[6] What

---

[1] *Liverpool Mercury*, 28 Apr. 1848. Moreover, it can be argued that in the 1850s parliamentary reform and administrative reform had not yet separated out into distinct and separate movements (John R. Greenaway, 'Parliamentary Reform and Civil-Service Reform: A Nineteenth-Century Debate Reassessed', *Parliamentary History*, 4 (1985), 168).
[2] 21 Dec. 1858, *Bright's Speeches*, 311, 313.
[3] 23 Nov. 1864, *Cobden's Speeches*, 495–6.
[4] See e.g. letter from W. R. Greg to Cobden, 11 May 1848, Cobden Papers, MCL.
[5] *Liverpool Mercury*, 15 Aug. 1848.
[6] *The Times*, 17 May 1849.

justice was there in a political system which gave Manchester the same number of representatives as Thetford?![7]

This problem, of course, was growing all the time, since, as George Cornewall Lewis noted, there had 'been a great disproportionate increase of the manufacturing and commercial classes since 1831, and ... if the balance was fairly struck then, they must be under-represented, as compared with the agricultural classes, now'.[8] It was this consideration that led Cobden to advise Bright in 1861 to hold back on the subject of parliamentary reform until the next batch of Census returns was published:

I suppose the North of England will shew an immense increase of population and wealth over the rural districts which will be a powerful appeal to the pride and self-respect of Lancashire, Yorkshire etc. not for ever to submit to be governed by the rural villages of Dorset, Bucks etc.—or rather by the accidental owners of these villages.[9]

Moreover, the entrepreneurial Radicals did not rest their case exclusively, or even principally, on arguments about the imbalance of *population*. In presenting his case for parliamentary reform in 1848, Cobden denied that his stand was based 'on any natural right at all'; nor would he employ 'the principle of population': 'I take the ground of property.' Manchester, Cobden pointed out, was assessed to the poor on an annual rental of £1,200,000, while Buckinghamshire was assessed at only £760,000; yet Buckinghamshire returned eleven MPs, as against Manchester's two. What right did a handful of landowners in Buckinghamshire have to tax the people of Manchester? Cobden also thought that a 'fair' system would give the West Riding of Yorkshire thirty Members in place of its current eighteen.[10] Despite his reputation as a demagogue, Bright (in 1858–9 especially) took the same line, invariably filling his speeches with wads of indigestible statistics about the disparity between the income tax yields of the small boroughs and the great cities.[11]

Because the urban Radicals set themselves up as the spokesmen of the populous boroughs, they provoked Conservative politicians into retorting that, if injustice there was, the main sufferers were the counties. As Disraeli said in 1852, the population of north Cheshire was appreciably larger than that of the boroughs of Macclesfield and Stockport (the latter being Cobden's original seat!), which returned twice as many Members.[12] This, though true, was a

---

[7] Dunckley, *Charter of the Nations*, 395. See Bright's reference to the 'great and free constituencies', 15 Mar. 1849, *Bright's Speeches*, 429.

[8] Lewis to James Wilson, 28 Nov. 1858, Barrington, *Servant of All*, ii. 103.

[9] Cobden to Bright, 10 Jan. 1861, Cobden Papers, Add. MS 43,651, fo. 211.

[10] 6 July 1848, *Cobden's Speeches*, 544–5.

[11] See Bright's speech at Glasgow, 21 Dec. 1858, *Bright's Speeches*, 307. See also *The Times*, 2 Dec. 1859.

[12] Maccoby, *English Radicalism*, 324. Perversely, Edward Baines, jun., was arguing in 1841 that 'equal electoral districts' would destroy the influence of the towns by increasing the

mere debating point. The Radicals were not drawing a contrast between boroughs and counties, since they needed no reminding that many boroughs were very small, agricultural in character, and under the effective control of one or more great territorial magnates. The important electoral division fell between the predominantly agricultural and the predominantly urban and industrial constituencies, the latter including county divisions like the West Riding.[13]

All of this mattered to businessmen for a variety of reasons. First, their scope for pursuing a parliamentary career was hampered. As G. C. Lewis, himself neither a businessman nor a Radical, confessed in 1858: 'It is only the larger towns and one or two counties which *regularly* return members of the industrial interest. Nearly all the counties and most of the smaller boroughs return members of the landlord class.'[14] Some middle-class politicians, like Laing, were forced to angle for the nomination of a small borough, with all that that implied in terms of dependence on an aristocratic patron. It also meant that agricultural issues tended to receive more, and commercial issues less, parliamentary attention than might otherwise have been the case. Walter Bagehot made precisely this point in *The English Constitution*: 'The cotton trade or the wine trade', he observed, 'could not, in their maximum of peril, have obtained such aid' as the landed interest were currently receiving through the Cattle Plague Act.[15]

In any case, Radicals were convinced that the 'progressive causes' which they supported drew their strength from the big cities. Thus Cobden was struck during the campaign for Repeal by the fact that Manchester, Birmingham, Glasgow, and Edinburgh were overwhelmingly in favour of reform, yet were 'counterbalanced' by boroughs with tiny electorates.[16] He was thinking along the same lines in 1862 when, writing to Gladstone, he observed:

The only opposition to the increase of our armaments has come from the members of the large and free constituencies. I had actually written a page on this very point showing how Finsbury, Lambeth, Glasgow, Manchester, Birmingham, Dundee, Westminster, Sunderland, etc., etc., etc., were found arrayed against these panics, while the members for aristocratically nominated counties, or territorial pocket boroughs, were always found supporting increased expenditure.[17]

representation of the counties (Edward Baines, *Household Suffrage and Equal Electoral Districts Shown to be Unfavourable to the Good Government and Purity of Elections . . .* (1841)).
[13] Gash has shown that this meant the over-representation of the South (excluding London) and the under-representation of the industrial North (Norman Gash, *Politics in the Age of Peel* (1953), 83).
[14] Lewis to James Wilson, 28 Nov. 1858, Barrington, *Servant of All*, ii. 103.
[15] Bagehot, *English Constitution*, 173. See Henry Ashworth's complaints about this, in letter to J. B. Smith, 14 Feb. 1866, John Benjamin Smith Papers, MS 923.2, S338, fo. 47.
[16] 28 Sept. 1843, *Cobden's Speeches*, 36. See also 8 Feb. 1844, ibid. 68, and Cobden's speeches of 27 Feb. 1846 and 18 Dec. 1849, ibid. 190–1, 213.
[17] Cobden to Gladstone, 26 Apr. 1862, Gladstone Papers, Add. MS 44,136, fo. 186.

Bright often made very similar points.

What neither man seems to have been ready to concede was that many of the big urban constituencies which they proudly presented as the heart of 'modern' Britain had very low levels of enfranchisement and socially exclusive electorates. In Manchester, for example, only about 4 per cent of the adult population had the parliamentary vote.[18] Or was it that very circumstance which made Cobden feel that they were especially well endowed with 'intelligence' as well as with wealth?

Finally, as Bagehot shrewdly recognized, a system which gave too little weight 'to the growing districts of the country and too much to the stationary' was a standing insult to manufacturers.

The great capitalists, Mr. Bright and his friends, believe they are sincere in asking for more power for the working man, but, in fact, they very naturally and very properly want more power for themselves. They cannot endure... that a rich, able manufacturer should be a less man than a small stupid squire.[19]

Why, then, did the urban Radicals (recognizing that their ranks were split on the question of extending the suffrage) not concentrate their efforts on securing a redistribution of seats? After all, in 1859 Bright was calling the question of distribution 'the very soul of the question of reform';[20] and in 1848 Cobden had observed that the redistribution of seats was 'the most essential change of any, for even with the present suffrage we might get on pretty well if the large towns had their fair share of the representation'.[21]

The difficulty resided in the fact that the precedent of 1832 had dictated that a redistribution measure would normally accompany a Reform Bill but could not be brought forward in isolation. It must also be remembered that redistribution would have aroused more opposition *within* the House of Commons than any other kind of parliamentary change, since the whole point of the exercise was to disfranchise many of the constituencies currently returning Members—something which did much to destroy Russell's Reform Scheme in 1854.[22] 'The House', Bright confessed to Cobden in 1857, 'will not vote any honest redistribution of seats—so many Members being affected by it, and their constituencies naturally resisting it.' From this he drew the deduction that franchise extension should take priority.[23]

---

[18] See Return of the Several Parliamentary Cities and Boroughs...', LVII (1866); 'Return Showing the Number of Electors in English and Welsh Boroughs in 1859–60...', LV (1860). See Gatrell, 'Commercial Middle Class', Ch. 3.

[19] Bagehot, *English Constitution*, 175.

[20] Frances Elma Gillespie, *Labor and Politics in Britain: 1850–1867* (Durham, NC, 1927), 153.

[21] Cobden to G. Wilson, 11 May 1848, George Wilson Papers.

[22] Southgate, *Passing of the Whigs*, 315–16.

[23] Bright to Cobden, 16 Apr. 1857, John Bright Papers, Add. MS 43,384, fo. 94. Unfortunately, Bright ignored his own advice eighteen months later: Angus Hawkins, *Parliament, Party, and the Art of Politics in Britain, 1855–1859* (Basingstoke and London, 1987), 158.

Throughout the 1840s and 1850s the Radicals concentrated, therefore, on a campaign to increase the influence of urban interests within a structurally unchanged electoral system. Nor was this by any means a totally hopeless enterprise. For whereas the 1831 Reform Bill had explicitly excluded from the county franchise those non-resident borough freeholders whose property was worth more than £10, the Whig Cabinet subsequently backtracked on this point.[24]

As a result, the so-called outvoters, many of them Dissenting townsmen with Radical convictions, were able to exercise a significant influence in several county constituencies. That this was not a negligible factor can be seen from the case of the West Riding (which Cobden represented between 1847 and 1857), where, according to one calculation, there were several thousand Liberal 'outvoters'.[25] By 1866 possibly as many as one-fifth of county votes derived from borough freehold qualifications.[26] Moreover, as we have seen, the number of such voters could be increased by the organized purchase of freeholds. In addition, thousands of urban dwellers in *un*enfranchised towns were obviously voting in county constituencies. Such urban 'infiltration' much annoyed the landed interest, as it was meant to do, and the Conservative Party later tried to put a stop to it.[27]

As far as the entrepreneurial Radicals were concerned, perhaps the most promising strategy for weakening the aristocratic hold over most of the counties and the small boroughs was to press for the secret Ballot. Cobden spoke on occasion of organizing a crusade on this issue, comparable to the campaign once run by the Anti-Corn Law League.[28]

The formal leader of the Ballot campaign, however, was not Cobden, but the enigmatic MP Francis Henry Berkeley. Only two points about his activities need be made here. First, the Ballot Society, founded in 1853 under Berkeley's leadership, drew heavily upon what Kinzer has called 'London men of business associated with the political radicalism which had long characterised the metropolis': men like Sir James Duke, a coal factor and insurance broker, and Wygram Crawford, a partner in a firm of East Indian merchants

---

[24] Smith (ed.), *Salisbury on Politics*, 201 n.

[25] F. M. L. Thompson, 'Whigs and Liberals in the West Riding, 1830–1860', *English Historical Review*, 74 (1959), 217 (9,288 out of an electorate of 37,513 voters).

[26] Smith, *Second Reform Bill*, 97. Seymour, on the other hand, plays down its importance (Charles Seymour, *Electoral Reform in England and Wales* (New Haven, Conn., 1915), 81–2).

[27] Including Palmerston: Palmerston to Russell, 10 Dec. 1851, Gooch (ed.), *Later Correspondence of Russell*, i. 216. The Conservatives' 1859 Bill aimed to take 90,000 urban voters out of the counties (Smith, *Second Reform Bill*, 42; Seymour, *Electoral Reform*, 273). Cranborne was still complaining about the situation in the 1860s (Smith (ed.), *Salisbury on Politics*, 200–1). But the 'outvoters' were never disenfranchised before 1918, though Disraeli *tried* to do something about it in 1859 and in 1867 (Seymour, *Electoral Reform*, 272–4).

[28] Cobden to Walmsley, n.d. (late 1852?), in Walmsley, *Life*, 283. Cobden to J. B. Smith, 26 Oct. 1852, John Benjamin Smith Papers, MS 923.2, S345, fo. 10.

and a director of the Bank of England.[29] Samuel Morley also contributed to
its funds. Secondly, the main argument deployed by Berkeley was that, under
a system of open hustings, one-third of county voters were deterred from
exercising the franchise at all, while those who did so were often put under
intolerable pressure by their landlords. Freehold owners, said Berkeley,
should be protected in the exercise of their vote, just as they would be in the
use of a carriage they had bought.[30]

Such arguments naturally proved attractive to the Manchester School, and
Cobden, Bright, and George Wilson all joined the Ballot Society as ordinary
members. Cobden, in particular, had always been obsessed with the need to
protect farmers against 'landlord intimidation'.[31] *Employer* intimidation in the
big cities was another matter. Cobden and Bright obviously deplored the
practice,[32] but they believed, with some justification, that most of the urban
constituencies in which large factories were located were far too populous to
be 'managed' in this way, even should the attempt be made. (However, given a
restricted franchise, many working men *favoured* open voting. It not only
enabled them to supplement their income from bribes; it also offered them
a way of exercising *some* pressure on their superiors, which is why the
metropolitan Radicals were against the Ballot as an *alternative* to franchise
extension.[33])

In addition, a reform that promised to reduce the turmoil and disorder
which characterized elections clearly had much to recommend it to respectable
middle-class opinion. And finally, as the Radical businessman William
Williams pointed out, the principle of the Ballot 'had been long approved by
vast numbers of the middle classes of society'; he had in mind bodies like
charitable institutions, scientific societies, the Bank of England, and the East
Indies Company, all of which employed this device.[34] Cobden, too, refuted
the standard objection that the Ballot was 'un-English' with the argument that

there is more voting by ballot in England than in all the countries in Europe. And why?
Because you are a country of associations and clubs,—of literary, scientific, and
charitable societies,—of infirmaries and hospitals,—of great joint-stock companies,—
of popularly governed institutions; and you are always voting by ballot in these
institutions.

He also reminded the House 'that railway directors [were] elected every

---

[29] Bruce L. Kinzer, *The Ballot Question in Nineteenth Century English Politics* (New York, 1982),
62.

[30] Parl. Deb., 3rd ser., vol. 118, 357–8: 8 July 1851.

[31] See 6 July 1848, *Cobden's Speeches*, 547.

[32] e.g. Cobden, 4 Dec. 1851, ibid. 559.

[33] See Ashworth's evidence to the Grey Committee, Report from Select Committee of House
of Lords on what would be the Probable Increase . . ., LXXXVII (1860), q. 3551. Kinzer, *Ballot
Question*, 47, 59–60.

[34] Evans, *William Williams*, 36.

year'.[35] No more impeccably middle-class way of conducting electoral contests, it seemed, could possibly have been devised.

But the *central* purpose of the Ballot question was to strike a further blow at 'feudalism'. 'Depend upon it,' Cobden told Walmsley in September 1852, 'the powers that be will give universal suffrage sooner than the ballot. You cut out the very heart of the aristocratic system in applying the principle of secret voting.'[36] Yet this in turn raises an interesting conundrum. At the very time that Cobden was writing his letter to Walmsley, he was also holding aloof from Joseph Hume's campaign to extend the franchise, using the argument that, in current circumstances, such a reform was 'impractical'.[37] Now, as Hinde comments, it seems both perverse and inconsistent to couple this argument with a commendation of the Ballot as an effective way of smashing landlord power. For why, on Cobden's own premisses, should the House of Commons, as at present constituted, be any more likely to concede the Ballot than to extend the suffrage? If open voting did, in truth, lie 'at the very heart of the aristocratic system', the aristocracy could presumably be counted upon to reject the Ballot.[38] And throughout the 1850s and 1860s that was indeed what happened, with Palmerston and Russell offering constant opposition to Berkeley's annual motion.[39]

This takes us to the crux of the matter: would the interests of the entrepreneurial Radicals benefit or suffer if the working classes were entrusted with power? The issue long continued to be a divisive one. The activities of the Complete Suffrage Movement, for example, had threatened to disrupt the League in the early 1840s.[40] Later, as we have seen, Cobden and Bright found themselves in acute disagreement during 1848 over the relative priority of franchise and financial reform,[41] a disagreement which was resumed in 1858–9, when once again Bright took the more 'democratic' and Cobden the more cautious stance.

The arguments were nicely balanced. In favour of the idea of franchise extension it could be claimed that no substantial reform of the fiscal system or of the civil administration would occur until the parliamentary system itself had been changed. Moreover, how could working-class opinion be effectively

---

[35] 6 July 1848, *Cobden's Speeches*, 547.

[36] 25 Sept. 1852, Walmsley, *Life*, 275.

[37] Hume, by contrast, thought the Ballot impracticable (Ronald K. Huch and Paul R. Ziegler, *Joseph Hume: The People's MP* (Philadelphia, 1985), 156).

[38] Hinde, *Richard Cobden*, 237. But, as Cobden argued, the Lords could not *trim* the Ballot; they had to either accept or reject it (Cobden to J. B. Smith, 26 Oct. 1852, John Benjamin Smith Papers, MS 923.2, S345, fo. 10).

[39] Kinzer, *Ballot Questions*, 68–9.

[40] The complete suffrage movement had included Joseph Sturge, John Bright, and Lawrence Heyworth, among other businessmen (Alexander Wilson, 'The Suffrage Movement', in Patricia Hollis (ed.), *Pressure from Without in Early Victorian England* (1974), 84–91).

[41] See Ch. 2.

mobilized on *any* reform issue as long as the middle-class Radicals refused to offer them any 'reward' for their assistance? Well might Joshua Walmsley argue that, without a commitment to franchise extension, the calls for financial reform would be seen by working men as mere 'selfishness' and would be boycotted accordingly.[42] As one speaker observed to a Sheffield meeting on administrative reform attended by class-conscious working men: 'The middle classes called on the working classes to assist them whenever they wanted anything (Cheers) . . . and now something was needed for them.'[43]

Some of the entrepreneurial Radicals believed that an enlargement of the franchise was desirable for other reasons, too. It would, they said, be an important step towards the abolition of corruption: 'The smaller boroughs are all held by the aristocracy in *fee simple*,' argued the Liverpool reformers. 'Boroughs *will* be bought so long as boroughs *can* be bought. The sole guarantee for the incorruptibility of a constituency is, that it shall be so large as to render its purchase an impossibility.'[44] Manchester's size and the impersonality of its social relations certainly seem to have acted as a barrier against the exercise of employer intimidation.[45]

Some businessmen went further, and called for the re-creation of a popular alliance, linking working with middle class, such as had helped carry the 1832 Reform Act. This was important, they said, since, in its absence, working men would be left to pursue their own class interests in isolation.

Let us not commit the folly of separating classes—of arraying shopkeepers and others of the middle order against *all* who subsist by weekly wages . . . [wrote the *Manchester Examiner*]. Without this community of feeling, we are by no means safe . . . Let the working classes feel that our feudal Establishment, our feudal aristocracy, our territorial laws, our army and navy, the grand sources of family aggrandizement, are all destined to be thoroughly and tranquilly reformed; and with that conviction on their minds, our intelligent operatives will become the surest guardians of future peace and order.[46]

Parliamentary reform, in short, could be presented as a device for maintaining middle-class authority and leadership over the lower orders.[47]

Now, it is hardly surprising that many politically conscious working men, especially Chartists and ex-Chartists, were by no means overwhelmed with gratitude at the prospect of being 'helped' in this spirit. Linton, for example, could sneeringly attack the middle-class Radicals as 'the party of financial and

---

[42] *Liverpool Mercury*, 28 Apr. 1848.
[43] *Sheffield Independent*, 23 June 1855.
[44] *Liverpool Mercury*, 30 Jan. 1849. Cobden agreed: 18 Aug. 1859, *Cobden's Speeches*, 587.
[45] Gatrell, 'Commercial Middle Class', 133–5.
[46] *Manchester Examiner*, 11 Mar. 1848.
[47] Cobden himself sometimes used this argument: 4 Dec. 1851, *Cobden's Speeches*, 562; also 23 Nov. 1864, ibid. 496. But W. R. Greg disputed the wisdom of this strategy, *Edinburgh Review*, 96 (Oct. 1852), 461–2.

parliamentary reformers, the infamous-peace party, the free-traders *in labour*, the mill-owning evaders of the factory-relief bill, the money lords, the comfortable Atheists on "Change".[48] Nothing beneficial to the working man, many ex-Chartists thought, could be looked for from this quarter.

Yet it was precisely the existence of this kind of class feeling which turned some of the entrepreneurial Radicals *against* any significant enlargement of the franchise—at least if this meant giving so many working men the vote that the existing electorate would be 'swamped'. The *Liverpool Mercury*, itself an advocate of a more democratic franchise, admitted that demagogues like Feargus O'Connor had done immense damage by spouting about 'the eternal and indissoluble antagonism of the interests of labour and capital' and by denouncing

merchants, manufacturers, and traders as a banded league of plunderers and villains, not to be conciliated but extirpated; it was not in flesh and blood that they, the middle classes, should agitate for a wider franchise. Aristocratic rule galled them; democratic rule promised to devour them.[49]

Cobden himself was almost certainly frightened away from the movement for parliamentary reform in 1848 by O'Connor's attempts to insinuate himself into the agitation of the London Radicals and by the later involvement of some Chartists in the Parliamentary and Financial Reform Association.[50]

Nearly all Radical businessmen believed in an identity of interests between capital and labour. This *could* be used as an argument for franchise extension, but it equally well served the opposite purpose. For if, as the leaders of the Birmingham Political Union had urged in the 1830s, the productive capitalists were already effectively 'representing' those whom they employed, what need was there for further change?[51] In practice, many of the entrepreneurial Radicals were anyhow inclined to caution because they feared that few working men were yet 'educated' to the point where they could fully understand the lessons of political economy and hence the nature of their own long-term interests. Thus, prior to 1860 or so, working-class calls for further factory legislation tended to be interpreted as signs of political immaturity, as did the development of trade unionism, which almost all adherents of the

[48] See Gillespie, *Labor and Politics*, 97. See the outbursts of Harney and Linton. Bright's hostility to factory legislation was often held against him (ibid. 87–8, 108, 97).

[49] *Liverpool Mercury*, 18 Apr. 1848.

[50] Wilson, 'Suffrage Movement', 95–8. Bright's attitude was more complex. He shared Cobden's view of O'Connor, but thought that Chartist riots did convince *some* middle-class people of the desirability of reform (Bright to G. Wilson, 12 June 1848, George Wilson Papers). Cobden's view had always been an 'instrumental' one: 'We must not turn the League into a suffrage party until there is something to be gained by it' (Cobden to Absalom Watkin, 11 Mar. 1842, Watkin, *Alderman Cobden*, 90).

[51] Clive Behagg, *Politics and Production in the Early Nineteenth Century* (1990), 102. See also ibid. 195–7.

Manchester School regarded as an economic fallacy rather on a par with Protectionism.

This explains why so many Radicals were attracted by the freehold purchase movement. Its beauty was that it seemed to provide a foolproof mechanism for ensuring that those who joined the political community had 'internalized' the value system of capitalism. 'What a privilege it is', enthused Cobden in 1844, 'for a working man to put his hands in his pockets and walk up and down opposite his own freehold, and say—"This is my own; I worked for it, and I have won it." '[52] To bring about such a situation would be desirable, he thought, quite apart from the contribution which the movement was making to a repeal of the Corn Laws: 'It is to that man of all others that I would wish to entrust the franchise.'[53] So delighted was Cobden with the notion of the members of the various freehold societies thriftily working out their own political emancipation that his normally sound judgement became clouded. For many years he continued to overestimate, quite absurdly, the political potential of the freehold movement, which never looked as if it could serve as a viable *alternative* to franchise extension.[54]

What all this implies is that Cobden, like most business Radicals, far from seeing the vote as a 'right', wanted to make its possession conditional upon acceptance of the policies which men of his class thought 'rational'. Financial reform, he told Bright in 1848, was needed in order to educate the wider public on such questions as armaments and colonies and so prepare them for a later extension of the franchise: 'There is a fearful mass of prejudice and ignorance to dispel upon these subjects,' he contended, 'and whilst these exist you may get a Reform of Parlt., but you will not get a Reformed policy.'[55] Indeed, Cobden saw that there was a risk that the 'Tory Aristocracy' might sponsor universal suffrage in the hope of taking 'their chance in an appeal to the ignorance and vice of the country, against the opinions of the teetotalers, non-conformists, and rational radicals, who will constitute 9/10ths of our phalanx of 40/- freeholders'.[56] Towards the end of his life Cobden modified his position. But even in his highly 'democratic' speech to his Rochdale

---

[52] 11 Dec. 1844, *Cobden's Speeches*, 123. The League argued that freehold purchase held out 'a hope, promise, and incitement of the most desirable and elevating description', and called it a 'means of self-emancipation' (18 Jan., 15 Nov. 1845, cited in Hamer, *Politics of Electoral Pressure*, 81, 85).

[53] 27 Feb. 1846, *Cobden's Speeches*, 194.

[54] See Cobden to Bright, 22 Jan. 1849, Cobden Papers, Add. MS 43,649, fo. 136. Prest, *Politics*, 110. Bright was more realistic (Bright to G. Wilson, 18 Sept. 1849, George Wilson Papers).

[55] Cobden to Bright, 23 Dec. 1848, Cobden Papers, Add. MS 43,649, fo. 116. For Cobden's views on 'the *floating mischief* in the country', see Cobden to Baines, 13 Apr. 1848, Baines Papers.

[56] Cobden to Bright, 1 Oct. 1849, Cobden Papers, Add. MS 43,649, fo. 144. For an example of Cobden's persistent tendency to link the franchise question to retrenchment, see Cobden to Watkin, 10 Dec. 1862, Watkin, *Alderman Cobden*, 195.

constituents in 1864, Cobden's faith in franchise reform owed much to a conviction that working men, if enfranchised, now had enough intelligence to take a strong stand for economy and retrenchment.[57]

Thus, the extension of the 'franchise' was seen by most Liberal businessmen as something of a gamble, to be undertaken or avoided as circumstances dictated. But might it not be possible to limit the risk by erecting 'safeguards' against democratic excess? W. R. Greg, who had been reduced to something like panic by Lord John Russell's mild reform proposals of 1852 (Bright thought they would do more harm than good), turned his attention to schemes for a 'taxation franchise'—though he felt that a necessary preliminary to this would be 'a fixed and determinate fiscal system' which no Government was likely to establish.[58] In an article in the *Edinburgh Review* in October 1852, Greg again floated this idea, only to reject it, before going on to suggest a whole range of 'fancy franchises' which would *'get'* at' the 'select' men among the artisan class 'without enfranchising the mass'.[59]

But there is little evidence that this sort of solution had much appeal to Liberal business MPs. True, Samuel Laing was arguing in 1866 for provisions that would reward intelligence and thrift, such as a special vote for those who owned realized property in a bank worth £30 or £40.[60] But few other major businessmen followed his lead.[61]

One reason for this was undoubtedly the fact that what was later known as a 'lateral' extension of the franchise had quickly become associated in everyone's mind with the political enemies of entrepreneurial Radicalism. It was actually Lord John Russell who had first floated the idea of 'fancy franchises' in his abortive 1852 Reform Bill, which included provisions for conferring the vote on men who paid 40s. a year in direct taxes but who would not otherwise

---

[57] 23 Nov. 1864, *Cobden's Speeches*, 493–6. In any case, it is arguable that many working-class Radicals had always favoured these goals.

[58] Greg to Gladstone, 4 Sept. 1852, Gladstone Papers, Add. MS 44,372, fo. 291. See Greg's other famous letters on this subject to Cobden and Gladstone, in Fraser, *Urban Politics*, 249–50, 262; also Greg to Cobden, 11 May 1848, Cobden Papers, Manchester Record Office. W. R. Greg to Gladstone, 4 Apr. 1852, Gladstone Papers, Add. MS 44,371, fo. 283.

[59] Greg, *Edinburgh Review* (Oct. 1852), 473–4, 478; Greg wanted an electoral system which was both restrictive and open ('Conservative Reform'), and which would also achieve finality: 'We cannot afford to have a perpetual series of Reform Bills' (ibid. 507). He suggested the establishment of 26 'National Constituencies', for which 'crotchety' men of eminence might choose to stand (ibid. 497–500).

[60] Parl. Deb., 3rd ser., vol. 182, 83: 12 Mar. 1866.

[61] But on 31 May 1865 the mayor of Burnley, obviously a businessman, wrote to George Wilson, suggesting a vote for everyone paying income tax (George Wilson Papers). And the sugar refiner R. A. Macfie, the future Liberal MP, delivered a paper to the Social Science Congress in which he proposed a 'plural' system whereby votes could be based on a variety of qualifications, including occupation of business premises and payment of income tax, as well as on a household franchise for those aged 24 or over and a freehold franchise for those over 40 (*Transactions of the National Association for the Promotion of Social Science*, 1865, p. 261).

qualify: mainly professional men.[62] Russell's equally abortive 1854 Bill added yet further categories: those earning a salary of £100 a year, paid quarterly; those drawing £10 a year from the Funds, bank stock, or East India Company shares; graduates; and depositors of £50 in savings banks for three consecutive years were all to qualify for the parliamentary vote. 'Fancy franchises' reappeared in Disraeli's reform measure of 1859; they included a vote for persons with investments yielding £10 per annum or with £60 in savings banks.[63]

Though they again featured in Disraeli's 1867 Bill, none of these attempts to provide 'safeguards' against the dangers of 'democracy' made much progress. They probably dropped out of favour partly because their 'novelty' shocked the House, partly because they ran into administrative problems: for example, the savings banks did not keep adequate registers of those holding deposits with them, and such lists as they did possess failed to distinguish between males and females.[64] Also, like the Unionist proposals during the Constitutional Crisis of 1910–11, these novel suggestions seemed a more alarming departure from traditional constitutional practice than the straightforward Radical solution. Perhaps, too, 'safeguards' of this sort simply drew attention to the dangers of a further extension of the franchise. If the working classes were so little to be trusted, should they be given the vote at all? This objection must have occurred to the entrepreneurial Radicals themselves.

The one successful move to counteract the effect of 'democracy' was the 'minority vote', which eventually became part of the 1867 settlement, at the instigation of the elderly Russell. But, interestingly, *The Economist*, which feared that any significant extension of the vote must damage business interests, had come out for this device several years earlier, believing that it alone could ensure that all classes were given a *fair share* of political power.[65] The merit of the 'minority vote', according to *The Economist*, was that it would enable 'the capitalists' in the large cities to carry the third Member in the three-Member constituencies, thereby avoiding the absurd situation of the work-people of a single wealthy contractor or manufacturer having 'a voice in the constitution equal to the united voices of all the merchants in the Royal Exchange'.[66]

---

[62] Smith, *Second Reform Bill*, 33. Earlier Russell had suggested to the Cabinet that the various trades and professions in each borough should form themselves into electoral colleges (ibid. 32). Thomas F. Gallacher, 'The Second Reform Movement, 1848–1867', *Albion*, 12 (1980), 153.

[63] Ibid. 34–7.

[64] Ibid. 167, 207, 151.

[65] *The Economist*, 17 Nov. 1860, p. 1260. *The Economist* much preferred this scheme to one of separate electoral rolls for different classes of voter, as advocated by a Manchester man of business Alderman Pochin (7 Apr. 1860, p. 367).

[66] Ibid., 3 Feb. 1866, p. 124 (each voter would have had only one vote).

Greg and *The Economist* were at the most pessimistic end of the spectrum of business opinion; as we shall see, not all the entrepreneurial Radicals were so alarmist. But the extent of the nervousness among the business community was quite sufficient to persuade Cobden of the need for circumspection. Parliamentary reform, he told Bright in 1848, 'would be working against wind and tide';[67] and two years later, in a letter to Samuel Morley, he criticized Walmsley for moving far beyond the natural speed of the middle classes.[68] Cobden's attempts to restrain the more impetuous Bright, particularly in 1848, have often been described. 'The citadel of privilege in this country is so terribly strong owing to the concentrated masses of property in the hands of the comparatively few', he explained, 'that we cannot hope to assail it with success unless with the help of the propertied classes in the middle ranks of society, and by raising up a portion of the working class to become members of a propertied order.'[69] Perhaps the nature of Cobden's disagreement with Bright emerges most clearly in a letter he wrote to their mutual friend William Hargreaves in April 1860:

The middle class, having the franchise, will never be very enthusiastic for a change which mainly lessens their power by dividing it among others. It is not in human nature to wish such a change, except once in a century when a generous fit comes over mankind in a moment of crisis, and *great common danger*. However, we must do what we can. Always taking care not to throw away the support of the majority of the middle class, *without whose cooperation no further reform can be effected*. They may gradually be brought to the side of those who are advocating an extension of the franchise, if we do not frighten them.[70]

How easy it still was to 'frighten' the middle class became apparent when, in the course of his attempts to 'get up' an agitation over parliamentary reform in 1858–9, John Bright inadvertently alienated many of the very people whose support he should have been enlisting by delivering a big speech at Birmingham (on 27 October 1858), the *tone* of which confirmed his reputation as a dangerous extremist.[71]

---

[67] Cobden to Bright, 22 Dec. 1848, Cobden Papers, Add. MS 43,649, fo. 109.

[68] Cobden to Morley, 19 Feb. 1850, Cobden Papers, Add. MS 43,668, fos. 66–7. To Smith he expressed the view that Walmsley and other metropolitan Radicals seemed 'to be landed in a mess of Chartism and red republicanism' (Cobden to J. B. Smith, 4 Mar. 1852, John Benjamin Smith Papers, MS 923.2, S345, fo. 4).

[69] Gillespie, *Labor and Politics*, 85. See correspondence in George Wilson Papers, from which it is clear that on this issue Bright had aligned himself with Walmsley.

[70] Cobden to Hargreaves, 30 Apr. 1860, Cobden Papers, Add. MS 43,655, fos. 112–13. In 1865 the *Bradford Observer* was right to be irritated at the National Reform Union's claims that Cobden, were he alive, would have endorsed their household suffrage programme (29 June 1865).

[71] Hawkins, *Parliament*, 158–9. It also involved a denunciation of the land system, the House of Lords, and the Anglican Establishment. Gallacher, 'Second Reform Movement', 162.

Yet, certainly in 1858–9, and arguably in 1866–7 too, Bright's position on parliamentary reform was essentially a very moderate one. He was certainly not advocating universal manhood suffrage; even in 1866 a £7 rating franchise would probably have satisfied him.[72] It is significant that the heart of Bright's proposal in the late 1850s was Redistribution and the Ballot. Consequently, Russell's private intimation that if these two items were abandoned, official Whiggery might be prepared to take up Reform, filled him with amused contempt. 'What is reform without a redistribution of seats and the Ballot?' was Bright's private comment to Cobden.[73] Not only did Bright pitch his arguments mainly at a middle-class constituency, he also pointed to his own position as an employer of labour to mock the fears of his opponents: 'I have a business which is more liable to injury from any disturbance of the public peace than your property,' he reminded the Commons in March 1859.[74]

By 1860 Bright had discovered yet another reason why the middle classes would benefit from an enlargement of the franchise. Because of their electoral exclusion, he argued, working men were in ignorance of the 'true' cause of their oppression, namely, 'the ruling class' and all its works; and so they lashed out blindly at members of the employing class with whom they came into daily contact. This sort of 'false consciousness', which made it impossible for working men to be instructed as to the true relationship between capital and labour, would continue, he warned, until such time as a Reform Bill had been carried.[75]

But Walter Bagehot, commenting on Bright's reform proposals, got beneath these surface arguments to what was really animating the Radical tribune. In an article published in January 1859 in the *National Review*, he pointed out that Bright's particular interest was Redistribution and that if this demand could be met on the basis of the current franchise, the Manchester School would clearly stand to benefit. But most societies, observed Bagehot, had what he called an 'uneasy class', which generalized its own dissatisfactions into a claim for 'equal rights for all mankind':

We cannot fail to observe that the new business-wealth of the present day (of which Mr. Bright is the orator and mouth-piece) has a tendency to democracy for the same reason. Such a symptom in the body politic is an indication of danger. So energetic a class as the creators of Manchester need to be conciliated; their active intelligence has rights which assuredly it will make heard. The great political want of our day is a

---

[72] Maurice Cowling, *1867: Disraeli, Gladstone and Revolution* (Cambridge, 1967), 293–5; see also discussion in Vincent, *British Liberal Party*, 215–27. The details of Bright's 1858 reform proposals had been worked out by his brother-in-law, the Edinburgh businessman Duncan McLaren. 'With your *head* and my *tongue* we will make something of it', Bright wrote on 15 November (Mackie, *McLaren*, ii. 147–8).

[73] Bright to Cobden, 24 Oct. 1858, John Bright Papers, Add. MS 43,384, fo. 142.

[74] Parl. Deb., 3rd ser., vol. 153, 791: 25 Mar. 1859.

[75] Cited in *The Economist*, 17 Nov. 1860, pp. 1257–60. How could this theory be reconciled with the story of industrial relations in Australia, *The Economist* pertinently asked?

capitalist conservatism. If we could enlist the intelligent creators of wealth in the ranks of those who would give their due influence to intelligence and property, we should have almost secured the stability of our Constitution.[76]

Had Parliament possessed the good sense to act on Bagehot's advice, the reform crisis of 1866–7 might never have developed in the way it did.

THE REFORM CRISIS, 1865–7

The complicated story of the Reform Act controversy of 1865–7 has often been told. Here the only purpose is to examine events from the perspective of those Radicals concerned with the maximization of the interests of the business community.

The first point to note is that the middle-class Radicals did not abandon their preoccupation with Redistribution during these years. Indeed, Bright frankly admitted in 1857 that 'it would be easy to double the number of electors, and at the same time to increase the aristocratic influence of Parliament'.[77] Admittedly, in 1866 he was encouraging the Whigs to defer introduction of a Redistribution measure, which he knew from bitter experience would be difficult to carry through the Commons; but this was a mere tactical device, since, as in 1858–9, Bright clearly hoped that a reformed Parliament might later consent to a truly 'advanced' reallocation of seats. In fact, he let the cat out of the bag when he privately admitted that Redistribution could 'be dealt with much better in a Parliament elected on the wider suffrage'.[78]

And even if Bright's stand on reform *had* shifted to some extent since 1859, his old League comrade George Wilson, now a leading light in the National Reform Union, was continuing to sing the old middle-class tunes: Manchester, he told a big public meeting in 1865, ought to have eighty-four MPs if the small boroughs retained their representation, a conclusion which he reached by comparing not only their populations but also their property values and income tax contributions: 'Where, then, was the "fair share" of the representation of property and income?', he asked.[79] This, of course, was exactly what Bright had been saying in 1858–9.

But an opponent of reform, Samuel Laing, a member of the 'Adullamite Cave', also chose to highlight the Redistribution issue when he criticized the

---

[76] Walter Bagehot, 'Parliamentary Reform', *National Review*, Jan. 1859, in *Collected Works*, vi. 234–5.

[77] Smith, *Second Reform Bill*, 22.

[78] Bright to Villiers, 27 July 1865, cited in Trevelyan, *Life of Bright*, 345. When, probably for reasons of expediency, Bright later affected to attach little importance to Redistribution, he drew upon his head the execration of the Liberal business MP Frederick Doulton (MP for Lambeth); see Parl. Deb., 3rd ser., vol. 182, 1715: 19 Apr. 1866. At a rally in Leeds in Oct. 1866 Bright made much of the grievance of the small boroughs 'in which the middle classes themselves are not independent' (*Bradford Observer*, 11 Oct. 1866).

[79] *Reynolds's Newspaper*, 21 May 1865.

abortive 1866 Bill for going about parliamentary reform in entirely the wrong way. Laing argued in the House on 12 March 1866 that the Returns recently laid before the House suggested that the case for lowering the franchise was much weaker than had previously been supposed, since it had now been demonstrated that as many as 40 per cent of the electorate in Nottingham and Leicester were working class. Yet the case for Redistribution, he said, was extremely strong.[80] Significantly, it was Laing himself who moved two important Redistribution amendments to Disraeli's Bill in 1867, the second of which would have given a third Member to six large boroughs at the expense of the grouped small boroughs.[81] Disraeli rejected this amendment on the grounds that it would give undue influence to commerce and industry![82] In a way, then, whatever their other disagreements, Bright and Laing had rather more in common with one another on the Redistribution question than either did with the Conservative Ministry.

The difference between Bright and people like Laing really arose from their different perceptions of the moral state of the working class. Militant trade union action had once again awoken fears in some quarters as to the consequences of entrusting power to working men, and, incidentally, had provided a *new* argument in favour of the Ballot: that it might usefully serve to protect *working-class electors* against 'trade union tyranny' in the event of a further franchise extension.[83] Pessimists like Lowe and Laing could still find the evidence they needed to sustain their suspicious view of working-class life.

The railway magnate Laing, in fact, merits closer attention. Unlike most members of the 'Cave', he did not come from landed society. True, he was now calling himself a follower of Palmerston. But the main thrust of his arguments was not a Whiggish insistence on the need to maintain the 'territorial Constitution'. What really worried Laing was the possibility that credulous working men, enfranchised before they had achieved maturity, would fall under the influence of quack 'political economists' who claimed that poverty and crime could be ameliorated by Act of Parliament. In no time at all, he warned, such a 'democratic' system of politics would land the country with an income tax of half a crown in the pound on income derived from property. Why run such risks? 'Industry had been made as free as the wind. All the trammels upon it had been removed: the food, clothing, and shelter of the people were all untaxed.' He observed that he had himself

been more allied to the doctrines of free-trade and non-intervention than the questions of pure politics; and he confessed he could not feel at ease as to the maintenance of those principles in a Parliament elected by a numerical majority of working men. As

---

[80] Parl. Deb., 3rd ser., vol. 182, 77: 12 Mar. 1866.
[81] See his speech of 26 Mar. 1867, ibid., vol. 186, 618–22.
[82] Smith, *Second Reform Bill*, 216–17.
[83] See Gillespie, *Labor and Politics*, 177.

they approached universal suffrage and manhood suffrage, the working classes were found to become Protectionists in feeling and practice, [as in the USA and in the Australian colonies]. That was natural enough, for it required foresight, knowledge, and education to induce a community to sacrifice Protection to higher and wider interests.[84]

The same set of attitudes can be seen in Robert Lowe. Admittedly, by agreeing to sit as Liberal MP for Lord Lansdowne's 'pocket borough' of Calne, Lowe allowed himself to be presented as a 'bought' defender of the aristocracy.[85] But his stand was really based on a devotion to political economy. For Lowe's experiences in 'democratic' Australia (he had lived there between 1842 and 1849) had convinced him that working men, once they had been given full political rights, would attempt to secure protection of their wages and living conditions, thus jeopardizing all the social and economic gains that had been achieved since 1832. In particular, he thought that the working class, if admitted to power, would neither accept middle-class leadership nor endorse such tenets of Liberalism as economy, laissez-faire, and a pacific foreign policy.[86] Moreover, Lowe deeply feared trade unionism, which he saw, of course, as nothing more nor less than an improper restraint on trade.[87] 'So far from believing that Democracy would aid the progress of the State, I am satisfied it would impede it,' he said. 'Its political economy is not that of Adam Smith.'[88]

Even the Conservatives' modest 1859 Reform Bill had alarmed him; he feared that it would hand over the representation of the great towns to the trade unions and reduce to nullities 'all the wealthy and intelligent men in those seats of manufacture and trade, thus undoing what was one of the great merits of the Reform Bill of 1832 to do'.[89] Thus, Lowe's main concern was that the advent of 'democracy' might put at risk the delicate governmental machinery by means of which a liberal commercial policy had been developed. He thought that an educated élite, even if its upbringing had been an aristocratic one, seemed likely to show greater respect for the imperatives of the market than did an emotional alliance of 'progressive capitalists' and working men. After all, it had been the Parliaments elected on a restricted franchise, despite their alleged aristocratic bias, which had created the conditions for capitalist growth, he claimed. No wonder Lowe was so astonished by the eventual outcome of the reform crisis: 'How was I to foresee that the

---

[84] Parl. Deb., 3rd ser., vol. 182, 1311–13, 1318–19: 13 Apr. 1866.
[85] In 1858 he was intriguing with Derby and the Conservatives; see Hawkins, *Parliament*, 209–10.
[86] Winter, *Robert Lowe*, Ch. 12.
[87] See his anonymous article 'Trade Unions', *Quarterly Review*, 123 (1867), 351–83.
[88] Cited in D. W. Sylvester, *Robert Lowe and Education* (Cambridge, 1974), 28.
[89] 26 Dec. 1859, cited in Southgate, *Passing of the Whigs*, 303.

middle classes which, to the great benefit of the country, have been intrusted with the electoral power would so tamely and miserably give it up and allow it to be transferred to the poorer classes,' he exclaimed.[90]

In talking and writing in this vein, Laing and Lowe were articulating the anxieties of many businessmen. But by the 1860s only a minority of the entrepreneurial Radicals felt like this. For, by the middle of the decade, if not earlier, most had persuaded themselves that the disenfranchised artisans (though perhaps not the 'residuum') had already demonstrated their fitness to exercise the franchise—morally, by their alleged nobility of behaviour during the Cotton Famine, and socially, by displays of self-control and thrift. Henry Ashworth, giving evidence to the Grey Select Committee in 1860, still felt apprehensive over trade unionism ('Drunkenness and strikes, I think, are about the monster grievances of the present age') and over the strength of class feeling among the Lancashire operatives, but he could also tell a story of growing working-class respectability.[91] The same applies to Bright, who in February 1861 was arguing that it would now be safe to enlarge the franchise because the previous thirty years had been 'an age of improvement in the condition, the character, and the intelligence of the people of England', brought about by 'thirty years nearly of peace' and fifteen years of free trade—an observation echoed four years later by the cautious Edward Baines.[92] Moreover, co-operation between middle-class Radicals and working-class leaders over the issues of Italy, Poland, and the American Civil War brought many trade unionists and employers closer together, and this in turn helped the cause of parliamentary reform.[93]

But if a decisive shift took place in the attitudes of Liberal businessmen in the Commons towards extending the electorate, this was mostly because the majority of working men were now demanding the franchise as the recognition of a social right, not as a weapon in the fight against property and capital. This made it that much easier for businessmen and middle-class spokesmen like Edward Baines, who was by no means a fire-eating Radical, to align themselves with the popular reform agitation of the mid-1860s. The entrepreneurial Radicals would also have been heartened to learn that when a popular reform meeting was held in Bradford in January 1864, it should have passed a resolution favouring 'a large extension of the franchise' in order to

[90] Parl. Deb., 3rd ser., vol. 188, 1548: 15 July 1867. Lowe claimed that until 1867 the middle class was 'the depository of political power in this country' (*Middle Class and Primary Education: Two Speeches* (Liverpool, 1868), 3).
[91] Report from Select Committee of House of Lords on what would be the Probable Increase . . ., LXXXVII (1860), p. 3560.
[92] Parl. Deb., 3rd ser., vol. 161, 105: 5 Feb. 1861. Fraser, 'Edward Baines', 204. See Baines's speech to the Bramley Reform Association, *Leeds Mercury*, 5 Jan. 1865.
[93] W. Hamish Fraser, *Trade Unions and Society: The Struggle for Acceptance 1850–1880* (1974), 125–7, 155. Wright, 'Leeds Politics'. *Idem*, 'Bradford'.

tackle church rates, the Irish Church, 'and the enormous expenditure and unequal taxation of the country'.[94]

Once reform measures had come before the House, it is interesting to observe how many Liberal manufacturers stepped forward to testify to the 'good character' of their employees. Such an MP was the Oldham industrialist John Platt, who announced himself as the employer of 5,000 adult males 'in one of the most important branches of mechanical enterprize, and one in which the best class of artizans in England were engaged [machine tools]':

Having had an experience of upwards of thirty years of the working class, he could say that, although it was quite true they had their failings, as well as any other class, he had no fear whatever of them. He was aware that there was one thing that frightened many employers and manufacturers—namely, the trades unions; but in regard to that point he took a different view from some persons. They would place more responsibility on the workmen by giving them votes and teaching them political economy in a practical sense; and by that means they would reduce the numbers who joined trades' unions.[95]

His fellow MP for Oldham, Hibbert, agreed. So did Frank Crossley, the Halifax carpet manufacturer.[96]

A delighted Bright urged the House to trust the judgement of those of its Members who, coming into daily contact with working men, well understood that franchise extension would 'increase the desire for education' and 'stimulate self-respect'. He added his own testimony:

I, living amongst a very dense population [sic], believe, and I think every employer of labour in this House will believe, that every interest in this country would be safer, more comfortable, and more happy in every particular if some 200,000, 300,000 or 400,000 persons were added to those who now possess the electoral franchise.[97]

Yet precisely what kind of franchise extension did these 'progressive businessmen' have in mind? This was a matter on which unresolved differences existed. Some big employers actually associated themselves with the 'democratic' Reform League, despite (or perhaps because of) its commitment to manhood suffrage and its close ties with politically active working men, especially in London (but also in the industrial Midlands and North). Among such employers were P. A. Taylor (of Courtauld's), T. B. Potter, Thomasson, and, at a discreet distance, Bright. Samuel Morley, too, contributed to the Reform League's funds (though, like Taylor, he also supported the National

---

[94] *Bradford Review*, 30 Jan. 1864. See Forster's big speech to his constituents on parliamentary reform (ibid., 9 Jan. 1864).

[95] Parl. Deb., 3rd ser., vol. 182, 865–6: 23 Mar. 1866.

[96] Ibid., vol. 183, 50–1: 27 Apr. 1866; vol. 182, 1407–8: 16 Apr. 1866. They took this line despite their continuing distrust of trade unionism. See the observations of the *Manchester Examiner*, 9 Feb. 1867 (cited by Gillespie, *Labor and Politics*, 233).

[97] Parl. Deb., 3rd ser., vol. 184, 613: 18 June 1866, cited in part in Smith, *Second Reform Bill*, 25.

Reform Union, with its programme of 'household suffrage'). In fact, it seems that the League heavily depended upon the financial backing of a handful of wealthy business sympathizers of Radical convictions. At the same time, *most* 'respectable' employers clearly tended to shy away from so 'dangerous' an organization.[98]

Far more reassuring to Liberal businessmen was the National Reform Union, which was a kind of revived version of the old Anti-Corn Law League, with George Wilson, appropriately enough, serving as chairman and with headquarters in Newall's Building. The NRU's origins lay in the Lancashire Reform Union, founded in 1859, which was, in its turn, an expression of a number of 'entrepreneurial conversions' to franchise extension occurring at about that time. Its business supporters included R. N. Philips, Bazley, Langworthy, E. Armitage, T. Ashton, and Henry Ashworth, all old Leaguers.[99] It later enjoyed considerable support from the Bradford 'millocrats'.[100] Cowling calls the NRU 'an attempt by a self-conscious bourgeoisie to provide leadership and exert power in the determination of public policy, and to display its strength by carrying the higher artisans along with it', adding, 'It had civic pride and corporate purpose.'[101] The NRU's mission, of course, was to persuade the working man that it was in his interest to combine with the middle class in an assault on aristocratic privilege.

Most NRU leaders were not that dissatisfied with Russell's mild Bill of 1866, with its £7 rental qualification in the boroughs, which they thought 'substantial and honest'.[102] The 'strengthening' of the middle class certainly bulked large in the calculations of a man like George Wilson, who, addressing a big rally in Manchester in 1865, emphasized that among the 23.5 million excluded from the franchise were 'five-sixths of the young men in warehouses, banks, railway companies, engineering concerns, and the intelligent working men'.[103] Indeed, most Radical businessmen, like Isaac Holden, the Bradford woollen manufacturer, wanted nothing more than a 'wise and moderate

---

[98] Howe, *Cotton Masters*, 242–3. Cowling, *1867*, 245–6; Fraser, *Trade Unions*, 151–2. In Bradford the League received help from wealthy mill-owners like Robert Kell and Alfred Illingworth (Wright, 'Second Reform Agitation', 185–6, and Reynolds, *Great Paternalist*, 213).

[99] Howe, *Cotton Masters*, 242–3.

[100] On the committed support of wealthy businessmen in Bradford, one of the main centres of the NRU, see Wright, 'Second Reform Agitation', 182–3.

[101] Cowling, *1867*, 243. The NRU's programme had four planks: household franchise, the ballot, 'an equal distribution of Members of Parliament, in proportion to population and property', and triennial parliaments. (See 1865 membership card in W. S. Nichols Papers, DB4/1/10.)

[102] The phrase 'substantial and honest' was used by one of the leading lights of the Bradford branch of the NRU, Alfred Illingworth (W. S. Nichols Papers, DB4/1/7).

[103] *Reynolds's Newspaper*, 21 May 1865. Nevertheless, the Union's meetings were sufficiently Radical in tone to upset a journal like *The Economist*. Commenting on a meeting chaired by Wilson in October 1864, it wrote: 'The Manchester Radicals are setting about the work of agitation in a fashion to disgust heartily all thinking reformers, amongst whom we claim to be reckoned' (29 Oct. 1864, p. 1339).

measure of Reform', which would 'safely widen the base of our representative system and . . . directly and personally interest a fair and considerable number of the thrifty and intelligent working men in the government and institutions of our country'.[104] The LFRA, by contrast, wanted the fullest possible extension of the suffrage, but only within the context of financial reform; and it criticized Bright and others for treating the issue of the vote 'merely as a sentimental grievance' or by reference to 'a supposed inherent right of all men to the suffrage without the performance of corresponding duties to the State'.[105] The Liverpool reformers much preferred the stand adopted by Bazley and George Wilson of the NRU, whom it praised for treating reform as a prelude to the fundamentally important task of reducing public expenditure.[106]

Now 'reform' presented in this cautious way met with a mixed reception from the poorer elements in the electorate. Understandably, many democratic Radicals were not impressed by it, and on several occasions class tensions threatened to break up the broadly based reform movement which had arisen in the mid-1860s. Thus, *Reynolds's Newspaper*, organ of the London working-class Radicals, burst out angrily, in the wake of the Manchester meeting at which Wilson had spoken, about the activities of 'dainty middle class agitators' and 'impostors': 'Nothing less than manhood suffrage ought to satisfy the enslaved orders. No demand for less can unite the oppressed millions.'[107] Such animosities were temporarily forgotten in a common indignation against Whig treachery and Tory opportunism. Indeed, the rejection of the Russell Reform Bill drew the Reform Union and the Reform League into an alliance.[108] But when the Union 'invaded' London in the spring of 1867, trouble again threatened to flare up until the emollient Samuel Morley stepped in to restore harmony.[109]

What held the two groups of reformers together more than anything else was the leadership of Bright, who enjoyed a high standing with them both—testimony either to the latter's tactical astuteness or perhaps to his intellectual woolly-headedness! In 1866 Bright was encouraging Wilson to draw up support in the 'Northern Towns'; but he prudently avoided identifying himself with the NRU,[110] though his brother, Jacob, was a prominent member of it. In fact, Bright's real objectives during 1866–7, apart from his concern to

[104] I. Holden to his Knaresborough constituents, 28 Mar. 1866, *Holden–Illingworth Letters*, 393–4.

[105] *Financial Reformer*, 1 Feb. 1866, p. 235; ibid., 1 June 1865, p. 102.

[106] Ibid., 1 Sept. 1868, p. 426.

[107] *Reynolds's Newspaper*, 21 May 1865. See also Wright, 'Second Reform Agitation', 189.

[108] However, see Beales's friendly letter to George Wilson, 12 Apr. 1866, George Wilson Papers. In the northern towns the relationship between the two organizations seems to have been very amicable.

[109] Cowling, *1867*, 260. Wright, 'Second Reform Agitation', 184–6.

[110] Bright to G. Wilson, 2 Feb., 30 Apr. 1866, George Wilson Papers.

carry *some* sort of reform measure, continue to mystify historians. Vincent draws a sharp contrast between this particular phase of his career and the earlier reform agitation of 1858–9, claiming that by the mid-1860s Bright had lost all confidence in the middle classes and was turning to the urban working man for support.[111] Cowling, on the other hand, has suggested that, far from wanting the establishment of 'democracy', Bright, in 1866 at least, would still have been quite happy with a £5 rating proposal.[112]

The disagreement is likely to continue, since the historical evidence can be read in several ways. But the position that Bright had totally abandoned his former middle-class constituency seems difficult to maintain. Although putting a greater emphasis upon working-class grievances[113] and sometimes even using the language of class (as Cobden had never done), Bright remained concerned to balance such remarks with appeals to the 'excluded' middle class like the following:

There is no greater fallacy than this—that the middle classes are in possession of power. The real state of the case . . . would be this—that the working men are almost universally excluded, roughly and insolently, from political power, and that the middle class, whilst they have the semblance of it, are defrauded of the reality.[114]

Moreover, Bright specifically denied Laing's argument that the 1832 Parliament had passed a series of reforms beneficial to the middle class; in fact, he protested, these reforms had been enacted only as a result of pressure from the very people whom the Reform Bill of 1866 was trying to enfranchise: 'The political gains of the last twenty-five years, as they were summed up [by Laing], are my political gains, if they can be called the gains in any degree of any living Englishman.'[115]

In conclusion, what, if anything, did the business Liberals achieve with respect to parliamentary reform? For 'Adullamites' like Laing (and Lowe) the events of 1866–7 proved a disaster. For these men had succeeded in destroying a moderate Reform Bill only to see the Conservatives carry a measure enfranchising three times as many new voters as Russell's would have done.[116] Moderate reformers like Baines also suffered a defeat. In 1864 Baines was proposing a Bill based on a £6 franchise which would, in his own estimation, have meant that 'the upper and middle class would still constitute

---

[111] On Bright's changing views on the franchise, see Vincent, *British Liberal Party*, 215–27.

[112] In February 1866 he was writing privately to Wilson in favour of a £6 rental franchise, accompanied by a provision for lodgers (2 Feb. 1866, George Wilson Papers). On Bright's ambition, see Cowling, *1867*, 33–5, 249–50, 293–5.

[113] Perhaps because he believed that the Tories 'care little for a middle class call for Reform. It is only numbers, and the aspect of force that will influence them' (see Bright's letter to G. Wilson, 27 June 1866, George Wilson Papers).

[114] Trevelyan, *Life of Bright*, 365.

[115] 23 Apr. 1866, *Bright's Speeches*, 367–9.

[116] Cowling, *1867*, 46.

two thirds of the voters in the boroughs';[117] as he rightly said of the measure which he introduced in that year, it was 'so limited as not in the slightest degree to warrant the fears of democracy which Lowe Horsman and Elcho conjure up'.[118] But events soon swept away all the safeguards which Baines had tried to erect, and his refusal to appear at the famous Woodhouse Moor rally in October 1866 signalled the start of a process which ultimately led to his displacement as a leader of Leeds Liberalism.[119]

By contrast, Bright enjoyed a 'good crisis'. His leadership of the reform agitation in the country clearly did much to persuade the Derby Ministry (and back-benchers on both sides of the House) that a settlement of the issue could no longer be delayed and that a Reform Bill—*any* Reform Bill—should be placed on the statute-book with the minimum of delay. Bright's activities in these years also brought him the national prominence which forced him into the inner leadership of the parliamentary Liberal Party, though this proved to be a mixed blessing to all concerned, not least to Bright himself!

Yet Bright—and, still more, the other Liberal businessmen—played only a peripheral role in the events which led to the Second Reform Act. Forster, it is true, forcibly impressed upon Gladstone in early 1867 that there should be no going back to the timid proposals of the previous year's Reform Bill.[120] And in the early summer of 1867 a delegation of entrepreneurial Radicals, including Bright, Baines, Bazley, Candlish, Cheetham, Cowen, Potter, J. B. Smith, Stansfeld, and Watkin, all of them MPs, along with George Wilson and a motley crew of clergymen, ironmasters, mill-owners, and manufacturers, made a decisive intervention when they met Gladstone to urge on him a moderate settlement of the problem of rate-paying along lines which eventually gave rise to the Childers Amendment.[121] Later, Smith and Platt were among the 'Tea Room rebels' who supported the principle of a household suffrage and did not want to support Gladstone's moves to establish a more restrictive set of electoral qualifications.[122] The effect of these various activities was to increase the likelihood of a Conservative-sponsored measure squeezing its way through a bemused House.

Yet businessmen who advocated some sort of rating franchise cannot have been happy with the final outcome. Bright himself had been entirely caught on

---

[117] Fraser, 'Edward Baines', 205.

[118] Ibid. 207. On Baines's growing moderation, see Steele, *Palmerston and Liberalism*, 179.

[119] Fraser, 'Edward Baines', 208. However, he did attend a Reform League banquet in Apr. 1867.

[120] Forster to Nichols, 21 Feb. 1867, W. S. Nichols Papers, DB4/1/14. Forster himself subscribed to the household franchise, or what he chose to call a 'hearthstone suffrage' (*Bradford Observer*, 11 Oct. 1866).

[121] Smith, *Second Reform Bill*, 174–6.

[122] The later revolt of 12 Apr. included the two Basses, Akroyd, Platt, and Doulton, as well as the two Grosvenors and other Whigs (Cowling, *1867*, 200). For McLaren's involvement in the 'Tea Room party', see Mackie, *McLaren*, ii. 163–5.

the hop by the Conservatives' volte-face,[123] and the Liberal MP and pottery manufacturer Frederick Doulton may well have had a point when he later twitted the Radical tribune with being 'afraid' of Disraeli's Bill.[124] Leave aside for a moment the consideration that, for the immediate future, the reform issue had been settled by Conservative Ministers in a way which greatly enhanced their party's electoral credibility. Were the *contents* of that Act satisfactory from the viewpoint of the entrepreneurial Radicals?

On one thing all historians are agreed: that the Conservatives, by successfully sponsoring reform, were at least able to shape, to a very large extent, the accompanying Redistribution measure. Indeed, D. C. Moore thinks that the most amazing aspect of 1867 is the fact that a Liberal-dominated Parliament was trapped into agreeing to a Redistribution scheme so unfavourable to Liberal interests. The Boundary Commissioners were instructed to enlarge the boroughs 'so as to include within [their] limits... all premises the occupiers of which ought, due regard being had to situation or other local circumstances, to be included therein for Parliamentary purposes'. This meant that suburban overspill areas became included within boroughs, thereby reducing the amount of 'urban contamination' in the counties—a long-standing Conservative objective.[125]

True, Disraeli's highly partisan Boundary Commission produced a report which was so unacceptable to the majority of MPs that a Select Committee had to be appointed at once. And the recommendations of this new Committee were later upheld by the House, against Disraeli's advice.[126] Yet none of this prevented the carrying of a redistribution scheme highly favourable to traditional ruling-class interests. Thus, the south-west region, with 76,612 borough electors, got forty-five MPs, while the north-west, with 232,431 voters, was allotted only thirty-two MPs, and London, with 263,991 voters, only twenty-two MPs. It has been claimed that this maldistribution, along with the incorporation of 100,000 suburban residents into the boroughs, 'buttressed the landed interest in both the counties and rural boroughs for another 17 years'.[127] Moreover, although the franchise scheme was a bold

---

[123] As late as mid-February 1867, Bright was privately expressing his conviction that the Administration was 'hostile to Reform' (Bright to Nichols, 16 Feb. 1867, W. S. Nichols Papers, DB4/1/18). Forster, on the other hand, was shrewdly predicting as early as October 1866 (at the Woodhouse Moor rally) that Disraeli might carry an extensive measure (*Bradford Observer*, 11 Oct. 1866).

[124] Parl. Deb., 3rd ser., vol. 188, 1593: 15 July 1867. But Cowling stresses the moderation of the League's ·leadership (e.g. *1867*, 19, 246–7).

[125] D. C. Moore, 'Social Structure, Political Structure, and Public Opinion in Mid-Victorian England', in Robert Robson (ed.), *Ideas and Institutions of Victorian Britain* (1967), 55–6. J. P. D. Dunbabin, 'Electoral Reforms and their Outcome in the United Kingdom, 1865–1900', in T. R. Gourvish and Alan O'Day (eds.), *Later Victorian Britain, 1867–1900* (1988), 100–1.

[126] Smith, *Second Reform Bill*, 219–25.

[127] Ibid. 225.

one, redistribution was extremely modest; thus Calne, with 600 electors and a population of 5,000, survived, while St Helen's remained disenfranchised. (How could the entrepreneurial Radicals be content with an electoral system under which Portarlington—by sixty-eight votes to fifty-one—sent a Tory soldier to represent its 2,874 inhabitants in the 1868 general election?![128]) Characteristically, when Disraeli ceded an extra Member to the four big English cities, he did so only at the expense of Luton, Keighley, Barnsley, and St Helen's—all likely Liberal seats.[129] By contrast, according to Cowling's calculations, the number of MPs representing agricultural and 'territorial' interests declined by only two or three, at the most.[130] No wonder that, even after the reform settlement had been ratified, the NRU continued to press for a new allocation of seats—as well as the Ballot, the equalization of the franchise, and the abolition of personal rating.[131]

Moreover, the Redistribution Bill also spread the Conservative vote very economically: thus, in 1868 the Conservatives won 101 borough seats from just over 2 million votes, the Liberals 263 seats from $8\frac{1}{2}$ million votes. Such an outcome is hardly surprising when one considers that the six largest boroughs had an electorate of 228,005, the six smallest 5,488.

But if, from the Liberal point of view, the Redistribution Bill was disappointingly modest, the franchise extension in 1867 was riskily ambitious. Moreover, one of its effects was to widen still further the discrepancy between the size of the county and the borough constituencies, the former increasing by only 38 per cent, the latter by 138 per cent.[132] Indeed, as F. B. Smith has shown, some of the largest increases in constituency size occurred in the big cities, especially Sheffield. This created difficulties for the Radicals in their urban strongholds by swamping them with new urban voters many of whom had no tradition of supporting the Liberal Party.[133]

Whether Derby and Disraeli had deliberately planned this innovation, knowing that it might bring them a party advantage, remains unclear. Certainly, some Conservatives really did believe that the further down the social scale one went, the more likely one was to find working men hostile to Liberalism. This was not the main consideration in the minds of Conservative

---

[128] *Financial Reformer*, 1 Dec. 1868, p. 469.

[129] Cowling, *1867*, 73. Hanham also agrees that in practice the Redistribution Bill 'did very little to remedy existing inequalities' (*Elections and Party Management*, xxiv).

[130] Cowling, *1867*, 76.

[131] J. D. Morton (the NRU agent) to Nichols, 11 Dec. 1867, W. S. Nichols Papers, DB4/1/19.

[132] Smith, *Second Reform Bill*, 238–9.

[133] Ibid. 237–8. In Leeds the electorate increased from 7,217 to 35,510 (Wright, 'Leeds Politics', 122). But the view that the extension of the franchise was itself responsible for the Conservative successes in industrial Lancashire in the 1868 general election is dismissed by John Vincent, 'The Effect of the Second Reform Act in Lancashire', *Historical Journal*, 11 (1968), 84–94.

leaders; but neither, it seems, was it entirely absent from their thoughts.[134] Some NRU members were certainly suspicious of a measure which ceded the household franchise '*unprotected by the Ballot*'; this, according to S. C. Kell, would 'hand over hundreds of thousands of the poorest and therefore most defenceless voters to the manipulations of unscrupulous election agents, armed with money and every other means of sinister influence'.[135]

Cowling thinks that the Conservatives gained from a generous franchise extension for rather different reasons. As some of them well understood, a lowered borough franchise was likely to damage the Whigs in *small* boroughs by bringing them into conflict with the Radicals: 'This induced a belief that one effect of franchise reduction would be to push the Liberal party a good deal further to the Left than it had gone hitherto—with the result that the Conservative party would establish total control of the respectable middle-classes as the working classes became more radical.'[136]

Another feature of the 1867 Act which displeased the urban Radicals was the 'minority vote', which obviously increased the chances of the Conservatives picking up one of the three seats in the major metropolitan boroughs. Bright took a dim view of a device which gratuitously threatened to create a Conservative MP for Birmingham![137] This was all the more annoying given the fact that the large boroughs had still been left grossly under-represented.[138] In the event, through the development of the 'caucus', the Liberals successfully kept all three Birmingham seats, but only at the cost of fostering a new type of 'machine politics' which few of the older generation of entrepreneurial Radicals can have found congenial.[139]

Such a line of argument should not be pressed *too* far. After all, the Liberals *did* win two of the three general elections fought on the basis of the 1867 Reform Act. Nor did the business Liberals suffer from the change in all parts of the country. In the north-east, for example, the period between the

---

[134] See Paul Smith, *Disraelian Conservatism and Social Reform* (1967), 90.

[135] S. C. Kell, *The Ballot. Shall the Vote be Free or Watched?—The Voters' Own or Some One's Else?* (Bradford, n.d. [1867]), 22–3. See also *Financial Reformer*, 1 Feb. 1866, p. 234.

[136] Cowling, *1867*, 65. But Charles Adderley told Disraeli in January 1866: 'Bass is in great terror of the amiable working class. Bass's hope is that a lower franchise wld reach a class of W'm more under their Masters' influence. He says the present £10 W'm are intolerable' (Smith, *Second Reform Bill*, 61).

[137] 8 Aug. 1867, *Bright's Speeches*, 412–14. Bright had earlier taken strong exception to this provision when it appeared in Russell's Bill of 1854 (diary, 13 Feb. 1854, Walling (ed.), *Diaries of Bright*, 160).

[138] Lord Frederick Cavendish, a friend of the Bradford reformers, approved of the minority clause on principle, but abstained on the vote because of his disapproval of the Government's failure to produce an adequate Redistribution measure (Cavendish to Nichols, 10 Aug. 1867, W. S. Nichols Papers, DB4/1/17).

[139] The 'minority vote' probably helped the Conservative Party in Manchester. On the other hand, in a traditionally Conservative city like Liverpool, it had the opposite effect.

passing of the Second Reform Act and the institution of the Ballot in 1872 represented the highpoint of manufacturers' influence.[140]

It is also possible that the 1867 Act hastened the process whereby men from commercial and industrial backgrounds entered the House of Commons, most of them (but by no means all—witness W. H. Smith) as Liberals.[141] Guttsman's analysis of the social backgrounds of MPs broadly confirms this interpretation.[142] In fact, scarcely had the 1868 election results been announced than grumbling began about the lowering of the 'tone' of the House. The blind economist and MP Henry Fawcett was particularly scathing about this development. Writing to Lord Cairns on 11 December 1868, Fawcett declared:

Intellectually it [House of Commons] is inferior to the last, and wealthy, uneducated manufacturers and merchants are more predominant than ever. Mill always predicted that this would be the case, thinking that the new voters would require two or three years to understand the power which has been given to them.[143]

At Cabinet level, too, businessmen began to appear in much larger numbers. Gladstone's first Ministry included Bruce, Bright, Forster, Stansfeld, and Goschen.[144] Finally, the weakening of the Whigs as a result of the events of 1866–7, plus the revolt of the 'Celtic Fringe', gave great heart to the entrepreneurial Radicals.

All in all, then, Bagehot had sound grounds, writing his 1872 Introduction to *The English Constitution*, for claiming that the Reform Act of 1867 had 'unmistakably completed the effect which the Act of 1832 began, but left unfinished':

The spirit of our present House of Commons is plutocratic, not aristocratic; its most prominent statesmen are not men of ancient descent or of great hereditary estate; they are men mostly of substantial means, but they are mostly, too, connected more or less closely with the new trading wealth.[145]

But the crucial question is whether, as Lowe and Laing from the 'Cave' and Cranborne from the Tory side of the House had predicted, the effect of the enlargement of the franchise represented so sudden a move towards 'democracy' as to imperil those legislative achievements of the preceding

[140] Nossiter, *Reformed England, passim.* See the discussion in Hanham, *Elections and Party Management*, 68–9, 74.

[141] Smith, *Second Reform Bill*, 6.

[142] Guttsman, *British Political Élite*, 82.

[143] Leslie Stephen, *Life of Henry Fawcett* (1885), 241–2. Malchow comments on the rush of businessmen into parliamentary politics in the 1860s and 1870s as indicating 'a "ripeness" of the commercial class for political co-optation' (*Gentlemen Capitalists*, 268).

[144] See Cowling, *1867*, 296.

[145] Bagehot, *English Constitution*, 279.

decades which had resulted from applying the lessons of 'political economy'. And here the evidence is ambiguous.

In the short run, Bright seems to have been vindicated. In the 1870s, and even beyond, most politically active working men, far from pressing their claims as a class, gave the impression of being broadly content with the panaceas which Bright, Gladstone, and other middle-class Liberal leaders were laying down on their behalf (a sizeable minority, of course, attached themselves to Disraelian Conservatism). The newly enfranchised treated the vote with pride, as a badge of political citizenship, and seemed more interested in attacking the extravagance and injustices of the aristocratic State than in pressing for even modest improvements in urban living conditions. Nor is this a matter for total surprise, since many plebeian and working-class Radicals had their own very good reasons for welcoming a regime of low taxation, a minimalist State, and a reduction in expenditure on the diplomatic service, the Civil List, and the like.[146]

In fact, a group of London Radicals, headed by Morley, came together in early 1868 to form the Financial Reform Union, the programme of which overlapped to a considerable extent that of the LFRA, although it drew upon a wider social spectrum for its support. In the general election later that year, this new pressure group intervened with its own address, calling on the electorate to vote for no candidate who was not prepared to pledge himself to reducing the Estimates by £10 million; 12 MPs signed the address, among them such familiar entrepreneurial Radicals as Jacob Bright, Candlish, Joseph Cowen, Charles Gilpin, Isaac Holden, Morley, Mundella, and Rylands, along with the indefatigable George Wilson.[147]

Enthusiastic 'reformers' had prophesied all along that this sort of thing would follow in the wake of an extension of the franchise, and they were also confident that 'the people' would be heavily involved in such activities. S. C. Kell, for example, had written earlier in the decade that just as the 'lower classes' had 'preceded the upper in the earnest advocacy of such holy and blessed movements as those against slavery, intemperance and war', so before very long they would 'pioneer the way for their so-called betters, in the sciences of politics and political economy'.[148]

Yet, whatever may have been the short-term consequences of reform, in the

---

[146] Eugenio F. Biagini, 'Popular Liberals, Gladstonian Finance and the Debate on Taxation, 1860–1874', in Eugenio F. Biagini and Alastair J. Reid (eds.), *Currents of Radicalism: Popular Radicalism, Organised Labour and Party Politics in Britain 1850–1914* (Cambridge, 1991), 134–62.

[147] *Financial Reformer*, 1 Mar., 1 May, 1 Sept. 1868. *Papers on Taxation and Expenditure Issued by the Financial Reform Union* (1869). The main difference in programme between the new organization and the LFRA was that the Union concentrated on retrenchment and declined to put 'Direct Taxation' on its banner. But a lecturer from the LFRA, John Noble, was involved in the building up of the London body, which maintained links with the Liverpool financial reformers.

[148] Kell, *Political Attitude*, 16.

long run the apprehensions of Lowe and Laing proved to be well founded. For the fact is that the electoral system to which the confused events of 1866–7 gave rise did not particularly suit the needs of the entrepreneurial wing of the Liberal Party. As Malchow argues, prior to 1867 the presence of businessmen at Westminster 'flattered the self-regard of the middle-class communities that returned them'; but a mass electorate put a premium on party loyalty and on wider national appeals, both of which undermined this older political culture.[149] Ironically, more businessmen may have been entering Parliament just at the moment when their effectiveness as a group was being reduced. Moreover, it is arguable that 1867 witnessed an abrupt transition from a predominantly aristocratic to a partly democratic political system; an intervening period of 'bourgeois domination' was skipped. Worse still, following the Second Reform Act, the British political system actually managed to *combine* elements of 'feudalism' and 'mass democracy'—the twin threats to the realization of the objectives of the entrepreneurial Radicals.

So far little has been said about Gladstone. This is a deliberate omission. For, whereas in the spheres of financial and administrative reform, Gladstone had creatively imposed upon his political contemporaries a series of imaginative solutions to current difficulties that were to be binding on the future, parliamentary reform largely eluded his control.[150] The *Morning Star*, Bright's journal, claimed in 1865 that Gladstone had 'been converted to Mr. Bright as Sir Robert Peel was converted by Mr. Cobden', and this, according to Cowling, led many Liberals to fear that Gladstone had been 'captured' by the Radical demagogue—which in turn, as Derby was quick to note, seemed likely to 'alarm the middle classes',[151] or at least their more timid members.

But Bright's friends, as well as Bright himself, always exaggerated their influence over Gladstone, who was pursuing his own characteristically tortuous course. If a link existed between the two men, it was that Gladstone, who had once promoted 'financial reform' as an *alternative* to constitutional change, eventually came to share Bright's belief in the social and educational progress that was supposedly raising the condition of the working man.[152] But, as Colin Matthew shows, Gladstone's starting-point as a parliamentary reformer was really his losing battle as Chancellor to rein in public expenditure. Once he

---

[149] Malchow, *Gentlemen Capitalists*, 352. However, the 'nationalization of politics' was a process which stretched over several decades, and it was not until the Edwardian period perhaps that the politics of 'local influence' finally succumbed to the politics of national programmes.

[150] Significantly, he told George Wilson on 3 Sept. 1866 that he thought he ought not, for the present, to involve himself in the reform question (George Wilson Papers).

[151] *Morning Star*, 4 Aug. 1865. Cowling, *1867*, 82.

[152] Wright, 'Second Reform Agitation', 192. Gladstone told the Commons in July 1867 that the working classes would 'adopt more universally the laws of freedom in their dealings among themselves in the labour market' only if 'they [were] placed in as close connection as possible with the representative system' (Cowling, *1867*, 29).

had accepted that the income tax, far from discouraging high expenditure, as he had once hoped, was actually having the opposite effect, Gladstone found himself faced with two alternatives: either to abolish the income tax entirely or to alter the composition of the electorate through a reconstruction of the entire political system. Opting for the latter course, he sought to enfranchise an élite of intelligent artisans by adhering to a £7 annual rental level of qualification.[153] Unfortunately for Gladstone, Disraeli's opportunistic extensions of the franchise, coupled with pressure from his own followers, forced him to shift his position, and he ended up endorsing a constitutional settlement which actually militated against the social and financial policies which he favoured.

Considering that Gladstone was able to embark on the first of his four premierships immediately after the resolution of the reform crisis, it may seem perverse to argue that he was in any way damaged by the 1867 Act. Yet damaged he certainly was. Not only had he been outmanœuvred by Disraeli in circumstances which temporarily threatened his leadership of the party;[154] but, more important still, the political settlement of 1867 did not at all accord with what Gladstone had been hoping to achieve, and, in a sense, he spent the rest of his political life deploring its consequences.[155] The electorate's rejection, in the 1874 general election, of his proposal to abolish the income tax is seen by many historians as symbolic.[156]

One final legacy of the Second Reform Act struggles must be noted. We have already seen how sceptical some Liberal businessmen were of the capacity of the newly enfranchised masses to understand the injunctions of political economy. Perhaps the most persuasive spokesman for that position, however, was a 'High Tory', Lord Cranborne (the future Lord Salisbury), one of three Ministers to resign in protest at Derby's and Disraeli's reform initiative.

Cranborne's position was, in fact, somewhat complicated. On the one hand, the peer's son stood fairly and squarely on a defence of the privileges of landed society; in sharp distinction to Laing, for example, he opposed the bestowal of new seats upon urban areas within the counties of Yorkshire, Cheshire, Lancashire, and Durham, calling this provision of Russell's Bill 'merely another device for increasing the already extravagant influence of the

---

[153] Matthew, *Gladstone 1809–1874*, 128, 140.

[154] For Gladstone's temporary despondency, see Gladstone to Nichols, 13 Apr. 1867, W. S. Nichols Papers, DB4/1/19.

[155] W. R. Greg, too, linked 'Beaconsfieldism' to the enlarged franchise (see 'A Modern Symposium': 'Is the Popular Judgment in Politics more just than that of the Higher Orders?', *Nineteenth Century*, 4 (1878), 174–81).

[156] Biagini, however, argues that most working-class Radicals, already great admirers of the 'People's William', sympathized with the proposal to abolish the income tax, and that the Liberal defeat in 1874 had little to do with the unpopularity of Gladstone's financial programme (Biagini, 'Popular Liberals', 154–62).

great towns'.[157] A desire to protect the agricultural districts from 'urban contamination' similarly led him to call for a sharp distinction to be drawn between the boroughs and the counties.

Yet Cranborne also insisted that *all* owners of property had a common interest in the maintenance of a restricted franchise. The reform issue, he said

is a struggle to decide whether the payers of direct taxation shall tax themselves, or shall be taxed at the will of those who do not pay it; whether the laws of property shall be made by the owners of property, or by those who have everything to gain and nothing to lose ... In short, it is a portion of the great political struggle of our century—the struggle between property, be its amount small or great, and mere numbers.[158]

Indeed, Cranborne spoke about the danger of entrusting political power to such men in terms strikingly similar to those employed by Lowe:

In proportion as you advance in democratic forms of Government, in that proportion is the doctrine of protection to native industry cherished. I would recommend free traders to study opinion in democratic nations—Australia, the United States, Canada, and France. ... I would appeal to the apostles of political economy to know what is the nature of the legislation by which this result is to be obtained. These are things which are not regulated by wishes, but by the inflexible laws of supply and demand. ... they will not succeed in the attainment of these objects which are so much in violation of the truths of political economy, but the attempt to do so might be more disastrous than the success of the measures themselves.[159]

The interesting thing is that, though he saw the importance of trying to conceal his prejudices, Cranborne continued to hold the commercial and industrial classes—indeed, the middle class as a whole—in aristocratic contempt, even though his prejudices had softened slightly since the 1850s.[160] Hence we have the paradoxical situation of a prominent Conservative developing a fully-fledged capitalist ideology likely to attract many businessmen but doing so from within a party which still possessed an aristocratic ethos and a largely aristocratic leadership. What Cobden, had he lived, would have made of this can only be imagined!

Meanwhile, what, in the shorter run, had the reform crisis meant to the entrepreneurial Radicals? Its main consequence was to expose a central ambiguity in their thinking. Most of them, Cobden and Bright in particular, had always looked with admiration to the United States of America, which they saw not only as the home of popular government and democracy (no aristocratic or ecclesiastical establishments) but also as the land of 'free

---

[157] July 1866, in Smith (ed.), *Salisbury on Politics*, 237.

[158] Apr. 1866, ibid. 219.

[159] Parl. Deb., 3rd ser., vol. 182, 231–3: 13 Mar. 1866. On this subject, see also Stewart, ' "Conservative Reaction" '.

[160] Smith (ed.), *Salisbury on Politics*, 59.

enterprise'. What the debates on parliamentary reform had forced them to consider was the possibility that 'democracy' and 'capitalism' might, at least in some historical circumstances, be antithetical, not complementary, forces.

This problem has been explored in recent years by both Marxists and 'neo-liberals'. Marxists have suggested that democracy gives the working class the illusion of political power, while in practice ensuring its permanent subordination: 'Democratic concessions fragment the working class into individual voters, fragmenting its collective power vis-à-vis capital, but constructing the misleading idea that the vote means real power.'[161] Some would say that this well summarizes Bright's position on the eve of the Second Reform Act. For what was Bright doing if not trying to incorporate the disenfranchised masses (or rather *some* of them) into the system and convert 'irrationally' discontented workmen into active citizens who could be relied upon to pursue various 'crusades' without challenging the privileges of capital?

Modern neo-liberals also see a congruence between democracy and capitalism, but they express the relationship differently. The essence of democracy, Sam Brittan argues, lies in the competitive struggle for votes, which he likens to the entrepreneur's quest for custom. In other words, the democratic process is itself a special kind of market, where votes are exchanged for policies. Unfortunately, say the neo-liberals, there can be nothing equivalent to 'budgetary control' in this system of 'dealing in votes', since, in the vote market, expensive policies always 'sell best'.[162]

How, then, can societies avoid the inflationary pressures to which democratic government allegedly gives rise? The answer has been sought by some neo-liberals in 'education'; that is, making voters 'internalize' market values so that they carry them into the polling booth. Others have recommended structural changes which would reduce the role of government (for example, privatization). Hayek has even suggested constitutional changes which would exclude 'unsuitable' people from the electorate: such as those under the age of 45 (!), along with variegated groups like Civil Servants and the unemployed, whose interests, he believes, run counter to that free operation of the market upon which the well-being of the entire community ultimately rests.[163]

Notions of this kind, of course, could hardly have arisen in mid-Victorian Britain, even though Cranborne, for one, seems to have been flirting with slightly similar ideas. As for the true entrepreneurial Radicals, they

---

[161] Stuart Hall, 'The Rise of the Representative/Interventionist State', in Gregory McLennan, David Held, and Stuart Hall (eds.), *State and Society in Contemporary Britain: A Critical Introduction* (1984), 10.

[162] Samuel Brittan, *The Economic Consequences of Democracy* (1977), Ch. 23. David Marquand, *The Unprincipled Society* (1988), 76–7. Some of these ideas are a development of the earlier insights of Schumpeter.

[163] Marquand, *Unprincipled Society*, 81. See F. A. Hayek, *Law, Legislation and Liberty*, vol. 3 (1979).

would surely have been horrified by the 'neo-liberalism' of their latter-day descendants. For these men were deeply committed to traditional notions of 'community' and the 'ancient Constitution',[164] notions which discouraged attempts at carrying the principles of political economy to their logical political conclusions. Whether this commitment was to the long-term benefit or the detriment of the British economy remains a matter for debate.

[164] 'I am in accord with our ancient Constitution', said Bright at Manchester, 20 Nov. 1866 (*Bright's Speeches*, 391). The same point is made in the *Financial Reformer*, 1 June 1865, p. 102.

7

The Problem of Education

'I have been tolerably well educated,' said Nicholas.

'Fine thing,' said the old gentleman, 'education a great thing—a very great thing—I never had any. I admire it the more in others. A very fine thing—yes, yes.'

(Dickens, *Nicholas Nickleby*)

According to Perkin, the 1870 Education Act (along with the 1862 Revised Code) 'provided the ideal entrepreneurial education for a docile and permanent labour force'.[1] It may, then, be significant that the author of that Act, W. E. Forster, was a businessman Radical who had recently been highly active in the Chambers of Commerce movement. Similarly, when, ten years later, education was made compulsory, this too owed its origin to a Liberal from a business background, A. J. Mundella.

But educational historians are now generally agreed that the main catalyst for the 1870 Act was not economic pressure. Nor did it owe much to the extension of the franchise which had taken place three years earlier. More important was the 'thunderclap from Manchester': the discovery, from a survey of that city, that the country was probably less well provided with elementary schools than the 'experts' had previously supposed. Taking advantage of the resulting mood of 'intolerability', Forster produced a reform measure which drew together ideas from a number of quite disparate sources, but was informed by a clear sense of what the Liberal Cabinet and the House of Commons would be prepared to tolerate.

Thus, there were no clear links between the needs of the business community and the creation of a national education system. Indeed, one reason that the 1870 legislation was enacted so belatedly was because of the strong opposition to compulsory education mounted by the 'voluntarists', led by Edward Baines of the *Leeds Mercury*, a quintessentially middle-class pressure group which included several prominent manufacturers. It may also be significant that the Forster Act immediately encountered the furious hostility of the 'secularists' of the Education League, an organization in which small-scale Birmingham industrialists predominated.[2]

---

[1] Perkin, *Origins*, 300.
[2] See Francis Adams, *History of the Elementary School Contest in England* (1882).

In fact, the contemporary Radical Right has recently sought to show that the post-1870 educational system was profoundly *inimical* to entrepreneurial values. Thus, E. G. West in his book *Education and the State* (published, significantly, by the Institute of Economic Affairs) has tried to demonstrate that the voluntary system was doing much better than generally accepted on the eve of the 1870 Education Act and that therefore State intervention, of the kind to which we have become accustomed, was neither necessary nor desirable. In short, an educational market of sorts was already becoming established in the mid-Victorian years, a market through which parental needs and wishes were being effectively met.[3]

Whereas West largely concerns himself with the *structure* of education, others have been more concerned with the damage done to the British economy by the *content* of education. Thus Martin Wiener in his famous book *English Culture and the Decline of the Industrial Spirit* heaps blame upon the public schools and the ancient universities for imbuing the whole of British society with mistaken notions of 'gentlemanliness'. This, he claims, has led to the neglect in Britain of scientific, technological, and vocational subjects (hence the depressed status of the engineer) in favour of a 'liberal education', particularly classics, with damaging consequences for Britain's economic performance.[4]

Yet there is a sense in which West and Wiener have adopted complementary approaches. For example, it is arguable that if educational choice had been left to the 'consumers' of education, a more 'practical' curriculum than the one which has prevailed for the last hundred years would have developed. Both men, in short, have a quarrel to pick with the 'experts' (or 'the education lobby', as West puts it) for foisting an inappropriate kind of schooling and training upon a largely passive populace. But this raises the question: Did the entrepreneurial Radicals of mid-Victorian Britain, whom they both admire presumably, have an alternative 'system' to offer?

THE ORGANISATION OF PRIMARY EDUCATION

The entrepreneurial Radicals certainly played their part (along with others) in protesting at the exclusiveness of the ancient universities, from which Dissenters were effectively debarred. But in the middle years of the century, such reforms were not at the top of the education agenda, the really live political issue being how best to provide a basic schooling for the children of the poor.

---

[3] E. G. West, *Education and the State: A Study in Political Economy* (1965), passim. For a discussion of West, see Marc Blaug, 'The Economics of Education in English Classical Political Economy: A Re-Examination' (1975), in *Economic History and the History of Economics* (Brighton, 1984), 150–83.
[4] Wiener, *English Culture*, passim.

Should primary education be left to private agencies, or should it be provided by the public authorities? Did parents have the right to neglect the education of their children? If not, and schooling were made compulsory, should not the cost of education be borne by the ratepayer or the taxpayer, since it would be inequitable to compel anyone to purchase a service for which he lacked the financial resources? Yet free education, some worried, might weaken that spirit of self-reliance upon which Britain's economic future ultimately depended. These were the all-important issues on which Victorian entrepreneurs, one might have supposed, would have held a distinctive point of view.

In fact, however, it was impossible to start with a tabula rasa, and the entrepreneurial Radicals, along with everyone else, could hardly tackle these issues *directly*. Instead, the immediate task was one of deciding what to do with the thousands of church schools, which offered the only education available to most youngsters. The politicians, in practice, were faced with three broad options. First, they could leave the churches (and any other private agencies that wished to enter the field) entirely free to carry on their work, with the state and local authorities staying strictly aloof ('voluntarism'). Second, they could separate education from religion by creating a network of publicly funded schools which would either concentrate on secular instruction ('secularism') or confine religious tuition to the reading of biblical texts, so as not to favour any one Christian denomination. Third, they might attempt some sort of a compromise between these two extremes: for example, leave schooling largely in the hands of religious organizations, yet provide a public subsidy conditional on the achievement of certain standards of efficiency in secular teaching, standards which could be ascertained either by inspection or by pupils' examination performance or by some combination of the two tests ('denominationalism').

The dilemma was further complicated by the inequality of resources commanded by the various religious denominations. The Church of England, nationally, possessed many more schools and commanded a much larger income than did its rivals,[5] hence, the denominational solution would have condemned large numbers of children of Nonconformist parents either to go uneducated or to attend Anglican schools where they would face the danger of proselytism. A 'conscience clause'[6] theoretically provided the necessary protection for Nonconformists trapped in 'single school districts'—that is to say, those mainly rural areas where the Church of England had a monopoly of educational provision. But the trouble with the 'conscience clause' was that, unless strictly enforced, it would be useless; yet, if enforced *too* strictly, it

---

[5] Blaug, 'Economics of Education', 164 and 180, n. 36.

[6] Introduced in 1859. See Henry Roper, 'Toward an Elementary Education Act for England and Wales, 1865–1868', *British Journal of Educational Studies*, 23 (1975), 204, n. 17.

might destroy the denominational character of the entire school, which would remove any incentive which the churches still had for raising funds for educational purposes. More worrying still, the payment of subsidies to church schools, either in the form of rate support or Exchequer grants, would be politically hazardous, since many ratepayers and taxpayers would furiously protest at being compelled to subsidize the 'errors' propagated by rival religious denominations; to Nonconformists this might even feel like the imposition of a new kind of church rate.

It was in the hope of avoiding these pitfalls that some educationalists advocated 'secularism': that is, the creation of publicly funded and controlled schools supplying a secular education (leaving religious instruction to be performed by the churches in 'out of school hours'). But this fell foul of the very widely held view (among Anglicans, Dissenters, and Roman Catholics alike) that an education uninformed by Christian doctrine and principles was worthless; moreover, few politicians wished to face the accusation that they were working to 'banish the Bible' from the schoolroom. Nor would simple non-denominational religious teaching, based upon readings from the Bible (what later became known as 'Cowper Temple religion'), be universally satisfactory, since this approach, while congenial to most Dissenters, was rejected by many Anglicans and by nearly all Roman Catholics. Here, in a nutshell, was the 'religious difficulty', which prevented the establishment of any effective or comprehensive educational system in England and Wales until the last quarter of the nineteenth century.

Now this religious difficulty obviously exercised the minds and consciences of Victorian businessmen, most of whom were devout Christians active in the affairs of their chosen church or chapel. So, not surprisingly, the entrepreneurial Radicals can be found dispersed throughout *all* the various educational camps. But, as we shall see, the most energetic of them were probably those Dissenters (led by Edward Baines) who subscribed to voluntaryism.

Unfortunately, the fervour of militant Dissent tended to bring Non-conformist businessmen into conflict with their Anglican counterparts, with fateful consequences. As Cobden realized as early as the 1840s, 'the voluntary education crotchet'[7] seemed likely to split the middle class right down the middle. Indeed, Cobden's own hold on his West Riding seat between 1847 and 1857 was shaky as a result of his unpopularity with the 'Bainesocracy'. By a stroke of good fortune, the dissolution of Parliament in 1852 came at a time when the threat of Protection momentarily drew all Liberals together in the face of the common enemy.[8] But once that threat had passed, the differences

---

[7] Cobden to George Wilson, 10 Mar. 1857, George Wilson Papers.

[8] D. Fraser, 'Voluntaryism and West Riding Politics in the Mid-Nineteenth Century', *Northern History*, 13 (1977), esp. 230.

between militant Dissenters and others not of their faith were bound to resurface. This led to incidents like the decision of the Executive Committee of the Liberation Society (the successor body to the Dissenters' Parliamentary Committee), on which several businessmen served, to prevent the election of the worsted manufacturer Edward Akroyd as Liberal Member for Halifax in the run-up to the 1865 election; their sole objection to Akroyd was that he was an Anglican who had shown little sympathy with the grievances of Nonconformists.[9]

Moreover, Dissenting fanaticism was capable of sowing discord even within the ranks of the Nonconformists themselves. The fury with which many Radicals in Bradford turned upon the ex-Quaker W. E. Forster, a doughty defender of the interests of the local business community, because of his involvement in the 1870 Education Act, shows to what lengths religious zealotry could go.[10]

But, aside from the religious difficulty, was a common front on the educational question, based upon rational economic criteria, *theoretically feasible*? Leaving aside their sectarian differences, were the principles of the entrepreneurial Radicals capable of being applied to educational problems?

'VOLUNTARYISM' AND THE CREATION OF AN EDUCATIONAL MARKET

Of the various available options, it is hardly surprising that, to many Non-conformist businessmen, voluntaryism proved to be the most attractive. For voluntaryism, the rejection of State religion on principle was both a coherent doctrinal creed and a practical embodiment of many of the secular ideals and aspirations of chapel-worshipping businessmen, combining, as it did, hatred of religious 'establishments' with a fervent commitment to those independent, self-regulating organizations which proliferated in the Victorian city.

R. J. Morris has clarified this aspect of things in an important article. The significance of the voluntary society in early Victorian Britain, he argues, lay in the way that it enabled the 'urban middle class elite to seek dominance over the industrial towns without the use of main force, not just by direct ideological influence, ... but also by reproducing in the voluntary societies forms of behaviour and social relationships which represented a paradigm for their ideal industrial society'. Interestingly enough, many of these societies— the subscription charities, for example—borrowed their organizational struc-ture in part from the joint stock company. But, declares Morris, the voluntary society was also important because it 'provided an expression of social power

[9] Hamer, *Politics of Electoral Pressure*, 110–11. Akroyd, incidentally, was the Liberal who had defeated Cobden at Huddersfield in the 1857 general election.
[10] Reynolds, *Great Paternalist*, 340–4. Michael Hurst, 'Liberal versus Liberal: The General Election of 1874 in Bradford and Sheffield', *Historical Journal*, 15 (1972), 669–713.

for those endowed with increasing social and economic authority' who were nevertheless 'excluded from effective exercise of state power by religious restrictions, franchise limitation, and often by the lack of any appropriate state agency'.[11] These were the ideological underpinnings of the creed of voluntaryism.

Now, many Nonconformist businessmen were bound to find attractive a creed which, when applied to education, seemingly harmonized their religious convictions with their economic interests. Take, for example, Edward Baines junior's famous 1843 pamphlet *The Social, Educational and Religious State of the Manufacturing Districts*. This was a protest against the educational clauses of Sir James Graham's ill-judged Factory Bill, which, it was feared, would give the Church of England a dominant position in the schooling of the poor. Baines, a leading Congregationalist layman, did, of course, see it in precisely this way; Graham, he fulminated, had declared 'war against all Nonconformists, whether Conservative or Liberal'.[12]

But Baines also disapproved of Tory-inspired factory legislation and, seeing Graham's measure as a gross affront to the 'manufacturing districts', districts in which Dissent, rather than Anglicanism, was the dominant form of Christianity, he passionately rushed to the defence of the northern industrial towns in the face of the 'libels' of their class enemies.[13] Thus, in Baines's eyes, the subsidization of Anglican education, the disparagement of industrial communities, and the irksome harrying of manufacturers by means of factory legislation all proceeded from the same source: an arrogant aristocratic establishment. Reading Baines's pamphlet, one is not always sure whether it is the chapel or the manufacturing system which is being defended, the two enterprises are proceeding simultaneously.

The passions aroused by the abortive Graham Bill had important consequences. Spurred on by the Baineses, father and son, the Congregational Union decided to break entirely free from the system of State-inspected and State-subsidized schools and to set up a separate school building fund, administered after 1845 by a specially constituted Board of Education. So successful was this initiative in its early days that men like the younger Baines and his fellow Congregationalist Samuel Morley persuaded themselves that the exertions of private agencies, in healthy competition with one another, would achieve far more for education than the halting efforts of the State.[14]

This, in turn, obviously fitted in with the belief of many Dissenting

---

[11] R. J. Morris, 'Voluntary Societies and British Urban Élites, 1780–1850', *Historical Journal*, 26 (1983), 95–118, esp. 110, 104, 113. See also *idem*, *Class, Sect and Party*.

[12] Baines, jun., *Manufacturing Districts*, 64.

[13] Ibid., esp. 59–62.

[14] The fullest account is to be found in Janet E. Allen, 'Voluntaryism: A "Laissez-faire" Movement in Mid-Nineteenth Century Elementary Education', *History of Education*, 10 (1981), 111–24. See also Binfield, *So Down to Prayers*, 85; Fraser, 'Edward Baines', 200–1; Morris, *Class, Sect and Party*, 274–5.

businessmen that 'free trade' in education naturally complemented free trade in industry. Baines made this clear in his appeal to Parliament and Government in 1854:

Throw the people on their own resources in Education, as you did in Industry; and be assured, that, in a nation so full of intelligence and spirit, Freedom and Competition will give the same social stimulus to improvement in our schools, as they have done in our manufactures, our husbandry, our shipping, and our commerce.[15]

Such a system, after all, had already proved its worth in respect of *secondary* and *higher* education, where, in Baines's words, private institutions 'really swarm[ed] through the land...created by the public spirit and liberality of the people themselves, without a word of encouragement or a sixpence of aid from their governors'.[16] By contrast, 'national education' (which to many had unpleasant 'Prussian' connotations) could be dismissed as a form of 'communism', being 'based on an entire distrust of individual energy and a hatred of free competition'.[17]

Financial considerations were also involved. State subsidies, Baines complained in 1862, meant 'the waste of public money, which added to taxation'. Such subsidies also artificially depressed 'the school fees paid by parents—the legitimate source for defraying the expenses of education throughout the country'.[18] Moreover, there were immutable 'physical laws', he claimed, which decreed that 'the private purse immediately and of itself closes when the public purse opens'.[19] In short, Baines believed, 'The system of education should be one of perfect freedom, and...the Government should leave the people, as in religion, the press, and industry, entirely to their own independent exertions.'[20] Lawrence Heyworth, the financial reformer, also expressed 'his conviction that the noble and generous principle of voluntaryism would ultimately succeed in giving to the people of this country all the education they would receive, and would give it to them of the best possible kind'[21]—a sentiment shared by Samuel Laing, the administrative reformer, and, at least initially, by Bright.[22]

Such boasting ceased abruptly when, at a specially convened conference in Manchester on 11 October 1867, the Congregational Union, Baines and Morley included, felt obliged to confess that voluntaryism had, despite the

---

[15] Edward Baines jun., *Education Best Promoted by Perfect Freedom not by State Endowment* (1854), 45.
[16] Baines jun., *Letters to Russell*, 43.
[17] *Leeds Mercury*, 2 Mar. 1850, cited in Binfield, *So Down to Prayers*, 87.
[18] Parl. Deb., 3rd ser., vol. 166, 198: 27 Mar. 1862 (Liddell).
[19] Baines, jun., *Letters to Russell*, 110.
[20] Parl. Deb., 3rd ser., vol. 164, 753: 11 July 1861.
[21] Ibid., vol. 116, 1296: 22 May 1851.
[22] S. E. Maltby, *Manchester and the Movement for National Elementary Education, 1800–1870* (Manchester, 1918), 91, n. 4. Bright too was, at least initially, a supporter (Parl. Deb., 3rd ser., vol. 91, 1088–1100: 20 Apr. 1847).

heroic efforts of its devotees, failed to cater adequately for the educational needs of the working class.[23]

But, from the very start, there had been ambiguities at the heart of voluntaryism; for what, exactly, was meant by 'free'? True, at secondary level a network of genuinely independent schools had come into existence.[24] But this was not so easy to achieve at elementary level. For if these schools charged 'realistic' fees, education would be priced out of reach of the poor, the very people who perhaps needed it most; hence, to bring education, theoretically at least, within the reach of *all*, the denominational societies needed to subsidize what they were providing out of charitable donations. This, after all, was what the Congregational Union found itself driven into doing. Now, such a quest for donations may indeed have stimulated healthy competition *between the different religious denominations*. But would parents 'value' a service which cost them little or nothing, in the way that they would value something which involved personal financial sacrifice?

There was also the consideration of responsiveness to parental demand. Most entrepreneurial Radicals were naturally contemptuous of educational endowments of all kinds. Their point of view was expressed with his usual pungency by Robert Lowe, who railed against an 'opium that puts all exertion to sleep'.[25] Endowed establishments, he argued, enjoyed an unfair advantage in the market-place (as his beloved Adam Smith had earlier noted), because they possessed both the resources and the prestige that enabled them to undercut private schools. However, such schools were themselves damaged by being sheltered from the full play of market forces in two ways. First, the teaching in these institutions tended to be bad, because, enjoying something like a monopoly, the teachers had no pecuniary incentive to bestir themselves, and this inevitably led to laziness and incompetence. Secondly, teachers and managers of endowed schools found it all too easy to ignore the wishes of pupils and parents in the matter of educational content. Indeed, trust deeds might positively prevent educational innovation, thereby 'freezing' the curriculum and making it impossible to bring in 'modern' subjects (as in the notorious Leeds Grammar School case).[26] The absurd domination of the public schools and of Oxford and Cambridge Universities by classical studies could also be blamed on to the existence of endowments.

Lowe's ambition was thus to enlarge the area of free trade in the English educational system (at the secondary level, at least) by making it more open than before to market forces. Appearing as a witness before the Taunton

---

[23] Allen, 'Voluntaryism', 122; Fraser, 'Edward Baines', 201–2; Roper, 'Toward an Elementary Education Act', 186, 196.

[24] Thomas W. Laqueur, 'Working-Class Demand and the Growth of English Elementary Education, 1750–1850', in Lawrence Stone (ed.), *Schooling and Society* (Baltimore, 1976), 192–205.

[25] Lowe, *Two Speeches*, 17.

[26] See Brian Simon, *Studies in the History of Education, 1780–1870* (1960), 105–7.

Commission, he declared: 'I myself see nothing for it but to make the parents of the children the ministers of education, and to do everything you can to give them the best information as to what is good education, and where their children can be well taught, and to leave it to work itself out.'[27]

Now at least the elementary education that was being funded out of charitable subscriptions did not suffer from the 'dead hand' imposed by trust deeds. Nevertheless, such 'voluntary' schools, though free from dependence on the State, were not truly 'paying their way'. (Nor, come to that, were the factory schools, which some manufacturers continued to supply for their juvenile employees.) And this reveals an interesting internal contradiction within voluntaryism. Baines himself had defined voluntaryism as a system covering 'all that is not Governmental or compulsory,—all that men do for themselves, their neighbours, or their posterity, of their own free will'.[28] But, self-evidently, the trouble with this vague definition was that it took in *both charitable and entrepreneurial activities*.

The secularists were quick to draw attention to this weak spot in their opponents' case. 'True' free trade, they argued, would 'destroy all charitable voluntary effort', since 'it would let the people alone until they demanded education, and then charge them a profitable price.'[29] A flustered Baines was forced to admit that, theoretically, 'the self-relying principle in the Voluntary system [*was*] inconsistent with the benevolent principle'. He then tried to resolve the dilemma in the following way: 'It is, indeed, possible', he admitted, 'for private charity to pauperize, though not so degradingly as public charity.' But was it likely, he asked, that 'benevolence [would] be put forth by individuals, to any great extent or for any long time, where there [was] no real need?'[30] The answer to this rhetorical question must surely be that such a state of affairs was only too easy to envisage!

The problem can be examined from a slightly different angle. Voluntary societies in the early Victorian town enjoyed success, as Morris says, because they successfully reconciled the conflict in the minds of the urban élites between the imperatives of the market and the values of paternalistic Christianity. The importance of voluntaryism was that it undertook 'useful' social work of a benevolent kind 'when government or profit seekers were unable or unwilling to act'.[31]

---

[27] Cited by E. G. West, 'Private versus Public Education, A Classical Economic Dispute' (1964), in A. W. Coats (ed.), *The Classical Economists and Economic Policy* (1971), 139.

[28] Baines, jun., *Education Best Promoted*, 28.

[29] John Watts, 'On National Education Considered as a Question of Political and Financial Economy', in *National Education not Necessarily Governmental, Secular or Irreligious: Shown in a Series of Papers Read at the Meetings of the LPSA* (1850), 109.

[30] Baines, jun., *Education Best Promoted*, 32. But the Congregationalists' schools mostly charged between 4*d*. and 6*d*. a week, compared to the 1*d*. charged in the National Schools; so some parental sacrifice was called for (Allen, 'Voluntaryism', 122).

[31] Morris, 'Voluntary Societies', 114.

Educational charities, however, differed in one important respect from, say, charities aimed at the relief of poverty or the reclamation of fallen women. For it so happened that there *was* a market (of sorts) in primary education in mid-Victorian Britain. Indeed, a rich profusion of schools, uninspected and unsubsidized, had grown up outside both the 'public sector' and the charitably subsidized Congregationalist network.[32] These were what contemporaries called 'adventure schools' or 'private venture schools', establishments founded to promote a modest livelihood for their proprietors and staff by supplying for a small fee a basic education for the children of the poor. By 1851 only 68 per cent of students had any part of their education financed by a public subsidy, and a decade later there were still 15,952 unassisted elementary schools, as against only 6,897 assisted ones, though the latter could accommodate more pupils.[33] Baines was able to celebrate the 'adventure schools' as illustrating

the efficiency of *free competition and self-interest* to produce excellence. If competition and interest stimulate manufacturers, merchants, artizans, farmers, professional men, and all this bustling world of industry, how is it that they should not equally stimulate *schoolmasters* and *school-committees*? They have stimulated, and are stimulating them.[34]

West agrees. Indeed, citing in his support the evidence gathered by the 1861 Newcastle Commission, he even goes so far as to contend that market forces had led to a growth of educational provision in the middle of the century to the point where the Forster Education Act of 1870 was unnecessary.[35]

These 'adventure schools', it is true, met with little favour in the eyes of professional 'educationalists', who grumbled not only about an absence of training and qualifications among the teaching staff, but also about the fragmentary nature of the education that was imparted, owing to an absence of pressure on parents to send their children to these schools *regularly*. Yet it was precisely this aspect of the 'adventure schools' which apparently recommended them to many working-class families: being 'close' to the communities which they served (like corner shops), they were acutely responsive to the rhythms of working-class life and to the practical needs of their 'customers'. Indeed, Laqueur has shown that working-class parents often preferred to pay four times as much in fees (say, 4*d.* to 8*d.* a week) rather than send their children to subsidized competitors which frequently had vacant places, because

---

[32] See Laqueur, 'Working-Class Demand', 195.

[33] Ibid. 202, 192. *Economist*, 15 Feb. 1862, p. 169. In 1861 the Duke of Newcastle estimated that there were 6,897 public elementary schools with 917,255 pupils being assisted by the Government, compared with 15,952 public elementary schools with 654,393 scholars not being assisted, as well as 671,393 children in Birkbeck, factory, and ragged schools, and 573,536 in private schools (Parl. Deb., 3rd ser., vol. 164, 498–500: 8 July 1861).

[34] Edward Baines, jun., *On the Lancashire Plan of Secular Education: A Letter to a Free Trade Member of the House of Commons* (Leeds, 1848).

[35] E. G. West, *Education and the Industrial Revolution* (1975), 106–8. Idem, *Education and the State*, 140–51.

they were attracted by the former's easy-going admission and withdrawal practices.[36]

Many working-class parents seem also to have liked a kind of schooling which did not 'waste' time on moral and religious indoctrination, but concentrated instead on supplying the rudimentary secular education which they thought was most 'useful' to their children's job prospects. Of course, this neglect of 'character training' and religion was what so shocked 'expert' bodies like the Manchester Statistical Society and which cut these institutions off from all state subsidies.[37]

But opposition to the 'adventure schools' did not come solely from the 'educational experts'. Most Victorian businessmen, too, found little to admire in them. Baines and his friends, for example, could not be expected to give backing to schools which skimped or ignored the teaching of religion.[38] Yet Baines's opponents, the secularists, also tended to be dismissive of schools whose educational standards they thought to be unacceptably low. For the secularists (many of them businessmen) believed that no marked educational improvement would take place until a nation-wide system of free 'common schools' had been set up, on the American model, with funding from the rates. 'We must both admit', Cobden had defiantly told Baines as early as 1848, 'that the *principle* of State education is virtually settled, both here and in all civilized countries.'[39] Why did many businessmen take this view?

THE SECULAR SOLUTION

From the start Cobden had been a consistent opponent of Baines's educational crusade; indeed, the strength of voluntaryism in the West Riding soon convinced him that he had chosen to represent the wrong constituency in 1847. No wonder, perhaps, that an Anglican like Cobden should have felt out of sympathy with this uncompromising manifestation of militant Dissent. But, in addition, he seems to have deplored sectarian bigotry because he realized that it was leading to the fracturing of the unity of his beloved 'commercial and industrial class'. In particular, the education issue threatened to divide Cobden and his friends from many Radicals with whom they otherwise enjoyed close political relations. For example, in 1851 Cobden met Samuel Morley, Henry Richard, and Edward Miall at Charles Gilpin's house; afterwards he sadly reported back to Sturge that the group had been unable to agree on education.[40] These differences of opinion were never satisfactorily resolved.

---

[36] Laqueur, 'Working-Class Demand', 195–7, 201.

[37] E. G. West, 'Resource Allocation and Growth in Early Nineteenth-Century British Education', *Economic History Review*, 23 (1970), 90.

[38] Baines, jun., *Letters to Russell*, 68, 71.

[39] Cobden to Baines, 28 Dec. 1848, Cobden Papers, Add. MS 43,664, fo. 205.

[40] Cobden to Sturge, 24 Mar. 1851, Cobden Papers, Add. MS 43,656, fo. 201. However, all affirmed the *principle* of religious freedom.

Cobden's attachment was to the National Public School Association (NPSA), created in 1850 out of an earlier organization, the Lancashire Public School Association (LPSA), whose origins go back to 1847. In the eyes of the Tory Chartist Joseph Rayner Stephens, the LPSA was the mouthpiece of the millocracy.[41] This was an exaggeration, for much of its initial impetus had been supplied by the Scotch Presbyterian chapel of William McKerrow of Manchester, while its educational programme owed a great deal to George Combe, the phrenologist, who admired the Massachusetts educational system, which he did much to popularize.[42] Yet it is true that two of the key figures among the 'Manchester reformers' were John Bright's brother, Jacob, and his brother-in-law, Samuel Lucas, both Mancunian businessmen, and that the active membership included Alexander Ireland, the business manager of the *Manchester Examiner*, Thomas Bazley, the wealthy textiles magnate, and the ubiquitous George Wilson of Anti-Corn Law League fame.[43] Indeed, many cotton lords clearly backed the new movement in the belief that it represented a *resumption* of the old anti-Corn Law campaign.[44]

The Manchester reformers subscribed to a form of 'secularism'—a word which was already acquiring a range of connotations and associations from which Cobden wished to dissociate himself. To a later generation of Birmingham Radicals, the creators of the National Education League, secularism, of course, involved an assault on the privileges of the Anglican Church. Cobden, by contrast, never ceased to look for an ecumenical solution to the educational difficulty, acceptable to moderate Anglicans and Dissenters alike. Thus, he insisted that the reorganized Association put the words 'Public School', not 'Secular' in its title, and he was quite happy to see schools, if they wished to do so, using an anthology of biblical texts in the classroom, provided that no single religious denomination was favoured. (Baines was quite justified in twitting the Manchester reformers for their vacillations on this issue.) In 1857 Cobden went even further, and reached a compromise with the local Anglicans, who were powerful and popular in industrial Lancashire, by endorsing Sir John Pakington's abortive Bill which aimed to give rate aid both to publicly organized and to denominational schools—arguably a precedent for Forster's later measure.[45]

But the crux of the Manchester reformers' case was that access to efficient schooling should become a right of citizenship, as was the case in America. True, these men shared in part the suspicions of the 'aristocratic State'

---

[41] See D. K. Jones, 'The Educational Legacy of the Anti-Corn Law League', *History of Education*, 3 (1974), 22.

[42] Howe, *Cotton Masters*, 218. P. N. Farrar, 'American Influence on the Movement for a National System of Elementary Education in England and Wales, 1830–1870', *British Journal of Educational Studies*, 14 (1965), 38–9.

[43] Jones, 'Educational Legacy', 18–19. Maltby, *Manchester*, passim.

[44] Howe, *Cotton Masters*, 217–19.

[45] Jones, 'Educational Legacy', 25.

entertained by the voluntaryists, and this was one reason why the NPSA advocated common schools, 'democratically' financed and controlled by *locally* elected bodies—which northern businessmen in many urban areas could realistically hope in time to influence or even capture. 'Convinced . . . of the impolicy, no less than of the unpopularity of a system of public schools under government control,' declared Samuel Lucas, 'they proposed to call into existence local authorities, periodically appointed by popular election.'[46]

None the less, the Lancashire reformers clearly viewed elementary education as a public service that should be 'insulated' from the market. Nor was this claim in any way economically irrational. It made perfect sense for Victorian entrepreneurs to argue that certain facilities (police, prisons, sewerage systems, even gas and water supply, as well as elementary education) should be provided by authorities which were accountable to the local ratepayers; only within such a framework could 'capitalists' pursue their avocations efficiently. In other words, the Lancashire reformers thought that the 'market' would operate to best advantage if certain basic amenities (the 'infrastructure', as we would say) were organized on a *non*-profit making basis. (Cobden drew an interesting analogy between his educational proposals and the powers which Manchester Corporation already exercised in respect of its waterworks.[47]) This, in turn, led the reformers to support compulsory education. Theoretically at least, Cobden saw no objection to parents being punished for neglecting their children's education, as happened in Switzerland: 'I should not be squeamish about any outcry there might be of the liberty of the subject, and so on,' he remarked—an uncharacteristic observation, on his part.[48]

Unfortunately for Cobden and his friends, the strength of voluntaryism, even among Lancashire's textile élite, to say nothing of its grip on the minds of the business community elsewhere, doomed the plans of the NPSA to failure. This happened for a number of reasons. For a start, the proposed rate-supported schools would quickly have become serious rivals to the educational agencies already in the field.[49] Indeed, Cobden frankly admitted that free schools would 'ultimately close all those schools that now call upon the poor children to pay 3*d*. or 4*d*. a week, and in which the difference of expense is now made up by the contributions of the congregations'. In these circumstances, he suggested, the local authority should purchase or rent the latter's schoolrooms, since it would be absurd to waste 'the vast capital invested in bricks and mortar for the erection of' new buildings.[50] But would this not have been an infringement of the rights of private property, as well as a threat

[46] *National Education*, p. v.
[47] 22 Jan. 1851, *Cobden's Speeches*, 593–4.
[48] Ibid. 595. Modern marketeers of course accept State aid in the form of 'vouchers'.
[49] For other reasons for its failure, see Howe, *Cotton Masters*, 224–9.
[50] 22 Jan. 1851, *Cobden's Speeches*, 594.

to the continuance of the voluntary religious societies? No mid-Victorian Government dared to countenance such a bold course of action.

Moreover, 'free education' was not a particularly popular cry, since many businessmen, and the 'shopocracy' in particular, wanted their public services to be *cheap*, whereas the plans of the NPSA would have involved considerable public expenditure. On this score the solution put forward by Forster in 1870—that of subsidizing church schools with Exchequer grants and 'filling in the gaps' with rate-supported ones—could be made to look much more attractive.[51] (In fact, none of the political economists, except, briefly, Senior, had advocated *free*, as distinct from subsidized, elementary education.)[52]

ENSURING VALUE FOR MONEY

Thus, by a simple process of elimination, it gradually came to be accepted that the least unsatisfactory of all the unsatisfactory solutions to the problem of primary education would involve paying some kind of public subsidy to the existing church schools. In fact, the first fateful step in this direction had been taken in 1833 when Parliament voted £20,000 to the two main educational societies, the Anglican-controlled National Society and the non-denominational British and Foreign Schools Society, for the support of buildings. (Russell extended this aid in 1846–7 so as to cover the cost of teacher training.)[53] It remained only for Parliament to sanction some system of locally funded schools in areas where existing educational provision was inadequate. And this occurred, belatedly, in 1870.

But how could the public be assured that it was getting good value for the money that it was funnelling through these outside agencies? In 1839 an inspectorate had been set up under the aegis of the Privy Council to maintain proper educational standards in the aided schools, but this did little to allay suspicions over the existence of waste and extravagance. Indeed, in its concern for 'standards', the inspectorate, it was feared, might positively *encourage*, rather than *discourage*, profligate expenditure. As it was, complained the critics, many schoolmasters were 'over-educated' for the necessarily menial job that they had to do, with the result that the instruction which they supplied to their pupils was too bookish, as well as too expensive.[54] In any case, by the start of

---

[51] Forster himself made this point when he stated that the programme of the National Education League (which bore some resemblance to that of the old NPSA) 'would entail upon the country an enormous expense' (Henry Roper, 'W. E. Forster's Memorandum of 21 October, 1869: A Re-examination', *British Journal of Educational Studies*, 21 (1973), 66).

[52] Blaug, 'Economics of Education', *passim*.

[53] See D. G. Paz, *The Politics of Working-Class Education in Britain, 1830–50* (Manchester, 1980).

[54] In one of his leaders in *The Times* (5 Oct. 1861) Lowe sneered at teachers 'capable of performing feats at which the hair of an Oxford First-classman might stand on end' (cited in A. J. Marcham, 'The Revised Code of 1862: Reinterpretations and Misinterpretations', *History of Education*, 10 (1981), 93).

the 1860s the very complexity of the system of Privy Council grants had made them very costly to administer.[55]

This was the problem facing Robert Lowe in 1859 when he became Vice-President of the Council, with responsibility for education. Though no businessman himself, he was a fanatical adherent of political economy who was determined to establish a market in education. Suspicious as ever of 'vested interests', Lowe soon came into conflict with the schoolteaching profession. For his own modest labours as an Oxford 'crammer' when a young man had convinced him that teaching was a repulsive activity that its practitioners would shirk if allowed to do so. To be kept up to the mark, they needed to be supplied with both incentives to succeed and penalties for failure. Once again, Adam Smith suggested to him that the remedy was to be sought in the extension of 'Free Trade'. In particular, Lowe hoped, through the removal of endowments, to secure fair and open competition between schools, so that there could be a free development of the curriculum.[56] All subjects, ancient and modern, he argued, should be given 'a fair and equal start', thus creating, as it were, a kind of market in academic disciplines.[57]

On arriving at the Department of Education, however, Lowe found that his hands were largely tied. It was simply not politically feasible, for example, to move against the endowments of the ancient public schools or those of Oxford and Cambridge Universities, where, in any case, reforms had already been set afoot. Lowe tried to shame these traditional institutions into modernizing themselves by opening up a debate on what would now be called 'curricular reform'. But that was as far as he could go.

Lowe *did* have power in the sphere of elementary education, but the elaborate and expensive system of Exchequer subsidies to schools which he inherited could not simply be dismantled. Instead, Lowe sought a mechanism that would prevent teachers and school managers from relapsing into the state of indolence and complacency that he assumed to be ingrained in their profession. As he put it in one of his *Times* editorials: 'The public have been paying their money for the education of the people without getting their money's worth.'[58] It was no good relying on the inspectorate in his view, since inspectors had formed a 'cosy' relationship with the very people whose efficiency they were supposed to be monitoring: 'What is the object of inspection?', he asked the Commons. 'Is it simply to make things pleasant, to give the schools as much as can be got out of the public purse, independent of their efficiency; or do you mean that our grants should not only be aids, subsidies, and gifts, but fruitful of good?'[59] Lowe's solution to the difficulty

---

[55] *The Economist*, 15 Feb. 1862, p. 170. *The Times*, 28 Sept. 1861.

[56] Winter, *Robert Lowe*, ch. 11. Sylvester, *Lowe and Education*, 14–19.

[57] 22 Jan. 1868, Lowe, *Two Speeches*, 16–17.

[58] 28 Sept. 1861, cited by A. J. Marcham, 'Recent Interpretations of the Revised Code of Education 1862', *History of Education*, 8 (1979), 129.

[59] Parl. Deb., 3rd ser., vol. 165, 205: 13 Feb. 1862.

was the institution of 'payment by results': making schools' capitation grants dependent on the examination performance of their pupils.

Lowe prepared the House for his imminent proposals for the overhaul of public elementary education with the ringing declaration: 'Hitherto we have been living under a system of bounties and protection; now we propose to have a little free trade.'[60] Surprisingly, perhaps, he did not act on his principles by giving any help to the 'adventure schools'. On the contrary, Lowe refused to allow these schools to put their pupils forward for the examinations upon which, after 1862, the new system of Exchequer block grants was largely based.[61] In fact, contrary to what is generally thought, school grants did not simply depend upon their pupils' proficiency in the three Rs; other conditions had first to be met before any public money at all was disbursed.[62]

But the new system of 'payment by results', created by the Revised Code of 1862 (for which, in fact, Lowe did not bear the entire responsibility[63]), did mean that the income of the endowed elementary schools would henceforth depend partly upon each individual school's record of attendance and partly on its pupils' examination performance in the three Rs as tested by the inspectors. In this way Lowe hoped to reassure the country that it was getting 'value for money' from its heavy educational expenditure. (Significantly, the educational grant fell from £813,441 in 1862 to £636,806 in 1865, much to Gladstone's, as well as Lowe's, satisfaction.[64]) *The Economist* warmly approved: 'A principal and predominant part of the pecuniary aid given by the State must be dependent on the production of definite results satisfactory to the State, and tested by the State,' it argued; the beauty of Lowe's arrangement was that it was designed 'to pay in direct proportion to ascertained excellence'.[65]

The Revised Code met with bitter hostility from nearly all teachers—but that was what Lowe had intended all along! Apart from anything else, teachers now had to haggle with their managers over salary levels, instead of enjoying a quasi-Civil Servant status: a valuable lesson for them in the laws of supply and demand, Lowe thought. 'Are you for efficiency or for a subsidy?', Lowe asked

---

[60] Ibid., vol. 164, 736: 11 July 1861.

[61] The Newcastle Commission had recommended that grants be given to unassisted and private schools on the criterion of examination results (Marcham, 'Revised Code', 90).

[62] Sylvester, *Lowe and Education*, 65.

[63] See Marcham, 'Recent Interpretations', 122–3; D. Mason, 'Peelite Opinion and the Genesis of Payment by Results: The True Story of the Newcastle Commission', *History of Education*, 17 (1988), 269–81.

[64] Laaden Fletcher, 'Payment for Means or Payment for Results: Administrative Dilemma of the 1860s', *Journal of Educational Administration and History*, 4 (1972), 18. Lowe almost certainly intended, through his Code, to effect a reduction of educational expenditure, as Marcham has argued ('Recent Interpretations', 125–32, and 'Revised Code', 87–92). But for a different view, see Laaden Fletcher, 'A Further Comment on Recent Interpretations of the Revised Code, 1862', *History of Education*, 10 (1981), 21–32.

[65] *Economist*, 22 Mar. 1862, p. 312; 29 Mar. 1862, p. 339.

the Commons. 'I believe we must appeal to the passions of the human mind—that we must enlist hope and fear to work for us—that we must hold out a prospect of sufficient remuneration if the children are properly taught, and of loss if they are not, or we shall do nothing.'[66] Lowe's educational reforms thus had the avowed intention of *raising productivity*, and represented an attempt to apply factory methods to the world of the teaching profession.

In all this, examinations had a dual function: they were a way of creating an 'internal market' in those areas of life where market forces could not operate fully, and they also served as a device whereby the *curriculum* of the elementary schools could be influenced. What subjects, then, did Lowe and other worshippers of 'business principles' during the mid-Victorian years want working-class pupils to learn?

SCHOOLING FOR CAPITALISM?

To put the question another way, did the entrepreneurial Radicals have a distinctive point of view as to why children should be sent to school in the first place?

In fact, many of the arguments which businessmen deployed in favour of education were the commonplaces of their day. To the Dissenters, the main purpose of literacy was obviously that it made possible the reading of the Bible and hence led to salvation. 'I have the strongest conviction that religion is the best element in education,' declared Baines, 'and ought to lie at its very basis.' But, as always, he refused to draw a clear distinction between Christianity and secular progress. 'However useful learning may be,' he wrote on another occasion, 'piety and virtue are *incomparably more useful*.' This was because the schools Baines was concerned to foster would be ministering to 'young children of the humbler class, many of whom have scarcely any domestic advantage, while they have many temptations', and so need to be provided with 'discipline'.[67]

The secularists appealed to social utility in a more *direct* way. Leaving small children to roam wild in the streets was, to use one of Cobden's favourite words, 'unsafe'. Almost to a man, the education enthusiasts stressed that education would sharply reduce the levels of poverty and crime, and so be beneficial to *all* members of the community. 'Why do people live in bad cellars, surrounded by filth and disease?', asked Cobden. 'You may say it is their poverty, but their poverty comes as much from their ignorance as their vices; and their vices often spring from their ignorance.' Education, he went on, would also teach people to be more thrifty, and, by encouraging rational recreation, would aid temperance.[68] In dissociating himself from Baines's

---

[66] Parl. Deb., 3rd ser., vol. 165, 205–6: 13 Feb. 1862.
[67] Baines, jun., *Education Best Promoted*, 32; *idem*, *Letters to Russell*, 68, 71, emphasis added.
[68] 25 Oct. 1853, *Cobden's Speeches*, 614.

voluntaryism, Joseph Pease similarly claimed that 'education would be the cheapest thing in the world, provided it was conducted on the right principle, for it tended to diminish crime, and to reduce the expenses of the convict establishments'.[69]

Speakers at the meetings held by the LPSA also took this line. The textile manufacturer Richard Gardner declared that 'the condition of the rising generation of the poor' was neither 'creditable to the wealth and civilization of the country, [n]or even compatible with its security'.[70] And Dr John Watts gave an interesting address 'On National Education Considered as a Question of Political and Financial Economy', in which, after briefly touching on the commercial advantages of improved education, he concentrated mainly on the avoidable 'costs' of ill health, mendicity, and, above all, crime. Moreover, as the Association reminded the wealthy and the highly placed, there could be 'no protection to property, no security for the maintenance of public order, like an educated people'.[71]

It is even more interesting to discover similar arguments being used in 1870 by A. J. Mundella, who, in his address to the Association of Chambers of Commerce, rested his case in part on the importance of reducing crime, drunkenness, and misery, as well as on the need to prepare the industrial work-force for a sharper phase of international competition.[72] W. E. Forster, when defending his 1870 Bill, spoke in similar terms.[73]

For Cobden himself, another important reason for advocating 'common schools', on the American model, was that this would strengthen the cohesion of British society:

One of the benefits we should derive from common schools would be, that it would cause that greater intermixture and blending of society that would arise from the middle and working classes sending their children to one common school, where they would become more familiarised in their common views, and tastes, and habits, and the boys would be brought up in genial sympathies and more intercourse than that which prevails at present in this country.[74]

The Manchester reformers, then, saw their 'common schools' as appropriate for middle-class as well as working-class youngsters. Education would also prepare people for citizenship: 'I want to have our self-government a habit of

---

[69] Parl. Deb., 3rd ser., vol. 164, 758: 11 July 1861.

[70] *National Education*, 13.

[71] Watts, 'On National Education', 92–113; *idem*, 'A Plan for the Establishment of a General System of Secular Education in the County of Lancaster', ibid. 199.

[72] Ilersic and Liddle, *Parliament of Commerce*, 131. On the other hand, in Nov. 1867 Mundella had successfully moved a motion calling for the adoption of a system of technical education similar to that of Germany and other Continental countries, 'in order to enable our manufacturers to maintain the position they have so long enjoyed' (ACC Papers, 27 Nov. 1867).

[73] Parl. Deb., 3rd ser., vol. 199, 466: 17 Feb. 1870.

[74] 1 Dec. 1851, *Cobden's Speeches*, 609.

appreciation—something our people will be proud of, not simply a habit.'[75] More particularly, in the course of his visit as a young man to the United States, Cobden had been forcibly struck by the high proportion of Americans who could read newspapers, thanks to its education system—something which was important to a Radical who wanted politics to be based not on coercion or influence, but on opinion.[76]

Cobden also claimed that, contrary to what most educational commentators of the day were saying, the problem of educational provision was not too bad in the towns but was a disgrace in the agricultural districts. In other words, Cobden wanted to rouse the countryside from its torpor, and characteristically saw lack of education as primarily a *rural*, not an urban, problem (that is, it was the fault of the aristocracy!).[77]

The assumption behind much of this talk was that the spread of education necessarily went hand in hand with a 'safe' extension of the franchise. But which should come first? Cobden's original position seems to have been that the creation of a national system of schools would pave the way for parliamentary reform, but he later withdrew that suggestion.[78] Perhaps Cobden realized that, in hinting at the prospect of political democratization, he was antagonizing some of the wealthy mill-owners like Hugh Mason, a supporter of the NPSA who feared 'democracy'.[79]

Mason's fears, of course, were shared by Lowe. But, once the franchise had been extended in 1867, Lowe started to rethink some of his basic attitudes, publicly recognizing, for example, that Disraeli's Reform Act had now placed on the State the duty of ensuring that the mass of the people received a satisfactory education and that public funds would have to be tapped to pay for this: 'I believe it will be absolutely necessary that you should prevail on our future masters to learn their letters' was his famous but usually misquoted phrase.[80] But most historians now believe that Lowe was almost alone in this belief, and it does indeed seem that the Forster Education Act owed little to the recent enlargement of the electorate.[81]

Be that as it may, businessmen were not alone in recognizing that before being given the vote, the working classes should first, either voluntarily or compulsorily, be prepared for their responsibilities. Still less had they originated the view that the purpose of education was to instil in the lower orders habits of deference and obedience; this had traditionally been the viewpoint of the Anglican Church and of dignitaries from landed society, with whom the

---

[75] 25 Oct. 1853, ibid. 614.

[76] 'England, Ireland and America', in *Political Writings of Cobden*, 96–8.

[77] See 22 May 1851, *Cobden's Speeches*, 602.

[78] Read, *Cobden and Bright*, 178–9.

[79] Howe, *Cotton Masters*, 225–6.

[80] Parl. Deb., 3rd ser., vol. 188, 1549: 15 July 1867.

[81] A. J. Marcham, 'Educating Our Masters: Political Parties and Elementary Education 1867 to 1870', *British Journal of Educational Studies*, 21 (1973), 180–91.

entrepreneurial Radicals normally had little in common. Thus, when the Tory *Quarterly Review* declared that the schooling of the poor should aim at providing 'a sound unambitious education, free from extravagance and fitted for the state of life to which the poor belong',[82] it found itself in incongruous alliance with the political economist Lowe.

Where some members of the business community, particularly the Mancunians, *did* make a distinctive contribution to the education debate was in their quickness to recognize the dangers of industrial competition from other states with better developed educational systems. For example, as early as 1835 Cobden, visiting America, had noted: 'If knowledge be power, and if education give knowledge, then must the Americans inevitably become the most powerful people in the world.'[83] This became an important theme in his educational propaganda for the NPSA: 'If we are to hold our own—if we are not to fall back in the rear in the race of nations—we must educate our people, so as to put them upon a level with the more educated artisans of the United States.'[84] Nor did the 'threat' come solely from the United States, as Cobden realized after observing the technical backwardness of many British businessmen as revealed in the Great Exhibition of 1851:

Did any reflecting man walk through the Great Exhibition without feeling that we were apt to be a little under a delusion as to the quality of men in other parts of the world, and their capacity to create those articles of utility of which we are apt to think sometimes we possess a monopoly of production in this country? Did nobody feel somewhat struck at the vast superiority of the French in articles of taste and delicate manipulation; and were we not equally struck to find ourselves so closely trod on the heels in everything that relates to the more rude utilities of life, in American productions, where we found ourselves beaten in shipbuilding, in locks, pistols, and many other things we had to show?[85]

Thomas Bazley, too, recognized that improved education would improve human capital, increasing both employers' profits and workmen's wages.[86] Or, as Cobden told the old Leaguer J. B. Smith, 'We shall be beaten by the Yankees unless we can raise the educational standard of our mechanic class . . . It will I hope alarm our capitalists a little.'[87]

Perhaps, however, Cobden and some of his friends were a little too far ahead of their times in sounding this note of alarm ('I don't think we can

---

[82] *Quarterly Review*, 111 (1862), 113.

[83] *Political Writings of Cobden*, 94.

[84] 25 Oct. 1853, *Cobden's Speeches*, 616.

[85] 1 Dec. 1851, ibid. 609; see also ibid. 615–16 (25 Oct. 1853).

[86] Howe, *Cotton Masters*, 220–1.

[87] Ibid. 221. See also the interesting observations in 'The Politico-Economical Value of a Sound Elementary Education of the Wage-Class', a paper given to the Social Science Congress in 1865 (*Transactions of the National Association for the Promotion of Social Science*, 1865, 347–56): 'Mind is the sole capital of a country,' etc. But the clergyman giving the paper balanced his reflections on improved industrial efficiency by also invoking 'reverence to God', etc.

wait,' Cobden had said in December 1851[88]). Few of the early speakers at the LPSA's meetings referred, except in the vaguest of terms, to the contribution which technical education might make to the future of British manufacturing. Revealingly, the Mancunian businessman Edmund Potter failed even to understand why some of his contemporaries had been so impressed by French industrial design, as demonstrated in their exhibits in the 1855 International Exhibition; these products, he sneered, had been put forward for show, in the hope of winning medals, not in response to demand; the only International Exhibition *he* was prepared to take seriously was the adoption by all nations of perfectly free trade. So long as British manufacturers could beat their overseas competitors in price and quality in free competition, this sort of complacency was bound to continue.[89]

It took the Paris Exhibition of 1862 to shake the confidence of a large section of the business community.[90] Thereafter, following Cobden's death, Mundella began to make progress in his campaign to line up the Chambers of Commerce behind the call for improved technical education.[91] Himself of Italian extraction, Mundella had for many years taken a close interest in the educational systems of Continental Europe, particularly Saxony. The next decade also saw the National Federation of Associated Employers of Labour calling for the establishment of fifty technical schools in as many industrial centres, even if each cost £2,000 a year. This would 'effect a revolution in our manufactures in the course of a few years, and would bring back the original outlay a hundred fold'. 'If England is ultimately beaten in the race,' said its journal, 'she will have herself to blame.'[92]

But what exactly were these businessmen demanding? It is important to remember that although literacy was a necessity for the growing number of clerical employees later in the century, the *first* phase of the Industrial Revolution probably saw a 'de-skilling' of labour.[93] True, many of the early industrialists like Greg and Ashworth had taken the lead in providing education for their juvenile employees in their own factories. But, as Michael Sanderson has shown, the Lancastrian mill-owners were antagonized by the

---

[88] 1 Dec. 1851, *Cobden's Speeches*, 610.

[89] Edmund Potter, *A Picture of a Manufacturing District: A Lecture Delivered in the Town Hall, Glossop, 15 January 1856* (1856), 9–12. By the late 1860s Potter had become a keen advocate of a strong Education Bill ('He did not care how strong'), but his objective was to make an 'impression' on trade unions so that their members would show greater economic rationality (Parl. Deb., 3rd ser., vol. 197, 1372–3: 7 July 1869).

[90] Following the London Trade Exhibition, Isaac Holden wrote to his wife, 21 May 1862: 'The French beat the English hollow in almost everything and every respect' (*Holden–Illingworth Letters*, 351).

[91] Bradford, already suffering from foreign competition in the worsted business, was quickly off the mark. See Firth, 'Bradford Trade', 20; Reynolds, *Great Paternalist*, 62; and Sigsworth, *Black Dyke Mills*, 57–8.

[92] *Capital and Labour*, 9 Sept. 1874.

[93] M. Sanderson, 'Literacy and Social Mobility in the Industrial Revolution in England', *Past & Present*, 56 (1972), esp. 75, 94, 102.

1833 Act, under which factory owners were *prohibited* from employing children who had failed to attend school for two hours a day for six days a week, and as a result began to call on the State to assume direct responsibility in this area.[94] By 1843, if Baines's statistics are to be believed, only 6,434 pupils were being educated in factory schools in the whole of Lancashire, Yorkshire, and Cheshire.[95] But may this not also be because most employers did not want the bother or the expense of running their own schools, in view of the fact that unskilled work at a cotton factory did not require any prior, specialized training?

Certainly it must be significant that few early Victorian businessmen explicitly put the case for education in strictly economic terms; as Richard Johnson has noted, 'Leaving literacy aside for a moment, there is little stress, before 1850, on teaching specific occupational skills', which could best be picked up on the factory floor.[96] Even Mundella wanted higher technical education to be grafted on to a general education, and in any case, as we have seen, he put heavy emphasis on traditional arguments for the provision of schooling. Moreover, most advocates of technical education were careful to make it clear that they wanted nothing more than the exposition of the general principles underlying trade and industry, such was their anxiety not to interfere in any way with unrestricted commercial competition.

Education might, of course, have prepared the working classes for life under capitalism in a *negative* way. One historian has asserted that the 'strategy was to build up a literate (but not skilled) upper working class content to do their allotted work without social or political ambition.'[97] Lowe's educational reforms could certainly be described in these terms. His 1862 Revised Code, for example, was clearly intended to provide a crash training programme in the three Rs which would fit the workers of a class-divided society for the unavoidable routine tasks awaiting them in later life. Lowe was not afraid to admit as much, telling the Commons: 'We do not profess to give these children an education that will raise them above their station and business in life, that is not our object, but to give them an education that may fit them for business.'[98]

---

[94] Sanderson, 'Education and Factory', 278–9.

[95] Baines, *Manufacturing Districts*, 26. But this is almost certainly an underestimate. Parliamentary returns indicate that by the mid-1850s there were still 46,000 children being educated in factory schools (*Transactions of the National Association for the Promotion of Social Science*, 1860, 382).

[96] Richard Johnson, 'Notes on the Schooling of the English Working Class, 1780–1850', in Roger Dale *et al.*, *Schooling and Capitalism: A Sociological Reader* (1976), 47.

[97] W. P. McCann, 'Elementary Education in England and Wales on the Eve of the 1870 Education Act', *Journal of Educational Administration and History*, 2 (1969), 21. Blaug demonstrates that the political economists all stressed the way in which schools improved the *behaviour* of pupils, not the cognitive value of what was taught (Blaug, 'Economics of Education', 172).

[98] Cited in Sylvester, *Lowe and Education*, 62. But, writing to Lingen in 1882, Lowe said that the three Rs had been picked out because they could most easily be examined: 'It was more a

Moreover, we have seen that the insistence on regularity of attendance often conflicted with the needs and wishes of working-class parents. From this it might be deduced that the movement to establish compulsory formal schooling on a national basis represented an attempt to 'control' the children of the poor and to socialize them in the virtues of subordination, dependability, and so on.[99] In the words of one historian, 'The first thing . . . children were taught at school was not reading or writing but to sit up straight, keep quiet and above all arrive on time.'[100] In other words, the move to organized schooling should perhaps be seen as preparation for the time-regulated routines of factory and office life. The *form* of education (the 'hidden curriculum') might have been more important than its actual *content*.

But this brings us to the final point: to what extent was there a deliberate attempt to inculcate a capitalist ideology by propagating, in simplified language, the doctrines of classical political economy? Historians of education have certainly noted one significant shift in the direction of deliberate propaganda. Whereas educational primers had once emphasized the virtues of 'obedience', 'loyalty', and so on, they point out, by mid-century this was supplemented—or even replaced—by attempts to inculcate the values of capitalism. In other words, there was a change from the older emphasis on subordination, being content and dutiful in that station of life to which God had ordained one, to comprehending rationally the working of the market economy.[101]

Robert Lowe fitfully played around with similar ideas. For example, he added political economy to the list of subjects taught in the Normal Schools in 1863. Two years earlier he had openly encouraged the schoolmasters in State-aided schools, 'in these days of strikes', to use their authority to get across to their charges the doctrine 'that wages do not depend on the will of a master, but have a law of their own to regulate them'. Proficiency in this topic, he suggested, would be of more use than a knowledge 'of the wars of the Roses, or of the history of the heresies in the early Church'.[102] Yet Lowe really had far too much common sense to suppose that industrial relations could be transformed by these methods.

It was quite otherwise with those who invented and propagated the new subject of 'social economy'. Here the organizing genius was the Utilitarian businessman William Ellis, who had become manager of the Indemnity

---

financial than a literary preference' (Christopher Duke, 'Robert Lowe—A Reappraisal', *British Journal of Educational Studies*, 14 (1965), 24).

[99] See Edward Akroyd's observations in *Political Parties*, 35.

[100] Morris, *Class, Sect and Party*, 254.

[101] See J. M. Goldstrom, 'The Content of Education and the Socialization of the Working-Class Child 1830–1860', in W. P. McCann (ed.), *Popular Education and Socialization* (1977), 93–109; *idem*, 'Richard Whately and Political Economy in School Books, 1833–80', *Irish Historical Studies*, 15 (1966–7), 131–46. Propaganda obviously took other forms; one thinks of the Society for the Diffusion of Useful Knowledge, the writings of Harriet Martineau, etc.

[102] *Parl. Deb.*, 3rd ser., vol. 164, 723: 11 July 1861.

Marine Insurance Co. at the age of 26; and the group's guru was Cobden's friend, the phrenologist George Combe. 'Social economy' represented nothing less than an attempt to reduce to simple didactic terms the principles of political economy. Ellis, in fact, prided himself on having accomplished what no previous writer had so much as attempted: bringing out the consequences of that science for individual conduct and social well-being. His various educational primers brim with moral maxims and practical advice: for example, on the folly of strikes, the value of prudence and forethought (appropriate counsel from someone employed in insurance!), and on how best to regulate one's expenditure for one's own and the common good.[103]

Ellis did not think of 'social economy' as appropriate only for the children of the poor, and he was delighted when University College School introduced the subject (briefly) into its curriculum, the first middle-class school to do so. Incidentally, Ellis held the public schools in profound contempt, the publication of *Tom Brown's Schooldays* confirming him in his belief that these institutions were given over to a demoralizing regime of flogging, fagging, and cramming. And, he sneered, the classical studies in which they specialized were 'relics of a once useful article' which now had little social utility.[104]

What Ellis meant by 'social utility' is quite clear from the arrangement of his various textbooks. He aimed to present political economy in such a way as to legitimize the market and to persuade the working-class youngster to seek his own betterment by observing market disciplines. Thus, his *Outlines of Social Economy* concluded with the reflection that, without knowledge of that subject, 'the causes of the privation and suffering by which [the working man] is surrounded and to which he is exposed, must ever remain a mystery to him; and he will never be able to discriminate between what he ought to bear with resignation, and what he may successfully struggle and secure himself of'.[105] In fact, Ellis had a great deal to say about 'bearing'; and the only 'struggling' of which he approved was the kind favoured by Samuel Smiles.

Convinced of the importance of his educational theories, Ellis worked hard to interest contemporary educationalists and prominent politicians, Cobden being among those whom he believed he had 'converted'.[106] Perhaps his most practical achievement was his part in the founding of the 'Birkbeck Schools', which enjoyed the patronage of James Wilson's aristocratic sponsor, the Earl of Radnor.[107]

---

[103] Edmund Kell Blyth, *Life of William Ellis* (1889), passim.

[104] Ibid. 168–9, 184–6, 166.

[105] [William Ellis], *Outlines of Social Economy* (1846), 76–7. On the principles of 'social economy', see *George Combe Education: Its Principles and Practices as Developed by George Combe*, ed. William Jolly (1877).

[106] Blyth, *William Ellis*, 152–6.

[107] For details of the Birkbeck schools, see W. A. C. Stewart and W. P. McCann, *The Educational Innovators 1750–1880* (1967), 326–41; Blyth, *William Ellis*, 112–13.

In 1852 Cobden visited one of these institutions, where he heard a fourteen-year-old monitor give a lesson on 'social economy' to a class of sixty boys, most of them younger than himself. 'One half the House of Commons might listen to these lessons with advantage,' he is said to have observed![108] Cobden's sympathetic interest may have had something to do with the introduction of the new subject into the curriculum of the Manchester Model Secular School, set up by the NPSA the following year. Under the enthusiastic leadership of its headmaster, Benjamin Templar, this institution developed a distinctive curriculum, which included the three Rs, physical science, drawing, human physiology, political economy, and practical morality (in lieu of religion). Its pupils were taught that industrial success depended upon 'a good moral character, and a well deserved reputation for honesty, truthfulness, industry, sobriety, and punctuality'.[109] The school's most active promoters included, along with a scatter of professional men, several cotton manufacturers, calico printers, and merchants, among them Bazley, Sir John Potter, and Elkanah Armitage—and, of course, Cobden.

When in 1858 the Manchester Secular School, in its anxiety to secure a Government grant, applied for recognition to the Committee of the Council on Education, some of Lancashire's leading industrialists (including Bazley) came forward to vouch personally for the good influence which it was exercising. In a joint testimonial these supporters declared:

The course of instruction pursued we consider of great practical importance, embracing as it does, in addition to the ordinary branches of day-school education, the exhibition of the uses and properties of matter,—of the organic laws and fundamental principles which create, preserve and affect health and wealth, and which vitally influence individual and social well-being.[110]

Also submitted were examples of school exercises produced (presumably) by some of the brightest pupils. Thus, a budding statesman (aged nine) gave the orthodox 'proof' of why strikes could never raise wage levels.[111] This, of course, was the very 'system' which Charles Dickens was mocking when he wrote *Hard Times*, in which the antisocial consequences of the 'Gradgrind philosophy' are dramatized through the depiction of the unspeakable Bitzer,

[108] Blyth, *William Ellis*, 93. Henry Morley and W. H. Willis, 'Rational Schools', *Household Words*, 144 (25 Dec. 1852).
[109] Jones, 'Educational Legacy', 29. Donald K. Jones, 'Socialization and Social Science: Manchester Model Secular School 1854–1861', in W. P. McCann (ed.), *Popular Education and Socialization* (1977), 115–17. On the Manchester Secular School, see also Combe, *Education*, 241–4.
[110] Copy of Correspondence between the Committee of the Model Secular School at Manchester and the Committee of the Council on Education, relating to the Subject of Admitting the Manchester Model Secular School to a participation in the Parliamentary Grant for Education, LXVI (1857–8), 7.
[111] Ibid. 32.

who had internalized only too thoroughly the values and lessons of 'social economy'.[112]

In his speech to the Reform Club on 7 January 1868, Forster himself discussed the need not only for the three Rs, but also for political economy. Yet, ironically, 'social economy' was probably one of the 'extra' subjects which Lowe's Revised Code, with its tendency to narrow the school curriculum to the three Rs, had helped to squeeze out.[113] In any case, those very aspects of the subject which struck Dickens and other contemporaries as objectionable helped to ensure that it never assumed a commanding position in the nation's educational system. 'Social economy', one of its foremost practitioners admitted, had always been unpopular with working-class parents, some of whom even withdrew their children from school rather than have them subjected to what they saw as 'nonsense', while a few supplied their own home instruction in order to neutralize the nefarious capitalist propaganda![114]

THE ENTREPRENEURIAL RADICALS AND HIGHER EDUCATION

But what of secondary and higher education? Given the fact that most Radical businessmen, the Dissenters in particular, felt excluded from the privileged world of the public schools and the ancient universities, how did they propose to remedy their grievances? Were they looking for the possibility of their children being given the opportunities which they themselves had 'missed', or did they want to *destroy* these endowed institutions?

Some of the old Free Trade campaigners certainly stuck faithfully to the old militant line. Thus, in 1843 R. H. Greg privately opined: 'Our public schools and universities want a "League" to reform them as much as the Corn Law gentlemen.'[115] And in 1854 The Revd Henry Dunckley called openly for 'the removal of the intellectual and religious monopolies which disgrace our age', and proposed the establishment of a new system of national education to be financed out of earlier educational endowments, as well as the abolition of the Anglican monopoly at Oxford and Cambridge:

Let idle placemen no longer live in academic state on funds which were intended to furnish the means of instruction to our rising youth, nor superstition and blind faith be permitted, beneath the cloak of medieval darkness, to emasculate the future mind of England. The property enjoyed by our universities, amounting to £741,000 annually,

---

[112] On the background of *Hard Times*, see Robin Gilmour, 'The Gradgrind School: Political Economy in the Classroom', *Victorian Studies*, 11 (1967), 212–13, 219.

[113] Roper, 'Toward an Elementary Education Act', 200.

[114] See the unintentionally comic account furnished by William Matthew Williams, a teacher at the Edinburgh Secular School, to the Social Science Congress of 1857 (*Transactions of the National Association for the Promotion of Social Science*, 1857, 512–15).

[115] R. H. Greg to R. P. Greg, 4 Dec. 1843, cited in Howe, *Cotton Masters*, 293, n. 105.

might, if economically applied, bring the boon of a sound, practical, and cheap university training within the means of the bulk of the middle classes.[116]

But, while urging the repeal of the 'religious tests', few Radical businessmen were prepared to follow Dunckley's lead. Why? This subject can be explored not just by examining what businessmen actually *said* about secondary and higher education, but also by seeing what plans they made for their own sons' education.

For those ambitious for their children's future, a prudent accommodation with the existing system obviously had much to recommend it. Edward Baines senior, for example, sent his eldest son, Matthew Talbot, to a series of local grammar schools; but when it became apparent that the young lad wished to be trained as a barrister, he had him moved to a private tutor and coached for 'the more liberal of the two universities', Cambridge—this at a time when the Test Acts had still not been repealed. The move proved to be a wise one, in that it probably helped Matthew Talbot in his political career. Elected from his father's old constituency, Leeds, in 1852 (he had previously been MP for Hull since 1847), M. T. Baines was made President of the Poor Law Board by Russell and then Chancellor of the Duchy of Lancaster in Palmerston's first Administration, thus becoming one of the very few genuinely middle-class politicians to attain high office in the mid-Victorian period.[117] By contrast, his rather more energetic younger brother, Edward Baines junior, whose education had been more typical of someone of his background, remained for fifteen years on the back benches.

Another pillar of Congregationalism, Samuel Morley, also temporized with the 'world'. On the one hand, he interested himself in the higher education of the middle classes by working to create a three-year residential education within reach of those to whom a standard university career was closed by giving his backing to Cavendish College in Cambridge, which aimed to provide the commercial middle class with an affordable university experience which would not violate their consciences.[118] But the ambivalence of Morley's views on secondary and higher education emerge in his notes for an undated speech, in which he urged the middle classes to take education more seriously. Education, looked at crudely, was a good investment, said Morley; but, while praising arithmetic and mathematics and modern languages (French and German), he was careful to add: 'No intention to disparage classical training—most important, absolutely essential for those who desire to extend their education; the very discipline is most valuable, but, keeping in mind the value

---

[116] Dunckley, *Charter of Nations*, 400, 403–4.
[117] On M. T. Baines's career, see Fraser, 'Edward Baines', 183–4.
[118] Hodder, *Life of Morley*, 401–3. Also Ian Campbell Bradley, *Enlightened Entrepreneurs* (1987), 50–1.

of adaptation, I would entreat you, while attending to the one, not to neglect the other.'[119]

Moreover, Morley entertained high ambitions for his *own* sons, all four of whom went to Trinity College, Cambridge. The great Dissenting business-man duly fell under the glamour of this institution. According to his uncritical biographer, Morley was always ready to make one of a party for the boat races, and 'took as keen an interest in the probability of First Trinity making a "bump" especially when, as was often the case, one of his sons was rowing in the boat, as if he were himself an old Trinity man'.[120] 'So often did he visit Cambridge during the time that his sons were at college, that their private tutor, or "coach", once said to him, "Why, Mr Morley, if you could only keep one term more, we would get the Vice-Chancellor to give you a degree"—a joke which Mr Morley greatly relished.'[121] All this while Morley was continu-ing to protest against the university tests, which, along with the Burials Act, he regarded as the greatest living Nonconformist grievance. But, significantly, he did this because he wanted 'the great middle class of the country' to be able to compete with all comers 'on fair and equal terms'.[122] Samuel Morley did not live long enough to see the fulfilment of his hopes: the elevation of his son Arnold to the Cabinet during Gladstone's last Ministry.

However, it should be emphasized that most Nonconformist businessmen were made of tougher stuff than this. Even the Ashworths of Bolton, whose social life took them very far away from the Quaker values of their youth, showed no interest in public schools or universities. Henry Ashworth sent his sons to a variety of educational establishments, mostly Quaker, taking them away in their mid-teens. He 'had no belief in universities', writes Boyson. 'He considered that they neglected scientific studies and produced a rankness of mind that it was the duty of true education to eradicate. He said in 1879 that few of the great discoveries and inventions of modern life had come from men who had been to universities.' His brother Edmund took the same view.[123]

Another distinguished Quaker who had fallen out of favour with the Society of Friends, John Bright, also showed some resolution in resisting the lures of 'gentrification'. His son William Leatham went to the famous Quaker school Grove House, in Tottenham, before entering business and becoming a partner in his father's cotton-spinning firm; he later served as a Liberal MP.

[119] Hodder, *Life of Morley*, 449.

[120] Ibid. 227–8.

[121] Ibid. 228–9. On this aspect of Morley's life and character, see J. P. Parry, *Democracy and Religion: Gladstone and the Liberal Party 1867–1875* (Cambridge, 1986), 214–15. But Morley did show a sturdier sense of independence than J. W. Pease (a second-generation Pease, admittedly), who accepted a baronetcy in 1882, only to pass over the chance of a peerage in 1894 (M. W. Kirby, *Men of Business and Politics: The Rise and Fall of the Quaker Pease Dynasty of North-East England, 1700–1943* (1984), 55, 59).

[122] Parl. Deb., 3rd ser., vol. 204, 67–8: 9 Feb. 1871. Hodder, *Life of Morley*, 345.

[123] Boyson, *Ashworth Cotton Enterprise*, 246.

No such success attended Richard Cobden's son, whose premature death devastated his parents; but, true to his father's principles, 'Dick' had been educated at a small private school, run on the Pestalozzi plan.[124]

Typical of the sort of proprietary school favoured by many Nonconformist businessmen until late in the nineteenth century was Amersham Hall in Buckinghamshire, so vividly described by Augustine Birrell, one of its pupils.[125] The headmaster, Dr Ebenezer West, specialized in the tuition of sons of Baptist clergymen; but clearly many businessmen also sent their sons to this idiosyncratic establishment. What one Radical manufacturer expected his son to be taught there can be seen from the interesting letter (undated, but presumably written around 1870) sent to West by Jeremiah Colman:

So far as his future life is concerned I presume it will be mercantile, at all events that is what I should desire, and that he should in due time take his place in my firm. For this purpose a knowledge of arithmetic is essential, and the power of writing a good business letter. Chemistry is desirable, and the modern languages also.[126]

According to Birrell, Amersham Hall taught a modified version of Latin and Greek, but the school was most successful in mathematics, though by the late nineteenth century its curriculum was already being largely moulded by the matriculation examination of London University. Yet the main legacy of the school was probably that it gave its pupils a sense that they sprang from the blood of martyrs. Birrell's experience was that he and his schoolfellows 'seemed for the most part to be stonily indifferent alike to the successes and the sufferings of their dissenting ancestors'.[127] But clearly, establishments like Amersham Hall continued throughout the nineteenth century to give wealthy and influential sections of the commercial and industrial middle class a strong sense of their 'differentness' from 'polite society'. So long as these feelings persisted, a significant fusion between church and chapel, landed and commercial wealth, could not be achieved.

Another strong impulse motivating the mid-Victorian entrepreneur in his approach to secondary and higher education was clearly civic pride—the same impulse that led to the creation of parks and amenities, and even to the development of what a later generation was to call 'gas-and-water socialism'. Such feelings had a tendency to override narrowly utilitarian considerations. So much is apparent in Thomas Bazley's attempts to upgrade Owen's College in Manchester to the status of a university. In his public appeal, Bazley did, it is true, praise the applied science departments of Owen's College, but he also stressed that most of its students attended the Arts Schools, where, he proudly announced, a new Chair of Classics was about to be

---

[124] See Hinde, *Richard Cobden*, 242.
[125] Augustine Birrell, *Things Past Redress* (1937), 40–6.
[126] Helen Caroline Colman, *Jeremiah James Colman: A Memoir* (1905), 243.
[127] Birrell, *Things Past Redress*, 42–3.

created. Moreover, Bazley went out of his way to deny that the College had any tendency... to render its studies subservient to the industry of Manchester'; and he dismissed the notion that 'because a college is situated in Manchester... its work must be secretly devoted to calico'.[128] Thus, whatever Matthew Arnold, who pillories Bazley in *Culture and Anarchy*, may have thought (and Arnold was *not* a particularly perceptive observer of this social world), the backers of Owen's College did not want an institution that was narrowly dedicated to commercial studies; indeed, as Howe shows, the College 'had little to do with rational economic calculations', and 'provided a broad, liberal education, not one geared specifically to the needs of textiles'.[129]

Cobden, too, eschewed a strictly utilitarian approach to education, though he was genuinely keen on breaking the monopoly in secondary and higher education accorded to classics and on developing 'modern' studies. In the bad-tempered exchange with aristocratic MPs alluded to earlier, he had incurred the derision of most of the educated world by making the far-sighted suggestion that a university Chair in the geography and history of the United States be endowed. But even then, Cobden's main objective was to stimulate interest in contemporary affairs, rather than impart 'useful knowledge'.

Lowe's position was even more complex. In his lecture on *Primary and Classical Education*, he had expressed anxiety at the spectacle of the educated classes being steeped in classics while ignorant of so many things which their social inferiors knew.[130] But his attitude to the public schools and the older universities softened considerably in the latter part of his career. For by then he had become obsessed with mitigating the damage which the 1867 Reform Act threatened to do to the country. The famous Order-in-Council on the Civil Service was self-consciously aimed at creating a privileged élite, a new aristocracy of talent to counter the democratizing tendencies of the day. Oxford and Cambridge might still need reforming, but they no longer seemed to pose a serious threat to liberal values; indeed, they might even have a beneficial role to play in the new strategy of resistance and containment. Moreover, although he disapproved of the narrow, archaic curriculum of the public schools, Lowe yet felt nothing but contempt for those middle-class parents who sent their children to schools specializing in a vocational commercial education centred on bookkeeping and the like. On this topic, if on few others, Lowe came very close to the position of his old adversary Matthew Arnold.[131]

---

[128] Thomas Bazley, 'Shall Manchester Have a University?', *Nineteenth Century*, 2 (1877), 113–23, esp. 120, 122.

[129] Howe, *Cotton Masters*, 293.

[130] Robert Lowe, *Primary and Classical Education: An Address to the Philosophical Institute of Edinburgh* (Edinburgh, 1867), 31–2.

[131] Winter, *Robert Lowe*, Ch. 10.

None of this is to deny that by the 1860s, and perhaps earlier, *some* manufacturers, worried over the growing intensity of foreign competition, were embracing the case for improved technical instruction as a means of safeguarding and extending home and overseas markets. Indeed, it was at about this time that a number of wealthy businessmen endowed colleges of higher technology (Frith's College in Sheffield, for example)—eloquent testimony to this new mood of concern. Moreover, the Nottingham hosiery manufacturer Mundella, who had made himself the spokesman for these concerns, succeeded in 1867 in placing technical education towards the top of the agenda of the Association of Chambers of Commerce, arguing that this was necessary if Britain were to keep up with the 'rapid progress and high excellence of Continental Manufacturers'. This resulted in the setting up of a subcommittee of the Association, the drafting of a report, and, later, the sending of a delegation to the Vice-President of the Privy Council.[132] Yet, as we have seen, when, a year after receiving this deputation, the Vice-President asked the Chambers of Commerce what practical remedies they were advocating, the Association in its reply argued *against* purely private provision of facilities, and also made it clear that it did not *merely* want practical commercial education.[133] This seems to have been the viewpoint of most manufacturers.

Finally, it is noteworthy that many Victorian entrepreneurs reacted angrily to the charge that men of their background were materialistic and philistine. They affected, it is true, to be indifferent to the strictures passed on them by Matthew Arnold in *A French Eton* and *Culture and Anarchy*; but the agitated way in which they did this suggests that the great Victorian 'Sage' had indeed succeeded in getting under their skin! Be that as it may, W. L. Sargant probably had a point when he denied that money grubbing was any more prevalent among manufacturers than among other classes in the community.[134] (Wiener's point is that it would have been better if the acquisitive instincts of English capitalists *had* been more highly developed.) In short, strict entrepreneurial values succumbed to what Howe has called 'the moralization

---

[132] ACC Papers, 27 Nov. 1867. Soon afterwards Forster persuaded the Bradford Chamber to accept a strongly worded motion on the need to establish technical educational institutions which, like those in Germany and other Continental countries, would teach the art of design and inculcate valuable scientific knowledge (Bradford Chamber of Commerce Minutes, 21 Jan. 1868, fos. 92–3).

[133] ACC Papers, 25 Jan., 3 Mar. 1868. The replies of the various affiliated Chambers were sent to the Vice-President of the Committee of the Council on Education and were printed as a parliamentary paper, along with a letter on technical education from Sir Jacob Behrens, *Parliamentary Papers*, LIV (1867–8), 37–52.

[134] Sargant, *Essays*, i. 42. Edward Baines, who spent much of his later years promoting the Yorkshire College, clearly did so from a variety of motives: a desire to make local industries more competitive, a commitment to the arts and sciences for their own sakes, and, not least, a strong pride in his city and county. See the material in the Baines Papers.

of the capitalist',[135] the rejection of pecuniary accumulation as an end in itself—a shift in attitudes with obvious implications for higher education.

CONCLUSION

Perhaps there was no area of public life in which the entrepreneurial Radicals achieved so little as that of education. One explanation would be that they lacked the sort of help from better-placed 'insiders' which had benefited them so much with regard to issues like the repeal of the Corn Laws and the passing of commercial reforms. Their one important ally was Robert Lowe, who arguably put forward the most clear-headed case for an education based upon rational economic principles, since 'payment by results' was a serious attempt to apply the values of the market to the nation's schooling. Yet, even in Lowe's case, a belief in the market was often tempered by an élitist strand of thinking which denied the central proposition of the market: namely, the assumption that consumers/parents know best what was in their own interest.

As for Gladstone, he was very little use at all to the entrepreneurial Radicals in educational matters. The Revised Code pleased the great Liberal statesman because it led to savings in public expenditure. But in other respects Gladstone, so often a friendly 'external' ally of the businessmen, had scant sympathy with their educational aspirations and attitudes; he made no pretence, for example, of being interested in 'social economy'![136] He did, of course, understand that the ancient universities would have to 'modernize' themselves if they were to survive; and he publicly expressed his confidence that 'the spirit of improvement' would govern Oxford and Cambridge now that they faced competition from the new unendowed colleges. But Gladstone also declared that 'the solidity of establishments founded on old endowments' generated traditions which, handed down from one generation to another, were a source 'at once of affectionate remembrances and of lofty aspiration'.[137] It may also be significant that Gladstone declined to give a government grant to Owen's College in Manchester, a decision which he later took as a precedent when asked for aid by the newly founded Aberystwyth College.[138]

Moreover, Gladstone specifically attacked the notion that 'the sole or main purpose of education [was] to stock the mind with knowledge as a shop is stocked with goods, and that the wants of life [were] to be met like the wants of customers'; preparing people for future employment was 'its lower, not its higher, purpose', the main goal being the improvement of the mind

---

[135] Howe, *Cotton Masters*, 314.

[136] Blyth, *William Ellis*, 157.

[137] *The Times*, 18 Apr. 1860. For Gladstone's later, more critical view of educational endowments, see *Revised Report of Proceedings at Dinner of 31 May 1876, held in Celebration of the Hundredth Year of the Publication of the 'Wealth of Nations'* (1876), 41.

[138] Matthew, *Gladstone 1809–1874*, 201–2.

itself. True, Gladstone followed up these remarks by recognizing the value of a business career: citing the example of ancient Greece and medieval Florence, he said that there was 'nothing in the pursuits of the merchant that ought to preclude the pursuit of mental refinement', and he called for a harmonious alliance between 'the pursuit of commerce and the interests of human cultivation'.[139] In all this Gladstone may have demonstrated more tact and fair-mindedness than did, say, Matthew Arnold, but it remained patently clear where the Liberal Leader's primary sympathies lay. In short, Bright's famous dictum that 'Oxford and tradition held [Gladstone] fast' applies more directly to the sphere of education than to any other area of public policy.

But it can also be argued that in matters of education the entrepreneurial Radicals were themselves in something of a muddle as to what they *wanted* to achieve. In part, they suffered from the old uncertainty (of which we have already seen several examples) as to which they valued more status or wealth. That the two things might not coincide was recognized by Lowe when he wittily suggested that the commercial middle class, whose main need was to raise its self-respect and its public ambitions, would do well to forsake its narrow concern with an education that merely prepared it for the counting-house and the manufactory.

Many businessmen seem to have reached this conclusion unaided, being principally motivated by 'pride of caste' and a determination to vindicate the 'manufacturing districts' against the 'aspersions' of critical outsiders. And this touchy class pride often found expression in an imitation of the older educational forms—in an anxiety, for example, to demonstrate that Manchester had a *real* university of its own, now that a faculty of classics had been attached to it. Indeed, with some businessmen (though not with as many as is sometimes claimed), the quest for a higher status for their 'order' tempted them to give their children a privileged education which, predictably, led to a rejection of family traditions.

What is more, Victorian businessmen found themselves unable to come to any common conclusion regarding the merits of different kinds of educational structure. It was easy to make airy declarations, as Behrens did in his presidential address to the Bradford Chamber of Commerce, about the desirability of converting 135 custom-houses into schools or colleges, 'instead of frowning as they do now upon commerce like so many robber castles of the middle ages'.[140] But what in practice was to be done? Even discounting the 'religious difficulty', there were actually perfectly sound *business* reasons why a merchant or industrialist might be either a voluntaryist (free schools naturally complemented the free market) or a secularist (the compulsory establishment of minimal educational standards in secular subjects would create an efficient

---

[139] *The Times*, 23 Dec. 1872.
[140] Bradford Chamber of Commerce 19th Annual Report, 1870, p. v.

work-force) or even a denominationalist (making use of the existing church schools offered the *cheapest* way out of the impasse).

More fundamentally still, 'business' views regarding educational *organization* often came into conflict with business views as to educational *content*, a dilemma which was also raised by the ownership of the Press.[141] For if, as Lowe and others believed, education, like newspaper opinion, was a kind of commodity, then it presumably made sense to organize that commodity with a view to the maximization of profit. But if *that* were done—in other words, if the 'customers' were given 'what they wanted'—might not the propaganda value of education be weakened? In short, how could profitability be combined with edification?

In West's view, such a combination might indeed have been achieved had education really been left to market forces, with maximum influence being exercised by the consumers/parents. This did not happen in the area of elementary education, he believes, because the 'suppliers' were (as always) better organized politically than were the dispersed 'consumers'.[142] More specifically, argues West, in the Victorian period a free market in education was hindered not only by the teachers, but, more important, by self-appointed experts who thought they knew best what constituted an appropriate educa-tion for the children of the poor. Thus, John Stuart Mill dismissed the very concept of an 'education market' with his famous aphorism: 'The uncultivated cannot be competent judges of cultivation.'[143] The Taunton Commission also followed this line of reasoning: the principle of supply and demand, it claimed,

fails when the purchasers demand the wrong thing and it fails also when they are incompetent judges of the right thing. The utmost, that it could do in the matter of education, would be to supply, not what is best, but what the parents believe to be the best.[144]

Kay-Shuttleworth, at the Privy Council, drew the appropriate moral: namely, that the State would have to *create* the demand for good education. Working-class parents were too ignorant to ask for it for their children; education was not a 'natural want', and 'all statesmen who have wished to civilise and instruct a nation, have had to create this appetite'.[145]

Both West and some of the socialist historians of education find this

---

[141] On the Press, see Conclusion.

[142] West, 'Resource Allocation', 94–5.

[143] John Stuart Mill, *Principles of Political Economy* (1848), Book V, ch. 11, sec. 8.

[144] Cited in West, 'Private versus Public Education', 139.

[145] Kay-Shuttleworth, 'Letter to Lord Granville, 29 July 1861', in *Four Periods of Public Education as Reviewed in 1832, 1839, 1846, 1862* (1862), 608. The Lancashire reformers sometimes made the same point: 'Unfortunately the free trade doctrine does not hold in the case of education until we have an already well educated generation of adults, who could properly appreciate, and would therefore properly pay for it' (*National Education*, 109).

attitude intolerably patronizing to working-class parents, who were not the fools that the educational 'experts' thought them to be. Indeed, it is arguable that working-class parents, immersed in the grim struggle for daily survival, took a sensibly 'practical' approach to their children's schooling. They had little interest in the niceties of religious dogma, 'character formation', or the 'duties of citizenship'; they were understandably preoccupied with ensuring that their children were taught the skills which would directly prepare them for the world of work.[146] In this way, it is suggested, the establishment of an uncluttered 'educational market' might have led to the kind of curricular reform which would have fended off Britain's later economic decline.

However, such claims seem somewhat implausible. For a start, they gloss over the very serious inadequacies of the 'adventure schools' (a fault also exhibited in some of the more sentimental socialist accounts).[147] They also underplay the educational deficiencies which drove Forster to introduce his Reform Bill in 1870. And, most important of all, they ignore those aspects of the 'adventure schools' which directly assailed the values of the office and the workshop. For example, the ease of entry and withdrawal, which encouraged irregularity of attendance, may have endeared these institutions to some working-class parents; but it is hard to see such features as being helpful to the 'enterprise culture'.

What sort of educational system *would* have stimulated economic growth in mid-Victorian Britain is a matter of continuing debate. All that can be said with certainty is that, notwithstanding the interesting opinions promulgated by, among others, Cobden, Forster, and Mundella, the entrepreneurial Radicals as a group failed to put together a distinctive educational programme. Indeed, in few areas of public life was their failure so palpable.

[146] Laqueur too talks about educational historians having been obsessed until recently with supply, not demand ('Working-Class Demand', 195) and also about the 'working class consumer of education' (ibid. 198).

[147] Hurt calls these schools 'no more than crèches' (J. S. Hurt, 'Professor West on Early Nineteenth-Century Education', *Economic History Review*, 24 (1971), 624–32, esp. 632).

8

The Labour Problem

I have ever been solicitous to bring out the self respect of our order, by inducing an honest display of pretensions to civil and social example, and that to foster the class pride of men who might otherwise have betrayed unworthy diffidence to their own usefulness—in other words to succour emulation. This pamphlet is intended quite as much to inform the Manufacturing Class themselves as any other class in the community of what is really the advanced position of the m[anu]f[acturin]g class as compared with any other class, and if it should advance them a step in the right direction, it will have done more good than it could possibly do by exposing the falsehoods of a Revd. Slanderer [Dr Vaughan].

(Ashworth to Cobden, 12 Dec. 1849)

Labour must be considered as a mere purchaseable article, like all other commodities, and ought to be bought and sold, and weighed and measured accordingly; . . . the honest fulfilment of contracts ought to be rigidly adhered to; and . . . all the law ought to do, so far as the adult is concerned, is to define the standard of measure and currency to be used. I believe this is a sound economical doctrine, and therefore, in practice, really benevolent. . . . The power of the trade union, then, *robs* . . . the worker of his right to work, and *robs* the capitalist of his right to purchase.

(Edmund Potter, 1860)

THE TEACHINGS OF POLITICAL ECONOMY

It may seem strange to relegate a discussion of the labour problem to the next to last chapter, and a short one at that. After all, many businessmen had no very firm views on, for example, the education question; but all were necessarily involved, in their day-to-day lives, in handling their work-force, and all would have had strong opinions on trade unionism and factory legislation. However, during the 1840s and early 1850s at least, most of the entrepreneurial Radicals took an entirely negative stance on both issues. Whereas in nearly all other areas of public life, Radical businessmen were dissatisfied with the status quo, and advocated changes (even if they could not always agree on what form change should take), in industrial matters most simply wanted to be left alone. Trade unionism and legislative restrictions on the working hours and conditions of factory operatives were seen as unwarranted interference with their rights as employers, to be resisted accord-

ingly. *Why Can I Not Do What I Will with My Own?* was the title of a pamphlet
supporting their position which well encapsulates businessmen's attitudes to
the labour problem. Only from the late 1850s onwards did the entrepreneurial
Radicals, led by the Nottingham hosiery manufacturer A. J. Mundella, start to
develop more positive policies.

In fending off all external encroachments on their business practices,
employers were motivated in varying proportions by self-interest, class pride,
and a theoretical commitment to the 'laws' of political economy. But it was
the latter which the Radicals tended to emphasize in their public pronouncements. Here, for example, is Henry Dunckley, the Anti-Corn Law cam-
paigner, lamenting the existence of factory legislation. 'The "Ten Hours'
Bill"', he wrote in 1854,

> was a retrogressive step. We see in this measure, however humane the motives which
> led to its adoption, an unjust interference with the rights at once of capital and
> labour.... The working man will not be and ought not to be, prevented from earning
> all the money he can.

'A mutually satisfactory contract' on wages and hours, declared Dunckley,
could always be reached between the employer and his hands, provided that
there was 'no outside interference'.[1] The Liverpudlian shipping magnate
William Brown deplored all factory legislation on similar grounds: 'Any injury
sustained by the masters must eventually fall on the men by the reduction of
wages,' he said.[2] Although women and children were generally recognized to
fall into a different category, James Heywood, MP for North Lancashire,
defended even child labour as being a blessing to poor working-class parents
who needed the extra money.[3]

The activities of trade societies were also held up to censure. Most
'masters' in mid-Victorian Britain, following the views expressed by the
political economists, dismissed them as an economic 'fallacy' akin to the old,
now discredited Protectionism.[4] For had it not been 'scientifically' proved
that no combination could raise wage levels, these being determined solely
by supply and demand? There was some uncertainty as to whether trade
unionism was merely futile or positively dangerous; but usually the two claims
were advanced simultaneously. Thus, during the famous Preston strike of
1853–4, a manufacturer ('Lancashire Man') told his 'hands' that he wished
'to buy [their] labour, fairly to pay for it, and to be as independent and
uncontrolled in the purchase as he is in the purchase of hats, clothes, or

---

[1] Dunckley, *Charter of Nations*, 383. See also Boyson, *Ashworth Cotton Enterprise*, 164.

[2] Parl. Deb., 3rd ser., vol. 111, 834: 6 June 1850.

[3] Ibid. 854–5. Only later was a distinction between women and children generally recognized.

[4] S. C. Kell reminded his readers of how long it had taken for the middle classes to see the
light on the Corn Laws, the country's false system of public finance, etc., and suggested that
patience should be shown to working men who persisted in clinging to their illusions about the
efficacy of trade unions (Kell, *Political Attitude*, 11–12).

shoes—free to buy where he likes, and where he can do so cheapest'.[5] Workmen who could not see the 'necessity' of this were treated as objects of pity and contempt. 'We regret to see the operatives so blind to their own interest,' said *The Economist*. 'They are led astray by interested advisers, who endeavour to make political capital by kindling discontent.'[6] The *Manchester Guardian* agreed. 'Hands have no right except for services rendered,' it said; and 'any decision as to the mode of management must arise with the master and be controlled by him. . . . Any suggestions made, or any outlays for profits are his property, and the workman has really no claim to any share of the profits arising therefrom.'[7]

These attitudes were slow to disappear. In 1869 Lowe was still referring to trade unionism as a mysterious conspiracy against the best interests of all classes of the community; working men who could not understand the folly of what they were doing he addressed in the tones of an exasperated schoolmaster faced by a class of recalcitrant schoolboys. Trade unionism, pontificated Lowe, was 'an enormous blunder, a gigantic miscalculation, based on fallacies the most obvious and mistakes the most easily detected'. 'The evidence in their favour [was] utterly futile.'[8] In a series of letters to *The Times* in 1869–70 Edmund Ashworth joined him in rehearsing the old verities on trade unionism: 'There is a danger of our falling back into the old guild system of Elizabeth,' he wrote. How could the Government justify the giving of 'a monopoly to a section of the community, whether large or small, to the utter exclusion of the remainder'? Trade unionism was 'the bane of English industry'.[9]

Moreover, *The Economist*, in its characteristically doctrinaire way, deprecated industrial 'combinations', in *whatever* quarter they arose, whether that of employers or 'hands': 'Combinations may have been effective to give victory to an army, to secure the control of the people by an hierarchy or the dominion of an aristocracy, but they do not give prosperity to trade. They are foreign to its nature and can only be ruinous.' This same article went on to deplore the support being given to the Preston employers during the great lock-out by manufacturers from all over Lancashire and Cheshire: 'We hope that the masters are not divided among themselves, and both adverse and favourable to combinations,' it said.[10]

---

[5] *Economist*, 31 Dec. 1853, p. 1464.

[6] Ibid., 24 Sept. 1853, p. 1074. 'The victims and the dupes' of those who gave them their orders, men who were committing 'a kind of moral suicide', it called the strikers (ibid., 3 Dec. 1853, p. 1352). For the employers' view of the strike, see *Preston Chronicle*, 28 Jan. 1854.

[7] *Manchester Guardian*, 14 Dec. 1853, cited in Kirk, *Growth of Working Class Reformism*, 267.

[8] *Quarterly Review*, 123 (1867), 364, 378. Likewise W. R. Greg (Fraser, *Trade Unions*, 73).

[9] *The Times*, 8 Nov. 1869, 9 Jan. 1870. See too Edmund Ashworth's evidence (5 June 1867) to the Royal Commission on Trade Unions ('Third Report of Commissioners into the Organisation and Rules of Trades Unions and Other Associations' (1867), 3910, qs. 4349–75).

[10] *Economist*, 31 Dec. 1853, pp. 1464–5.

As the events at Preston made clear, employers could put on impressive displays of solidarity during a crisis.[11] But they were usually sensitive to the accusation that such collectivist behaviour contradicted the rugged individualism which they professed to practice.[12] Thus Cobden reluctantly accepted that employers *might* be justified in forming defensive organizations so long as these did not become permanent. But, he added, employers should make clear 'that they hold all such combinations whether of capitalists or labourers to be unsound in principle and that they seek only to establish such a state of things as shall leave every individual free to make his own bargain without interference from any other parties'.[13] Edmund Potter, the wealthy calico printer, went further, and declared that he was 'not yet willing' to meet trade union encroachments with counter-organizations, which, he said, might come to have as deadening an effect on employers as trade unions did on *their* members.[14] Indeed, one reason why Lowe so disliked trade unionists was that they provoked employers to follow their own bad example.[15]

So the entrepreneurial Radicals set out with an ideological distaste for both factory legislation and trade unionism. *The Economist* actually thought that the two things were linked. During the Preston strike, for example, it hinted that the operatives were acting against their own interests at the behest of landowners who had already shown their hatred of the manufacturing districts by sponsoring restriction of hours.[16] Since legislative harassment of employers had also had the effect of exerting downward pressure on wage levels, *The Economist* believed that there was an obvious solution to industrial unrest: the operatives should abandon the chimera of a 10 per cent wage increase and instead combine *with* their masters to get rid of the Factory Acts![17]

But quite as important as this doctrinaire commitment to political economy was the sense of injured pride which clearly influenced the attitude to industrial questions taken up by many employers.[18] 'It is the duty of Manufacturers, as a body, to sustain the right estimation of the class to which they belong,' the Central Committee had proclaimed in 1844.[19] As in the 1830s,

---

[11] H. I. Dutton and J. E. King, *'Ten Per Cent and No Surrender': The Preston Strike, 1853–1854* (Cambridge, 1981), 80–1 and passim. But, once again, attempts to organize employers across a large area of the country tended to run into the obstacle of regional pride; see *Bradford Observer*, 14 June 1855.

[12] Joyce, *Work, Society and Politics*, esp. ch. 4.

[13] Cobden to W. F. Ecroyd, 9 Nov. 1853, cited in Howe, *Cotton Masters*, 164.

[14] J. G. Hurst, *Edmund Potter and Dinting Vale* (Manchester, 1948), 46.

[15] *Quarterly Review*, 123 (1867), 351–2. Nor were such views held only by those who were doctrinaire. For the Wolverhampton Chamber of Commerce's objection to *all* 'combinations', see 11th Report of Commissioners into Trades Unions, 94–5.

[16] *Economist*, 24 Sept. 1853, p. 1074.

[17] Ibid., 8 Oct. 1853, pp. 1128–9.

[18] Howe thinks that such status considerations rated more highly than economic advantage in the minds of the mill-owners (*Cotton Masters*, 184–5).

[19] *Report of the Central Committee*, 4. The Master Spinners of Preston were similarly worried in 1839 about 'the frequent misrepresentations made in the House of Commons and elsewhere

manufacturers passionately resented any attempt to stigmatize their behaviour as greedy and immoral or to criminalize minor infractions of the Factory Acts.[20] This feeling of resentment was slow to evaporate. Thus, Thomas Bazley, angry about the 1860 Bleaching and Dyeing Works Bill, protested at the aspersions being cast on what he called a highly 'respectable class of men' with a strong commitment to the interests of their workpeople.[21] William Brown took the same line: if one excluded Liverpool, which was not a manufacturing town, Lancashire was 'one of the most virtuous [counties] in the kingdom'; why, then, was it being discriminated against?[22] Heywood proudly went on the *offensive*: the factory system, he declared, 'was a benefit to the country, as conferring a moral education upon the population'.[23]

'It was not the rate of wages so much as dictation and interference with all his internal arrangements that perplexed and annoyed' the 'capitalist', said Edmund Potter in 1869.[24] When employers spoke like this, they particularly had in mind the 'impertinence' of a landlord-dominated Parliament. In the opinion of the Halifax textile owner Edward Akroyd, it was especially unfair that factory masters had 'been singled out by Parliament from all other classes of employers' and subjected to minute and, he thought, often harmful and irrational regulations.[25] Indeed, as long as country gentlemen stood up in Parliament to express their 'sympathy for the working classes of the towns' and presented petitions on their behalf,[26] Radical MPs would continue to feel a strong sense of injustice. What about the condition of the farm labourers, they justifiably asked?[27] There was also anger at 'sentimental' philanthropists and theoreticians who pontificated about the problems of the manufacturing districts without any practical experience of industrial life.[28]

But it was the behaviour of the inspectorate which aroused most indignation. 'It was very hard upon the millowners', said John Cheetham, 'to be bound by the opinion of the Inspectors, who were not practical men, and

relative to the master spinners', and drew attention to 'the propriety of disabusing the public mind of the impressions thereby made upon it' (Papers of Master Cotton Spinners of Preston and Neighbourhood, Lancashire County Record Office, DDX 1116).

[20] W. G. Carson, 'Symbolic and Instrumental Dimensions of Early Factory Legislation: A Case Study in the Social Origins of Criminal Law', in Roger Hood (ed.), *Crime, Criminology and Public Policy* (1974), 107–38. This important article deals with the genesis and aftermath of the 1833 Factory Act; but its terms are as applicable to the controversies of the 1840s and early 1850s.

[21] Parl. Deb., 3rd ser., vol. 158, 979: 9 May 1860.

[22] Ibid., vol. 111, 836: 6 June 1850.

[23] Ibid., vol. 141, 445: 4 Apr. 1856.

[24] Ibid., vol. 197, 1371–2: 7 July 1869. See also *Economist*, 10 Mar. 1855, p. 251.

[25] *NAPSS* (1857), 155.

[26] e.g. E. Ball: Parl. Deb., 3rd ser., vol. 128, 1290: 5 July 1853.

[27] Ibid., vol. 111, 853–4: 6 June 1850 (Trelawny); ibid., vol. 216, 826–7: 11 June 1873 (Fawcett).

[28] Bright complained bitterly that those who wanted these controls 'were in a state of child-like ignorance', knowing nothing about such industrial processes (though this particular rebuke was aimed at William Williams, the metropolitan Radical) (ibid., vol. 139, 1369: 25 July 1855).

who, in fact, knew little or nothing about the matter.'[29] Bright, in a particularly violent explosion in March 1855, spoke of 'the insulting nature of the inspectorship' and of 'the insolence and annoyance' of Horner's character (Leonard Horner was the Chief Factory Inspector); and he threatened 'to leave the country, and to live somewhere else, where labour and capital were allowed to fight their own battle on their own ground, without legislative interference'.[30] It was precisely to protest against 'undue restrictions and interference' that the Factory Law Amendment Association (soon to be transformed into the National Association of Factory Occupiers) was set up in 1855. The Association formally accused inspectors of casting 'imputations on the manufacturers as a class'.[31] Such was the bitterness of their resentment that one of the cotton lords could speak of inspectors who 'went to the mills as if the proprietors were the greatest scum of the earth'.[32]

A similar combination of attitudes affected the views of the entrepreneurial Radicals on the issue of trade unionism. Cobden warned Ashworth to deal with the striking Preston workers in a kindly spirit.[33] But even Cobden found it impossible to countenance action which encroached upon managerial prerogatives.[34] Most businessmen took the same view. Thus, during the Preston strike the cotton masters explicitly stated that the dispute was less one of wages than a 'question of mastery', a rejection of 'the spirit of tyranny and dictation'.[35] Similarly Edmund Ashworth, in his later protests against trade unionism, complained about his personal loss of authority: 'He must not interfere with the men either as to quantity or quality of work.'[36] 'All this interference with the management of business', wrote Ashworth, 'is so harassing to an employer, whose interest, powers of invention and adaptation are required to please his customers, that it may well account for the decline of an industry so trammelled.'[37]

Although it is often said (and rightly) that hostility to trade unionism and opposition to factory legislation among employers was replaced from the mid-

---

[29] Parl. Deb., 3rd ser., vol. 141, 376: 3 Apr. 1856.

[30] Ibid., vol. 137, 613: 15 Mar. 1855.

[31] B. L. Hutchins and A. Harrison, *A History of Factory Legislation* (1903; 1966 edn.), 117.

[32] Ibid. 114–15. See Bazley's remarks at the convening meeting of the National Association of Factory Occupiers (ibid. 116). See also Kirk, *Growth of Working Class Reformism*, 247.

[33] Cobden believed that the Preston strikers were 'dupes' who needed to be given 'a valuable *lesson*' (Cobden to Ashworth, 29 Nov. 1853, Cobden Papers, Add. MS 43,653, fos. 218–19). But he later advised Ashworth 'to deal guardedly with the labourers' side of the question. In exposing the misdoings even of the leaders, do it in a kindly spirit "more in sorrow than in anger", and don't attribute bad motives even to the worst of them' (Cobden to Ashworth, 17 June 1854, ibid., fo. 227).

[34] Howe, *Cotton Masters*, 167.

[35] Fraser, *Trade Unions*, 99. For why the Preston mill-owners resisted attempts at outside mediation, see William Ainsworth's letter, Papers of Master Cotton Spinners of Preston and Neighbourhood, DDX 1116/3/1.

[36] *The Times*, 6 Dec. 1869.

[37] Ibid., 9 Jan. 1870.

1850s onwards by a more flexible attitude, even one of acceptance, the mood did not shift that swiftly. Take, first, the question of factory legislation. The Crimean War actually provided the Lancashire textile owners with yet another argument against the hated inspectorate. In the words of *The Economist*:

It is not wise . . . in subordinates of the Government—Factory Inspectors and others— to provoke comparisons between private enterprise and Government exertions, direct- ing the national anger and contempt pointedly against an existing Administration.

And Aspinall Turner of the Manchester Commercial Association declared that 'they did not want inefficient men to conduct either the warfare at Balaklava, or inefficient, superannuated men to conduct their manufacturing industry' at home.[38]

The formation of the National Association of Factory Occupiers was aimed at preventing invidious enactments and at the amendment, though not the total repeal, of the Factory Acts.[39] Employers also bitterly criticized legislation enforcing the fencing of machinery.[40] As late as 1864 the Bradford millocrats were vigorously, and successfully, fighting off an attempt to bring certain categories of employees in warehouses under the protection of the Factory Acts, saying that they objected 'strongly to the annoyance of being under the supervision of inspectors' when no good grounds for this interference had been established.[41] As for trade unions, these continued to be viewed with suspicion, and episodes like the 'Sheffield Outrages' speedily reawakened employers' ancestral mistrust of workers' 'combinations'.

THE SOFTENING OF ENTREPRENEURIAL ATTITUDES?

Yet, despite the obduracy of many employers, others became more relaxed in their attitudes towards both trade unionism and factory legislation.

In the 1830s and 1840s trade unions had quite widely been viewed (not entirely without reason) as conspiratorial organizations of wild, desperate men duped or coerced by 'paid agitators'.[42] But in the calmer atmosphere of the later 1850s some employers began to discern that trade unions performed certain valuable services. For example, their restrictive practices often stabilized prices, thereby allowing large employers to resist cut-throat competition from small firms paying low wages. Also the extension of piece-work in some

---

[38] *Economist*, 10 Mar. 1855, pp. 251–2.

[39] Hutchins and Harrison, *Factory Legislation*, 116. Andrew H. Yarmie, 'British Employers' Resistance to "Grandmotherly" Government, 1850–80', *Social History*, 9 (1984), 149.

[40] Hutchins and Harrison, *Factory Legislation*, 117–19. In Apr. 1856 the Association carried a Bill which watered down an earlier measure regulating the fencing of machinery.

[41] Bradford Chamber of Commerce 14th Annual Report, 1865, pp. 25–9. The protests took the form of drawing up a petition, sending delegations to London, and circulating all MPs.

[42] Patrick Brantlinger, 'The Case against Trade Unions in Early Victorian Fiction', *Victorian Studies*, 13 (1969), 37–52.

industries made co-operation very useful in the establishment of agreed price-lists, of which the most famous was the Blackburn Standard List, inaugurated in 1853.[43]

It has been argued that in areas like the textile belt of Lancashire, which experienced mechanization at an early stage, a 'mature' system of industrial relations quickly developed,[44] in which the new, more 'respectable' union officials had a key role.[45] In fact, the situation in Lancashire was far messier than this. Throughout the entire mid-Victorian period, many cotton lords kept up a bitter rearguard campaign against union recognition, and the industrial history of these years is scarred by a succession of bitter disputes, running from the Preston strike of 1853–4 to the Padiham dispute of 1859 and beyond. Significantly, few of the cotton unions go back any further than the mid-1880s.[46]

At the same time a certain mellowing of attitude can be discerned, not only on the part of union officials, but also on the part of some manufacturers. Some sectors of engineering were similarly affected. As early as 1851, an anti-union employer like the machine tools manufacturer John Platt was discussing the manning of new machines with the union leader William Newton.[47] By 1869 even Edmund Potter, the scourge of unionism, was ready to admit that the labour leaders were an intelligent and responsible body of men who often exercised a restraining influence on their rank and file: 'If all the Trades Unionists were as well educated and as courteous as their leaders, the matter would be very different.'[48] This was a complete reversal of the earlier view.

The change of attitude was reflected in the deliberations at the Social Science Congress, which in 1860 set up a special committee to report on the whole question of trade unionism. This committee produced a carefully balanced report. On the one hand, it deprecated any interference with employers' management prerogatives; but at the same time it recognized that trade unions could play a stabilizing role in industrial relations. In 'well-organized' trades, it said, strikes were only called as a last resort. 'The leaders of trades' societies are known and responsible men; they have the confidence of their own class,' the committee concluded.[49]

This softening of tone is thought by some historians to owe much to the 'Christian Socialists', two of whom, Ludlow and Maurice, sat on the Social

---

[43] Fraser, *Trade Unions*, 101–4. Joyce also stresses the establishment of generally orderly industrial relations against a backdrop of prosperity in the Lancashire textile industry (*Work, Society and Politics*, 64–6).

[44] Joyce contrasts this situation with that of the West Riding (*Work, Society and Politics*, 73–6).

[45] Ibid. 63–6; Fraser, *Trade Unions*, ch. 2.

[46] The case is developed at length in Kirk, *Growth of Working Class Reformism*, ch. 6.

[47] Fraser, *Trade Unions*, 100.

[48] Parl. Deb., 3rd ser., vol. 197, 1372: 7 July 1869.

[49] Report of the Committee on Trades' Societies Appointed by the National Association for the Promotion of Social Science (1860), p. xv.

Science Committee, while another member of the group, Tom Hughes, served as one of its two secretaries.[50] This coterie also seems to have been instrumental in improving the way in which trade unionism was described and discussed in the Press.[51]

True, the destruction of the theory of the 'wage fund' (the main theoretical obstacle to the recognition that trade unions really could improve the wages of their members) still lay some distance in the future.[52] Wage levels, according to the current orthodoxy, were determined solely by market forces. But it was now conceded by some outside observers that trade unions, by 'testing' the market, could usefully inform their members what the 'going-rate' actually was—something that individual workmen were powerless to do, as John Stuart Mill pointed out.[53] The Social Science Congress agreed: trade unions, through careful enquiry and discussion, often helped to determine what ought to be the market price of labour.[54] 'The effect of trades' societies as an education in the art of self-government is [also] important,' it said.[55] Likewise, the Bradford mill-owner S. C. Kell, a severe critic of most forms of trade union activity, was prepared in 1861 to concede that such organizations could legitimately keep their members informed about the overall state of trade, 'so that at any time a surplus of operative force existing in one place may be sent to some other district, where a similar kind of labour is in greater demand, before that surplus has had time to reduce wages'.[56] By 1869 even *The Times* was admitting that trade unionism had come to stay, and had some potential for good as well as for evil.[57]

Other Radicals eventually came round to the view that it was not consistent with their principles for the law to discriminate against trade unions, imposing upon these bodies restrictions and penalties from which employers were free. Paradoxically, the deep-rooted hostility to 'class legislation' and the commitment to market principles characteristic of middle-class Radicalism could sometimes lead to views that were, in some respects, *favourable* to trade unions. By October 1873 even Robert Lowe had come to take a critical view of the existing Master and Servants Act: 'I hold that there is no sound distinction', he wrote in a Cabinet Memorandum, 'between contracts to buy and sell labour and contracts to sell any other commodity, and the sooner this

---

[50] Fraser, *Trade Unions*, 83–4.

[51] Ibid. 76–85, 201–4.

[52] Ibid. 170–80. And even then, most employers took little notice of the theoretical refinements of Mill, Thornton, and Jevons, which they regarded as mere quibbles (Yarmie, 'British Employers' Resistance', 143).

[53] Fraser, *Trade Unions*, 170.

[54] Report of Social Science Committee, p. xii.

[55] Ibid., p. xv.

[56] Kell, *Political Attitude*, 13–14.

[57] Fraser, *Trade Unions*, 204. But the following year, *The Times* asked tentatively: 'Which is the better state of things—moderate wages with everything cheap, or high wages with everything dear?' (10 Jan. 1870).

absolute equality between all persons contracting irrespective of the subject matter of the contract is recognised, the better.'[58]

But to some prominent Radical businessmen, a recognition of the 'inequalities' which disfigured society entailed even more far-reaching reform proposals. By the late 1860s a few of them were not only prepared to defend union rights, but were also presenting themselves as 'friends of Labour' and trying to help working men secure parliamentary representation. Prominent in this group were Forster (one of the authors of the Social Science Congress Report[59]), Mundella, and Samuel Morley.

Once again, Morley provides an interesting case. As a major employer—by 1880 he employed some 3,000 people in his factories, another 4,000 as domestic outworkers, and over 1,000 in warehouses and offices[60]—he took an interest in industrial relations, and positively supported trade unions, though he continued to believe strongly in a 'harmony of interests' between workmen and their masters, a point of view which, as we have seen, also influenced his attitude towards parliamentary reform. Morley well illustrates Vincent's paradoxical assertion that in the mid-Victorian years the most doughty parliamentary fighters for social reform and for workers' rights were the great employers.[61] In this respect his position was not unlike that of his fellow hosiery manufacturer Mundella.[62]

Indeed, according to Vincent, the distinguishing feature of the 'Commercial Liberals' was that so many of them belonged 'to the world of controversial humanitarianism', a humanitarianism which, like their radicalism, was rooted in a 'tender-mindedness in primary social attitudes'.[63] Such a description well fits the members of the Quaker Pease family, several of whom served as president of the Peace Society, as well as being zealous opponents of slavery, capital punishment, and cruelty to animals.[64] It would also cover Morley, who,

---

[58] Jonathan Spain, 'Trade Unionists, Gladstonian Liberals, and the Labour Law Reforms of 1875', in Eugenio F. Biagini and Alastair J. Reid (eds.), *Currents of Radicalism: Popular Radicalism, Organised Labour and Party Politics in Britain 1850–1914* (Cambridge, 1991), 124. This article argues that such shifts of attitude meant that the Liberal front bench was able to make a genuine and important contribution to Disraeli's labour law reforms.

[59] Fraser, *Trade Unions*, 82–3. Forster was heavily influenced by the ideas of the Christian Socialists, which he had encountered through his friendship with both Kingsley and Lord Goderich. The experience seems to have strengthened him in his support for a strategy of co-operation between employers and trade unions in which he had long believed. See his remarks to the Congress, *NAPSS*, 1859, p. 715. Edward Akroyd was also a member of the Social Science Committee, but his views on trade unionism did not greatly change as a result.

[60] Bradley, *Enlightened Entrepreneurs*, 46.

[61] Vincent, *British Liberal Party*, 74.

[62] Though Mundella felt that Morley was becoming irresponsibly Radical in 1872, when he met with trade union leaders and formulated an 'advanced' labour programme (Armytage, *A. J. Mundella*, 117).

[63] Vincent, *British Liberal Party*, 75.

[64] Kirby, *Men of Business and Politics*, 58.

amidst a plethora of humanitarian commitments, was a keen drink reformer, proudly wearing his blue riband within the precincts of Westminster.[65]

These 'progressive' businessmen also took a relaxed—even benevolent—view of factory legislation. But they were not alone in this. For, as Howe argues, the 'class détente' which followed Repeal signified a greater social acceptance of manufacturers, and this, in turn, reduced employer resistance to State controls.[66] By 1857 Akroyd could even find kind words to say about Shaftesbury, and was referring to 'the philanthropic zeal and powerful eloquence of Mr. Richard Oastler' and 'the premature and lamented death of Mr. Sadler'—magnanimity of which he would have been incapable ten years earlier.[67] Hutchins and Harrison go so far as to talk of a 'conversion of public opinion' between 1845 and 1860 which was 'curiously rapid and complete'.[68] Mundella, addressing the Commons in 1874, certainly claimed that something of this kind had occurred: 'Forty or 50 years ago,' he said, factory legislation 'was regarded as county against town, the landed gentry against the manufacturing interest, and as Tory against Whig.... Happily there is no such feeling in existence to-day.'[69] It was certainly a sign of the changing times when an industry like the potteries industry actually petitioned to be brought under the control of factory legislation, as happened in the early 1860s.[70]

Contributing perhaps to this 'conversion' was a reaction against the wildly alarmist talk which opponents of 'restriction' had used in the 1840s when predictions of industrial collapse in the face of foreign competition abounded. One thinks of the famous recantations of Graham and Roebuck on the occasion of the debate on the 1860 Bleaching and Dyeing Works Bill.[71] Four years later John Crossley (Francis's brother) addressed the Commons in a similarly penitential mood: 'He had looked upon the first Factory Act with great fear, because he had believed that it would not answer, but he could now bear testimony to its good effects in every direction.' Mundella, who actively worked to extend the factory laws, also dwelt upon the recent prosperity of the economy. His critic, Bazley, he said, was 'living refutation of his own arguments.... Have not the manufacturers grown both in influence and wealth? Are not many of them rich beyond the dreams of avarice?'[72]

---

[65] Bradley, *Enlightened Entrepreneurs*, 51.

[66] Howe, *Cotton Masters*, 189. On the establishment in 1855 of the Manchester Steam Users' Association, which avoided external interference, see Peter W. J. Bartrip, 'The State and the Steam-Boiler in Nineteenth-Century Britain', *International Review of Social History*, 25 (1980), 77–105.

[67] *NAPSS*, 1857, p. 151.

[68] Hutchins and Harrison, *Factory Legislation*, 121.

[69] Parl. Deb., 3rd ser., vol. 218, 1741: 6 May 1874.

[70] Hutchins and Harrison, *Factory Legislation*, 152. See Parl. Deb., 3rd ser., vol. 175, 1710: 14 June 1864.

[71] Ibid., vol. 158, 984, 989–91: 9 May 1860.

[72] Ibid., vol. 175, 1727: 14 June 1864; ibid., vol. 218, 1769: 6 May 1874.

There were, in any case, 'economic' arguments in support of the proposition that factory reform might be positively beneficial. Legislative restriction, it was now often said, provided 'a protection of the good manufacturer
against the bad'.[73] 'The result of factory legislation was to compel the bad
factory owner to do what the good factory owner would do readily of his own
accord.'[74] It was also self-interest—namely, a fear of 'unfair competition'—
which clearly underlay the motion passed by the Association of Chambers of
Commerce in 1869 calling upon the Government to bring workshops under
the operations of the Factory Acts.[75] Finally, the argument was now being
voiced that it was not so much the shorter working day which was harming
Britain in the field of international competition as the fact that her operatives
were working for too *many* hours, to the neglect of their basic education. 'Yes,
Sir, it is brains that we must cultivate in future in order to maintain our
national industry,' declared Mundella.[76]

Significantly, the MPs who used these arguments were the Radicals who
also wanted trade union reform: Forster (a supporter of the original Ten
Hours Act),[77] Morley, and Mundella, the leader of the movement to establish
a statutory fifty-four-hour week. But it was as businessmen that these men
chose to present themselves. Introducing his 1873 Factory Acts Amendment
Bill (also backed by Morley), Mundella, for example, told the Commons that
he spoke as a textile employer who had always taken account of the 'economic
side of the question'. 'The limit proposed by this Bill', he assured his
audience, 'would economize fuel, gas, and wear and tear of machinery, and
the result would be as much, if not more, work in the 54 than in the 60
hours.'[78] He later went on to cite many businessmen and trade organizations
which had publicly taken his side.[79] Similarly, Forster in 1869 can be found
backing a Bill to safeguard union rights (Hughes and Mundella were co-
sponsors) in his capacity 'as an employer of labour himself';[80] and two years
later he warned other businessmen, as someone who was 'not merely . . . a
member of the Government or of the House, but [also] a master manufacturer',
that they should not give the impression that 'they were legislating for their
own class'.[81] After 1868 there was a sizeable bloc of recently elected Liberal
business MPs who held such views, especially on the subject of trade union

[73] Parl. Deb., 3rd ser., vol. 175, 1725: 14 June 1873 (e.g. Adderley).
[74] Ibid., vol. 219, 1459: 11 June 1874 (Anderson).
[75] ACC Papers, 24 Feb. 1869.
[76] Parl. Deb., 3rd ser., vol. 218, 1749: 6 May 1874.
[77] Ibid. 1801: 6 May 1874. See also Reynolds, *Great Paternalist*, 38, 130. In 1855 Forster
parted company with most of the worsted manufacturers in dissociating himself from the National
Association of Factory Occupiers (*Bradford Observer*, 14 June 1855). For Forster's admiration of
Oastler, see Forster to M. Balme, 7 Dec. 1867, W. Riding Archives, Bradford, DB4/9/13.
[78] Parl. Deb., 3rd ser., vol. 216, 820–1, 826: 11 June 1873.
[79] Ibid., vol. 218, 1768–9: 6 May 1874.
[80] Ibid., vol. 197, 1386: 7 July 1869.
[81] Ibid., vol. 207, 285: 19 June 1871.

rights: P. A. Taylor, R. M. Carter, Peter Rylands, J. J. Colman, and Samuel Plimsoll among them.[82]

In fact, by the 1870s it was the blind economist Fawcett, rather than any of the manufacturers or merchants, who had become the most uncompromising parliamentary critic of factory law extension. This laid him open to the rebuke of Mundella, who spoke dismissively of Fawcett's 'vague, senseless crotchet' and hoped that 'the House would not be led awry by theories, however eloquently urged by men who had no practical acquaintance with the subject'.[83]

To Mundella, the old Cobdenite arguments had been not so much abandoned as reformulated. Recognition of trade unions, he said in 1869, was

purely a question of Free Trade in labour. It was only by slow degrees that he had shaken off the prejudices of his class, and had come to the conclusion that the only way in which masters and workmen could come to a good understanding was by placing them upon a perfect footing of equality before the law.... He did not think it right that the capitalist should have the sole control of the market, and that the labourer should have no control whatever.... Combination was as fair for the men as for the masters.

Education was needed before most workers could understand the principles of political economy, said Mundella, but this would not be achieved by repression.[84]

Yet Mundella's views were by no means shared by all, or even most, Radical businessmen. The old attitudes died hard. This had already become apparent in 1860 when the Social Science Congress debated its committee's report on trade unionism. The new 'softer' line was fiercely attacked by Edmund Potter, Thomas Bazley, and the Ashworth brothers.[85] Indeed, Mundella's promotion of trade union legislation and the extension of factory hours helped to revive some of the 'traditional' entrepreneurial positions. Mundella's Factory Acts Amendment Bill of 1873, for example, was widely opposed by the Lancashire mill-owners.[86] A year later Bazley was still saying that, 'having destroyed the Corn Law monopoly, the House should be very careful of setting up another, and especially one so injurious as a monopoly of

[82] Spain, 'Trade Unionists', 115–17.

[83] Parl. Deb., 3rd ser., vol. 219, 1465, 1467: 11 June 1874.

[84] Ibid., vol. 197, 1373–5: 7 July 1869. Plimsoll also spoke out strongly in favour of trade union legalization (ibid. 1366–70), though apparently in language which disgusted the House (Armytage, *A. J. Mundella*, 70).

[85] Report of Social Science Committee, 603–4, 606–7, 613–14, 619–20.

[86] Parl. Deb., 3rd ser., vol. 216, 822–3: 11 June 1872. In July 1867 Moffatt had moved a resolution in the House that it was 'not prepared, without further evidence, to interfere with the free exercise of labour to so great an extent as is contemplated by the present measure'—i.e. the Factory Acts Extension Act (although the Amendment was subsequently withdrawn) (ibid., vol. 189, 476: 30 July 1867).

Labour'.[87] Nor was opposition confined to rhetoric. In 1872, 130 MPs (101 of them Liberals) voted against giving unions the right to picket.[88] This was the occasion on which, against the advice of their own Government, many Radicals supported the Lords' hostile amendments to the Criminal Law Amendment Bill. Included in this group were Baines, Illingworth, and McLaren, while other prominent businessmen such as the Bass brothers, Brassey, Dixon, and T. B. Potter were conspicuously absent.[89] In fact, even in the late 1860s and the early 1870s there were still Liberal businessmen like Edmund Potter who continued to argue that 'all combinations which prevented competition were in their nature antagonistic to Free Trade'.[90]

It was all very well for Mundella to laugh at his manufacturing opponents as a 'stage army':

They came before us first as individual employers; next, as a federation of employers; next, as the Chamber of Commerce; and now as the Factory Employers' Association. But the same gentlemen play the same leading characters, and form the *dramatis personae* in all the principal parts.[91]

Yet these opponents had become an organized force in December 1873, with the formation of a new pressure group, the National Federation of Associated Employers of Labour (NFAEL), which was supported by John Laird, L. J. Crossley, the Ashworth brothers, Titus Salt, and Akroyd, as well as Bazley and Edmund Potter, its two most prominent parliamentary spokesmen.[92] Ironically, Mundella's Nine-Hour Bill may well have done much to set off the train of events leading to the formation of this body.[93]

How seriously is the NFAEL to be taken? From the start, it ran into ideological conflict with some of the very organs of the Press whose 'economic principles' would seem to have coincided with its own. *The Times*, for example, feared that it heralded the start of an intensified struggle between the two 'armies' of capital and labour.[94] Could this antagonistic view of industrial relations be reconciled with the orthodox view that the interests of capital and labour were inseparable?[95] Moreover, *The Economist*, with superb consistency,

---

[87] Parl. Deb., 3rd ser., vol. 218, 1773: 6 May 1874. See also Crossley's fears of foreign competition (ibid. 1776).

[88] Armytage, *A. J. Mundella*, 112. Yarmie, 'British Employers' Resistance', 151.

[89] Fraser, *Trade Unions*, 164.

[90] Parl. Deb., 3rd ser., vol. 197, 1370–1: 7 July 1869. For other expressions of hostility towards trade unionism, see the remarks by McLaren (ibid., vol. 207, 284: 19 June 1871) and J. B. Potter (ibid. 287).

[91] Parl. Deb., 3rd ser., vol. 218, 1766: 6 May 1874.

[92] Fraser, *Trade Unions*, 117–18. Andrew H. Yarmie, 'Employers' Organizations in Mid-Victorian England', *International Review of Social History*, 25 (1980), 228. *Idem*, 'British Employers' Resistance', 155.

[93] Yarmie, 'Employers' Organizations', 226–7.

[94] Ibid. 229. On the views of the Iron Trades Employers Association, founded in the previous year, see Joyce, *Work, Society and Politics*, 72.

[95] The issue is discussed in *Capital and Labour*, 31 Dec. 1873, pp. 3–4.

continued to voice doubts about the morality of all trade combinations and the threat that they posed to the operation of the free market. It also shrewdly pointed out some of the practical snags which the new Federation was likely to encounter: 'The class of employers, we believe, is quite as strong as the class of labourers, but a federation of employers will commonly be weaker than a federation of labourers.' Employers could not discipline their members through the control of providence funds as unions could, and attempts to create a central war chest to help resist strikes would quickly run into difficulty. 'Sound capitalists now make provision for strikes of labourers as for all other trade events,' and the existence of a central fund would simply mean that imprudent employers would find themselves artificially protected.[96]

But perhaps the rhetoric of the Federation and of its journal, *Capital and Labour*, may give a somewhat misleading impression. Joyce thinks that the employers who joined the organization did so because they opposed *aggressive* trade unionism, not because they disapproved of unions as such.[97] More generally still, the businessmen who denounced all interference with market forces seldom practised what they preached. Trade unionism was an established fact. As a result, like the proliferating body of trade associations, the Federation had a purely defensive role. *Capital and Labour* itself insisted on this fact: the Federation, it said, had no offensive functions, but was merely a 'rampart . . . to keep back an advancing army'.[98] Moreover, again like the trade associations, it could only sustain the enthusiasm of its members when some specific threat existed to unite it. Within a few years it had dwindled away.[99] This is hardly surprising. For, as the experience of the Bradford Chamber of Commerce shows, the whole question of trade union rights and obligations tended to reduce the business community to paralysis.[100]

On the question of factory legislation something more like a consensus emerged. Thus, whereas in 1850 Bright was confidently predicting that the legislature would shortly have to retrace its course,[101] the Federation in the 1870s simply wanted to prevent restriction of hours and working conditions being *extended* in what it regarded as a reckless way; few businessmen had any fault to find with that objective.

Yet a wide area of disagreement still existed within the business community —indeed, a dichotomy tended to develop. There is a poignancy in Mundella's

[96] *Economist*, 27 Dec. 1873, p. 1558.
[97] Joyce, *Work, Society and Politics*, 70–1.
[98] *Capital and Labour*, 31 Dec. 1873, p. 4.
[99] Joyce, *Work, Society and Politics*, 70–1. Yarmie also stresses the body's heterogeneity ('Employers' Organizations', 233).
[100] The Bradford Chamber of Commerce simply could not reach a collective opinion on the 1869 Trade Union Bill; see Bradford Chamber of Commerce 19th Annual Report, 1870, p. 53; Bradford Chamber of Commerce Minutes, 25 May 1869, 7 Mar., 25 Apr. 1871, fos. 205, 455–6, 473.
[101] Parl. Deb., 3rd ser., vol. 111, 850–1: 6 June 1850.

story of how he led a deputation to the Home Secretary in 1872 to call for the fifty-four-hour week and almost bumped into another deputation of Yorkshire mill-owners protesting against any such innovation![102] Such divisions of opinion were hardly calculated to increase the influence at Westminster of MPs who claimed to be speaking on behalf of the business community.

THE THEORETICAL DILEMMA

But underlying these disagreements lay a deeper dilemma. An instructive exchange had occurred at the Social Science Congress in 1859, when Fawcett spoke of labour as a mere commodity and welcomed industrial conflict as a necessary stage in the determination of a proper wage level. Forster begged to differ. Speaking as a worsted manufacturer, Forster argued that his prime concern was not to cheapen labour, but rather to 'get his work done well, and to pay such wages as would accomplish that object'.[103] His fellow woollen magnate Edward Akroyd, the creator of Akroydon, whose views on industrial relations were much 'drier', took a broadly similar approach. 'Political economy will not help us to avoid strikes and their attendant evils,' he said. 'Nay, the danger is aggravated by the rigid application of this science.' Fawcett's justification of the strike as a test of the market price of labour was unhelpful, said Akroyd:

Precisely at this point of our difficulty, when the hard maxims of political economy afford no relief, social science steps in, and lights our path to a peaceful adjustment of the question. I mean the only true social science, based upon Christianity, and teaching us to do unto others as we would they should do unto us.[104]

In fact, as we have seen, many manufacturers were even ready, on pragmatic grounds, to establish a collaborative relationship with representatives of their work-force. Yet, though this could be seen as an 'enlightened' way of creating industrial harmony and stability, and so of boosting profits, might not such practices also function as a conspiracy against the consuming public, since the latter might have to pay, in the form of higher prices, for the concessions which had been made to labour?

This issue can best be explored through an examination of what is usually called 'employer paternalism'. Now the money spent on running factory schools could perhaps be justified as a way of enriching the human resources of the work-force and of increasing productivity, though even this could be

---

[102] Armytage, *A. J. Mundella*, 125.

[103] *NAPSS* (1859), 716.

[104] Ibid. 720. The paternalist mill-owner Hugh Mason was saying in 1868 that 'it would be impossible for him to buy the labour of his workpeople, and for the workpeople to sell him that labour, the same as an ordinary commodity over the counter of a shopkeeper. . . . The bond which united them was not the cold bond of buyer and seller' (quoted in Kirk, *Growth of Working Class Reformism*, 294).

seen as a dangerous distortion of the market. But what about the provision of a more elaborate network of social services? Addressing the Social Science Congress in 1857, Akroyd explained that he ran a dining-room for his mill-hands, which they managed through a committee, as well as a library, a news room, allotments, and so forth, and that he also made arrangements for the supply of tea, coffee, soup, and coal at low prices during the winters. Yet what he was doing clearly troubled his conscience. 'As a political economist myself,' said Akroyd defensively, 'I am fully aware of the objections which may be justly raised against any unwise interruptions of the ordinary channels of supply and demand.' He then went on to defend such arrangements by claiming that they helped working men 'feel that their own and their employer's interests are identical' and that they served to 'teach them to do their duty in that station of life to which it shall please God to call them'.[105]

Yet such professions of 'paternalism' obviously ran counter to the image which many employers had of themselves. Cobden, as we have seen, attached great importance to the virtues of 'manly independence'. Just as he resented being patronized by landed society, so he assumed that the working man would resent being patronized by *his* social superiors. This formed a large part of Cobden's case against factory legislation. In his *Open Letter to Lord Ashley* he wrote: 'Mine is the masculine species of charity which would lead me to inculcate in the minds of the labouring classes the love of independence, the privilege of self-respect, the disdain of being patronised or petted, the desire to accumulate and the ambition to rise.'[106] Significantly, Mrs Gaskell makes her mill-owner Mr Thornton say in *North and South*: 'I choose to be the unquestioned and irresponsible master of my hands, during the hours that they labour for me. But those hours past, our relation ceases; and then comes in the same respect for their independence that I myself exact.'[107]

However, many of Cobden's mill-owning friends *did* feel a wider sense of responsibility towards those whom they employed, behaving in a way not unlike that of an enlightened landlord towards his dependants. This was particularly the case in the late 1850s and 1860s when many cotton masters put on elaborate trips and tea parties for their work-force, in addition to providing them with a whole range of social amenities: acts of generosity which in turn elicited testimonials and thank-you presents from the grateful operatives.[108] But such acts of philanthropy can also be found at an earlier

[105] *NAPSS* (1857), 531. On the 'feudal' and paternalistic establishments of Akroyd and Ripley, see Joyce, *Work, Society and Politics*, 144. On Forster's factory at Birley-on-Wharfedale and Francis Crossley's good works in Halifax, see Reynolds, *Great Paternalist*, 178. See also J. A. Jowitt (ed.), *Model Industrial Communities in Mid-Nineteenth Century Yorkshire* (Bradford, 1986).

[106] Cited in Georgina Battiscombe, *Shaftesbury: A Biography of the Seventh Earl 1801–1885* (1974), 149.

[107] Elizabeth Gaskell, *North and South* (1855), ch. 15. However, Mr Thornton experiences a change of heart and becomes a practitioner of welfare paternalism before the end of the novel.

[108] Kirk, *Growth of Working Class Reformism*, 292–300.

period. We have already seen how in the debate on the Ten Hours Bill even John Bright boasted of the educational and other services he was voluntarily providing for his 'hands'.[109] And Cobden himself took 600 of the work-force from his Chorley enterprise to the seaside resort of Fleetwood to celebrate the repeal of the Corn Laws, paying expenses and the day's wages.[110] As for the Ashworths, they were not only noted for their fierce commitment to the orthodoxies of political economy, but also, paradoxically, had long been admired as 'paternalist employers'.[111] Similarly, Titus Salt, a founding member of the NFAEL, was also the creator of the 'model' village of Saltaire.

Some historians have treated Salt as a protagonist of what they call the 'New Paternalism', which allegedly flourished in the more relaxed class atmosphere of the late 1850s.[112] But even in the early decades of the century there had been paternalist employers of this type operating in the 'industrial villages' which were so important at this stage of the Industrial Revolution: the Gregs, Ashworth, Thomas Ashton, and so on.[113] These men may never have been typical of their class, but their activities do testify to the concern on the part of many manufacturers to disprove their opponents' allegations that they were mere heartless money-grubbers. (Whether they made a significant contribution to the lowering of class tensions and the 'integration' of manual workers into the capitalist system is obviously quite another question.[114])

Yet, as David Roberts observes, few of these employers actually used the 'paternalist rhetoric' so prevalent in their day. Henry Ashworth, for example, insisted that his 'benevolence' arose out of calculated self-interest. Such men and their apologists did not speak 'of the duties of property, the need of rank, or the value of deference'.[115] Indeed, the whole purpose of these exercises in improving industrial relations was to help the independent and self-reliant workman to help himself.[116] As Joyce puts it, the paradox of 'employer paternalism' was that, although it often 'overstepped the strict limits of laissez faire', yet, 'viewed in other terms', it was the 'logical outcome' of laissez-

---

[109] Parl. Deb., 3rd ser., vol. 89, 1146–7: 10 Feb. 1847. See ch. 1.

[110] H. I. Dutton and J. E. King, 'The Limits of Paternalism: The Cotton Tyrants of North Lancashire, 1836–54', *Social History*, 7 (1982), 61.

[111] On the Ashworths, see Boyson, *Ashworth Cotton Enterprise*, passim. Roberts, *Paternalism*, 172–3. For a contemporary account, see Taylor, *Notes of a Tour*, letter 2.

[112] Joyce, *Work, Society and Politics*, ch. 4. More sensibly, Richard Price calls it 'the Revitalisation of Paternalism' (*Labour in British Society: An Interpretative History* (1986), 59–67).

[113] Roberts, *Paternalism*, 172–8. See S. Greg, *Two Letters to Leonard Horner, Esq., on the Capabilities of the Factory System* (1840).

[114] Dutton and King, while giving examples of employer paternalism in North Lancashire ('Limits of Paternalism', 60–1), argue that the masters were not really *committed* to this strategy, nor were the mill-hands conciliated by it (ibid. 72–3). For another highly critical view of the prevalence and effectiveness of 'employer paternalism', see Koditschek, *Class Formation*, 425–30 and Morris, *Class, Sect and Party*, 118–19.

[115] Roberts, *Paternalism*, 175.

[116] Price, *Labour in British Society*, 64.

faire.[117] Thus, in Richard Price's words, although 'the imagery of the family replaced the language of political economy in middle-class representations of social relations', these 'paternal feelings could only be aroused voluntarily'.[118]

'Welfare paternalism', then, was an uneasy combination of ideas and aspirations. But the fact that so many employers resorted to it at all suggests that Cobden's concept of 'manliness' and 'independence' was too austere. Certainly, in the day-to-day running of a factory, principles and values were often brought into play which owed little to the teachings of political economy. (Why, for example, was it degrading for the working man to be dependent upon the State, but not for him to depend upon his employer?) Admittedly, a desire to discipline and reward employees by enlightened techniques of 'social control' goes some way to explaining such behaviour, but it does not provide the total explanation.

Joyce has perhaps come nearest to solving the problem. In the case of the newly risen, he argues, 'paternalism shored up the flimsiness of social station', while for the fully established it provided proof of their 'worth' and of their willingness and ability to copy some of the aspects of the life-style of a land-owning class which they 'both envied and despised'. And underlying these confused motivations was the 'almost messianic faith' felt by many industrialists in the 'civilising power of industry, itself an aspect of the nineteenth-century God of Progress'.[119] As so often happened in mid-Victorian Britain, a somewhat insecure pride in what had been achieved by manufacturing industry took precedence over 'the laws of political economy', and perhaps even over the long-term interests of capitalism itself.

---

[117] Joyce, *Work, Society and Politics*, 137–8.

[118] Price, *Labour in British Society*, 63–4.

[119] Joyce, *Work, Society and Politics*, 140–1. In the 1860s, he argues, many employers started to consider themselves 'Captains of Industry', a faith bolstered in part by a religious sense of 'calling' (ibid. 141).

Conclusion

COBDEN, GLADSTONE, AND THE WHIGS

Despite all the warnings about the dangers of 'Whig history', many students of the Victorian period seem only too eager to dive headlong into the world of modern, class-based politics, in which a 'bourgeoisified' Conservative Party is locked in conflict with the Labour Movement. This sort of approach has led to attempts to bury the Whigs with indecent haste.[1] But a similar approach has also been adopted towards the entrepreneurial Radicals. As with the Whigs, the historiography has been unduly preoccupied with the Radicals' ultimate 'failure', to the neglect of what they were currently doing. Such an approach can be found even in Malchow's excellent study *Gentlemen Capitalists*, none of whose four 'representative' businessmen came from the industrial towns of northern England and only one of whom was a manufacturer. The very process of selection, it almost seems, has been designed to produce 'capitalists' possessing considerable 'gentlemanly' potential. In many respects, this is perverse. Of course, entrepreneurial Radicalism ultimately failed in its mission; and Cobden and Bright lived long enough to discern this melancholy truth. But, then, all political creeds can be said to 'fail' in the long run.

In putting over the view that the failure of entrepreneurial Radicalism in general and of Cobden in particular was somehow preordained, political historians have pursued a variety of different arguments. For example, some claim that Cobden was never truly 'representative' of the class for which he was the self-appointed spokesman, even if the economic crisis of the 1840s temporarily concealed this truth. That there was distrust of Cobden from the very start is not in doubt.[2] The campaign for the incorporation of Manchester, for example, had drawn its support mainly from the 'shopocracy', with many of the staider elements of the business community holding aloof.[3] The methods of the League leaders in the 1840s later caused further suspicion among the respectable middle class. For although the Mancunian merchants and manufacturers were Free Traders almost to a man, many resented the highly political and demagogic way in which the Repeal case was being

---

[1] T. A. Jenkins, *Gladstone, Whiggery and the Liberal Party 1874–1886* (Oxford, 1988).

[2] Hinde, *Richard Cobden*, 70. During the Stockport campaign of 1837, Cobden's support had come mainly from the shopkeeping class (Edsall, *Cobden*, 46–7).

[3] On this subject, see Cobden to Bright, 16 Sept. 1848, Cobden Papers, Add. MS 43,649, fos. 78–9. But on the links between Cobden and plebeian Radicalism, see Eugenio F. Biagini, 'Popular Liberals', 135–9.

argued—hence the establishment in 1845 of the Commercial Association, a breakaway from the Chamber of Commerce which the League now controlled.[4] Hence, too, the persistent hostility to Cobden and his friends on the part of the *Manchester Guardian*, which took a more 'Whiggish' view of the world. This has led one of Cobden's biographers to the blunt conclusion that the Radical leader 'was not typical of his class and there was a good deal of mutual dissatisfaction between him and his fellow manufacturers'.[5]

Moreover, according to some recent writers, Cobden's perspectives on economic problems differed from those of other northern manufacturers in that, as the son of a Sussex tenant farmer, he was as much concerned with the development of agriculture (and pursuing a *private* vendetta against landlordism) as he was with promoting the interests and satisfying the needs of the textile industry. In any case—or so it is often said—Cobden approached political problems as a 'moralist', to whom issues of economic advantage were always secondary.

Fortunately for Cobden—so goes this interpretation—his reputation as the man who had emancipated industry from the trammels of the Corn Laws was at its height in 1847, when the country went to the polls. It was again a piece of good fortune that when Parliament was next dissolved, in 1852, the country polled under a threat of a return to Protectionism. This led to a reuniting of the Free Trade party and silenced, for the time being, the more 'conservative' of Cobden's and Bright's growing band of middle-class critics.

Meanwhile, some historians claim, nothing had come from the attempts of the old Anti-Corn Law League leaders to find the 'big idea' that would sustain their campaign against the aristocracy. Financial reform, parliamentary reform, and the freehold purchase movement were all broached—without much success.[6] As for the involvement of Cobden and Bright in the peace movement, this not only lacked popular support but was also repudiated by most of their one-time middle-class followers.[7] It took the Crimean War to expose this weakness. But thereafter the claims of Cobden and Bright to represent the industrial and commercial classes lacked all credibility.[8] Since no other middle-class politicians were prepared to take their place, entrepreneurial politics quickly ran into the sands. Thus the rejection of Bright and Milner Gibson by their Mancunian constituents in the 1857 general election marked the effective end of the influence of the Manchester School and the start of the 'Palmerstonian era', during which the great mercantile and industrial cities were prepared to pay obeisance to the old

[4] For a measured assessment of the origins and nature of the 'split', see Howe, *Cotton Masters*, 204–5.

[5] Hinde, *Richard Cobden*, 70–1.

[6] This is the theme of McCord's interesting essay, 'Cobden and Bright in Politics, 1846–1857'.

[7] For a discussion of this issue, see Ch. 2.

[8] McCord, 'Cobden and Bright', 107–9. Fraser, *Urban Politics*, 205–6.

aristocratic Premier.[9] Many studies of entrepreneurial Radicalism stop short
at about this point.

But, as we have seen, this sort of interpretation gives a misleading impression
of Cobden's personality and political role. The Radical leader's reactions
during the American Civil War, for example, suggest that economic 'principle'
tended to have the ascendancy over morality when the two appeared to be in
conflict, rather than vice versa. And although Cobden's love of the Sussex
Weald and his knowledge of agriculture cannot be doubted, this did not
prevent him from siding with the manufacturing north in the 'battle' between
the two civilizations.[10] True, Cobden soon became disillusioned over the
failure of the industrial and commercial class to fulfil its destiny, and his
correspondence increasingly dwells upon the timidity, social deference,
snobbishness, and so on of the entire business community, including his
fellow Mancunian capitalists. In his later years he can even be found wearily
discussing the defects of 'John Bull' as though something were amiss with the
'national temperament'—surely a contradiction of his central beliefs.

Yet Cobden never forgot that, but for the support, financial and otherwise,
of merchants and manufacturers, the campaign for the repeal of the Corn
Laws could never have succeeded.[11] Confronted by the criticisms of the
metropolitan Radicals in 1852, Cobden wrote back defiantly: 'The Northern
capitalists are, with all their imperfections, the most liberal of their order
in the United Kingdom. I speak particularly of the mill-owners and manufacturers of Lancashire and Yorkshire.'[12] And although some historians
believe that in his final years Cobden despaired of his former middle-class
supporters to the point where he began to pin his hopes upon 'the masses',[13]
there is much evidence to suggest otherwise. For example, as late as 1862,
Cobden could still write to Ashworth about the central role which the
Chambers of Commerce would necessarily play in the war against feudalism.

Moreover, as we have seen, the creed of entrepreneurial Radicalism did not
lose its relevance or its influence as speedily as is commonly supposed; still
less was everything in Cobden's career futility and anticlimax once the Corn
Laws had been repealed. Even the electoral set-back of 1857 did not mean
the effective demise of the Manchester School. For, despite the debacle of
1857, Cobdenite Radicalism was still a flourishing cause in the 1860s, and the
tradition it represented, far from disappearing from national politics, survived
to resurface in new forms with Chamberlain in the mid-1870s and with Lloyd
George three decades later. Within a couple of years the defeated Radical

---

[9] e.g. Gatrell, 'Commercial Middle Class', Ch. 10; Fraser, *Urban Politics*, passim.
[10] See Chs. 1 and 4.
[11] Howe, *Cotton Masters*, 212–13. Textile manufacturers produced 56% of the 1844 Fund,
70% of the 1846 Fund, though these figures exclude subscriptions below £100.
[12] Cobden to Walmsley, 15 Jan. 1852, Walmsley, *Life*, 234.
[13] e.g. Read, *Cobden and Bright*, 158–61.

MPs had all returned to the House, and if they no longer threatened the stability of the Government, this good news had never reached the ears of the harassed Liberal Whip, Brand. In many ways, the mid-1860s saw a revival of Radicalism, this time with W. E. Forster of Bradford as its central figure.

Similarly, historians have been far too ready to take uncritically the complaints made by Cobden and Bright about the alleged 'servility' of the urban middle classes: the readiness of the big capitalists, out of snobbery, to abase themselves before the elderly aristocratic Prime Minister, Palmerston. On the contrary, it is quite possible, as we have seen, to interpret the encounters between the Prime Minister and the businessmen of the northern cities that he visited in the late 1850s and early 1860s in a quite different way. Palmerston seems to have been eager to ingratiate himself with his audience, and went out of his way on these occasions to sing hymns of praise to commercial and industrial progress—'aping', if you like, the northern business class.

True, Cobden's hopes of a revolutionary assault on the citadel of landed privilege and power never materialized. But the reasons for this are complex. Undoubtedly, there is something to be said for the view that capitalism was developing from the 1850s onwards in ways which were distinctly unhelpful to entrepreneurial politics. The impersonality of life in the very large towns, where class segregation had early established itself, militated against attempts by the likes of Cobden to act as the 'natural' leaders of the 'middle and industrious classes'. London had always been barren territory for these rebels. Moreover, by the end of the 1850s neither Leeds nor Manchester provided them with a congenial environment. Perhaps the cause survived longest in smaller factory towns like Rochdale. The creed of entrepreneurial Radicalism, with its emphasis on the role of the self-made risk-taking capitalist, was also damaged by the later spread of the limited liability company, leading to a divorce between ownership and management. Another aspect of that transformation which weakened entrepreneurial politics was the growth of a metropolitan business culture, centred on the Stock Exchange, which drew many manufacturers away from the active management of their firms into a life of investment and speculation.[14]

But it was not only economic developments that doomed entrepreneurial Radicalism to defeat. Equally important was the reaction of other politicians to the Radicals. In a way, Cobden and his friends, like other revolutionaries before and since, rather wanted their 'enemies' to show recalcitrance. Unfortunately, landed society did not play into their hands by blankly opposing all the demands which the businessmen were making. On the contrary, as Perkin rightly emphasizes, the aristocratic Ministries of mid-Victorian Britain frequently identified themselves with the very policies most likely to please

---

[14] Malchow, *Gentlemen Capitalists*, 349.

(and disarm) their business critics. Similarly, MPs from landed society tended to identify with the interests of their middle-class constituents.[15] The way in which Lord Morpeth watered down his original commitment to factory reform under pressure from his manufacturing constituents in the west Riding well illustrates this point.[16]

This flexibility on the part of certain members of landed society was bound to influence the political attitudes of many businessmen. Since the mid-1840s, perhaps earlier, there had been politicians from the commercial world like James Wilson who believed in the good sense and benevolence of a section of the Whig aristocracy and were prepared to work in a junior capacity as allies of the established élite. In particular, the triumph of Repeal seemed to furnish proof that no further 'organic' (in particular, no further franchise) reforms were necessary. The sort of businessmen whose views were represented by the *Manchester Guardian* saw nothing much wrong in leaving the details of government in aristocratic hands, provided that the Government created a suitable framework for the promotion of economic growth and pursued congenial commercial policies. This 'division of labour' made a good deal of sense to industrialists who, because of their conditions of work, found it difficult to abandon their factories and warehouses for the dubious pleasures and rewards of parliamentary politics. ' 'Tis a perfect paradise for the aristocracy in this country, if they knew only how to behave themselves,' Cobden once drily observed. 'Whom have they to govern? Practical, industrious, intelligent men, whose thoughts centred in their business, and who would gladly leave to those above them the toil of government, if those were willing to allow commerce and industry fair play.'[17] Many businessmen wanted, above all, a framework of *stability* within which they could conduct their business operations; and one reason for Palmerston's popularity as Premier is that he provided precisely that. No wonder that whenever his Governments ran into trouble, there was a fall in the price of consols on the London Stock Exchange.[18]

Many of the middle-class men who *did* make their way in national politics were, for this very reason, prepared to accept a subaltern role by working *within* the established political system. For example, Lowe admitted to Delane in 1861 that, in his anxiety for promotion, he was willing to undertake 'work too hard or too dangerous for aristocratic hands'.[19] An exasperated Bright felt that 'Bob Lowe' was showing quite the wrong entrepreneurial spirit in thus turning *his own career* into a kind of 'commodity':

[15] Perkins, *Origins*, esp. 376–7. Joyce, *Work, Society and Politics*, 2; Howe, *Cotton Masters*, 94. For similar conclusions covering a slightly later period, see James Cornford, 'The Transformation of Conservatism in the Late Nineteenth Century', *Victorian Studies*, 7 (1963), 35–66.

[16] Mandler, *Aristocratic Government*, 234.

[17] Speech at Birmingham, 13 Nov. 1845, *Cobden's Speeches*, 172.

[18] Steele, *Palmerston and Liberalism*, 5.

[19] Cited in Marcham, 'Revised Code', 95, n. 112.

He has bargained himself into *two* Govts in *one* Parlt . . . He has brought his wares to a good market—and his politics have been a good investment so far, and if the people of Manchester wish politics to be a trade, and their Member to have transactions on his own a/c, they could not do better than take Lowe as their representative.[20]

However, it is a moot point whether the Whig Ministries really did merit the trust which many contemporary businessmen reposed in them. The sceptics cited the Whigs' 'hereditary incapacity' at finance, evidenced by Wood's tenure of the Exchequer, the continuation of the income tax, and the growth of public expenditure. Against this could be set the abolition of the Navigation Acts, the equalization of the sugar and timber duties, the Encumbered Estates Act, and, later, the legalization of limited liability. The issue is complicated by the existence within early nineteenth-century Whiggery of a variety of political approaches. It has recently been argued that the 1830s and 1840s saw the reinvigoration of aristocratic government by prominent Whigs anxious to demonstrate their anxiety to serve all the people by distancing themselves from middle-class calls for 'economic reform'. By the late 1840s, however, this tradition was becoming exhausted, and, especially after the merger with the Peelites in the Aberdeen coalition in 1852, the Whigs lost their distinctive identity as they evolved into 'liberals'.[21]

However, that still leaves at issue the problem of exactly who was permeating whom. It could be argued that the great Whig families co-opted sympathetic businessmen into their ranks and adopted a range of domestic policies with which, left to their own devices, they would possibly have ignored. Their reward was the retention of their dominant political position; indeed, Whiggery, against all the odds, managed to survive well into the 1880s. But did the outcome leave them with the trappings of office but without the substance of power? Similar uncertainty surrounds the position of the business community. The 'commercial and manufacturing class' saw many, though by no means all, of the laws by which it set store brought onto the statute-book through Whig sponsorship. But, in the process, Cobden's hopes of raising the esteem of his order and overthrowing the aristocracy suffered a serious set-back.

Gladstone, too, must take much of the credit—or the opprobrium, depending on one's point of view—for the eventual demise of Cobdenite politics. As we have seen, Gladstone did not embody the 'entrepreneurial ideal' in any straightforward way. But what successes the entrepreneurial Radicals enjoyed owed much to Gladstone's backing. Most of the Radical causes which he sponsored (the 'liberation of commerce', for example) were successful; those of which he disapproved (like the destruction of educational endowments) fared less well. For Gladstone was not only 'the greatest schoolmaster of the

---

[20] Bright to George Wilson, 22 Mar. 1857, George Wilson Papers.
[21] Mandler, *Aristocratic Government*, passim.

day', as the Liverpool financial reformers called him;[22] he also formed an indispensable link between the world of industry and commerce, on the one hand, and established centres of aristocratic power, on the other. It is a mark of Gladstone's political ambiguity that in retrospect one hesitates as to whether to call him a friend of entrepreneurial Radicalism or the subtlest of its enemies.

For although many of Gladstone's policies met the demands of the entrepreneurial Radicals, it is highly significant that the Liberal Leader never embraced Cobden's class analysis. As Gladstone explained to his brother in August 1859: 'The Liberal side of the House is certainly at this time the more pacific and economical: but the manufacturing and mercantile classes have had much to do with promoting wars and likewise annexations or assumptions of territorial power and responsibility which are in some respects as dangerous and bad.'[23] True, Cobden himself eventually came to accept the broad truth of this diagnosis; but he did so with a sense of shame and sadness at the failure of 'his' order to fulfill its historic destiny. Gladstone, on the other hand, took comfort from this confirmation that, in the great public issues which divided the country, class did not face class in simple hostility.

For Gladstone saw it as his role, not to lead the 'middle classes' into battle against their aristocratic oppressors in vindication of the entrepreneurial ideal in politics, but to preside over a 'national settlement' which would rest upon class harmony. Even in those of his speeches in which he most openly 'wooed' the business community, he seldom neglected to make this point clearly, as when he opened the Peel monument in Manchester in October 1853. *The Times* got the message which Gladstone was trying to convey when it spoke of the existence of a new spirit of civic pride and class harmony: 'The nation governs itself, and its measures are the fruit of common deliberation, compromise and time.' (In an adjoining editorial, it rapped Cobden over the knuckles for his Peace Movement, which had been 'from the first the ruin of Mr. Cobden's reputation as a statesman'.)[24] The 1853 budget was intended to be precisely such an embodiment of the spirit of class compromise.

Similarly, when Gladstone presented himself to the electors of South Lancashire in 1865, having 'escaped' the archaic aristocratic world of Oxford University, he was quick to remind his northern audience of 'the duty of establishing and maintaining a harmony between the past of our glorious country, and the future that is still in store for her'.[25] And later, at a prize-giving ceremony at Liverpool Royal Institution School, he dextrously balanced his praise of modern commerce with warnings about the danger of confusing

---

[22] *Financial Reformer*, Nov. 1864, 541 (Jeffery).
[23] William Gladstone to Robertson Gladstone, 18 Aug. 1859, Shannon, *Gladstone*, 391.
[24] *The Times*, 14 Oct. 1853.
[25] Shannon, *Gladstone*, 547.

true education with commercial instruction: 'There is no training for the conflicts and toils of life . . .', he insisted, 'which does greater justice to the receiver of it than the old training of the English public schools and Universities.'[26] Thus, Gladstone may, as Bagehot claimed, have possessed 'the speculative hardihood, the eager industry of a Lancashire merchant' underneath 'the scholastic polish of his Oxford education',[27] but there was much more to Gladstone than that!

As a 'class reconciler', Gladstone was in many ways following in the footsteps of his hero Sir Robert Peel. But it was Peel's fate to be required to operate within the context of a Conservative Party unwilling to perform this conciliatory role. From this constraint Gladstone, after 1846, was free. Thus, Gladstone was able to preside over a *genuine* synthesis of commercial and aristocratic ideals and to forge a party machine which could secure its implementation.[28] This he was able to do, in large measure, because he had an authentic footing in both worlds, which Peel did not—still less Palmerston! For, in setting out to conciliate the classes, Gladstone was reconciling both the two different branches of his own family and also the two different sides of his own personality.

Given the reluctance of most mid-Victorian businessmen to embrace the revolutionary politics which Cobden so uncompromisingly upheld and given the very limited possibilities inherent in the cautious tactics of 'permeation' which found favour with figures so otherwise diverse as James Wilson and Samuel Morley, it is little wonder that Gladstone should have exercised a fascination over the great commercial centres. Perkin finds this fascination entirely understandable. Gladstone's policies, he argues, 'were those which the middle class would have pursued for themselves if they could have in their midst a leader as appealing and representative as Gladstone. . . . [Indeed], as long as entrepreneurial society lasted in a form still recognizably true to its ideal, it found its chief political expression in Gladstone and the Liberal Party'.[29]

But more convincing is Anthony Howe's witty remark that 'the "ghost" of the League was finally exorcised by the priestcraft of Gladstone',[30] for it seems to have been by a mixture of showmanship and magic that he was able to persuade so many Radical members of the commercial and industrial class,

[26] *The Times*, 23 Dec. 1872. See further, Ch. 7.

[27] *National Review*, July 1860, reproduced in Bagehot, *Collected Works*, iii. 419. See Lord Stanley's diary entry of 4 Mar. 1865, in John Vincent (ed.), *Disraeli, Derby and the Conservative Party: Journals and Memoirs of Edward Henry Lord Stanley, 1849–1869* (Hassocks, 1978), 229.

[28] Boyd Hilton makes the point that Gladstone needed conflict, even if it had to be artificially created; but this was to be a conflict which divided the classes, not one which set them against one another (*Age of Atonement*, 353).

[29] Perkin, *Origins*, 380.

[30] Howe, *Cotton Masters*, 244.

particularly Bright, that he was their 'natural' leader, when closer reflection should have shown them that this was not the case. But if deception was involved, then it was as much self-deception on the Radicals' part as any conscious attempt by Gladstone to mislead.

All this suggests that the trouble with Perkin's account of the 'triumph of the entrepreneurial ideal' is that it is too bald. To take only one example, is it really plausible to say of the reformed public schools that 'they embraced the new entrepreneurial ideal and its morality and instilled them into the sons of the aristocracy and gentry'?[31] Most historians would argue the very opposite. In other words, to use Perkin's own metaphor, his *Origins of Modern English Society* undoubtedly underestimates the extent of the 'transmission losses'[32] which occurred when landed society set itself up as the interpreter of middle-class interests.

It is true that businessmen who secured election to Parliament were affected by the processes of political integration which tended to break down 'class feeling'.[33] Nevertheless, many members of that class continued to dislike the idea of 'ruling by proxy' and, out of a sense of class pride, still wanted political power for their own order. After all, the notion that one class can 'rule' through the instrumentality of another is in many ways intrinsically un-attractive. The British Labour Movement developed earlier this century because thousands of working men and women were determined to take control of their fate and not be 'represented' by their well-meaning middle-class 'friends' in the Liberal Party. (Similarly, the feminist movement rests on the fundamental assumption that women cannot trust men to act as guardians of their interests.) Many mid-Victorian businessmen felt likewise, and by the 1860s they had achieved a modicum of success in asserting themselves in the political arena. They dominated local government in most of the manufactur-ing towns; they had established a significant presence on the magistrates' bench in industrialized counties like Lancashire. It had even become politically expedient to give them high office in the national government itself. In 1859 Palmerston tried hard to entice Cobden into the Cabinet, failing which he had to be content with giving junior ministerial office to some of the lesser fry from the business world. Six years later Russell 'landed' Forster, and was even prepared to make a commitment to parliamentary reform in order to achieve this goal. When Gladstone became Prime Minister, Bright, too, was at long last brought in from the cold.

But when Cobden refused to abandon the back benches, he may well have had a premonition about the troubles which lay in store for entrepreneurial

---

[31] Perkin, *Origins*, 298.

[32] Ibid. 272.

[33] This point is emphasized in W. C. Lubenow, *Parliamentary Politics and the Home Rule Crisis: The British House of Commons in 1886* (Oxford, 1988), esp. Conclusion.

Radicalism now that office lay within its reach. Here, after all, was a group which had started off with the belief that, given the political will, business methods could be applied to public life. Land and labour were to be treated as commodities just like raw materials and manufactured goods, and market values (which embodied 'rationality') were to be exalted over tradition and inherited privilege. Yet how exactly was this to be achieved? The eventual failure of entrepreneurial Radicalism owed less to the opposition it encountered from non-business groups than to the *practical* problems involved in the application of entrepreneurial principles.

THE ENTREPRENEURIAL DILEMMA

Businessmen often agreed on what they were trying to achieve, but differed over *means*. A good example of this is the debate surrounding the extension of the franchise. John Bright and the 'Adullamite' Samuel Laing had a surprising amount in common; they simply disagreed over whether a vertical extension of the suffrage could be safely attempted. Laing, like other cautious business-men, feared that manual workers would quickly use their new-found power to attempt to secure an artificial protection of their own wages and working conditions. Bright took the opposite view: bringing the better-educated sec-tion of the working class within the pale of the Constitution and giving them citizens' rights would, in his view, be the most effective way of exposing the fallacies of trade unionism and *attaching* working men to market values.

The difference was as much the result of a difference of temperament as of anything else. Many of the northern industrialists felt they knew their employees well and had enough authority over them to be sure that the new electors would not abuse their vote. Samuel Laing, however, was a pessimist, as was Robert Lowe; such men believed that everyone (but ill-educated working men more than most) lacked the capacity to behave rationally and so would soon 'go wrong' if temptations were placed in their path. To put it another way, Bright perhaps thought that competition and market values were 'natural' and would be embraced by everyone once they had been disabused of their 'errors'; while others, like Laing, were conscious of the fragility of the commercial progress that had been achieved since 1832, and feared that, unless very great care were taken, society would regress. What distinguished Lowe was the intensity of his pessimism; but his political philosophy did not differ greatly in substance from Bright's.

There were other occasions when the problem was in knowing quite what political economy really enjoined. This was particularly true in the 1850s and the 1860s, when more technical issues of legal reform and of economic management forced themselves on the attention of Parliament. The desirability or otherwise of limited liability split the business community (and indeed other groups, too), because, in Professor Taylor's words, it could be 'viewed both as emancipatory in removing restrictions on the mobility of capital and as interventionist in according privileges to corporate enterprises which were denied to the individual entrepreneur'. One man's laissez-faire was another man's intervention.[34] Moreover, in whose interest was limited liability supposed to operate: that of the business corporation itself, the individual investor, or the traders who had dealings with the incorporated firm?

Then there were areas of public life in which 'competition' proved difficult to implement, because businessmen were unsure whether they were entitled to propagate their own beliefs and values as though they were goods being brought to the market or whether, in so good a cause, they could swallow their usual principles and go in for some straightforward subsidized propaganda. We have seen how this dilemma baffled Edward Baines. The raising of money to found voluntary schools that could supply the kind of education favoured by businessmen like himself seemed an obvious course of action to take. But it laid its organizers open to the objection that education, like everything else, would be valued only if the parent/consumer were prepared to make pecuniary sacrifices in order to acquire it; what was available 'free' or at below cost price would be neither valued nor worthy of esteem.

A similar dilemma confronted the entrepreneurial Radicals when they embarked on the purchase and control of newspapers. Cobden and his friends played a notable part in the 'liberation' of the Press from its existing fiscal restraints. They also ventured into the risky world of newspaper management by founding the *Morning Star*, with a view to propounding what they regarded as 'sound doctrine'. '*The cheap daily press will do more than any other human agency to form the public opinion of this Country,*' Cobden declared.[35]

Yet, while worrying about how best to ensure that 'their' paper was '*permanently honest*', in Bright's words,[36] the 'Manchester men' tended to view 'information' and 'opinion' as marketable commodities and the expanding press as a spectacular example of capitalist enterprise. Consequently, they wanted their paper to be commercially successful; indeed, many of their business friends would not support the *Star* at all unless there was a reasonable prospect of making a profit.[37] To employ C. P. Scott's later aphorism, the entrepreneurial Radicals believed that 'righteousness' should be not only 'readable', but also 'remunerative'.[38] Certainly, no one realized more acutely than Cobden how difficult it would be to combine profitability with

[34] Arthur J. Taylor, *Laissez-Faire and State Intervention in Nineteenth-Century Britain* (1972), 12.

[35] Koss, *Rise and Fall*, 125, Cobden's emphasis. As a letter-writer, Cobden was a great underliner.

[36] Ibid. 108. On Bright's anxieties as to whether his paper could 'be *permanently honest*' without alarming the persons who had put up the risk capital for it, see Bright to G. Wilson, 4 Aug. 1855, George Wilson Papers.

[37] Cobden to Sturge, 30 Sept. 1855, Cobden Papers, Add. MS 43,656, fo. 359.

[38] Alan J. Lee, *The Origins of the Popular Press in England 1855–1914* (1976), 173.

'edification'; for 'honest' newspapers tended to be a bad investment. Indeed, the *Morning Star* lost more than £80,000 before it finally folded in 1868,[39] despite Cobden's earnest insistence that the editorial team be prepared, if necessary, to compromise their principles so as to attain a large enough readership to ensure commercial viability.[40]

Other wealthy newspaper proprietors, however, seem not to have been too concerned with making big profits, though they felt uncomfortable about the prospect of sustaining large *losses*; business success was not their main concern. Thus, when in 1868 Samuel Morley purchased the *Daily News* (which by then had amalgamated with Bright's *Morning Star*), he did this, or so he later declared, 'not to make money, but to advocate principles', and he was 'almost disappointed' when his investment yielded a healthy dividend.[41] It seems that Morley preferred to incur a loss on a form of propaganda designed to make society 'better educated' about 'economic laws' (among other things), even though this entailed shielding his paper from the laws of competition which he generally advocated for the rest of society.

Then too there were areas of public life, like Civil Service reform, to which the application of market principles seemed quite inappropriate. How, in that case, could the evils of patronage and monopoly be eradicated and standards of efficiency kept high? The answer seemed to lie partly through the creation of what we would today call 'internal markets' and partly through the institution of competitive examinations. Both devices were adopted by Robert Lowe and combined in his Revised Code of 1862. Interestingly enough, reflecting in old age on the significance of his career, Lowe listed 'the principle of payment by results' as part of the legacy of political economy, along with the repeal of the Corn and Navigation Laws, currency reform, and the institution of limited liability.[42] Examinations accorded well with the 'spirit of the age', and were particularly welcomed by many of the entrepreneurial Radicals.

But while many businessmen, like Morley, saw examinations and market competition as being merely different aspects of the same fundamental process, others saw them rather as *alternative* mechanisms of control. Henry Ashworth, for example, came out against limited liability because he did not want the penalties for business failure to be in any way lowered, and he justified his position as follows:

---

[39] Koss, *Rise and Fall*, 90.

[40] Cobden to Sturge, 30 Sept. 1855, Cobden Papers, Add. MS 43,656, fo. 362. Byles's *Bradford Observer* commented in 1867 that a newspaper was not a mere machine for making money, but served higher moral purposes (James, 'Byles and *Bradford Observer*', 115).

[41] Hodder, *Life of Morley*, 247. See also Koss, *Rise and Fall*, 306–7; Lee, *Origins of Popular Press*, 163, 214.

[42] Robert Lowe, 'Recent Attacks on Political Economy', *Nineteenth Century*, 4 (1878), 868. He also included, of course, 'open competition for public appointments'.

Let it be borne in mind that our mercantile pursuits, unlike our learned professions, are not sheltered by law from open competition; nor is access to them rendered difficult by tests of fitness or other privileged exclusions; on the contrary, they are free and open to all who may choose to enter upon them, and are subjected only to those conditions and penalties, moral and pecuniary, which overtake disaster in the conducting of them.[43]

In other words, precisely because entry into a mercantile career was *not* controlled by an examination system, the full unfettered play of market forces was necessary to keep its practitioners up to scratch.

But examinations were obviously human contrivances for encouraging certain kinds of excellence and for discouraging others. No one understood this more clearly than Lowe. Yet it was some time before the businessmen who started off as enthusiastic supporters of competitive examinations saw the precise purposes to which they were being put by Gladstone and the Northcote–Trevelyan group of reformers. For, far from opening up public institutions to a meritocratic élite, the examinations set by the Civil Service Commission (with a marking scale which favoured classical studies) were clearly operating in such a way as to *reinforce* traditional privilege. Many businessmen, when they saw this, turned in disgust against examinations as such—which, after all, most did not employ in their own firms—and recommended instead the end of 'tenure' and a more brutal hiring and firing policy as the only way of improving administrative efficiency.

Thus the application of 'business methods' to public life turned out to be a far from simple affair. Nor did the principles of 'political economy', even when these could be ascertained, always serve as an infallible guide. True, businessmen liked on appropriate occasions to parade their knowledge of the 'dismal science', though it may be doubted whether many had made a close study of it. On the other hand, as 'practical men of business', they often expressed irritation towards those whom they saw as mere theoreticians. For example, Professor Fawcett's academic disquisitions on the evils of factory legislation in the late 1860s and early 1870s struck many employers as pedantic nonsense.[44]

CHRISTIANITY, 'PATERNALISM' AND ENTREPRENEURIAL VALUES

A literal obedience to the imperative of market forces worried businessmen for other reasons. Themselves pious, practising Christians in most cases, they were sensitive to the accusation that the dictates of political economy were at variance with the teaching of the Gospel. As a small boy, Bright had felt

---

[43] First Report of Royal Commission on Mercantile Laws, XXVII (1854), 195.
[44] See Ch. 8.

himself to be the 'heir of martyrs'; and, symbolically, his first major speech had been made against the levying of church rates ('a witness to inherited resentment').[45] And most of the League leaders were Dissenters of one kind or another (the Ashworths, like Bright, were Quakers).

Cobden, it is true, made light of the dilemma. Although an Anglican by profession, Cobden was also a secular optimist who managed to persuade himself that the principles of commercial freedom were but an application of the Christian faith. Perhaps that is why he so badly wanted to demonstrate that the liberation of commerce would result in universal peace. Free Trade, he was convinced, was a cause which could be promoted, with almost equal legitimacy, from within a Chamber of Commerce or from the pulpit, because the 'laws' of political economy were simply aspects of the 'great natural law', which had divine—nay, even scriptural—sanction. Cobden could, without any embarrassment, refer to the 'sacredness' of the Free Trade principle.[46] To buy in the cheapest and sell in the dearest market, he once said, was merely to carry out 'to the fullest extent the Christian doctrine of "Doing to all men as ye would they should do unto you"'.[47]

Conversely, the Corn Law was, in Cobden's opinion, a 'law which interfere[d] with the wisdom of the Divine Providence, and substitute[d] the law of wicked men for the law of nature'.[48] The situation was well described by Dunckley: 'It may be difficult to say whether he [Cobden] was more attached to commercial freedom because it would tend to promote peace, or to a peaceful policy because it would tend to promote commercial freedom'.[49] In general, perhaps, Cobden tended to put the emphasis on economic factors. For example, despite his genuine abhorrence of the methods needed to acquire and retain an empire, he greeted the outbreak of the Indian Mutiny by waxing indignant about its *costs*: 'Looking at the question as a political economist I believe we sh[oul]d be in 10 years a richer and more prosperous people without a yard of territory in India than we shall be if we succeed in retaining that "Empire" and even China into the bargain.'[50]

---

[45] Vincent, *British Liberal Party*, 196–7. Trevelyan, *Life of Bright*, 37–41. 'I am avowedly a member of the Nonconformist body,' Bright told the Commons in 1847. 'My forefathers languished in prison by the acts of that Church which you now ask me to aggrandize' (Parl. Deb., 3rd ser., vol. 91, 1100: 20 Apr. 1847).

[46] 15 Jan. 1846, *Cobden's Speeches*, 187.

[47] 27 Feb. 1846, ibid. 198. Compare Dickens's satirical treatment of this issue in *Hard Times* (1854), Ch. 9.

[48] 28 Sept. 1843, *Cobden's Speeches*, 35.

[49] Dunckley, *Jubilee of Free Trade*, 62–3. The blend of economics and morality is also to be found in Cobden's 14 June comment in his journal (Morley, *Cobden*, ii. 302–3).

[50] Cobden to Fitzmayer, 3 Sept. 1857, Cobden Papers, Add. MS 43,665, fo. 71. Compare Bright's concern with India as a potential supplier of raw cotton. On Cobden's calculation that it would be the manufacturers and merchants who would have to bear the main brunt of war, see his letter to Edward Baines, 1 Mar. 1848, Baines Papers.

In fact, doctrinaire members of the Manchester School sometimes accompanied this emphasis on the primacy of economics with a scepticism about the role of 'altruism' in public life. 'You may reason ever so logically, but never so convincingly as through the pocket,' Cobden once observed.[51] Nor did these observations apply only to other people's motivation. Henry Ashworth declared that outside family life his *own* motivating force was self-interest: 'I deny that either the landlord or myself is a patriot or a benefactor.... We both act from one cause, we have both one motive—that of enlightening self-interest.'[52] A fellow Quaker agreed: 'I am a manufacturer in a considerable way of business,' said Bright; 'but I never professed to keep on my manufactory for the benefit of my work-people, or for the sake of clothing my customers. My object is, by the expenditure of capital and by giving labour to a business, to procure for myself and family a comfortable income, with a hope of realising something like a competency at a late period of my life.'[53] What inspired these 'confessions' was, of course, a desire to expose the landowning class's spurious claim to be somehow performing a public service.

However, whatever the Weber thesis might say, few manufacturers or advocates of the manufacturing system were happy with this kind of materialistic approach; nor was Cobden's blithe belief in an identity between 'morality' and 'entrepreneurial values' shared by all his followers.[54]

One way of coping with the resulting ethical conflict was to draw a sharp distinction between the world of work, where the laws of competition were supposed to reign supreme, and the world of the family, where the values of mutual love and support were paramount. Indeed, some of the ideological defenders of 'capitalism', like Herbert Spencer, made that distinction a central element in their social thought. The fallacy of socialism, they argued, was that it sought to import into society at large the ethics of the family, something which could only have disastrous results.[55] In short, the most fanatical of marketeers, whether in Britain or in the United States, have always unreservedly conceded that certain areas of human life should be insulated from market forces. The 'buying and selling' of votes, for example, was thought by the entrepreneurial Radicals to be an immoral practice (and one which they associated with their 'feudal' opponents);[56] likewise with the

---

[51] Cobden to Bright, 23 Dec. 1848, Cobden Papers, Add. MS 63,649, fo. 116.

[52] Boyson, *Ashworth Cotton Enterprise*, 223.

[53] 26 Mar. 1845, *Bright's Speeches*, 440.

[54] The 'Christian economics' propounded by Thomas Chalmers, which Boyd Hilton so brilliantly analyses in his *Age of Atonement*, made little impact on the 'entrepreneurial Radicals', few of whom had been brought up in this particular Evangelical tradition. In fact, as Boyd Hilton himself argues, this mode of thought 'mainly appealed to the comfortably well-off *nouveaux riches* who, opposing privilege, nevertheless defended the existing social order: notably the salaried, professional, and *rentier* classes most susceptible to the ideas of the evangelical intelligentsia' (197).

[55] See Peel, *Herbert Spencer*, 221–2.

[56] Kell, *Ballot*, 11.

purchase of commissions in the Army, a practice condemned even by an 'entrepreneurial' newspaper like the *Daily News*.[57] By drawing such boundaries, a peaceful co-existence between Christianity and entrepreneurial values became conceivable.

From the start, it was also recognized that the entrepreneurial instincts and the 'law of competition' must be subject to certain limitations and restraints or the very cohesion of society would be jeopardized. 'Entrepreneurialism', if allowed unbridled expression, could easily find outlet in antisocial behaviour (commercial fraud, for example) offensive to most people's moral sense.[58] Hence, in practice, market competition in Britain had never been, and was never to become, completely 'free'. Only within the framework of law could competition legitimately take place, and, even in an age which set great store by 'freedom of contract' and the doctrine of *caveat emptor*, many legislative restrictions remained in place.

But were such legislative restrictions sufficient? Christian businessmen continued to worry about the apparently conflicting injunctions emanating from their religion and from the doctrines of political economy—what Malchow calls 'the contrasting ethic of the chapel and the board-room'.[59] Here were moral dilemmas which could not easily be avoided; they formed, of course, a familiar theme of mid-Victorian fiction. In short, did the Christian businessman have particular moral obligations to those whom he employed, as well as to society at large?

Samuel Morley, for one, believed in the seriousness of such obligations, a belief reinforced by his education. Morley had grown to manhood heavily influenced by The Revd T. Binney of King's Weigh House Chapel, who 'had a hold upon business men from the fact that in his earlier days he had himself been engaged in commerce, and had acquired a knowledge of the world which too many ministers lack'.[60] Encouraged by this experience, Morley attempted to run his business affairs in the light of Christian principles; that he enjoyed so much worldly success seemed proof that spiritual concerns and economic rationality could be harmoniously reconciled. Morley, in other words, undoubtedly saw the pursuit of a business career as a 'vocation'; but this did not mean that profit making played an important part in God's design for the world. In fact, making money for its own sake he genuinely abhorred. 'The strength of a nation lies not in the wealth, but in the virtue, of its people,' he once remarked.[61] And, in a letter to the *Daily News*, he took issue

---

[57] The *Daily News* observed (15 Mar. 1855) that the nation would have 'no more buying and selling of commissions, no more trafficking in commands as if they were so many bales of cotton' (cited in Spiers, *Radical General*, 167).

[58] Norman Russell, *The Novelist and Mammon: Literary Responses to the World of Commerce in the Nineteenth Century* (Oxford, 1986).

[59] Malchow, *Gentlemen Capitalists*, 8.

[60] Hodder, *Life of Morley*, 60.

[61] Ibid. 456.

with those economists who contended that no man was bound to give more for a commodity than it was worth, be that commodity an article or labour, arguing that this ignored man's responsibility to his fellow men.[62] Finally, with regard to the distribution of his many philanthropic donations, his biographer notes that Morley 'was not, as many rich men are, a worshipper of success. He had a very tender sympathy for men who failed.'[63] 'A servant of Jesus Christ' reads the inscription on his tombstone.[64]

Many other Nonconformist politicians displayed a similar disposition. For example, J. J. Colman, the 'mustard magnate' (like Morley, a Congregationalist), saw 'work' as a form of religious service,[65] the purpose of which was not the mere amassing of wealth. In a paper entitled 'The Race for Riches', written in 1855, Colman declared:

Let the merchants and tradesmen of England remember that riches are not the true mark of nobility any more than title is. A man returning his few hundreds a year may be much better and wiser than one who returns many thousands. The race for riches must not be the moving spring of action, for if it is it will surely bring unhappiness and misery in the end. Enterprise is wholesome enough but it must have a good foundation to rest on.[66]

But did these edifying sentiments represent a departure from a proper commitment to entrepreneurial values and capitalist norms?

The case of the Quaker banking and industrial dynasty, the Peases, dramatizes the dilemma. Following family tradition, argues Maurice Kirby, the Peases attached little importance to strictly entrepreneurial considerations in the determination of their business strategy. Unfortunately, this devotion to Christian ethics seems to have contributed to the eventual collapse of their firm.[67] Generosity in supporting a range of charities and 'good causes' may have been responsible for the economic difficulties experienced by other businessmen, too.[68] Can a wider moral be drawn from such cases?

---

[62] Hodder, *Life of Morley*, 357–9.

[63] Ibid. 313. On Morley the philanthropist, see David Owen, *English Philanthropy 1660–1960* (Cambridge, Mass., 1964), 401–8.

[64] Hodder, *Life of Morley*, 492. It is striking how many Dissenting MPs of this stamp came in time to admire Gladstone, an admiration which, in Morley's case, was 'difficult to distinguish from hero-worship', according to his biographer. It was not simply appreciation of Gladstone's policies and executive capacity which elicited these feelings: the 'G.O.M.' 'always looked at the moral side of things', Morley would say (ibid. 404, 246).

[65] Colman, *Jeremiah James Colman*, 136.

[66] Ibid. 432–3.

[67] Kirby, *Men of Business and Politics*, Ch. 6; *idem*, 'The Failure of a Quaker Business Dynasty: The Peases of Darlington, 1830–1902', in David J. Jeremy (ed.), *Business and Religion in Britain* (Aldershot, 1988), 156–7.

[68] Malchow, *Gentlemen Capitalists*, 374: 'It is to Protestant anxiety rather than aristocratic pretension that one must often look for an explanation for the significant withdrawal of resources from Victorian business to other uses.'

In a provocative essay, Roy Campbell concedes that Christianity, by emphasizing the need for high standards of commercial ethics, contributed to efficient business practice, as well as to general social morality during the Victorian years. At the same time, a persistent note of disapproval of wealth creation may have done something, he observes, to discourage businessmen and to shake their faith in their particular 'vocation'. Similarly, the Christian duty to make social provision for the work-force and to use profits for philanthropic purposes was often emphasized to the point of neglecting the employer's other moral duties: to his consumer and (within the joint stock company) his shareholders.[69] In fact, locked into an intense sectarian rivalry as to who had the best record in 'Christian good works',[70] many active Dissenting businessmen of the kind likely to go into parliamentary politics on the Liberal side tended to apologize (needlessly?) for the capitalist economic order to which they belonged. Cobden strove manfully to combat this sense of inferiority, but with only partial success.

Some manufacturers were also unsettled by the gibes of critics like Thomas Carlyle, Ruskin, and Matthew Arnold. W. E. Forster may have been an untypical mill-owner in many ways, but his experience is nevertheless interesting. In late 1847 the Carlyles visited him at his Yorkshire home. On their departure, Forster wrote to a friend that one effect of intense discussion with the 'Sage' had been

to make me desire to sift my faith, not, I trust, in a frivolous sceptical temper, but in order to get yet firmer foothold, to strengthen my convictions, so that I may in future be able to meet him or his likes, not with a mere logical opinion, but with a living faith which might prove its own power.[71]

Other Bradfordian businessmen came under the influence, literary and in some cases personal, of Ruskin.[72]

As a result of such encounters, many manufacturers sought to appease their critics by trying to live up to Carlylean ideals. To achieve this goal (and to demonstrate Christian piety), self-made entrepreneurs often threw themselves into a whole array of 'compensatory activities': endowing educational and cultural institutions, founding churches, and taking the lead in the provision of fine public buildings for their localities. Even so, they tended to suffer from a chronic sense of insecurity. Note, for example, how anxious the Birmingham gunsmith W. L. Sargant was to dispel the notion that people in his 'order'

---

[69] R. H. Campbell, 'A Critique of the Christian businessman and his paternalism', in Jeremy (ed.), *Business and Religion in Britain*, 27–46.

[70] The Anglican Akroyd and the Congregationalist Crossleys, the two biggest employers in Halifax, ran rival 'model communities', the former naming his streets after Anglican cathedrals, the latter after Nonconformist heroes like Cromwell and Gladstone! (Jowitt (ed.), *Model Industrial Communities*, 186).

[71] Reid, *Life of Forster*, i. 212.

[72] Hardman, *Ruskin and Bradford*, passim.

were more avaricious than anyone else.[73] Arguably, then, the 'civic gospel' of the 1870s and 1880s owed much to the businessman's sense of guilt.[74]

But did what Howe has called the 'moralisation of the capitalist'[75] really contribute to greater economic efficiency? As we have been, Campbell is sceptical on this score. On the other hand, Koditschek, in his study of Bradford, has persuasively argued that ultimately the liberal entrepreneurs *gained* by the abandonment of their 'initial predisposition to envision the social world entirely in competitive market terms'. 'In the last analysis, particularly during moments of crisis,' writes Koditschek, a 'more limited, less heroic conception of hegemony, in which culture and politics regained some autonomy in relation to the competitive individualism which properly ruled the market-place, proved more effective in underwriting the social stability that was necessary for entrepreneurship as an economic form to thrive.'[76]

CLASS PRIDE

Nevertheless, many entrepreneurial Radicals suffered from cultural inhibitions, in the sense that their prime concern was not to maximize their earnings as producers, but rather to assert their social dignity in the face of their aristocratic detractors, from whom many were separated by a high cultural barrier. For although, even in the early nineteenth century, it was by no means uncommon for second-generation manufacturers to be sent to a public school or to an Oxford or Cambridge college,[77] few of the entrepreneurial Radicals who made a name for themselves in politics had received anything more than a basic education.

[73] Sargant, *Essays*, i. 42.

[74] But for a very different view, that the 'civic gospel' was 'at root an entrepreneurial gospel', see the important article by Jones, 'Public Pursuit of Private Profit?'.

[75] Howe, *Cotton Masters*, 314. It is anyhow arguable that, in the 1830s and 1840s, the urban middle class lacked a coherent ideology. Political economy was one element in its creed, but so were evangelicalism, utilitarianism, a belief in individuality, a sense of hierarchy and paternal responsibility, and so on (Morris, *Class, Sect and Party*, 167).

[76] Koditschek, 'Dynamics of Class Formation', 547–8. In the early 19th century, Morris suggests, social breakdown was likely to occur in the absence of a middle-class élite of merchants and professional men who could mediate between the employer and his hands. This (whether they realized it or not) was helpful to *all* sections of the middle class, since the pursuit of profit and capital accumulation, untempered by other considerations, would not have maintained the stability of the capitalist order (*Class, Sect and Party*, Ch. 13, esp. 327).

[77] See examples of Lancashire textile masters going to public school and university in Howe, *Cotton Masters*, 57. A banker like Goschen, it is true, had been to Rugby and then to Trinity College, Cambridge; but then City bankers inhabited a social world which largely cut them off from the manufacturers of the Midlands and the North (José Harris and Pat Thane, 'British and European bankers, 1880–1914: An "Aristocratic Bourgeoisie"?', in Pat Thane, Geoffrey Crossick, and Roderick Floud (eds.), *The Power of the Past* (Cambridge, 1984), 215–34; W. D. Rubinstein, *Men of Property: The Very Wealthy in Britain since the Industrial Revolution* (1981), passim; Y. Cassis, 'Bankers in English Society in the Late Nineteenth Century', *Economic History Review*, 38 (1985), 210–29).

Many businessmen were Dissenters who would anyhow have been out of place at a public school (or even at the local grammar school); and, in the period prior to the repeal of the University Test Acts, study at Oxford or Cambridge would have been wellnigh out of the question. The Quakers, of course, ran their own establishments, and many famous businessmen had attended one of these: John Bright, for example, went to a series of Friends' schools, including Ackworth, near Pontefract, and W. E. Forster received his schooling at Grove House, Tottenham.

Other businessmen underwent a far more modest education. Although his father was then in possession of a considerable fortune, Samuel Morley was taught by a Congregational minister at a Nonconformist boarding-school at Melbourn in Cambridgeshire;[78] and Titus Salt, along with his sister, went at the age of 11 to a day school connected with Salem Chapel, Wakefield, where 'the instruction imparted was what was recognized as "a plain commercial education"', including history, geography, and drawing.[79] Isaac Holden, a Methodist, began work in a weaver's shed at the age of 10, receiving his education at night schools.[80] Nor did Cobden, an Anglican, fare any better; he was sent by his uncle to a poorly run boarding-school in North Yorkshire, from which he was rescued and sent out to work at the age of 15, the normal age for someone employed in industry or commerce to start earning his crust.[81] Most businessmen still regarded going on to university or college as a 'luxury'. Even in the 1860s W. L. Sargant, himself a manufacturer, could write that by the age of 13 a boy had 'been taught all that a man of business wants: reading, writing, spelling, arithmetic, geography, and a little history'; everything else was merely to make a gentleman of him.[82]

In any case, manufacturers and merchants would hardly have learned much that was relevant to their chosen careers by prolonging their education. Of course, the Nonconformist academies may have inculcated values (industry, honesty, fair dealing, and so on) which *indirectly* contributed to their pupils' later business success. In this connection it is interesting to note the verdict on Ackworth, passed by one of its headmasters: 'The aim of "getting on in life" was put before the pupils as an ideal... They were successful in business, several founding firms of world-wide repute.'[83] But to be a prosperous cotton spinner, contractor, or wool stapler, one did not need to have mastered the kind of technical knowledge that was available only in educa-

---

[78] Hodder, *Life of Morley*, 12; he started work in the family firm at the age of 16 (ibid. 18).

[79] Balgarnie, *Sir Titus Salt*, 23–5. On the importance of the Dissenting academies, see Joyce, *Work, Society and Politics*, 31.

[80] 'Memoir of Isaac Holden'. The rudimentary education of the Bradford mill-owners and the 'autodidacticism' which this produced is well discussed in Koditschek, *Class Formation*, 189–95.

[81] Morley, *Cobden*, i. 4–5.

[82] Sargant, *Essays*, ii. 247–8.

[83] I. H. Wallis, *Frederick Andrews of Ackworth* (1924), cited in Simon, *History of Education*, 112.

tional institutions, calico printing being a rare exception.[84] An ability to read, write, and keep accounts largely sufficed. Thus, what success these men enjoyed, they could reasonably ascribe to hard work, good judgement, and, not least, family connections.

Few major Victorian entrepreneurs lacked *any* education. The great contractor Thomas Brassey who, so ran the rumour, could not write his own name and totted up the dibs on his five fingers, was in no way typical.[85] On the other hand, few businessmen had undergone what their contemporaries would have considered a proper education; that is to say, few of them knew more than a smattering of Latin and Greek, while many were totally ignorant of the classical languages.

This 'deficiency' affected individuals in different ways. Sargant wrote revealingly about how people of his 'order' often suffered a chronic lack of self-confidence. If a young man was to enter an established business with the expectation of becoming its principal, he observed,

he may well complain in after life, if he is removed [too] soon [from school]. He will find afterwards that he is at a great disadvantage when he gets into the society of better educated men. He will frequently not understand what they are talking of, or their illustrations and allusions: a Latin quotation in a book, or a Latin name in a museum, abashes him.[86]

Indeed, Robert Lowe, who was far from recommending a classical education for the commercial middle class, nevertheless felt that the narrowly vocational schooling which was that all such people tended to receive had made them needlessly modest and reluctant to assert their own legitimate class interests. Even in Cobden and Bright, hardly men lacking in self-confidence, one detects a kind of defensiveness underlying their professions of contempt for a public school and 'varsity' education.[87]

As Sargant again noted, such feelings of injured pride often made the manufacturer with little formal schooling 'intent on bringing up his own sons in a very different fashion'.[88] But, more commonly, in the early and middle Victorian years at least, this sense of exclusion and the touchiness it engendered led to middle-class attacks on aristocratic privilege, which, at the same time, betokened a kind of class pride.

Even the Chamber of Commerce movement, which obviously existed to serve the immediate economic needs of merchants and industrialists, was

---

[84] Howe, *Cotton Masters*, 287–90.

[85] *Ancestor*, 2 (1902), 233.

[86] Sargant, *Essays*, ii. 200.

[87] See Cobden's famous remarks in a speech at Rochdale, 23 Nov. 1864, *Cobden's Speeches*, 491–2. Bright's reflections on classical studies can be found in Leech (ed.), *Letters of Bright*, 291–3.

[88] Sargant, *Essays*, ii. 200.

animated by such class feeling. In February 1862 its President said 'that he trusted commercial men would be more true to themselves, and he believed that, if they would act through this Association, they might do much good'.[89] As for the Bradford Chamber, one of its original aims, its organizers later recalled, had been that of 'raising the tone of mercantile honour amongst its members'.[90] No wonder that Bradford businessmen sometimes found themselves torn between a sense of what this 'honour' enjoined and the dictates of 'political economy'. For example, the Bradford Chamber was pressed by the Halifax delegates in 1864 to commit itself to standard terms of credit. The mill-owner Robert Kell protested at the very idea: 'The Chamber could not fix prices between the buyer and the seller. . . . They might as well attempt to fix the price of cabbages or the price of tea, or interfere between the manufacturer and those in his employ to fix the rate of wages.' But other members of the Chamber felt that a gesture in the direction of a uniform business code would mean the stamping out of dishonourable behaviour and the raising of its members' 'credit' in a spiritual sense.[91]

Once again it was Cobden who most eloquently articulated these sentiments. 'Our countrymen, if they were possessed of a little of the *mind* of the merchants and manufacturers of Frankfort, Chemnitz, Elberfeld, etc., would become the De Medicis, and Fuggers, and De Witts of England, instead of glorying in being the toadies of a clod-pole aristocracy, only less enlightened than themselves!,' he wrote in 1838.[92] The publication of Smiles's *Industrial Biography* momentarily gave him heart: 'The captains of industry are invading the domain that was formerly held sacred to the warrior or statesman,' he told Ashworth. 'A century ago who would have dreamed of erecting statues to Cromptons, Wedgwoods, or even Watts?'[93] In fact, two of the favourite words in Cobden's (and Bright's) vocabulary were 'self-respect' and 'manliness'.[94] Birmingham's adoption of Bright as its parliamentary candidate, for example, was welcomed by Cobden in 1857 as 'noble and manly'.[95]

Unfortunately, the members of the Manchester School came in time to feel that 'manliness' was precisely what their own order lacked. The adulation shown by the Mancunian middle class to the Queen on her visit to their city was stigmatized as lacking in 'self-respect'. Thus, like the Marxists of a later

---

[89] ACC Papers, 19 Feb. 1862.
[90] Bradford Chamber of Commerce 20th Annual Report, 1871, p. 9.
[91] Bradford Chamber of Commerce Minutes, 27 Jan., 17 Feb. 1864, esp. fos. 155–6, 163.
[92] Cobden to F. Cobden, 6 Oct. 1838, cited in Morley, *Cobden*, i. 134.
[93] Cobden to Ashworth, 11 Nov. 1863, Cobden Papers, Add. MS 43,654, fo. 274.
[94] Cobden to Bright, 11 Aug. 1857, Cobden Papers, Add. MS 43,650, fo. 256. The theme of 'manliness' is interestingly portrayed in the character of the mill-owner Mr Thornton in Gaskell, *North and South*, Ch. 20. Samuel Smiles, too, believed the 'highest object of life . . . to be to form a manly character, and to work out the best development possible, of body and spirit—of mind, conscience, heart and soul' (*Self-Help*, 367).
[95] See Cobden to J. B. Smith, 12 Aug. 1857, John Benjamin Smith Papers, MS 923.2, S345, fo. 61.

generation, Cobden suffered repeated disappointment in those to whom he assigned the task of historical emancipation.

There were several reasons why it proved to be so difficult to imbue manufacturers and merchants with class pride, or rather to make this sentiment a unifying, rather than a divisive, factor. Landowners at least shared a commitment to a set of traditions, and possessed certain inherited privileges which they could come together to defend. Likewise, working-class organizations rested on certain ideals of communality and social solidarity. But Cobden was trying to foster a sense of class unity among businessmen who not only *believed* strongly in an ideology of mobility and individualism, but who were also in many cases actually locked into fierce competition with one another.[96] For example, at a trivial level, the Brights, who had moved into carpet manufacturing, were involved in the 1860s in a lengthy patent suit against the Crossleys of Halifax.[97] To these economic divisions must be added status rivalries within a middle-class community which, in the larger cities, was highly heterogeneous.[98]

Obviously, these rivalries were exacerbated by religious disagreements. Sectarianism, in fact, was always threatening to cut across the endeavours of the entrepreneurial Radicals. Samuel Morley, for example, had started off as a keen admirer of Cobden, who had encouraged him to go into politics, calling him the 'head at once of the Administrative Reformers and the Dissenting politicians'.[99] But it was primarily with a view to removing 'Dissenters' grievances' that Morley and others like him entered the House of Commons, his own particular fields of interest being educational reform, the abolition of university tests, the Burial Bill, and so on (as well as bankruptcy law reform).[100]

The conflict between Church and Dissent, historians are agreed, was fundamental to the political arena for most of the nineteenth century.[101] On the one hand, this conflict to some extent gave shape and purpose to the assault made by resentful businessmen on the established aristocratic state, and, as such, it continued to provide the impetus for a kind of entrepreneurial politics well into the twentieth century. On the other hand, sectarian radicalism

---

[96] The point is well made by Malchow, *Gentlemen Capitalists*, 5.

[97] Vincent, *British Liberal Party*, 199. When the award went to Bright Bros., John Bright wrote to his wife: 'In this case we have been ill treated by the Halifax people—they have not behaved as gentlemen or Christians, and they deserve the fate they have received' (8 Mar. 1864, John Bright Family Papers).

[98] Morris sees the Leeds middle class as hierarchically organized, with merchants and professional men at the top, retailers and small masters at the bottom, and manufacturers in the middle (Morris, *Class, Sect and Party*, Ch. 13, esp. 321).

[99] 7 Mar. 1857, Hodder, *Life of Morley*, 142.

[100] The compulsory collection of church rates, which ended in 1868, had also been an issue with which he had been much concerned through his connection with the Liberation Society.

[101] Fraser, *Urban Politics*, 265.

also led not just to internal dissension within the Liberal Party, but, more generally, to the weakening of Cobdenite 'class politics', since religion, by dividing the urban élite in all the major English cities, helped to keep off the political agenda those issues on which the 'true' entrepreneurial Radicals would have preferred to focus. Brian Harrison has argued, with reference to nineteenth-century humanitarian movements, that Victorian society owed much to the disagreements that divided it, since it was 'sewn together by its inner conflicts'.[102] Nothing better illustrates this thesis than the sectarianism which gave many Victorian businessmen a social identity and a purpose in public life, yet at the same time inhibited their full expression. Thus, although the assault on the established Church signified a sort of attack on the traditional political élite, it did so only in a partial, indirect way. For whatever affinities Morley and other Nonconformist businessmen of his type may have had with Cobden, they differed from him in not seeing entrepreneurial values as providing the basis for a new political *system*. The difference was a vital one, and had important practical consequences.

Cobden tried to overcome these difficulties by *shaming* his order into self-respect. But, to an even greater extent than the pioneers of the Labour Movement, he came up against the obstacles of sectionalism and regionalism. As we have seen, the political perspectives of the major industrial towns were shaped by their relative importance *vis-à-vis* the surrounding countryside. The manufacturers of the Lancashire textile belt could afford to defy the local landed classes; but those from the West Riding felt it necessary to negotiate some kind of alliance with theirs. The actual structure of the industrial economy also produced differences of political strategy. In the West Midlands the small scale of the productive units made for easy intercourse between artisans and small masters, and this found expression in a 'democratic' ideology. In Manchester, by contrast, the heavy capitalization of the cotton industry had at a relatively early stage produced a marked social differentiation not only between masters and men, but also between the major manufacturers and the shopocracy. There, entrepreneurial politics came to be characterized as much by distrust of the 'masses' as by resentment of the pretensions of the aristocracy.

At a purely economic level, the disagreements between the great urban centres were even more pronounced. Commercial districts had needs that were different from, and sometimes opposed to, manufacturing districts; dock towns clashed with inland towns; the traders had a major grievance against the railway interest; and so on.

More generally, commercial rivalries were accentuated by that intense civic pride which was so important a feature of Victorian middle-class life. The

---

[102] Brian Harrison, citing L. Coser, 'Religion and Recreation in Nineteenth-Century England', *Past & Present*, 38 (1967), 123.

protracted row between Liverpool and Manchester about harbour dues is a good example of this.[103] Gladstone, who had a good understanding of both cities, observed in October 1864:

As long as I can recollect there has been a friendly rivalry and competition between Liverpool and Manchester. Sometimes Manchester and Liverpool have had their little controversies and little contests, but these contests are like the quarrels of man and wife, woe be to him that attempts to interfere therein.[104]

The rather comical vendetta between Leeds and Bradford shows with even greater clarity the lengths to which civic rivalry could go.[105] Such antagonisms had tangible economic origins. But they perhaps signified something more profound. Many entrepreneurs suffered from insecurity, as a result of a stunted education. So their sense of self-worth was crucially bound up with 'their' town, whose rise in the world paralleled their own. The fact that many—perhaps most—successful manufacturers in the 1850s and 1860s had not been born in the town of their adoption simply made their subsequent identification with it all the more fierce.[106]

On the political front Cobden tried hard to put such emotions to constructive uses, as when he urged the Mancunians not to be behind the citizens of Birmingham in acquiring their own self-governing corporation.[107] But more often than not inter-city conflict led only to bitter divisions. Thus, Bright and other textile manufacturers felt a prejudice against financial reform in the late 1840s because the movement had originated in Liverpool—a prejudice which Cobden worked hard to eradicate.[108] Conversely, the Manchester School suffered in the 1850s from resentment at the 'dictatorial' behaviour of Newall's Building, just as there was later to be a distrust of the 'Caucus' as a Brummagem invention.

It is also significant that Sargant, in his *Essays of a Birmingham Manufacturer* (1869), was most anxious to defend industrialists against the claims to

---

[103] See above, Ch. 5.

[104] *Financial Reformer*, Nov. 1864, 542: speech at Manchester Free Trade Hall. Liverpool's long adherence to the Navigation Acts had not endeared it to the other entrepreneurial Radicals.

[105] The Bradford Chamber, e.g., was furious when *The Times* printed stories of widespread business failures in its city on the strength of an article in the *Leeds Intelligencer*. Solemn resolutions were passed condemning the calumny, representations made to *The Times*, etc. (Bradford Chamber of Commerce 4th Annual Report, 1855, 14–15). On the rivalry between the two cities, see also *Bradford Observer*, 9 Mar. 1865; and for an earlier example, *Leeds Mercury*, 6 Feb. 1830.

[106] Interesting material relating both to the personal insecurity of the pioneering Bradford mill-owners and to their 'immigrant status' is to be found in Koditschek, *Class Formation*, esp. Ch. 6.

[107] Cobden, *Incorporate your Borough*, 4. During the Corn Law struggle, Cobden was very anxious to dispel the notion that the League was dominated by Mancunian mill-owners, and wanted the other manufacturing districts to be more prominently involved (Cobden to Edward Baines, jun., 12 Oct. 1841, Baines Papers).

[108] See Cobden's letters to Bright of Dec. 1848, Cobden Papers, Add. MS 43,651.

superiority being made by merchants. 'In Liverpool it is common to speak of Liverpool gentlemen and Manchester men,' he wrote. But, Sargant retorted, 'In manufactures, there is direct and untiring competition, between man and man, between nation and nation. Without lively and sound brains, a manufacturer is beaten out of the field.' Liverpool, by contrast, was too absorbed in speculation (at least according to Sargant), while the 'cockneys' of London lacked public spirit and suffered from complacency and a ludicrously inefficient municipal administration.[109] All these remarks were made in a semi-jocular vein, but they express the jealous spirit of rivalry which separated the big cities. The Association of Chambers of Commerce was an attempt to overcome such regionalism, but it was to some extent crippled by the very prejudices it was trying to combat.

The Chambers of Commerce were also faced with a dilemma of another kind. Some of the more intellectual figures associated with the movement, like Leone Levi and Jacob Behrens, were groping their way towards what a later generation would call 'corporatism'. Behrens, for example, in commending tribunals of commerce to the Bradford Chamber, suggested that in future it might be' necessary to establish a 'constituency' for the election of businessmen to serve on such bodies. This, he mused, would mean the re-creation of the old medieval guilds 'if we can succeed in finding for them a new foundation more in accordance with the present state of society'. Perhaps, if the registration of all firms and partnerships were to be achieved, said Behrens, 'the names of every banker, manufacturer, or merchant entered upon the register would furnish the desired constituency, not only for the Tribunals of Commerce, but also for the Chambers of Commerce, who feel that they have become institutions of too important a character to continue the mere voluntary associations which they are at present'.[110]

But was this an acceptable goal for the entrepreneurial Radicals? Might not such organized bodies of producers build up their strength until they were in a position to exploit the consumer and strike bargains with the State? Cobden's original aim, of course, had been to achieve the very opposite! Thus, when Robert Lowe (the consistent exponent of a 'consumers' capitalism') and James White warned the Commons in March 1865 of the dangers of a new 'protectionism' emanating from the Chambers of Commerce movement, they had some grounds for their fears.[111]

But this, in turn, raises the wider question of the attitude of Radical

---

[109] Sargant, *Essays*, i. 5, 11–12, 14–27. This disparaging use of the word 'cockney' to describe things metropolitan is often found in Cobden. One of Baines's objections to equal electoral districts in 1841 was founded on a recognition that it would increase the number of London MPs from 18 to 45, something he regarded as inimical to social progress (Baines, *Household Suffrage*, 12).

[110] Behrens, 'Tribunals of Commerce', 8–9.

[111] See Ch. 5.

businessmen towards the State. How far was the old hostility really being replaced by a more flexible or pragmatic approach?

ENTREPRENEURIAL POLITICS AND THE STATE

Now, the argument among businessmen about the role of the State is more complex than is often recognized. It certainly cannot be reduced to a conflict between *laissez-faire* and intervention or to a contest between individualism and collectivism. Quite reasonably, the overwhelming majority of Victorian businessmen believed in a market economy and wanted to keep State powers to a bare minimum. On the other hand, they also recognized that for there to be a market within whose framework competition could take place, the State would sometimes have to intervene. In particular, a market economy required what a later generation would call an 'infrastructure', which, some felt, could most efficiently be financed out of public funds. For example, most businessmen favoured the State acquisition of the telegraph service, because they wanted to be rescued from dependence upon an inefficient private monopoly.[112] (*The Economist*, too, conceded that the Post Office did its work more cheaply and fairly than many private companies—quite apart from which, the revenue which it generated meant that the pressure on the income tax payer was lightened![113]) Controls over the railway companies could be defended in much the same way. The public provision of decent drainage and sewerage and the maintenance of law and order also found favour with many businessmen, particularly with commercial managers accustomed to running large enterprises. Such men did not share the obsession of the small trader with 'economy', but set greater store by efficient administration and cost-effectiveness, and saw that the removal of social evils at source would in the long run reduce business costs.[114]

The production of goods, as distinct from the provision of services, was quite another matter. Cobden struck a sympathetic chord with many businessmen when he questioned the validity of government manufactories. The entrepreneurial Radicals saw great advantages in the Government using competitive tenders to meet its various needs, rather than trying to supply them for itself. But, once again, where market forces were not 'doing the trick', many businessmen were not afraid to invoke government aid. A good example of this is the demand by Lancashire mill-owners for a State policy to foster cotton growing in the Empire, especially in India, in order to minimize the dangers of reliance upon the southern states of America. Thomas Bazley

---

[112] See M. J. Daunton, *Royal Mail: The Post Office since 1840* (1985), 82–4. Cohen, 'Towards a Theory of State Intervention'.
[113] *Economist*, 11 Apr. 1868, p. 413.
[114] Jones, 'Public Pursuit of Private Profit?', 242–3.

recognized that this seemed to be flying in the face of economic orthodoxy, but he defended the position of the Cotton Supply Association as follows:

The law of supply and demand has not unfrequently [sic] been appealed to on this subject, and no doubt, where no countervening obstacles exist, its operation is true and certain; yet it must not be forgotten that under this law the demand has frequently to be diminished to meet a limited supply, whilst, to prevent loss and suffering in our contemplated difficulties, it is necessary that the supply of cotton should be enlarged adequately for the existing means of consumption, and for that reasonable extension which increasing labour and capital require.

Even Bright supported Bazley on this issue.[115]

Otherwise, attitudes towards the State depended on the sympathy with which businessmen felt they were being treated by its agents. Thus, despite the remarkable congruity of legal and economic thought and despite the view, expressed by Hayek and others, that the establishment of the rule of law, with its concomitant virtues of universality and predictability, was the precondition for rational economic decision making, the *structure* of the legal system was not to the liking of Victorian businessmen, who, as we have seen, tried whenever possible to avoid initiating civil actions to recover debts, and so on.

Similarly, in the early and middle decades of the nineteenth century, businessmen preferred to see powers entrusted to local authorities rather than central government, no doubt because in many urban areas they could already hope to influence—even control—public policy. Only from the 1860s onwards did businessmen lose much of their former suspicion of State institutions, seeing them no longer as creatures of aristocracy and 'Old Corruption'. This change of view closely mirrored their growing confidence in their own role in national politics. A similar evolution of attitudes was later to take place within the working-class movement around the turn of the century.[116]

Moreover, many of the entrepreneurial Radicals were less concerned with raising principled objections to State activity as such than with puzzling out what they wished to achieve with political power once they had attained it. Two areas of policy proved particularly troublesome.

The first was fiscal policy. Here businessmen knew what they disliked. They resented the privileged position which land enjoyed in the early years of the century, and, to a lesser extent, continued to enjoy. They also felt it unfair that earners of 'precarious' incomes should not be treated more leniently. But they could never decide on what positive alternatives they favoured. Some welcomed the income tax; others favoured its abolition. The notion of a

---

[115] *Transactions of the National Association for the Promotion of Social Science*, 1861, p. 732. Also Howe, *Cotton Masters*, 199–202. Bradford was engaged in a similar enterprise through its Wool Supply Association (Sigsworth, *Black Dyke Mills*, 61–2).

[116] See Pat Thane, 'The Working Class and State "Welfare" in Britain, 1880–1914', *Historical Journal*, 27 (1984), 900, 891.

'property tax' had its attractions. But although such a tax would have allowed some businessmen to work off their spleen against landowners, it threatened capital accumulation, as *The Economist* pointed out, and it would also have had the effect of encouraging manufacturers to hold on to their working capital, long after it had become 'rational' for them to sell out.[117] Faced by these dangers, most businessmen opted for what was economically 'safe', rather than pursue an ancestral hatred. But that left them with little to advocate other than 'economy'. It was into this policy vacuum that Gladstone came, holding out his own nostrums, which attracted the support of most businessmen, but did not truly embody entrepreneurial values.

In matters of education, the commercial middle classes had even less idea what they wanted to achieve. For this they should not be blamed. Even with hindsight, it is not clear what sort of educational system would most have encouraged economic growth and strengthened the institutions and value system of capitalism. Britain, it is worth noting, was far from alone in prioritizing the 'liberal arts' at the secondary and higher levels of education; a move in this direction can be discerned in other European countries in the latter half of the nineteenth century.[118] Moreover, contrary to what is often alleged, the argument that public schools discouraged pupils from going forward into business careers is open to question; in fact, from the middle of the century onwards ex-public schoolboys were entering commerce and industry in increasing numbers.[119] Indeed, the 'public school code', with its emphasis on 'honour', proved to be highly appropriate to many business occupations, like finance ('My word is my bond').

Yet, even assuming that the needs of the economy, especially from the 1860s onwards, really did require a more developed system of primary education and a proliferation of technical and commercial colleges to raise the proficiency of the industrial work-force, how was all this to be brought into existence? *Parental demand* by itself was unlikely to be effective, just as consumer demand alone would probably not have led to the provision of the sophisticated urban infrastructure upon which industry increasingly came to depend. Nor could manufacturers necessarily be expected to give a lead in the matter. Indeed, some economic historians believe that late Victorian businessmen, by concentrating on the traditional staple industries, instead of diversifying into the new science-based industries, were behaving quite rationally, in that they were making larger profits out of exploiting established markets than they could have done by opening up new ones. Yet this, if true, would suggest

---

[117] *Economist*, 17 Dec. 1859, pp. 1399–1400. Ibid., 31 Dec. 1859, pp. 1454–5.

[118] See the essays in Detlef K. Muller, Fritz Ringer, and Brian Simon (eds.), *The Rise of the Modern Educational System: Structural Change and Social Reproduction 1870–1920* (Cambridge, 1987), esp. 7–8 on the 'generalist shift' and 159 on the economic functions served by a public school education.

[119] T. W. Bamford, *The Rise of the Public Schools* (1967), 221.

that market rationality was a poor guide to the long-term needs of the British economy.[120] Did that mean that some trust should be given, after all, to the much-derided 'educational experts'? These are imponderable questions.

One final point. Did businessmen even know where their real interests lay? Cobden and Bright could not make up their minds on this issue. On the one hand, they often presented the 'commercial and manufacturing classes' as what Marx would have called a 'universal class', a class that, in promoting its own interests, was simultaneously promoting the good of the community as a whole. Such a conviction figured prominently in the propaganda of the Anti-Corn Law League.[121]

On the other hand, Cobden often spoke with great contempt about what flesh-and-blood businessmen were doing and saying.[122] Such statements reflected his belief that no 'class could be trusted to legislate in favour of its own interest, for it generally mistook its own interest'.[123] Hence, Cobden's famous remark in December 1845: 'We will save the Duke of Richmond's order from the Duke of Richmond.'[124] This rather amusingly inverts the more commonly expressed view that no class can be allowed to control legislation because it will all too easily identify—and *further*—its own interest! But what Cobden presumably meant was that the pursuit of self-interest would be conducive to the common good—but only if people 'correctly' apprehended where their self-interest lay, which would not happen automatically. On occasion, Bright, too, ventured the opinion that even 'the most intelligent manufacturers' held erroneous opinion on subjects which affected their own interests—or at least, that they had done so, before enlightenment subsequently dawned.[125]

Yet although Cobden often took a pessimistic view of the *short-term* future, he held to a generally optimistic view of the world. Free Trade was destined to triumph sooner or later; and people of all social classes and all nations would eventually throw off the vestiges of barbarism and live together in peace and amity.

Lowe, by contrast, had the strongest distrust of men's capacity to behave rationally, fearing that they would undoubtedly fall back into a state of selfish lethargy unless constantly goaded into greater effort. One of his favourite

---

[120] Donald N. McCloskey, 'Did Victorian Britain "fail"?', *Economic History Review*, 23 (1970), 446–59; Alan Sked, *Britain's Decline: Problems and Perspectives* (Oxford, 1987), 14–15.

[121] The middle class, Cobden once asserted, 'have no interest opposed to the general good, whilst, on the contrary, the feudal governing class exists only by a violation of sound principles of political economy' (cited in Perkin, *Origins*, 372).

[122] e.g. in his campaign to stop the establishment of a colony in Labuan, he was remarkably unimpressed by the fact that the Manchester and Glasgow Chambers of Commerce had petitioned the Government to do precisely this (Parl. Deb., 3rd ser., vol. 105, 1068–9: 1 June 1849).

[123] Ibid., vol. 134, 784: 27 June 1854.

[124] 17 Dec. 1845, *Cobden's Speeches*, 179.

[125] *Economist*, 17 Nov. 1860, pp. 1259–60.

expressions was that it was no part of his duty to 'make things pleasant all round'. No one who came into even superficial contact with Lowe ever supposed otherwise! Moreover, in Lowe's view, political economy was a *science*: and 'the object of science is not to please or to conciliate. It has no policy. It knows no compromise. If false, no popularity can redeem it; if true, no unpopularity can hurt it.'[126] On the contrary, one feels, the more unpopular political economy was, the greater the presumption, in Lowe's mind, that it must be objectively valid.[127] A similar spirit underlay his approach to examinations. Doubtless he had a passionate commitment to a mechanism that would destroy favouritism and nepotism in the interests of efficiency and merit; but it is equally clear that he derived a deep sense of personal satisfaction from the spectacle of weak candidates being 'ploughed'![128]

But more than a misanthropic view of the world was involved here. For Lowe sensed—perhaps correctly—that it might be a mistake to see political economy as necessarily serving as the ideology of the commercial and industrial middle classes. Lowe himself, as he cheerfully conceded, lacked business experience, and felt little sympathy for those who possessed it—which was why some business MPs attacked him in June 1857. Indeed, Lowe later felt that the reason why the middle class surrendered so abjectly during the reform crisis was that it lacked confidence in itself, a weakness he ascribed to the short-sightedness and lack of culture of businessmen. 'Every man was thinking too much of his own business, of his own affairs, of his till and his counting-house, and too little of the great events passing around them,' he argued. The business community lacked the capacity for 'combined action' precisely because it had received too narrowly commercial an education. So one lesson which Lowe drew from the events of 1866–7 was that not only did the masses need educating, but so did the middle classes themselves. The latter needed to be taught that 'money [was] not ... the be all and end all of life'. 'They want to have their morale raised, their sense of honour developed.'[129]

In any case, Lowe tended to distrust businessmen as a class, and for the very reason that he also distrusted trade unionists: because he feared that, as producers, they were well placed to impose themselves upon what he once called 'the greatest corporation of all—the community at large'.[130] School-

---

[126] *Nineteenth Century*, 4 (1878), 862.

[127] Though Gladstone, too, inclined to adopt this stance. See Gladstone to Lowe, 13 Aug. 1873, Morley, *Life of Gladstone*, ii. 464–5.

[128] Witness the well-known story of his Oxford University days (Winter, *Robert Lowe*, 10).

[129] Lowe, *Two Speeches*, 4–5, 18.

[130] Parl. Deb., 3rd ser., vol. 140, 1351: 25 Feb. 1856. In his draft report to the Hubbard Select Committee on the Income Tax, Lowe deprecated what he saw as 'an attempt to favour one class of property at the expense of another', and insisted on fair play for both the holder of rent charges and the Fund-holder (Report of Select Committee on Income and Property Tax, VII (1861), pp. xxiv–xxv). Another illustration of Lowe's inveterate habit of attributing self-interested

teachers and dons fell under the same suspicion. It was the *consumer* whom Lowe saw himself as trying to protect. Gladstone put it well when he assured Lowe, in an otherwise critical letter: 'You have fought for the public, tooth and nail.'[131] But in Lowe's view of the world, consumers were a mass of individuals, divorced from all localities. How apt it was, therefore, that Lowe should have ended his Commons career as the representative of London University, an 'invisible' constituency of the educated, which owed its entire existence to the operations of an examining board!

This suggests a paradox. We have seen that 'entrepreneurial values', meaning a commitment to the rules and spirit of a market economy, were quite widespread in nineteenth-century Britain and by no means confined to the business community. Perhaps these 'entrepreneurial values' should be differentiated from what I have called 'entrepreneurial politics', meaning the struggle of new business groups, especially the northern industrialists, to achieve political influence and social status commensurate with their economic power. If so, it is possible—the thought had certainly occurred to Lowe—that economic progress had its own logic, which manufacturers themselves simply could not be relied upon to appreciate.[132] In other words, perhaps the failure of entrepreneurial *politics*, far from hindering the establishment of entrepreneurial *values*, may indirectly have assisted their dissemination.

motives to any businessman with whom he found himself in disagreement is described by Malchow, *Gentlemen Capitalists*, 285.

[131] Gladstone to Lowe, 13 Aug. 1873, Morley, *Life of Gladstone*, ii. 464.
[132] See Joyce, *Work, Society and Politics*, 28.

Bibliography

UNPUBLISHED PAPERS

Aberdeen Papers (British Library).
Papers of the Association of British Chambers of Commerce (Guildhall Library, London).
Baines Papers (West Yorkshire Archives, Leeds).
Bradford Chamber of Commerce Minutes (West Yorkshire Archives, Bradford).
Brand Papers (House of Lords Records Office).
John Bright Papers (British Library).
John Bright Family Papers (University College London).
Bright–Hargreaves Papers (British Library).
Broadlands Papers (Palmerston) (Southampton University).
Cobden Papers (British Library).
Cobden Papers (Manchester Central Library).
Gladstone Papers (British Library).
Glynne–Gladstone MSS (St Deiniol's Library, Hawarden).
Layard Papers (British Library).
Manchester Chamber of Commerce Papers (Manchester).
Minutes of Master Spinners' Association (Lancashire Record Office).
W. S. Nichols Papers (West Yorkshire Archives, Bradford).
John Benjamin Smith Papers (Manchester Record Office).
George Wilson Papers (Manchester Record Office).

OFFICIAL PAPERS

Report on Navy Estimates from Select Committee on Navy, Army, and Ordnance Estimates, XXI (1847–8).
Report of the Third Select Committee on Miscellaneous Expenditure, XVIII (1847–8).
Second Report from Select Committee on Army and Ordnance Expenditure, IX (1849).
Report of the Select Committee on Army and Ordnance Expenditure, X (1850).
Report of the Select Committee on Income and Property Tax, IX (1852).
Second Report of Select Committee on Income and Property Tax, XX (1852).
Report of Select Committee on Decimal Coinage, 422 (1853).
First Report of Royal Commission on Mercantile Laws, XXVII (1854).
Report on the Organization of the Permanent Civil Service, XXVII (1854).
Reports and Papers Relating to the Civil Service, XX (1854–5).
Copy of Correspondence between the Committee of the Model Secular School at Manchester and the Committee of the Council on Education, Relating to the Subject of Admitting the Manchester Model Secular School to a Participation in the Parliamentary Grant for Education, LXVI (1857–8).

Return Showing the Number of Electors in English and Welsh Boroughs in 1859–60, LV (1860).

Report from Select Committee of House of Lords on what would be the Probable Increase . . ., LXXXVII (1860).

Report of Select Committee on Income and Property Tax, VII (1861).

Report of Select Committee on the practicability of adopting simple and uniform Systems of Weights and Measures, VII (1862).

Report from Select Committee on Trade with Foreign Nations, VII (1864).

Royal Commission into Law Relating to Letters Patent for Inventors, XXII (1864).

Correspondence with the Association of Chambers of Commerce, 1864, LVIII (1864).

Return of the Several Parliamentary Cities and Boroughs . . ., LVII (1866).

Third Report of Royal Commission on Organization and Rules of Trades Unions, XXXII (1867).

Report of Select Committee on Tribunals of Commerce, XII (1871).

Report of Select Committee on Tribunals of Commerce, IX (1873).

Third Report of Royal Commission on the Judicature, XXIV (1874).

NEWSPAPERS AND JOURNALS

Annual Register.
Blackwood's Magazine.
Bradford Observer.
Bradford Review.
Capital and Labour.
Daily News.
The Economist.
Edinburgh Review.
Financial Reformer.
Household Words.
Illustrated London News.
The League.
Leeds Mercury.
Liverpool Mail.
Liverpool Mercury.
Manchester Daily Times.
Manchester Examiner and Times.
Manchester Guardian.
Morning Star.
Nineteenth Century.
Norfolk News.
Norwich Mercury.
Papers on Taxation and Expenditure.
Preston Chronicle.
Punch.
Quarterly Review.
Reynolds's Newspaper.
Saturday Review.

Sheffield and Rotherham Independent.
The Times.
Transactions of the National Association for the Promotion of Social Science (NAPSS).

BOOKS

(Place of publication is London unless otherwise stated.)
ADAMS, FRANCIS, *History of the Elementary School Contest in England* (1882).
Administrative Reform Association papers.
Administrative Reform: The Re-Organisation of the Civil Service by Subordinate therein (1855).
AKROYD, EDWARD, *The Present Attitude of Political Parties* (1874).
ANDERSON, OLIVE, *A Liberal State at War: English Politics and Economics during the Crimean War* (1961).
ARMYTAGE, W. H. G., *A. J. Mundella 1825–1897: The Liberal Background to the Labour Movement* (1951).
ARTHURS, H. W., *'Without the Law': Administrative Justice and Legal Pluralism in Nineteenth-Century England* (Toronto, 1985).
ASHWORTH, HENRY, *International Maritime Law, and its Effect upon Trade* (Manchester, 1864).
——, *Recollections of Richard Cobden M.P. and the Anti-Corn Law League* (1876).
ATIYAH, P. S., *The Rise and Fall of Freedom of Contract* (Oxford, 1979).
AUSUBEL, HERMAN, *John Bright: Victorian Reformer* (New York, 1966).
AYERST, DAVID, *Guardian: Biography of a Newspaper* (1971).
BAGEHOT, WALTER, *The Collected Works of Walter Bagehot*, ed. Norman St John Stevas (1968), vol. 3.
——, *The English Constitution* (1867; 1963 edn.).
BAINES, EDWARD, *Household Suffrage and Equal Electoral Districts Shown to be Unfavourable to the Good Government and Purity of Elections...* (1841).
——, *The Social, Educational and Religious State of the Manufacturing Districts* (1843).
BAINES, EDWARD, jun., *Education Best Promoted by Perfect Freedom not by State Endowment* (1854).
——, *Letters to the Right Hon. Lord John Russell on State Education* (1846).
——, *On the Lancashire Plan of Secular Education: A Letter to a Free Trade Member of the House of Commons* (Leeds, 1848).
BALGARNIE, R., *Sir Titus Salt Baronet* (1877; new edn., Settle, 1970).
BAMFORD, T. W., *The Rise of the Public Schools* (1967).
BARRINGTON, EMILIE I., *The Servant of All: Pages from the Family, Social and Political Life of My Father James Wilson...* (2 vols.; 1927).
BATTISCOMBE, GEORGINA, *Shaftesbury: A Biography of the Seventh Earl 1801–1885* (1974).
BECKETT, J. V., *The Aristocracy in England 1660–1914* (1986).
BEHAGG, CLIVE, *Politics and Production in the Early Nineteenth Century* (1990).
BEHRENS, J., *Tribunals of Commerce: A Paper Read before the Members of the Bradford Chamber of Commerce of their Annual Meeting, 19 January 1865* (Bradford, 1865).
Sir Jacob Behrens, 1806–1889 (privately printed, n.d.).

BERESFORD, M. W., *The Leeds Chamber of Commerce* (Leeds, 1951).

BIAGINI, EUGENIO F., and REID, ALASTAIR J., *Currents of Radicalism: Popular Radicalism, Organised Labour and Party Politics in Britain 1850–1914* (Cambridge, 1991).

BINFIELD, B. CLYDE, *So Down to Prayers: Studies in English Nonconformity 1780–1920* (1977).

Birmingham Income Tax Reform Association, *Papers* (Birmingham, 1857).

BIRRELL, AUGUSTINE, *Things Past Redress* (1937).

BLACKBOURN, DAVID, and ELEY, GEOFF, *The Peculiarities of German History: Bourgeois Society and Politics in Nineteenth-Century Germany* (Oxford, 1984).

BLAKE, ROBERT, *The Conservative Party from Peel to Churchill* (1970; 1972 edn.).

—— , *Disraeli* (1966; 1969 edn.).

BLYTH, EDMUND KELL, *Life of William Ellis* (1889).

BOND, BRIAN, *The Victorian Army and the Staff College 1854–1914* (1972).

BOYSON, RHODES, *The Ashworth Cotton Enterprise: The Rise and Fall of a Family Firm 1818–1880* (Oxford, 1970).

Bradford Chamber of Commerce Annual Reports (Bradford Central Library).

BRADLEY, IAN CAMPBELL, *Enlightened Entrepreneurs* (1987).

BRIGGS, ASA, *Victorian Cities* (1963; 1968 edn.).

—— , *Victorian People* (1954; 1965 edn.).

BRIGHT, JOHN, *The Public Letters of the Right Hon. John Bright*, ed. H. J. Leech (1895).

—— , *Speeches on Questions of Public Policy by John Bright, M.P.*, ed. James E. Thorold Rogers (popular edn., 1883).

BRITTAN, SAMUEL, *The Economic Consequences of Democracy* (1977).

BROWN, LUCY, *The Board of Trade and the Free Trade Movement 1830–42* (Oxford, 1958).

BUXTON, SYDNEY, *Finance and Politics: An Historical Study, 1783–1885* (1888).

CARLYLE, THOMAS, *Past and Present* (1843; Ward Lock & Co. edn., 1910).

Central Committee, *Report of the Central Committee of the Association of Mill Owners and Manufacturers Engaged in the Cotton Trade for the Year 1844* (Manchester, 1845).

CHAPMAN, RICHARD A., and GREENAWAY, J. R., *The Dynamics of Administrative Reform* (1980).

CHECKLAND, S. G., *The Gladstones: A Family Biography 1764–1851* (Cambridge, 1971).

CHILDERS, SPENCER, *The Life and Correspondence of the Right Hon. Hugh C. E. Childers, 1827–1896* (1896).

CHILSTON, VISCOUNT, *W. H. Smith* (1965).

CHURCH, ROY, *Economic and Social Change in a Midland Town: Victorian Nottingham 1815–1900* (1966).

Civil Service, Examinations for, and Promotion therein, Considered by a PRACTICAL MAN (1855).

COBDEN, RICHARD, *Incorporate Your Borough* (1838).

—— , *The Political Writings of Richard Cobden* (1886).

—— , *Speeches on Questions of Public Policy by Richard Cobden, M.P.*, ed. John Bright and J. E. Thorold Rogers (1870; 1908 edn.).

COLMAN, HELEN CAROLINE, *Jeremiah James Colman: A Memoir* (1905).

COMBE, GEORGE, *Education: Its Principles and Practices as Developed by George Combe*, ed. William Jolly (1877).

CONACHER, J. B., *The Aberdeen Coalition, 1852–1855* (1968).

—— , *Britain and the Crimea, 1855–56* (1987).

CORNISH, W. R., *Intellectual Property: Patents, Copyright, Trade Marks and Allied Rights* (1981).

COTTRELL, P. L., *Industrial Finance, 1830–1914* (1980).

COWLING, MAURICE, *1867: Disraeli, Gladstone and Revolution* (Cambridge, 1967).

CROSBY, TRAVIS L., *English Farmers and the Politics of Protection 1815–1852* (Hassocks, 1977).

—— , *Sir Robert Peel's Administration* (Newton Abbot, 1976).

CROUZET, FRANÇOIS, *The First Industrialists: The Problem of Origins* (Cambridge, 1985).

CUDWORTH, WILLIAM, *Manningham, Heaton and Allerton* (Bradford, 1896).

DAUNTON, M. J., *Royal Mail: The Post Office since 1840* (1985).

DICKENS, CHARLES, *Miscellaneous Papers* (1914).

DODD, WILLIAM, *The Factory System Illustrated*, ed. W. H. Chaloner (1968; original edn., 1842).

DRIVER, CECIL, *Tory Radical: The Life of Richard Oastler* (New York, 1946).

DUNCKLEY, THE REVD HENRY, *The Charter of the Nations; or Free Trade and its Results* (1854).

—— , *Richard Cobden and the Jubilee of Free Trade* (1896).

DUTTON, H. I., and KING, J. E., *'Ten Per Cent and No Surrender': The Preston Strike, 1853–1854* (Cambridge, 1981).

'Economist', *Letter to Robertson Gladstone, Esq., on the Publications of the Financial Reform Association* (1849).

EDSALL, NICHOLAS C., *The Anti-Poor Law Movement, 1834–44* (Manchester, 1971).

—— , *Richard Cobden: Independent Radical* (Cambridge, Mass., 1986).

ELLIOT, ARTHUR D., *Life of George Joachim Goschen, First Viscount Goschen* (1911).

ELLIS, WILLIAM, *Outlines of Social Economy* (1846).

ELLISON, MARY, *Support for Secession: Lancashire and the American Civil War* (Chicago, 1972).

ERICKSON, ARVEL B., *The Public Career of Sir James Graham* (Oxford, 1952).

EVANS, D. MORIER, *The Commercial Crisis 1847–1848* (2nd edn., 1849).

EVANS, DAVID, *The Life and Works of William Williams . . .* (Llandyssul, 1939).

FABER, GEOFFREY, *Young England* (1987).

FINER, S. E., *The Life and Times of Sir Edwin Chadwick* (1952).

FINLAYSON, GEOFFREY B. A. M., *The Seventh Earl of Shaftesbury 1801–1885* (1981).

Fortunes Made in Business, Vol. 2 (1884).

FRASER, DEREK, *Urban Politics in Victorian England* (1976; 1979 edn.).

FRASER, W. HAMISH, *Trade Unions and Society: The Struggle for Acceptance 1850–1880* (1974).

GARRARD, JOHN, *Leadership and Power in Victorian Industrial Towns 1830–80* (Manchester, 1983).

GASH, NORMAN, *Mr Secretary Peel: The Life of Sir Robert Peel to 1830* (1961).

—— , *Politics in the Age of Peel* (1953).

—— , *Reaction and Reconstruction in English Politics 1832–1852* (Oxford, 1965).

GILLESPIE, FRANCES ELMA, *Labor and Politics in Britain: 1850–1867* (Durham, NC, 1927).

GOOCH, G. P. (ed.), *The Later Correspondence of Lord John Russell 1840–1878* (1925).

GREENLEAF, W. H., *The British Political Tradition*, Vol. 2: *The Ideological Heritage* (1983).

GREG, S., *Two Letters to Leonard Horner, Esq., on the Capabilities of the Factory System* (1840).

GREG, W. R., *The One Thing Needful* (2nd edn., 1855).

GREVILLE, CHARLES C. F., *A Journal of the Reign of Queen Victoria from 1832 to 1852* (1885).

GUEDALLA, PHILIP (ed.), *The Palmerston Papers, Gladstone and Palmerston, 1851–1865* (1928).

GUTTSMAN, W. L., *The British Political Élite* (1963; 1968 edn.).

—— (ed.), *A Plea for Democracy. The 1867 Essays on Reform and Questions for a Reformed Parliament* (1967).

HAMER, D. A., *The Politics of Electoral Pressure: A Study in the History of Victorian Reform Agitations* (Hassocks, 1977).

HAMMOND, J. L., and BARBARA, *Lord Shaftesbury* (4th edn., 1936).

HANHAM, H. J., *Elections and Party Management: Politics in the Time of Disraeli and Gladstone* (1959; 1978 edn.).

HARDMAN, MALCOLM, *Ruskin and Bradford: An Experiment in Victorian Cultural History* (Manchester, 1986).

'Harry Holdfast', *A Short Letter to Mr. Cobden in Reply to his Long Speech at Manchester, from his Quondam Admirer* (1849).

HAWKINS, ANGUS, *Parliament, Party, and the Art of Politics in Britain, 1855–1859* (Basingstoke and London, 1987).

HAYEK, F. A., *Law, Legislation and Liberty*, Vol. 3 (1979).

HENNOCK, E. P., *Fit and Proper Persons: Ideal and Reality in Nineteenth-Century Urban Government* (1973).

HILTON, BOYD, *The Age of Atonement: The Influence of Evangelicalism on Social and Economic Thought, 1795–1865* (Oxford, 1988).

HINDE, WENDY, *Richard Cobden: A Victorian Outsider* (New Haven, Conn., 1987).

HIRST, FRANCIS W., *Gladstone as Financier and Economist* (1931).

HODDER, EDWIN, *The Life and Work of the Seventh Earl of Shaftesbury* (1887), Vol. 2.

—— , *The Life of Samuel Morley* (1887).

The Holden–Illingworth Letters (Bradford, 1927).

HOWE, ANTHONY, *The Cotton Masters 1830–1860* (Oxford, 1984).

HUCH, RONALD K., *The Radical Lord Radnor: The Public Life of Viscount Folkestone, Third Earl of Radnor (1770–1869)* (Minneapolis, 1977).

—— and ZIEGLER, PAUL R., *Joseph Hume: The People's MP* (Philadelphia, 1985).

HUNT, BISHOP CARLETON, *The Development of the Business Corporation in England, 1800–1867* (New York, 1936; 1969 edn.).

HURST, J. G., *Edmund Potter and Dinting Vale* (Manchester, 1948).

HUTCHINS, B. L., and HARRISON, A., *A History of Factory Legislation* (1903; 1966 edn.).

HYDE, FRANCIS EDWIN, *Mr. Gladstone at the Board of Trade* (1934).

ILERSIC, A. R., and LIDDLE, P. F. B., *Parliament of Commerce: The Story of the Association of British Chambers of Commerce, 1860–1960* (1960).

JENKINS, T. A., *Gladstone, Whiggery and the Liberal Party 1874–1886* (Oxford, 1988).

—— (ed.), *The Parliamentary Diaries of Sir John Trelawny, 1858–1865* (1990).

JEREMY, DAVID J. (ed.), *Business and Religion in Britain* (Aldershot, 1988).

JOWITT, J. A. (ed.), *Model Industrial Communities in Mid-Nineteenth Century Yorkshire* (Bradford, 1986).

JOYCE, PATRICK, *Work, Society and Politics: The Culture of the Factory in Later Victorian England* (Brighton, 1980).

KAY-SHUTTLEWORTH, 'Letter to Lord Granville, 29 July 1861', in *Four Periods of Public Education as Reviewed in 1832, 1839, 1846, 1862* (1862).

KEBBEL, T. E., *A History of Toryism* (1886).

KELL, S. C., *The Ballot. Shall the Vote be Free or Watched?—The Voters' Own or Some One's Else?* (Bradford, n.d. [1867]).

—— , *The Political Attitude of our Law-Making Classes towards the Unenfranchised and the Duties Incumbent upon these in Consequence* (Bradford, 1861).

KINZER, BRUCE L., *The Ballot Question in Nineteenth Century English Politics* (New York, 1982).

KIRBY, M. W., *Men of Business and Politics: The Rise and Fall of the Quaker Pease Dynasty of North-East England, 1700–1943* (1984).

KIRK, NEVILLE, *The Growth of Working Class Reformism in Mid-Victorian England* (1985).

KITSON, CLARK G., *The Making of Victorian England* (1962).

KODITSCHEK, THEODORE, *Class Formation and Urban-Industrial Society: Bradford, 1750–1850* (Cambridge, 1990).

KOSS, STEPHEN, *The Rise and Fall of the Political Press in Britain*, Vol. 1: *The Nineteenth Century* (1981).

KYDD, SAMUEL H. G., *The History of the Factory Movement* (1857; rev. edn., New York, 1966).

Lancashire Public School Association, *National Education not Necessarily Governmental, Secular or Irreligious: Shown in a Series of Papers Read at the Meetings of the LPSA* (1850).

LEE, ALAN J., *The Origins of the Popular Press in England 1855–1914* (1976).

LEVI, LEONE, *Chambers and Tribunals of Commerce and Proposed General Chamber of Commerce in Liverpool* (Liverpool, 1849).

LEWIS, GILBERT FRANKLAND (ed.), *Letters of Sir George Cornewall Lewis* (1870).

LINDSAY, W. S., *A Confirmation of Admiralty Mismanagement . . . with Reply to the Charges of Sir C. Wood* (1855).

Liverpool Financial Reform Association Pamphlets.

—— , *Report on Taxation: Direct and Indirect: Adopted by the Financial Reform Association, Liverpool, and Presented to the Annual Meeting of the National Association for the Promotion of Social Science, held at Bradford, October, 1859* (Liverpool, n.d.).

LOWE, ROBERT, *Middle Class and Primary Education: Two Speeches* (Liverpool, 1868).

—— , *Primary and Classical Education: An Address to the Philosophical Institute of Edinburgh* (Edinburgh, 1867).

LUBENOW, W. C., *Parliamentary Politics and the Home Rule Crisis: The British House of Commons in 1886* (Oxford, 1988).

—— , *The Politics of Government Growth: Early Victorian Attitudes towards State Intervention 1833–1848* (Newton Abbot, 1971).

MACCOBY, S., *English Radicalism, 1832–1852* (1935).

McCORD, NORMAN, *The Anti-Corn Law League 1838–1846* (1958).

MACHIN, G. I. T., *Politics and the Churches in Great Britain 1832 to 1868* (Oxford, 1977).

MACKIE, J. B., *Life of Duncan McLaren* (Edinburgh, 1888).

MALCHOW, H. L., *Gentlemen Capitalists: The Social and Political World of the Victorian Businessman* (Basingstoke and London, 1991).

MALTBY, S. E., *Manchester and the Movement for National Elementary Education, 1800–1870* (Manchester, 1918).

MANDLER, PETER, *Aristocratic Government in the Age of Reform: Whigs and Liberals, 1830–1852* (Oxford, 1990).

MARQUAND, DAVID, *The Unprincipled Society* (1988).

MARTIN, A. PATCHETT, *Life and Letters of Robert Lowe, Viscount Sherbrooke* (1893).

MARX, KARL, and ENGELS, FREDERICK, *Selected Works* (Moscow, 1958).

—— ——, *On Britain* (Moscow, 1962 edn.).

MASTERMAN, JOHN, MP, *Report of Proceedings at the Public Meeting of Merchants, Bankers, and Traders of the City of London, Held at the London Tavern on Wednesday, Dec. 3, 1851, for a Reform of the Board of Customs* (1851).

MATTHEW, H. C. G., *Gladstone 1809–1874* (Oxford, 1986; 1988 edn.).

—— (ed.), *The Gladstone Diaries*, Vol. 6: *1861–1868* (Oxford, 1978).

MAXWELL, HERBERT, *Life and Letters of Fourth Earl of Clarendon* (1913).

MILL, JOHN STUART, *Principles of Political Economy* (1848).

MONYPENNY, WILLIAM FLAVELLE, *Life of Benjamin Disraeli Earl of Beaconsfield*, Vol. 2: *1837–1846* (1912).

MOORE, BARRINGTON, *Social Origins of Dictatorship and Democracy* (1966; 1969 edn.).

MORLEY, JOHN, *The Life of Richard Cobden* (London, 1881; 1896 edn.).

——, *Life of William Ewart Gladstone* (3 vols.; 1903).

MORRIS, R. J., *Class, Sect and Party. The Making of the British Middle Class: Leeds, 1820–1850* (Manchester, 1990).

MUELLER, HANS-EBERHARD, *Bureaucracy, Education, and Monopoly: Civil Service Reforms in Prussia and England* (Berkeley, Calif., 1984).

MULLER, DETLEF K., RINGER, FRITZ, and SIMON, BRIAN (eds.), *The Rise of the Modern Educational System: Structural Change and Social Reproduction 1870–1920* (Cambridge, 1987).

MUNFORD, W. A., *William Ewart, M.P. 1798–1869: Portrait of a Radical* (1960).

NOSSITER, T. J., *Influence, Opinion and Political Idioms in Reformed England: Case Studies from the North East 1832–74* (Hassocks, 1975).

OFFER, AVNER, *Property and Politics 1870–1914: Landownership, Law, Ideology and Urban Development in England* (Cambridge, 1981).

OMNIUM, JACOB, *A Letter on Administrative Reform* (1855).

OWEN, DAVID, *English Philanthropy 1660–1960* (Cambridge, Mass., 1964).

PARKER, CHARLES STUART (ed.), *Sir Robert Peel: From his Private Papers*, Vol. 2 (1899).

PARRY, J. P., *Democracy and Religion: Gladstone and the Liberal Party 1867–1875* (Cambridge, 1986).

PAZ, D. G., *The Politics of Working-Class Education in Britain, 1830–50* (Manchester, 1980).

PEEL, J. D. Y., *Herbert Spencer: The Evolution of a Sociologist* (1971).

PERKIN, HAROLD, *The Origins of Modern English Society 1780–1880* (1969; 1972 edn.).

PETO, SIR S. MORTON, *Taxation: Its Levy and Expenditure Past and Present* (1863).

POTTER, EDMUND, *A Picture of a Manufacturing District: A Lecture Delivered in the Town Hall, Glossop, 15 January 1856* (1856).

PREST, JOHN, *Politics in the Age of Cobden* (1977).

PRICE, RICHARD, *Labour in British Society: An Interpretative History* (1986).

PROUTY, ROGER, *The Transformation of the Board of Trade, 1830–1855* (1957).
RATHBONE, ELEANOR F., *William Rathbone: A Memoir* (1905).
RAY, GORDON N., *The Letters and Private Papers of W.M. Thackeray* (1946).
READ, DONALD, *Cobden and Bright: A Victorian Political Partnership* (1967).
—— , *Peel and the Victorians* (Oxford, 1987).
REID, T. WEMYSS, *Life of William Edward Forster* (1888).
Revised Report of Proceedings at Dinner of 31 May 1876, held in Celebration of the Hundredth Year of the Publication of the 'Wealth of Nations' (1876).
REYNOLDS, JACK, *The Great Paternalist. Titus Salt and the Growth of Nineteenth Century Bradford* (1983).
RIDLEY, JASPER, *Lord Palmerston* (1970; 1972 edn.).
ROBBINS, KEITH, *John Bright* (1979).
ROBERTS, DAVID, *Paternalism in Early Victorian England* (New Brunswick, NJ, 1979).
ROSE, MARY B., *The Gregs of Quarry Bank Mill: The Rise and Decline of a Family Firm, 1750–1914* (Cambridge, 1986).
RUBINSTEIN, W. D., *Men of Property: The Very Wealthy in Britain since the Industrial Revolution* (1981).
RUSSELL, NORMAN, *The Novelist and Mammon: Literary Responses to the World of Commerce in the Nineteenth Century* (Oxford, 1986).
SABINE, B. E. V., *A History of Income Tax* (1966).
SARGANT, W. L., *Essays of a Birmingham Manufacturer* (Birmingham, 1869).
SAVILLE, JOHN, *1848: The British State and the Chartist Movement* (Cambridge, 1987).
SEMMEL, BERNARD, *The Rise of Free Trade Imperialism* (Cambridge, 1970).
SEYMOUR, CHARLES, *Electoral Reform in England and Wales* (New Haven, Conn., 1915).
SHANNON, RICHARD I., *Gladstone*, vol. 1: *1809–1865* (1982).
—— , *Gladstone and the Bulgarian Agitation 1876* (1963).
SHEHAB, F., *Progressive Taxation: A Study in the Development of the Progressive Principle in the British Income Tax* (Oxford, 1953).
SIGSWORTH, ERIC M., *Black Dyke Mills. A History* (Liverpool, 1958).
SIMON, BRIAN, *Studies in the History of Education, 1780–1870* (1960).
SKED, ALAN, *Britain's Decline: Problems and Perspectives* (Oxford, 1987).
SMILES, SAMUEL, *Self-Help* (1859, 1910 edn.).
SMITH, F. B., *The Making of the Second Reform Bill* (Cambridge, 1966).
SMITH, PAUL, *Disraelian Conservatism and Social Reform* (1967).
—— (ed.), *Lord Salisbury on Politics: A Selection from his Articles in the* Quarterly Review, *1860–1883* (Cambridge, 1972).
SOUTHGATE, DONALD, *'The Most English Minister . . .': The Policies and Politics of Palmerston* (1966).
—— , *The Passing of the Whigs 1832–1886* (1962).
SPIERS, EDWARD M., *The Army and Society, 1815–1914* (1980).
—— , *Radical General: Sir George de Lacy Evans 1787–1870* (Manchester, 1983).
SPINNER, THOMAS J., Jun., *George Joachim Goschen. The Transformation of a Victorian Liberal* (Cambridge, 1973).
STEELE, E. D., *Palmerston and Liberalism, 1855–1865* (Cambridge, 1991).
STEPHEN, LESLIE, *Life of Henry Fawcett* (1885).
STEWART, ROBERT, *The Foundation of the Conservative Party 1830–1867* (1978).
—— , *Party and Politics 1830–1852* (1989).

——, *The Politics of Protection: Lord Derby and the Protectionist Party 1841–1852* (Cambridge, 1971).

STEWART, W. A. C., and MCCANN, W. P., *The Educational Innovators 1750–1880* (1967).

STRACHAN, HEW, *Wellington's Legacy: The Reform of the British Army 1830–54* (Manchester, 1984).

SWEETMAN, JOHN, *War and Administration: The Significance of the Crimean War for the British Army* (Edinburgh, 1984).

SYLVESTER, D. W., *Robert Lowe and Education* (Cambridge, 1974).

TAYLOR, ARTHUR J., *Laissez-Faire and State Intervention in Nineteenth-Century Britain* (1972).

TAYLOR, W. COOKE, *Notes of a Tour in the Manufacturing Districts of Lancashire* (based on 2nd edn. of 1842; reissued 1968).

TENNANT, [CHARLES], *The People's Blue Book: Taxation as it is and as it ought to be* (1857).

TREVELYAN, GEORGE MACAULAY, *The Life of John Bright* (1913).

VINCENT, JOHN, *The Formation of the British Liberal Party 1857–1868* (1966; 1972 edn.).

—— (ed.), *Disraeli, Derby and the Conservative Party: Journals and Memoirs of Edward Henry Lord Stanley, 1849–1869* (Hassocks, 1978).

WALLING, R. A. J. (ed.), *The Diaries of John Bright* (New York, 1930).

WALMSLEY, HUGH MULLENEUX, *The Life of Sir Joshua Walmsley* (1879).

WARD, J. T., *The Factory Movement, 1830–1855* (1962).

—— (ed.), *Popular Movements c.1830–1850* (1970).

—— and WILSON, R. G. (eds.), *Land and Industry* (Newton Abbot, 1971).

WATERFIELD, GORDON, *Layard of Nineveh* (1963).

WATKIN, A. E., *Absalom Watkin: Extracts from his Journal 1814–1856* (1920).

WATKIN, SIR E. W., *Alderman Cobden of Manchester* (n.d.).

WEAVER, STEWART ANGAS, *John Fielden and the Politics of Popular Radicalism, 1832–1847* (Oxford, 1987).

WEISSER, HENRY, *April 10: Challenge and Response in England in 1848* (Lanham, Md., 1983).

WEST, E. G., *Education and the Industrial Revolution* (1975).

——, *Education and the State: A Study in Political Economy* (1965).

WIENER, MARTIN J., *English Culture and the Decline of the Industrial Spirit 1850–1980* (Cambridge, 1981).

WILLIAMS, W. E., *The Rise of Gladstone to the Leadership of the Liberal Party, 1859 to 1868* (Cambridge, 1934).

WINTER, JAMES, *Robert Lowe* (Toronto and Buffalo, 1976).

WRIGHT, G. HENRY, *Chronicles of the Birmingham Chamber of Commerce, A.D. 1813–1913, and of the Birmingham Commercial Society A.D. 1783–1812* (Birmingham, 1913).

ARTICLES

ALLEN, JANET E., 'Voluntaryism: A "Laissez-faire" Movement in Mid-Nineteenth Century Elementary Education', *History of Education*, 10 (1981), 111–24.

ANDERSON, OLIVE, 'The Administrative Reform Association, 1855–1857', in Patricia Hollis (ed.), *Pressure from Without in Early Victorian England* (1974), 262–88.

ANDERSON, OLIVE, 'The Janus Face of Mid-Nineteenth-Century English Radicalism: The Administrative Reform Association of 1855', *Victorian Studies*, 8 (1964–5), 231–42.

——, 'Loans versus Taxes: British Financial Policy in the Crimean War', *Economic History Review*, 16 (1963–4), 314–27.

ANDERSON, PERRY, 'Origins of the Present Crisis', *New Left Review*, 23 (Jan.–Feb. 1964), 26–53.

ANNAN, N. G., 'The Intellectual Aristocracy', in J. H. Plumb (ed.), *Studies in Social History* (1955), 241–87.

ARNSTEIN, WALTER L., 'The Myth of the Triumphant Victorian Middle Class', *The Historian*, 37 (1975), 205–21.

ARTHURS, H. W., ' "Without the Law": Courts of Local and Special Jurisdiction in Nineteenth Century England', in Albert Kiralfy, Michele Slatter, and Roger Virgoe (eds.), *Custom, Courts and Counsel* (1985), 130–49.

AYDELOTTE, WILLIAM O., 'Constituency Influence on the British House of Commons, 1841–1847', in William O. Aydelotte, *The History of Parliamentary Behaviour* (Princeton, NJ, 1977), 225–46.

——, 'The Country Gentlemen and the Repeal of the Corn Laws', *English Historical Review*, 82 (1967), 47–60.

——, 'The House of Commons in the 1840s', *History*, 39 (1954), 249–62.

BAGWELL, PHILIP S., 'The Railway Interest: Its Organisation and Influence, 1839–1914', *Journal of Transport History*, 7 (1965), 65–86.

BARTRIP, PETER W. J., 'The State and the Steam-Boiler in Nineteenth-Century Britain', *International Review of Social History*, 25 (1980), 77–105.

BATZEL, VICTOR M., 'Legal Monopoly in Liberal England: The Patent Controversy in the Mid-Nineteenth Century', *Business History*, 22 (1980), 189–202.

——, 'Parliament, Businessmen and Bankruptcy, 1825–1883: A Study in Middle-Class Alienation', *Canadian Journal of History*, 18 (1983), 171–86.

BIAGINI, EUGENIO F., 'Popular Liberals, Gladstonian Finance and the Debate on Taxation, 1860–1874', in Eugenio F. Biagini and Alastair J. Reid, *Currents of Radicalism: Popular Radicalism, Organised Labour and Party Politics in Britain 1850–1914* (Cambridge, 1991), 134–62.

BLAUG, MARC, 'The Economics of Education in English Classical Political Economy: A Re-Examination' (1975), in *Economic History and the History of Economics* (Brighton, 1984), 150–83.

BRANTLINGER, PATRICK, 'The Case against Trade Unions in Early Victorian Fiction', *Victorian Studies*, 13 (1969), 37–52.

CAIN, P. J., and HOPKINS, A. G., 'Gentlemanly Capitalism and the British Expansion Overseas. I. The Old Colonial System, 1688–1850', *Economic History Review*, 39 (1986), 501–25.

————, 'Gentlemanly Capitalism and British Expansion Overseas. II. New Imperialism, 1850–1945', *Economic History Review*, 40 (1987), 1–26.

CALKINS, W. N., 'A Victorian Free Trade Lobby', *Economic History Review*, 13 (1960–1), 90–104.

CAMPBELL, R. H., 'A Critique of the Christian Businessman and his Paternalism', in David J. Jeremy (ed.), *Business and Religion in Britain* (Aldershot, 1988), 27–46.

CARSON, W. G., 'Symbolic and Instrumental Dimensions of Early Factory Legislation:

A Case Study in the Social Origins of Criminal Law', in Roger Hood (ed.), *Crime, Criminology and Public Policy* (1974), 107–38.

CASSIS, Y., 'Bankers in English Society in the Late Nineteenth Century', *Economic History Review*, 38 (1985), 210–29.

COHEN, IRA J., 'Towards a Theory of State Intervention: The Nationalization of the British Telegraphs', *Social Science History*, 4 (1980), 155–205.

CORNFORD, JAMES, 'The Parliamentary Foundations of the Hotel Cecil', in R. Robson (ed.), *Ideas and Institutions of Victorian Britain* (1967), 268–311.

——, 'The Transformation of Conservatism in the Late Nineteenth Century', *Victorian Studies*, 7 (1963), 35–66.

DAUNTON, M. J., '"Gentlemanly Capitalism" and British Industry 1820–1914', *Past & Present*, 122 (1989), 119–58.

DUKE, CHRISTOPHER, 'Robert Lowe—A Reappraisal', *British Journal of Educational Studies*, 14 (1965), 19–35.

DUNBABIN, J. P. D., 'Electoral Reforms and their Outcome in the United Kingdom, 1865–1900', in T. R. Gourvish and Alan O'Day (eds.), *Later Victorian Britain, 1867–1900* (1988), 93–125.

DUTTON, H. I., and KING, J. E., 'The Limits of Paternalism: The Cotton Tyrants of North Lancashire, 1836–54', *Social History*, 7 (1982), 59–74.

EDSALL, N. C., 'A Failed National Movement: The Parliamentary and Financial Reform Association, 1848–54', *Bulletin of the Institute for Historical Research*, 49 (1976), 108–31.

FAIRLIE, S., 'The Nineteenth-Century Corn Law Reconsidered', *Economic History Review*, 18 (1965), 544–61.

FARRAR, P. N., 'American Influence on the Movement for a National System of Elementary Education in England and Wales, 1830–1870', *British Journal of Educational Studies*, 14 (1965), 36–47.

FERGUSON, ROBERT B., 'The Adjudication of Commercial Disputes and the Legal System in Modern England', *British Journal of Law and Society*, 7 (1980), 141–57.

FIRTH, GARY, 'The Bradford Trade in the Nineteenth Century', in D. G. Wright and J. A. Jowitt (eds.), *Victorian Bradford* (Bradford, 1981), 7–36.

FISHER, J. R., 'Issues and Influence: Two By-Elections in South Nottinghamshire in the Mid-Nineteenth Century', *Historical Journal*, 24 (1981), 155–65.

FLETCHER, LAADEN, 'Payment for Means or Payment for Results: Administrative Dilemma of the 1860s', *Journal of Educational Administration and History*, 4 (1972), 13–21.

——, 'A Further Comment on Recent Interpretations of the Revised Code, 1862', *History of Education*, 10 (1981), 21–32.

FRASER, DEREK, 'Edward Baines', in Patricia Hollis (ed.), *Pressure from Without in Early Victorian England* (1974), 183–209.

——, 'Politics and Society in the Nineteenth Century', in D. Fraser (ed.), *A History of Modern Leeds* (Manchester, 1980), 270–300.

——, 'Voluntaryism and West Riding Politics in the Mid-Nineteenth Century', *Northern History*, 13 (1977), 199–231.

GALLACHER, THOMAS F., 'The Second Reform Movement, 1848–1867', *Albion*, 12 (1980), 147–63.

GARRARD, JOHN, 'The Middle Classes and Nineteenth Century National and Local

Politics', in John Garrard *et al.* (eds.), *The Middle Class in Politics* (1978), 35–66.

——, 'Parties, Members and Voters after 1867', in T. R. Gourvish and Alan O'Day (eds.), *Later Victorian Britain 1867–1900* (1988), 127–50.

GHOSH, P. R., 'Disraelian Conservatism: A Financial Approach', *English Historical Review*, 99 (1984), 268–96.

GILMOUR, ROBIN, 'The Gradgrind School: Political Economy in the Classroom', *Victorian Studies*, 11 (1967), 207–24.

GOLDMAN, LAWRENCE, 'The Social Science Association, 1857–1886: A Context for Mid-Victorian Liberalism', *English Historical Review*, 101 (1986), 95–134.

GOLDSTROM, J. M., 'The Content of Education and the Socialization of the Working-Class Child 1830–1860', in W. P. McCann (ed.), *Popular Education and Socialization* (1977), 93–109.

——, 'Richard Whately and Political Economy in School Books, 1833–80', *Irish Historical Studies*, 15 (1966–7), 131–46.

GORDON, SCOTT, 'The London *Economist* and the High Tide of Laissez-Faire', *Journal of Political Economy*, 6 (1955), 461–88.

GOWAN, PETER, 'The Whitehall Mandarins', *New Left Review*, 162 (1987), 4–34.

GREENAWAY, JOHN R., 'Parliamentary Reform and Civil Service Reform: A Nineteenth-Century Debate Reassessed', *Parliamentary History*, 4 (1985), 157–69.

GUROWICH, P. M., 'The Continuation of War by Other Means: Party and Politics, 1855–58', *Historical Journal*, 27 (1984), 603–31.

HALL, STUART, 'The Rise of the Representative/Interventionist State', in Gregory McLennan, David Held, and Stuart Hall (eds.), *State and Society in Contemporary Britain: A Critical Introduction* (1984), 7–49.

HARRIS, JOSÉ, and THANE, PAT, 'British and European Bankers, 1880–1914: An "Aristocratic Bourgeoisie"?', in Pat Thane, Geoffrey Crossick, and Roderick Floud (eds.), *The Power of the Past* (Cambridge, 1984), 215–34.

HARRISON, BRIAN, 'Religion and Recreation in Nineteenth-Century England', *Past & Present*, 38 (1967), 98–125.

HART, JENIFER, 'The Genesis of the Northcote–Trevelyan Report', in Gillian Sutherland (ed.), *Studies in the Growth of Nineteenth Century Government* (1972), 63–81.

——, 'Sir Charles Trevelyan at the Treasury', *English Historical Review*, 75 (1960), 92–110.

HAWKINS, ANGUS B., 'A Forgotten Crisis: Gladstone and the Politics of Finance during the 1850s', *Victorian Studies*, 26 (1983), 287–320.

——, ' "Parliamentary Government" and Victorian Political Parties, *c.*1830–*c.*1880', *English Historical Review*, 104 (1989), 280–301.

HILL, CHRISTOPHER, 'The Norman Yoke', in *Puritanism and Revolution* (1958), 50–122.

HILTON, BOYD, 'Peel: A Reappraisal', *Historical Journal*, 22 (1979), 585–614.

HUGHES, EDWARD, 'Civil Service Reform 1853–5', *History*, 27 (1942), 51–83.

——, 'Sir Charles Trevelyan and Civil Service Reform, 1853–5', *English Historical Review*, 64 (1949), 206–34.

HURST, MICHAEL, 'Liberal versus Liberal: The General Election of 1874 in Bradford and Sheffield', *Historical Journal*, 15 (1972), 669–713.

HURT, J. S., 'Professor West on Early Nineteenth-Century Education', *Economic History Review*, 24 (1971), 624–32.

JAMES, DAVID, 'William Byles and the *Bradford Observer*', in D. G. Wright and J. A. Jowitt (eds.), *Victorian Bradford* (Bradford, 1981), 115–36.

JOHNSON, RICHARD, 'Administrators in Education before 1870: Patronage, Social Position and Role', in Gillian Sutherland (ed.), *Studies in the Growth of Nineteenth Century Government* (1972), 110–38.

——, 'Notes on the Schooling of the English Working Class, 1780–1850', in Roger Dale *et al.*, *Schooling and Capitalism: A Sociological Reader* (1976), 44–54.

JONES, DONALD K., 'The Educational Legacy of the Anti-Corn Law League', *History of Education*, 3 (1974), 18–35.

——, 'Socialization and Social Science: Manchester Model Secular School 1854–1861', in W. P. McCann (ed.), *Popular Education and Socialization* (1977), 111–39.

JONES, LINDA J., 'Public Pursuit of Private Profit? Liberal Businessmen and Municipal Politics in Birmingham, 1865–1900', *Business History*, 25 (1983), 240–59.

JOWITT, J. A., 'Copley, Ackroydon and West Hill Park: Moral Reform and Social Improvement in Halifax', in J. A. Jowitt (ed.), *Model Industrial Communities in Mid-Nineteenth Century Yorkshire* (Bradford, 1986), 37–61.

——, 'Parliamentary Politics in Halifax, 1832–1847', *Northern History*, 12 (1976), 172–201.

KEMP, BETTY, 'Reflections on the Repeal of the Corn Laws', *Victorian Studies*, 5 (1961–2), 189–204.

KIRBY, CHESTER, 'The Attack on the English Game Laws in the Forties', *Journal of Modern History*, 4 (1932), 18–37.

KITSON CLARK, G. S. R., 'The Electorate and the Repeal of the Corn Laws', *Transactions of the Royal Historical Society*, 1 (1951), 109–26.

——, 'The Repeal of the Corn Laws and the Politics of the Forties', *Economic History Review*, 4 (1951–2), 1–13.

KODITSCHEK, THEODORE, 'The Dynamics of Class Formation in Nineteenth-Century Bradford', in A. L. Beier, David Cannadine, and James M. Rosenheim (eds.), *The First Modern Society* (Cambridge, 1989), 511–48.

LAQUEUR, THOMAS W., 'Working-Class Demand and the Growth of English Elementary Education, 1750–1850', in Lawrence Stone (ed.), *Schooling and Society* (Baltimore, 1976), 192–205.

McCANN, W. P., 'Elementary Education in England and Wales on the Eve of the 1870 Education Act', *Journal of Educational Administration and History*, 2 (1969), 20–9.

McCLOSKEY, DONALD N., 'Did Victorian Britain "Fail"?', *Economic History Review*, 23 (1970), 446–59.

McCORD, NORMAN, 'Cobden and Bright in Politics, 1846–1857', in Robert Robson (ed.), *Ideas and Institutions of Victorian Britain* (1967), 87–114.

MacDONAGH, OLIVER, 'The Nineteenth-Century Revolution in Government: A Reappraisal', *Historical Journal*, (1958), 52–67.

MACINTYRE, ANGUS, 'Lord George Bentinck and the Protectionists: A Lost Cause?', *Transactions of the Royal Historical Society*, 39 (1989), 141–65.

MANDLER, PETER, 'Cain and Abel: Two Aristocrats and the Early Victorian Factory Acts', *Historical Journal*, 27 (1984), 83–109.

MARCHAM, A. J., 'Educating our Masters: Political Parties and Elementary Education 1867 to 1870', *British Journal of Educational Studies*, 21 (1973), 180–91.

——, 'Recent Interpretations of the Revised Code of Education 1862', *History of Education*, 8 (1979), 121–33.

MARCHAM, A. J. 'The Revised Code of 1862: Reinterpretations and Misinterpretations', *History of Education*, 10 (1981), 81–99.

MASON, D., 'Peelite Opinion and the Genesis of Payment by Results: The True Story of the Newcastle Commission', *History of Education*, 17 (1988), 269–81.

MATTHEW, H. C. G., 'Disraeli, Gladstone, and the Politics of Mid-Victorian Budgets', *Historical Journal*, 22 (1979), 615–43.

MOORE, D. C., 'The Corn Laws and High Farming', *Economic History Review*, 18 (1965), 544–61.

——, 'Social Structure, Political Structure, and Public Opinion in Mid-Victorian England', in Robert Robson (ed.), *Ideas and Institutions of Victorian Britain* (1967), 20–57.

MORRIS, R. J., 'Voluntary Societies and British Urban Élites, 1780–1850', *Historical Journal*, 26 (1983), 95–118.

NEWBOULD, IAN D. C., 'Whiggery and the Dilemma of Reform: Liberals, Radicals and the Melbourne Administration, 1835–9', *Bulletin of the Institute of Historical Research*, 53 (1980), 229–41.

PARTRIDGE, M. S., 'The Russell Cabinet and National Defence, 1846–52', *History*, 72 (1987), 231–50.

QUINAULT, ROLAND, '1848 and Parliamentary Reform', *Historical Journal*, 31 (1988), 831–51.

RAVEN, JAMES, 'British History and the Enterprise Culture', *Past & Present*, 123 (1989), 178–204.

ROPER, HENRY, 'Toward an Elementary Education Act for England and Wales, 1865–1868', *British Journal of Educational Studies*, 23 (1975), 181–208.

——, 'W. E. Forster's Memorandum of 21 October, 1869: A Re-examination', *British Journal of Educational Studies*, 21 (1973), 64–75.

RUBINSTEIN, W. D., 'Wealth, Élites, and the Class Structure of Modern Britain', *Past & Present*, 76 (1977), 99–126.

SANDERSON, MICHAEL, 'Education and the Factory in Industrial Lancashire, 1780–1840', *Economic History Review*, 20 (1967), 266–79.

——, 'Literacy and Social Mobility in the Industrial Revolution in England', *Past & Present*, 56 (1972), 75–104.

SAVILLE, JOHN, 'Sleeping Partnership and Limited Liability, 1850–1856', *Economic History Review*, 8 (1955–6), 418–33.

SPAIN, JONATHAN, 'Trade Unionists, Gladstonian Liberals, and the Labour Law Reforms of 1875', in Eugenio F. Biagini and Alastair J. Reid (eds.), *Currents of Radicalism: Popular Radicalism, Organised Labour and Party Politics in Britain 1850–1914* (Cambridge, 1991), 109–33.

STEELE, E. D., 'Imperialism and Leeds Politics, c.1850–1914', in Derek Fraser (ed.), *A History of Modern Leeds* (Manchester, 1980), 327–52.

STEWART, ROBERT, '"The Conservative Reaction": Lord Robert Cecil and Party Politics', in Lord Blake and Hugh Cecil (eds.), *Salisbury: The Man and his Policies* (1987), 90–115.

——, 'The Ten Hours and Sugar Crises of 1844: Government and the House of Commons in the Age of Reform', *Historical Journal*, 12 (1969), 35–57.

STRACHAN, HEW, 'The Early Victorian Army and the Nineteenth-Century Revolution in Government', *English Historical Review*, 95 (1980), 782–809.

THANE, PAT, 'The Working Class and State "Welfare" in Britain, 1880–1914', *Historical Journal*, 27 (1984), 877–900.

THOMPSON, E. P., 'The Peculiarities of the English', in *The Poverty of Theory* (1978), 35–91.

THOMPSON, F. M. L., 'Whigs and Liberals in the West Riding, 1830–1860', *English Historical Review*, 74 (1959), 214–39.

TRAINOR, RICHARD, 'The Gentrification of Victorian and Edwardian Industrialists', in A. L. Beier, David Cannadine, and James M. Rosenheim (eds.), *The First Modern Society* (Cambridge, 1989), 167–97.

——, 'Peers on an Industrial Frontier: The Earls of Dartmouth and of Dudley in the Black Country, c.1810 to 1914', in David Cannadine (ed.), *Patricians, Power and Politics in Nineteenth-Century Towns* (Leicester, 1982), 70–132.

VINCENT, JOHN, 'The Effect of the Second Reform Act in Lancashire', *Historical Journal*, 11 (1968), 84–94.

WARWICK, PAUL, 'Did Britain Change? An Inquiry into the Causes of National Decline', *Journal of Contemporary History*, 20 (1985), 99–133.

WEBB, IGOR, 'The Bradford Wool Exchange: Industrial Capitalism and the Popularity of Gothic', *Victorian Studies*, 20 (1976–7), 45–68.

WEST, E. G., 'Private versus Public Education, A Classical Economic Dispute' (1964), in A. W. Coats (ed.), *The Classical Economists and Economic Policy* (1971), 123–43.

——, 'Resource Allocation and Growth in Early Nineteenth-Century British Education', *Economic History Review*, 23 (1970), 68–95.

WILSON, ALEXANDER, 'The Suffrage Movement', in Patricia Hollis (ed.), *Pressure from Without in Early Victorian England* (1974), 80–104.

WRIGHT, D. G., 'Bradford and the American Civil War', *Journal of British Studies*, 8 (1969), 69–85.

——, 'Leeds Politics and the American Civil War', *Northern History*, 9 (1974), 96–122.

——, 'The Second Reform Agitation', in D. G. Wright and J. A. Jowitt (eds.), *Victorian Bradford* (Bradford, 1981), 165–98.

YARMIE, ANDREW H., 'British Employers' Resistance to "Grandmotherly" Government, 1850–80', *Social History*, 9 (1984), 141–69.

——, 'Employers' Organizations in Mid-Victorian England', *International Review of Social History*, 25 (1980), 209–35.

ZIMMECK, META, 'Gladstone Holds His Own: The Origins of Income Tax Relief for Life Insurance Policies', *Bulletin of the Institute of Historical Research*, 58 (1985), 167–88.

DISSERTATIONS

GATRELL, V. A. C., 'The Commercial Middle Class in Manchester c.1820–1857', Ph.D. dissertation, Cambridge University, 1971.

Index